THE ROAD NOT TAKEN

A military historian and foreign policy analyst who has been called "one of the world's leading authorities on armed conflict," Max Boot is the author of *The Savage Wars of Peace: Small Wars and the Rise of American Power*, *War Made New: Technology, Warfare, and the Course of History, 1500 to Today*, and the *New York Times* bestseller *Invisible Armies: An Epic History of Guerrilla Warfare from Ancient Times to the Present Day*. The Jeane J. Kirkpatrick senior fellow in national security studies at the Council on Foreign Relations in New York, he is also a regular contributor to the *New York Times*, the *Los Angeles Times*, *Foreign Policy*, *USA Today*, and many other publications.

OTHER BOOKS BY MAX BOOT

Invisible Armies:
An Epic History of Guerrilla Warfare
from Ancient Times to the Present

War Made New:
Technology, Warfare, and the Course of History,
1500 to Today

The Savage Wars of Peace:
Small Wars and the Rise of American Power

Lansdale arrives at Tam Son Nhut Airport in Saigon, August 29, 1965, to begin his second tour in Vietnam. His embassy rival, Philip Habib, is at left. (AP)

THE ROAD NOT TAKEN

EDWARD LANSDALE AND THE AMERICAN TRAGEDY IN VIETNAM

MAX BOOT

First published in the US by Liveright Publishing Corporation in 2018
First published in the UK by Head of Zeus in 2018

9 7 5 3 1 2 4 6 8

A catalogue record for this book is available from the British Library.

ISBN (HB): 9781788542678
ISBN (E): 9781788542661

Book design by Brooke Koven

Printed and bound in Germany by CPI Books GmbH

Head of Zeus Ltd
First Floor East
5–8 Hardwick Street
London EC1R 4RG

WWW.HEADOFZEUS.COM

To Sue Mi Terry,
for supporting me

And to the Council on Foreign Relations,
for supporting my work

CONTENTS

PART THREE • *Nation Builder (1954–1956)*

PART FOUR • *Washington Warrior (1957–1963)*

PART FIVE • *Bastard Child (1964–1968)*

PART SIX • *The Beaten Man (1968–1987)*

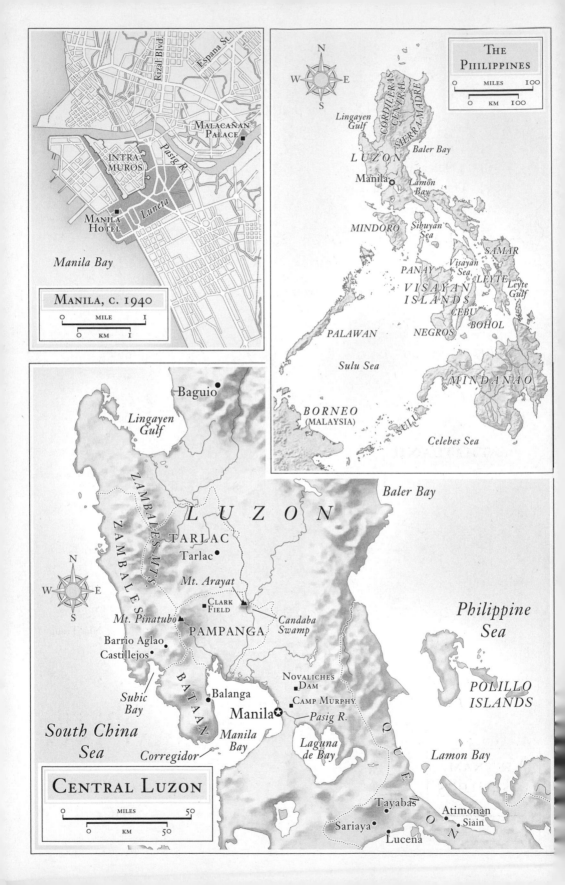

MANILA, C. 1940

Espana St.

Rizal Blvd.

Pasig R.

MALACAÑAN PALACE

INTRA-MUROS

Luneta

MANILA HOTEL

Manila Bay

MILE 1

KM 1

THE PHILIPPINES

MILES 100

KM 100

N
W E
S

CORDILLERAS CENTRAL

SIERRA MADRE

Lingayen Gulf

Baler Bay

LUZON

Manila

Lamon Bay

MINDORO

Sibuyan Sea

SAMAR

Visayan Sea

PANAY

VISAYAN ISLANDS

LEYTE

Leyte Gulf

CEBU

BOHOL

PALAWAN

NEGROS

Sulu Sea

MINDANAO

BORNEO (MALAYSIA)

SULU

Celebes Sea

CENTRAL LUZON

Baguio

Lingayen Gulf

L U Z O N

Baler Bay

ZAMBALES MTS.

ZAMBALES

TARLAC

Tarlac

Mt. Arayat

CLARK FIELD

Candaba Swamp

Mt. Pinatubo

PAMPANGA

Barrio Aglao

Castillejos

BATAAN

Subic Bay

Balanga

Novaliches Dam

Camp Murphy

Manila

Pasig R.

Corregidor

Manila Bay

Laguna de Bay

South China Sea

Philippine Sea

POLILLO ISLANDS

Q U E Z O N

Lamon Bay

Tayabas

Atimonan

Siain

Sariaya

Lucena

N
W E
S

MILES 50

KM 50

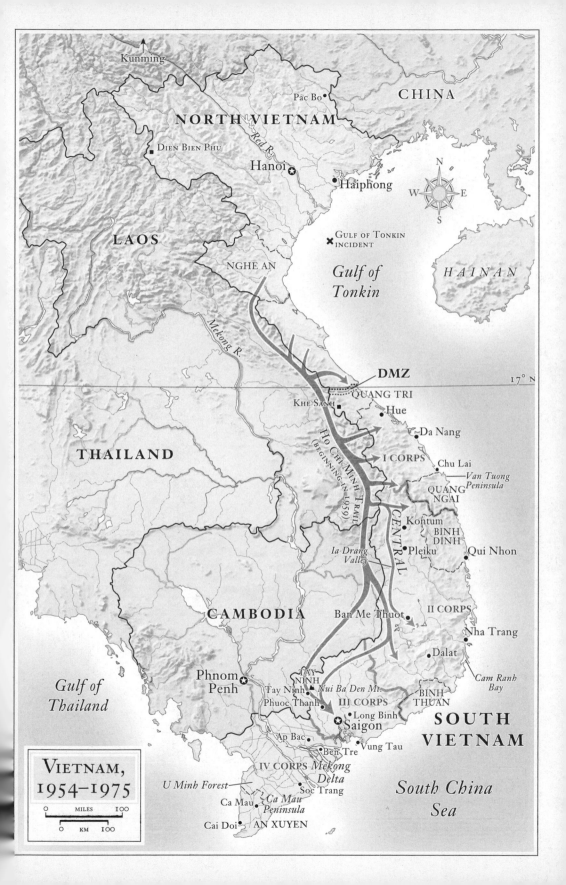

Kunming

CHINA

NORTH VIETNAM

Pac Bo

Dien Bien Phu

Red R.

Hanoi

Haiphong

LAOS

Gulf of Tonkin
INCIDENT

NGHE AN

Gulf of
Tonkin

HAINAN

Mekong R.

17° N

DMZ

QUANG TRI

Khe Sanh

Hue

THAILAND

Ho Chi Minh Trail
(BEGINNING IN 1959)

Da Nang

I CORPS

Chu Lai

Van Tuong
Peninsula

QUANG
NGAI

Kontum

BINH
DINH

CENTRAL

Pleiku

Qui Nhon

Ia Drang
Valley

CAMBODIA

Ban Me Thuot

II CORPS

Nha Trang

Dalat

Gulf of
Thailand

Phnom
Penh

TAY
NINH

Nui Ba Den Mt.

Tay Ninh

Phuoc Thanh

III CORPS

Long Binh

Saigon

Cam Ranh
Bay

BINH
THUAN

SOUTH
VIETNAM

Ap Bac

Vung Tau

Ben Tre

IV CORPS

Mekong
Delta

U Minh Forest

Soc Trang

South China
Sea

Ca Mau

Ca Mau
Peninsula

Cai Doi

AN XUYEN

Vietnam,
1954–1975

0   MILES   100

0   KM   100

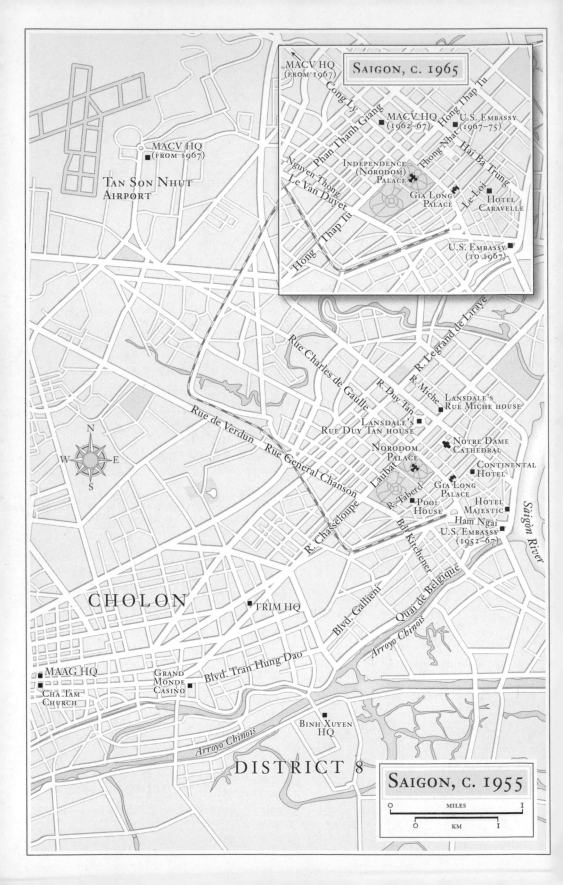

SAIGON, C. 1965

MACV HQ (FROM 1967)

Cong Ly

Phan Thanh Giang

MACV HQ (1962–67)

Hong Thap Tu

U.S. EMBASSY (1967–75)

Nguyen Thong

Thong Nhut

Hai Ba Trung

Le Van Duyet

INDEPENDENCE (NORODOM) PALACE

GIA LONG PALACE

Le-Loi

HOTEL CARAVELLE

Hong Thap Tu

U.S. EMBASSY (TO 1967)

MACV HQ (FROM 1967)

TAN SON NHUT AIRPORT

Rue Charles de Gaulle

R. Legrand de l'Iraye

R. Duy Tan

R. Miche

R. Miche

LANSDALE'S RUE MICHE HOUSE

Rue de Verdun

Rue General Chanson

LANSDALE'S RUE DUY TAN HOUSE

NOTRE DAME CATHEDRAL

NORODOM PALACE

CONTINENTAL HOTEL

N W E S

Laubat

GIA LONG PALACE

R. Chasseloupe

R. Taberd

POOL HOUSE

HOTEL MAJESTIC

R. Chasseloupe

Bd. Kitchener

Ham Ngai

U.S. EMBASSY (1952–67)

Saigon River

CHOLON

Blvd. Gallieni

Quai de Belgique

TRIM HQ

Arroyo Chinois

MAAG HQ

GRAND MONDE CASINO

Blvd. Tran Hung Dao

CHA TAM CHURCH

BINH XUYEN HQ

Arroyo Chinois

DISTRICT 8

SAIGON, C. 1955

0   MILES   1

0   KM   1

DRAMATIS PERSONAE

FILIPINOS

Oscar Arellano — Head of CIA-sponsored Operation Brotherhood in South Vietnam.

Patrocinio "Pat" Yapcinco Kelly — Lansdale's guide to Huklandia; mistress; second wife.

Ramon "Monching" Magsaysay — Defense minister, 1950–53; president, 1953–57.

Manuel "Manny" Manahan — Newspaper publisher; Magsaysay aide.

Juan "Johnny" Orendain — American-educated lawyer.

Elpidio Quirino — President, 1948–53.

Carlos Romulo — Ambassador to Washington, 1952–53, 1955–62; presidential candidate, 1953.

Manuel Roxas — President, 1946–48.

Frisco "Johnny" San Juan — Head of the CIA-sponsored Freedom Company in South Vietnam; a leader in the CIA-sponsored National Movement for Free Elections (NAMFREL) in the Philippines.

Luis Taruc — Huk military leader, 1942–53.

Napoleon "Poling" Valeriano — Philippine Army officer who worked with Lansdale in Vietnam in 1950s and 1960s.

VIETNAMESE

Bao Dai — Emperor of Vietnam, 1926–45; chief of state, 1949–55.

Bui Diem	South Vietnam's ambassador to the United States, 1967–72.
Cao Van Vien	Chief of South Vietnam's Joint General Staff, 1964–75.
Duong Van Duc	South Vietnamese officer who oversaw pacification of Ca Mau Peninsula, 1955.
Duong Van Minh ("Big Minh")	General who led anti-Diem coup in 1963.
Ho Chi Minh	Vietminh leader, 1941–54; North Vietnam leader, 1954–69.
Le Quang Vinh ("Ba Cut")	Warlord of the Hoa Hao sect.
Le Van Vien ("Bay Vien")	Leader of the Binh Xuyen criminal empire.
Le Duan	North Vietnamese leader, driving force behind the war against South Vietnam.
Le Van Kim	South Vietnamese officer, commanded pacification of Quang Ngai and Binh Dinh provinces, 1955.
Jean Leroy	French-Vietnamese Catholic warlord.
Ngo Dinh Diem	Prime minister and then president of South Vietnam, 1954–63.
Ngo Dinh Nhu	Ngo Dinh Diem's brother and chief adviser.
Tran Le Xuan ("Madame Nhu")	Wife of Ngo Dinh Nhu.
Nguyen Duc Thang	South Vietnamese general, minister of revolutionary development in the mid-1960s.
Nguyen Ngoc Tho	Vice president of South Vietnam, 1956–63; prime minister, 1963–64.
Nguyen Khanh	South Vietnamese general; president, 1964–65.
Nguyen Loc Hoa	"Fighting priest" who led the village of Binh Hung.

Nguyen Van Hinh	Chief of staff, South Vietnamese armed forces, 1952–54; pro-French.
Nguyen Van Thieu	South Vietnamese general; president, 1965–75.
Nguyen Van Vy	Nguyen Van Hinh's successor as chief of staff; pro-French.
Nguyen Cao Ky	South Vietnamese air force commander; prime minister, 1965–67; vice president, 1967–71.
Pham Duy	Folk singer.
Pham Xuan An	North Vietnamese spy and Lansdale friend.
Pham Xuan Giai	South Vietnamese officer in charge of psychological warfare, 1950s.
Tran Van Don	South Vietnamese general; a leader of the 1963 anti-Diem coup.
Tran Van Soai ("Nam Lua")	Hoa Hao warlord.
Trinh Minh Thé	Cao Dai warlord.
Vo Nguyen Giap	Vietminh, North Vietnamese military commander, 1945–75.

AMERICANS

George Aurell	Chief of the CIA's Far East Division and CIA station chief in Manila, 1950s.
Charles T. R. "Bo" Bohannan	Intelligence officer who worked for Lansdale in both the Philippines and Vietnam.
McGeorge Bundy	National security adviser, 1961–66.
Ellsworth Bunker	Ambassador to South Vietnam, 1967–73.
Frank Church	Democratic senator from Idaho who chaired hearings on intelligence in 1975.

William Colby	CIA chief of station in Saigon, CORDS chief, and CIA director, 1973–76.
J. Lawton Collins	Army chief of staff; U.S. ambassador to Saigon, 1954–55.
Lucien "Luigi" Conein	CIA officer who worked for Lansdale in Vietnam in the 1950s and 1960s.
Myron Cowen	Ambassador to the Philippines, 1949–52.
Thomas Dooley ("Dr. America")	Navy doctor who wrote the best seller *Deliver Us from Evil*, about the 1954–55 exodus of refugees from North Vietnam.
Michael J. Deutch	Engineer and economist; member of Lansdale's Vietnam team in 1965–66.
Allen Dulles	CIA director, 1953–61.
Elbridge Durbrow	Ambassador to South Vietnam, 1957–61.
Daniel Ellsberg	Member of Lansdale's team in Saigon, 1965–66; Pentagon Papers leaker.
Graves Erskine	Marine general; head of Pentagon's Office of Special Operations, 1953–61.
Philip Habib	Chief of the political section, U.S. embassy in Saigon, 1965–66; later under secretary of state.
William King Harvey	Head of the CIA's Task Force W (dealing with Cuba), 1961–62.
Donald Heath	Ambassador to Saigon, 1952–55.
Richard Helms	CIA officer; CIA director, 1966–73.
Gabriel L. Kaplan	CIA operative, member of Lansdale team in the Philippines, 1950s.
Sam Karrick	Army officer and Christian Science practitioner who worked for Lansdale in Vietnam in the 1950s and 1960s.
Helen Lansdale	Lansdale's first wife.

Henry "Harry" Lansdale — Lansdale's father.

Sarah "Sadie" Lansdale — Lansdale's mother.

Edward "Ted" Lansdale — Lansdale's older son.

Peter "Pete" Lansdale — Lansdale's younger son.

William Lederer — Navy captain; coauthor of *The Ugly American*.

Henry Cabot Lodge Jr. — U.S. ambassador to Saigon, 1963–64, 1965–67; also U.S. senator, UN ambassador, and Republican vice presidential nominee.

Robert McNamara — Secretary of Defense, 1961–68.

Hank Miller — U.S. Information Agency officer who worked for Lansdale in Vietnam in the mid-1960s.

John W. "Iron Mike" O'Daniel — Chief of the Military Assistance Advisory Group in Saigon, 1954–55.

Edward Philips — Lansdale's grandfather.

Rufus "Rufe" Phillips III — CIA and USAID officer, Lansdale team member.

L. Fletcher Prouty — Former Lansdale aide at the Pentagon who later accused him of complicity in the JFK assassination.

Joseph Redick — CIA linguist who worked for Lansdale in Vietnam in the 1950s and 1960s.

G. Frederick Reinhardt — Ambassador to South Vietnam, 1955–57.

Walt Rostow — Senior JFK and LBJ national security official.

Robert Shaplen — *New Yorker* correspondent, Lansdale friend.

Howard R. Simpson — U.S. information officer in Saigon in the 1950s and 1960s.

Raymond Spruance   Admiral; U.S. ambassador to the Philippines, 1952–55.

David T. Sternberg   Disabled CIA officer who worked for Landsale in the Philippines.

Maxwell Taylor   Army chief of staff, JFK aide, chairman of the Joint Chiefs of Staff, and ambassador to South Vietnam, 1964–65.

John Paul Vann   U.S. military adviser to the South Vietnamese army.

William C. Westmoreland   U.S. military commander in South Vietnam, 1964–68.

Samuel T. "Hanging Sam" Williams   Chief of Military Assistance Advisory Group—Vietnam, 1955–60.

Samuel V. Wilson   Lansdale aide at Pentagon; Special Forces officer.

Frank Wisner   Chief of Office of Policy Coordination, 1948–51; CIA deputy director for operations, 1951–59.

Barry Zorthian   Head of Joint U.S. Public Affairs Office in Saigon, 1964–68.

Any life when viewed from the inside is simply a
series of defeats.

—GEORGE ORWELL[1]

Buddhist monk Thich Quang Duc burns himself to death in Saigon,
June 11, 1963. One of the most famous and influential photographs in
history, it helped to bring down Ngo Dinh Diem. (AP)

The Day of the Dead:
Saigon, November 1–2, 1963

We are launched on a course from which there is no respectable turning back: The overthrow of the Diem government.

—HENRY CABOT LODGE JR.

WHAT caused the tragedy of the Vietnam War? Historians can always point to deep forces to explain that defining event in twentieth-century American history: geography and demography and environment, ideology and economics and sociology, race and class and religion. Implicit is the assumption that whatever happened *must* have happened, that there was no conceivable alternative. Such a deterministic outlook is alluring but ultimately not compelling; it ignores the role of contingency and the impact of decisions made by human and hence fallible historical actors. At various points from 1954 to 1975—from the beginning of America's predominant influence in Indochina to its apogee in the 1960s and its humiliating end—events might very well have taken a different course. There were many turning points along the way. One was especially significant.

When veterans and old-timers, former officials and retired reporters, analysts and historians try to explain how the United States became so deeply embroiled in Vietnam, they often point the finger of blame at one particular twenty-four-hour period: from midday on Friday, November 1, 1963, to midday on Saturday, November 2. What happened in those hours would wind up dashing a vision best enunciated by the American adviser and intelligence officer Edward Lansdale of how Communist advances might be resisted by building up a viable South Vietnamese state that could win the loyalty of its people. The events of November 1–2 opened a Pandora's box of body counts, bombing runs, free-fire zones, and search-and-destroy missions that would lead ultimately to the destruction of South Vietnam along with the presidency of Lyndon Johnson. It would maim the foreign-policy credibility of the Democratic Party, at least temporarily, and terminate the postwar consensus in American foreign policy. More important than anything, it would also lead to the destruction of countless lives, American and Vietnamese, both fighters and (in the case of the Vietnamese) bystanders.

As with many grand historical events that look inevitable only in retrospect, there was scant premonition of what was to come when dawn arrived in Saigon at 5:42 a.m. on November 1, 1963.[1] It was a typically sultry fall morning, a half day off for Catholics to mark All Saints' Day. But since only about 10 percent of South Vietnam's population was Catholic, life for most went on as normal. This city of two million people, then still renowned as the "Paris of the Orient," was, as usual, crowded, noisy, bustling, and odoriferous. Its streets were nearly impassable with the traffic of cars and trucks, ox carts, three-wheeled *cyclopousses* both pedaled and motorized, not to mention armored personnel carriers, jeeps, and other military vehicles. Pedestrians took their lives into their hands whenever they stepped off a sidewalk.

It was not just the traffic but also the sights and sounds that could be overwhelming for an outsider. A newly arrived American, a Navy nurse named Bobbi Hovis, noted that "a curious chorus of voices—high-pitched, strident, and overwhelming to the ear—was ever present, and the chanted, spoken, shaken, rattled and drummed sounds of Saigon identified a distinctive community of vendors."[2] She also identified the noisome odors of the city, much reduced in the modern megalopolis but then quite pungent—a mixture of the fermented fish sauce called *nuoc mam* and the smell of waste, human as well as animal. Given the "almost totally inadequate sanitation facilities," it was common to see people urinating or defecating in the streets. "With the searing sun beating down upon the walls and sidewalks . . . ," Hovis recalled years later, with an almost visible wrinkle of her nose, "much of Saigon took on the odor of an enormous outhouse."[3]

Things were considerably more sedate and less miasmic behind the cream-colored stucco walls of the Gia Long Palace, formerly the residence of the French lieutenant governor of Cochin China (southern Vietnam), where servants bustled along the hushed hallways and French was still the language of choice. Here President Ngo Dinh Diem spent long hours over countless cigarettes and small cups of tea, regaling fidgety visitors with his worldview. Here, too, in a "long, high room full of books and mementoes, with a view over the garden,"[4] his powerful counselor and brother, Ngo Dinh Nhu, unfurled complex conspiracies to protect the embattled regime and strike at its critics. He was assisted in this task by his wife, the attractive and sharp-tongued Madame Nhu. Known as the Dragon Lady to her legions of unadmirers, she favored a beehive hairdo and served as official hostess for the unmarried president.

The very fact that the Ngos were in residence at the Gia Long Palace was a sign of the turmoil afflicting their increasingly isolated, family-dominated regime. (In addition to Ngo Dinh Nhu, two other brothers wielded considerable power: Ngo Dinh Thuc, the archbishop of Hue, and Ngo Dinh Can, the political boss of the central region.) The previous year, two disaffected air force pilots had bombed the Independence Palace, official residence of the presidents of South Vietnam. The entire left wing was demolished. Madame Nhu suffered minor injuries and three staff members were killed, but Diem emerged unscathed. A bomb had penetrated the very room where he was reading but failed to detonate, a piece of good fortune that the devoutly Catholic president ascribed to "divine intervention." Subsequently he and his family were forced to relocate to the Gia Long Palace while the neo-Baroque Independence Palace was torn down and a new, modernist structure was built on the site.

Life had not gotten any easier for the Ngos in 1963. On May 6, the increasingly paranoid Diem had issued an edict banning the public display of religious flags, which, he feared, served to elevate the power of religious groups at the expense of the state. Following the orders of Diem's overzealous brother, Archbishop Thuc, police in Hue began tearing down flags and banners that Buddhists were posting to celebrate the Buddha's 2,527th birthday, Vesak Day. The Buddhists were understandably upset, given that just two days earlier Catholics had paraded with their own banners to honor Thuc's twenty-five years as an archbishop. An angry crowd gathered outside the radio station in downtown Hue on the evening of May 8, 1963. One of their number pulled down the flag of the Republic of Vietnam from the rooftop and replaced it with a Buddhist flag. Other protesters prepared to storm the radio station to force it to play a special message in honor of Vesak. Soldiers and police arrived on the scene, and an angry confrontation ensued. Suddenly there was a loud explosion and gunshots that left nine protesters dead and fourteen wounded. The regime claimed a Communist bomb was responsible, but most observers blamed the security forces. The resulting revulsion against the increasingly authoritarian government was fomented by a minority of militant, urban-based Buddhist monks who accused Diem of anti-Buddhist bias even though the majority of his cabinet members, province chiefs, and generals were Buddhists or Confucians, not Catholics.

The confrontation took a horrifying turn for the worse on June 11. That morning, as a protest against the government, a seventy-three-year-old Buddhist bonze known as Thich Quanc Duc sat down in the lotus position in the middle of a Saigon street while another monk poured gasoline over his head and saffron robe. Then Thich Quanc Duc lit a match and stoically burned to death, never crying out even as his skin blackened and peeled off. Watching this revolting and riveting spectacle was a throng of onlookers, including the Associated Press reporter Malcolm Browne. Tipped off by press-savvy monks, Browne snapped an iconic image of this self-immolation that was transmitted around the world and convinced many, not least in the Kennedy administration, that Diem was locked in an unwinnable confrontation with his country's Buddhist majority that would make it all the harder to resist Communist subversion. Rarely had a single photograph had such a catalyzing effect.

Diem tried to conciliate his Buddhist opponents by guaranteeing them freedom to practice their religion, but he was undermined by the obduracy of the Buddhist hard-liners and of his own brother and sister-in-law. Ngo Dinh Nhu and his wife were convinced, wrongly, that the Buddhist movement was directed by Communist agents,[5] and they were determined to crush the protests by force. Madame Nhu's contemptuous references to the bonze's "barbecue" only exacerbated the confrontation.[6] Adopting the harder line urged by his brother, Diem dispatched his security forces to raid thirty pagodas—out of nearly five thousand in the entire country—that were centers of resistance to his rule. The raids, on the night of August 20–21, led to hundreds of arrests, and they sparked outrage in official American circles. The Kennedy administration, dominated by its own family nexus consisting of the president and the attorney general, wanted Diem to reconcile with the Buddhists, not to confront them—to release all political prisoners, not to round up more of them.

This was the post–World War II era in which the United States, newly emerged as a superpower and embroiled in a high-stakes Cold War, did not long tolerate trouble from small states, whether allies or enemies, without trying to change their leaders, preferably through the use of cloak-and-dagger covert action. The Eisenhower administration had notoriously connived at coups in both Iran (1953) and Guatemala (1954) and, less successfully, in Congo, Iraq, and Indonesia. John F. Kennedy would try to topple Fidel Castro in Cuba, Patrice Lumumba in the Congo, and Rafael Trujillo in the Dominican Republic. Now many of the president's aides had decided that, with his opposition to the Buddhist movement, Diem had made himself a liability in the struggle for freedom. Ironically, they placed their confidence in the

South Vietnamese generals who thought that he had been too soft, rather than too hard, on the Buddhists.

◆

LATE IN the day on Saturday, August 24, 1963, the newly arrived American ambassador in Saigon received an "eyes only" cable from Washington—one of the rare diplomatic messages that can change history. "The US Government cannot tolerate situation in which power lies in Nhu's hands," it said. "Diem must be given chance to rid himself of Nhu and his coterie and replace them with best military and political personalities available. If, in spite of all of your efforts, Diem remains obdurate and refuses, then we must face the possibility that Diem himself cannot be preserved." The cable concluded by granting the ambassador wide latitude to instigate a coup: "You will understand that we cannot from Washington give you detailed instructions as to how this operation should proceed, but you will also know we will back you to the hilt on actions you take to achieve our objectives."[7]

This controversial communiqué had been instigated by an anti-Diem clique at the National Security Council and State Department while President Kennedy and other senior administration officials were away from Washington. On this lazy late-summer weekend, the president, reached at his retreat in Hyannis Port, approved the cable with little debate despite the earlier misgivings of the CIA director, the secretary of defense, and the chairman of the Joint Chiefs of Staff, among others, who were out of touch and not consulted.

The cable's message, however controversial and ultimately counterproductive, found a receptive audience in the stately personage of Henry Cabot Lodge Jr., a patrician New Englander who was a former senator, United Nations ambassador, and Republican vice presidential nominee. On August 22, just a day after the pagoda raids, he had landed at Saigon's Tan Son Nhut Airport[8] to assume the duties of American ambassador at the personal request of his fellow Bostonian (and old political rival) who now occupied the Oval Office. Lodge arrived with his own entourage of journalists and an anti-Diem bias that was only reinforced by the latest crackdown on Buddhist critics.

Far from querying this suggestion to overthrow an allied head of state, Lodge avidly embraced his new role as kingmaker. It was, in fact, a role that he had previously played in American politics as one of the Republican paladins who had persuaded General Dwight D. Eisenhower to seek the presidency in 1952. Lodge had then served as Ike's campaign manager. Having successfully changed America's course, Lodge thought it would be child's play to do the same in the small country—a backward and primitive place, he clearly thought—where he was now posted as the representative of a superpower. Lodge's "frequently pinched nostrils made it seem as if he were constantly smelling something rotten," an American visitor later wrote, and Lodge did not hesitate to clean up the malodorous situation he had now discovered.⁹ He cabled back, "Believe that chances of Diem's meeting our demands are virtually nil. . . . Therefore propose to go straight to general with our demands, without informing Diem."¹⁰ The State Department assented to his suggestion. A few days later, he added, "We are launched on a course from which there is no respectable turning back: The overthrow of the Diem government."¹¹

Lodge was disappointed to learn, however, that for all his encouragement, the generals were not yet up to the job of toppling their head of state—they were too disorganized and too suspicious of one another to carry off the operation in August. And many of them were less enthusiastic about removing Diem than Lodge was. Failing to overthrow Diem, Lodge instead chose to freeze him out.

The two French-speaking mandarins, one from Boston, the other from Hue, had an initial meeting on August 26 at which they wore matching white sharkskin suits. The lanky American towered over the much shorter Vietnamese, symbolically replicating the unequal relationship between their two countries. This conversation was, by Lodge's own account, fairly cordial, with the president engaged in a "remarkable discourse" lasting two hours "about his own family and extent to which Viet-Nam was an underdeveloped country."¹² Their next conversation, which occurred on September 9 and which would represent the last time the two men would speak privately for the next six weeks, was not so cordial. The ambassador presented a peremptory demand that the president remove his autocratic brother, Ngo Dinh Nhu, from the country for at least the next few months and end all censorship of the press, an ultimatum that Diem unsurprisingly rejected. Lodge left fuming about Diem's "medieval view of life" and his lack of interest in Lodge's proposed changes.[13] Thereafter, the two men did not speak, as Lodge pursued a "policy of silence" designed to cause the Ngo dynasty "a certain amount of apprehension" and possibly get them into "the mood to make a few concessions."[14]

The silent treatment was interrupted only by a state dinner at Gia Long Palace on September 29 that Lodge attended along with two distinguished visitors, Secretary of Defense Robert McNamara and General Maxwell Taylor, chairman of the Joint Chiefs of Staff. Diem tried to warm up their frosty relationship by inviting the ambassador to spend the day and night of October 27 at the president's villa in the cool mountain air of Dalat, in the Central Highlands.[15] Diem thought this outing, which included "a sumptuous Vietnamese dinner," signaled a rapprochement with Washington. He had no presentiment that at Tan Son Nhut Airport in Saigon, on his way to Diem's villa, Lodge personally had given Lieutenant General Tran Van Don, a former army chief of staff, his go-ahead to prepare a coup against the president.[16]

Rather than engage with Diem, Lodge and his superiors in Washington preferred to punish him—and the rest of South Vietnam—by cutting off American economic, though not military, aid. This was seen by the South Vietnamese generals as the withdrawal of the "Mandate of Heaven" from Diem, and a sign that his continuance in office would endanger the American aid upon which the entire regime depended for its very survival.[17] Most of President Kennedy's senior advisers remained opposed to a coup—all but Secretary of State Dean Rusk—and the president himself remained skeptical. But not skeptical enough to override Lodge or even order him home. Not only was Lodge the "man on the spot," but he was also a man with a political constituency, one that the president feared could be mobilized against him in 1964. The last thing that Kennedy wanted was to give Lodge cause to run against him as the Republican nominee for president. Lodge was simply too powerful to be fired. And he was too self-confident to be reined in; Henry Kissinger, then a young professor at Harvard, was not alone in thinking him "insufferably arrogant and not very bright."[18] So the ambassador, who was determined to oust Diem at all costs, had his way, notwithstanding the serious doubts in Washington about the course on which he was embarked.

Lodge and Diem met one final time, on the morning of November 1, when Lodge escorted Admiral Harry Felt, the visiting chief of the U.S. Pacific Command, to the Gia Long Palace. The two men, along with aides, saw Diem from 10 a.m. to 11:15. Diem then asked to speak to Lodge alone for twenty minutes. He delivered a conciliatory message that Lodge summed up as: "Tell us what you want and we'll do it."[19]

His entreaty came too late. The cable containing Diem's offer was not dispatched to Washington until 3 p.m. on November 1, 1963. By that time an American-supported coup against Diem was already well under way—an event that would undo everything the Kennedy administration was trying to accomplish in Vietnam and thrust America deeper into the disorienting vortex of a grisly and seemingly interminable guerrilla war.

◆

AT 12:30 p.m. that day, Navy nurse Bobbi Hovis wandered out of the U.S. Naval Station Hospital at 263 Tran Hung Dao in downtown Saigon. Normally this was siesta time in this tropical city, but the streets were abuzz with activity: "Only a hundred yards from me I saw a gun emplacement and barbed-wire barricades. Sandbags surrounded the emplacement, and I found myself staring into the barrels of guns pointing directly at me. Troops were working quickly setting up more concertinas, sandbags, and guns."

The go signal had just been given to various military units commanded by officers who had vowed to overthrow Diem. Vietnamese marines were in the lead, supported by airborne and armored units. Almost the entire panoply of South Vietnam's American-trained armed forces was arrayed against the president, save for the Special Forces and the palace guard. No sooner did the troops enter Saigon than they began attacking in the direction of the well-fortified presidential palace. Standing on a fourth-floor balcony at the hospital, Hovis "had an excellent view of a city about to explode":

> Swarms of bullets flew down the street. Everywhere I looked, I saw tree limbs snapping and flying in all directions. Lead was ricocheting off building walls. People were taking cover in doorways, while others braved exposed balconies and rooftops. If a volley came too close, they scrambled for cover. When the bullets moved out of their immediate range, once again heads popped up. . . .
>
> The noise from the street fighting eventually gave way to the booming explosions of aircraft rockets. American-made T-28 fighter bombers moved in from the south, swooping low over the presidential palace. Green tracers fired from .50 caliber machine guns streaked the horizon. The palace responded with a return of antiaircraft fire, creating black smoke that arose in puffs and spread out against the deep blue sky. . . .
>
> The scene was surrealistic, the illusion of relative safety totally shattered. This was something out of a movie or a book, I thought. It took a few moments for me to adjust to the reality.[20]

What made the unfolding scenario all the more bizarre, although Hovis did not know it at the time, was that the Diem brothers were convinced that the coup was their own handiwork. Too devious for his own good, Nhu had contrived a mock coup, code-named Operation Bravo, that was supposed to smoke out traitors in the ranks. It would then be suppressed by loyal army units that would affirm their loyalty to President Diem and bring him back by popular acclamation. The brothers thus were slow to understand that a real coup was under way, not a stage-managed replica.

When he finally understood that he was under all-out assault by his own army, Diem in desperation telephoned Lodge at 4:30 p.m., wanting to know where the United States stood. By his own account, Lodge smoothly deflected the question with the practiced ease of the veteran politician that he was: "I do not feel well informed to be able to tell you. I have heard the shooting but am not acquainted with all the facts. Also it is 5:30 a.m. in Washington and U.S. government cannot possibly have a view." The short, frustrating phone call ended with the two men talking past each other.

Lodge's final words were, "If I can do anything for your physical safety, please call me."

Diem replied, "I am trying to re-establish order." He then hung up.[21]

Lodge's tone of puzzled innocence was, of course, exceedingly duplicitous. He had been involved every step of the way in encouraging the coup plotters, giving careful direction to the CIA agents who met with the disaffected generals. His chief liaison was Lucien Conein, a French-born CIA officer who had served behind Nazi lines in occupied France and had first come to Indochina in 1945. Conein was famous for his extensive gun collection and for his close contacts with all sorts of Vietnamese characters, ranging from generals to gangsters—categories that were not mutually exclusive. A fellow CIA officer wrote after first meeting him, "Conein impressed me as a dangerous man, a kind of John Dillinger on our side. There was a hint of barely restrained violence about him that his alert, blue eyes under bushy eyebrows, as well as his abrupt, blustery manner and short temper, did nothing to belie."[22]

Conein had been intimately involved in coup plotting since a fateful July 4 meeting with Lieutenant General Tran Van Don. That meeting, like seemingly every other important gathering, had taken place in the Caravelle Hotel, the city's most modern hostelry, opened in 1959 and boasting a top-of-the-line air-conditioning system, a backup generator, vast stretches of marble, and bulletproof glass along with a rooftop terrace bar where at night revelers could watch air strikes in the distance across the Saigon River—"like aristocrats viewing Borodino from the heights," the journalist Michael Herr was to write.[23] The Caravelle became a favorite watering spot for American war correspondents, diplomats, spies, and contractors as well as upper-class Vietnamese of all stripes. (In 1960 a group of anti-Diem activists issued an attack on the president that became known as the Caravelle Manifesto after the place where it was composed.) Subsequent meetings took place at a complicit dentist's office, where both Conein and Don pretended to be patients.[24]

The generals harbored numerous grudges against Diem—but the president's suppression of civil liberties was not one of them. Tran Van Don, for one, was aggrieved that Diem had delayed his formal promotion to lieutenant general until the day after a fellow coup plotter, Duong Van Minh, had been elevated to that rank, thereby vaulting "Big" Minh ahead of him in seniority. Because Diem did not fully trust him, Don was then relieved of his command of I Corps, an important combat command, and given a meaningless post in Saigon as "Commander of the Army," without actual command authority.[25] Another coup plotter, Brigadier General Ton That Dinh, the military governor of Saigon, was upset that the president had refused to appoint him interior minister, a post he coveted.[26] The coup leader, Big Minh, so called because at six feet he was considerably taller than the average Vietnamese, was yet another spurned job seeker. A graduate of the French École Militaire and the U.S. Army's Command and General Staff College in Fort Leavenworth, Kansas, he was described by one American reporter as a "heavy, fierce-looking soldier whose single tooth is a proud badge of the Japanese torture he suffered during World War II."[27] He took command of the conspiracy in large part because, despite his bravery in fighting for Diem against various internal enemies in 1955, the president had removed him from a combat command and made him head of a meaningless "Field Command," which left him with far too much idle time on his hands. As Tran Van Don later acknowledged, "One of Ngo Dinh Diem's greatest errors was to give some of his most efficient and highly regarded generals meaningless jobs. Not only did they become bitter, but they used their time to think, make plans, and perfect strategies."[28]

As soon as the coup started, the generals got word to Lou Conein. The buccaneering CIA man strapped on a .38-caliber revolver and grabbed a brown bag filled with five million piastres (about seven thousand dollars). He then jumped into a jeep driven by a Vietnamese sergeant and raced off to the Joint General Staff Headquarters, leaving behind a U.S. Special Forces team to guard his family from potential retribution by Diem loyalists. Once at the military headquarters, Conein established a secure telephone line to the U.S. embassy, located six blocks from the Gia Long Palace, and spent the rest of the day and night providing play-by-play as the coup unfolded.

Half of the division commanders outside Saigon remained loyal to the president, but they could not move their units to the capital, because the rebels had cleverly blocked the roads and rivers or spirited away needed boats and trucks. The few senior officers who refused to join the uprising were summarily executed by the coup plotters. Few of the ordinary soldiers mobilized against the president knew that they were part of a coup; many were told they were *safeguarding* the president. The biggest obstacle to the rebels' designs was Diem's palace guard, fifteen hundred strong and armed with tanks, artillery, and machine guns. These men fought stubbornly to defend the palace while Diem and his brother sheltered in a bunker beneath the courtyard.

Diem tried phoning the generals, offering to negotiate reforms. He had said the same thing during the last army coup attempt, in 1960. Back then, he had used the delay to bring in loyal army units from outside Saigon to crush the uprising. This time the generals would not fall for the same ruse.

The battle for the palace raged all night beneath a full moon. The flash of guns and the pop of magnesium flares nearly turned darkness into daylight as rebels and loyalists clashed at point-blank range amid narrow alleys and streets. The close-quarters combat seesawed first one way, then the other. Finally, in the early morning hours, after 33 people had been killed and 236 wounded, the defenders waved a white flag. The rebels went inside, expecting to take the president and his brother into custody, only to find that they had disappeared. They had slipped out of the palace the previous night through an unguarded gate, then driven, in a commonplace Citroën 2CV instead of the presidential limousine, to a supporter's house in Cholon, Saigon's sprawling Chinatown. Nhu reportedly had suggested that they split up because the president would have a better chance of escaping without his widely loathed brother, who was seen as the regime's Svengali. But Diem feared that Nhu, if caught by himself, would be executed on the spot. They had ruled together, Diem decided, and now they would flee together.

Around 6:45 a.m., Diem called Lodge to see whether the Americans might be able to do something to help him. Lodge held out the possibility of asylum abroad but refused to do anything to help Diem get there. Lodge's aide, Major General John Michael Dunn, offered to go to Cholon himself to bring the Ngo brothers out. Lodge refused. "We can't," the ambassador said. "We just can't get that involved."[29]

Having nowhere else to turn, Diem called the general staff headquarters to tell the generals that he and his brother were at the caramel-colored Cha Tam Church in Cholon and that they were ready to surrender. At first, Diem demanded full military honors but then settled for a promise of safe passage to exile. Big Minh sent a convoy with American-made jeeps and an M-113 armored personnel carrier to bring the brothers back to headquarters. When the convoy returned at 11 a.m., it brought back both men—but they were no longer breathing.

Minh told Lou Conein that they had committed suicide. As a Catholic, Conein didn't believe it.[30] He immediately understood that they had been killed, and photographs of their corpses confirmed it. Both had been shot in the head with a pistol, and Nhu had also been stabbed multiple times with a bayonet. The tart-tongued Madame Nhu was lucky to escape a similar fate; she was traveling in Beverly Hills, California, with one of her daughters when her husband and brother-in-law were murdered.

The brothers' killer was Captain Nguyen Van Nhung, a bodyguard to Big Minh and a "professional assassin who liked to keep a record of the people he killed by scratching a mark on his pistol for each victim."[31] Before the convoy left for the church, Minh had given a hand signal to Nhung, who had carried out his orders with ruthless efficiency. Neither the president nor his brother had any chance to defend himself; their hands were tied behind their backs when they were murdered. Big Minh had wanted to be sure that Diem would not stage a comeback. He got his wish—and the entire world would have to live with the consequences.

The Diem regime ended, along with the life of its leader and his brother, on the morning of November 2, 1963—All Souls' Day. Or, as it is known in some Catholic cultures, the Day of the Dead.

◆

WHEN WORD of Diem's death reached Washington, President Kennedy was meeting with his senior advisers in the Cabinet Room. The Kennedys over time have acquired a reputation for cultivating a tough-guy persona, but there was nothing hard about the president's reaction to this unexpected news. General Maxwell Taylor wrote, "Kennedy leaped to his feet and rushed from the room with a look of shock and dismay on his face which I had never seen before."[32] Secretary of Defense Robert McNamara confirmed, "When President Kennedy received the news, he literally blanched. I had never seen him so moved."[33] Rather naïvely, Kennedy had not expected that a plot which he had sanctioned would lead to the death of a fellow Catholic president.

Two days later, Kennedy dictated for the record a short memo, not declassified until decades later, in which he confessed, "I was shocked by the death of Diem and Nhu." Kennedy recalled meeting Diem years before in Washington and finding him to be an "extraordinary character." Kennedy privately paid tribute to Diem for the way in which "he held his country together to maintain its independence under very adverse conditions." Kennedy concluded that the "way he was killed" was "particularly abhorrent" and held himself responsible for the coup: "I feel we must bear a good deal of responsibility for it beginning with our cable of early August in which we suggested the coup."[34]

Tragically, JFK was not to live long enough to see for himself the problems caused by Diem's demise. He himself would be felled by an assassin's bullet within three weeks. The new South Vietnamese government, run by a military junta chaired by Big Minh, lasted all of three months. On January 30, 1964, power was seized by another general, Nguyen Khanh, who had played only a minor role in the anti-Diem coup. He, in turn, was forced out the following year. Each time the top man changed, so too did many lower-level officials, including the important provincial and district governors. Prime ministers changed more often than the seasons. By the time that Henry Cabot

Lodge returned to Vietnam in 1965 for his second tour as ambassador, he wrote, "I found the Saigon government in a state of grave instability and turmoil."[35] A small measure of calm was restored shortly thereafter with the ascension of yet another general, Nguyen Van Thieu, who had been part of the anti-Diem coup. At first ruling jointly with Air Vice Marshal Nguyen Cao Ky and then by himself, he would remain in power until 1975, shortly before the destruction of the Republic of Vietnam.

Long before then, South Vietnam's political credibility and governmental effectiveness, already weakening in Diem's final year, had suffered a blow from which it never recovered. The generals who succeeded Diem were just as authoritarian, unpopular, and aloof—and considerably more illegitimate, ineffective, and corrupt. None had much success in dealing with threats ranging from the Buddhists to the Communists. Within four months of Diem's death, more Buddhists had self-immolated than during his entire nine-year reign, but with Diem gone these voluntary autos-da-fé were no longer headline news.[36] The Communists also stepped up their offensive, with the number of attacks in the Mekong Delta soon reaching a new high. A leader of the National Liberation Front, the Communist front organization, called Diem's death a "gift from Heaven for us."[37]

With Communist infiltrations increasing, Diem's emphasis on protecting the rural populace in "strategic hamlets"—a tried-and-true pacification tactic that had worked for the British from the time of the Boer War at the turn of the century to the Malayan "Emergency" in the early 1950s—was set aside in favor of conventional, big-unit operations. The burden of stopping the Communists shifted from the presidential palace in Saigon to the nearby U.S. embassy and the U.S. Military Assistance Command—Vietnam. As the authors of the Pentagon Papers later wrote, "Our complicity in [Diem's] overthrow heightened our responsibilities and our commitment in an essentially leaderless Vietnam."[38] With Communist forces on the offensive, Kennedy's successor, Lyndon B. Johnson, reluctantly decided in 1965 he had no choice but to send American soldiers into combat. Within four years, half a million American troops were trapped in a quagmire. William Colby, a former CIA director and station chief in Saigon, was later to call Diem's overthrow "the worst mistake of the Vietnam War," a judgment shared by both Lyndon Johnson and Richard Nixon,[39] if resisted by other analysts who maintain that the tragedy of America's defeat was inevitable whether Diem remained in power or not.

The course that the United States was now embarked on was not just a mistake; it was a catastrophe that would profoundly alter American foreign policy for decades to come, and it might conceivably have been avoided if only Washington policymakers had listened to the advice of a renowned counterinsurgency strategist who had been present at the creation of the state of South Vietnam. His guidance had been disregarded not only about the wisdom of the Diem coup itself but also, crucially, in the years immediately preceding and following that pivotal event. He had argued, in vain, the need to scale back the amount of firepower expended against the insurgents and to make Saigon's government more accountable, legitimate, and popular to the people it aspired to rule. Victory may have been out of America's grasp in any case; North Vietnam was a formidable foe and South Vietnam a weak ally. But it is no exaggeration to suggest that the whole conflict, the worst military defeat in American history, might have taken a very different course—one that was less costly and potentially more successful—if the counsel of this CIA operative and Air Force officer had been followed.

Who was this singular visionary, this unhonored strategist, this sidelined adviser who wanted to follow, as Robert Frost put it, the road not taken?

His name was Edward Geary Lansdale.

INTRODUCTION

The Misunderstood Man

*There are few individuals in my knowledge more damned and
at the same time applauded. . . . History's going to have to por-
tray Lansdale's real part.*

—Lieutenant General Victor H.
"Brute" Krulak, U.S. Marine Corps[1]

The legendary Edward Lansdale, a covert operative so influential that he was said to be the model for Graham Greene's *The
Quiet American* and for one of the main characters in *The Ugly American*, remains, even more than four decades after the conclusion of the
Vietnam War, one of the most fascinating and mysterious, yet misun-
derstood, figures in post-1945 American foreign policy.

He was portrayed by David Halberstam in his 1969 classic, *The
Best and the Brightest*, as a "particularly futile and failed figure": a "classic Good Guy, modern, just what Kennedy was looking for," who
"allegedly knew and loved Asians" but "talked vague platitudes one step
away from the chamber of commerce." In Halberstam's telling, he was
an expert on "how to fight guerrilla wars the right way" who became
"part of a huge American mission which used bombing and artillery
fire against Vietnamese villages."[2] Stanley Karnow, in his 1983 *Viet-*

nam: A History, drew Lansdale in equally unflattering hues as "a deceptively mild, self-effacing former advertising executive," an ineffectual "romantic" who "overlooked the deeper dynamics of revolutionary upheavals" and who "seemed to be oblivious to the social and cultural complexities of Asia."[3] Tim Weiner, in his Pulitzer Prize–winning 2007 book, *Legacy of Ashes: The History of the CIA*, was more scathing still, deriding Lansdale as a "Madison Avenue . . . con man" who dreamed up impractical schemes to overthrow Fidel Castro.[4] By contrast, Neil Sheehan, in another Pulitzer Prize–winning volume, *A Bright Shining Lie: John Paul Vann and America in Vietnam* (1988), lauded Lansdale as a Machiavellian genius, a "legendary clandestine operative" who ruthlessly and effectively bulldozed opposition to Ngo Dinh Diem in order to consolidate the nascent state of South Vietnam. Sheehan wrote with what some might consider flattering exaggeration: "South Vietnam, it can truly be said, was the creation of Edward Lansdale."[5]

Taking up the theme of Lansdale as a "dirty tricks" specialist, the late L. Fletcher Prouty, a retired Air Force colonel who had once worked for Lansdale at the Pentagon, went so far as to suggest that he was part of a right-wing conspiracy that was responsible for the murder of John F. Kennedy.[6] These sinister animadversions were picked up by the director Oliver Stone in his conspiratorially themed 1991 film, *JFK*, which features a shadowy Lansdale stand-in referred to only as General Y running the assassination on behalf of the "military-industrial complex."

This is symptomatic of the long concatenation of misunderstanding and misinformation that still clouds Lansdale and his legacy. His was an epochal, if ultimately tragic, story—one that sheds considerable light not only on the course of the Vietnam War, a conflict whose bitter legacy still haunts American foreign policy, but also on such vital issues as how the United States can effectively fight insurgencies abroad, how it can deal with autocratic allies, and how it can most effectively dispense military and political advice to foreign partners of dubious reliability. But Lansdale's struggles and achievements, while important to postwar history and relevant to contemporary debates, remain but dimly understood.

Halberstam, Karnow, Sheehan, and Weiner were—and, in the case of the latter two, still are—superb journalists and historians, but none has captured the totality of Ed Lansdale, and, by extension, of this particular part of the Vietnam War itself. The accounts of the first three were circumscribed because the authors knew Lansdale only in the 1960s, a frustrating decade for him, not at the peak of his effectiveness in the 1950s. The time is right, then, for a deeper look at Lansdale, one that is intended to do for him what Sheehan so memorably accomplished for John Paul Vann in *A Bright Shining Lie* or what Barbara Tuchman so effectively did for General "Vinegar Joe" Stillwell in *Stillwell and the American Experience in China*.

Like those earlier works, *The Road Not Taken* is meant to be not only a biography of a pivotal, yet strangely unknown, figure; it is also a work of history with often surprising diplomatic, political, and military implications that seeks to recast our understanding of recent American history—and, indeed, of contemporary American policy debates. As the subtitle suggests, this book is concerned both with Lansdale *and* with the "American tragedy in Vietnam," but in order to understand his impact on Vietnam, one must first appreciate what he did elsewhere, not only in the Philippines, where he served prior to arriving in Saigon in 1954, but also in "the Washington jungle," where he struggled to make a mark in the eight years, 1957 to 1965, between his two Vietnam tours.

◆

THE STARTING point for this examination must be to clear away the mythology that surrounds Lansdale and obscures his real legacy. He was, for a start, almost certainly not the model for the young American intelligence operative Alden Pyle in *The Quiet American* (1955); Greene wrote a draft of his novel before Lansdale had even arrived in Saigon. Yet the identification of Lansdale as "the Quiet American" adheres like indelible ink, because the views that Greene ascribes to Alden Pyle are an identifiable caricature of the views held by Lansdale. He *was* the model for Colonel Edwin B. Hillandale, practically the only admirable character in Eugene Burdick and William Lederer's scathing indictment of U.S. foreign policy, *The Ugly American* (1958), but unlike the fictional Hillandale, the real-life Lansdale did not speak Tagalog or any other foreign language. More importantly, Lansdale was not, as he has so often been depicted, an inveterate practitioner of, or advocate for, assassinations and "dirty tricks." In fact, although he had a weakness for fanciful propaganda coups, such as hiring an astrologer to predict a bleak future for North Vietnam, he was deeply suspicious of most covert action, seeing it as a shortcut designed to deal with deep-rooted problems that demanded a political, not a military, solution. And, as this book will show, he had no connection with the assassination of President Kennedy, a charge that is nothing short of historical blasphemy, for the thirty-fifth president was a man he worked for, admired, and respected.

The very fact that Lansdale is even mentioned in connection with a supposed right-wing plot to kill the president, credible evidence of which has never come to light, is symptomatic of how little he is understood still. What motive would the military and CIA have had to kill Kennedy? Conspiracy-mongers most often claim it was either revenge because Kennedy didn't do enough to support the Bay of Pigs invasion or an act of preemptive warmongering because Kennedy wanted to pull American troops out of Vietnam. What Kennedy would have done had he lived is unknowable, and there is still much debate among historians about whether he was serious about downsizing the U.S. military commitment to South Vietnam. But of one thing there can be no doubt: Lansdale was not an advocate for a larger U.S. military presence in Indochina. He argued that the American emphasis should be on building up legitimate, democratic, and accountable South Vietnamese institutions that could command the loyalty of the people, and he thought that sending large formations of American ground troops was a distraction from, indeed a hindrance to, achieving that all-important objective. As for the Bay of Pigs, Lansdale had never been a fan of the operation in the first place. He wanted to oust Castro not with a D-Day-style invasion staged by exiles but rather by fomenting a popular internal uprising, a strategy that was very much in keeping with his philosophy.

Contrary to the journalistic clichés, Lansdale was neither a "dirty tricks" artist nor an unworldly dreamer, neither Machiavellian mastermind nor arch-bumbler. He was an idealist and realist both—a canny strategist who recognized the need both for tough military action against insurgents and for political and social action designed to address the roots of an uprising. The doctrine of "Lansdalism," as his teachings were labeled by some journalists, was founded on the bedrock of the Declaration of Independence and the Bill of Rights. He believed that the "basic political ideas" set out in those documents would have far more appeal in Asia than either colonialism or communism—and could help cement alliances between the United States and Third World peoples struggling for self-rule. His ideas were ridiculed at the time by self-styled sophisticates such as Graham Greene, but they look more credible when seen from the vantage point of the twenty-first century, when democracy has spread across Asia to such disparate lands as Japan, South Korea, Taiwan, Indonesia, Malaysia, Burma, and Nepal.

The larger implications are obvious—and they make *The Road Not Taken* more than just one man's story. Lansdale's yin-yang approach, of hunting down guerrillas and terrorists while trying to attract the support of the uncommitted, is the basis of modern "population-centric" counterinsurgency doctrine as applied by the United States in Iraq and Afghanistan, by Britain in Northern Ireland, by Colombia against the FARC, by Israel in Lebanon, the West Bank, and Gaza, and by many other countries with varying degrees of success. The most commonly cited influences on counterinsurgency thinking include David Galula of France, Robert Thompson and Gerald Templer of Great Britain, and David Petraeus of the United States. But Lansdale was fighting insurgents as early as any of them—first in the 1950s in the Philippines, where he helped to put down the Huk Rebellion, and then in South Vietnam, where, even if he did not create the state, he helped to consolidate its authority in its uncertain early days.

Lansdale was a master of political warfare and propaganda whose tactics in fighting global communism could, I propose, usefully be studied by officials today fighting global jihadism. He was also one of the most storied military and political advisers in history. Among twentieth-century advisers, his influence was rivaled only by that of T. E. Lawrence, and his example is arguably more important for the present day because, while "Lawrence of Arabia" was an insurgent, Lansdale was a counterinsurgent par excellence. His practices could be emulated by contemporary advisers in countries ranging from Mali to Mexico.

Lansdale's greatest gift was for establishing a rapport with foreigners even if he did not speak their language. His close connection with President Ramon Magsaysay of the Philippines and President Ngo Dinh Diem of South Vietnam was crucial to all that he accomplished in those countries—and stands in stark contrast to the inability of subsequent American representatives to establish ties of trust with leaders not only in the Philippines and South Vietnam but also, in the modern age, in Iraq and Afghanistan. One of the great failures of post-9/11 American foreign policy was the inability to deal adequately with Hamid Karzai and Nouri al-Maliki, who were installed as president of Afghanistan and prime minister of Iraq, respectively, by the United States and its partners and then grew so estranged from the United States that many in Washington came to see them as the chief obstacles to American success. The frustrating U.S. experience in Afghanistan and Iraq, with its uncanny and disturbing echoes of America's relations with Diem–era South Vietnam, might have taken a different course if U.S. ambassadors and commanders had studied Lansdale and his techniques for winning the trust, and shaping the policies, of foreign leaders.

In the final analysis, however, Lansdale's story was more sanguinary than sanguine and some of his most valuable lessons are ultimately cautionary. His experience shows how difficult it can be to apply counterinsurgency theory in practice and how hard it is to move a giant bureaucracy such as the U.S. government, which too often is driven by internal imperatives to follow self-destructive policies. In fact, Lansdale was truly "the American T. E. Lawrence." Like his eccentric and rebellious predecessor, whose dreams of Arab nationhood were suborned by British and French imperialists, Lansdale ended his days with a haunting sense of failure.

◆

LANSDALE'S IMPROBABLE saga—the story of how this laid-back advertising man from California became a guerrilla-warfare guru, covert-action specialist, and one of the most unconventional generals in the nation's history—has been told before but only in broad brushstrokes and never with the kind of accuracy, detail, in-depth knowledge, and context so pivotal and intriguing a figure demands. He has been the subject of a biography by the army chaplain and college professor Cecil Currey and of an academic monograph by the historian Jonathan Nashel, in addition to numerous descriptions in larger volumes devoted to the Vietnam War, the Philippines, the CIA, Fidel Castro, the Kennedy assassination, and other topics—including this author's own *Invisible Armies: An Epic History of Guerrilla Warfare from Ancient Times to the Present.* Lansdale, moreover, published an engaging, if evasive, memoir of his experiences in the Philippines and Vietnam between 1950 and 1956, and his close associate Rufus Phillips published a more complete account of their work together in Vietnam. Yet no book or article has ever given Lansdale adequate credit for his pioneering role in the history of counterinsurgency, for his prescient advice to policymakers during the Vietnam War, or for the applicability of his teachings in a new era of advisory work for the U.S. and allied militaries. Lansdale's legacy stands as a rebuke both to anti-interventionists who assume that fragile states should stand or fall on their own and to arch-hawks who believe that massive commitments of American military forces are necessary to win any war.

The Road Not Taken is based on a thorough review of the relevant documents, many of them unavailable to any previous writer. The most important of these new sources are letters written by Lansdale to his first wife, Helen (provided to the author by their son Pete Lansdale), and to his longtime mistress and second wife, Pat (provided by her granddaughter Patricia Pelaez-Yi), which cast a fresh and unexpected light on some of his most consequential decisions, such as his return to the Philippines for a second, history-altering tour in 1950. I am the first person after Lansdale himself who has ever read both sets of letters, to Helen and to Pat, many of them written contemporaneously. Together, they provide the most intimate and complete account that will ever be available of Lansdale's thinking—and they reveal the hitherto unrevealed importance of his love affair with Pat to the narrative of his life. I was also given access for the first time to family correspondence between Lansdale and his brothers (thanks to his niece Ginger Brodie), which provides fresh information about their upbringing, including their father's shocking (and hitherto unknown) abandonment of their mother, which occurred when Lansdale was but a young man.

These personal missives, which show the inner man, are an invaluable supplement to Lansdale's official papers and the papers of those he worked with, many of them newly declassified. Once-secret documents obtained by the author provide more information than ever before available about Lansdale's role in such crucial events as the 1953 Philippine election, which made his close friend Ramon Magsaysay president, the creation of the state of South Vietnam in 1954–56, and Operation Mongoose in 1961–62 to oust Fidel Castro. Among the most important of these documents is the full report of his Saigon Military Mission from 1954 to 1955, roughly a fourth of which was excerpted by the *New York Times* in 1971 along with the Pentagon Papers but the full text of which, amounting to fifty-six pages, was not declassified until 2014. The full text of the Pentagon Papers itself, some seven thousand pages in all, was not released until 2011.

To ferret out the full written record—or as much of it as possible— the author has reviewed documents from more than thirty archives in four countries across three continents. Many archival requests uncovered unexpected treasures. In late March 2015, for example, I found myself sitting in the spacious, sunlit reading room of the U.S. National Archives in Maryland, poring over Lansdale's voluminous office files from the Department of Defense in 1960–61. I was holding the actual documents left in their original manila folders by Lansdale's own secretary. Those files had been declassified and made available to researchers for the first time just the previous day.

To supplement the written record, the author has walked in Lansdale's footsteps. In both Vietnam and the Philippines, I have visited many of the places where he made his reputation, from the still-bustling streets of Manila and Saigon (now Ho Chi Minh City) to important locations in the provinces, such as the "Holy See" of the Cao Dai religion in Tay Ninh Province, which looks much as it did when Lansdale first moved to Vietnam in 1954. I have seen for myself the countryside of both countries, where rice farmers continue to eke out a living as their ancestors had done in Lansdale's day—and since time immemorial. Mount Arayat in Luzon and Dien Bien Phu in northern Vietnam are by and large quiet today, eerily so, but in Lansdale's time they were abattoirs where Communist and anti-Communist troops fought to the death. Visiting such remote locales gave me a sense of the challenges of topography and weather that confronted combatants on both sides, along with a sense of atmosphere that informs the following account.

My work in the archives and in the field was supplemented by a careful reading of the latest academic literature and interviews with numerous individuals who knew Lansdale. These included Americans such as the Pentagon Papers leaker Daniel Ellsberg; the former ambassador Frank Wisner, son of a legendary CIA figure who mentored Lansdale; the former CIA director John Deutch, whose father also worked with Lansdale; Lansdale's own sons, Pete and Ted, and their wives, Carolyn and Carol; Pat Kelly's grandchildren, Patricia Pelaez-Yi, Leah Pelaez-Ramos, Manny Pelaez, and Francisco Kelly; and the retired covert operatives Victor Hugo, Richard Smith, Jerry French, Calvin Mehlert, and Samuel Wilson, all of whom once worked for Lansdale. In addition, I also sought out former aides to Presidents Ngo Dinh Diem and Nguyen Van Thieu who sat down with me in their exile in California, Maryland, and Virginia, and Filipinos such as Frisco San Juan and Ramon Magsaysay Jr. who sat down with me in Manila. Many of them spoke to a historian for the first time, thanks to the invaluable help provided to me by Rufus Phillips, a former CIA officer who was one of Lansdale's closest associates and who served as head of rural pacification programs in South Vietnam in the early 1960s. "Rufe" spent countless hours with me, both in person and via email, to set me straight about myriad matters big and small.

What I have found is that some of the tales of Lansdale's successes, as told by previous authors—successes such as installing Ramon Magsaysay as defense minister of the Philippines in 1950, or luring the chief subordinates of South Vietnam's army chief of staff out of the country in 1954 before they could carry out a coup against Ngo Dinh Diem—do not bear close scrutiny. Too many chroniclers have taken at face value Lansdale's own, embellished accounts of his deeds when responsibility should more accurately be spread to include other pivotal actors. But while *The Road Not Taken* debunks some of Lansdale's supposed achievements, it also controverts those who claimed that he was naïve or ill-informed, a credulous huckster bent on uncritically imposing American concepts on foreign societies he did not understand. Lansdale was a close student of both the Philippines and Vietnam, the two countries where he primarily operated. Far from being ignorant, he was a shrewd observer and operator who understood more than he often let on—and more than many of his critics did. Indeed, the kind of detailed, on-the-ground knowledge that he acquired should serve as a model for other soldiers, intelligence officers, journalists, aid officials, and diplomats who are dispatched to foreign lands.

The Road Not Taken is not meant to be a brief for or against Lansdale, nor for or against the big causes—counterinsurgency and nation building, intelligence gathering and covert action, the Vietnam War and the Huk Rebellion, the Cold War and the secret war on Fidel Castro—with which he is forever associated. It is intended, rather, to be a sympathetic, but dispassionate, account that will give a new generation of readers a better appreciation for Lansdale's wisdom, as well as for his shortcomings and blind spots, to better understand his counterinsurgency era and our own.

PART ONE

AD MAN

(*1908–1945*)

Lansdale (head down) and colleagues at the Theodore
Segall Advertising Agency in San Francisco, c. 1940. (RSPP)

1

In Terrific Flux

At all times and under all circumstances overcome evil with good.

—HARRY LANSDALE, QUOTING MARY BAKER EDDY

A T the turn of the twentieth century, the United States had just begun to assume a leading role on the world stage and, in particular, in Asia, where Edward Lansdale would spend most of his storied, if not unblemished, career. America's growing military might was heralded by the Great White Fleet—sixteen new battleships, their hulls painted a glistening white—which departed on March 16, 1907, on a circumnavigation of the world. The battlewagons' progress out of their anchorage at Hampton Roads, Virginia, noted a reporter, was marked by "the glistening of spotless hulls, the curl of foam-crested bow waves, the cheering of sailors afloat and friends ashore, [and] the breeze-blown strains of 'Auld Lang Syne' floating across the waters." The spectacle was a thrilling one for a former assistant secretary of the navy attired in "top hat, frock coat, striped trousers" as he paced across the deck of the presidential yacht, the *Mayflower*. Theodore Roosevelt was positively bursting with pride. "Did you ever see such a fleet? Isn't it magnificent? Oughtn't we all feel proud?" he exclaimed to the gathered dignitaries, adding for good measure that the enlisted men were "perfectly bully."[1]

The battleships and their "bully" sailors were still making their way up the Pacific coast of South America when on February 6, 1908, in far-off, landlocked Detroit, Edward G. Lansdale emerged into the world, a child of the nascent American Century. "Teddy" Lansdale obviously was too small to be aware at the time of the naval voyage ordered by another Teddy; the Great White Fleet would return to Hampton Roads on February 22, 1909, when he was just a year old. But like other American boys of his generation, he would have imbibed, along with his Cream of Wheat and Grape Nuts, a sense that American power was spreading to every corner of the globe like milk filling up a bowl of cereal.

The inexorable growth of American military might was hardly the only change that Edward Lansdale observed during the years of his youth. He came into the world just as the Wild West outlaws Robert Leroy Parker ("Butch Cassidy") and Harry Longabaugh ("the Sundance Kid") were dying in a shoot-out in rural Bolivia, and just as the first Model T, the automobile of the masses, was rolling off an assembly line in Detroit. Both were small but significant symbols of the transition from the old America to the new—from a land of pioneers seeking their fortune on the lawless frontier to a country of cities and suburbs, factories and offices, managers and employees. As Jack London wrote in *The Iron Heel*, a dystopian novel published in 1908, the year of Lansdale's birth, "Never in the history of the world was society in so terrific flux as it is right now. The swift changes in our industrial system are causing equally swift changes in our religious, political, and social structures. An unseen and fearful revolution is taking place in the fiber and structure of society."[2]

Edward Lansdale was in many ways a rather typical product of early twentieth-century, middle-class America, a society struggling to cope with this "fearful" transformation that was just beginning. There was nothing elite about him: unlike the "Wise Men," as the leading shapers of postwar American foreign policy came to be known, Lansdale was not a product of a New England prep school and the Ivy League; he would never work at an investment bank or a white-shoe law firm. His background was much more ordinary—middle-class, decidedly not upper crust. His childhood years were spent mainly in Detroit and Los Angeles, far from the corridors of what would become known as the Eastern Establishment. Like many other men of his generation, he grew up proud of his country, reluctant to speak about himself, more interested in work than in family, a chain smoker and a regular drinker, a firm believer in the value of self-reliance and assiduous toil. And yet there were aspects of his character—including his outspoken aversion to authority, his extreme informality, his embrace of "the Orient," his rejection of the racism so prevalent in American society—that set him apart from his peers. There is seldom a straight line between childhood influences and adult behaviors, but there are clues in Lansdale's upbringing to explain the man he became—and the impact he exercised on America's deepening involvement in Asia.

◆

ON HIS father's side, Edward Lansdale could trace his family's roots in America back to late seventeenth-century Maryland, specifically to Montgomery County, close to what would become the District of Columbia. The family surmised that their ancestors had come originally from north Lancashire, England, where "Lansdale" and such variations as "Lonsdale," meaning "of Lunesdale" or the vale of the Lune River, are common place-names and family names. Edward was one of four children, all boys, born to the peripatetic automotive executive Henry Lansdale and his homemaker wife, Sarah, whose own family had arrived from England far more recently and had settled in the West. The oldest of the siblings was Henry Philips (later simply Phil), who was born in 1906, eighteen months before "Teddy" (Ed's childhood nickname).[3] The younger boys were Benjamin Carroll, born in 1909, thirteen months after Ed, and David Brooke, the baby of the family, born in 1916, eight years after Ed.

A major influence on their development was their maternal grandfather, Edward Philips, a legendary, Horatio Alger–type figure in the family. Born in England in 1850, he left home around age nine following the death of his father, a physician. His impoverished mother could not support her brood, forcing Edward, like Oliver Twist, to scrape a living on the streets of London's East End. As a teenager, he enlisted in the British army, but he did not like the onerous and brutal service, and so he deserted and made his way to the "land of opportunity." He started off in Cleveland, where census records show him in residence by 1870 as an ironworker.

It was probably in Cleveland that he met and married Sarah Adelaide Walker, who would become Ed Lansdale's grandmother. By 1879, Ed and Sarah Philips, like an increasing number of newcomers, had made their way to California. After unsuccessful stints panning for gold in the Yukon and ranching in northern California, Edward Philips settled in San Francisco, where he made a fortune helping to rebuild the city after the great earthquake and fire of 1906. Once a penniless orphan, Edward Philips died in 1930 a wealthy man.[4]

Grandfather Philips was a pugnacious, charming, and sometimes infuriating character who had no patience for the hypocritical conventions of polite society. Phil Lansdale recalled that he was an "extreme extrovert" who "tackled life with explosive energy." He was also "semi-literate," and liked to appall his daughter, Phil's mother, by telling her "not just vulgar jokes but filthy jokes."[5]

Edward Lansdale inherited a "spirit of independence and wild humor" from his grandfather.[6] He did not, however, follow his grandfather into the business world as his siblings did. His older brother, Phil, started his own advertising agency in Orange County, California, and later the nationwide chain 4-Day Tire Stores, becoming a multimillionaire. His younger brother Ben was a brilliant engineer who wound up owning a more modest automotive wholesale business in Sunnyvale, California, while the still younger David Lansdale spent his entire career as a midlevel manager with Scott Paper Company, manufacturers of toilet paper and tissues.

Ed, for his part, would show indifference to moneymaking throughout his life, choosing instead to pursue advancement in a less remunerative but even more cutthroat business—counterinsurgency—in which he would preach ideals of brotherly love at odds with his grandfather's self-centered outlook. But, in a paradox that would define his personality, he would not be above employing ruthless tactics that Edward Philips, a hard-nosed businessman, would have approved of.

◆

BY CONTRAST with Grandfather Philips, who, according to Phil Lansdale, "was unable to complete a sentence without a four-letter word or three,"[7] Ed Lansdale's father, Henry (known as Harry), was a straight arrow. Phil recalled that he saw their father, a devout Christian Scientist, swear and take a drink only once in his entire life. "Dad dressed immaculately and his language was immaculate," Phil later wrote.[8]

The son of a plumber in Washington, D.C., Harry had dropped out of Business High School in the District of Columbia after just two years (1897–99) to support himself, employing the shorthand he had learned in school to work as a clerk and stenographer. He received his first big break in 1903, at age twenty, when he was hired as secretary to the brilliant and mercurial John H. Patterson, founder of National Cash Register—still in business today as NCR, a computer maker. Harry's brief career at National Cash Register ended abruptly in 1906 when Patterson demanded to know how long he had been working there. "Three years," the young man replied. "That's long enough," said Patterson, and fired him on the spot.[9] (Thomas J. Watson Sr., who would become the first great CEO of IBM, would be cashiered by Patterson seven years later in similarly abrupt fashion.)

In 1905, the year before he was fired, Harry married Edward Philips's daughter Sarah (known as Sadie), whom he had met while she was living with relatives in Washington. Now he was out of work and had a wife and his first son to support. Desperate for a job, Harry found employment working for Harry Leland, founder of the Cadillac Automobile Company. He was still working at Cadillac when Ed was born. But he would not stay long. Over the next quarter century the peripatetic Harry Lansdale would move from one automotive firm to another, many of them, such as Krit and Hare's Motors, now long forgotten. Ironically Harry did not enjoy steady success until the Great Depression, helping in the 1930s to form the National Automotive

Parts Association, better known as NAPA Auto Parts, which he would run as general manager and vice president until his retirement in 1955.

"We never knew," Ed Lansdale was to say, "whether we were going to be rich or poor next week."[10] As boys, Ed and his brothers knew what it was like to be an outsider, because the fluctuations of their father's career kept the family moving from one part of the country to another at a time when regional variations were much greater than they became after the advent of superhighways, television, and chain stores.

◆

THE FIRST "horseless carriage" appeared on the streets of Detroit in 1894—a rickety vehicle with no top and no hood and an average speed of seven miles per hour. Its designer and builder, Charles B. King, shocked the public with his bold prediction that these contraptions would "in time supersede the horse."[11] That day was to arrive sooner than all but a few dreamers could have imagined. By 1916, when Teddy Lansdale was an eight-year-old boy living in Detroit, the city was home to thirty-five factories supplying over half the world's automobiles.[12]

The Lansdale family lived in Highland Park, a municipality enclosed by the city of Detroit, located only six miles from downtown. It was a rough, blue-collar neighborhood where Teddy stood out in his fancy, middle-class wardrobe, which made him look, he said, like a "Little Lord Fauntleroy." When young Teddy had to walk to school in Highland Park in his velvet suit sewn by his mother's sister, Aunt Adelaide, past Eastern European autoworkers and their families, each block was a fight for survival.[13] "I was barely large enough," he recalled, "to hold up the lid of an ash can as a shield in the boyhood gang tussles on the streets, which started with rocks, then progressed to . . . 'bee-bee guns.'"[14]

◆

TEDDY LANSDALE was just as much of an outsider in the family's next destination—Bronxville, the suburban "village" in Westchester County, New York, where the family lived from 1920 to 1922. Anxious to preserve its status as "the most desired residential village near New

York City," as the local newspaper called it, Bronxville welcomed only white, native-born Christians. Houses were typically sold with "gentlemen's agreements" designed to keep Jews and Negroes from moving in. Among the wealthy families lured by Bronxville's appeal were the Kennedys, who moved there in 1929, to a brick mansion on a six-acre estate, when the future president was twelve years old.[15]

Moving to this small, homogenous suburb from polyglottal Detroit must have been quite jarring. One of Teddy's few memories of this town, where he lived from the ages of eleven to thirteen, was that he was set upon by a gang of more privileged kids from a nearby private school. To escape, he ran into the Lansdale yard, where he and his older brother Phil returned fire with "snow rocks"—rocks encased in snow and ice to look like snowballs. "Their iced snowballs stung," Ed later wrote. "Our iced rocks stunned." The attackers beat a hasty retreat before this tactical escalation, which showed that Lansdale could already be ruthless when the occasion called for it.[16]

◆

YOUNG LANSDALE, by then known as Ed rather than Teddy, continued to stand out just as much when he moved to Los Angeles in 1922, wearing his East Coast, baggy-kneed "knickers"—which the other kids at his junior high school considered effeminate, or "sissy," attire[17]—but he would soon become a quintessential Californian.

L.A.'s population would swell from 576,763 in 1920 to 1.5 million in 1940, not counting what a guidebook described as a "large transient population of tourists, job-hunters, climate-seekers, elderly retired persons and Hollywood hopefuls." Newcomers were attracted not just by economic opportunity—by the chance to find a good job and buy a home of one's own—but also by the lure of warm weather, free beaches, and palm trees and aromatic orange groves. Lacking established social structures, Los Angeles was unusually open to ideas, good and bad, to original thinkers and hucksters alike. As a guidebook gushed, it presented "a new sense of freedom" that would tempt newcomers to sample "new pleasures, new habits of living, new religions." Lansdale imbibed this "sense of freedom" as he was growing up; it helped to mold his conviction that, with his guidance, foreign lands could shake off the constraints of history as easily as his hometown had done.

Los Angeles also served to shape Lansdale's predilection for breezy manners and open-neck clothes instead of the more constricting suits and military uniforms most of his contemporaries were wearing and the more stuffy, formal way in which they typically behaved. Los Angeles, after all, was a place where, as a guidebook noted, "boys blaze forth in multihued silk shirts" and "men go hatless, women stocking-less." Lansdale would grow up to become a quintessential maverick who, long before the birth of Bill Gates or Steve Jobs, developed an aversion not just to wearing neckties but also to the regimentation that formal business attire denoted.

◆

WHEN HE was a boy, Ed's interest in American history was fired by his father, who recalled as they watched a parade of returning World War I veterans "what his great aunt had told him about seeing her grand-father march with other Revolutionary veterans when she was a little girl. It sound[ed] to me like some recent yesterday, as did other family comments of, 'Oh, yes, he was the one who fought at Yorktown.'"[18] Looking back on his long-ago boyhood, the elderly Ed Lansdale noted that such remarks "telescoped our country's history for me in an inti-mate and wondrous way, bringing our first Fourth of July up until it seemed almost yesterday."[19]

Although he appreciated history, Ed was an indifferent student. He especially struggled with foreign languages—an ironic handicap for someone who later became renowned for his understanding of foreign societies. But like his father, he loved to read, especially pulp novels by Edgar Rice Burroughs and Zane Grey. His reading, however, extended well beyond these juvenile favorites. His most cherished tomes were a "collection of writings from the American Revolution . . . bound in green suede leather." Most likely he was reading the nine volumes of *American Archives*, a compilation of the writings of the Founding Fathers published between 1837 and 1853. From its pages, Lansdale developed a devotion to the Revolutionary firebrands Samuel Adams and Thomas Paine, both masters of the art of propaganda that he would later practice in both its civilian guise of "advertising" and its military version, "psychological warfare."[20]

Lansdale would often cite a celebrated, if likely apocryphal, exchange between Thomas Paine and Benjamin Franklin. "Where liberty is, there is my country," said Franklin. Paine supposedly replied, "Where is not liberty, there is mine."[21] Paine's words formed Lansdale's personal credo, while the Declaration of Independence, which Paine advocated and Adams signed, would form the intellectual heart of his counterinsurgency doctrine.[22]

His embrace of the Founding Fathers can be seen as his reaction to the "terrific flux" of American society in the early years of the twentieth century. Some would react to this great dislocation by adopting new philosophies such as progressivism, socialism, fascism, or communism; others, by reasserting religious faith. Neither a communist nor an active Christian, Lansdale would be guided by a personal doctrine of "Americanism" that he traced back to the verities of the Revolutionary generation.

◆

A FIRM belief in Horatio Alger–like individualism and self-help, which was typical of self-made men in those pre–welfare state days, was inculcated into all of the Lansdales. As a businessman used from an early age to supporting himself, Harry did not believe in providing his boys with an allowance. He forced Edward and his brothers to do chores such as washing the dishes and to take jobs such as delivering newspapers to earn spending money and even to buy their own clothes. As a demonstration of their father's insistence on self-reliance, Phil Lansdale recalled how his father taught him to swim on Maceday Lake, northwest of Detroit: "He walked out to the end of the pier. He pushed me in the lake, and walked back into the house." Phil "learned how to swim instantly but . . . wouldn't speak to Dad for weeks."[23]

It was not just his father who set an example for Edward Lansdale of how to be "independent" and how to "stand on your own"—lessons that would prove valuable when he was dispatched later in life with little preparation or institutional support to unfamiliar societies.[24] So did his mother Sarah, Edward Philips's daughter, a warm-natured woman who did not have much education but who was a resourceful homemaker and a doting parent.[25] At a time when women were just being given the right to vote and women drivers were still a rarity, she would race trolley cars in her single-cylinder Cadillac and think nothing of driving thousands of miles with her sons from the East Coast, when the family lived there, to visit her native California in the summer.[26] Sadie Lansdale was a much more steady presence in her boys' lives than their hardworking father, who was seldom home. She passed along a healthy dose of self-confidence to her boys. "She was absolutely convinced," Ben Lansdale wrote, "that they were the smartest of all children, good in every way, and with the ability to accomplish whatever they set out to do."[27]

Sadie was also an amateur painter, a hobby that Ed picked up. Ben, who drew too, said his brother was "a very good amateur artist" whose "pictures were dynamic, quite unlike the wooden, static things I painted." As an adult, Lansdale would produce sketches and paintings that he would give away as a mark of friendship.

Another Lansdale ploy would be to play the harmonica in order to break down barriers with skeptical Asians—a practice made famous by *The Ugly American*, which has the Lansdale stand-in, Colonel Edwin B. Hillandale, using his mouth organ to charm Filipinos in the provinces and, back in Manila, joining in late-night jam sessions with a dance band, "playing his harmonica close to the mike, improvising like Satchmo himself."[28] It was Lansdale's father who first taught him to play the harmonica. His mother thought, his brother Ben recalled, that "it would be nice if we boys learned to play musical instruments a little more highly toned." Ed studied violin with an instructor, but "he never really got his heart into it and consequently never became a very accomplished player."[29] Later, the harmonica sometimes would be the only weapon Lansdale carried.

◆

RELIGION PLAYED a significant role in Lansdale's upbringing. Sarah Lansdale had been raised a Protestant, Harry a Catholic. They had been married in a Protestant ceremony, but both converted at some point early in their marriage to a new faith, Christian Science, under the influence of Sadie's unmarried sister, Adelaide.

At the beginning of the twentieth century, the Church of Christ, Scientist, founded in Boston by Mary Baker Eddy in 1879, was a controversial new religion. It became notorious for rejecting medical science and trying to cure disease with faith healers known as practitioners. Eddy's attack on medicine grew out of her conviction that physical suffering was imaginary. The only thing that was real, she taught, was God, "the immortal Mind," and "by knowing the unreality of disease, sin, and death, you demonstrate the allness of God."[30] In Eddy's view, all disease and other misfortunes could be cured by faith and prayer. She taught that positive thinking could banish evil and transform the world.

All the Lansdale boys were required to attend Christian Science Sunday school, and although none became devout Christian Scientists when they grew up, all of them, and Ed especially, were to be affected by church teaching in ways they may not have realized. Late in his life, Harry Lansdale was to quote to his son David a passage of Mary Baker Eddy's *Science and Health with Key to the Scriptures* (1875) that was particularly meaningful to him: "At all times and under all circumstances overcome evil with good. Know thyself and God will supply the wisdom and the occasion for a victory over evil."[31] *Overcome evil with good*: that was Edward Lansdale's unspoken mantra throughout his years on the front lines of the Cold War. His deeply held assumption that he could transform Pacific societies to live up to America's ideals had its origins not only in his reading about the American Revolution and in his Los Angeles upbringing but also in the mind-over-matter teaching of his parents' faith.

Christian Science was important to Ed Lansdale in another way: it gave him sympathy for the underdog and added to his empathy for minorities. Christian Science had only a hundred thousand adherents at the time of Mary Baker Eddy's death in 1910.[32] In the early days, before the passage of years and the publication of its prestigious newspaper, the *Christian Science Monitor*, had enhanced its legitimacy, the faith was every bit as controversial as contemporary movements such as the Unification Church and the Church of Scientology. In a typical attack, the Reverend A. Lincoln Moore of the Riverside Baptist Church in New York thundered in 1906 that "Christian Science is unchristian, anti-Christian, anti-biblical, Christless, Godless—in brief, Pagan."[33] Such anti–Christian Science bigotry translated into schoolboy taunts when Lansdale was growing up. He later recalled that "it's not a very popular religion and you're looked at askance wherever you go."[34]

◆

ED LANSDALE's growing identification as an outsider, both religiously and geographically, made him unusually cosmopolitan and tolerant for his day. He emphatically rejected the anti-Chinese prejudice that his mother exhibited. "When I went to college at the University of Michigan," Ed's brother David remembered, "I made good friends with a Chinese guy. . . . I wanted to bring him out to the house for dinner, and my mother wouldn't let me. She wasn't going to have a 'Chinaman' in her house. Isn't that something?"[35]

While Sadie's bigotry seemed outlandish to David in the 1980s, it was hardly unusual for a white Californian of the 1920s and 1930s weaned on lurid and falsified tales of crime, depravity, and drug addiction in San Francisco's Chinatown. In 1906–07, shortly before Lansdale's birth, the San Francisco Board of Education mandated that all Chinese, Japanese, and Korean children attend a segregated "Oriental School." In 1913, the California legislature, terrified of the so-called "yellow peril," voted to deny landownership to Japanese immigrants. Japanese Americans were spit upon in the streets and denied service in barbershops, where they were told, "We don't cut animals' hair."[36] Even people as liberal, enlightened, and worldly as John F. Kennedy casually referred to Asians as "chinks."[37]

Not Edward Lansdale. He was never contaminated by the bacillus of racism. "Asians were a minority who had a very rough time," he recalled, but he never "joined with the majority's denigration of the minority."[38] Growing up in Los Angeles, which by 1930 had the second-highest non-white population of any major city in the country,[39] he knew and got along with many people of Asian and Latin American ancestry. Far from harboring, like his mother, anti-Asian prejudice, he was imbued from an early age, his best friend from college remembers, "with the romance of the South Seas, the Orient." At his college fraternity house, he even wore a sarong—a typical article of clothing on many Pacific islands and in Southeast Asia—in place of pajamas or a nightshirt.[40]

Language, skin color, ethnicity: none of it made much of a difference to Edward Lansdale. As a religious and geographical outsider, as well as a maverick by temperament, he invariably identified with minorities even if he belonged to the ethnic majority. He saw people of other racial and ethnic backgrounds as individuals, and sought to appeal to them as equals. This made Lansdale an unusual, and unusually effective, agent of American power—if not always a successful one.

2

Enfant Terrible

*Not knowing what to do after [my mother] told me, I went
down to the pool and swam and swam and cried and cried in
the water.*

—DAVID LANSDALE

LATER in life, Edward Lansdale would emerge as one of the foremost American authorities on Vietnam and the Philippines. He
would also become a virtuoso politico-military adviser, a crack propagandist, and an expert on counterinsurgency warfare, a field that has
been described as the "graduate level" of warfare—"far more intellectual than a bayonet charge," in the words of T. E. Lawrence.[1] Those
were not skills he learned, by and large, in the classroom. Unlike Lawrence of Arabia, to whom he has been compared, Lansdale was not
drawn to the region where he would make his name by any academic
inquiry, which helps to explain why he did not make his first acquaintance of Asia until he was in his mid-thirties. By contrast, Lawrence
first visited the Middle East in 1909 as an Oxford undergraduate to
work on his senior thesis on Crusader castles, and returned after graduation to work as an archaeologist on an excavation sponsored by the
British Museum. Lansdale would be, at best, an undistinguished stu-

dent who did not display the intellectual brilliance—or the psychological fragility—of T. E. Lawrence, who admitted that "madness was very
near" for him.[2] But Lansdale's school years did teach him lessons in
character and leadership, striving and hustling that would help make
possible his later exploits.

After graduating from Berendo Junior High School in the mid-
Wilshire district of Los Angeles, Edward Lansdale entered the tenth
grade at Los Angeles High School in 1923, the same year that *Time*
magazine published its first issue, Adolf Hitler staged his unsuccessful Beer Hall Putsch, and Calvin Coolidge assumed the presidency.
L.A. High was the oldest high school in Southern California, dating to
1873. For thirty years, from 1895 to 1925, its direction had been determined by the legendary principal William Harvey Housh, like many
Californians an immigrant from the Midwest. By the time that Housh
retired, wrote the *Los Angeles Times*, "an enormous percentage of the
leading men of this city were Los Angeles High School students and
came under the benign influence of Mr. Housh."[3] Lansdale was one of
the last students touched directly by the taskmaster principal, with his
moralistic approach to education.

The school's motto, "Home of the Mighty Romans," seemed particularly appropriate for a student like Lansdale who, in the manner of a
Roman proconsul, would one day set out to defend his country's interests abroad. So, too, the high school's focus on civics seemed apt for
someone like Lansdale who was already becoming a devoted believer
in the principles of the American Revolution. As one of Housh's successors put it in a handbook for students, "The backbone of the course
of study is cultural rather than technical. Efficient and loyal citizen-
ship has been the key note of the many generations that have graduated
from the old pioneer school."[4] Lansdale imbibed the lessons in citizen-
ship the school had to offer. He joined the junior ROTC program and
he became an Eagle Scout, "winning," his brother Ben recalled, "row
upon row of merit badges across his chest."[5]

Ed did better in high school than he would do in college, earning
mostly B's and a few A's. His worst grade was an F in Latin, demonstrating for neither the first nor the last time his inability to learn for-

eign languages. His greatest achievement was to complete enough extra coursework to graduate a semester early, in December 1926.[6]

◆

GOING FROM an old institution of learning to a new one, Lansdale entered the University of California at Los Angeles, better known as UCLA, early in 1927—a year that would see Charles Lindbergh's celebrated solo flight across the Atlantic and the release of the first full-length motion picture with sound. The university was but eight years old and the campus was still located, as it had been since its inception in 1919, on a 25-acre plot on the outskirts of downtown Los Angeles. It would not move to its present location in Westwood—the name bestowed by the real estate developers Harold and Edwin Janss on an empty 383-acre tract near the Pacific Ocean—until Lansdale was a junior. When the new campus opened for 5,500 students on September 20, 1929, only the iconic Royce Hall, modeled on a basilica in Milan, and three other buildings had been completed. The grounds still had not been landscaped and were devoid of trees and shrubs. Construction materials were piled everywhere, and when it rained the dust turned into mud.

The newness of UCLA when Lansdale went there is significant: his achievements in college in some ways would prefigure his accomplishments in the newly independent nations of South Vietnam and the Philippines. Both in college and afterward, he was an institution builder. At UCLA, he built up a magazine, a fraternity, and an ROTC unit. "We were very proud of the fact that we were starting a new tradition," Lansdale's best friend and fraternity brother, Hubert "Pooley" Roberts, recalled.[7]

Lansdale and Roberts decided to work on a new humor magazine, *The Claw* (a name inspired by UCLA's mascot, the Bruin), which was being started in the fall of 1928 by a third student, Rehbock "Reh" Lewis. An English major, Lansdale fancied himself a humorist and, despite his lack of experience, somehow persuaded Lewis to hire him as the new magazine's editor, with Pooley Roberts working under him as associate editor. Roberts was later to comment that Lansdale was a "pretty good politician" with "the facility for almost naively getting what he wants from other people."[8]

The university administration at first forbade the magazine's publication on campus and suspended Lewis for a year for producing such risqué material, even though *The Claw*'s humor was pretty tame, at least by later, *Harvard Lampoon* standards. Typical jests, most of them in the Borscht Belt (or possibly Chinese fortune cookie) style, included such one-liners as " 'I hate to go to class—I haven't touched my German for two days.' 'What's *her* name?' "[9] Eventually Reh Lewis was reinstated as a student, and *The Claw* was approved for sale in the student bookstore. Lansdale and Lewis ran the modest operation from an office above Crawford's drugstore in Westwood Village, and Lansdale was involved in every aspect of the work, from typesetting to selling advertisements and copies (twenty-five cents an issue).[10]

Cartooning was a particular passion of Ed's. He developed "a distinctive style of his own,"[11] recalled Pooley Roberts. To supplement his meager income, he would use a black wax crayon to draw cartoons depicting campus events on big sheets of butcher paper. He would put up his cartoons in a local restaurant in exchange for a free meal, in a barbershop in exchange for a haircut, and in a clothing store in exchange for clothes.

In 1930, Lansdale got tired of running *The Claw* and turned over his editorship to Roberts. He set his sights on running for president of their fraternity. He worked quietly to develop a group of supporters among the 150 "brothers," and he wound up besting a rival for the post. Once again Roberts noticed that Ed had an "ingenious charm" that gave him "the ability to integrate with other people without their realizing that they were being used by him for some purpose or other." The secret of Lansdale's appeal even at this early age, Roberts discerned, was "that he showed an interest in you. We egotists mostly like to talk about ourselves, and he would draw people out, let them talk about themselves."[12] Not only did Lansdale succeed in winning the presidency of his fraternity, but he managed to affiliate the UCLA chapter with the prestigious national fraternity Phi Gamma Delta, whose members were known as "Fijis."[13]

By his senior year, Lansdale had also risen to cadet colonel of the ROTC regiment as well as president of the UCLA chapter of the Scabbard and Blade, a national military honor society. He was an energetic cadet who received his reserve commission as a second lieutenant in the U.S. Army in 1929, followed by a promotion to first lieutenant in 1932. He had shown interest in the military from a young age; as a high school student, he had participated in summertime Citizens' Military Training Camps. His brother Ben, however, recalled that Ed "was less than an ideal soldier," for he was "rather rebellious of the army traditions that seemed to be the mainstay of the training."[14] Lansdale would continue to question the military way of doing things even as he rose to become a general.

Lansdale could not afford to devote all his time to *The Claw*, Phi Gamma Delta, and the ROTC. He had to make money to stay in school. UCLA may have been tuition-free for state residents, but students did need enough money to live on. That was not easy to come by, given that Ed was attending college at a time when his father's shock-absorber business was failing and before he prospered with NAPA Auto Parts. Times were so tough after 1929 that some students supposedly banded together to split the cost of a hamburger, each pitching in a nickel for a bite.[15]

Lansdale tried to stay in college by working as a waiter at an upscale Hungarian restaurant in Westwood Village. To show up on time, he had to wear his tuxedo to class and sprint across the campus after a 5 p.m. lab. Along with some of his fraternity brothers, Lansdale also worked as an extra on Hollywood pictures. They especially liked musicals. "We'd get to dress up, sing songs, dance with nice looking girls, get a meal and something to drink and get paid for it," Lansdale recalled.

With all of his extracurricular activities, classes became almost an afterthought. His grades were terrible—mostly C's with a few B's and D's. He earned only one A during his entire undergraduate career—for English 1B in the fall of 1927. As if to make up for it, in the spring semester of 1928 he got a D in that same course.[16] By the end of the 1930–31 school year, his fourth on campus, Lansdale was still short of the credits required for graduation. Rather than try to scrape by for another semester, he decided to leave school and seek his fortune as a writer or illustrator in New York.

◆

LANSDALE ARRIVED in New York in September 1931 at a time of existential crisis. The bill for the excesses of the Roaring Twenties began coming due in October 1929 when the New York Stock Exchange crashed. By 1932, one in three New Yorkers was unemployed.[17] Some of the newly homeless took to living in makeshift shantytowns that sprang up across the city; they were called, here as elsewhere, Hoovervilles in sardonic tribute to the incumbent president. The literary critic Edmund Wilson wrote in December 1931 that people "seemed gaunt, gray, unsure of themselves and gloomy" and that "the life, the excitement had partly gone out of the city—the heart had been taken out of it."[18] Many intellectuals flocked to the Communist Party for salvation, while other Americans were drawn to demagogues like Huey Long and Father Charles Coughlin. In 1932, the future New York mayor Fiorello La Guardia wondered, "Are we going to admit that Mussolini is right, that Republics and parliamentary forms of government are failures?"[19]

That this did not happen was due in no small part to the recovery, more psychological than physical, wrought by Franklin Delano Roosevelt when he moved from the New York governor's mansion to the White House in 1933. Roosevelt's legislation creating the Securities and Exchange Commission, the Tennessee Valley Authority, the Federal Deposit Insurance Corporation, the National Recovery Administration, the Public Works Administration, the Civilian Conservation Corps, the Social Security Administration, and much else besides was "more than a New Deal," commented Secretary of the Interior Harold Ickes. It was "a new world."[20] Although its economic impact was mixed (GDP reached its pre-Depression level in the mid-1930s, but employment did not recover until the mid-1940s),[21] the New Deal had a profound impact in altering the views of Americans such as Edward Lansdale of what their government was capable of doing. All but a small minority of Roosevelt haters—and Lansdale was not that—came out of the 1930s convinced that government had a bigger obligation to shape the economy than had been commonly accepted in the more laissez-faire 1920s. The very landscape of New York was reshaped by the New Deal: federal money funded the creation of the Queens–Midtown Tunnel, the Bronx–Whitestone Bridge, the Brooklyn–Battery Tunnel, La Guardia Airport, McCarren Park Pool in Brooklyn, the Central Park Zoo, and other projects.[22]

The mobilization for World War II only a few years later would reinforce what was generally perceived to be the lesson of the New Deal, causing confidence in big government to soar to heights never reached before or since. Edward Lansdale's personal experience of the Great Depression and its long recovery while he was living in New York and later in California helped midwife his faith in the power of the American government to rebuild and reshape devastated societies.

◆

WHEN HE first moved to New York, Lansdale hoped to find work on a newspaper, but one of his prospective employers folded just before he arrived, while another was laying off staff. With barely fifty cents in his pocket (or so he remembered, no doubt with a bit of poetic license), he was rescued from penury by the family friend Harry Greenly, a fellow Christian Scientist who had known the Lansdales when they lived in Bronxville. Greenly was now chairman of the Official Classification Committee, which set freight rates for railroads across the country, and he gave Lansdale a job as one of his clerks. It was boring, "lousy" work, Lansdale discovered, but he was good enough at it to become chief clerk within a year.[23] In his spare time, he drew *New Yorker*-style cartoons that were never published and wrote plays that were never staged.

Initially Lansdale lived in a modest apartment at 288 West Fourth Street, in the West Village. One day he ran into a fellow "Fiji"—a member of the Phi Gamma Delta fraternity—who was broke and in need of a place to stay. Lansdale put him up, and thus wound up visiting his new roommate's sister in an apartment where she lived with other young women in Greenwich Village, a legendary haunt of college students, bohemians, mafiosi, junkies, gays and lesbians, and artists and writers.

One of the women sharing this Grenwich Village walk-up was Helen F. Batcheller, a small-town girl from western New York with "brilliant blue" eyes who was working as a secretary for a hardware company.[24] Ed and Helen soon struck up a romance. They later claimed that she was only a year older than he was—a claim repeated by his previous biographer.[25] In fact, she was seven years older: she had been born on March 5, 1901.[26] But it did not seem to make much difference at the time. In 1932, when they met, he was twenty-four, she was thirty-one, and they soon made a handsome couple. A picture from the early 1930s shows them looking like movie stars of the period, with even a hint of Myrna Loy and William Powell: Lansdale, just under five feet ten inches tall and less than 160 pounds, is slim and handsome. He is not yet sporting the mustache he would soon grow to appear older, and he is looking at the camera with a cool, even gaze, wearing a three-piece suit and a fedora tilted back at a rakish angle, holding a railing with one hand while the other encircles Helen's waist. Helen, just five feet three inches tall and 115 pounds,[27] has short, curly hair and is wearing a simple, nondescript dress. That Helen is leaning on his right arm masks the fact that his right shoulder is lower than his left—his only obvious physical imperfection. Helen was pretty, but she already had a few strands of white hair and within a few years would go prematurely gray even as Ed remained handsome and youthful-looking.

Those, however, were considerations for the future. In the present—in the impoverished but bustling New York of the early 1930s—Ed and Helen were, so far as can be discerned from the vantage point of nearly a century on, enormously happy in the way that only the newly infatuated can be. Ed had dated in high school and college but had never had a terribly serious relationship before. Pooley Roberts recalled that "he was a very attractive appearing man, and many girls would have been very happy to be his steady,"[28] while another college friend said, "He got around socially with the young ladies, in an innocent sort of way."[29] His relationship with Helen was something more serious.

For middle-class young people of the period, the inevitable next step was matrimony. The ceremony was performed at the Episcopalian Church of the Ascension, near Helen's apartment, on September 3, 1933, almost exactly two years after Lansdale's arrival in New York.[30] Christian Scientists have a tradition of not staging weddings or funerals in their churches, so the choice of venue was not necessarily significant, and yet in this case it did signal that Lansdale was starting to leave the religion of his youth. Although he would remain a nominal Christian Scientist, he would later describe himself as "not a religious person."[31] Helen, who had been raised a Presbyterian, would be converted to Christian Science by her mother-in-law, Sadie Lansdale.

From the beginning there were warning signs that the marriage's course would be less than smooth. Lansdale's exuberant and adventurous personality made a marked contrast to his wife's more reserved and cautious nature. While Ed later traveled by himself across insurgent-infested areas of the Philippines and Vietnam, Helen never even learned to drive a car (in spite of Ed's constant pleading, "You'd better learn to drive"),[32] and she was too afraid to fly to attend a son's wedding because as a girl she had been traumatized by a scary ride in an open-cockpit biplane at a county fair.[33] "Helen was not a very warm-natured person, not a fun-loving gal at all," said Ed's brother David.[34] "Helen was a very quiet, home-type young woman," recalled Pooley Roberts,[35] while Phil Lansdale commented, "She didn't have much curiosity. She felt sorry for herself much of the time. She was a very small person, prematurely gray, and I didn't find her very stimulating or very interesting."[36] In fairness, others had a more favorable impression of Helen. One of her friends told the author that, although she was "quiet," she was a "wonderful," "lovely," and "beautiful" woman.[37]

How did two such different people wind up together? David Lansdale asked his brother that very question half a century later. Ed replied that "we were both in New York together and we were both lonely" and got married "just for companionship."[38] That statement, uttered in 1984 by an old man long after Helen's death, sounds more dismissive than the explanation that probably would have been offered by his younger self while still in the throes of passion. Yet it contains an element of truth, especially if one reads into it an oblique reference to the physical attraction the two felt and the enjoyment they no doubt derived from the steady availability of sex for the first time in their lives—a far more intense experience than the furtive gropings of youth.

There was, however, more to the union than sheer physical attraction or even a desire for companionship. There was, in fact, more than Ed, who hated to speak about his private life even with his brothers, would let on. Ed and Helen shared a secret—a family scandal—that few if any outsiders knew about. It may well have been this history of familial betrayal that, as much as anything else, drew these two young New Yorkers together.

◆

AT EIGHT O'CLOCK in the morning on May 14, 1851, a train with twelve passenger cars had pulled out of New York City. Aboard were President Millard Fillmore, along with much of his cabinet and many other dignitaries. The train made slow progress as it snaked toward western New York with enthusiastic crowds gathering at every stop to hear a legendary orator, Secretary of State Daniel Webster, address them from the observation car. They were there to commemorate the opening of the Erie Railroad, at 445 miles the longest in the world and the first to connect the Atlantic Ocean with the Great Lakes.

The next day, the train reached the railroad's terminus in Dunkirk, New York, a small but prosperous port on Lake Erie settled in the early nineteenth century and named after the French town that would become famous as the embarkation point for the British Army in 1940. "On the arrival of the excursion party at Dunkirk," a local historian later wrote, "it was welcomed by every exhibition of joy that could be manifested by the people assembled. Salutes, processions, barbecues, banquets and fireworks; a great bonfire illuminated the night, the harbor was filled with shipping, flags and bunting were everywhere displayed."

When Helen Frances Batcheller was born in Dunkirk fifty years later, the terminus of the railroad had long since moved to Buffalo. After the railroad decided in 1869 to close its repair and manufacturing shops in Dunkirk, the enterprising engineer Horatio Brooks, who had brought the first locomotive to Dunkirk in 1851, decided to lease the property. Thus was born the mighty Brooks Locomotive Works, which would manufacture hundreds of steam engines annually and employ thousands of workers. The first general superintendent was David Russell, Helen's great-grandfather, who made a fortune that was still extant when Helen was born. His granddaughter, Nellie, married young and was deserted by her husband, Willard Oscar Batcheller, son of a salesman of undertaker supplies from Worcester, Massachusetts, shortly after they had brought Helen Frances (known in her youth as Fanny) and her brother, Russell, into the world. Nellie herself died soon thereafter, in 1909, of tuberculosis.

Having lost their mother and never knowing their father, Fanny and her brother were raised by their grandparents, David Russell's daughter, Mary Jane Russell Herrick, and her husband, Lee Herrick, who had been foreman in the carpenter shop at the Brooks Works before his retirement. They owned a large house filled with crystal, china, and silver, and their needs were attended to by servants. Mary Jane died in 1927, at age seventy-five. Helen was then twenty-six, and she no doubt expected that she would become a wealthy heiress living a life of ease in her hometown. Yet according to family lore, the attorney handling the estate made off with her inheritance. Helen was now left to fend for herself. In search of work, she moved to New York City, where she met a handsome younger man recently arrived from Los Angeles with dreams of writing for a living.[39]

◆

ED LANSDALE was reeling at the time from his own family drama—one that he kept a secret from all of the previous writers who have chronicled his life, for he came of age at a time when extramarital affairs were far more scandalous and divorce much less common than they have since become. Ed's father, Harry Lansdale, had moved to Detroit in 1930 to take a position with NAPA Auto Parts. For the first six months, he lived alone in the Statler Hotel, while his wife, Sarah, remained behind in Los Angeles with fourteen-year-old David, the only one of their children still at home. Opportunity led to temptation, and the forty-seven-year-old executive started an affair with Ethel

Dow, a forty-one-year-old cashier in the hotel coffee shop who was ten years younger than his wife.[40]

David, the only one of the Lansdale boys to leave a written account of his reaction to the news, remembers that it was "a terrible shock." He received the news during the 1932–33 school year, when he was a high school senior in Ann Arbor, Michigan, and Ed was dating Helen in New York. David remembers his mother telling him one day, "Your dad is in love with another woman." "Not knowing what to do after [my mother] told me," wrote David, who was on the high school swim team, "I went down to the pool and swam and swam and cried and cried in the water." Given the strict family code of privacy and self-reliance, shared by most Americans of the time, David "couldn't talk about it" with his mother or his brothers—"we never discussed family problems with each other or anyone else."[41] Ed was older than David—in 1933 he was twenty-five—but there is little doubt that the news came as a terrible blow to him as well. It likely made him all the more eager to marry Helen to restore a measure of stability in his life, to create a new family to replace the one he had lost.

Setting an example that eventually would be followed by his son Ed, the wayward father waited until after Sarah died, in 1954, to marry his girlfriend, Ethel. (Harry himself would die five years later, leaving Ethel a well-off widow.) But Sarah and Harry Lansdale never lived together again after 1930. While Harry settled down in Detroit with his new paramour, Sarah spent much of the rest of her life flitting between her sons' houses, never quite settling down anywhere again. We can only guess at the toll the separation took on her; she seems never to have spoken of it to her children. But a hint of her feelings was evident in the fact that she made a point of avoiding the use of "Ethyl gas" in her car.[42] Sarah's Christian Science faith must have helped her to get through this crisis. *This is not really happening*, she must have told herself; *it's only an untrue and therefore unreal figment of the mortal Mind*.[43]

Having lost most of his own religious faith, Edward Lansdale did not have the solace of Christian Science teaching to comfort him in dealing with upheaval. All he could do was focus on his work and his bride as he built a new life for himself a continent apart from his parents. The problem was that his work was not very satisfying. He was not planning to go into the railroad business. He needed a new occupation—and he needed to find it while the Great Depression was still ravaging the economy.

◆

WITH NO sign of significant relief on the economic horizon, Edward Lansdale's aspirations of becoming a writer, playwright, or cartoonist would be interred without even a marker in the mass grave that collectively buried the dreams of a generation of young Americans. Conceding defeat, he was determined to leave New York—and his mind-numbing job compiling railroad timetables—as soon as he could. He finally resigned in 1935 from the Official Classification Commission, and, after four years in New York, moved with his bride back to Los Angeles to accept a position in the advertising office of Silverwoods department store. In becoming an adman, he was entering a profession that was already influential and well established, even if it had not yet scaled the heights of influence and glamour that it would reach with the advent of television commercials in the 1950s.

Advertising, the business in which Lansdale would learn many of the skills that he would later employ as a CIA operative, had grown along with mass-circulation newspapers and magazines since its nineteenth-century origins in the marketing of patent medicines. The outbreak of World War I led the Woodrow Wilson administration to harness advertising for its own purposes. The Committee on Public Information, led by the journalist George Creel, launched a propaganda blitz to whip up support for crushing the "barbaric Huns." Its role in the war effort gave advertising a patriotic patina and enhanced its social standing, laying the groundwork for the even more ambitious employment of psychological warfare in World War II. In 1919, an article in the *New Republic* glorified "the advertising man" as the "genius of America," the "enfant terrible of the time," "the cornerstone of the most respectable American institutions; the newspapers and magazines depend on him; Literature and Journalism are his hand maidens. He is the Fifth Estate."[44]

That Edward Lansdale got an opportunity to enter the Fifth Estate after the failure of his grander literary aspirations was due to nepotism in its purest form: the advertising manager of Silverwoods department store was none other than Phil Lansdale. Ed's older brother had worked in advertising at a variety of clothing stores in Southern California after flunking out of the University of Arizona in 1929. Phil wanted an assistant, and he knew that his brother was a good writer, so he enticed him to return to Los Angeles to work for him and learn the business.

However valuable the experience he gained, Lansdale had no desire to stay at Silverwoods for long. The salary was small and the headaches of working for his demanding older brother, who became notorious for going through copywriters, were large. It did not help that Helen Lansdale resented Phil for not giving her new husband the money or recognition she thought he deserved.

◆

DURING THE summer of 1937, at a time when the nation was riveted by Amelia Earhart's disappearance over the Pacific in the midst of an around-the-world flight, Lansdale drove north to the Bay Area looking for work. San Francisco had long since been overtaken by the parvenu to the south, at least in population. But in the late 1930s denizens of San Francisco still regarded their metropolis as the first city of the West Coast, and with considerable justification. A New Deal guidebook written by local writers boasted, "When the other cities of the Coast were still hamlets in forest clearings or desert cow-towns, San Francisco was 'The City.' It is 'The City' still." The crowning glories of San Francisco—the Golden Gate Bridge to Marin County and the Bay Bridge to the East Bay—had just been completed when Lansdale arrived.[45]

San Francisco saw itself as the capital not just of the West Coast but of the entire Pacific basin, where Lansdale would spend much of his career. That ambition was symbolized by the Golden Gate International Exposition, a world's fair that Lansdale undoubtedly visited in 1939 or 1940 along with millions of others. Held on Treasure Island, a man-made island in San Francisco Bay, its theme was "A Pageant of the

Pacific." A Court of the Pacific included pavilions devoted to Australia (featuring a collection of kangaroos, wallabies, and wombats), French Indo-China (with many items "from the ancient city of Angkor," which could be viewed to the accompaniment of "Annamite and Cambodian music"), and other Pacific destinations.[46] Condescending though the exhibits may seem to modern eyes, they were emblematic of the fascination with East Asia that Lansdale shared with many other Californians of his era. While another part of the exposition celebrated "The Peacemakers," the American role in the Pacific was not destined to be a peaceful one. It is entirely fitting that, after the exhibition closed, Treasure Island became a Navy and Marine base—part of the constellation of military installations around the Bay Area that would enable the United States to wage not only World War II in the Pacific but also subsequent wars in Korea and Vietnam.

While Lansdale had spent almost his entire life in big cities, none would entrance him the way San Francisco did. He was far from alone in concluding that, with its cosmopolitan mix of people, it was the most attractive of American cities. Standing at noon on Market Street, he marveled at the crowds spilling out of office buildings into the thoroughfares. "It's the first time I ever saw such a happy working crew," he recalled. "I was amazed looking at those faces and listening to their voices that these were happy people, living and working in San Francisco, so I decided I wanted to work here and bring my wife up to live in this place, far more so than in Los Angeles."[47]

◆

THE OPPORTUNITY for Lansdale to live and work in San Francisco would be provided by Theodore H. Segall, a Jewish immigrant from Romania and a high school dropout who in 1925 had started one of the city's first advertising agencies, serving predominantly Jewish retail clients such as Fred Benioff Furs, Milens jewelers, and Schwartz & Grodin men's clothing store. Segall had seen Lansdale's work for Silverwoods, and he thought Lansdale would be a good fit. Indeed, he was. Before long, Lansdale was working on the accounts of, as he later wrote, "6 men's stores, a restaurant chain, a candy manufacturer, a food processor and wholesaler, a county chamber of commerce, and various political campaigns . . . all at the same time."[48] Among his accomplishments was to help develop a popular "Hero of the Week" program sponsored by Segall clients on a local radio station, which presented tales of local do-gooders such as a crossing guard who saved two children from being run over by an oncoming automobile.[49]

In July 1941, Lansdale moved to a larger agency with a tonier list of clients, increasing his salary from $3,600 to $4,800 a year at a time when the median income for a man in the United States was less than $1,000 a year.[50] His new boss was another Jewish high school dropout, Leon Livingston, the son of a German immigrant who had launched his own agency in 1923. More successful than Segall, he lived in a mansion atop Pacific Heights and operated from a penthouse office in one of San Francisco's first skyscrapers.[51]

Lansdale was now working for such prestigious clients as Wells Fargo bank, Italian Swiss Colony wines, and Levi Strauss jeans. But he was hardly cowed by his new boss. He recalled Livingston walking into his office: "I'd be sitting at my desk with my feet crossed and leaning back in my chair with my eyes closed and he'd say, 'You aren't paid for sleeping here.' And I'd just open an eye and I'd say, 'Leon, you're disturbing my thought. I'm thinking, see? Get out of my room.'"[52]

On another occasion, Lansdale openly disagreed with his boss at a meeting with a client. Levi Strauss was trying to expand to the East Coast for the first time. Livingston suggested the company spend its money on billboards, for which his agency would get healthy commissions. Lansdale jumped in to say that was a bad idea. He argued that Levi Strauss should put its money into hiring extra salesmen to push their jeans into the major eastern clothing stores before doing any advertising. Afterward Livingston was so furious with Lansdale for throwing away thousands of dollars in commissions that he refused to walk on the same side of the street with him, telling Lansdale he was being a fool, to which the account executive replied, "No, that's honest advice. I believe what I told them." All worked out well in the end: later that day, a Levi Strauss executive called to say they were adopting Lansdale's suggestion to hire more salesmen for an East Coast rollout, but they were also going to increase their advertising spending, so the agency would not lose any commissions.[53]

Both honesty and insolence would become Lansdale trademarks—he would seldom hesitate to tell the truth as he saw it, even if it offended a superior.

◆

THE LANSDALE family grew concomitantly with Ed's advertising career. He and Helen had their first child, Edward Russell Lansdale (who would become known as Ted and later Ed), on June 2, 1939. A second and final son, Peter Carroll Lansdale (Pete), arrived on November 7, 1941. The family was living in a narrow, three-bedroom bungalow, with thick stucco walls and low ceilings, located at 880 Thirty-Fourth Avenue in San Francisco's Richmond district, an "urban suburb" close to Golden Gate Park and the Pacific Ocean.[54]

Precisely a month after Pete's birth, on December 7, 1941, a cool, seasonal Sunday with limpid skies and temperatures in the low sixties,[55] the entire family was in the modest backyard of their house getting some sun and fresh air, with the newborn in a baby carriage. The carefree weekend was interrupted by the unexpected appearance of one of Lansdale's former colleagues, who had been drafted into the army (conscription had begun in October 1940). With considerable agitation, he told them to turn on the radio. Thus they learned that Japanese warplanes had just bombed Pearl Harbor and other military installations on Oahu.

"The news seemed to be completely alien to my place and time there," Lansdale recalled. "It came as a surprise to me to find myself a bit later that day bearing a growing feeling that it was a time when all Americans had to get into the fight for our country . . . and that included me. The more I thought about it, the more it took shape as an iron-clad duty, not to be questioned."[56] But Lansdale had resigned his reserve army commission in 1937 to concentrate on his advertising career, and he had not succeeded in winning back his commission in 1939 after Germany's invasion of Poland. Now thirty-three years old, he would have to fight simply to "get into the fight."[57]

3

An Institution
Run by Its Inmates

*They kept using me to go out, getting new information and
meeting new people all the time, which seemed to be my forte.*

—EDWARD LANSDALE

THE coming of total war transformed untold millions of American lives, creating a lasting caesura that would unalterably separate the first half of the twentieth century from the years that followed. Housewives became factory workers. Executives became bureaucrats. Mechanics became Marines. Students became soldiers. In many cases, the experiences of war, whether traumatic or mundane or some of both, made it impossible for these men and women to go back to the lives they had lived in peacetime. Yet even by the standards of wartime, Edward Lansdale's journey from adman to CIA officer, from a career in advertising to a career in nation building, counterinsurgency, and psychological warfare, was particularly unusual.

Although Lansdale wanted to volunteer after the attack on Pearl Harbor, he found it hard to do so. The army refused to take back this overage volunteer because he had been diagnosed with an enlargement of his thyroid gland—in medical terminology a "simple colloid goiter moderate."[1] He was also unemployed, since Leon Livingston, an ardent liberal who was described by his daughter as "patriotic" but "anti-military,"[2] had fired Lansdale on the spot in a fit of pique after he announced his intention to enlist. Chagrined to be losing his star employee, Livingston told him, "If you're looking to fight, go join the Russian army. At least they have better looking uniforms than ours."[3] "So," Lansdale recalled, "Christmas 1941 found us—the country at war, and me jobless, with a family to house and feed."[4] No other advertising agency would hire him because he told prospective employers that he would quit the minute he was accepted into the army.

Salvation came from Carroll Harris, president of a typographic firm that Lansdale had worked with. In 1942, Harris appeared in an army colonel's uniform. Lansdale heard he was "connected with something very hush-hush in San Francisco," and he asked to join up.[5] A member of the Army's Military Intelligence Service, Harris promised to see what he could do to help in Washington. Upon returning from Washington, Harris told Lansdale that while the Army could not hire a civilian, he had some "friends" who could provide him with work right away. He asked Lansdale whether he had ever heard of a fellow named Donovan, first name Bill, a swashbuckling World War I combat hero and wealthy New York lawyer who was setting up a new intelligence agency known at first as the Coordinator of Information (COI) and then, after June 1942, as the Office of Strategic Services (OSS). Thanks to the intervention of Harris—"a kindly liberal who wants me to infuse idealistic ethics in intelligence work," Lansdale later wrote[6]—he was put under contract by the OSS in July 1942, working initially out of the Military Intelligence Service office at 74 New Montgomery Street in San Francisco.

Many years later, Ben Lansdale remembered his older brother confiding in him "that someday he would like to become a secret agent to help our government win some future war."[7] Now Ed Lansdale would have the opportunity to realize this youthful ambition.

◆

THE OSS was, in many ways, an ideal organization for the neophyte operative. It was as unconventional and informal as he was. As one

OSS agent later wrote, "OSS is the last refuge of men and women who want to do something but don't fit the regulations."[8] Lansdale fit in right away. In 1943, he visited OSS headquarters in Washington, and managed to get in despite not having any of the appropriate badges or passes. The colonel he was meeting with was "quite taken" with his feat. "How did you do that?" he wanted to know. "Misdirection," Lansdale explained. "Getting the guard interested in something else going on and a conversation we had at the time, while holding out what looks like a pass and isn't."

The colonel told Lansdale that he had been working on personnel files, before exiting his office in order to check on something urgent. Left alone, Lansdale immediately opened a drawer and took out his own personnel file. The colonel came back with a stopwatch to congratulate him: "Fastest time I ever saw anybody do that. You were moving even before I had left the room."[9] By breaking the rules, paradoxically, Lansdale had passed the test for admittance into the OSS, which, like all intelligence agencies, existed to lie, cheat, and steal for its country.

◆

THE HEAD of the OSS office in San Francisco turned out to be Navy Commander William H. Vanderbilt III, scion of one of America's richest families and a former governor of Rhode Island. He was typical of the upper-crust individuals whom Donovan had recruited, leading to jokes that OSS stood for "Oh So Social." The OSS, however, did not limit itself to hiring pedigreed Wall Street bankers and lawyers. Its recruits included the Harvard professor Arthur Schlesinger Jr., the film director John Ford, the Arctic explorer Vilhjalmur Stefansson, the Red Sox catcher Morris "Moe" Berg, as well as, in the words of one of Donovan's agents, "safecrackers, paroled convicts, remittance men, professional wrestlers and boxers, circus stars, code experts, military characters, nightclub frequenters, and a miscellany of others."[10] Donovan's credo was to hire anyone "of great ability" and "later on we'll find out what they can do."[11]

Lansdale had already demonstrated a talent for getting along with people who were very different in background from himself. As was his wont, this middle-class Californian soon struck up a fast friendship with Vanderbilt, a veritable blue blood from the East. Eventually, in March 1943, Lansdale would be granted a medical waiver and accepted back into the Army as a first lieutenant working in military intelligence, but even in that new capacity he would continue to do work on the side for the OSS. "It was an unusually harmonious relationship," he later recalled, made possible by his friendship with Vanderbilt. Lansdale's service in World War II would anticipate his simultaneous work in the 1950s for the CIA and the Air Force.[12]

The OSS was full of military personnel and it was, at least in theory, under the control of the Joint Chiefs of Staff, but it was positively disdainful of military hierarchy and protocol. In the field, OSS men seldom saluted, dressed as they pleased, and often sported copious facial hair, ranging from full beards to walrus mustaches, all in violation of military regulations.[13] "The OSS is the only institution that is run by its own inmates," one of its operatives said.[14] In short, it would be an ideal incubator for a maverick recruit who would become notorious for his disdain for bureaucracy.

While the regular military had a conservative outlook typified by rock-ribbed Republicans such as Douglas MacArthur, the OSS was, at heart, a New Deal agency with a progressive, idealistic ethos that would carry over to the CIA. A war correspondent wrote that "race, color and previous condition of servitude cut no ice whatever" in the OSS "as long as one actually wanted to get into the fray and help to win it."[15] The OSS, in other words, was as color-blind as Lansdale himself, and no doubt his service reinforced his willingness to cast aside prevailing racial and ethnic prejudices.

◆

THE OSS bore the unmistakable personal imprint of "a short man with mild blue eyes," "a soft Irish voice," "pudgy hands," a "thick-set neck," and an "easy slow-going manner" that concealed reservoirs of "enormous energy."[16] His name was William J. Donovan, but he was invariably known as Wild Bill. An inveterate risk taker, he had risen from an impoverished Irish Catholic background in Buffalo to graduate from Columbia University and Columbia Law School, where one of his classmates was a seemingly indolent patrician from Hyde Park named Franklin D. Roosevelt. Donovan had then earned the Medal of Honor, the Distinguished Service Cross, and a Purple Heart, among other decorations, while exhibiting near-suicidal bravery as an officer with the American Expeditionary Forces in France in 1918. After the war, he served as a federal prosecutor in western New York and, harboring dreams of becoming the first Catholic president, ran unsuccessfully as a Republican candidate for lieutenant governor and governor. He then moved to New York City, where he established himself as one of the preeminent lawyers on Wall Street. Donovan married the daughter of one of the richest men in Buffalo, but he cheated on her compulsively with a long line of lovers, and he spent so extravagantly that he was in constant financial difficulties in spite of his substantial income.

Despite their political differences, Roosevelt in 1941 acceded to his old law school classmate's request that he be allowed to establish America's first civilian intelligence agency. Running a growing government bureaucracy, which eventually came to number twelve thousand employees, did nothing to curb Donovan's disdain for established procedures or the dictates of prudence and safety. He often said, "I'd rather have a young lieutenant with guts enough to disobey an order than a colonel too regimented to think and act for himself."[17] Lansdale would certainly never hesitate to disobey an order.

Donovan was famous for his receptivity to unconventional ideas. Stanley P. Lovell, a chemist who headed the OSS's Office of Scientific Research and Development, and whom Donovan referred to as his own Professor Moriarty, wanted to lace Hitler's food with estrogen to make his mustache fall out and his voice turn soprano. Lovell also developed a chemical dubbed "Who? Me?" that replicated the "revolting odor of a very loose bowel movement." His madcap idea was to distribute it to children in Japanese-occupied cities of China so that they could squirt "Who? Me?" on the trouser seats of Japanese officers who happened to walk by. The theory was that this would cost the Japanese, who valued cleanliness, "a world of 'face.'"[18]

It is important to keep such outlandish schemes in mind to understand how Lansdale could later entertain seemingly madcap ideas for undermining the Communist leaders Luis Taruc, Ho Chi Minh, and Fidel Castro. David Bruce, who was to become a distinguished diplomat after his OSS service, wrote, "Woe to the officer who turned down a project because, on its face, it seemed ridiculous, or at least unusual."[19] Bruce himself had to spend weeks investigating the possibility of attacking Tokyo with bats that had incendiary bombs strapped to their backs.[20] If it did nothing else, Lansdale's OSS service reinforced his openness to projects that seemed ridiculous to outsiders.

Another Donovan characteristic, which Lansdale later exhibited all too well, was a tendency to pick counterproductive bureaucratic fights. As a new agency, the OSS threatened existing competitors such as the Army's Military Intelligence Service, the Office of Naval Intelligence, and especially the Federal Bureau of Investigation. Donovan feuded incessantly with FBI director J. Edgar Hoover not only over which agency would operate intelligence networks in Latin America but also over which one would have the right to burgle foreign embassies in Washington. (The FBI won both battles.) Their internecine battle could become brutal: Hoover accused the OSS of harboring Communist and Fascist spies and compiled a dossier on Donovan that included details of his numerous extramarital liaisons. Donovan retaliated by putting together his own file on the FBI, including rumors that its director was a homosexual or, in the argot of the day, a "fairy."[21]

The OSS also fought with the State Department, in part because its operatives abroad developed a habit, which would carry over to the CIA, of disregarding American ambassadors and deciding on their own what actions to take. A classic example was the actions of the OSS officer Beverly Bowie, formerly an editor at *National Geographic*, in Bucharest in 1944. One of the first Americans in liberated Romania, he became a regular guest at meetings of the newly established cabinet. "Before they vote on anything," he explained, "they ask me what I think. I go into a trance and figure out what Franklin D. Roosevelt would do, then give 'em the answer. They pass all my laws unanimously. I never thought running a country was so easy."[22] Bowie was exaggerating for comic effect, but Lansdale would operate in somewhat similar fashion. He too would find it easy to virtually run the countries where he would be assigned, even while grappling with the kind of bureaucratic disputes that also bedeviled Wild Bill Donovan.

◆

THE OSS became legendary for the work of its operatives behind enemy lines—daring commandos such as the three-man Jedburgh teams that parachuted into occupied Europe in June 1944 to prepare for D-Day. This was not, however, the kind of work that Lansdale did; he labored for Research & Analysis (known as "the Chairborne Division")[23] and Secret Intelligence, not the more glamorous Special Operations division and the Operational Groups, which carried out sabotage in occupied lands. His war was spent operating out of San Francisco and later New York, gathering intelligence and recruiting agents. "Not much in the way of heroics," Lansdale commented, "but it was truly fascinating work for me."[24]

Much of Lansdale's time was spent trying to expand the government's scant knowledge of, in his words, "the vast and hitherto almost unknown places where we were putting forces." These included such unfamiliar destinations as Kwajalein, Eniwetok, and Aitape, and that was simply in the Pacific theater. The United States, Lansdale noted, lacked "very basic information on geography, terrain, man-made features on the terrain, [and] the people involved." He filled in some of the blanks.[25]

Lansdale did not just gather information but also offered suggestions on how to turn it into a weapon. In 1943, for example, he circulated a memorandum on Japanese proverbs. "The Japanese, like all Orientals, love proverbs," he wrote, and then went on to argue that "a surprising number of these sayings—clothed with credibility by centuries of usage—can be made applicable to modern events and can be, in the opinion of this section, used effectively against the Japanese." For instance, he suggested, the Japanese saying "The biggest serpent has no terrors for the eagle" could be "startlingly pertinent" if "Japan is portrayed as the serpent and growing United Nations air power as the eagle."[26] It was an early sign of the interest in folklore that would become a hallmark of his later assignments in the Philippines and Vietnam.

Lansdale proved relentless and creative in finding new sources of information. He not only interviewed foreign-born students at thirty-seven different universities to obtain information about their homelands;[27] he also talked to a couple of Sufi murshids (or teachers), practitioners of a mystical sect of Islam, to learn "about social structures of South Asian and Middle Eastern countries." One of them "submitted his thoughts on the nature of the war then going on in the deserts of North Africa" in blank verse. Lansdale passed along this epic poem to Washington for further "study."[28]

"Each individual" he interviewed "was a gold mine," Lansdale later said—"if the interviewer was a good miner."[29] Lansdale was. Such was his reputation for "industry, tact, ingenuity and good judgment" (in the words of a fellow officer) that he was assigned in 1944–45 to an intelligence post with the Army Transportation Corps in New York City, where he became "responsible for the quality and quantity of work produced by hundreds of interrogators at eight Ports of Embarkation."[30] The interrogators would interview sailors and other travelers about what they had seen while abroad and pass some of them along for recruitment as intelligence agents. A small sign of Lansdale's success can be glimpsed in his record of promotions: having been commissioned a first lieutenant in February 1943, he advanced to captain in December of that year and to major in January 1945.[31] "They kept using me to go out, getting new information and meeting new people all the time, which seemed to be my forte," he recalled.[32]

Lansdale was developing a reputation not only as a savvy interviewer and skilled intelligence gatherer—Lansdale the listener—but also as someone who "seemed to get along very well with Asians." For that reason he was called upon in 1942 by the Office of Naval Intelligence to help quell a potential mutiny among Sumatran sailors aboard Dutch merchant ships in West Coast ports. Some of the Sumatrans—Sumatra, then part of the Dutch East Indies, is today part of Indonesia—had heard Queen Wilhelmina's radio broadcast in support of FDR's Four Freedoms (freedom of speech, freedom of worship, freedom from fear, freedom from want). They "decided that they were part of the Four Freedoms," Lansdale recalled, "and they were all going to go home and have their own freedom." Lansdale was a fervent supporter of the Four Freedoms himself, but he believed that the exigencies of wartime took precedence over all else. In this particular case, it was important to keep Allied supplies moving on Dutch ships. To head off a strike, Lansdale said, "I managed to meet various seamen in port and I had drinking bouts with them. At one of those I was rather exuberantly made a member of the Batak tribe of Sumatra. The Bataks among the seamen from then on kept me very well advised on what their plans were and also listened to me as I talked them out of having a strike and to continue on in the war effort until the day of victory."[33]

Such rapport building soon would be reprised in the Philippines and later in Vietnam.

◆

EDWARD LANSDALE's record during World War II suggests that he could have become a successful case officer for what is today known as the CIA's Directorate of Operations, the unit charged with recruiting and running spies. But that is not the direction in which his postwar career was to take him. He was to become a covert warrior, not an intelligence gatherer. His focus would be on changing the facts on the ground rather than merely ferreting them out.

That transformation began in the late summer of 1945 amid events so consequential that their ripples continue to buffet the world to this day. On August 6, a B-29 bomber dropped an atomic bomb over Hiroshima and, in a blinding flash and mushroom cloud, killed more than 130,000 people. On August 9, another B-29 dropped an atomic bomb on Nagasaki, killing at least 60,000 more people. Five days later, at 7:03 p.m. on August 14, the moving electric sign on the New York Times Building flashed the welcome news: "Official—Truman announces Japanese surrender." While the vanquished Japanese succored the wounded and buried the dead in two of their major cities, half a million celebrants packed into Times Square responded with a "victory roar" that "beat upon the eardrums until it numbed the senses," the *Times* reported. "For twenty minutes, wave after wave of that joyous roar surged forth."[34]

The revelry in Times Square, and all across the country, had barely ended when portents of troubles to come began to appear like storm clouds on the far Pacific horizon. On August 17, 1945, Indonesian nationalists led by Sukarno declared independence from the Netherlands—a declaration that Dutch leaders were intent on resisting by force. On August 25, an American intelligence officer named John Birch was shot and killed in a confrontation with Chinese Red Army troops. (His death would later be commemorated by some conservatives as the first casualty of the Cold War.) On September 2, the veteran revolutionary Ho Chi Minh, speaking to cheering throngs in Hanoi, proclaimed a new republic. The French did not recognize this new state and vowed to keep control of Indochina by any means necessary. And then, on September 8, American troops in "full battle array"[35] landed at Inchon, the port of Seoul, to accept the surrender of Japanese troops in Korea—but only in the south. The northern half of Korea was occupied by Soviet troops. Before long, the Korean Peninsula would be cleaved, just like Germany, into two antagonistic states, one pro-Soviet, the other pro-Western. Such events would make a mockery of the whimsical headline the *New York Times* had run on August 15, 1945, the day after Japan's surrender, above a picture of four young WACs (Women's Auxiliary Corps) in Guam: "The Outlook in the Pacific is Bright and Pretty." In truth, the outlook was decidedly cloudy with political tsunamis in the forecast.

Lansdale was soon to learn this for himself. Just as millions of American servicemen were at long last preparing to return home, he was shipping out in September 1945 for the first time on a long-term overseas assignment. Thanks to "the caprice of Army clerks who shuttled millions of Americans in uniform around the world at seeming random,"[36] as he later put it, he was headed to Asia, where he would encounter not the old enemy, Japanese imperialism, but the new one— Communist expansionism—and his duties would expand far beyond those of a regular intelligence officer. His success at finding a niche within the OSS and the Army's Military Intelligence Service during World War II ensured that he would not have to return at war's end

to what now appeared to have been a humdrum life as a San Francisco advertising man. He was eager for adventures to come on the
far side of the Pacific in the places that he could only have imagined
while visiting the Golden Gate International Exhibition on Treasure
Island five years before, in what by now must have seemed like a long-
vanished age.

PART TWO

COLONEL LANDSLIDE

(1945–1954)

Colonel Lansdale and Defense Minister Ramon Magsaysay,
October 1952, on one of their inspection trips to the
Philippine countryside. (MSFRIC)

4

The Time of His Life

Filipinos and I fell in love with each other.

—EDWARD LANSDALE

Nation building—the wrenching process of bringing disparate people together under a new government—is as old as civilization. The very first nation builders were the ancient kings of Mesopotamia and Egypt, who five thousand years ago constructed the first civilizations. Every great conqueror, from Alexander to Napoleon, was in some form a nation builder. The two great victors of World War II—the Soviet Union and the United States—were no different. Each attempted to spread its own form of government and political ideology, different as they were, to new nations being born across Asia and Africa from the debris of old colonial empires.

This was both a heady and a nerve-racking time, with American proconsuls installed in Tokyo and Berlin, and American emissaries fanning out around the world to refashion nations on democratic lines. Truman's secretary of state, Dean Acheson, was to title his memoirs *Present at the Creation.* Many others who were active in those years felt the same way. "We have, and we know we have, the abundant means to bring our boldest dreams to pass—to create for ourselves whatever world we have the courage to desire," said Archibald MacLeish, the poet and Librarian of Congress.[1]

Anything seemed possible at the dawn of the postwar world.

◆

EDWARD LANSDALE's introduction to the excitement and frustrations of nation building came in the fall of 1945 when he arrived in the Philippines. His first glimpse of the land where he would make his reputation came near midnight on October 9, 1945, only two months after the nuclear bombs had finally stilled the war engines of the Japanese Empire. An electrical storm was raging, and he was exhausted after a sixteen-day voyage from San Francisco along with four thousand other soldiers aboard the USS *Uruguay*. During the crossing, the titanic transport ship had hit the tail end of a typhoon and everyone aboard thought they were going to sink. They were, in fact, lucky to make it to land.[2]

The land in which they were arriving was both alien and strangely familiar—the United States refracted through a funhouse mirror. The Philippines was a largely Catholic country where English was the language of government, the upper crust went by nicknames like Babe and Pinksy, Rotary and Shriners and Lions clubs were a well-established part of the social firmament, and Tin Pan Alley tunes were as popular as they were in New York. A young American officer who had arrived in Manila just a few months before Lansdale remarked in wonder, "Why the girls here paint their lips, their finger nails and even their toe nails, just as in the States."

The Philippines was not, of course, just the same as the United States. As Stanley Karnow was to point out in his book *In Our Image: America's Empire in the Philippines*, the vast majority of the ordinary people were far less touched by American influences than were the elites. In rural areas, most farmers lived under a quasi-feudal regime, laboring on the estates of a small number of wealthy landowners whose property holdings descended from the days of Spanish rule. Even the more Americanized upper class was bound by extended kinship ties that were alien to the more individualistic Americans and that underlay a pervasive culture of corruption. But superficially, at least, there was much that would have made a newcomer like Lansdale feel at home.[3]

The transformation of the Philippines into a faraway simulacrum of the United States had begun nearly half a century earlier. While the United States had declared war on Spain in 1898 as a result of American outrage over Spanish abuses in Cuba, the peace treaty that ended the conflict also gave the United States, almost as a lagniappe, sovereignty over another former Spanish colony, the Philippines. The young insurgent leader Emilio Aguinaldo y Famy led violent resistance to American rule in a savage conflict with some similarities to the future war in Vietnam—including the domestic opposition that both wars aroused. The Anti-Imperialist League united worthies such as Mark Twain, Grover Cleveland, and Andrew Carnegie, who were horrified to read that American troops were torturing Filipinos (including the use of the "water cure," a technique learned from the Spanish, and later called waterboarding) and killing even noncombatants.

Yet while the United States was to lose in Vietnam, it won in the Philippines. An important difference was that North Vietnam was adjacent to the People's Republic of China, which provided copious weapons and training to the Vietminh and later the Vietcong, whereas the Philippine *insurrectos*, fighting on islands whose approaches were dominated by the U.S. Navy, had no real outside support. The *insurrectos* also lacked leaders of the caliber of Ho Chi Minh and Vo Nguyen Giap; Aguinaldo made no attempt to win over the bulk of the population by pushing for social and land reforms, as the Vietcong would later do, because such revolutionary steps would have alienated his upper-class supporters.

By the time the conflict had mostly ended, in 1902, the United States had lost 4,234 dead and 2,818 wounded. Some 200,000 Filipino civilians died as a result of disease and mistreatment from both sides. Brigadier General J. Franklin Bell, a future Army chief of staff, extinguished the last resistance on Luzon by herding more than 300,000 civilians into "zones of protection," similar to the "concentration camps" that British forces were constructing at virtually the same time to defeat a Boer uprising in South Africa, in order to cut them off from the guerrillas.

As in South Africa, many in the Philippines died because of the lack of proper medical care and nutrition in these makeshift holding pens.

It would be a mistake, however, to imagine that American forces simply terrorized Filipinos into acquiescence. While U.S. troops relentlessly pursued guerrillas, the first civilian governor, William Howard Taft, who arrived in 1900, set up schools and hospitals, imported idealistic young American teachers known as Thomasites (they arrived on the transport ship *Thomas*), improved public sanitation, wiped out infectious diseases, built roads, and took other steps to win over the population. Lansdale would later cite the efforts of the Thomasites and other well-intentioned Americans as the ideal of the "True American" that the United States needed to inculcate into its representatives abroad to win the Cold War: "a person of integrity, with the courage of his convictions, with competence in some technical field, with devotion to getting things done, and with Christian affection for his fellow man." ("Admittedly," he added, in a self-aware postscript, "this is an ideal which human weaknesses make it difficult to achieve.")[4]

U.S. rule was paternalistic and racist (Taft referred to Filipinos as "our little brown brothers" and ordinary soldiers called them "goo-goos" or "niggers"), but it was also in important respects more liberal than contemporary European colonial regimes. Washington did not allow American companies to set up agricultural concerns to exploit local labor and land such as the vast rubber plantations owned by the French in Indochina, the Dutch in the East Indies, and the British in Malaya. There was no need to exploit the Philippines when the American homeland was so abundantly provided with natural resources of its own. The Filipinos elected a national legislature in 1907, and by the 1920s they had taken over most administrative and military posts. In 1935, President Roosevelt created the Philippine Commonwealth, which enjoyed autonomy in its domestic affairs, while promising complete independence in 1946.

Filipino-American ties were tested and ultimately strengthened by the Japanese attack that began within hours of the bombing of Pearl Harbor on December 7, 1941. While some Filipinos cooperated with the Japanese occupiers, few became enthusiastic adherents of the

Greater East Asia Co-Prosperity Sphere. Filipinos resented the fact that they had to bow to their new conquerors or else suffer "a slap in the face, a kick in the ass, or a blow from a gun butt."[5] By war's end some two hundred thousand Filipinos had joined guerrilla bands to resist Japanese rule in cooperation with scattered survivors from the defeated American forces. They were inspired, these Filipinos, by the injunction of Commonwealth President Manuel Quezon y Molina, who told his people before evacuating Corregidor, "Keep your faith in America, whatever happens."[6]

General Douglas MacArthur kept his own faith in the Philippines even after being evacuated to Australia in 1942. One of the most brilliant and obdurate, vainglorious and controversial figures in modern military history, he was the son of General Arthur MacArthur, who commanded U.S. troops in putting down the "Philippine Insurrection," and he himself had spent a substantial portion of his life in the Philippines. Although known to American soldiers (including his often exasperated aide, Major Dwight D. Eisenhower) for his aloof, autocratic, and self-dramatizing ways, MacArthur endeared himself to Filipinos by treating them as equals at a time when racism was still pervasive among Americans in the archipelago. Determined to make good on his pledge to "return," MacArthur insisted over the objections of his Navy counterparts that U.S. forces had to liberate the Philippines on their island-hopping campaign toward the Japanese mainland. And on October 20, 1944, MacArthur did wade through the surf to a beach on the island of Leyte to proclaim, "People of the Philippines I have returned. . . . Rally to me!"

Nearly three months later, on January 9, 1945, U.S. troops landed at Lingayen Gulf on northern Luzon in order to drive to Manila, 110 miles to the south. The Japanese army commander in the Philippines, Lieutenant General Tomoyuki Yamashita, wanted to abandon Manila, a flat, sprawling city of seven hundred thousand people, because he did not believe it could be successfully defended; he preferred to harass the American invaders from bases in Luzon's jungle-covered mountains. But Rear Admiral Sanji Iwabuchi, the commander of a naval defense force, had other ideas. With twenty thousand soldiers and sailors under his command, he was determined to defend Manila to the last man. He forced U.S. troops to fight for Manila block by block in vicious street fighting accompanied by artillery duels that razed much of the city between February 3 and March 3. After just a week of fighting, one resident of Manila reported that the "view down San Andres [Street] was like a scene from Dante's Inferno. Strewn with bloated corpses, wrecked cars, dead animals, piles of rubble, twisted metal roofing, and urban debris, we could not get oriented because there was not a single landmark we recognized."[7]

An estimated one million Filipinos perished during the Japanese occupation. Of that total fully 10 percent—one hundred thousand— died in the ruins of Manila when the hour of liberation was at hand. An American general who toured the city on March 3 found that it had all but "ceased to exist." For days afterward, noted the historian D. Clayton James, "the horrible stench of thousands of unburied corpses pervaded the downtown area." But then, "like the miraculous appearance of green shoots on the charred earth of a forest recently ravaged by fire, signs of life and activity began to reappear" as Filipinos emerged from "hiding in blasted buildings and homes."[8] Even though American artillery fire had played a significant role in Manila's destruction—arguably a greater role than Japanese vindictiveness—few Filipinos blamed their liberators and most were grateful for American help in rebuilding. Filipinos and Americans immediately began working together to deliver food, stop the spread of contagious diseases, reopen schools, restart the water supply, and do everything else needed to bring a devastated metropolis back to life. By March 13, 1945, the lights were coming back on across Manila.

◆

EDWARD LANSDALE landed in the Philippines just seven months after the conclusion of the Battle of Manila and only three months after the last Japanese units on Luzon had surrendered. He saw the war's impact even before setting foot ashore. In Manila harbor, Lansdale counted thirty sunken ships: "There were sterns pointing straight up to the sky out of the water, hulls side up looking like elephants submerged and taking baths, just sticks of masts above the water, and some twisted and buckled rusty plates like reddish warts above the water where ships had been blown apart."

Lansdale made the trip to a U.S. Army camp outside Manila aboard a crowded troop train. He and the other soldiers were packed like cattle into cars that were normally used to transport sugarcane. As the train chugged along at 15 mph, someone "started 'moo-ing' like a lonely cow and the moo-ing was taken up all along the line." From the "trainload of moos," Lansdale could see that the "strikingly beautiful" countryside had not been affected by war to the same extent as the harbor. He saw "palm huts on stilts with vivid green banana fronds making a border for a blue, blue sky marbled with towering fluffs of cumulus clouds, and before this background of sky and hut and fronds was spread a rice paddy intersticed with small raised dikes and the green rice sprouts making a staccato vertical pattern broken by big old water buffalo plodding along, with a copper skinned old man, all bent, straw big brimmed coolie hat on his head, following after."

When the train reached Manila, such bucolic scenes were replaced by further reminders of the legacy of conflict. "Stone walls along the roads were gouged and holed," Lansdale wrote, "tall apartment houses and hotels and public buildings—the ones that earned Manila the name 'Pearl of the Orient' showed gaping holes, sagging concrete floors open to view, and with rusty iron girders all twisted and bent and dangling out of crumbled concrete twenty stories up like dried worms baked in the sun while still wriggling."

Lansdale and the other troops finally settled into a camp located fifty-five miles outside Manila, near a major air base, Clark Field. There were still many unexploded shells scattered around. "Ordnance teams are blowing them up constantly and I'm writing now [to] the accompaniment of boom-boom-boom," Lansdale wrote on October 12, 1945. Also loitering about were some Japanese holdouts who either had not heard of their nation's surrender or who refused to believe it. Lansdale saw fourteen Japanese soldiers—"a very bedraggled group of forgotten men"[9]—come in from the hills just outside his camp and surrender rather than starve in the jungle.

Most American soldiers in the Philippines were eager to depart now that the war was over. "Everything is confusion and indifference here now," Lansdale noted, "the correct attitude being: the war is over now, so let's go home."[10] Lansdale possessed a very different outlook. Before he had shipped out from the United States, Ed had a brief conversation with his brother Ben, an engineer in uniform, who had visited the Philippines during the war to study the impact of proximity fuses in artillery shells.

Ben remembered Ed asking him "what musical tunes were popular among the Filipino troops and when I didn't know, he played a few tunes on his pocket-size harmonica and asked me if I had heard any of those." Ben said he hadn't paid attention to what Filipinos were singing because "that wasn't part of my military duties." He wondered why Ed cared.

Lansdale replied that he "wasn't going there to shoot at people or to try to make them change their minds by force, but rather to understand them and to help guide them into a type of democracy that would live and have meaning to the people. And one way to understand and to communicate with the people is by knowing their songs, something they hold dear to their hearts."[11]

If we are to credit Ben's recollection of this conversation, Ed Lansdale was from the start of his sojourn in Asia intensely interested in the people he would meet and how he could help them to build a better nation.

◆

MAJOR LANSDALE was initially assigned as chief of the relatively small intelligence division (G-2) for Army Forces Western Pacific. (Under the Napoleonic staff system adopted by the U.S. armed forces, the personnel staff is designated G-1, intelligence is G-2, operations G-3, logistics G-4, and so on.) In this position he performed myriad jobs. He helped to coordinate security for the 1946 inauguration of Manuel Roxas y Acuña, a close associate of the late Manuel Quezon, as the last president of the American-dominated Commonwealth of the Philippines and the first president of the independent Republic of the Philippines.

He helped to train an intelligence division for the new Philippine army. He resolved some "300-odd cases of internees of doubtful nationality," such as Chinese slave laborers imported into the Philippines by the Japanese. In the latter case, one of his friends, Major O. J. Magee, wrote, "He found the root of the trouble quickly, pulled, kicked and pounded his way through obstacles of inertia, high politics, pomposity and ignorance, and soon had an honest system operating smoothly."[12]

All the while, Lansdale was struggling to understand the country in which he now found himself living—something that remarkably few soldiers of any nationality bother to do when deployed abroad. The rare exceptions tend to be celebrated ones. They include the French field marshal Hubert Lyautey in Indochina and Morocco, the British commanders Robert Clive and Frederick Roberts in India, and T. E. Lawrence in Arabia. Only a few contemporary Americans such as Douglas MacArthur in the Philippines and Japan would have made the list; in years past, the most noted American military students of foreign societies had been Indian fighters such as George Crook and Christopher "Kit" Carson. While their fellow officers preferred unintellectual pastimes such as polo or hunting, drinking or card playing, these renegades undertook the difficult and sometimes dangerous work of acquainting themselves with alien cultures and in the process often became alienated from their own societies.

Lansdale followed their example by getting his "staff of home-sick Americans to change their habits of estimating an enemy's order-of-battle and combat intentions and, instead, to take a hard look at the country where we were. An estimate of the war-ravaged socio-economic conditions in the Philippines, soon to be an independent nation relying on itself, was sorely needed. So we worked on the task, giving the results not only to Washington but also to Malacanan [Palace] where they were of use to the Philippine President and his Cabinet."[13] By the beginning of 1947, Lansdale and his staff had compiled twenty-seven major studies that offered the most thorough survey of conditions in the Philippines during that period. A typical study, completed in June 1946, began by noting, "The situation is far worse than what was envisioned in 1941." The Philippines faced war damage estimated at $700 million to $800 million, with nearly 80 percent of schools and 60 percent of power plants having to be rebuilt. The citizenry also confronted rampant "lawlessness" and a skyrocketing cost of living, making "many necessities of life . . . nearly impossible to obtain, except through the black market." "On the other hand," the survey noted, "the situation is far more encouraging than it was right after the liberation in the Spring of 1945." "Money and supplies" had poured in from the United States to help alleviate "the first, or disaster, phase of rehabilitation." The health situation had improved, the ports were again functioning, "transportation is nearly normal again," and "public water-works are in good shape."[14] Following this summary came page after page of in-depth information, illustrated by striking photographs.

Although the details were unique to the Philippines, roughly similar conclusions could have been reached about many other places in post-1945 Asia, including China, Burma, Indonesia, Malaya, Korea, Thailand, and Indochina—all of which, like the Philippines, would be convulsed by insurgencies that arose out of the chaotic, impoverished, and unsettled postwar conditions. Lansdale recognized the danger before most of his contemporaries. His reports were not focused on tracking enemies, the traditional mission of military intelligence. Rather, he was tracking societal conditions to ensure that new enemies did not arise out of the rubble of old wars.

◆

JAPAN, WHICH in the historian John Dower's phrase "embraced defeat," was one of the few Asian nations that did not experience an armed uprising after the end of the war, but U.S. forces stationed there still faced a daunting array of difficulties. Lansdale was to get a firsthand glimpse of the challenges of rehabilitating America's former adversary in 1946. That summer the military government of the Ryukyus, a chain of islands stretching south from the Japanese mainland toward Taiwan, was to pass from the U.S. Navy to the U.S. Army. Okinawa, the biggest of the Ryukyus, was well known to American soldiers as the scene of one of their bloodiest battles of World War II. The other Ryukyus, some of them little more than tiny unpopulated atolls jutting out of the blue-green waters of the East China Sea, were terra incognita to most Americans—or, for that matter, most Japanese. In the spring of 1946, Major Lansdale was dispatched, at his own initiative, to learn more about the thirty-two islands located north of Okinawa, with an estimated population of 190,000.

While his formal mission was simply to gather information, Lansdale was, in fact, part of a larger endeavor on the part of the American armed forces, which were then engaged in one of the most successful examples of nation building on record by converting the Japanese from foes to friends. That process was just beginning when Lansdale set out for the Ryukyus. Assigned to accompany him was an agent from the Army Counterintelligence Corps, James Clark, an Army photographer, Technician Fifth Grade David Greene (addressed as "corporal" or "tech corporal"), and a Nisei interpreter, Technician Fourth Grade Matsue Yagawa (addressed as "sergeant"). No other transportation being available, they had to travel on leaky wooden Japanese boats, first the *Koei-maru* and then the *Taekuku-maru*, which were normally used to haul rice and other goods between the islands.

They set off from Okinawa at the end of April 1946 aboard the eighty-foot-long *Koei-maru*, which Lansdale described as "a sort of overgrown rowboat and a very ratty, dirty and ancient one." Lansdale had to share the "tiny" captain's cabin with two other Americans. In addition to the Americans, the boat carried Japanese crew members, a Japanese government official, a Japanese sugar dealer, and the "silver-toothed" Japanese captain and shipowner, who, Lansdale was amused to note, "laughs at everything. If the ship were sinking, he'd probably stand on deck and laugh until the tears came." Lansdale did not speak a word of Japanese, but still had "quite a conversation" with his Japanese shipmates "using our phrase books."

As they chugged along, the whole boat shaking from the vibrations of the diesel engine, Lansdale sat early one morning on the "deck" ("boards over the hold with canvas cover"), wearing nothing but shorts, smoking a cigarette (most likely a Chesterfield, his favorite brand), enjoying the "pleasantly warm" weather, and looking out over the endless ocean. Lansdale "started wondering how strange it was to be in a little Jap island boat that the U.S. had been trying to sink not long ago—and going up to look at islands which few people have even heard of." (His casual use of "Jap" shows that the contemptuous wartime argot had not entirely vanished with the coming of peace.) Along the way, Lansdale saw such natural wonders as an active volcano on the island of Suwanosejima, which had "ruddy flames and plumes of smoke" and "spit up white hot chunks of magma from time to time as we approached it across the strait." But his primary interest was in the natives, not nature, and he found plenty to fascinate him in these remote and isolated societies. Hanging "onto a bulkhead with one hand" while "writing with the other," he would produce an extensive report on food availability, public health, government, education, social organizations, and other aspects of the islands. It was not just subjects of military concern that caught his attention and led him to put pen to paper. On Suwanosejima, he was entranced by the locals who "danced and sang for us the other night—old ladies first, beating hard drums and a dry nasal song, then the younger women with kids strapped on their backs—the kids looking wide-eyed at the Americans as their mothers jogged in a circle."

Lansdale's observations were part of a long history of American fascination with the islands of the Pacific stretching at least as far back as *Typee: A Peep at Polynesian Life* (1846), Herman Melville's first book, which was based on his experiences as a deserter from a whaling ship in the Marquesas Islands. Interest in the region only increased with Commodore Matthew Perry's "opening" of Japan in 1853–55, the clipper trade with China, and the fin de siècle acquisition of Hawaii, Samoa, the Philippines, Guam, and Wake Island, followed four decades later by the island-hopping campaign in World War II. A naval lieutenant just a year older than Lansdale was even then writing a collection of short stories that would come to define Pacific island culture for most Americans. James A. Michener's *Tales of the South Pacific* would be published in 1947 and, after rocketing to the top of the best-seller list, would win the Pulitzer Prize and become the basis for the popular musical *South Pacific*. Lansdale's experiences could have made a fitting sequel—"A Tale of the North Pacific."

In a journal he kept, Lansdale recounted how his party made land-fall at the town of Naze, capital of the island of Amami Oshima, on May 2, 1946. He observed "dark masses of high hills on each side, above was alive with stars, and nearby in the waters, were rowboats and sampans with fishermen using copper-colored flares to attract the fish." The boat's engine was shut off, and they "glided along silently over the batches of copper reflections." Nearly all of the Ryukyus had been bombed or strafed regularly by American warplanes between March and August 1945. These attacks destroyed a third of the fishing fleet and roughly half of all standing structures. "The business section of Naze was wiped out," one of Lansdale's reports noted, and farmers were unable to work their fields "because of the frequency of the air raids." Although fishermen were going out once again and farmers were planting sweet potatoes, Lansdale noted, "the islands are existing on a bare subsistence level." The inhabitants were reduced to eating grass soup.

The crisis, as in many other places in Europe and Asia, was compounded by the kind of corruption that the director Carol Reed and screenwriter Graham Greene would memorably depict in the 1949 film noir classic *The Third Man*, set in a seedy and decrepit Vienna. In a village on Amami Oshima, Lansdale discovered the local version of the black marketeer Harry Lime, played by Orson Welles in the movie. His name was Kinoje Degushi, and his position was subgovernor (or mayor). Misusing his authority, he had stolen substantial supplies of rice and sold them on the black market. Lansdale did not bother to notify his headquarters and ask for instructions. He took matters into his own hands by confiscating all of the rice and redistributing it to the residents. Then he convened the people in the schoolhouse, which he converted to a makeshift courthouse, to sit in judgment on their subgovernor.

With Kinoje sitting forlornly beside him, Lansdale, speaking through his Japanese American translator, Matsue Yagawa, delivered an indictment of the subgovernor, saying he wasn't doing his job, because he was letting the people go hungry. As Lansdale was speaking, Matsue whispered to him that Kinoje was trying to inch open the drawer of the school desk in front of him to grab a gun. The army counterintelligence agent and photographer were getting nervous; they asked for, and received, Lansdale's permission to prepare their rowboat for a hasty departure. Lansdale, who had a .45-caliber automatic pistol in a shoulder holster, told Matsue to tell the subgovernor, "I know he's got a gun in there and I'm waiting for him to get it . . . and take a shot at me so I can kill him right in front of the people." Upon hearing this, Kinoje jumped up to show that he had no gun and surrendered on the spot.

Lansdale and his small team marched their prisoner down to the boat to transport him to jail, one of the few buildings that remained standing in Naze. As they were leaving, Matsue asked Lansdale how fast he was on the draw. Lansdale had to admit that he'd never taken his pistol out of its shoulder holster. On examining the gun, he discovered it was lodged so tightly in the new holster that he couldn't even "tug it loose." "Oh Geez," Matsue said nervously. "I thought you were lightning fast. I was getting ready to duck and everything but you'd just have been creamed on the spot." Lansdale was no gunfighter, but he was a master of psychology and had just tricked the subgovernor into submission.

While they were sailing back to Naze with their prisoner, Lansdale and his men passed a small copse of Japanese fishing boats. The fishermen had already heard of how Lansdale had arrested the corrupt official, and they were yelling thanks. In Naze, local people came up to express their gratitude and to offer gifts. The mayor gave him a scroll, and the local prostitute, "the one bad girl for all these islands," gave him "a little handkerchief with dirty pictures on it, all nicely folded up."

Lansdale, naturally, found the trip to be "exciting." He exulted, with the typical pride of the Western imperialist or nation builder, "In some places, I was the first white man people had seen—in most places, the second white man." "And," he added excitedly, "coming in on a Jap boat, I learned more about the islands than anyone previously. . . . I'm the only officer above the grade of 2nd Lt. or Ensign who ever rode a rice boat in these waters." While on the move, he wrote, "I'm really having the time of my life—except I seem to stink of moldy rice by now."

Helping the people of these exotic, faraway islands while advancing the interests of his own country was a heady tonic for a thirty-eight-year-old former advertising man who only five years before might easily have imagined that he would spend the rest of his life peddling consumer products—Levi's jeans and Wells Fargo bank accounts and Swiss Colony wines—while living in the comfort of Northern California. His initial success in the Ryukyus confirmed Lansdale's conviction that, by getting involved in their internal affairs, he could help the people of Asia as they confronted the challenges of the postwar world. "Look where I am," he thought. *And look at what I can do.*[15]

◆

BACK AMID the wartime damage and tropical beauty of the Philippines, Lansdale continued his efforts to learn as much as possible about the archipelago. "I have always felt that if you are going to report on something," Lansdale later said, "don't take the word of other people, go out and eyeball it and see and then talk to people. You get a far different feeling for the problem and the situation."[16] He made it a point to get out of Manila as often as possible to explore the countryside. Usually he went on Sundays, a day of rest for many of his fellow soldiers but not for him. In a journal he kept intermittently, he described a typical Sunday—October 27, 1946—which illustrated not only how widely he traveled but also how many friends he had accumulated in such a short time.

"I was glad to get away from Manila," Lansdale wrote, which he did by borrowing a jeep to pick up his friend Engracio Fabre, recently appointed commissioner of immigration by President Roxas. Together they "drove over to a house in the Santa Cruz district just off Rizal [Boulevard]" to pick up Congressman Fortunato Suarez from the city of Lucena. "When Suarez came out finally in a rumpled white pongee suit, complete with shirt and tie, his packages piled on top of all Fabre's packages, we then set off again and picked up a Congressman from Samar at a nearby house." Their next destination was yet another congressman's house, where they were surprised to find a political meeting in progress at 7:30 a.m. on Sunday. "So I sat," Lansdale wrote a few days later, "and looked wise while speeches in Tagalog sputtered all around me." After an hour of this, "we all shook hands and swore eternal friendship and the four of us who went in then went out and drove to . . . breakfast at the Selecta, which consisted of thick doughy hotcakes and coffee."

By 11 a.m., Lansdale and his three friends were on the highway heading south toward Quezon Province, a narrow isthmus wedged between the Sierra Madre mountains to the north and the Sibuyan Sea to the south. The drive in the topless vehicle was bumpy and uncomfortable. Soon it started to rain. "In seconds we were working through mud and a passing truck threw a big gob of it into my face," Lansdale wrote. "Suarez, dozing in his white pongee in the rear seat, let out a wild yell and I turned and saw that he was covered with mud. He and the others then started laughing at the fun of getting splattered with mud, so I just kept on going. We entered the coconut country and my good humor came back, with the sight of green trees again." By 1 p.m., with the rain still falling hard, they stopped for lunch "at a fairly clean looking panciteria," where they sat in their "muddy and soggy clothes and ate a sourish pancit soup and rice and a strong-tasting fish and washed it down with coffee." When they got on the road again, "the rain suddenly turned into a regular S.E. monsoon, with sheets of water blowing in horizontally. I strapped my raincoat tightly about my wrists, but even then the rain blew up my left sleeve where my arm was raised to the steering wheel and I was soon sopping wet inside my rain-proof."

Finally they reached the town of Lucena, the capital of Quezon Province nestled precariously on the edge of Tayabas Bay, where, Lansdale wrote, he "delivered Suarez to his wife, who gave me a glass of tepid beer which I drank while my clothes kept a steady drip-drip on the living room floor." Then on to Fabre's hometown of Sariaya, "where I discussed the local copra situation with [Rufino] Rodriguez, the local big-shot planter, then I met the governor and was invited to a banquet." At Fabre's house, "suddenly the strain of the . . . week and the long drive hit me, so I went in and lay down on his parents' bed, on a straw mat, and 'took a nap.' Fabre tried to wake me later to attend the governor's banquet, but without luck. I slept right on through until 5 the next morning, when I woke up, had a cup of coffee and drove the 150 km. back to Manila for a conference with the general at 9 a.m."[17]

◆

LANSDALE DID not spend all his time hobnobbing with influential politicos. He was just as eager to meet the Negritos, Stone Age hunter-gatherers living on Luzon and other islands across Southeast Asia. Existing apart from other Filipinos, the Negritos had little interest in the quarrels between the Japanese and the Allies or later the Communists and the government, but with their knowledge of the rain forests of central Luzon they could be invaluable scouts and intelligence collectors for whichever side won them over. They occupied a cultural and geographical niche somewhat similar to that of the Montagnards, the hill tribes of Vietnam, which the French were then employing against the Vietminh and which the Americans would later employ against the Vietcong.

In October 1945, shortly after his arrival in the Philippines, Lansdale set off to find out what had happened to a Japanese armored column near Clark Field. Some Negritos, only three to four feet tall and clad in loincloths, showed up at his camp. Lansdale cooked them dinner while trying to figure out how to communicate with them since the only word of English they knew was "okay." They didn't even speak Tagalog, only their own tribal dialect. "This problem was finally solved by each of us drawing pictures in the sand and acting out parts," Lansdale recalled. In this way he figured out that the Americans had done something to the daughter of the tribal chief and specifically something to her belly. At first Lansdale assumed she had been abducted and raped by GIs. But "after three or four hours of talk," he finally figured out that the chief's daughter had been hit accidentally by an American artillery barrage meant to stop a Japanese armored column from escaping into the Zambales Mountains. "With that," Lansdale concluded, "I took off my GI watch that I had and I strapped it on the wrist of the tribal president as an expression of an American's sympathy about his daughter. He seemed pleased. I showed him how to wind the watch and how to listen to it. He didn't know how to tell time but I showed him."[18]

Thus began a long process that eventually resulted, with Lansdale's encouragement, in the Philippine armed forces utilizing some of the Negritos as intelligence gatherers and scouts against the Communist rebels known as the Huks.

◆

THE NEGRITOS were not the only Filipinos won over by Lansdale. So was practically everybody he met. One of his Filipino friends later said, "Ed had a way, he could make a friend of everybody except Satan, I think. And he was the one American that was liked by practically every Filipino."[19] An American correspondent in the Philippines noted that "he had a good way of talking with the Filipinos on the basis of man to man, no condescension, no talking down. They appreciated that after so many years of the Japanese and American colonials."[20]

Lansdale amply returned their affection. "Filipinos and I fell in love with each other. Almost everything I did there was done with tremendous brotherly love," he later said.[21] But some Filipinos—and, more to the point, Filipinas—he loved more than others.

5

In Love and War

*Pat [Kelly] showed me all these things up in the mountains that
I would have never known otherwise, and very few people have
ever known.*

—EDWARD LANSDALE

E D Lansdale's closest Filipino friend initially was Juan C. Orendain, an American-educated lawyer with the quintessentially
American nickname Johnny, who happened to be as informal and
friendly as Lansdale himself. He "joins with me," Lansdale wrote
on January 11, 1946, "in a quiet crusade against neckties": "Johnny
is now . . . the only man to show up at Cabinet meetings without tie
or coat, while some of the fussier ministers glare at him."[1] Lansdale
became very close not only with Johnny but also with his wife, Louise,
and their children, who called him "uncle" and for some of whom he
served as godfather.

Beyond their dislike of formal attire, Orendain and Lansdale were
bound together by a romantic vision of America as a force for good.
Orendain related to Lansdale the story of how as a little boy on the island
of Panay he met his first Americans during the Philippine–American

War of 1899–1902. "Rumors of the approach of 'savage' Americans had spread dramatically. Johnny was sure that they ate little boys like him for breakfast." The whole family tried to flee, but Johnny and a smaller brother got tired and sat down to rest. "Suddenly what Johnny took to be a giant in blue was standing before the boys. He was smiling and holding out something to Johnny in his hand. It was an apple. Thus Johnny met two things brand new to him, an American and an apple. Johnny took the apple to his parents and neighbors hiding in the hills and convinced them that the Americans were friendly. They returned home. Soon afterwards, an American sergeant started a school in the barrio, with Johnny among the students."[2]

Orendain later went to law school at Stetson University in Florida, where he learned to make the best apple pies Lansdale had ever tasted, and grew up conditioned to think almost as well of the United States as Lansdale himself did. That made Orendain a natural object of suspicion under the Japanese occupation. At the very first dinner that Lansdale shared with the Orendain family in 1945, he heard the story of how during the war they were "stopped by Japanese troops and their five-year-old son sang to the soldiers the only song he knew, 'God Bless America.' The non-English-speaking soldiers patted him on the head for the pretty song and fortunately didn't ask him for his name, which was MacArthur Orendain."[3]

One day in early 1946, a few months after Lansdale's arrival in the Philippines, Orendain stopped by his quarters with a friend in the car—a good-looking war widow in a white dress. Her full name was Patrocinio Yapcinco Kelly, but she was known simply as Pat Kelly. She was then working for a Manila newspaper. Before long she would go to work at the U.S. War Damage Commission. Later she would spend many years working for the U.S. Information Agency at the U.S. embassy in Manila. Talking to her, Lansdale saw at once that she was "full of fun"—and full of good information, too.

Lansdale was intensely interested in a Communist-dominated rebel group that had once fought against the Japanese and was now beginning to fight against the independent government of the Philippines. They had been known as the Hukbong Bayan Laban sa Hapon, or People's Anti-Japanese Army, but, in emulation of Mao Zedong's forces, they had recently changed their name to Hukbong Mapagpalaya ng Bayan, or People's Liberation Army. The Huks (pronounced *hooks*) were led by urban Marxist intellectuals, but their foot soldiers were ordinary young farmers fed up with the abuses of the Philippines' feudal system, in which a handful of wealthy families owned the land and the vast majority of peons had to work it for negligible recompense. Pat Kelly had gone to high school with Luis Taruc, the Huks' military leader, in Tarlac City, north of Manila, in an area of central Luzon, the Philippines' principal island, where the Huks were particularly strong. Lansdale was eager to meet Taruc and other Huks. Pat volunteered to serve as his guide. Together they would venture out to the roughest backcountry of Luzon in dangerous and uncomfortable circumstances. Thus was born a friendship and soon a romance.

"I can still see you the first time I ever saw you, sitting up so, in a white dress, in Johnny's jeep," Ed wrote to Pat a few years later. "You interested and excited me then, Pat, although I didn't know how deeply in love with you I was until we went to Baler [Bay]." (The trip, to a beach 140 miles northeast of Manila, took place later in the year.)[4]

Meeting Pat would spark the most intense and extended love affair of Lansdale's life. It would also lead him indirectly to his greatest success in the Philippines, his acute and sympathetic understanding of the Filipino people being intensified and extended by his relationship with this highly perspicacious and alluring Filipina.

◆

As LONG as Western men have been journeying to the Orient (a term that once encompassed all of Asia and North Africa), they have, inevitably, fallen in love with the women they found there. The practice has a provenance as ancient as the stories of Antony and Cleopatra, Paris and Helen of Troy. As soon as Europeans reached the Americas, Africa, and Asia beginning in the fifteenth century, conjugal relations with local women followed. The Age of Discovery, in other words, was also an age of sexual discovery, with all kinds of tropes and innuendos that are now considered racist. What was the erotic fascination of the foreign and hence mysterious East? A good part of the appeal, as the onetime *New York Times* Beijing bureau chief Richard Bernstein notes, lay in "an Eastern erotic culture that had always been more frank and less morally fastidious about sexual needs than the Western Christian erotic culture, which valued exclusivity with a single lifetime partner and associated sex for pleasure with sin."[5] Countless travel accounts echoed the observations of François Pyrard, a French sailor who spent five years in captivity in the Maldives Islands in the early seventeenth century. He wrote that "the women of all India are naturally much addicted to every kind of ordinary lewdness."[6] This image of the East as an erotic playland was further reinforced by the Victorian explorer Richard Francis Burton, who translated two erotic masterpieces, *The Arabian Nights* and the *Kama Sutra*, into English. Like later advocates of "free love," Burton inveighed against the "silly prejudice and miserable hypocrisy" of Europe and advocated "the comparatively unrestrained intercourse between men and women" which supposedly existed "among savages and barbarians," because it "relieved the brain through the body."[7]

Many years later, the literary scholar Edward Said would accuse Western explorers of being invidious "Orientalists" who exploited the people they came into contact with. There is an element of truth in the charge, but many were also driven by genuine enthusiasm for discovery, and the exploitation was not entirely one-sided—many poor Asian women saw relationships with Westerners as an opportunity for economic betterment and an escape from tightly constricted lives in traditional societies.

While conceivably beneficial to both sides, the possibility for tragedy always lurked in these cross-cultural romances. The best-known work on this theme is Giacomo Puccini's 1904 opera *Madame Butterfly*, which was based on actual incidents that had occurred in late nineteenth-century Japan. The protagonist is Pinkerton, an American naval officer living in Nagasaki who, through a marriage broker, finds a fifteen-year-old Japanese girl, Cio-Cio-San ("butterfly" in Japanese). The two get married before Pinkerton sails off for America. He is gone three years. The whole time, as any opera lover knows,

Cio-Cio-San pines for him and refuses an offer of marriage from a Japanese prince. But when Pinkerton finally returns, he brings back a new American wife. Once they learn that Cio-Cio-San has given birth to Pinkerton's son, the couple unfeelingly decides to adopt the boy. Hiding her own emotions, Cio-Cio-San agrees to give up her son, but when Pinkerton arrives to collect him she cuts her own throat, leaving the child clutching an American flag. No doubt there were many such heartbreaks—even some suicides—that resulted from liaisons between Western men and Asian women. Pat Kelly was made of sterner, more substantial stuff than Puccini's Cio-Cio-San, but her own East–West romance with Edward Lansdale would have its own share of frustration and heartbreak.

◆

PART OF Pat's appeal for Ed was the timeless attractions of youth and beauty. She was fourteen years younger than Lansdale's wife: born on March 13, 1915, she was thirty-one years old in 1946, black-haired and attractive, while Helen was forty-five and prematurely gray. Ed himself was thirty-eight, equidistant in age between the two women, and he was lonely stationed abroad without his family. It was natural that he would take a liking to the "beautiful as well as brainy"[8] younger woman, who was full of knowledge about the problems that most concerned him—issues of which his wife, back home, was entirely unaware. And all the more so because Pat was possessed of a livelier personality than his Stateside wife, according to those who knew both women.

Helen Lansdale was an old-fashioned, self-conscious "lady" who had gone to a finishing school and behaved according to the prim standards of the early twentieth-century provincial American upper class, Dunkirk, New York, branch. Her mise-en-scène was a world in which women wore white gloves, ate small, crustless snacks known as "tea sandwiches," and made polite, uncontroversial conversation. She was not happy that her husband's work interfered with her dream of having an intact family in genteel conditions back in the United States.[9]

Lieutenant General Samuel V. Wilson, who served as Lansdale's deputy at the Pentagon in the early 1960s, later said,

I do not recall Helen Lansdale as being intellectually inclined or curious about what was going on in the world in general, especially in the realm of U.S. foreign policy and national security. . . . She was more of a 19th rather than 20th Century lady, more comfortable with the social customs and cultural mores of that period. And Ed, while deeply steeped in history, was more of a 20th Century figure who was constantly probing the future. She was looking back, he was looking forward. Helen was family-oriented, would have been at her happiest in a small cottage with a white picket fence and raising children. Ed enjoyed a secluded rendezvous, a mountain hideout or a small hidden beach—but only to rest up and gather his strength for the next adventure.[10]

Pat—more curious, intellectually sophisticated, opinionated, and outgoing—was instinctively in greater sync with Ed's personality and interests. She had, according to Rufus Phillips, another of Lansdale's associates, a "very vibrant Filipino personality" and was "a lot of fun to be around." She was also full of "shrewd observations" on Philippine politics, if also, on occasion, "pretty acerbic" and "sarcastic."[11] Pat's grandchildren would say she had "great looks and an outgoing personality,"[12] adding that, unlike most Filipino women of her time, who were raised to be quiet and meek, she "commanded" a room.[13] Little wonder, then, that Pat "bewitched" Lansdale.[14]

◆

PAT WAS one of six children of Fernando Yapcinco and Maxima Alcedo. Both parents were half Chinese and half Filipino, hailing from Pampagna Province, in central Luzon. Her father was one of the first surveyors in the Philippines, and he traveled all over the country doing work for the government. Pat was born in the Visayas when her father was working there; her family thereafter joked that she was a vampire because Filipinos believed that vampires dwelled there. Tarlac Province, where Pat grew up, was a land of lush vegetation, towering mountains, and sprawling sugar and rice plantations. It had been a center of resistance to Manila ever since a 1660 uprising against Spanish rule.

The existence of the plantations and the propensity to revolt were not unrelated: Tarlac suffered all the inequities of the Philippines' feudal landownership system. Tarlac was dominated by two intermarried clans: the Aquinos and the Cojuangcos. In Pat's youth the leading political figure was "Don" Benigno S. Aquino Sr., a future speaker of the National Assembly, and the leading landowner was "Don" José Chichioco Cojuangco, scion of a wealthy sugar clan. Aquino's son Benigno Jr. ("Ninoy") married Cojuangco's daughter Corazon ("Cory"), thus producing a political dynasty: Both his wife, Cory, and his son Benigno Aquino III would become president. Pat's lineage was far more modest, but in a country where literacy was a status symbol, she was far closer in background to the wealthy Aquinos and Cojuangcos than to the desperately poor, uneducated sharecroppers who toiled on the plantations.[15]

When the Japanese attacked the Philippines in 1941, Pat was working in the library of the *Manila Tribune*. That she was working at all made her unusual among Filipino women of that era. That she waited until she was twenty-six years old to marry made her doubly unusual; at that time, recalled her granddaughter, many Filipinas were getting married as young as sixteen.[16] Her husband was James Kelly, an orphan of Irish Filipino ancestry and thus another offspring of East–West romance. He died of tuberculosis in 1944, a victim of the shortage of medical care in that year of total war, leaving Pat not only his last name but a daughter, Patricia, born just a few months before his demise. Philippine society frowned upon single mothers and working mothers, and Pat was both, but she was not overly concerned about social conventions. After her father's death in 1949, Pat would become head of her whole family, displaying her business acumen by running a family-owned store and modest real estate holdings in Tarlac while performing a full-time job in Manila. Pat, then, was an independent woman who beguiled Lansdale in ways his more domestic wife had never done.[17]

Lansdale's love letters reveal just why he was so taken with his new paramour. He told Pat that "you had the brightest mind I'd met in the Philippines" (a comment that might seem racist if taken out of context, but in fact Lansdale was greatly impressed by many Filipinos), "you are the most intensely interesting person I've met," and "you're uncanny in your great gift for understanding people." Sounding like many a smit-ten lover, he was enchanted "with those legs of yours," "that glorious lilt of hips and fanny you achieve somehow in your walk," "that favor-ite spot of mine behind your knee," "that hoydenish impish smile of yours," "that delightful glint in the eye that you have and that makes you so much fun to be with."[18] As if attempting to channel Cole Porter, he called her "the most delectable, intriguing, and wisest half of me."[19] In turn, Pat teased Ed constantly and he loved it. "If I didn't enjoy your needling so much, I'd give you a spanking,"[20] he said. Like Ed, Pat culti-vated a hard-boiled exterior but could be very emotional. He called her "sophisticated a bit on the outside and so warm and spicy inside that worldliness." "Hecks sake," he wrote in the innocent slang of the 1940s, "no wonder I tumbled for all time."[21]

"I have it bad, my beloved," he wrote to her two years after their first meeting. "Yes, I love you. . . . You're so very very much in my thoughts and in my being."[22] He recalled moments they had shared together: "How can I forget that drizzle at Baler Bay . . . or the cold night near the Experimental Farm at Baguio when you were so warm all snuggled close or that next-to-last visit to Atimonan [a beach town] when we were so hungry for each other."[23] He remembered, too, "those noons again by the Manila Hotel and my head in your lap and I could almost feel you under my head and see how you looked from a lap's eye view."[24] In another letter, he recalled "the honest way you used to drink bour-bon and water—when we weren't working on gin,"[25] and the way she would put "half a jar of mustard on one hamburger."[26]

His interest was not transitory, nor limited to physical passion. "You're the one person I want to share my life with . . . ," he wrote, adding, "If it's love, it's something I've never known before. I'm just not a whole person away from you, and cannot understand why God brought us together when I had previous obligations"—an oblique ref-erence to his existing marriage—"unless He meant us for each other."[27]

◆

IT IS not always clear, in retrospect, when Lansdale was traveling with Pat Kelly around the Philippines or when he was traveling by himself or with male friends such as the Associated Press reporter Spencer Davis, with whom he formed a lifelong friendship. Ed's periodic journal entries make no mention of Pat, because they were meant to be read by his wife and brothers. But it is clear that she was along on many of his post-1945 expeditions, and it was her role as an invaluable intermediary and interpreter, not only of language but also of customs and mindsets, that would account for so much of his success with the Filipino people. He was later to say, "Pat showed me a lot of the back country that the Huks went through. . . . She showed me all these things up in the mountains that I would have never known otherwise, and very few people have ever known."[28]

What he found was that central Luzon, a low-lying, agricultural region of rice paddies and sugar fields interspersed with barrios (villages) stretching 125 miles north of Manila Bay to Lingayen Gulf and bounded by the Zambales Mountains to the west and the Sierra Madre to the east, was increasingly dominated by the Huks. This area, home to more than a million people, even came to be known as Huklandia.

"Central Luzon is still a place where fear starts as the sun sets each day," Lansdale wrote on March 19, 1947.

> Farmers hurry home out of the rice paddies and cane fields. Buses stop for the night in the nearest town and the highways become empty, except for occasional pairs of armored cars hurrying along on patrol. In the larger towns, police sling their carbines and rifles on their shoulders and hurry into the center of town, usually opposite the marketplace, where they stand nervously under a street lamp in a group and peer into the shadows and stop every passing vehicle. Home folks finish their suppers and then hurry to close the doors of wooden homes or put the door panels in the nipa shacks . . . and make sure the lights are set for all night long.

Yet Lansdale kept going through the threatening darkness: "It's strange to roam around at night and see lights in all the houses and to realize that people are sleeping next to the flickering candle, coconut oil or carbide lamps, hoping the light will keep evil-doers away from their bedsides."[29]

In entering these Huk-dominated areas, Lansdale was armed with little more than his smile and his harmonica; his pistol would not have protected him from an ambush. Usually his personality was disarming enough. "You don't kill a guy laughing at you, being nice to you," he later said.[30]

An example of how he operated came in a trip to Huklandia in 1947. "I stopped in one town on the Pampagna River one hot noon to get a coke at a little sari-sari [convenience] store," he recounted. "The town had supplied a lot of men to the Huks, so most of the men were either dead by now or hiding out with the Huks in the swamps or hills. As I drank the hot coke, a group of local people gathered around and stared at me, more sullenly than most do." He was "taking a bitch puppy from a family in Pampagna to relatives in Tarlac"—almost certainly to Pat and her family—so he got the puppy out of the jeep and gave him the last of his coke. "I winked at some small boys watching me as I did this," Lansdale wrote, "and they smiled shyly. I smiled back, and then all those standing around suddenly smiled." The ice broken, Lansdale "wound up sharing lunch with a family, sitting on the split bamboo floor of their nipa house." Although he didn't say so, odds were that Pat was along to act as translator and guide.[31]

Lansdale benefited, of course, from being in a land in which *Yanquis* were generally looked upon with affection. Yet even though most Filipinos were pro-American, life-threatening dangers abounded for an outsider. On Sunday, June 8, 1947, a "beautiful morning," Lansdale was inspired to paint his "yearly landscape." He stuck his "water colors, cold beer, sandwiches, camera, and .45 pistol in the jeep, put on a sport shirt and walking shorts, and drove"—along with Pat—"about 10 miles north of Manila to Novaliches dam." Since it was "sizzling hot," he and Pat popped open cans of beer as soon as they stopped. They were just taking their first sips when behind them they heard someone say "ps-s-s-st Joe." "So I turned around for a look," Lansdale wrote. "There, 10 feet behind me was a Filipino with a big handkerchief across his face and with an M-1 [carbine] raised to his shoulders on a dead bead with my head."

"Hey, take it easy," Lansdale told him, while starting to reach for the .45 pistol beside his seat. He thought better of it when he realized the bandit wasn't alone. There were five men altogether, all armed. So he and Pat obeyed their instructions to exit the jeep with their hands raised. As four of the bandits began unloading the jeep, "the one with the M-1 kept inching up closer behind me," Lansdale wrote. "I sensed that he was extremely nervous and probably out on his first holdup." He remembered that a U.S. Army lieutenant had been murdered in this area the previous year under similar circumstances, and he "started to get scared."

The bandits were speaking Tagalog, which Pat no doubt translated for Ed. "The nervous guy with the M-1 behind me said something about killing the *kano* (me) and then searching the body," Ed wrote. "You are in bad trouble now, just doing this to me," he replied. "Don't get into really bad, serious trouble doing anything more."

The bandits took Lansdale's new Rolex watch and his wallet along with Pat's Semca wristwatch and handbag and all of their other possessions. Then they blindfolded Ed and, leaving Pat behind, made him climb into the jeep before taking off cross-country. Just as Lansdale was wondering what was going to happen next, the jeep stopped. He was afraid that he was going to be killed on the spot. To prevent that from happening, he recounted, "I asked them for one of my cans of beer. They opened one and gave it to me, so I told them they might as well drink up my beer." This calmed the bandits, and it was to become a standard Lansdale ploy when meeting hostile men. (Many years later he explained that you need to give potential killers "something else to think of fast, and I would ask them if they needed cigarettes or need some food or did anyone want a drink.")[32] Taking advantage of the change in mood, Lansdale "told them it was a lousy trick to make me walk so far back on a hot day and to give me another open can of beer for the walk." Lansdale finally decided to risk taking off his blindfold and climb out of the jeep. The young, nervous bandit with the M-1 was still talking about killing him, but an older bandit took charge and escorted Ed down "a muddy trail next to a rice paddy."

Lansdale walked five miles back to the dam to reunite with Pat and to call Filipino and American MPs. The only way we can be sure that Pat was present during the robbery, given the care that Ed took to excise any mention of her from his letters home, was the police report that he filed. Paragraph four read, "At the time of the robbery, I was accompanied by Mrs. P. Y. Kelly, who was also robbed of her possessions."[33]

◆

THIS ARMED robbery hardly dissuaded Lansdale from trying to get close to the Huks. He went to great lengths to track down their leader, Luis Taruc. One of the few genuine peasants in the Huks' leadership, Taruc had gone to an American-run school and, like Johnny Orendain, had formed an emotional attachment to American history. "I cherish Jefferson and Abraham Lincoln, especially Lincoln," Taruc later told an interviewer.[34] But Taruc had been influenced by an American soldier in a very different way than Orendain had been. As a boy, he had met an American sergeant who was a dedicated Communist and set him on the path, after brief labor as a tailor, to becoming a Communist himself. During World War II, Taruc led Huk guerrillas against the Japanese occupiers. In 1946, he won a seat in the Philippines Congress as a candidate of the Democratic Alliance, a leftist political party. But President Manuel Roxas accused him and other Huks of being terrorists and refused to seat them. Denied a chance to influence his country's future via the political process, Taruc and the other Huks took to the hills in late 1946 to resume guerrilla warfare. Not yet thirty years old, Taruc was appointed the Huks' military supremo.

He and his comrades found a receptive audience among subsistence farmers who had long-standing grievances against a landowning elite that kept them in a state of semifeudal peonage. Many ordinary Huks wanted reform, not a revolution, but they were led by Marxist ideologues who enforced a strict discipline on their ranks. Those who were suspected of disobeying commands were subject to summary "liquidation" as "traitors." The Huks had little if any direct contact with Chinese or Soviet organizers, so instead they studied the American reporter Edgar Snow's 1937 book *Red Star over China*, about Mao Zedong's movement, for pointers on how to conduct a revolution.[35] Just like their

Chinese and Vietnamese counterparts, the Huks sent cadres into the barrios to hold covert political rallies and to gather intelligence, food, and recruits. Meanwhile, armed guerrillas in mobile columns ambushed military units and terrorized government officials and their supporters.

Lansdale thought he might be able to meet Taruc if he visited the home of his sister in a small town in central Luzon. He knew that Taruc's sister was pregnant and losing her teeth, so he brought along some calcium tablets and a message that he "would sure love to talk to her brother if he ever sneaked into town." He found her house dark, but the door was partially open, so he stuck his head inside and asked, "Anybody home?" The answer came when he felt gun barrels poking into his ribs. Taruc's bodyguards were in the house, and they were convinced Lansdale was a spy. The first thing he could think to say was, "Don't shoot, look at the floor. . . . If you're going to shoot me, do it outside. . . . Don't get the floor bloody and the women have to scrub up after you."

Talking fast, Lansdale argued that he was too valuable to kill. He pointed out that the Huks risked sending couriers through military checkpoints to Manila to give their press releases to news agencies so that they could be published in the United States and eventually read by President Truman. Lansdale suggested that talking to him was a much simpler way to get the president's ear because, he claimed rather presumptuously (and prematurely), his reports were read by Truman himself. So he whipped out a pad of paper and asked them, "What do you want to tell the president of the United States?"

The Huks obligingly proceeded to air their grievances. Once they were done, their anger spent, they told him that Taruc's sister was in the bedroom. Lansdale went in to introduce himself and give her the pills. He learned that Taruc had gone out of the back window just as he had come in the front door.[36] Lansdale never did succeed in meeting the elusive rebel leader, but he did manage to walk away from another close call thanks to his quick thinking.

◆

IN ADDITION to meeting the Huks for himself, Lansdale was interested in studying how the American-trained Philippine army fought them. On Saturday, March 29, 1947, he set out for central Luzon to see "where men were killing men in dubious battle." A battle was being waged on Mount Arayat, a "lonely mountain that rises with volcanic abruptness from the central plain where no mountain should be." It was being used as a Huk base, and now it was under attack by the Military Police Command of the Philippine army. Lansdale had been invited to "come up and see the fun" by Major Napoleon "Poling" Valeriano, like Pat Kelly an invaluable interpreter of local politics and culture who was to become one of his closest associates in both the Philippines and Vietnam.

Valeriano was a 1937 graduate of the Philippine Military Academy (modeled on West Point), the U.S. Cavalry School at Fort Riley, Kansas, and the U.S. Army Command and General Staff College at Fort Leavenworth, Kansas. He was also a survivor of the Bataan Death March who had escaped from a prisoner-of-war camp to join guerrilla resistance against the Japanese.[37] Since the start of the Huk Rebellion, he had developed a reputation as one of the most able and ruthless officers in the entire Philippine army. He was in charge of the Nenita unit, a "hunter killer" team whose purpose, he explained, was "to seek out and destroy top leaders of the Huk" and "by disciplined, ruthless action to strike terror into the guerrillas and their supporters."[38] It had been nicknamed the "skull squadron" by rebels who accused Valeriano's men of taking Huks' heads as trophies. Although friends with Poling, Lansdale did not share his lust for battle. "I have broken bread and shared cans of beer with folks on both sides of this squabble," Lansdale said, "and I couldn't square with myself if I had to sit and listen to the orders being issued to kill people I knew."

Instead of joining the army troops as they advanced up Mount Arayat, Lansdale went down a carabao (water buffalo) track by himself (or accompanied only by Pat Kelly) and made camp that night in "a flat place with a five foot tree growing in it." He strung his mosquito net from tree to jeep, ate his rations, and watched as "the base slope of Mount Arayat lighted up with flashes." "I slept most of the night," Lansdale wrote, "except for the heavier firing when I awoke long enough for a cigarette and to wonder if there were any Huks on the mountain and what a bad spot they were finding themselves in."[39]

As these comments suggest, Lansdale was sympathetic to the ordinary Huks and skeptical of the heavy-handed tactics being employed against them by the Philippine army—similar to those being employed by the French and later the Americans in Vietnam. "Most of the Huks . . . believe in the rightness of what they're doing, even though some of the leaders are on the communist side of politics," he wrote. "And there is a bad situation, needing reform, which still exists in central Luzon. Agrarian reforms still seem to exist only on paper and I suppose armed complaint is a natural enough thing after the guerrilla heritage of most of these folks."[40]

As for the Military Police Command, the force on the front lines against the Huks, he thought it was "so riddled with politics it can only make weak passes at the Hukbalahaps who are in open rebellion in Luzon. And, the Philippine Army itself is involved in one scandal after another as its officers sell off the U.S. surplus they are supposed to be guarding for the Republic."[41] Both sides were guilty, he believed, of deplorable excesses: "Cruelty and a lust for murder are commonplace. Philippine Army MPs take but few prisoners. They merely shoot their newly captured Huks, often in the back of the head. It is hard to prove sedition, the true crime, against these folks, so why waste time with legal proceedings? On the other hand, MPs live but a few agonized moments after the Huks capture them. Both MPs and Huks have told me they learned to kill during the Jap occupation."[42]

Lansdale realized that the blunderbuss approach of the security forces was creating more enemies than it was eliminating—exactly the same problem the U.S. armed forces would later face in Vietnam. The problem was that as a lowly army major he did not yet have the power to force his Filipino counterparts to adopt a different approach.

◆

THE YEAR 1947 would bring significant changes in Ed Lansdale's professional and personal life. In August his family—Helen Lansdale and their two boys, Ted, age eight, and Pete, age six—arrived from California to live with him in a military housing compound in Manila. Relations between Ed and Helen were predictably tense after a two-year separation, and they did not improve upon Helen's arrival.

Manila undoubtedly had made real strides since the dark days of the immediate postwar period. Lansdale wrote in early 1948 that a U.S. military officer from 1945 would have gotten lost in "the city of today": "He would be mostly amazed at the six-lane divided concrete boulevard which they've made out of the bumpy Espana Street," and he "would see few Army vehicles, hear less shooting," and he would "go to new night clubs" like the Riviera, Town House, and El Cairo.[43] But there were still many lingering signs of the war, including the ubiquity of pontoon bridges and Quonset huts, which were intended to be temporary but remained in place years after Japan's surrender. There were also reminders of the ongoing rebel war, including a growing population of rural residents who, driven out of their homes by mounting violence between the Huks and the army, had become squatters in Manila.

Helen Lansdale, newly arrived from the San Francisco Bay Area, was disgusted by the privations posed by her new surroundings. She wanted to keep everything "beautiful" and "immaculate,"[44] said a friend of hers, and that was impossible to achieve in the tropics. "She was a nice person," Ed's associate, Rufus Phillips, said many years later, "but I think not suited for living abroad under fairly chaotic circumstances. . . . She liked an ordered existence."[45] To make matters worse, Helen fretted about Ed's safety while he was off on expeditions to Huklandia. She became upset when he came home from a trip with bullet holes in his vehicle, so he stopped telling her about his adventures.[46] But she was reminded of the danger they lived in when, as Ed recalled, "the Philippine army would escort us from parties with armor, light tanks, scout cars, and heavy weapons."[47]

Ed's Filipino friends would joke upon meeting Helen, "What! Ed's wife? Why, he never told anyone he was married." "Since Helen and the boys arrived," Ed wrote, "I have discovered that that is the Number One humor line in Manila."[48] This jest was, of course, not very funny to a wife who must have increasingly suspected that her husband was cheating on her, for his relationship with Pat was an open secret around town. Peter C. Richards, a British-born Reuters correspondent who was a good friend of Lansdale's, recalled that he and his wife socialized with both Pat and Ed *and* Helen and Ed: "We got along well with him and his wife as a couple, and we got on well with him and Pat as a couple. And you might say almost simultaneously. I don't know how that worked, but it worked all right. That was their problem, not ours."[49]

◆

WHILE COPING with a new domestic situation, which forced him to juggle a wife and mistress in a scenario ripped from a French bedroom farce, Edward Lansdale also had to get used to new professional responsibilities. In 1947, he switched from the Army to the newly established U.S. Air Force, which he believed would offer "more elbow room for fresh ideas,"[50] even if he had no intention of learning to fly. "I wanted a share of the thinking that would help guide my country in the troubled days I saw looming," he later wrote, and he figured that "in an air age" the Air Force "would assume the mantle" of intellectual leadership from the Army.[51] At the same time that Lansdale was switching services, he was also changing jobs—much against his will. But his desires did not carry much weight when balanced against those of the most powerful American in all of Asia.

By then a five-star general, Douglas MacArthur was Supreme Commander for the Allied Powers in Japan and Commander of Army Forces in the Pacific. He was focused primarily on the rebuilding of Japan, which he directed from a walnut-paneled office on the sixth floor of the Dai Ichi Insurance Building in Tokyo, across from the Imperial Palace, yet he remained keenly interested in the Philippines. He would have Philippine newspapers flown to him every day, and he would mark up, with visible annoyance, all the anti-American comments he read. Lansdale, reading the same newspapers in Manila, summed it up: "As far as the Manila press was concerned, the 'big white brothers' are just so many s.o.b.'s." The newspapers now were full of criticism that, as Lansdale noted, "GI drivers were racing through the streets killing off pedestrians or bumping into jitneys (which were probably built out of stolen Army jeeps)." Another sore point was the location of U.S. military bases—"The Filipinos want military bases in the Philippines, but not near anybody and certainly not near Manila."[52] GIs did not help their own cause with wanton displays of racism against "Flips," as they often called the locals.

For MacArthur, who was obsessive about managing his public image and was contemplating a run for the presidency in 1948,[53] the criticism became intolerable when it reached the American press. On October 20, 1946, the *New York Times* correspondent Richard J. H. Johnston (derided by Lansdale as a "20-day expert on Manila")[54] published an article claiming, "With morale at its lowest ebb, their carelessness in dress, their unconcealed dislike for the Filipinos and their slovenly demeanor, the American troops on occupation duty in the Philippines are being openly referred to as 'ambassadors of ill will.'" No doubt pacing his office as usual and, we'd like to imagine, smoking one of his trademark corncob pipes, MacArthur demanded something be done about the upsurge in anti-Americanism. Since the current Army public information officer (PIO) in Manila, a full colonel, wasn't getting the job done, he had to be replaced.

MacArthur's chief of staff, Major General Paul J. Mueller, flew to Manila to find a more capable public affairs man. He called on Major Lansdale and told him, "I have checked with the top of the Philippine government, with all the newspapers, with the top social people in the Philippines, with the top business people, and the only American in this command that they all know is you. The only one they speak favorably of as someone they can talk to is you. None of them know the guy who is PIO now including the editors of the papers and the radio stations and they all know you as a friend."[55]

A few days later Lansdale inexplicably began getting calls about press matters. He went straight to Major General George F. Moore, commander of the Philippines Ryukyus Command (as Army Forces Western Pacific had been renamed), to tell him that the calls should be referred to the PIO.

"Didn't we tell you?" Moore said. "You are the PIO because MacArthur wants it that way."

It was not an honor that pleased Lansdale. He had enjoyed his time in intelligence and viewed this new assignment as an unrewarding diversion that, given the lowly status of public affairs in the military hierarchy, would be a career dead end. (While he was in G-2, he used to joke "that public relations was the lowest form of life in the army.")[56] He protested that as a mere major he was too low-ranking to deal with the heads of the other staff sections, who outranked him. A career army officer who had received his commission in the Coast Artillery Corps a year after Lansdale was born, Moore told Lansdale that those were the orders and they were not subject to discussion. That approach never worked well with Lansdale, who insolently replied, "I went into this army for patriotic reasons and I'll leave for the same goddamned reasons. I'll quit. It's up to you." General Moore was unused to being talked to that way by mere majors. Just as unexpected was Lansdale's next demand: that Moore agree in writing to back up Lansdale in any dispute he might have with more senior military officers. Given MacArthur's diktat, Moore had no choice but to sign the unusual contract that Lansdale drew up.[57]

Armed with this authority and a promotion to the temporary rank of lieutenant colonel, Lansdale set up a new public affairs office in downtown Manila, at a remove from the military headquarters, so that he could be "very close to the newspapers and the media and the businesses—the Philippine people, in other words." He made clear to reporters and editors that if they had any questions, they could call him directly rather than dealing with the military or embassy bureaucracies, and that he would "respond very quickly."[58]

In what would come later to reflect his overarching philosophy, he instructed his new staff, "It is time we changed our thinking about our public relations. We have been on the defensive. . . . Now is the time to take the initiative. . . . We should keep the journalists (particularly the Americans) so busy with favorable news that any bad breaks for the U.S. Army will be merely incidental and not be blown up beyond their importance."[59] In another memo, he wrote, "We must make certain that everyone understands that this is the Army of a friendly nation, stationed among friends. . . . That's the guiding principle. Worth repeating. . . . We are soldier sons of people who have fought for liberty and man's highest ideals. Let's keep our own honor bright, our ideals high."[60] These were some of the earliest written expressions of the principles that would hereafter guide Lansdale's counterinsurgency strategy. Whether acting as an intelligence officer, public relations officer, or a more amorphous politico-military adviser, as he would eventually become, Lansdale always focused on winning over the population by acting in a brotherly fashion.

"We changed the attitude 180 degrees overnight almost," Lansdale said with his trademark hyperbole. "It got so that after I was there about a week that the only news about Americans that they ever had would be if I had said that was a true story."[61] Lansdale and his subordinates even went around Manila removing "barbed wire barriers from city streets that U.S. military folks had put up to make parking spaces for themselves."[62]

In his new job Lansdale spent a lot of time on the social circuit. "Being PIO means," he explained, "that you go on everyone's dinner list, someplace down the table between the hostesses' embarrassing cousin from Cebu and the Vietnamese representative. It means, too, a coat and tie in a climate worthy of a T-shirt and shorts only. 'You meet such nice people' a PIO is told between bouts of dysentery, alcohol poisoning, and plain indigestion. Sometimes that's true."[63] On one night alone in July 1948, he was invited to "the opening of an art exhibit at the National Museum, a cocktail party for the S.F. trade delegation at the Manila Hotel, a reception for Americans at the Embassy, a housewarming party at Conchita Mestre's over on Singalong, and a party at the newly opened Sky Room at the Jai Alai." "The only difference in the parties," he commented sardonically, "is that you get fried chicken livers at the Philippine Army parties and sliced turkey at American parties."

All of these social events "are the meat and potatoes of a public relations man," Lansdale noted, "but they sure as hell are weary after a time." One weekend, he wrote, "I got so fed up on social affairs that I sneaked off to the provinces . . . down south to the beach near Siain, Tayabas, where the barrio folk are friendly and a guy can go without shaving and just lie around under the coconut palms on the beach."[64] Unstated was that Pat Kelly undoubtedly accompanied him on such short, but clearly restorative, jaunts.

◆

BY 1948, with his tour of duty winding down, his work had made him a local celebrity. "Hellsfire," he wrote, "I've even made the movie ads for premieres of Tagalog movies, with pix of me talking into microphones, and had editorials saying what a fine upright lad I am."[65] When Lansdale and his wife and kids sailed for San Francisco on November 19, 1948, he recalled, "a hundred or so Filipino friends heaped flowers upon my family and me and embraced us as the Philippine Constabulary band marched out on the pier next to the U.S. Army band and surprised me with a serenade of my favorite Filipino songs." He found the sendoff to be "heartwarming," but it "puzzled the other passengers." "As we sailed off, a group of them asked me, 'What in the hell did you do to deserve that?'"[66] In response, all that the modest major could do was shrug his shoulders.

In fact, he knew the answer—that he had succeeded in integrating and ingratiating himself with all levels of Philippine society. During the previous three years, he had traveled from the streets of Manila, jammed with pedestrians and jitneys, to the dense jungles and isolated nipa huts of the boondocks. He had met bandits and congressmen, Negrito tribesmen and farmers, soldiers and Huks. He had seen for himself how both the insurgency and the government operated. He had become, in short, one of the leading experts on the Philippines not just in the U.S. armed forces but in the entire U.S. government.

The following year, Lansdale could boast, in answer to a question on a military personnel form—"Have you any qualifications, as a result of training or experience, which might fit you for a particular position?"—that he had demonstrated the "ability" to win the "confidence [of] Orientals," and that he was known on a first-name basis by everyone from the president of the republic "down to farmers in [the] provinces."[67] That may seem a self-serving judgment, but it was echoed by Philippine observers. The *Philippine Armed Forces Journal*, for example, wrote in January 1948 that "the present friendly relations which exist between the United States army forces in the Philippines and the Filipino public" was "traceable in a large measure to Major Edward G. Lansdale." The newspaper praised him for having a "winning personality and knack for winning friends" and for "not a whit of any holier-than-thou attitude." Those who spoke with Lansdale, the article said, "invariably have become his most vociferous boosters."

No one, of course, was a bigger booster than Pat Kelly, now separated from her beloved by the expanse of the Pacific Ocean.

6

The Knights Templar

*I've written the career branch in Washington giving them 100
reasons why I should be returned to the Philippines pronto,
except I didn't tell them the main reason.*

—EDWARD LANSDALE

THE army transport ship *General A. W. Greely* was carrying
Edward Lansdale and his family back to a United States that
had changed considerably since his departure in the fall of 1945. In
those three years, more than ten million service members had left the
military to enter college on the GI Bill, to take new jobs, to marry, and
to live in new suburbs such as Long Island's Levittown. The austerity
of the war years had given way to the so-called baby boom and to a
buying spree as once war-rationed Americans shopped for boxy cars
from Ford and Chevrolet, big electric refrigerators and blenders from
General Electric and Oster, and other luxury goods that came to define
the postwar world. In that year, 1948, Americans were just starting to
watch television, which by the time of the Vietnam War would shape
public perceptions of the fighting in ways that no one could have imagined. In that infant age of television, however, Americans were tuning
in to see not battlefield reports but, rather, *Texaco Star Theater*, hosted

by the comedian Milton Berle, or a puppet show called *Howdy Doody*, which would later be regarded by the baby boomers as an emblem of a more innocent era. (Lansdale was slightly behind the times; he would not watch his first television shows until late 1949.)[1]

Harry S. Truman, the Missouri haberdasher turned politician, remained president, as he had been when Lansdale first set out for the Philippines, but now by the will of the voters rather than by the caprices of a death at Warm Springs, Georgia. On November 2, 1948, just a few weeks before the *Greely* steamed out of Manila harbor, Truman had been elected against all odds over the Republican nominee, Thomas E. Dewey, leading to, among other things, Lansdale's losing a bottle of beer in a bet with Pat Kelly on the outcome of the election.[2]

Truman was no longer presiding over a country giddy over the end of the greatest war in history. Americans were now increasingly apprehensive about a new conflict with an expanding Communist axis that carried the risk of World War III and a nuclear conflagration of unimaginable horror. The paranoia of the times led to reports of "flying saucers"—a potential enemy from another planet—and to even more widespread reports about an enemy lurking within American society. Loyalty oaths and investigations for suspected "disloyalty" were the order of the day, with J. Edgar Hoover and other "Red hunters" quick to seize on the hysteria to justify ever-expanding investigations. The headlines brimmed with news about Alger Hiss, a former State Department official accused of espionage, and about the Hollywood Ten, movie industry figures who went to prison for refusing to testify about their Communist associations.

◆

YET AS the *Greely* steamed across the vast blue-green expanse of the Pacific, Lansdale's thoughts were not on politics or world affairs. His letters reveal that all he could think about was his "darling Patching," as he called Pat. "It's rough and windy and hard to write with the paper fluttering and the deck dropping out from under me," he wrote to her early one morning shortly after sailing out, "but you seemed so close to me this morning that I got up about an hour ago and stood on deck to watch the sun come up the way you used to in Atimonan, and thought about you."[3] (Atimonan is located on Lamon Bay, about a hundred miles southeast of Manila.)

Before leaving, he had committed to memory every last detail of "the most adorable bewitcher I've ever known."[4] Now everything he saw aboard the ship reminded him of the lover he had left behind: "I watch a cloud and it starts turning into your face. I note an ankle on the companionway in front of me and start comparing it with those legs of yours disappearing up the back stairs at WDC [the War Damage Commission in Manila, where she worked]. Someone laughs and I see that hoydenish, impish smile of yours and then hear your quizzical 'why?' when I'd start grinning back."[5] Even something as prosaic as a bowl of cream of tomato soup reminded him so much of Pat that, he wrote, "I couldn't eat the rest of my dinner and went out and walked the deck, thinking of you laughing about such a thing."[6]

Hopelessly smitten with his paramour, he kept thinking of a hundred things he wanted to do with his faraway lover—"to cruise down to Mindanao with you, drive up to the northern end of Luzon, maybe really go to Sorsogon [the southernmost province of Luzon] after all, but most of all just to be with you happy, happy that you're close and new things are ahead and we'll share them."[7] He found it "strange how lonely it is for me with hundreds of people around"—including his own family—"none of them with your precious magic." "I have to fight with myself to put something else in letters to you," he confessed, "other than I love you, I love you, I love you, I love you, over and over again, yet that's what I want to say."[8]

Pat wasn't the only person with whom Lansdale shared his feelings. He came clean with Helen, too, and even asked her for a divorce. Believing that the relationship would be transient and that being home could attenuate his feelings for his distant mistress, she refused. "My wife only agrees to a separation for now. No more. To keep any 'hussy' from 'getting' me," the dejected husband wrote to Pat on July 5, 1949. In another letter, he told Pat that Helen is "asking how many illegitimate children I have and threatens to investigate, while offering me love, for the children's sake."[9]

Lansdale could have gone ahead with a contested divorce despite his wife's wishes, but he chose not to do so. "I haven't made a clear cut break yet because I didn't have you by my side giving me the peculiar courage this seems to call for," he told Pat. "You know how loyal I am to people—and this has been rather terrific on me. Particularly when you write that you're sort of falling out of love. I don't believe it, Pat my beloved, and we're going to spend a lot of our lives together. . . . I haven't even kissed anyone else since I met you and that's a pleasure that's hard for someone like me to forgo. . . . You're my woman and I want you!"[10]

Often throughout the winter and spring of 1949 Ed berated himself for not being able to get a divorce. "I'm mad at myself for giving in to the conventions of polite society and getting so far away from you," he told Pat.[11] A month later, after a long night of heavy drinking, he assured her, "I'm hoping that my own present affairs straighten out as quickly as possible—because we belong together."[12] He formally asked Pat to marry him. "I want you to know I love you and love you and love you and love you and if you were here I'd chew you up," he assured her.[13]

By the summer of 1949, the sobering realities of American law began to dissipate his dream of divorce. "I want you for keeps," he wrote Pat, "but lawyers tell me I cannot beat the rap, with my kids, etc., today."[14] In the late 1940s, getting a contested divorce was no easy matter.[15] California, like other states in the days before no-fault divorce laws, required the plaintiff to prove grounds for dissolving the marriage, such as adultery, extreme cruelty, desertion, incurable insanity, or willful neglect. It was certainly understandable that Ed shied away from such a proceeding, knowing that it could adversely affect his career prospects in the Air Force, to say nothing of the well-being of his two sons. Whatever he told Pat, he also was likely conflicted in his own mind about breaking up his marriage as his parents' marriage had been sundered. Like many children of divorce, he would not have been eager to emulate his father's example of leaving his mother, having seen for himself the emotional damage inflicted on the family.

Although Pat was hurt by Lansdale's failure to get a divorce, she also fretted, and for good reason, about how she would be treated as a

Filipina if she moved to a country where Japanese Americans had been interned in camps only three years before and racial minorities continued to suffer severe discrimination. Lansdale saw for himself the virulence of Jim Crow when in the fall of 1949 he briefly moved to Alabama to attend an Air Force course. He immediately noticed "the 'colored entrance' signs on restaurants and hotels" and the segregated compartments on trains.[16] Lansdale tried to reassure Pat: "You are a beautiful and wonderful person, with ability to make friends and find happiness any place. That's all that really counts anywhere in the world."[17] But in the United States of the late 1940s, where immigration laws had stanched the flow of Asian immigrants since 1924, Asian Americans were few outside of Hawaii and the West Coast, and Pat's skin was not the right color for much of white society.

◆

IN LIEU of a divorce, Helen and Ed agreed on a trial separation. She stayed at their house in Larkspur, a bedroom community in Marin County across the bay from San Francisco, where the family had moved in 1943. And she kept their two sons, now ten and eight years old, with her. They were joined for long stretches by Ed's mother, Sarah, long since abandoned by her own husband.

Ed moved by himself in February 1949 to his next assignment, teaching strategic studies at the newly created Air Force Intelligence School at Lowry Air Force Base in Denver. During the war, when it had served as a training ground for bombardiers, Lowry had swelled to a population of more than twenty thousand people. More recently it had become a demobilization center, a last stop for airmen returning to civilian life. It was Lansdale's bad luck that he went from the tropical Philippines to the frigid Rocky Mountains during a particularly severe winter. In December 1948–January 1949, there were eighteen snowstorms in twenty-seven days and temperatures fell to a dangerous forty below zero. In some states, snowdrifts were more than thirty feet high. On the way from San Francisco to Denver in February 1949 aboard a gleaming new train, Lansdale noted, "Snow and more snow and freezing cattle now in huddles in the snow."

"I'm just about the loneliest guy in the world the way I miss you tonight and keep on missing you," Ed wrote to Pat not long after arriving at Lowry.[18] "I've been feeling mighty low and blue ever since arriving here. The bluest I get is at 5:30 a.m. when I have to crawl out of a warm bed into a cold room, then go out into the night . . . and get breakfast at the Officers' Club a half mile away."[19]

In his new job, Lansdale was expected to talk about the Soviet economy, U.S. national debt, and other subjects about which he knew little. He would regularly go to the Denver Public Library for long hours of research. An added inconvenience for someone who loved to "loaf" in the morning was that he had to report for duty at 5:45 a.m. and begin lecturing at 6 a.m.—"just about the time you're rolling over for some more sleep," he wrote Pat, "or coming home from the Luneta you rascal."[20] (The Luneta is a large park near the Manila waterfront.) "Bleary-eyed and sleepy,"[21] he complained of his new job in his usual humorous way: "The school blithely loads me up with more lectures, talks, graduation speeches, briefings, seminars, forums, and other stuff than one guy can handle. . . . All I can do is shout an enraged 'what!' when told what the subject will be—and then be a good soldier and study like hell."[22]

While Lansdale did follow orders, he let his superiors know that he was unhappy with his oppressive workload.[23] Little wonder, then, that by the time Lansdale read a borrowed copy of Elliott Arnold's *Everybody Slept Here*, a lurid melodrama about intersecting lives and loves in wartime Washington, fellow officers at Lowry had already added marginal comments saying "This is Ed" and "Ed, note" alongside "descriptions of one of the characters who just doesn't fit into the Army—his reports were too honest and he fought with all the brass for what he believed in."[24] Lansdale was developing a reputation as a military malcontent.

Stuck in the freezing weather, doing a job he didn't particularly like, separated from his family, all that Lansdale could think of was how to get back to the Philippines. "These months away from you seem like an unpleasant dream," he wrote his inamorata, "and my life has lost so much of its flavor that I've crawled into myself with you."[25] He got particularly nostalgic when the mess hall at Lowry would play

Latin tunes such as sambas or guarachas that were also popular in the Philippines. When he heard that familiar music, he told Pat, "I can hardly eat or taste my food, you seem so close so suddenly."[26] Lansdale remained so smitten that he turned down an advance from a "gal" who wasn't "knockneed, pidgeontowed, bowlegged, pianolegged, peglegged or deformed with elephantiasis"—who was, in fact, in the language of the time, "quite a little provocative baggage." That he told Pat of this opportunity spurned was evidence of his fidelity—and of his desire to pique her jealousy.[27]

From the start, Lansdale was scheming to escape the dreary Air Force assignment, but it wasn't easy. "If I do a good job," he noted, "it means that I'll have to stay here for a long time and no Philippines. If I do a lousy job, I get stuck running a laundry or in the Arctic Circle."[28] "I've written the career branch in Washington giving them 100 reasons why I should be returned to the Philippines pronto," he told Pat, "except I didn't tell them the main reason: P. Mathilda Y.K.yA., whom I love, adore and cherish, and who seems to be running around having the time of her life as soon as my back is turned and who needs me there to feed sandwiches to and to put her head right down in my lap for old-fashioned bug hunting (hey, I never found one, did I?)."[29]

◆

WHILE LANSDALE was pining to return to his "precious minx"[30] in Manila, the Cold War was escalating with a virulent intensity that threatened the stability of the entire world. Winston Churchill had famously warned, as far back as 1946, that "an iron curtain has descended across the Continent." The U.S. response to the Soviet Union's seizure of Eastern Europe and to its support for Communist movements in other parts of the world came to be known as the containment doctrine. It grew out of the so-called Long Telegram sent from Moscow in 1946 by the diplomat George Kennan, who elaborated on his thesis in an article he published in the journal *Foreign Affairs* the following year under the byline "Mr. X." He argued that the United States had to enter into a "policy of firm containment, designed to confront the Russians with unalterable counter-force at every point where they show signs of encroaching upon the interests of a peaceful and stable world."[31] This became the intellectual underpinning of the Truman Doctrine—the president's announcement, on March 12, 1947, that he was asking for $400 million in assistance to Greece and Turkey to help fight Communist subversion. The following year, Secretary of State George C. Marshall unveiled a $12 billion initiative to rebuild Europe—an act of both selfless generosity and cold strategic calculation that came to be known as the Marshall Plan. The Soviet Union tried to test the West by blockading West Berlin in 1948, but Truman rose to the challenge by dispatching the U.S. Air Force to deliver supplies to the beleaguered city for nearly a year. In April 1949, the United States and Canada joined with ten nations in Western Europe to form the North Atlantic Treaty Organization to resist Soviet aggression.

Yet despite these Western countermeasures, the threat from the Soviet bloc only seemed to be growing. On September 23, 1949, President Truman announced that the Soviet Union had tested an atomic bomb, breaking the American nuclear monopoly. Just eight days later, Mao Zedong announced the formation of the People's Republic of China. America, it seemed, had entered a new age of insecurity. Two of the most powerful nations in the world were aligned against it and one of those nations possessed the ultimate weapon. Many feared that Armageddon was imminent. The well-informed British diplomat Harold Nicolson reflected the anxiety of the times when on November 29, 1948, he wrote in his diary that "Russia is preparing for the final battle for world mastery and that once she has enough bombs she will destroy Western Europe, occupy Asia, and have a final death struggle with the Americas." He judged the odds of peace being maintained at "not one in ninety."[32]

In trying to figure out how the United States could have lost ground to the Communists, many Americans blamed a fifth column of traitors such as Alger Hiss, a paladin of the Eastern Establishment who was convicted on January 21, 1950, of perjury for denying that he had spied for Moscow. On February 9, Joseph McCarthy, the scowling junior senator from Wisconsin, appeared before the Women's Republican Club in Wheeling, West Virginia, to charge that the U.S. government was permeated by "traitors from within." McCarthy even claimed to have a list of 205 State Department employees "that were known to the Secretary of State as being members of the Communist Party," thereby setting off the frenzy that became known as McCarthyism.[33] The seemingly precise figure actually derived from a four-year-old internal investigation of security risks at State that included alcoholics, homosexuals, and others, not just Communists. In a subsequent letter to President Truman, McCarthy reduced the number of State Department "Reds" to 57. The number would continue to fluctuate, like the weather, seemingly at random.[34]

McCarthy was an Irish Catholic small-town judge and a dipsomaniac with a vengeful streak and an exaggerated war record as a Marine tail gunner (he had not actually flown in combat). "Ignorant, crude, boastful, unaware of either intellectual or social refinements,"[35] in the words of a reporter who socialized with him, he was also an opportunist of genius with an unerring feel for how to stir up fear and to exploit the anti-Communist mood of the day. He would ask witnesses appearing before his subcommittee such loaded questions as "What have you got against this country?"[36] With McCarthy, always prone to hyperbole and innuendo, denouncing "a conspiracy so immense . . . as to dwarf any previous venture in the history of man,"[37] hysteria was in the air. As David Oshinsky, author of the foremost history of McCarthyism, notes, "Indiana forced professional wrestlers to sign a loyalty oath," "Ohio declared Communists ineligible for unemployment benefits," and "Tennessee ordered the death penalty for those seeking to overthrow the *state* government."[38]

Few were as immune to this paranoia as Lansdale seemed to be—or as levelheaded in trying to achieve a balanced outlook that avoided the extremes of both the most paranoid anti-Communists, who saw a Red under every bed, and the most idealistic liberals, who sometimes made it sound as if the whole Communist threat was a figment of McCarthy's unhinged imagination. When news broke of Stalin testing an atomic bomb, Lansdale wrote to Pat, "The Russian atomic explosion had the US newspapers in a tizzy. . . . Some of the officers here asked me what 'significance' it had—so I told them it was a Russian plot to get our pay raised. Sure enough, our Pay Bill passed through the Senate tonight. Now I get $4 more a month."[39] Yet at the same time that he refused to panic about Communist advances, Lansdale had no illusions about the totalitarian depravity of Communist rule. In early 1949, he wrote, "It's going to be a bloody future for a lot of Chinese. There's been a lot of thinking, among folks I've talked to here, that the Chinese Communists are simple agrarian socialists (shades of the Huks!), and that it will be simple to continue doing business with China in the same old way. I think they will continue doing business with the U.S., etc.—but will be building up a real communist nation all the time—and it's going to be a real sorry headache for us some day."[40]

Like many others at a time when any government employee deemed a security risk was liable to be fired or even prosecuted, Lansdale worried that he, too, might get into trouble with the Red hunters. In April 1949, for example, while stationed at Lowry, he was nervous when a guest seminar he gave at the University of Colorado was mentioned in the *Denver Post*. "These days, they take officers out and shoot them for mentioning foreign countries in public—and I mentioned practically the entire Far East," Ed wrote to Pat. "The reporter was friendly enough to mention my 'hedge' words, so maybe my statements were careful enough not to get me shot at sunrise. However, if you hear any shooting in the general direction of Denver, that's me, smiling and gallantly refusing a blindfold because they aren't your panties and smoking a last cigarette while leaning against the wall in front of the firing squad."[41]

However exaggerated and undocumented, McCarthy's charges continued to find a ready reception in a nation staggered by a continuing series of Communist blows—of which the most costly was the invasion of South Korea by North Korean forces in the predawn darkness of June 25, 1950. By September 1950, after having suffered heavy casualties, the U.S. forces had been pushed back to a shrinking perimeter around the port city of Pusan, on the southwest corner of the peninsula. General Douglas MacArthur's audacious landing at Inchon, behind enemy lines, on September 14, 1950, abruptly reversed the course of the conflict and sent North Korean troops reeling back across the thirty-eighth parallel. But the brief prospect of victory disappeared as rapidly as the leaves of autumn when on November 26 some three hundred thousand Chinese troops launched human-wave attacks on MacArthur's overconfident and overstretched forces. For the second time in less than a year, American and South Korean troops had to retreat in confusion. Eventually the lines stabilized again along the thirty-eighth parallel, the prewar boundary between North and South Korea. A long, costly, dispiriting stalemate was in the offing.

◆

CONFRONTING WHAT appeared to be an increasingly successful Communist offensive around the world, the Truman administration expanded its commitment to containment. The linchpin of its response was NSC-68, a top-secret paper completed in April 1950 by the Department of State's Policy Planning Staff under Paul Nitze, a wealthy and brilliant former Wall Street banker with a dark view of Soviet intentions. Along with his boss, Secretary of State Dean Acheson, he called for a massive buildup of American military power. Defense spending would nearly triple between 1950 and 1953.[42]

There was also a covert part of the American buildup, which had begun with the establishment of the Central Intelligence Agency in 1947. This was the successor to the OSS, which had been disbanded, over Bill Donovan's vociferous objections, at the end of World War II because President Truman did not want to establish an "American Gestapo."[43] But the CIA in its early years was primarily concerned with espionage and analysis, whereas influential figures such as George Kennan, head of the State Department's Policy Planning Staff in 1947–48, believed it was necessary to do more to covertly resist the Soviet Union and its proxies. National Security Council Directive 10/2, issued on June 18, 1948, created a new Office of Special Projects—shortly to be renamed the Office of Policy Coordination (OPC), an even more anodyne euphemism—to wage war in the shadows.

The head of the OPC was Frank G. Wisner, a wealthy Mississippian who had just turned forty. He had a gap-toothed smile, a compact frame, boundless energy, and a bald head bursting with ideas. Known to his friends as Wis, he had been brought up with an aristocratic ethos: "We were told that to whom much is given, much is expected," one of his nieces recalled. He was a fierce competitor who tried to win at everything from football to mah-jongg. He had even been invited as a sprinter and hurdler to the 1936 Olympic trials; he was not able to go, because his father thought it would be more character-forming to work in a Coca-Cola bottling plant that summer. After graduating from the University of Virginia Law School, Wisner went to work on Wall Street at a major law firm before joining the Navy and, in 1943, the OSS. He was galvanized by his experiences as an OSS operative in Romania from August 1944 to January 1945 when he watched the Red Army impose its brutal control, which included shipping trainloads of ethnic Germans to Russia to work in slave-labor camps. Wisner was later diagnosed as a manic-depressive; he would commit suicide in 1965. But in the late 1940s no traces of his mental illness were visible to associates. "Highly intelligent, experienced, energetic, and impeccably well-connected, he was uniquely well qualified for the job," the future CIA director Richard Helms was to write.

The OPC's remit was as wide as the Cold War itself. NSC 10/2 had given it authority over "propaganda, economic warfare; preventive direct action, including sabotage, anti-sabotage, demolition and evacuation measures; subversion against hostile states, including assistance to underground resistance movements, guerrillas and refugee liberation groups, and support of indigenous anti-communist elements in threatened countries of the free world." To finance its operation, the OPC had a pipeline straight into the Marshall Plan. Countries that participated in the Marshall Plan had to match the American contribution in their own currency. Five percent of those funds was secretly set aside for the OPC's use, amounting to $200 million a year ($1.9 billion in today's dollars).

This secret fund, nicknamed "candy," was symptomatic of the lack of controls over the OPC. This ultra-secret agency was supposed to "take its policy direction and guidance from State and the National Military Establishment," and once a week Wisner duly met with officials of both. But the State Department and Pentagon representatives were hawks who had no interest in reining in the OPC's covert plots against the Soviet bloc. In practice, therefore, Wisner had a large degree of discretion to create his own marching orders. That did not change substantially even when the OPC was merged into the new CIA Directorate of Plans in August 1952, with Wisner taking over as the CIA's deputy director for plans—another euphemism, since the new organization was concerned not with planning but with acting. Policymakers in those days tended to give the CIA ample running room in order to preserve "plausible deniability" of its actions, and Congress was not interested in providing serious oversight for similar reasons.

Wisner was well positioned to take advantage of all this freedom because of his social connections with a group of senior government officials, such as Allen Dulles, Charles "Chip" Bohlen, and George Kennan, and journalists such as the columnists Joseph and Stewart Alsop and the *Washington Post* publisher Philip Graham, all of whom lived near one another in Georgetown. This Georgetown circle has been described as "one of the most extraordinary clubs the world has known, a natural aristocracy," and Wisner was a charter member. He could craft new missions for his outfit in late-night conversations over steaks and martinis with his privileged peers.

Similar to Lansdale in his contempt for bureaucracy and his willingness to take risks, in love with adventure for its own sake, and fired by anti-Communist zeal, Wisner was firmly in the mold of Will Bill Donovan. He dismissed the CIA's intelligence analysts as a "bunch of old washerwomen, exchanging gossip while they rinse through the dirty linen." He did not want to chronicle history; he wanted to change it. He created at the OPC and later at the Directorate of Plans, the future CIA director William Colby was to write, "the atmosphere of an order of the Knights Templar, to save Western freedom from Communist darkness—and from war."

Before long, thanks to Wisner's "intense drive," his organization would become bigger than the rest of the CIA combined. In 1949, the OPC had just 302 personnel and a budget of $4.7 million. Three years later, it had nearly 6,000 full-time and contract employees and a budget of $82 million.[44]

◆

As THE OPC was expanding its operations, Edward Lansdale was still struggling to find a way to get back to the Philippines. At the end of October 1949, after graduating from a monthlong Air Force instructor's course in Alabama as the third-best student out of ninety-eight,[45] he took a short leave of absence to go to Washington. "Hq. there balked at my scheme to get back to the Philippines," Ed explained to Pat Kelly, "and I have to see what I can do to unbalk them."[46] The task of unbalking was made considerably easier when Lansdale ran into an old friend, Colonel George Chester, an army intelligence officer for whom Lansdale had worked back in Manila. Chester had been highly impressed by Lansdale—he described him, in purple prose, as having "the highest potential value of any AF [Air Force] Officer I have known, with a steel trap mind and a driving purpose in a relaxed body. . . . I would rather have Col. Lansdale with me than any other Officer I know."[47] When Lansdale explained his dilemma, Chester, who unbeknownst to Lansdale had just joined the OPC, told him "yes, something was coming on, he would stick [Lansdale's] name in the hopper and see if there would be some way of getting out of" a return to duty as an instructor at Lowry Air Force Base.

A couple of weeks later, by which time Lansdale was back in Denver, an Air Force colonel from the OPC personnel office came to see him and started talking to him about "a group forming in Washington for Cold War duty." Lansdale's "ears pricked up." It sounded exactly like what he was looking for. He volunteered immediately. While in later years it could take a recruit years to be vetted, hired, and trained by a more bureaucratized CIA, in those days the hiring process was expedited by the urgency of the moment and the lack of bureaucratic layers. Only a few weeks later, in November 1949, Lansdale relocated to Washington to report for duty at OPC.

◆

JUST AS they did not accompany him to Denver, Helen Lansdale and the boys did not make the trek cross-country. On his own in the capital, Lansdale took up residence in the bachelor officers' quarters at Fort Myer, Virginia. From his bedroom window, he could peer across the river to see "all the tombs for the dead and living that distinguish the city of Washington." His neighbors on this military compound included a number of the nation's most-senior generals. One day, he said hello to a man walking by, "wondering where I knew him from. After he'd waved good morning with a big smile it came to me."[48] The passer-by was none other than General Omar Bradley, the chairman of the Joint Chiefs of Staff.

Washington was still an overgrown, not to mention segregated, village in those days, one that had four daily newspapers but no truly good restaurants—and no Beltway.[49] Lansdale would walk forty-five minutes across Arlington Memorial Bridge into Washington each morning to the OPC's offices in seedy, rat-infested temporary wooden buildings erected along the Reflecting Pool near the Lincoln Memorial. The occupants of the "Tempos" shivered in the winter and sweltered in the summer. Employees who brought their lunches to work had to suspend the food from strings on the ceiling to guard against rodents and ants. The future CIA director Allen Dulles called the Tempos "a damned pig sty," but they would be the agency's home until the opening in 1961 of Dulles's dream palace—a new "campus" complex in suburban Langley, Virginia.[50]

Although assigned to a civilian intelligence agency, Lansdale did not stop serving in the Air Force. He had just been promoted to lieutenant colonel and soon would become a full-bird colonel. He would spend the next six years working for two masters, civilian and military, covert and overt, while trying to serve one interest—that of the United States.[51]

Lansdale's efforts to fit in were further complicated by his lack of an Establishment pedigree in an organization that was as full of Ivy League, upper-crust spies as the OSS had been. Admittedly, one of the defining features of the American establishment was its openness to talent. Even John J. McCoy, president of the World Bank, high commissioner in Germany, and chairman of the Council on Foreign Relations—a man who would come to be seen as the very symbol of the foreign-policy elite—hailed from a relatively modest background, having been raised by his widowed mother, a hairdresser in Philadelphia. For most of these men (and it was a male-only club in those days), an elite education, rather than elite birth, served as an entrée to the world of influence. McCoy, for example, had gone to Amherst College and Harvard Law School. Lansdale would be unusual not because he came from a middle-class background but because he had managed to rise without having spent any time in the Ivy League or on Wall Street.

◆

SWORN TO secrecy, Lansdale could not tell either his faraway wife or his overseas mistress about his new assignment except in the most general terms; it was a vow he would keep for more than three decades, until, nearing the end of his life in the 1980s, he finally confessed to a biographer that he had worked for the CIA—a fact that by then was common knowledge. The OPC, however, was more secret than the CIA; its very existence was not declassified until decades after the fact. In speaking to friends and family, Lansdale offered not a hint of what he was up to. "My job is merely the usual headquarters stuff of wrestling papers around and sitting behind a desk to make the room look full," Ed wrote to Pat Kelly. "I'd like to tell you that I have a key spot in the nation—such as advising Mrs. Barkley [wife of Vice President Alben W. Barkley] on how to handle her old man for best results—but I'm out of practice in such matters—so I have no such importance."[52] (The seventy-one-year-old vice president, nicknamed "Veep" by his young grandson, had captivated the nation in 1949 when, following the death of his first wife, he married a thirty-seven-year-old widow.)

Although the matters Lansdale was working on were more important than he let on, there is no doubt that he was sincere in his frustration with Washington bureaucracy. He complained to Pat about "the long hours and the crazy gobbledygook official language I have to deal in." "Once in a while," he wrote, "I get mad and let loose in straight, plain, blunt English and scare the pants off all the nice little gentlemen. I only hope the Russians get just as balled up in official dealings as we do."[53]

While Lansdale told Pat that he hoped his relocation to Washington would be "a big step to the Philippines,"[54] initially he worked on Soviet affairs for the OPC, which had been impressed that he had delivered lectures on the Soviet economy at Lowry Air Force Base. This was indicative of the scattershot nature of the new intelligence agency, since Lansdale did not speak Russian and had no real expertise in the

Soviet Union. He was, in any case, eager to focus on the Philippines, and his superiors were willing to approve his transfer to the OPC's Far East Division in 1950 because they were increasingly worried about the drift of events in the archipelago. Thanks to the exigencies of the Cold War, he was drawing one step closer to returning to Manila—and his beloved Patching.

7

"A Most Difficult and Delicate Problem"

Extreme care must . . . be exercised in the methods used to persuade the Philippine Government to take necessary action.

—NATIONAL SECURITY COUNCIL

THROUGHOUT history, rulers have tried to crush rebellions with fire and sword. Sometimes it has worked. But just as often it has backfired by engendering more support for the rebels. Examples of this phenomenon abound, from the days of the Jewish Revolt against Rome in AD 66 to the early days of America's war in Iraq from 2003 to 2007. Indeed, many guerrilla groups have staged raids in the express hope of provoking an overreaction. During World War II, for example, Josip Broz Tito would attack German forces in Yugoslavia in no small measure because he knew they would destroy nearby villages in retaliation—and thereby force the villagers to take to the hills to join his partisans.

The Philippine army cannot be compared in brutality to the Nazis, but a similar phenomenon could be discerned during its ham-handed assaults against the Hukbalahap movement, typified by the offensive on Mount Arayat that Edward Lansdale had witnessed in 1947. President

Manuel Roxas had sent the Philippine constabulary to crush the uprising with a "mailed fist."[1] But just as in Vietnam later, the guerrillas, with their excellent intelligence system and informers within the government ranks, usually knew of the army's attacks well beforehand—and the lumbering pace of the army's advance, announced by thunderous artillery barrages, gave them ample time to escape. The soldiers would vent their fury on the peasants left behind, stealing their rice and livestock, looting their homes, abusing their women. The consequences were predictable. As the Huk leader Luis Taruc wrote,

> Every time a peasant was arrested and tortured as one of our suspected supporters, able-bodied men from his barrio fled to the hills. They would rather join the Huks than suffer the same fate. For every barrio woman raped by undisciplined and demoralized soldiers or civilian guards, more peasants, including women, would be driven by hatred and indignation to join the rebels. For every barrio looted and burned to the ground by troops carrying out their superiors' scorched-earth policy, a new Huk unit was founded. Every prisoner "shot while trying to escape" led more strong young men and girls from the nearby barrios to join the dissidents.[2]

After Roxas's death from a heart attack in 1948, his vice president and successor, the sickly and stout Elpidio Quirino, tried a different approach. He declared a cease-fire and offered amnesty to the Huks if they would disarm. Taruc traveled to Manila to engage in high-level negotiation. But the talks broke down when it was time for the Huks to give up their arms. Instead, they restarted the guerrilla war.

Quirino gave the Huks a gift of inestimable value by stealing the 1949 presidential election. In the wake of this fraudulent election, the Hukbalahap movement spread across Luzon and into neighboring islands such as the Visayas, as Filipinos increasingly came to conclude that political change could not be achieved peacefully. The Huks' slogans were "Bullets Not Ballots" and "Land for the Landless." Both were potent appeals. Huk strength increased to fifteen thousand fighters, backed by a support network of as many as a million people (out of a total population of twenty million).

On April 28, 1949, a Huk unit a hundred strong ambushed a convoy carrying Aurora Quezon, widow of the late president, less than ninety miles from Manila. She was killed along with her daughter and son-in-law and eight others while traveling to dedicate a memorial to her late husband in his hometown of Baler. In Washington, Edward Lansdale was shocked at the news and worried about Pat Kelly's safety traveling on nearby roads. "The ambush just seemed to point up that jittery feeling I get sometimes when thinking of you traveling around with me—although Lord knows I seemed to get you into more trouble that way than is normal for a human being," he wrote to her.[3]

The insurgency appeared to be an inexorable force that threatened to topple the government in Manila, just as another Communist movement had just toppled the Nationalist government in China. On March 20, 1950, Huks overran seventeen towns and villages in central Luzon.[4] Five months later, on August 26, five thousand guerrillas struck twelve towns and villages in the same area. Tarlac City, the hometown of both Luis Tarluc and Pat Kelly, bore the brunt of the latter assault. Twenty-three soldiers and seven civilians were killed at Tarlac's military base, Camp Makabulos. Among the victims were soldiers lying sick or wounded in hospital beds. The attackers also raped army nurses and freed nearly fifty prisoners from the Tarlac jail while making off with 140,000 rounds of ammunition.[5]

When Lansdale read about the Tarlac raid back in Washington, his immediate reaction once again was not of a soldier or spy but of a man removed by more than eight thousand miles from the woman he loved. He wrote her, "Please, Pat, how did the raid affect you? Are you or the family planning on moving to Manila? If so, can I help out somehow, financially or in some other way? When I read the news, I did some quiet praying and you've been very much in my thoughts every moment since. You are precious to me, brod, and I don't want anything to happen without my being close by to help."[6] Pat, it turned out, was safe—but her security, along with that of her neighbors, was precarious. The army had to deploy heavy forces to prevent Manila itself from falling. President Quirino was so fearful of attack that he anchored a gunboat on the Pasig River, bordering the grounds of the colonial-era Malacañang Palace, so that he and his family could make a quick escape in the event the compound was overrun.[7]

Although a dedicated anti-Communist, Quirino was also an ineffective one. He was part of the problem, not the solution. A senior State Department official wrote on April 20, 1950, in scathing and undiplomatic, if accurate, language, that he "has demonstrated no capacity whatsoever to understand the problems of his country or the indicated solutions. His overweening vanity and arrogance compel him to ignore advice from those who do understand. His pettiness and vindictiveness prevent even his closest advisers from telling him anything unpleasant, or anything they believe he does not want to hear. His insistence on making all decisions himself has resulted in a virtual paralysis of his Government."[8] Similar issues would plague South Vietnam in the future under a series of leaders who would insist on reserving to themselves all the key decision so that no rivals could emerge. Secretary of State Dean Acheson feared that, as a result of its "shocking deterioration," the Philippines might be on the verge of a "total collapse."[9]

It was no easy matter to stave off disaster. The State Department memo outlined two basic options: "bring pressure to bear upon President Quirino for internal reform" or "encourage the Filipinos to force a change in the presidency." A third option was also on the table: send U.S. troops to fight the Huks, just as they had already been sent to Korea and as they would be sent a decade later to Vietnam. The U.S. ambassador in Manila, Myron Cowen, urged Dean Acheson to give serious consideration "to stationing US combat troops (not less than a reinforced division) in the Philippine Islands."[10] The Truman administration, however, was anxious to avoid another major troop deployment, because U.S. forces were already committed in Korea and policymakers were cognizant of "the extreme sensitivity of Philippine officials and the people in general on the question of their national sovereignty."[11] The preferable path was to push the Quirino government in a more constructive direction, but this was, as the NSC recognized, "a most difficult and delicate problem": "Extreme care must therefore be exercised in the methods used to persuade the Philippine Government to take necessary action."[12]

To put the Philippine economy in order, President Truman on June 27, 1950, dispatched to Manila a blue-ribbon panel of advisers led by the banker Daniel Bell. After an intensive study of local conditions, the Bell mission recommended a series of tax, legal, bureaucratic, and agricultural reforms in return for a U.S. grant of $250 million over five years. Quirino accepted the deal in November 1950 but implemented few of the promised changes.[13]

There remained the thorny issue of how to improve the Philippine military's ability to put down the Huk Rebellion. The Pentagon had already dispatched a Joint U.S. Military Assistance Group (JUSMAG) composed of sixty-nine officers and enlisted men to Manila. The problem was that, as Vinton Chapin, the chargé d'affaires at the U.S. embassy, noted, "the JUSMAG is composed of officers who . . . are well-equipped to advise with respect to ordinary matters of military organization and operations but who have inadequate knowledge of and experience with political subversion and guerrilla warfare of the type with which the Philippine Government is faced."

The United States would encounter similar problems in South Vietnam just a few years later, with conventionally minded American military advisers creating a South Vietnamese army designed for countering a conventional military invasion, not the guerrilla threat that Saigon actually faced. To address this shortcoming in the Philippines, Chapin recommended "that there be assigned to the JUSMAG a substantial number of officers having actual experience in guerrilla and anti-guerrilla operations, and particularly in operations involving Communist-led forces."[14] He suggested sending personnel who had served in China or Greece. Unknown to him, there was already an officer who had made a close study of the Huk movement at the OPC headquarters in Washington.

◆

WHILE HE was working in Washington, Edward Lansdale would take every opportunity to meet visiting friends from the Philippines. In

February 1950, for example, he was delighted to find that Johnny Oren-dain, the lawyer who had introduced him to Pat Kelly, was in town. The two men stayed up all night talking and the next night took part in high-spirited revelry at the Fort Myer Officers Club along with some of Lansdale's other friends, ranging from a Czech concert pianist to a Nevada miner. They "woke up the club"—"a deadly old hole"—"with laughing and singing and a serious Brahms concert in the dining room," Ed wrote to Pat. This was the kind of gathering that the gregarious Lansdale liked best—"a wondrous mixture of high and low brow and all of us slightly drunk."[15]

The following month, Lansdale heard from another visiting friend, Lieutenant Colonel Mamerto Montemayor of the Philippine army. He was in town along with a congressman from Manila on a mission to win more aid for Philippine war veterans. Lansdale, he suggested, should meet his traveling companion. That night the three men had dinner together. The strapping congressman, a veteran of the guerrilla war against Japan who was now chairman of the National Defense Committee of the Philippine House of Representatives, was a "husky, intense man, his restlessness evident in his foot-jiggling." He confided to Lansdale how worried he was about the "current morale of Filipino soldiers," which was "sinking under the combination of physical and psychological attacks, the latter perniciously erosive since the Huks pictured the Philippine government as totally corrupt and told the soldiers they were suckers for risking their lives to defend it."

The congressman told Lansdale that "he wanted to go back and talk to the president of the Philippines" about a program of action to combat the Huks. So that night Lansdale took the congressman back to his quarters at Fort Myer, sat down with a manual typewriter, and asked him exactly what he wanted to do. When the congressman told him, Lansdale put the thoughts into his own language. "His ideas," Lansdale later wrote, "were infused with a practicality about the use of troops against guerrillas and a compassion for the people on the land, which stemmed from his own experiences as a successful leader of guerrillas in World War II, in areas where Huks now were operating." The end product was virtually identical to a program of action that Lansdale had just crafted and presented to his superiors at the OPC.

In any counterinsurgency or, for that matter, any military operation, success is seldom possible without inspired leadership. Right there and then, Lansdale decided that this burly congressman "should be the guy to handle [the campaign] out in the Philippines, because of his feelings towards the people and towards the enemy; he understood the problem, which very few Filipinos ever understood and very few Americans either."[16]

◆

HIS NAME was Ramon Magsaysay (pronounced *mahg-sigh-sigh*). Born on August 31, 1907, just six months before Lansdale, he grew up in an environment vastly different from the early twentieth-century America of Lansdale's boyhood. Part of Magsaysay's legend was that he was one of the common people. He even lived as a boy in the Philippine version of a log cabin—a shanty made of bamboo and cogon grass, which had been built by his father. But though the Magsaysays were poor by American standards, they were better off than most of their neighbors in Zambales Province in central Luzon, home of the giant Subic Bay U.S. naval base and the volcanic Mount Pinatubo.

Ramon, known as Monching, was the second-oldest of eight children born to the carpenter Exequiel Magsaysay and his wife, Perfecta, the daughter of a wealthy landowner. As a teenager, Exequiel had been a member of the Katipunan secret society, which fought for Philippine independence first against the Spanish and then the Americans, but after the end of the war of independence in 1902 he had made his peace with the *Yanquis*. He even went to work as a teacher at an American-run trade school. He was fired from this post in 1913, however, after he gave a failing grade to the son of the school superintendent. His oldest son would inherit his father's strict code of honesty.

After losing his teaching job, Exequiel relocated with his family to the village of Castillejos, about ninety miles from Manila, where he and the rest of the clan ran a sari-sari store along with a carpentry and blacksmith shop. To supplement his income, Exequiel worked as the foreman of a public works gang. Like Teddy Lansdale, Monching was expected to earn his own money and in his case contribute to the family's livelihood, so he would get up at five in the morning to toil on road construction alongside his father's workers. This was the origin of a burly physique that, along with his height—five feet ten inches, the same as Lansdale, but tall for a Filipino of his day—would make Magsaysay an imposing presence.

Eventually the Magsaysay family would prosper, building a rice mill and acquiring thousands of acres of agricultural land, along with the first tractor in the entire province. But Monching never lost his down-to-earth attitude. His favorite reading material was *Popular Mechanics*; he became a self-taught mechanic of considerable skill. Like Lansdale, he was an indifferent student who never received a college degree in spite of spending five years, on and off, at two different colleges. As an adult, he would feel defensive about his lack of education; this would make him lean heavily on trusted advisers.

In 1933, the same year that Ed and Helen Lansdale wed, the twenty-six-year-old Monching married Luz Banzon, an eighteen-year-old schoolgirl from a wealthy family. (Her father was a prominent land-owner and former mayor of Balanga, capital of Bataan Province.) By 1939, when World War II broke out, Magsaysay was comfortably settled with his growing family as the branch manager for the Try Tan bus line in his native Zambales Province. With the onset of war, Magsaysay joined the army as a captain running a motor pool, and he did not stop fighting after the army was defeated and the country occupied, taking to the hills to join a group of guerrillas operating under American officers. By the fall of 1944, he had risen to command more than ten thousand guerrillas in Zambales. His men had already cleared the province of Japanese by the time U.S. troops arrived in January 1945. Yet, unlike many other guerrilla officers, the modest Magsaysay refused to give himself a field promotion. He remained a captain until after the liberation, when his American superiors promoted him to major and awarded him the Bronze Star.

Fresh from these triumphs, Magsaysay was installed as military governor of Zambales by the U.S. forces. He held the job for only five weeks in early 1945, but that was enough to catapult him into a position of prominence. He further solidified the loyalty of his guerrillas by lobbying the U.S. and Philippine authorities to provide them back pay and other compensation for their wartime efforts. When his men took up a collection to show their gratitude, Magsaysay characteristically insisted that the money, all thirty thousand pesos, be returned to those who had donated it. But he did accede to his men's urging that he run for Congress in the first postwar election in 1946. Campaigning in uniform, he defeated five other contenders, most of them men with far more impressive résumés.

Magysaysay stood out in this era of extravagant corruption, similar to the Gilded Age in America, as one of the few honest men in Philippine politics. He was, to be sure, not totally free of the stench of sordid politics; he was a close ally of the speaker of the House, Eugenio Perez, who had accumulated a fortune in office. But Magsaysay lived in the same simple house that he and his family had occupied before the war, and he wore the same unstylish clothes—khaki pants and casual white shirts—that he had sported as a student. In 1948, he was selected as chairman of the National Defense Committee and the next year won reelection handily.

Yet many in Manila still disdained Magsaysay as a country bumpkin who had risen on a good war record and a ready smile but "had nothing in his head." Even his friends had to concede "he was not an intellectual, in fact he was anti-intellectual. . . . He hated to read anything more than half a page double-spaced." Later, after Magsaysay became president, a story spread around Manila that, when his secretary of finance told him that one of his plans for economic uplift was blocked by the law of supply and demand, Magsaysay replied, "Let's repeal the damned law!" Even if this story is apocryphal or if Magsaysay was speaking in jest, he was plainly in need of wise guidance if he was to advance any further within the sharp-elbows corridors of Philippine politics. Aware of Magsaysay's talents and deficits, Edward Lansdale believed he could provide him the help he needed to become defense minister, in the process turning the tide against the Huks.[17]

—

BEFORE HE could guide Magsaysay to power, however, Lansdale first had to convince others in Washington of the Filipino's utility. In March 1950, two days after he had first met the unvarnished Filipino soldier-turned-politician, Lansdale convened a lunch at the Hotel Washington where he introduced the visiting congressman to his superiors—Frank Wisner and Colonel Richard G. Stilwell, head of the OPC's Far East Division (and a future four-star general)—along with Livingston T. Merchant, assistant secretary of state for Far Eastern affairs, and General Nathan Twining, vice chief of staff of the Air Force. They were as impressed as Lansdale had been by Magsaysay after the Filipino, who spoke English fluently, gave a speech, carefully crafted by Lansdale, in which he laid out his ideas. At Lansdale's urging, the OPC decided to throw its support behind Magsaysay. "I went broke taking them all to lunch," Lansdale said, but it was worth it.[18]

The outbreak of the Korean War in June 1950, however, delayed action in the Philippines. It was not until August that Colonel George Chester and Livingston Merchant flew to Manila as emissaries of the OPC to tell President Quirino to fire the incumbent minister of defense, Ruperto Kangleon, another former guerrilla and a close friend of the president's, and replace him with Magsaysay.[19] Given the extent to which Quirino was dependent on U.S. support—if he did not get more money from Washington, the Philippine government would not be able to pay its bills—he had to hew closely to the Americans' demands. But it was not just the Americans who were pushing for Magsaysay; so was Eugenio Perez, the powerful speaker of the House and Magsaysay's political patron. Quirino was not opposed to the idea: he had already offered, back in March, to make him defense minister. Magsaysay had declined, because he doubted that he could be effective in this new role, given the pervasive corruption and other problems plaguing the government.[20]

It would be an exaggeration, then, to give the impression, as have so many previous accounts, that Lansdale single-handedly engineered Magsaysay's selection. His voice was but one among many. His greatest influence may have been in convincing the hesitant congressman that he should take the position and that he could be effective with American support. As usual with major historical events, Magsaysay's selection as secretary of national defense—announced on his forty-third birthday, August 31, 1950—was the product of multiple factors. It was not solely the work of one midlevel intelligence officer in Washington. That officer, however, would play a much larger role in helping Magsaysay to carry out his new duties.

◆

THE OPC agreed to send Edward Lansdale to Manila to work as Magsaysay's personal adviser while operating separately from the CIA station. His "cover" would be working at JUSMAG as an intelligence adviser to Quirino. Some of his colleagues told Lansdale, "That's the lousiest cover we have ever heard of, to go out as an intelligence chief." He replied, "Why not? I'm not going to be doing intelligence work. I can do that on the side and it will all be germane."[21] For a man who lived a covert life both professionally (as an intelligence officer) and privately (as Pat's lover), Lansdale was remarkably indifferent to the demands of subterfuge. The most open and public of spooks, he became used to hiding in plain sight.

When his superiors balked at giving him what he felt he needed in terms of support, Lansdale was irate, threatening—in one telling of the story—to come "back with my pocket full of grenades and . . . to throw grenades at you."[22] In another rendition of this tale, Lansdale did not mention any hand grenades; he simply said that "he slammed and locked the door and said he would not let them leave until they gave him" what he needed.[23] Whatever Lansdale's exact words, there is little doubt that he was vehement and insubordinate. His OPC superiors understandably concluded that Lansdale was a "wild man." But the OPC, like the OSS before it, was used to outsize characters and tolerated their foibles and excesses far better than the more regimented military did. Rather than cashier him on the spot for his impertinence, his superiors gave him what he wanted.[24]

His entourage was to be a modest one, and not without its comical characters. Eventually swelling to a grand total of six operatives, the Lansdale team consisted at first only of Army Captain Charles T. R. Bohannan and a communications specialist, Lieutenant A. C. "Ace" Ellis, both on the OPC payroll. They would be joined in the Philippines by Lansdale's cigar-chomping secretary, Helen Jones, who had worked for him previously at G-2. She had come out to the Philippines in the 1930s and won a Medal of Freedom for working with Philippine guerrillas during the war to smuggle food, clothing, and medicine into Japanese prisoner-of-war camps.[25] While Jones took care of administrative tasks, the "even-tempered" Ellis allowed Lansdale to communicate directly with Washington without having to let the regular CIA station at the embassy know what he was up to.[26]

Bohannan, known as Bo or Boh, was the most important member of the team initially, aside from Lansdale himself. He was a thirty-five-year-old anthropology PhD and a specialist in Navajo folklore who in the 1930s had worked for the Smithsonian Institution. He first arrived in the Philippines as an infantryman in 1944, leading a scouting force behind Japanese lines just ahead of the main U.S. invasion. He developed a reputation as a "tough" and "fearless" leader while gaining the kind of combat experience that Lansdale lacked. He was evacuated home after being wounded in an attack on a cave full of Japanese troops. He returned to the Philippines in 1946 as an army counterintelligence officer and stayed until 1949. Like Lansdale, he fell "in love with the people and the islands."[27]

Bo was highly intelligent—"one of the smartest guys I ever met in my life," recalled Army Major General Victor J. Hugo Jr., who as a young second lieutenant worked with Bohannan in the 1950s. He also happened to be one of the few military or intelligence officers who was even more unconventional than Lansdale himself. A character whose eccentricities might have come straight out of *Catch-22* or *M*A*S*H*, he became notorious for attending important meetings barefoot and squatting in the corner rather than sitting on a chair. He never wore socks; he went everywhere, even in uniform, in woven leather huarache sandals. He also favored a bush jacket with used brass shotgun shells for buttons. Initially he lived in normal military quarters in Manila, but eventually he trucked a couple of semicircular, corrugated steel

Quonset huts to a vacant lot and combined them into a makeshift house for himself and his wife, Dorothy, a schoolteacher who joined him in Manila in 1952.[28] "People would think he was crazy or something—that he wasn't right in the head," Lansdale recalled.[29] But as someone who could be eccentric himself, Lansdale got along just fine with Bohannan.

◆

BY THE time Lansdale was ready to leave for the Philippines in September 1950, he was trying to reconcile with Helen even though he was still telling Pat Kelly that he was "terrifically, terribly and awfully lonely" without her.[30]

Just a few months earlier, Ed had bought a decrepit, two-story house in northwest Washington, D.C., for nine thousand dollars. The address was 4503 MacArthur Boulevard, an appropriate location given the impact that Douglas MacArthur had had on his career.[31] Although the Lansdale home was located next to Georgetown, it was in the far less exclusive Palisades, a narrow neighborhood running along the Potomac River far removed from this more genteel preserve of power. At the time, it was a working-class to middle-class area full of narrow, wooden, single-family houses built, like Lansdale's house, around the turn of the century, and a few brick, two-story apartment buildings erected more recently. Five doors down from the new Lansdale house was an eyesore—a gasoline station.[32] Behind the backyard, however, was a large public field where the Lansdale boys could play, and around the corner was an elementary school they could attend.

Helen had sold their place in Larkspur and was relocating to Washington just as Ed's orders for the Philippines finally came through— and shortly after he had started to remodel the house himself. Helen "was appalled," Lansdale later wrote, "at the sight of our new home in Washington, in which I had only progressed as far as chopping down walls to make larger rooms and ripping out the plumbing for modernizing. Standing in the shambles, I broke the news that I was leaving within hours for the war in the Philippines. It wasn't the most pleasant moment of my life."[33] When he set out this scene in his deliberately opaque 1972 memoir, Lansdale naturally omitted the most unpleasant fact of all from his wife's perspective: the knowledge that her husband was about to return to the place where her rival lived. Lansdale left filled with guilt, which he ascribed to "the condition in which I had left that house."[34] No doubt his guilt was also due to his knowledge that his reconciliation with his wife was stillborn as he rushed back to the homeland of his mistress. Helen would have been livid if she had known that Ed was writing to Pat Kelly that his desire to be with her was "the real reason behind all my plans to get out there,"[35] thus underscoring—even allowing for romantic exaggeration—the crucial influence of this extramarital relationship on his career trajectory.

◆

THIS TIME, Lansdale's journey to the Philippines did not necessitate spending weeks aboard an uncomfortable troop transport. "I rode to the scene of conflict," Lansdale wrote, "sunk down in a pillowed lounge chair aboard a Pan-American Clipper, a Boeing B-377 Stratocruiser that cruised between fifteen and twenty-five thousand feet above the water." In those days there was only one class of service aboard the Pan Am Clipper: "strictly first."[36] A 1950 Pan Am promotional film showed happy passengers in suits smoking and playing bridge in the lounge aboard the Stratocruiser while enjoying amenities such as a seven-course dinner prepared by a white-jacketed steward in the "largest and most efficient flying kitchen in the world."[37]

Just as Lansdale dissembled in his memoir about the true source of tension with his wife upon his departure, so too he concealed how his sudden upgrade in travel had come about. "Some unknown benefactor in the travel section in Washington had decided to hurry me to my destination," Lansdale artfully wrote, "bypassing the delays of military traffic, which at the time was concentrating on getting troops to Korea, and sending me to the Philippines by U.S. commercial carrier."[38] In truth, he knew perfectly well the name of his benefactor. Frank Wisner, the energetic OPC chief, was impatient to get his operative to Manila to turn the tide of yet another war that the "Free World" appeared to be losing. And the OPC, unlike the armed forces, had the freedom and the funds—all that "candy"—to travel first-class.

8

"All-Out Force or All-Out Friendship"

I learned to stick a toothbrush and razor in my pocket, since often days would pass before we returned to Manila again.

—EDWARD LANSDALE

EDWARD LANSDALE reached Manila on a typical, tropical "sun-filled day" in early September 1950 to find its one million residents blithely unaware that an insurgency was threatening their future. The streets, he noted, "were crowded." Jeepneys—jeeps converted into buses—darted hither and yon. "People along the sidewalks were laughing and happy," Lansdale wrote, and "everywhere radios blared at their top decibel output." The air of unreality was further heightened when he moved, along with Charles "Bo" Bohannan and A. C. "Ace" Ellis, into a pleasant bungalow at the Joint U.S. Military Assistance Group (JUSMAG) compound. The neighborhood resembled an American-style suburb of tract houses, manicured lawns and all; Filipinos dubbed it "the country club." The only reminder of a security imperative was a sentry box with a single bored Philippine soldier and a wire fence topped with a single strand of barbed wire.

It did not take Lansdale long to detect an undercurrent of darkness just beneath the sunny surface. He asked one well-connected news-paper editor (probably his friend Manuel Manahan) whether people were afraid of the Huks. The newspaperman startled him by refusing to say anything until he had led Lansdale to the "farthest corner" of his garden, "a patch of darkness behind some bushes." Here he confessed that "Hell yes, he was afraid" of "Huk trigger squads." He was even afraid to talk to Lansdale "because the security of American offices, such as those at JUSMAG and the Embassy, was a sour joke." Huk agents, he warned, had access to the contents of safes in both locations. This warning led Lansdale to hide his own private papers in the most secure location he knew: the tightly guarded liquor locker at JUSMAG.

Even more baleful was the news that greeted Lansdale when he trav-eled to Tarlac City, eighty miles north of Manila, to spend "a night with friends"—a guarded reference to Pat Kelly, with whom he no doubt had a joyous reunion. (Within a month of his arrival, he was telegramming her: "PUT ON COFFEE POT SEE YOU SUNDAY YOUR ADOBE. BIG HUG YOU LOVING RASCAL.")[1] Only a few weeks before, as we have seen, a group of Huk fighters had slaughtered wounded soldiers in their hospital beds and raped military nurses in Tarlac, yet Lansdale was dismayed to hear the locals speak "of the Huks with considerable admiration." This was because the Huks had been careful not to harm civilians. They had targeted only soldiers, who were seen as instruments "of the privileged few" rather than as "the defenders of the people."

On his way back to Manila the following morning, Lansdale saw another part of the problem—a traffic jam in front of a police check-point where "money was being handed over by the drivers, a little unofficial and illegal tribute they paid to enter the city." He wondered, "What must the people be thinking about all those in uniform repre-senting authority!"[2]

◆

THE NEWLY appointed defense minister, Ramon Magsaysay, had given up his predecessor's spacious office downtown to move into a former card room above the officers' club at Camp Murphy, the armed forces' headquarters on the outskirts of the city. Lansdale was climbing the stairs when he heard "the thump of running feet" punctuated by "gasps and heavy breathing." "Somebody was muttering 'sonnamabeech' over and over again." He thought the defense minister "must be some sort of a nut on physical education—maybe he is running in place or something up there." Once he walked in, he saw that the defense minister was chasing a civilian around the room, "swinging his big fist at the man every time he got close." Though it surely must not have been the first time, Magsaysay was upset that the "sonnamabeech" had tried to bribe him.[3]

Once his good humor was restored, Magsaysay invited his new American friend home for dinner in the same small house on Arellano Street, in the impoverished Singalong district, that he had built in the 1930s. Lansdale noticed there "were no street lights in his neighborhood"; the only illumination was provided by "several pungent *tinghuy* lamps with their wicks floating in coconut oil held in the half-shells of coconuts" hanging over a sidewalk sari-sari store, a sign that many sections of Manila had not progressed beyond the gas-lit era that America had left behind decades ago. Yet even in the dim light Lansdale could see an unusually large number of men on the sidewalk. Their hair was long, flowing down to their shoulders—the sign of a guerrilla because "haircuts are hard to come by when a man is on the run." Magsaysay's aides were noticing the same thing. A few of them stood guard outside his house to prevent the defense minister from being kidnapped or killed.[4]

After dinner, at which Lansdale for the first time met Magsaysay's wife, Luz, and their three children, Ed suggested that the family relocate for their own safety. The defense minister could have moved into a house at Camp Murphy, but he did not want to pull rank and bump some officer out of his home. So, for the three months until a new house was ready for him, he agreed to bunk with Lansdale at the JUSMAG compound while Luz and their children went to stay with her family in Bataan, the mountainous peninsula on Manila Bay where American and Filipino troops had held out in 1942.[5]

Thus Lansdale became not only Magsaysay's adviser but also his roommate. He referred to his new friend as Monching, and soon they grew as close as brothers, becoming used, as he said, "to revealing our innermost thoughts to each other." The two men would stay up late into the night, sitting around the rattan dining table or sprawled out on the rattan couch and easy chairs, talking over the problems of the Philippines and brainstorming possible solutions. "They were learning from each other," Magsaysay's son would say.[6] "As he would worry over an event and what he should do about it," Lansdale recalled, "I would try to sum it up for him again. Then I would ask what it would look like to his children, and to his children's children. This perspective often threw a clear light on the problem as he talked it back to me."[7]

So successful was Lansdale in impressing his ideas on Magsaysay that before long they talked in virtually identical terms even when apart. A group of visiting French officials, after talking to both men separately, wanted to know how Lansdale "controlled" this "native"— "by money, by blackmail, how?" Lansdale had to laugh. "I guess some people in Europe and Asia simply never will understand the very real and open friendship there was between us," Lansdale wrote a decade later. "Neither of us ever had reason to talk differently when apart from each other. We shared a trust in each other, believed in much the same principles of life, and had warm affection for each other's country and country-men. This plain and fundamental truth has always seemed to escape those seeking some sophisticated explanation."[8]

Because the defense minister lived there, Filipino officers would come by Lansdale's house. While waiting to talk to Magsaysay, they would chew the fat with Lansdale or Bohannan and in the process offer insights into the country's problems. Lansdale realized these conversations were so valuable that he began hosting regular "coffee klatsches," which came to resemble a Filipino version of FDR's "brain trust." Convened in Lansdale's cottage was a thoroughly eclectic assemblage, including, he wrote, "the most thoughtful of the staff officers and combat commanders" of the Philippine army, along with "veterans of the guerrilla resistance in World War II, journalists, civil specialists in government bureaus, and community services leaders." Each gathering was limited to no more than a dozen participants, "so that the guests could sit comfortably close and share in the conversation." Participants were encouraged to lean back and prop their feet up on the coffee table. "The relaxed informality helped keep the talks free and flowing," Lansdale said. In this respect, the meetings became a perfect reflection of Lansdale's California sensibility, far removed from the sort of rigid protocol normally found in military meetings. Lansdale was an unobtrusive, but essential, presence in these sessions, which quickly wound up catalyzing the entire counterinsurgency campaign.[9]

◆

THE VERY first night that Magsaysay moved into Lansdale's house, he expressed his frustration, his feet jiggling and his fist pounding in frustration on a cot, with the lethargy and corruption of the "clique-ridden officer corps." Magsaysay wanted to root out the worst offenders, but he couldn't even identify them. When he went out on an inspection tour, Lansdale recalled, "he would find that officers had been tipped off about his coming, had everything tidied up, and had their stories ready for briefing him glibly about the local situation." Magsaysay knew he was being Potemkinized, presented with an overly "rosy picture," but the high command told him that for security reasons he could not make unannounced inspections. Lansdale encouraged him to assert the full power of his office, noting that "as secretary of national defense, he had ample authority to visit units in any manner he personally desired, including surprise inspections if he wished." Magsaysay's face lit up when he heard this.

At 4:30 the next morning, not long after Lansdale had finally gone to bed after a late-night bull session, he felt a hand shaking him awake. "Hey, what's up?" he asked. His new roommate replied, "You'll see. We're going to the provinces." Lansdale was "still half asleep" when the two of them drove over to Camp Murphy. They woke up some pilots and took off in two tiny L-5 light observation aircraft known affectionately as flying jeeps. Each of these turboprop airplanes had just two seats. With Magsaysay in one plane and Lansdale in the other, they flew off at the defense minister's direction, finally landing in a corn field next to a highway in central Luzon. The pilots stayed behind with the aircraft while Magsaysay and Lansdale went into town, the former wearing a loud Hawaiian shirt and straw hat, the latter in his khaki uniform and blue Air Force garrison cap.

The bizarre-looking duo must have seemed as out of place as Martians, thumbing down a truck and riding as hitchhikers to the local constabulary headquarters. Here they found a sergeant asleep at his desk. Magsaysay woke him and demanded to be taken to his commanding officer. The sergeant was dubious until Lansdale stepped forward to inform him "that the sport-shirted civilian was the new secretary of national defense." As if this were a Filipino forerunner of *Hogan's Heroes*, the sergeant saluted and dashed out. Looking around, the visitors saw that a gun cabinet was unlocked; the rifles inside were "a tempting target for Huk guerrillas in the neighborhood." Magsaysay grabbed a couple of rifles and told Lansdale to hide behind the door. As the captain in command barged in, "Magsaysay thrust the muzzle of his rifle into the captain's back," and shouted, "Stick 'em up!" The surprised officer's hands shot into the air. "Boys, I don't know how you've managed to stay alive so long," the dismayed defense minister said.

Magsaysay was determined to relieve the slovenly captain, but back in Manila he learned that General Mariano Castañeda, the armed forces chief of staff, didn't want some politician meddling in personnel matters. The chief only grudgingly agreed to transfer the captain after the defense minister lost his temper on the telephone. This brought home to Magsaysay the importance of being able to relieve—and promote—officers. Both areas were problematic, because officers were being advanced on the basis of seniority rather than combat performance and then kept in their jobs no matter how corrupt or incompetent they were. To fix this problem, Lansdale interceded directly with Elpidio Quirino, persuading the president to issue a memorandum making clear that the defense minister had the right to promote and demote for just cause. The next year, with Lansdale's help, Magsaysay would even succeed in getting rid of the politically well-connected but ineffectual Castañeda. "I got the president to empower the secretary of national defense . . . to permit him to be the real leader of the military effort," Lansdale recalled.

Armed with this authority, Magsaysay, along with Lansdale, kept up a frenetic pace of field inspections. "I learned to stick a toothbrush and razor in my pocket," Lansdale wrote, "since often days would pass before we returned to Manila again." It is hard to imagine the more rank-conscious and aloof George C. Marshall, who as U.S. defense secretary was then Magsaysay's counterpart, undertaking such flying visits devoid of any trappings of office. But Magsaysay, as relaxed and unpretentious as Lansdale, was right at home. On these expeditions, he invariably carried his favorite weapon—a .30-caliber paratrooper's carbine with a folding stock. A crack shot, he would practice by hitting beer bottles. When Magsaysay would get hungry on the road, his favorite foods were canned corn ("the big kernel type") and canned corned beef, which he would split with Lansdale. "But what he really enjoyed," Lansdale later said, "was a fish-fry up along a mountain stream in the foothills of the Zambales, with the fish roasted over hot coals, rice heaped up on banana leaves on the ground for everyone to dig into with their fingers, and all his local pals from his old guerrilla band . . . reminiscing about the days of the Japanese occupation; everyone with shoes off, happy in the shade of the trees."

With astonishing alacrity, the odd couple of Magsaysay and Lansdale began to change the mindset of the armed forces. Bo Bohannan and Napoleon Valeriano of the Philippine army later wrote, "No commander, even in the most isolated outpost, could go to bed at night sure that he would not be awakened before dawn by an irate Secretary of National Defense. . . . And the commander could also be sure of a personally administered 'shampoo,' a sort of verbal but violent Dutch rub, if he didn't know the answers [to Magsaysay's questions]; it would be twice as severe if he tried to bluff." Thus troops began to act more diligently for fear of the consequences if they were caught napping.[10]

◆

MAGSAYSAY TOOK considerable personal risk on these forays into areas where the Huks were active, but then no one ever doubted his courage. His bravery helped make possible the first big coup of the anti-Huk campaign. On the very day that he was sworn into office, Magsaysay had been told by President Quirino that a senior Huk leader known as Comandante Arthur was disaffected and wanted to meet with a senior government official. Magsaysay's aides feared a trap, but the defense minister insisted on going. "Arthur" turned out to be Taciano Rizal, a member of the Hukbalahap politburo and grandnephew of the Philippine national hero José Rizal, a poet and revolutionary who had been executed by a Spanish firing squad in 1896. Over a series of meetings, Magsaysay persuaded Rizal to surrender and to provide information about the location of Huk politburo members, divided between the "ins" who lived in Manila and the "outs" in the countryside.

When Magsaysay told Lansdale of his talks with Rizal, the American suggested a typically offbeat idea—either bold or bizarre, depending on one's perspective—to capture the entire Huk high command. "I recalled the Filipino guerrillas of World War II and the compelling attraction the arrival of a U.S. submarine held for them," Lansdale said. "Perhaps the Huk guerrilla leaders would find the reputed arrival of a Soviet submarine equally irresistible. Through Rizal, we could get credible word to the Huks of the arrival of such a submarine and use it as the magnet to draw Huk leaders to a rendezvous, where we could capture them." Bohannan and Lansdale even began practicing Russian phrases so that they could impersonate Russian naval officers, Lansdale wrote, but "my pleas to U.S. officials to lend me a submarine for a couple of days seemed only to arouse their suspicions that I had gone insane." Magsaysay and a sobered Lansdale had to scale back their ambitious plans to focus on capturing only the politburo members living in Manila. Rizal identified a female courier who delivered to them baskets of fruits and vegetables containing hidden messages. In the early morning hours of October 18, 1950, twenty-one strike teams from the Military Intelligence Service fanned out to stage simultaneous raids on Huk hideouts throughout Manila. They arrested 105 suspects, of whom six were identified as politburo members. Just as important, they seized tons of documents, cash, weapons, and radios.[11]

"Comrades, I have bad news, very bad news." Thus did a Huk officer deliver tidings of the politburo raids to a group of insurgents hiding in the jungle, among them William J. Pomeroy, an American Communist and former GI who had married a Filipina. The news left the guerrillas, Pomeroy was to write, feeling like miners "when the tunnel behind them caves in and the choking dust rushes through the dark hole underground" or like divers "when their air hoses are cut deep down in the jagged caverned coral reefs." But bad as this blow was, it was far from fatal. Few insurgent movements have ever been defeated by having their leaders captured or killed—especially when, as in the case of the Huks, that leadership was collective and not based around a cult of personality. As Pomeroy noted, "Our movement is not a mortal creature with a head that dies when severed at the neck. It is a living organism that grows and multiplies, by fusion and by fission, closing over its wounds and continually reshaping itself."[12]

Undaunted, the Huks struck back on November 25, 1950. One hundred of their fighters attacked Barrio Aglao in Zambales Province, where Magsaysay had lived as a youth; they killed twenty-two people, kidnapped ten more, and burned down thirty-four houses. As soon as he heard of the attack, Magsaysay rushed to Aglao with Lansdale. They arrived, Lansdale wrote, to find smoke still rising "from the burned houses" and bodies lying "strewn over the ground." Magsaysay was so enraged that he personally led the pursuit of the Huk raiders, accompanied by his former World War II fighters "armed with shotguns, knives, and pistols." When it became apparent that the attackers were not going to be caught, Magsaysay was forced to return to Manila, "heartsore and weary," in Lansdale's words. "The memory of Aglao stayed with Magsaysay. In the nights immediately following, vivid nightmares would tear him from his sleep."[13]

Such a searing assault might have led another leader to resort to the kind of heavy-handed repression that would have generated greater support for the rebels. Magsaysay avoided this trap. Under Lansdale's guidance, he pushed a strategy heavy on psychological warfare and "civic action"—a term that Lansdale plausibly claimed to have coined.[14]

◆

ED LANSDALE, along with many other OSS and OPC operatives, had long been fascinated by "psywar," a discipline that had grown concurrently with the advertising industry. In World War II, President Roosevelt had assigned "white" propaganda operations—those openly attributable to the U.S. government—to the Office of War Information, while "black" operations, whose true source was not revealed, were the responsibility of the OSS's Morale Operations branch. The Office of War Information did everything from dropping leaflets on Axis soldiers urging them to surrender to setting up the Voice of America to bolster morale at home and abroad. Its output, though often bombastic, was essentially factual. Morale Operations, by contrast, specialized in spreading false rumors through covert radio stations, leaflets, newspapers, and other means. Typical rumors included claims that, in the words of one historian, "Luftwaffe pilots were refusing to fly . . . , former Nazi leader Rudolf Hess was leading a detachment of Allied troops in France, and Wehrmacht rations had been found to have been poisoned."[15] In the postwar world, a similar division between white and black propaganda was maintained. The new U.S. Information Agency, in whose Manila office Pat Kelly worked, took responsibility for the white side, the OPC and then the CIA for the dark side. Frank Wisner was particularly fascinated with propaganda, which he promulgated through such sources as Radio Free Europe and Radio Liberty, the Congress for Cultural Freedom, and the National Student Association. He likened this information operation to a "Mighty Wurlitzer" organ that could play any tune he desired.[16]

Given Lansdale's own advertising background, it is hardly surprising that he immersed himself in psychological warfare. At his urging, Magsaysay created civil affairs sections in each battalion in direct counterpart to the political commissars that performed similar duties for the Huks. Lansdale was one of the few Americans of this period who had read Mao Zedong's works. He knew that the Communist leader instructed his guerrillas to "keep the closest possible relations with the common people," "be courteous and polite," and "pay for all articles."[17] It was no coincidence that new army civil affairs offices set out, Lansdale explained, "to make the soldiers behave as the brothers and protectors of the people in their everyday military operations, replacing the arrogance of the military at highway checkpoints or in village searches with courteous manners and striving to stop the age-old soldier's habit of stealing chickens and pigs from the farmers."[18]

Conventionally minded officers were often reluctant to undertake civic action, which they viewed as a political rather than a military mission. "To persuade them to try it," Lansdale wrote, "I pointed out that one reward of brotherhood was the willingness of people henceforth to talk more openly with the soldiers. If a commander were to practice civic action honestly and thoroughly, I guaranteed that it would increase his unit's 'raw take' of tactical intelligence by 100 percent in a week. It often took less time than that."[19]

Civic action, rather than the "search and destroy" missions that would become so common the following decade in Vietnam, became a hallmark of the campaign against the Huks. Soldiers were issued candy and chewing gum to hand out to kids and told to carry more food than they needed. This way they would not have to requisition rations from the populace and instead could give extra food to farmers who had been forcibly "taxed" by the Huks. Magsaysay, showing an instinctive sympathy for the underdog, also directed army judge advocate generals to represent poor farmers in property disputes against rich landlords. At Lansdale's urging, he even created what would today be called an inspector general's office, run by Colonel Jose "Joe" Banzon, a cousin of Magsaysay's wife and yet another friend of Lansdale's. Banzon would investigate complaints about the troops or other information provided by average Filipinos utilizing a cheap ten-centavo telegram. Magsaysay often told his troops, "I want every enlisted man of the Philippine army in uniform to serve as a public relations man for the Army and for our government."[20]

Such efforts to woo the population have a long pedigree, stretching back to the "bread and circuses" that the Roman Empire provided to keep its subjects compliant. But an emphasis on the softer side of warfare was a relatively recent development in modern Western military doctrine, which had been relentlessly focused on conventional warfare since the days of Marlborough and Napoleon. Tactics designed to win what another contemporary counterinsurgency commander, General Gerald Templer in Malaya, called "hearts and minds" were still seen as novel in Lansdale's day, and it was his success in the Philippines, along with Templer's success in Malaya, that would help convince many regular soldiers of their importance.

There was, in fact, a remarkable, if largely coincidental, resemblance in the campaigns designed by Lansdale and Templer in different Southeast Asian nations at virtually the same time. Like Lansdale, but unlike the more brutal French forces in Indochina, Templer emphasized the political side of counterinsurgency. "The shooting side of the business is only 25 percent of the trouble," he famously said, "and the other 75 percent lies in getting the people of this country behind us." To win popular support, Templer promised independence "in due course" once the Communist insurgency was defeated. And, like Lansdale, Templer frowned upon the use of artillery or air strikes—blunt weapons that tended to kill more civilians than insurgents. But Templer also understood, as did Lansdale, that measures to win over the undecided populace had to be accompanied by well-aimed actions to capture or kill hard-core guerrillas. Templer's most sweeping tactic was to forcibly relocate hundreds of thousands of Chinese squatters into heavily fortified "New Villages," where they could be prevented from supplying the guerrillas with food, money, or intelligence.[21]

Lansdale and Magsaysay did not go that far, but they did start their own, much smaller-scale resettlement plan. Known as EDCOR (Economic Development Corps), it offered fifteen to twenty acres of free farmland on the distant island of Mindanao in the southern Philippines to guerrillas who defected. Because of budgetary limitations, fewer than 250 Huks were resettled. Yet such was the publicity that Lansdale generated for EDCOR that its psychological impact was much greater. EDCOR's very existence helped combat the Huks' appeal of "Land for the Landless." Soon Huks were appearing in army camps asking to surrender and demanding to know how soon they could get a farm. Meanwhile, Malayans began complaining that the New Villages in which they were being resettled didn't have electric lights "like EDCOR in the Philippines." British officials came to the Philippines to investigate; they were startled to discover how small EDCOR actually was.[22]

CIVIC-ACTION AND resettlement programs were the salubrious side of the Philippine counterinsurgency campaign. But this was still a war and inevitably there was a more violent, coercive part to the military's operations. Magsaysay's slogan, most likely ghostwritten by Lansdale, was "All-Out Force or All-Out Friendship," and the two parts were equally important.[23]

Employing millions of dollars in American military assistance, Magsaysay enlarged the size of the army to fifty-three thousand troops, and transformed it from a ragtag vestige of the colonial era, creating Battalion Combat Teams, twelve hundred strong, to be its main striking force in place of the smaller and less effective Philippine constabulary units, which had been on the front lines before.

Lansdale also wanted to create airborne assault teams that could be dropped to block the escape of Huk units on the ground, thus anticipating the "air cavalry" tactics employing helicopters that the U.S. Army would use in Vietnam in the 1960s. Helicopters were still a novelty in the early fifties and not available in the Philippines, but Lansdale got the U.S. Army high command to contribute a battalion's worth of parachutes and instructors skilled in "smoke jumping" into forests in the Pacific Northwest. However, JUSMAG vetoed the idea because its commanders believed that it was too risky—even though, as Lansdale ruefully noted, "I was the only one among them who had gone on foot over the ground where the operation was to take place."[24] JUSMAG was more supportive of Lansdale when he argued "that a somewhat more liberal use of [American-made] napalm should be given to the Philippine armed forces," but this proposal was blocked by Ambassador Cowen. He feared that the United States would assume moral responsibility "if any innocent Philippine citizens were inadvertently burned by the careless use of napalm."[25] The Philippine army was forced to use less effective, locally made napalm.[26] That Lansdale, who would become well-known for his opposition to the excessive use of firepower in Vietnam, favored the use of airborne assault teams and napalm in the Philippines shows that he was capable of being more ruthless than most of his admirers or critics imagined—or than he himself cared to recall in later years.

Magsaysay and Lansdale had more luck with another innovative concept for offensive action suggested in one of their coffee klatsches by Captain Rafael "Rocky" Ilito, a Filipino graduate of West Point who came up with the idea of creating Scout Ranger units—five-man teams of volunteers that would infiltrate enemy-dominated areas to monitor Huk movements. They could then either ambush a small Huk detachment or call in larger army units to deal with a bigger formation. This concept echoed the British SAS in World War II and anticipated the U.S. Army's Long-Range Reconnaissance Patrols ("Lurps") in Vietnam. William Pomeroy, the American Huk, wrote, "There was a time when the forest was wholly ours and we lived in it as within a fortress, issuing forth at will to spread panic among our foes." But, with the introduction of the Scout Rangers, "the forest is like a breached wall, through which the government troops pour at their will."[27]

Later on in Vietnam, U.S. forces would kill far too many civilians, usually out of sheer carelessness and an abundance of caution rather than outright malevolence, and they would inflate "body counts" by claiming that everyone they killed was a Vietcong fighter. To prevent such abuses in the Philippines, Magsaysay and Lansdale imported cheap box cameras from Japan and handed them out to the troops. Patrols were ordered to photograph any enemy casualties. "This did two things," Lansdale later said. "First of all it kept the casualty figures down to a point of reality that became remarkably accurate. And secondly . . . it taught the troops not to go out and shoot women and children and then claim them as enemy casualties."[28] By minimizing civilian casualties, Lansdale made sure that military operations did not backfire, a strategy that his many successors in Vietnam failed to heed.

◆

BY NO means focused only on military solutions, Lansdale felt the need to understand the belief system of the Filipino people and discovered that much of the populace, including his friend Magsaysay, was intensely superstitious. (The defense minister became angry when Lansdale scoffed at his belief in "ghosts and ghoulies.")[29] To take advantage of this credulity, a psywar squad from the Philippine army "planted stories among town residents of an *asuang* [vampire] living on the hill where the Huks were based," Lansdale wrote.

> Two nights later, after giving the stories time to circulate among Huk sympathizers in the town and make their way up to the hill camp, the psywar squad set up an ambush along a trail used by the Huks. When a Huk patrol came along the trail, the ambushers silently snatched the last man of the patrol, their move unseen in the dark night. They punctured his neck with two holes, vampire-fashion, held the body up by the heels, drained it of blood, and put the corpse back on the trail. When the Huks returned to look for the missing man and found their bloodless comrade, every member of the patrol believed that the *asuang* had got him and that one of them would be next if they remained on that hill. When daylight came, the whole Huk squadron moved out of the vicinity.[30]

Lansdale was proud of this ruthless stratagem, which he recounted to many audiences in future years. It would become, indeed, a core part of his legend—recounted, for instance, in the 2007 National Book Award–winning novel, *Tree of Smoke*, by Denis Johnson, the son of a U.S. Information Agency officer who spent part of his childhood living in Manila. One of the book's characters, the former Air Force colonel-turned-CIA officer Francis X. Sands, cites the vampire story as evidence that it's important to wage war "at the level of myth," because the enemy is "more scared of his gods and his devils and his aswang than he'll ever be of us."[31] What such celebratory accounts left out was that this operation constituted, even in the early 1950s, a war crime because the Philippine soldiers deliberately killed rather than captured an enemy fighter and then mutilated his corpse.

Another "combat psywar operation" that Lansdale instigated was less controversial, importing U.S. Navy bullhorns that had been used by beachmasters in amphibious landings and distributing them to Philippine officers. When a Philippine infantry company was pursuing a Huk squadron, the company commander went up in an aircraft. He grabbed a bullhorn and, based on intelligence reports he had received, began calling out the names of individual Huks, pretending that he recognized them from the air. As the airplane was about to fly away, he made a final broadcast: "Thank you, our friend in the squadron, for all the information." The suspicious Huks wound up executing three of their own men in the search for a nonexistent traitor. Picking up on the "eye of God" theme, Lansdale had psywar teams sneak into towns whose inhabitants were known to be sympathetic to the Huks. The soldiers would paint a baleful eye on a wall facing the house of each suspected Huk sympathizer. "The mysterious presence of these malevolent eyes the next morning had a sharply sobering effect," Lansdale wrote.[32]

Another, far more lethal example of Lansdale's deviousness was to provide the Huks with booby-trapped ammunition. Before long, he wrote, "Huk rifle barrels were exploding from the use of faulty ammunition" and hand grenades started "exploding right in the hands of Huk ambushers." Either type of accident would send red-hot shrapnel flying into the guerrilla's body, causing serious injury or death. Booby-trapped rifle ammunition would be likely to produce a fatal head wound, while a booby-trapped grenade would, at a minimum, reduce the arm to a bloody stump. If nothing else, these sabotaged weapons taught the Huks not to continue buying ammunition from corrupt suppliers who had been secretly funneling them government stockpiles.[33]

◆

COLLECTIVELY ALL of these measures—the field inspections to improve the army's honesty and effectiveness, the expansion of the army's size and its reorganization into Battalion Combat Teams, the creation of the Scout Rangers to hunt down rebels in the jungle, the raids to capture the Huk leadership in Manila, the expansion of civic action, the resettlement of surrendered rebels, the use of psywar tactics such as the "eye of God" and the "vampire" killing, the booby-trapped weapons—took a serious and growing toll on the Huks. By the middle of 1951—while, in Korea, weary American troops, now commanded by General Matthew Ridgeway rather than the cashiered Douglas MacArthur, were repelling the latest Chinese and North Korean offensive—the Philippine insurgents were on the defensive for the first time since the beginning of their struggle in 1946. "It is no longer victory that preoccupies us," wrote William Pomeroy. "It is survival."[34]

U.S. Ambassador Myron Cowen, a lawyer turned diplomat, knew where to give the credit. "Through a combination of guile, good luck, and brute force, Magsaysay and Lansdale inflicted severe defeats on the Huks," he wrote to Secretary of State Acheson on September 19, 1951.

[Lieutenant] Colonel Lansdale has been the right hand of the Secretary of National Defense Magsaysay and he has in a large measure been responsible for Magsaysay's success in breaking the backbone of the Huk military forces and in dispersing the Philippine Communist organizational setup. It is inconceivable to me that the Philippine situation would be as favorable as it is without Colonel Lansdale's superb performance. He has lived day and night with Magsaysay at very real risk to himself. He has guided and advised him. He has provided a driving power and when necessary a restraining one and furthermore he has been a better source of intelligence than all the rest of our intelligence efforts put together.[35]

This was high praise from the American diplomatic establishment. But to convert the tactical successes that Lansdale and Magsaysay had achieved into a lasting strategic victory would require more than mere military action. It would require political action centered on two upcoming elections—the 1951 legislative and regional election and the 1953 presidential election. If these votes were as corrupt as previous ballots had been, the government could not win the confidence of the people. If, on the other hand, the elections could be conducted honestly, the Huks would lose a valuable rallying cry.

Magsaysay, however, was only in charge of the army. How could he and his American adviser stop the president, Elpidio Quirino, and his corrupt Liberal Party machine from stealing more elections? And if they could not prevent more election fraud, how could they possibly defeat the Huks? Two men were now matched against an entire political system.

9

The Power Broker

At times I feel like Boss Hague, at others Rasputin.

—Edward Lansdale

THE CIA manipulated its first foreign election only half a year after the agency's establishment in 1947. To keep Italy, economically and morally lacerated after two decades of Fascist wantonness, from going Communist, the newly formed National Security Council approved a program of covert action to buttress the conservative premier Alcide De Gasperi and his Christian Democratic Party against the Popular Democratic Front established by the Communist and Socialist parties in an election scheduled for April 18, 1948. The CIA provided as much as ten million dollars in cash to finance the Christian Democratic campaign. In addition to bankrolling anti-Communist politicians, the CIA worked in cooperation with the State Department and the Voice of America to launch an all-out propaganda blitz to warn Italians against embracing Communism. Anti-Communist appeals from well-known entertainers such as Bing Crosby and Dinah Shore were supplemented by shipments of the film *Ninotchka*, Greta Garbo's 1939 satire of Soviet life. The newspaper publisher Generoso Pope, who subsequently founded the *National Enquirer*, chipped in with a campaign asking fellow Italian Americans to send letters and telegrams to their friends and relatives in the old country urging them to vote against Communism. Jay Lovestone, an American labor activist and erstwhile Communist with close ties to the CIA, mobilized his Italian labor union contacts to assist in the campaign.

The result, from Washington's perspective, was entirely satisfactory: the Christian Democrats won 48.5 percent of the vote in 1948, up from 36 percent in 1946, and acquired an absolute majority in parliament. It is not clear, admittedly, how much of the outcome was due to CIA efforts. American economic aid such as the Marshall Plan, signed into law just weeks before the vote, and efforts by the Vatican to mobilize church members were also of considerable importance—to say nothing of De Gasperi's own appeal. But in the minds of policymakers the 1948 Italian election established a covert-action template that could be followed successfully in other elections where the Communist threat loomed large. Arthur Krock of the *New York Times* spoke for many when he commended officials for the "perfect handling of the American interest . . . in the peninsular roughhouse."[1]

Such operations became much easier to execute after the establishment, just two months after the Italian election, of Frank Wisner's Office of Policy Coordination, expressly designed and amply funded for waging "political warfare." Thus, by the time that Lansdale submitted a request to his superiors at the OPC to influence the 1951 Philippine congressional campaign, the institutional resources for such a project were in place—along with the determination to use them. America, it was clear, was far removed from pre-1941 isolationism. Yet the manipulation of foreign politics remained a controversial project within the American foreign-policy establishment. Naturally, it was more contentious still in the countries whose destiny lay in the balance. Before long, Lansdale would find himself at the center of political storms in both Washington and Manila.

◆

THERE WAS, admittedly, a crucial difference between the situation in Italy in 1948 and that in the Philippines in 1951. In the former instance, the Truman administration had been worried about Communists' winning power outright at the ballot box, because the Italian Communist Party was the largest in Western Europe. In the Philippines, by contrast, the Communist Party was prevented by law from contesting the election. The concern was that abusive, corrupt, and reactionary anti-Communists would win the election by fraud and thereby inadvertently strengthen the Communists' attempts to foment a revolution.

Charged with safeguarding the vote was the ineffectual Philippine Commission on Elections. In the summer of 1951, Lansdale hatched a scheme with Ramon Magsaysay to have the commission request the assistance of the armed forces. President Elpidio Quirino's Liberals had been the worst offenders among vote stealers the last time around, so Lansdale was careful to ensure that the request from the election commission came while Quirino was out of the country receiving medical care at Johns Hopkins Hospital in Baltimore.

To further safeguard the elections, Lansdale set up an OPC-funded organization, the National Movement for Free Elections, known by its acronym, NAMFREL. It was ostensibly run by three Filipino war veterans. Its real guiding light, in addition to Lansdale himself, was another CIA operative, named Gabriel L. Kaplan. He first came to Manila in 1951 on behalf of a CIA-backed Committee for a Free Asia, which eventually changed its name to the Asia Foundation. Later he would masquerade as the representative of yet another CIA front, the Catherwood Foundation.

A short, stocky man with a taste for giant Churchill cigars, Gabe Kaplan was a liberal Republican lawyer and politician from New York who had failed in a bid for Congress in 1938 and for the state supreme court in 1940. He used to say of his unsuccessful campaigns, "Fortunately I'm Jewish. But even that wasn't enough. I needed just a bit of Italian blood besides." (The dominant New York City politician of the day, Fiorello La Guardia, was both Jewish and Italian.) Kaplan was recruited for the OPC by a fellow liberal Republican lawyer from New York, Desmond FitzGerald, who had joined the Office of Policy Coordination's Far East Division after battling alongside Kaplan against the corrupt Democratic Party machine. He thus became one of the few Jews in an organization that still resembled a WASPy men's club. Kaplan's New York political experience proved invaluable in foiling Tammany Hall's Philippine counterparts. He also brought exactly the same perspective to dealing with Filipinos that Lansdale himself had, treating his contacts with "trust and respect," rather than trying to bribe or blackmail them in the way that CIA case officers normally were taught to do. But he was more outspoken than his quiet boss: "Gabe was short but very glib of tongue," Frisco "Johnny" San Juan, one of the founders of NAMFREL, recalled decades later. "You put him in a room, he would always dominate the conversation."[2]

Employing NAMFREL volunteers as well as Philippine troops, the unlikely tag team of Lansdale and Kaplan orchestrated an ambitious scheme to protect the election. "Philippine Army troops guarded public meetings to guarantee free speech and later patrolled the vicinity of polling places to prevent harassment of voters and electoral officials," Lansdale recalled. "The polling places themselves were guarded by high school and college ROTC cadets, who were often taken to the precincts by army transports or by members of Namfrel; and the latter also served as poll-watchers under the direction of the Commission on Elections." While some cheating undoubtedly occurred in 1951, it was much less than in 1949. That most of the winning candidates belonged to the opposition party—the Nacionalistas—attested to the election's honesty.

To heighten the impact of the voting, Lansdale orchestrated a typical bit of black propaganda. After the Military Intelligence Service arrested a Huk agitprop cell in Manila, Lansdale used their communications channels to write his own propaganda on behalf of the insurgency. His theme was "Boycott the Election!" based on the assumption that the 1951 vote would be as dirty as its 1949 predecessor. He produced an entire fake directive along those lines "typed on a captured Huk typewriter on captured paper, with authenticating identification." So realistic was Lansdale's missive that soon it was echoed by the entire Huk propaganda apparatus. When the election turned out to be honest, the Huks were discredited.[3]

◆

LANSDALE WAS shrewd enough to apprehend that one honest election by itself was hardly enough to win the war. Six months after the 1951 election, he wrote to his wife, Helen ("Tike"):

> It looks like the Huks are really crumbling, the first country in the world to defeat the Communists this way. It isn't over yet, but the end is in sight if we can just keep the pressure up. . . . Trouble is, democracy is not building up fast enough to replace the void created as communism crumbles, which presents new and complex problems. . . . There are indications that same old tricks of using forceful coercion on the electorate are being planned, even though this was licked in the last election of 1951. Friends are getting worried and jittery again and running in here with their tales of woe . . . and are getting bucked up, fannies slapped and sent out as men again.[4]

To maintain momentum, Lansdale decided that his friend Ramon Magsaysay would be the ideal candidate to replace Quirino as president, but he knew that it was important not to have Magsaysay campaign for office prematurely, so as to sustain the nonpartisan aura of the defense secretary. When speculation began about a Magsaysay-for-president campaign, Lansdale wrote to Helen, "[I] had him say he was too busy with a big job to have time to think of politics— go 'way and let me work.'"[5] All the while, Lansdale was plotting to raise Magsaysay's political profile so as to position him for the presidential race.

Lansdale orchestrated a campaign-style trip for the defense minister to the United States and Mexico in June 1952. Magsaysay traveled on a four-engine Lockheed Constellation aircraft lent to him by the U.S. military. He was accorded practically the treatment of a head of state, welcomed with nineteen-gun salutes in San Francisco, Washington, and New York. He even met with President Truman, Secretary of State Dean Acheson, Secretary of Defense Robert Lovett, General Omar Bradley, and major newspaper and magazine publishers. Newspapers hailed him as an "imaginative administrator" (*New York Times*), "a Pacific dynamo" (*New York Herald Tribune*), and other encomia.

The only glitch occurred on Magsaysay's airplane en route to Mexico City to address a Lions International convention. Lansdale's team had prepared a speech for Magsaysay. Its author was David T. Sternberg, a chain-smoking, wheelchair-bound CIA officer who had initially arrived in the Philippines in 1939, endured Japanese incarceration during the war, and now worked for the CIA while posing as the *Christian Science Monitor* correspondent in Manila. Frisco San Juan described him as a "genius": "His physical condition sharpened his mind. He was at a disadvantage physically but first-class mentally."[6] Sternberg's draft speech stressed the need for "the highest type of fighting ideals and principles" to defeat "the Communists." But Magsaysay had been sold on a competing draft written by a "right-wing party hack" in the Philippines that Lansdale described as a "tirade of negative invective against the Huks"—"one of those 'they eat little babies for breakfast' type of things" in which "the only good Huks were dead Huks." There was no mention of the spirit of "brotherly protection and friendship" that animated the anti-Huk campaign Lansdale had devised. Yet aboard the airplane Magsaysay told Lansdale that this was the text he was planning to deliver.

"The hell you are," Lansdale said. "You are going to use this speech that was written for you and that is you to a T."

Peeved, Magsaysay shot back, "All right, I am going back to Manila then. To hell with them, I don't need to give a speech anyhow."

Lansdale replied firmly, "You are going down and you are going to give that speech." Then, "shocked and angry," he grabbed the other speech from Magsaysay's hands and tore it into shreds.

As the argument escalated, Magsaysay shoved Lansdale, and Lansdale "slugged him real hard, and he went down." Or so he recalled years later; in another version of the tale, he merely said they had a "brief tussle." In both versions of the story, the two men looked up and saw that their fight had been witnessed by Quirino's wide-eyed adult daughter, Vicky Quirino Gonzalez, who was traveling with the party.

She said to Lansdale in horror, "Papa told me about you!"

Lansdale replied that this was a "brotherly fight," adding, "I am fighting because I love this guy very much." Magsaysay saw things the same way. The two men quickly patched up their quarrel, and Magsaysay wound up delivering the speech that Lansdale wanted.

In fact, Magsaysay did pretty much everything that Lansdale wanted, not because he was a paid American agent but because he had such faith in his friend's acumen. Magsaysay's confidence was justified, at least judging by the consequences of the trip. He returned to Manila "as a conquering Caesar," in the words of two early biographers.[7]

◆

THE CHALLENGE was to convert Magsaysay's popularity into a viable campaign—and to prevent Quirino from stealing the election. Magsaysay was a member of Quirino's Liberal Party, but he knew that the president would not step aside for him. There ensued complex negotiations with the barons of the Nacionalista Party, the former president José Laurel and Senator Claro Recto, to secure its nomination for Magsaysay. This was not a natural alliance. Laurel and Recto were as anti-American as Magsaysay was pro-American. Moreover, they had served under the very Japanese occupation regime (Laurel as president, Recto as a cabinet minister) that Magsaysay had fought. But they were also professional politicians who could spot a winner when they saw one.

Lansdale was in the thick of all the wheeling and dealing. At one point, the Nacionalistas produced an agreement that would have given Magsaysay the nod in return for a promise that the party, not the president, would select his cabinet members. Magsaysay was willing to sign anything he needed to win, but Lansdale "prevailed on Magsaysay," according to Magsaysay's biographer José Abueva, "not to cut corners which would later compromise his moral position as a reform leader."[8] Finally, on November 16, 1952, Magsaysay and the Nacionalistas signed a secret agreement: they would support him in return for his resignation from the Liberal Party and his pledge to give them a say, but not a veto, in cabinet appointments. The agreement also pledged support for Magsaysay from a third party, the Citizens Party led by Senator Lorenzo Tanada, a prominent former Liberal known as a corruption fighter.

Lansdale subsequently detailed these negotiations in a top-secret cable to Allen Dulles, who had taken over as CIA director in February 1953. (The OPC had been merged with the CIA in 1952.) Referring to Dulles only as "Director, KUBark," and signing himself "Geoffrey S. Villiers" (a pseudonym apparently picked at random from a telephone directory), Lansdale recalled that Tanada had come to him in 1952 "stating that he was 'reporting for orders to save democracy in the Philippines.'" The marching orders Lansdale gave were to support Magsaysay, and subsequently "Citizens Party personnel helped construct the opposition structure under Magsaysay."[9]

The secret agreement was so politically explosive that Lansdale could not leave it even in his preferred hiding spot, the JUSMAG liquor locker. Fearing it would be used to blackmail Magsaysay, he gave the only copy for safekeeping in a sealed envelope to Raymond Spruance, a retired admiral and World War II hero who had taken over as ambassador in February 1952. Spruance placed it in his bedroom safe, not trusting the main embassy safe for such a sensitive document. A few months later, after knowledge of the letter's existence leaked out, he returned it to Lansdale, who secreted it under the floor of his house. Two decades later, and long gone from the Philippines, Lansdale said, "It's still there today, as far as I know."[10]

◆

RAMON MAGSAYSAY resigned from the cabinet on February 28, 1953, with a blast at President Quirino. His resignation letter, carefully crafted by a group of supporters, including no doubt Lansdale, said, "It would be useless for me to continue as Secretary of National Defense with the specific duty of killing Huks as the administration continues to foster and tolerate conditions which offer fertile soil to Communism."[11]

Now that Magsaysay was openly a candidate, Lansdale helped organize a Magsaysay for President Movement modeled on a similar campaign that had drafted Dwight Eisenhower for president in 1952.

Lansdale even composed a slogan for the candidate, "Magsaysay Is My Guy"; Magsaysay became known as "the Guy" throughout the country. Lansdale collaborated with the jazz musician and future foreign minister Raul Manglapus to compose a campaign song, "The Magsaysay Mambo." Its first two verses:

> *Everywhere that you would look*
> *Was a bandit or a crook*
> *Peace and order was a joke*
> *Till Magsaysay pumasok [entered]!*

> *That is why, that is why,*
> *You will hear the people cry:*
> *"Our democracy will die*
> *Kung wala si [without] Magsaysay!"*[12]

Lansdale had a master disc sent to the United States, where thousands of vinyl records were produced by the CIA and smuggled back into the Philippines.[13] The song became so popular, Lansdale wrote to Helen on May 18, 1953, that "it has made a big hit around here, all the kids singing it, and of course radios turned on full blast so that the neighbors half a mile down the road can enjoy the pretty music. Some of the newspaper lads here claim I wrote the thing. As they say in Brooklyn," he concluded wryly, "perish forbid." When some of the officers at the mess at Clark Air Base asked Lansdale whether he had "heard that hit tune in the Philippines called the Magsaysay Mambo," he simply played "dumb."[14]

Lansdale had become, he wrote home, the ringmaster of "a twenty-ring circus, with each ring needing an eye kept on it and with me having to run several of the rings at the same time to boot."[15] He was getting used to being woken up early to be confronted with problems he had not expected when he went to bed the night before. As he told Helen,

It might be the use of napalm against Moro outlaws or the financial troubles of a newspaper or the replacement of a good combat commander or putting on a radio program at a moment's notice to how to bring two Filipinos together despite mutual distrust or hearing about the latest rumor campaign to discredit me or how a close friend's wife is being seduced by a band leader or a special operation against the Huk leadership or how to bring security for civilians along the eastern shore of Laguna de Bay or doping out the intentions of intriguing politicos or, most often, the 1953 presidential campaign here.

With a mock-humble flourish, Lansdale concluded, "It will be good to just have to wonder whether I get orange juice or grapefruit on the breakfast table."[16]

Far removed from the duties of an ordinary military officer or even secret agent, Lansdale had become a political power broker. "At times I feel like Boss Hague, at others Rasputin," he wrote to Helen, adding cryptically, "but without entering into things the way they did."[17] This was not a model that most American government representatives would aspire to: Frank Hague had presided over a corrupt political machine as mayor of Jersey City, New Jersey, from 1917 to 1947, and became notorious for proclaiming, "I am the law," while Grigori Rasputin was a licentious mystic who gained a sinister hold over the Romanov family in the last days of the Russian czar. Presumably when Lansdale said that he was not "entering into things the way they did," he meant that he did not abuse his power as Hague and Rasputin did. But that he would even invoke the comparison shows that his hidden influence was expanding in a way that many of his countrymen—to say nothing of ordinary Filipinos—would not have approved of.

◆

IN RECOGNITION of the success he was having orchestrating the anti-Huk campaign, Lansdale was promoted by the Air Force to full colonel in January 1952, ahead of his peers. He was in many ways eclipsing the CIA station chief, Ralph B. Lovett, a mild-mannered and soft-spoken retired army one-star, as well as JUSMAG's new commander, Major General Albert Pierson, a veteran of the New Guinea and Philippine campaigns in World War II. Lansdale was even assuming more prominence than Ambassador Ray Spruance, the victor of the Battle of Midway, who was dubbed "the Sphinx" by Filipino newspapermen because he was so reluctant to speak in public.[18] (One of the ambassador's aides recalled, "On the rare occasions when we were able to talk him into making a speech he approached it with far more nervousness than he ever did the Japanese fleet.")[19] Lansdale was dismayed by "the lack of firm and positive U.S. representation here" and decided he had no choice but to fill the vacuum—even if he was supposed to be a *covert* operative. "I've found myself time and again having to speak up strongly on U.S. policy—when Spruance or Pierson should," Ed wrote to Helen. "That's strictly between us, because a colonel can really be jumped on for some of the things I've had to say and do recently."[20]

Soon Filipino reporters were kidding Lansdale that he was running for president himself after having already served as the real secretary of national defense.[21] He was becoming so famous that he was recognized wherever he went. He wrote to Helen in the spring of 1953, "I've never been in Fura before, but as I drove up the only street, folks leaned out my windows, yelling hello, Ed, and Magsaysay is my Guy (a campaign slogan) at me and inviting me in to eat. A few days earlier, I was stuck for the night down in Southern Luzon and rather than drive a not-too-safe-highway at night, stopped off at a hotel run by Chinese (as most are). I scribbled some name on the register (making it up at the moment) and the hotel manager read it, smiled, and said happy to have you with us Col Lansdale."[22]

It wasn't just in the provinces that Lansdale was acquiring an outsize reputation. Carlos Romulo, the Philippine ambassador to Washington, who was contemplating a presidential bid of his own, told his staff, Lansdale wrote, "that nobody could be elected President here if I opposed the guy . . . a pleasant false belief, huh?"[23]

False or not, this belief in Lansdale's omnipotence became increasingly widespread, and it led to a backlash both in Washington and in Manila. Criticism of Lansdale broke into the open in early 1953, just as the Eisenhower administration was assuming office, when *Bataan* magazine published an article, subsequently circulated by Quirino's office,

warning of a "master mind"—"a certain army colonel"—who was creating "an American Army party organized to foist a 'man on horseback'
on the Filipinos."²⁴ In case there was any doubt as to the identity of the
"master mind," the *Manila Evening News* ran its own article making
clear that "the American colonel attacked in Bataan Magazine is the
propaganda chief of the JUSMAG." The Huks got into the act, too.
They "have coined a phrase of 'Jusmagsaysay' to indicate he's my boy,"
Lansdale reported.²⁵

Among those irate at Lansdale's machination, not surprisingly, was
Elpidio Quirino himself. The onetime prodigy of Philippine politics,
he had climbed what Disraeli called "the greasy pole" ever since, as a
young lawyer from a small town in backwoods Luzon, he had first been
elected to the House of Representatives in 1919 at age nineteen. His
steady ascent had taken him to the Senate and then the vice presidency,
followed, after Manual Roxas's death in 1948, by the ultimate prize, the
presidency itself. His more than three decades in politics were full of
considerable achievements. He had helped secure from Washington the
passage of a law in 1934 to grant the Philippines independence, which
would come in 1946, and he had helped draft the constitution. During
the war, unlike many of his political rivals, he had refused to cooperate
with the occupiers. He had been captured and imprisoned by the Japanese, and his wife and three children had been killed during the bloody
Battle of Manila. In the postwar years, he had presided over impressive
reconstruction efforts even if his term was also marred by the pervasive
corruption that had allowed the Huk insurgency to flourish.

In 1953, Quirino was only sixty-three years old but looked older.
He had but three years to live and had to spend two valuable months of
the 1953 campaign receiving treatment in Baltimore for a variety of ailments, including heart, stomach, and kidney problems. But even from
his hospital bed, he was not too sick to fight back against those who
were seeking to usurp his hard-won hold on power. "I swear to God,"
Quirino vowed, "I will destroy those who will try to destroy me."²⁶

Quirino knew that Lansdale was not only a close adviser to Magsaysay but also a CIA officer, and he tried to kick Lansdale out of the
country. Lansdale was forced to cut short a vacation with his family

in Florida in early 1953 to rush back to the Philippines at the personal request of Allen Dulles and his brother, Secretary of State John Foster Dulles. These two dedicated Cold Warriors believed that it would be easier for Quirino to bar Lansdale from the country than to expel him. High-level U.S. pressure kept Quirino from carrying out his threat. Acting on behalf of the CIA—a potent, if concealed, force in American foreign relations that now rivaled and even eclipsed the State Department—Lansdale was free to continue exerting his quasi-covert influence.

In the end, given how pro-American most Filipinos were, the attacks on Lansdale's leading role did not sting nearly as much as they would have in other countries. On the stump, Magsaysay would boldly declare, "Quirino and the other Liberals charge that I have American advisers. Sure I do. . . . These are the best friends we've ever had, and I'm proud to have them as my associates."[27] Magsaysay even had an aide who looked a bit like Lansdale, right down to the mustache, stand on the campaign platform with him when the real Lansdale wasn't around to make clear that he had the American imprimatur.[28]

◆

QUIRINO AND his supporters were not the only ones unhappy about Lansdale's growing prominence in Filipino politics. So were some of Lansdale's own colleagues in the U.S. government who opposed American operatives' intervening so deeply in the politics of a sovereign country and the CIA's playing such a prominent role in American foreign policy. "A lot of our little guys . . . seem to be trying to pull me down as much as the politicos here, figuring I guess that now is a good time," Lansdale complained in the spring of 1953.[29]

Some of those trying to pull him down were not, in truth, so little, and their objections, far from being petty or spiteful, raised an important and enduring debate about the role of America's intelligence agencies. They included David K. E. Bruce, the under secretary of state, a man who would serve every president between Truman and Ford. Like Lansdale, he was an OSS veteran, albeit from a moneyed, Old South milieu far removed from Lansdale's more modest upbringing. (Bruce's first wife was the daughter of Andrew Mellon, the nation's richest man; his second wife, Evangeline Bruce, became a legendary Georgetown hostess.) Bruce wanted Lansdale sent home in December 1952 because he was so closely identified with Magsaysay. He suggested in telegram shorthand that the "relationship established between US and Magsaysay threatens become prejudiced to US interests in Philippines and to those of Magsaysay if not altered to meet present circumstances. Full US support for SecDef in his campaign against Huks is quite different from support for potential presidential candidate already committed to oppose admin in which he serves. Believe we must find way of making this position clear to Magsaysay, who must also realize any widespread conviction that he is hand-picked candidate of US wld not further his own polit career."[30]

This was the beginning of a larger critique of covert action that Bruce would develop in the years ahead. In 1956, he and the former defense secretary Robert Lovett would submit, at President Eisenhower's request, a secret review of the CIA that was harshly critical of its tendency toward "King Making" in pursuit of those twin goals "of 'frustrating the Soviets' and keeping others 'pro-western' oriented." Anticipating an argument that would become a staple of political discourse in the 1970s after the CIA's covert activities were publicly revealed, Lovett demanded to know, "What right have we to go barging around into other countries, buying newspapers and handing money to opposition parties or supporting a candidate for this, that or the other office?"[31]

Another skeptic was George Aurell, a cautious and ineffectual bureaucrat who was the head of the CIA's Far East Division. A CIA colleague recalled that Aurell "had never been able to accept the fact that so much social engineering was involved in the activities of Lansdale and Kaplan," whom he would sneeringly describe as "great crusaders." Aurell would say, in reference to EDCOR, "What in hell is an intelligence agency doing running a rural resettlement program? I'm glad to help fight the Huks, but is it our job to rebuild the nation?"[32]

His criticisms of "nation building" would be echoed in Washington during conflicts ranging from Vietnam in the 1960s to Afghanistan and

Iraq in the 2000s. Many policymakers would advocate a narrow, tactical approach to battling insurgents—kill or capture as many as possible and don't worry about fixing societal problems. Lansdale, by contrast, was convinced that without creating functioning state institutions there was no way to defeat a determined insurgency. He was aware of the difficulties of improving governance in a Third World country—he confronted them every day—but still he was frustrated with colleagues who "failed to grasp the political nature of 'people's warfare,' such as the Huks had attempted to wage." He found himself citing Mao to argue, "All military actions are meant to achieve political objectives while military action itself is a manifested form of politics."[33] When it came to CIA involvement in the 1953 Philippine presidential election, Lansdale wrote to his superiors, "In brief, it was because we saw no other ready solution to the defeat of Communism in the country."[34]

Now he just had to convince the new CIA director.

◆

ALLEN WELSH DULLES had a diplomatic pedigree like few others. His maternal grandfather, John Watson Foster, had been President Benjamin Harrison's secretary of state. His "Uncle Bert" was Robert Lansing, Woodrow Wilson's secretary of state. His older brother, John Foster Dulles, became Eisenhower's secretary of state. But although Allen and Foster Dulles pursued similar career paths, they had very different personalities. Foster was brilliant and hardworking but also dour, moralistic, pompous, and reserved. Winston Churchill, one of many who did not care for him, said he was a "bull who always brought his china closet with him."[35] Allen was more charming, a genial raconteur and practiced seducer—in short, more like Lansdale himself. His "Santa-like 'Ho-ho-ho' laugh"[36] somehow made the covert machinations he directed seem less menacing. Foster would be respected by his colleagues; Allen would be beloved.

After graduating from high school at fifteen, Foster was valedictorian of the Princeton class in 1908 and afterward enjoyed a meteoric rise at the Wall Street law firm of Sullivan & Cromwell. Soon he would become the highest-paid lawyer in the country and the Republicans' chief foreign-policy spokesman. Allen followed his brother to Princeton and after graduation entered the Foreign Service—but only because the United States had no civilian intelligence service. Like Edward Lansdale, Allen was a devotee of Rudyard Kipling's *Kim*, one of the first and most popular novels of espionage, and he aspired to follow in Kim's footsteps.[37] Posted during World War I in Vienna and Bern, Switzerland, Allen developed the case officer's skill at cultivating sources and evaluating their information. In 1926 Allen, who had attended law school at night, left the government to become a high-paid international lawyer at his brother's firm. His recreational interests were tennis, talking foreign policy over brandy and a pipe, and womanizing. He would torture his long-suffering wife by writing letters telling her of all the enjoyable hours he had spent on his frequent trips abroad with a variety of beautiful women. "I don't feel I deserve as good a wife as I have," he confessed, "as I am rather too fond of the company of other ladies."[38]

Allen Dulles's life changed for good in 1942 when another New York lawyer with a roving eye—Wild Bill Donovan—recruited him for what would become the OSS. Before long, Dulles was back in his old stomping ground in neutral Switzerland, which in World War II, as in World War I, proved to be a playground for secret agents. Much like Lansdale, Dulles had, in the words of his biographer Peter Grose, a "marvelous, low-key way of speaking" that endeared him to most people he met.[39] Also like Lansdale, Dulles did not believe in excessive secrecy; he made sure that his status as an American spymaster became common knowledge in Bern so that potential sources would know where to go with their information. Before long German officials dissatisfied with the Nazis were showing up in the sitting room of his cozy apartment. He was able to gain information about the Holocaust, rocket and nuclear development, plots to kill Hitler, and much else besides. He even helped to negotiate the surrender of the German army in Italy. Even more than Lansdale, Dulles also combined romance with espionage. Both Mary Bancroft, an American newspaper heiress, and Countess Wally Castelbarco, daughter of the Italian American conductor Arturo Toscanini, became his agents and his lovers.

After the war, Dulles briefly returned to the practice of law but, like Frank Wisner and many other veterans, he found civilian life a bore. In January 1951, he became the CIA's deputy director for plans; in August, deputy director of the entire agency; and then in February 1953, following Eisenhower's election, director of central intelligence. Nicknamed the Great White Case Officer, he loved the romance of espionage and hated the paperwork. The Soviet mole Kim Philby, who knew Dulles when he was MI6 liaison officer in Washington, said that Dulles "was nice to have around: comfortable, predictable, pipe-smoking, whisky-sipping company," and that "his unprofessional delight in cloak-and-dagger for its own sake was an endearing trait."[40]

While Eisenhower set the general direction of foreign policy, a field in which he was far better schooled than most of his predecessors and successors, he delegated much of its implementation to the brothers Dulles. They spoke on the telephone daily and gathered every Sunday at their sister Eleanor's place in northern Virginia to plot by her pool. Foster distrusted the Foreign Service and preferred to implement sensitive operations or handle important relationships through Allen's CIA people because they labored under less oversight.[41]

The Dulles brothers' plans to liberate the "captive peoples" of the Communist bloc—an Eisenhower campaign slogan in 1952—went awry when Communist secret police forces rolled up CIA-organized networks in, inter alia, Poland, Ukraine, Albania, China, and Tibet. That left the Dulles brothers to focus on lands where Communism had not yet taken root. Allen Dulles proclaimed, "Where there begins to be evidence that a country is slipping and communist takeover is threatened, we can't wait for an engraved invitation to come and give aid."[42]

With Eisenhower's blessing, Dulles charged ahead in June 1953 with Operation Ajax, a joint undertaking with Britain's MI6 to overthrow Prime Minister Mohammad Mossadeq of Iran, who was threatening to nationalize oil fields belonging to the British-owned Anglo-Iranian Oil Company (now British Petroleum) and who, it was feared in Washington, was soft on Communism. Kermit "Kim" Roosevelt Jr., Theodore Roosevelt's grandson, was tasked with returning real power to the Shah of Iran. That is precisely what occurred in Tehran in August

1953, while the Philippine election campaign was heating up, although historians continue to debate how much of the credit or blame should go to the CIA. Later that year, Eisenhower would give the go-ahead to Operation Success to topple Guatemala's leftist president, Jacobo Arbenz. In 1954, a CIA team under Colonel Richard Haney would contrive a "spontaneous uprising" to drive Arbenz out of power.

Such coups were not without cost. After taking power in 1979, Iran's Islamist revolutionaries would cite the anti-Mossadeq uprising, which actually had been supported by the clerical establishment, to justify their anti-American animus. And among those embittered by the overthrow of Arbenz was a young Argentinian physician named Ernesto "Che" Guevara who was in Guatemala City as it was being bombed by unmarked American aircraft; this experience helped turn him into a Marxist revolutionary. But the Eisenhower administration never imagined that its regime-change operations would eventually produce such "blowback." To the contrary, the CIA campaigns in Iran and Guatemala were seen as proof that covert action was an economical and effective alternative to waging war. As one of Eisenhower's biographers put it, he had a "fundamental belief that nuclear war was unimaginable, limited conventional war unwinnable, and stalemate unacceptable. That left the CIA's covert action capability."[43]

It is hardly a surprise, then, that Allen Dulles was inclined to support Lansdale as much as he did Kim Roosevelt and other swashbuckling covert-action specialists. He loved to take favorite field officers to the White House and introduce them to Eisenhower, saying, with a twinkle in his eye, "Mr. President, here's my best man!"[44] Intensifying a post-1945 shift in the exercise of American influence—quite a change from prewar days, when the United States did not even have a civilian intelligence agency—the Eisenhower administration did not cavil at using covert operatives to manipulate foreign elections. But even Dulles cautioned Lansdale that he had to "realize the delicacy of his position" and "conduct himself with extreme discretion."[45]

It helped that the senior American representative in the Philippines was also a supporter of Lansdale's. Ambassador Ray Spruance was no professional diplomat. A career military man who was not given to dissembling, he hated Quirino with a passion and admired Magsaysay for his "courage, honesty, and patriotism."[46] To win Spruance's favor, Lansdale hosted him on inspection trips to the provinces, "which," Lansdale noted, "he loves since he can get into old khakis and walking shoes."[47] After hearing that Spruance liked melons, Lansdale even took him to a cantaloupe patch in the Candaba Swamp that had just been liberated by Filipino troops.[48] This campaign paid off: in December 1952, the ambassador wrote to his superiors in Washington that Lansdale's presence was "essential in view of his personal contacts and the current situation."[49]

◆

YET THE schism between the sanctioned diplomats of the Establishment and the new guild of covert operatives intent on saving "Western freedom from Communist darkness" continued to widen. Despite the support of Dulles and Spruance, Lansdale still complained of "sniping at me (verbally) by several folks at our Embassy to whom I am somewhat lower than a skunk."[50] Major General Albert Pierson did more than just snipe. He insisted that Lansdale's continued presence in JUSMAG was an embarrassment and a violation of the embassy's decree that U.S. personnel stay neutral in the election. (Spruance, who knew and approved of Lansdale's behind-the-scenes machinations, had issued a disingenuous "warning" on March 13, 1953, to "all Americans resident here to refrain scrupulously from any kind of participation in the election.")[51] Pierson was not able to expel Lansdale from the country any more than Quirino could. But he did manage to expel Lansdale from JUSMAG's organizational chart and its housing compound. Lansdale would soon get his revenge; his complaints to Allen Dulles contributed to Pierson's dismissal and replacement in August 1953 by another general, Robert M. Cannon, who was more accommodating.[52]

In search of a new cover, Lansdale transferred to the Thirteenth Air Force at Clark Air Base, where he masqueraded as deputy command historian. He received a room in the bachelor officers' quarters in a concrete building that he described as "shaped coyly like a long cracker box, ultra modern and functional, but still a cracker box." Lansdale also rented a "little one-bedroom sawali house in Angeles close by, to put up guests and visitors," he informed Helen. (Sawali is a woven bamboo used to build nipa huts.) "Angeles is still quite a honky-tonk town and I dislike it as much as ever (the first town I ever really knew in the Philippines). The amusing rumor is that I've taken a house in town for nefarious love affairs . . . a rumor that is actually helpful. How about flying over for a weekend and give the rumor mongers something to really talk about?"[53] Lansdale knew, of course, that his wife hated to fly and hated the Philippines, so she would never take him up on his offer. Moreover, he was still passionately in love with Pat Kelly and still seeing her regularly. Given his continuing relationship with Pat, it's likely that the gossip was right and that Ed's house in Angeles really was nothing more than a love nest, even as Ed was also working to repair his relationship with his distant wife. Helen was trying to promote a rapprochement with her faraway husband by sending him notes she had taken during Christian Science classes. "The lessons recently scare this poor old sinner, but then maybe I need the scaring," Lansdale told her.[54]

To the extent that Lansdale had any religious faith, it would have come in handy in dealing with mounting personal attacks during this period that were not just bureaucratic in nature. Tony Quirino was the president's brother and political enforcer, performing much the same role that Ngo Dinh Nhu later would play for his brother Ngo Dinh Diem in South Vietnam. During the 1953 campaign, Quirino was recalled to active duty as a lieutenant colonel in the Philippine army and given charge of a special command in the Military Intelligence Service manned by his thugs. His men got on Lansdale's tail a couple of times in Manila, making plain to Lansdale that he was "to be shipped home in a coffin." Lansdale recalled "one wild nighttime chase all through Manila before I eluded them."[55] Another time, he was shot at in his car with a .30-caliber rifle. "Incredibly," he wrote, "the bullets missed me."[56] As a precaution, he had to change his license plates and repaint his vehicle.[57] "It's not much fun to be under attack all the time," Lansdale admitted, "telephones tapped, followed night and day, threatened, asked by your commanding general to get out, have the general commanding the base I'm supposed to move to say he doesn't want a 'trouble maker.' "[58]

In light of the controversy that now surrounded him, Lansdale thought, "Maybe it's just as well if I hole up for a few days and be quiet as a little mouse."[59] It was an understandable reaction, a form of self-preservation. But Lansdale could not stay out of the action for long—not when an election with momentous consequences for the future of the Philippines and the Cold War was about to occur. Before long he would be the mouse that roared.

10

"A Real Vindication"

This is the way we like to see an election carried out.
—President Dwight D. Eisenhower

UNTIL the late nineteenth century, most politicians considered the act of campaigning to be sordid and unseemly. As late as 1896, William McKinley refused to go on the campaign trail at all, preferring to receive visitors at his home in Canton, Ohio. The Philippines, like most other countries, had even less history of stumping for votes. It did not hold its first legislative elections until 1907, and its first presidential election had to wait until the creation of a commonwealth in 1935. Most of the leading politicians were scions of the landed elite who disdained what was perceived as the grubby process of asking the hoi polloi for votes as much as America's Founding Fathers did. In the 1935 campaign, Manuel Quezon won the presidency after delivering only two speeches. In 1941, he won reelection without making a single speech.[1]

Ramon Magsaysay was different. A man of the people, he kept up a frenetic pace of campaigning in 1953, traveling by airplane, car, train, boat, and even carabao to places that no previous presidential candidate had ever visited. "Breakfast was at twelve noon, lunch at six in the evening, and supper at two or three o'clock the next morning," wrote one of his supporters.[2] Many members of his entourage got sick and run-down as the unrelenting pace continued—but not the tireless candidate. He kept going, trying to shake as many hands as possible, in no small part to draw a contrast between his youthful energy and Elpidio Quirino's advanced age and infirmity. Everywhere he went, he was greeted by adoring crowds shouting, *"Mabuhay*, Magsaysay!" (Hurray, Magsaysay!)

Magsaysay was no great orator or deep thinker, but he had a talent for connecting with ordinary people in a way that Lansdale's next protégé, Ngo Dinh Diem, could never master. One of his biographers wrote that Magsaysay "was perfectly at ease mingling with the people, shaking their hands, flashing his smile, talking in simple English, or in Tagalog or Ilocano, impressing everybody with his tall, big frame and rugged looks, heartily enjoying his meal with whoever happened to be his hosts."[3] At the same time that Magsaysay was courting the common people, he was also wooing powerful interests, including sugar and coconut growers, the American and Chinese business communities, regional power brokers, and the Catholic Church.[4]

His ability to balance both parts of his coalition—the man in the street and the dealmaker in the boardroom—was a sign of his political skill. So, too, was his ability to parry the Liberals' insults. They accused him of being stupid and ill-informed—"fit only to be a garbage collector," in one caustic critic's stinging rebuke. When he heard this, Magsaysay grinned and fired back, "A garbage collector is just what this nation needs, to clean out the dirt and filth of graft and corruption."[5]

The biggest threat to Magsaysay's election was the worry that a third-party ticket led by the Liberal defectors Carlos Romulo and Fernando Lopez, who had resigned as Quirino's ambassador to Washington and vice president respectively, might split the anti-Quirino vote. But that danger was removed on August 21, 1953, when, following tortuous backroom negotiations, Romulo and Lopez decided to end their long-shot campaign and endorse Magsaysay in exchange for cabinet and congressional seats for their supporters.[6]

Thereafter, Magsaysay's victory seemed assured, provided that

Quirino's men did not steal the election—or even try to assassinate him. Security was a constant worry for Magsaysay's aides, given the way their candidate exposed himself. His welfare was looked after by a bodyguard of fifty former guerrillas—his old troops—bristling with weapons. One of them later recalled, "We ate dust on roads so hidden under it that you could not see the car ahead. I lost ten pounds in ten days, during one phase of the campaign."[7] But even if Magsaysay's guards could keep him alive, could anything be done to prevent Quirino from stuffing the ballot boxes in his favor?

◆

WHILE THE campaign was reaching a climax, Edward Lansdale, having already played the role of a Boss Hague or Rasputin, was still lying low, trying to stay out of the public eye. It was, in some ways, a stroke of fortune that in June 1953 he was invited by a visiting American general to go to Indochina on a trip that, as we shall see, would last three weeks. When he returned, he once again took up a pivotal behind-the-scenes role in supporting his friend Monching. He had been officially instructed by Washington that he could go ahead and help "on clean elections," but he was supposed "to have nothing to do with candidates." He thought these instructions were nonsensical—"How in hell can a guy fight for a free election without getting close to a candidate and having him do the in-fighting on the dirtiest phases of fraud?"—so, as was his wont, he skirted the rules.[8] George Aurell, the CIA's Far East Division chief, later complained that Lansdale got "money for political funding, propaganda schemes and so forth" by disguising them as "requests for new filing equipment or air-conditioning repairs."[9]

Lansdale used "cut-outs," that is, covert intermediaries, to advise Magsaysay "on the conduct of the campaign" and to provide him "with his major speeches and themes."[10] (David T. Sternberg, the wheelchair-bound CIA officer, continued to be the main author of Magsaysay's speeches.)[11] His philosophy was always "helping the Filipinos to help themselves." Therefore, he wrote of his CIA team (code name Kugown) in a top-secret report for Allen Dulles: "We taught, encouraged, but kept our direct assistance as covert as possible."[12]

Years later, Lansdale was to claim that the "U.S. government gave no funds, secret or otherwise, to any of the candidates in the 1953 Presidential election in the Philippines."[13] He dubbed widespread tales of secret American spending a "fantasy" and a "fairy tale," and said disingenuously, "I only wish I were wealthy enough to have disbursed so many millions."[14] (Of course no one was claiming that Lansdale used funds from his own checking account.) In internal government documents, however, he was more forthcoming. In 1961, for example, Lansdale wrote to Deputy Secretary of Defense Roswell Gilpatric that "Magsaysay's own story of receiving 3-million-dollars from the U.S. to help him campaign was untrue and was told by him only to impress political leaders into supporting him, yet it still has currency." And what was truth? "Since I had those U.S. funding responsibilities in 1953," Lansdale continued, "I know how much smaller U.S. expenditures actually were and for what, and so do the proper U.S. fiscal authorities." He added, "Almost all U.S. political actions and the relatively small U.S. funds were expended" on ensuring "'free elections' through truly secret balloting and an honest count."[15] Note that in this secret memorandum, not declassified until 2014, Lansdale did not dispute that he had provided funding to Magsaysay; he merely said that he had provided a lot less than three million dollars.

Lansdale later recalled being offered five million dollars by Allen Dulles for use in the campaign. But he was "uneasy about this amount of money and asked if he was supposed to buy votes with it." He "felt that such an action would be of short-term value [only], and that the important thing was to teach the Filipinos new ways of governing themselves that would stay with them forever." In the end, Lansdale accepted one million dollars in cash, which he stashed in the JUSMAG liquor locker, but he claimed to have spent no more than sixty thousand dollars.[16]

Even if Lansdale did not hand Magsaysay bags of greenbacks, he served as a conduit between the campaign and American citizens and companies.[17] American firms provided an estimated $250,000 to Magsaysay, equivalent to $2.2 million in 2017 dollars. Some of the donors no doubt were content with keeping the Philippines from going Communist; others probably desired special favors from a president they had helped to elect.[18]

◆

WITH MAGSAYSAY'S campaign now running smoothly, Lansdale's main focus, given his awareness of a long tradition of political chicanery, was on preventing Elpidio Quirino from rigging the election. He uncovered, he later wrote, "plots to assassinate Magsaysay, the use of thugs to intimidate political workers, the location of a shipment of a million fake ballots printed in Hong Kong and secreted in the Philippines in readiness for stuffing ballot boxes, and the surreptitious moves of political bosses to gain control of the electoral machinery."[19] Of course, Lansdale himself was hardly innocent of charges of manipulating the election, but he drew a clear distinction in his mind between campaigning to win votes and intimidation of voters or stuffing of ballot boxes.

To head off such a possibility, Lansdale mounted an effort even more ambitious than the one he had assembled in 1951. He enlisted the papal nuncio, Cardinal Vagnozzi, as well as numerous civic groups such as the Jaycees, the Rotarians, and the League of Women Voters. All were told, in coordination with NAMFREL (the National Movement for Free Elections), to be on the lookout for election shenanigans. Meanwhile, Lansdale waged what he described as "a long, bitter, semi-covert struggle . . . to prevent the Armed Forces from becoming the personal instrument of the Quirinistos through officers subservient to the person of Quirino rather than the nation." Lansdale and his team relayed messages that army officers who worked against Magsaysay could expect to suffer the consequences after the election, while those who resisted Quirino's pressure could expect to be rewarded with promotions and assignments. He also launched "black" operations to block the Quirino machine; he later said he had arranged for the burning of warehouses that contained bogus ballots.[20]

Because Tony Quirino was threatening newspaper publishers in order to stop the publication of articles unfavorable to his brother, the relentlessly entrepreneurial Lansdale decided to put out a newspaper of his own. The *Free Philippines* was named after a publication of the same name that had been published covertly during the Japanese occupation. An eight-page tabloid, it was produced between September 28 and November 17, 1953, at first as a weekly and then, as the election approached, as a daily. Each issue had an average run of one hundred thousand copies. This newspaper exposed election "skulduggery" such as the "ominous transfers of honest constabulary commanders from big vote areas and their replacement by more pliable commanders" and "large-scale distribution of ink eradicator to henchmen who had access to the polls." Lansdale thought this publication, secretly financed by the CIA, had a significant impact: "The fact that the entire editorial staff of the *Free Philippines* kept active, despite armed coercion and economic pressure, stirred up first admiration and finally emulation in other newspapermen."[21]

Lansdale also took care to marshal foreign press coverage to counteract the pro-Quirino press. For example, a Scripps-Howard newspaper correspondent "asked for help in his pre-election reporting." Lansdale sent him to Negros Occidental Province, where a friend of Ed's could provide "first hand contact with citizen action against armed coercion."[22] Lansdale and his team arranged oleaginous profiles of Magsaysay in *Time*, *Life*, and other American publications that were widely read in the Philippines. A typical example was an April 20, 1953, article about Magsaysay in *Life* entitled "An Honest Man with Guts"; it described him as "the only man who could prevent the country from slipping." Lansdale had the CIA's "Mighty Wurlitzer"—its propaganda apparatus—playing at full blast during the 1953 campaign.

◆

ELECTION DAY came on Tuesday, November 10, 1953, and by the following morning it was obvious that Magsaysay was going to win—he was ahead of Quirino by a margin of three to one. But in those precomputerized days, it took a long time to count the ballots from such a sprawling country. There were still no official results by Wednesday evening. The following day, Thursday, November 12, Lansdale and Magsaysay sought to escape the pressure aboard the *Marguerite*, a motor yacht belonging to Rear Admiral Richard Cruzen, a noted polar explorer who was commander of U.S. naval forces in the Philippines. Along with Magsaysay's family and some of his cronies, they cruised through Manila Bay past Corregidor while waiting for the results to come in. The day was gray, with, Lansdale noted, "clouds coming down low on the bay over towards Arayat and Bataan." The clouds lifted, at least metaphorically, when they received word shortly after midday that Quirino had conceded. More than 4.2 million out of 5.6 million registered voters cast ballots, and Magsaysay received a decisive 68.9 percent of the total.

Lansdale was exultant, calling it "a real vindication of the things we believe in." For the first time in ages, he was "able to sit down and draw a big breath." His immediate hope was to catch up on his sleep. "There's a bunk here and I'm going to roll into it and see what that almost unknown luxury, a nap, feels like," he told Helen. "The work has come out beautifully, constructively for the U.S." He was particularly impressed that the election was largely violence-free: "Moral pressure had built up so greatly that the goons and toughies simply became ashamed of themselves at the last moment, and started becoming disobedient to their leaders, who were ordering all sorts of desperate measures. . . . I think the Philippines grew up maybe a couple of generations worth overnight in doing so."[23]

Upon learning of the results, President Eisenhower delivered a coded compliment to the CIA's man in Manila, whose full meaning would have been apparent only to someone like the president who had been briefed on Lansdale's covert mission. "This is the way we like to see an election carried out," he said.[24] Vice President Richard Nixon, who arrived with his wife, Pat, in Manila a couple of weeks after the election, delivered his own congratulations in a meeting with Lansdale and his six-man team in which he said that the CIA's mission in the Philippines had accomplished its objectives. Lansdale noted that Nixon, as a politician himself, had "almost an instantaneous grasp of the nuances of the problems faced and solved" by his team—"as though he were one of us."[25]

For his achievements in the Philippines, Lansdale was to receive the

National Security Medal, a decoration created by President Truman to recognize accomplishments in intelligence. Lansdale would become only the fourth recipient, after the former CIA director Walter Bedell Smith, covert operative Kim Roosevelt, and Rear Admiral Joseph Wenger, a legendary naval cryptologist, and he won the medal before it was bestowed on J. Edgar Hoover, Wild Bill Donovan, or Allen Dulles himself. His citation commended him for "directing a brilliant campaign to arrest and reverse the spread of Communist influence," adding that his "ingenuity in devising plans, and his perseverance in carrying them through to a successful conclusion" added "greatly to the strength of the free world in a critical area."[26] Since the medal was classified, it was locked up in a CIA safe. Lansdale could wear a ribbon on his uniform, but he could not say what it was for. When asked, he would joke, because it was blue and gold, that Ulysses S. Grant had pinned it on him for his service during the Civil War.[27]

Lansdale also received growing public accolades, including an article in *Time* magazine on November 23, 1953, which said that "the Magsaysay victory was a U.S. victory" and that "U.S. Colonel Edward Lansdale of the Air Force" had become "virtually his mentor and publicity man." As a result of the election, Lansdale gained a new nickname, apparently invented by the Indian ambassador to Manila. He became known as Colonel Landslide, a name that would follow him, both mockingly and reverently, from Asia to America for years to come. "Big joke, huh," Lansdale snorted.[28]

◆

IN THE 1972 movie *The Candidate*, Robert Redford plays a handsome and privileged young candidate, Bill McKay, who, against the odds, wins a U.S. Senate race in California. In the last scene, McKay escapes his own victory party along with his chief political consultant, Marvin Lucas, played by a bearded Peter Boyle. McKay asks Lucas, with a hint of desperation in his voice, "Marvin . . . what do we do now?" A raucous press throng then invades the room, and the movie ends before Marvin can reply. Unlike the fictional Marvin Lucas, Edward Lansdale would be forced to supply an answer to that question.

Lansdale was understandably eager to move on from the Philippines after the 1953 election triumph, but his friend Monching, by now dependent on his guidance, would not let him go. A few days after the vote, Lansdale and the president-elect were aboard another ship, this time a Philippine navy patrol boat called the *Bohol*, trapped on the outer edge of a typhoon. As they were getting showered by the waves, Lansdale threw his blanket over Magsaysay to keep him dry and Magsaysay grabbed Lansdale's hand and asked his American friend "to stick with him through the selection of a cabinet, making up his legislative and executive programs, dealing with [Syngman] Rhee and Chiang [Kai-shek], etc."[29] Confronted with such an emotional appeal, Lansdale had no choice but to accede.

Before long he was working as hard as he had before the election, his days often beginning at five in the morning and not ending until midnight. "Nuts," he realized, "I'm suddenly in the middle of tough economic and other affairs with someone who suddenly feels lost and has turned to me for help, apart from all the other advisers who've now moved in on him."[30]

◆

INAUGURATION DAY, Wednesday, December 30, 1953, was hot and muggy, like most days in the Philippines, with the temperature soaring to nearly ninety degrees Fahrenheit.[31] Magsaysay wanted to drive to the ceremony not in the black presidential Chrysler Imperial limousine used by his predecessor but in a more fun and racy Ford convertible. Elpidio Quirino persuaded him to stick with the official car. Together they rode from the Malacañang Palace to the Luneta, a waterfront park packed with at least two hundred thousand spectators. But Quirino could not persuade Magsaysay to switch clothes. Instead of a suit, the new president wore the distinctive embroidered Philippine shirt known as the *barong Tagalog* to take the oath of office and deliver his inaugural address. Magsaysay, sweat pouring down his face, was then borne away from the platform on the shoulders of a cheering crowd, his head bobbing up and down on the ocean of humanity, his clothes getting torn by his admirers.

Back at the Malacañang Palace, a series of ornate buildings on the banks of the Pasig River that had served as the home of Philippine and American governors-general before becoming the official residence of Philippine presidents, Magsaysay threw open the doors to the public. More than fifty thousand people swarmed in during the next two days. Strangers ten deep stood around the presidential dining table to watch Magsaysay eat his inaugural lunch. A news report noted, "Whole families picnicked on the flower beds; kids shied pop bottle caps at shimmering chandeliers inside the palace; mothers nursed their babies on satin-covered furniture in the drawing rooms."[32] Lansdale was reminded of stories about Andrew Jackson's populist inauguration in 1829, when his backwoods supporters mobbed the White House, breaking china and furniture to get at the ice cream, cake, and whisky-laced punch.

In keeping with his determination to be, as he vowed in his inaugural address, "President *for* the people," Magsaysay implemented Lansdale's suggestion that he continue his habit of soliciting complaints and suggestions by means of the ten-centavo telegrams he had introduced as defense minister. To administer this program, Magsaysay set up a new Presidential Complaints and Action Commission under Lansdale's friend Manuel Manahan. A new day seemed to be dawning in which, as Magsaysay told the throngs assembled to watch his swearing-in, the Philippines would at last see "a government sensitive to your needs, dedicated to your best interests, and inspired by our highest ideals."[33]

◆

LUIS TARUC, the Huks' supremo, heard of the 1953 election results while on the run in the swamps of Luzon. He and a small group of fighters had managed to evade the army dragnet, but they could not outrun their own hunger and thirst. The security forces by then were in firm control of the barrios where Huk sympathizers had once provided the guerrillas with food. Taruc wrote that the remaining Huks "came near starvation," reduced to eating "snails and edible grasses."[34]

Once he knew that Ramon Magsaysay had won the election, Taruc began to think it was time to give up the armed struggle. He was encouraged in this belief by no less than his own mother, whose appeals for his surrender were heard for months on the radio—another of Lansdale's brainstorms. On February 10, 1954, little more than a month after Magsaysay's inauguration, Taruc met secretly in the sugarcane fields near Clark Air Base with two emissaries of the president— Manuel Manahan, who had been secretly recruited by Lansdale eight years earlier to gain the confidence of the elusive guerrilla chief,[35] and Benigno "Ninoy" Aquino Jr. of the *Manila Times*. "The people have spoken. They have overwhelmingly elected President Magsaysay," Taruc told them. "It is for us to accept their verdict."[36] Aquino, a brash young reporter who had dropped out of college to become a war correspondent in Korea, later continued the talks alone on behalf of Magsaysay. Taruc wanted an unconditional amnesty for himself and his followers; Magsaysay wanted to try Taruc and his followers while holding out the possibility of executive clemency.

The negotiations between Taruc and Aquino, the forty-one-year-old peasant and the twenty-one-year-old child of privilege, culminated on May 17, 1954, in a dramatic early-morning meeting in the barrio of Santa Maria in Taruc's native Pampanga Province. Aquino went in alone at 6:30 a.m. Army troops who had surrounded the town told him that if he did not emerge by nine they would "blow the place to smithereens." Aquino recounted what happened next:

> Taruc was waiting at the foot of Mt. Arayat, an extinct volcano. His lean figure was surrounded by the people of the barrio; like them, he wore a gray peasant shirt, brown pants, and wide-brimmed straw hat. The only question I asked was: "Do you accept the president's terms?" Taruc said: "I accept." He shook my hands warmly and said farewell to the barrio folk, many of them weeping. Minutes later we were speeding towards Manila, escorted by army jeeps.[37]

Lansdale thought that Aquino was a "pushy" upstart who had rushed in to take credit for the long, hard work that he and Manahan had put in to win over Taruc.[38] Aquino would use this feat to launch his political career, which would culminate two decades later when he became the leading dissident challenging the dictatorship of Ferdinand Marcos. Taruc, for his part, would be tried and convicted of sedition, murder, and rebellion. He would spend nearly fifteen years behind bars, claiming all the while that Magsaysay had reneged on a pledge to free him.

The Huk Rebellion was over. The Philippines had become one of the few places in the postwar world where a major Communist uprising was defeated without intervention by foreign troops, as in Malaya, or without a bloodbath, as in Indonesia or Guatemala. The anti-Huk campaign represented one of the CIA's biggest covert-action successes ever, and it was achieved largely by one man's deft manipulation of local politics rather than through costly American spending or heavy-handed American military action.

It helped, of course, that the Philippines was a group of islands where the insurgents could be isolated from outside support. The Huks never received meaningful assistance from either China or the Soviet Union. But then neither did the young Fidel Castro, and he managed to take power just a few years later in another island nation. The Philippines might very well have gone the same way as Cuba if it had continued to be ruled by a corrupt and ineffectual clique. This did not happen, because Magsaysay and Lansdale worked so closely and effectively together to counter the Huks in both the military and the political realms. Some of Lansdale's methods, such as faking vampire deaths, booby-trapping ammunition, or producing phony Huk directives, would strike critics as "dirty tricks." On the whole, however, the campaign that Lansdale masterminded was remarkably sparing in human and financial terms compared with those being waged in other countries, including French Indochina.

Having orchestrated one of the classic counterinsurgency campaigns of the postwar world, Lansdale had secured renown as a maestro of counterguerrilla warfare and a virtuoso of nation building. Now he had to figure out what to do for an encore.

PART THREE

NATION
BUILDER

(1954–1956)

Ngo Dinh Diem stands triumphantly in a South Vietnamese army
jeep while touring Qui Nhon, capital of Binh Dinh Province, May 1955,
after the completion of a Lansdale-directed pacification campaign. (RPPP)

11

La Guerre sans Fronts

*It is a secret, hit-and-run business which bewilders the usual
person used to an enemy who fights in an orthodox manner.*

—EDWARD LANSDALE

"IN Indochina I drained a magic potion, a loving cup which I have
shared since with many retired *colons* and officers of the Foreign
Legion, whose eyes light up at the mention of Saigon and Hanoi."[1] So
wrote the English novelist and part-time intelligence agent Graham
Greene of his first visit to Vietnam, in early 1951. It was a sentiment
shared by countless Westerners, including Edward Lansdale, who first
arrived in French Indochina for a three-week visit with an American
advisory mission in June 1953 while on a brief sabbatical from the
Philippines.[2]

Lansdale's letters, written both to his family and to Pat Kelly, were
as rapturous as those of any tourist visiting a captivating country for
the first time, and they will sound familiar to anyone who has ever
been to Indochina. "For years now, I've been fascinated with views
of the undercut islands of Cam-ranh Bay," he wrote, "and finally saw
them this morning from the air." He found the scenery of southern
Vietnam, then known as Cochin China, "much the same as the Phil-

ippines," a "mangrove and swamp delta land from several rivers, the largest of which is the Mekong." In the north, a region known historically as Tonkin, he observed that "the mountains are weirdly sharp and angular above the flooded and muddy rice paddies, with river channels meandering sort of aimlessly a few inches below the paddies, and with hundreds and hundreds of hamlets or villages spotting the place like islands."

Like many other tourists, he complained about the inconveniences of travel in the tropics in these pre-air-conditioned days. He found the weather "exceptionally hot and muggy" and "gasped like a fish out of water on the bed at night." In Hanoi he stayed at the French colonial-style Metropole Hotel, opened in 1901, where Somerset Maugham wrote one of his travelogues, Charlie Chaplin honeymooned, and Graham Greene penned part of *The Quiet American*. Its bartender "could produce a reasonable facsimile of almost any civilized drink except water."[3] Yet it was precisely ice-cold water that Lansdale thirsted for. The only cold drink he was offered was champagne, which was poured "whether it was 9 in the morning or 3 in the afternoon." "Between a glass of champagne or a cold coke on a hot day," Lansdale opined, sounding like the epitome of *Homo americanus* circa 1953, "I'll take the latter any time."

Lansdale noted, in common with many other visitors, that Saigon to the south was often compared to "a big French provincial town." "I've never seen France," he admitted, "so I don't know." (One of Lansdale's quirks was that he would never visit Europe.) He was charmed by the "sidewalk cafes, broad boulevards, and lots of trees." He noted that "Little Renaults shoot around with horns blowing," but the rest of the city was distinctly Asian: " 'Cyclos' are the main transport, a tricycle rickshaw with the passenger out in front where the Renaults can hit him first." Like Graham Greene, who developed a taste for the local prostitutes, Lansdale took notice of the beautiful women: "Most of the folks in the street are Vietnamese women in sleazy Chinese satin pajamas, all white or black. They sweep the streets, dig ditches, drive cattle, lay bricks or pour concrete; the men are either away fighting or tending shop (or, as I suspect, loafing at home)."

Lansdale found Hue, in central Vietnam, to be "a sleepy little place of rice paddies where irrigation is run by foot-pedal pumps (folks sitting on a contraption which looks like a one-wheeled bicycle on stilts) and where [Emperor] Bao Dai has his palace, an old replica of the Palace at Peking, with miles of outer walls and whole villages inside." When he visited the coastal city of Nha Trang, which reminded him of "Santa Barbara with big mountains just behind the town and a beautiful beach," he jumped into the ocean to go swimming.

It would have been easy for Helen or Pat reading his missives to miss the fact that he was traveling in a war zone and not on an ordinary sightseeing trip. That, indeed, may have been the point: not wanting to worry his family, Lansdale typically played up the comic and innocuous aspects of his travels. He dismissed a small wound he received, "to the great glee of the French with me," when a hand grenade went off too close to him: "A scratch on the finger from a grenade fragment which healed so well that I can't even find it now to show anyone if I felt like it." In fact, hand grenades tossed by the Vietminh were a danger even in Saigon, where cafés had erected nets to protect their outdoor tables.

In his typical sardonic style, Lansdale made light of the war raging around him: "Aside from forts and barbed wire," he wrote, "this is a beautiful place." No doubt Lansdale shared with Graham Greene that "feeling of exhilaration which a measure of danger brings to the visitor with a return ticket."[4] It was a rather more serious matter for ordinary Vietnamese, who had no way out. They were trapped in a war that would continue, on and off, for more than twenty years and that would claim millions of casualties.[5]

◆

By THE time Edward Lansdale appeared on the scene, the French Indochina War was already more than seven years old and the American war had not yet begun, but signs that the first war might be ending and the second about to start were already becoming clear to astute observers. A battered France, in the final throes of losing its last colonial possessions, was fighting an increasingly futile struggle against a movement known as the Vietminh, an abbreviation for Viet Nam Doc

Lap Dong Minh Hoi (the Revolutionary League for the Independence of Vietnam), which, like the Huks in the Philippines, had been founded as a nationalist movement resisting foreign rule during World War II. Originally pledged to fight both the French and the Japanese, the Vietminh was ostensibly a coalition of nationalist groups, but it was dominated by the Workers Party of Vietnam, as the Communist Party had renamed itself. Its charismatic leader, Ho Chi Minh, had already established himself as the most famous Vietnamese in the world—a distinction he holds to this day.

Debate has often swirled about whether Ho was a communist or a nationalist. The evidence shows that, like many other insurgents, he saw no contradiction between the two convictions. "The two," wrote a French diplomat who knew him well, "complemented each other, merged."[6] Ho handled the dual identities, nationalist and communist, as adroitly as he handled his many aliases.

The man who would become Ho Chi Minh was born in 1890, three years before the birth of Mao Zedong, as Nguyen Sinh Cung in the central Tonkin province of Nghe An, long known for its stubborn and rebellious people—"the buffaloes of Nghe An," they were called.[7] When he reached age ten, his name was changed, in conformity with Vietnamese custom, to Nguyen Tat Thanh (He Who Will Succeed). The son of a Confucian scholar and part-time farmer, Nguyen Tat Thanh attended a prestigious French school in Hue. He was, however, expelled in 1908 for joining demonstrations by peasants upset at their high tax burden—a sign of the growing opposition to France's colonial rule, which had begun in the 1850s.

In 1911, he shipped out of Saigon aboard a merchant vessel bound for Marseille. He would not see Vietnam again for three decades. In the intervening years, he visited Africa, Asia, Europe, and North and South America while working as a gardener, cook, pastry chef, and snow sweeper, among other occupations. By 1917, he had settled down in Paris, where he was won over to Marxism, a conversion inspired by Lenin's call for Communist parties to make common cause with nationalist movements in Asia and Africa to smash imperialism and capitalism. Reading Lenin's "Theses on the National and Colonial

Questions," the man now known as Nguyen Ai Quoc (He Who Loves His Country) recalled, "I was overjoyed to tears."[8] In 1920, he took part in a meeting that formed the French Communist Party.

Three years later, he moved to Russia to work for the Communist International (Comintern), the Soviet organization charged with subversion abroad. He received further instruction in revolutionary ideals and practices at the Communist University of the Toilers of the East, better known as the Stalin School. Here he became, in the words of a French Communist, an "accomplished Stalinist," but he was mercifully devoid of Stalin's megalomania, fanaticism, and paranoia. Short and thin, with a wispy beard, Nguyen impressed everyone he met with his "goodness and simplicity"[9]—traits that would eventually make him a widely beloved figure in Vietnam who would become known as Bac Ho (Uncle Ho). Only his large black eyes, "lively, alert, and burning with extraordinary fervor," hinted at the zeal with which Ho pursued his twin passions, nationalism and communism.[10]

In 1930, by now living in Hong Kong, Nguyen helped create the Vietnamese Communist Party. It had a total of just 255 members inside Vietnam, making it smaller than rivals such as the Vietnamese Nationalist Party (VNQDD).[11] The French police would imprison every Communist they could identify; many would be tortured and executed, creating a fierce anti-French hatred that one day would be transposed to the Americans. Nguyen himself was arrested, though not by the French, but by British authorities in Hong Kong in 1931, and thus received gentler treatment. He was held for eighteen months and then deported. In 1938, after another sojourn in Stalinist Moscow, Nguyen moved to southern China, where he established a fresh base to export revolution to Vietnam.

In the city of Kunming, in 1940, he was introduced to a comrade who would before long become his top general. Vo Nguyen Giap was a younger man (born in 1911), who had spent time in prison in Vietnam for nationalist agitation but had also earned a law degree and had taught history at a private school. In traveling to China, he had left behind his wife, who would be arrested by French authorities and die in prison, a fate previously suffered by his father and sister. Their deaths would harden his hatred of the colonial regime in spite of his Franco-phone upbringing.

Giap was "extraordinarily intelligent"—"one of the most brilliant products of our French schools," a French diplomat called him.[12] An autodidact in military affairs, he would become one of the greatest military commanders of modern times. His hero may have been Napoleon, but his model was Mao Zedong. Both Nguyen and Giap worked diligently to implement Mao's three-stage model of revolution: a "localized guerrilla war," followed by a "war of movement" waged by a mix of conventional and guerrilla forces, and finally a "general uprising" that would bring down the regime. This concept of "people's war" waged in the countryside by peasants was more appropriate for rural countries such as China and Vietnam than the kind of urban uprising that Lenin had carried out in Russia.

The opportunity to launch an insurgency against French rule in Indochina presented itself when France was conquered by Nazi Germany in the spring of 1940. Japanese troops, Germany's allies, duly arrived in Indochina a few months later, and even though the Germans allowed the Vichy regime to stay in existence until March 1945, French power and prestige never recovered. The weakness of the Vichy regime allowed Nguyen to return in 1941 to Vietnam for the first time in thirty years and establish the Vietminh as a "popular front" to galvanize a nationalist uprising. Along with Giap and a few other comrades, he established a headquarters near the village of Pac Bo in northern Vietnam, just across the border from China in a remote area of dense jungle and steep mountains. As a security measure, he adopted a new pseudonym: Ho Chi Minh (He Who Enlightens). In contrast to the colonial splendors enjoyed by foreigners at Hanoi's Metropole Hotel, his new home was a damp and cold cave, where he slept on branches and bathed in a local stream; his meals consisted of rice with a little meat or fish. A naturally abstemious man, rugged despite his frail appearance, he told his comrades, "We must be able to tolerate all hardships, surmount the worst difficulties, and struggle to the end."[13]

Two years later, in 1942, Ho Chi Minh traveled back to China to seek the help of both China's Nationalists and Communists in his struggle against the French and the newly arrived Japanese. The Kuomintang regime, far from helping him, imprisoned him for eighteen months as a dangerous subversive before finally releasing him in 1943 because of his vow to help in the anti-Japanese struggle. Ho did not arrive back in Pac Bo until 1944. In 1945, he received a team of OSS operatives who helped to train his men and even provided him with quinine and sulfa drugs, which may have saved his life after he contracted malaria and dysentery. Like most people who met him, the OSS officers were impressed by Ho's "clear-cut talk" and "Buddha-like composure";[14] the rebel leader shared Ramon Magsaysay's personal magnetism, a quality that his future rival, Ngo Dinh Diem, singularly lacked. The OSS men did not notice how skillfully Ho deflected questions about whether he was a Communist. That's what "the French label . . . all Annamites who want independence," he replied disingenuously.[15]

◆

As soon as the Japanese surrendered on August 14, 1945, following the annihilation of Hiroshima and Nagasaki, Ho Chi Minh shrewdly moved to fill the power vacuum in Indochina. On September 2, in a Hanoi bedecked with red bunting, the new Democratic Republic of Vietnam was proclaimed with Ho Chi Minh its president. For the occasion, the fifty-five-year-old Ho, demonstrating a flair for proletarian symbolism, wore a plain khaki suit with a high collar of the kind favored by both Stalin and Mao, along with cheap rubber sandals—"his standard uniform as head of state for the next twenty-four years," noted Fredrik Logevall in *Embers of War,* his superb history of the French Indochina War.[16] To maintain a patina of democratic legitimacy, Ho held an election early the next year and included a few opposition politicians in the government. But the Vietminh accrued all real power into their own hands while persecuting members of non-Communist parties.

Ho realized that his nascent state soon would be imperiled by the arrival of Chinese troops in the north and British troops in the south, tasked by the Allies with overseeing the surrender of Japanese forces. Before long, he knew, the supercilious French would be back as well.

To forestall this eventuality, he vainly tried to enlist the United States as an ally. He even quoted liberally from the Declaration of Independence in proclaiming Vietnam's own independence. But his appeals to President Truman—there were at least eight letters from Ho between October 1945 and February 1946—went unanswered. Administration officials had little enthusiasm for the return of French colonialism, but they also had no desire to aid a veteran Comintern operative. Many analysts would later see this as a squandered opportunity, although in those days, before Tito's 1948 break with Stalin, few Americans could have imagined that a Communist leader could be independent of the Soviet Union.

Failing to get American help, Ho Chi Minh could not prevent the return of the French. On November 23, 1946, in an attempt to drive the Vietminh out of the port of Haiphong, French warships and aircraft opened fire on the Vietnamese quarter, killing thousands of civilians. The French then secured Hanoi after a brief battle, but Vietminh units slipped out to continue the struggle—a pattern that would recur in the years ahead. The French forces could inflict casualties, but they could not achieve victory. The French war machine, like the American one that would come after it, was simply too slow, too ponderous, and, above all, too clankingly loud to annihilate the elusive Vietminh fighters in *la guerre sans fronts* (war without fronts). The guerrillas would inevitably hear the attackers coming and scatter long before they could be pinned down.

In frustration, the French resorted to old colonial habits, torturing prisoners and bombing villages that were suspected of harboring insurgents. In the process, they made many of the same mistakes the Philippine army had made in its losing battles against the Huks before the reforms instituted by Magsaysay and Lansdale—only on a much bigger scale. What made the situation even more dismal from the French perspective was that the government they were asking the people to support was far more illegitimate than that of Elpidio Quirino. Quirino may have been elected president in a crooked election, but at least he was a Filipino and he did have a real base of support. Few if any Vietnamese, by contrast, backed the continuation of the French colonial regime. The only course of action that could have made the anti-Communist cause truly popular would have been transferring complete authority to a genuinely independent Vietnamese government, or at least promising to transfer such authority in the near future, as the British were then doing in Malaya. But this the French resolutely refused to do.

Having already alienated much of the Vietnamese population, the French suffered a blow from which they would never recover with the ascendance in 1949 of the Communists in neighboring China. Mao Zedong sent military advisers and weapons to the Vietminh. Outside assistance or lack thereof is usually the surest indicator of the fate of any insurgency, and the Vietminh, unlike the Huks, now had it in abundance.

In October 1950, Giap threw thirty thousand of his newly trained and equipped troops against the isolated French posts along the 200-mile border between Vietnam and China. By the end of the month, the French Far East Expeditionary Corps had lost control of the border, along with six thousand troops and enough weaponry to equip an entire Vietminh division.[17] It was, as a French correspondent noted, an "appalling, stupefying, unbelievable defeat."[18] An indomitable new French general, Jean de Lattre de Tassigny, momentarily retrieved the situation and stymied Giap's Red River offensive in 1951, securing for the time being Hanoi, Haiphong, and the rice-growing regions of the north. But on November 19, 1951, de Lattre left Vietnam, suffering from cancer. He would die in France two months later, leaving behind a grieving widow and a stalemated war effort. As an American diplomat in Paris put it, invoking a phrase that would become associated with Vietnam, "France could see no light at end of tunnel."[19] French leaders had already abandoned hopes of victory; they were simply looking for "an honorable way out"[20]—a quest that would also obsess American policymakers in years to come.

◆

THE STALEMATE in Indochina was of growing concern to Washington because the United States, having long ago abandoned a posture of neutrality, was now paying 80 percent of the bill for the French war effort. In 1953, the Joint Chiefs of Staff decided to send Lieutenant General John W. O'Daniel, commander of the U.S. Army in the Pacific, to Indochina to assess whether the French had adequate war plans and, if not, to assist in the creation of better plans. Only five feet six inches tall but with a foghorn voice and a swagger that made him appear much larger, "Iron Mike" O'Daniel was, in the words of one newspaper correspondent, a "jut-jawed, gravel-voiced, outspokenly colorful leader of combat troops" who had compiled an impressive record in World War I, World War II, and Korea. The origins of his nickname remain in dispute, but "by one account, he won it in France in World War I as a lieutenant when he fought for 12 hours at St. Mihiel, although hit in the face by a German machine-gun bullet." Thereafter his face looked as if it "might have been carved out with an axe." In World War II, he led the Third Infantry Division from Italy to France and into Germany. When asked by a British general how much ground the division had lost in a German counterattack at Anzio, O'Daniel replied, "Not a goddamned inch, sir." While an outstanding combat soldier in the mold of George S. Patton, O'Daniel was, like Patton, no diplomat; after serving as military attaché in Moscow from 1948 to 1950, he caused a ruckus by publicly describing Moscow as a "vast slum." Nor was he an expert in either nation building or counterinsurgency. But he found such an expert when he briefly stopped at Clark Air Base in the Philippines on the way to Indochina.[21]

O'Daniel sat down with Colonel Edward Lansdale on the night of June 19, 1953, and was so impressed by what he had to say that he asked the CIA man to accompany him to Vietnam. Lansdale was in the midst of managing Ramon Magsaysay's presidential campaign, but, thinking he would be gone only two or three days, he agreed. This was at nearly midnight. "What time are you going over there?" Lansdale asked. "Wheels up at 0900 in the morning," O'Daniel replied.[22] Lansdale barely had time to pack a suitcase and let his colleagues know he would be leaving before he was off to Saigon. He would spend much of the next three weeks scrambling for clean clothes.[23]

Over those weeks Lansdale would travel all over Indochina. "The Vietminh have forces nearly everywhere and have friends where they don't have forces," he wrote. "It is a secret, hit-and-run business which bewilders the usual person used to an enemy who fights in an ortho-dox manner. Here the enemy fires from the ground where you don't expect him, tosses a grenade or fires a bazooka at you when you are in a safe rest area, or comes howling in on your fort in a Chinese mob attack, when he's supposed to be miles away. I've been living with such problems now since the middle of 1950, so a lot of the strange pattern seemed all too familiar."[24]

What did not seem so familiar to Lansdale was the extent to which the French army occupied static defensive positions—quite different from the active combat patrolling and civic action conducted in the Philippines under his prodding. "The chief feature of the landscape in Vietnam," he found, "is the nearest fort, a slender stone pillar two stories high with a flag on it, looking as though it were just put there for a movie version of Beau Geste. Some of the forts get quite elabo-rate, halfway between log-and-dirt versions of the Maginot Line and some frontier stockade in the French-and-Indian wars over on our con-tinent. The Communist enemy, the Vietminh, are the Indians . . . the French, Vietnamese, Cambodians and Laotians are too often reminis-cent of Braddock . . . brave and gallant folks, but not as cunning as their enemy."[25] (General Edward Braddock was the unfortunate commander of a British column that was ambushed and nearly wiped out by French and Indian fighters near present-day Pittsburgh in 1755.)

Echoing Lansdale's concerns, O'Daniel was convinced that if only the French troops would leave the forts and take the fight to the enemy, they could prevail in short order. A French officer who met with O'Daniel found that he viewed Indochina as a "simple problem" that could be "solved" with an *attitude agressive*.[26] The only thing that gave O'Daniel pause was all the defeatism he encountered: in his ini-tial meetings, the French briefers used the word "difficult" to describe the situation "50 or 100 times." "I finally made it a rule in my group," O'Daniel said, "that anybody that even spoke the word 'difficult' would be fined a dollar and I think by the end of the visit we were out of the habit of using it." If only the Vietminh could be banished as easily as the word "difficult"![27]

O'Daniel recommended to the French commander, General Henri-Eugène Navarre, that he reorganize his forces to create seven new divisions to strike at the Vietminh. In the end, only seven extra battalions would be sent by a war-weary nation. O'Daniel also won a commitment from Navarre to launch a general offensive in the north in September 1953 and in the meantime to organize various "raids," "clearing operations," and "breaking out operations." The ambitious, verging on delusional, goal these two generals came up with was to defeat the Vietminh by 1955. In return, O'Daniel promised to go home and endorse an extra four hundred million dollars in U.S. aid that the French desperately wanted.[28]

There is no evidence to indicate that Lansdale shared Iron Mike's faith in the potential of offensive action by itself to deliver victory in short order. His focus lay elsewhere: he wrote the "guerrilla warfare" and "psychological warfare" annexes of the blueprint that O'Daniel presented to the French. His psychological warfare memo recommended that the war be turned from a "colonial" struggle into a "war of free and independent Vietnamese, advised and aided by the French Union, fighting to free the country of Chinese-Communist controlled forces, which are made up of brother Vietnamese." "With this political basis," Lansdale argued, "victory can be gained." But he recognized there was scant chance that the French would grant true independence; he found to his dismay that the French were waging a "white man's war against the Asians," one that was very different from the way in the Philippines "Asians [were] fighting Asians." "The Vietnamese were the orderlies, the guys sitting out at front desks stamping papers, going through the pro forma stuff without any real responsibilities."[29] Lansdale was later to say, "I didn't see how Navarre was going to win, unless he made radical changes to get the Vietnamese nationalists much more deeply involved."[30]

Nevertheless, Lansdale argued that "aggressive psychological warfare need not wait upon the establishment of a political basis" for the war effort. He advocated the creation of "a strong troop education program on behavior towards civilians; each wrong act by a soldier makes more enemies, [while] good behavior makes promises and propaganda accepted as truth by the civilian population." Even this, however, was too ambitious a goal for the French forces, which continued, as if 1950s Indochina were nineteenth-century colonial Africa or Asia, to treat civilians with casual brutality and contempt.[31]

Lansdale's other memorandum advocated "waging guerrilla warfare against the Viet-minh" primarily in the far north, where conventional French troops were no longer able to operate. He called for raising more guerrilla forces composed of mountain tribes to hamper Viet-minh supply lines from China in order to "start pricking the bubble of Viet-Minh superiority, and give a big morale boost to loyal Vietnamese."[32] As Lansdale acknowledged, the French were already conducting some operations along these lines with secret CIA support, but while French-supported tribes were able to tie down Vietminh forces to guard rear areas, they never came close to cutting Giap's supply lines. Eventually, after the end of the French Indochina War, these tribal fighters would be left behind to be slowly hunted down by the vengeful Vietminh.[33]

◆

BY MID-JULY 1953, after three hectic weeks in Indochina, Lansdale was back in the Philippines to supervise the denouement of the presidential campaign. "My house boy is eating a cut up avocado in a glass tumbler, with sugar and canned milk on it, the foothills of the Zambales range are green with new kunai grass, and the distant gunfire is all small arms stuff . . . ," Lansdale wrote to his family, "so it's good to be back where a war has become small time and might be over some day before long if we are wise enough."[34] He was also glad to be back with Pat Kelly. During his time in Vietnam, he told her, "I've just worn out shoes running around and haven't even had a chance to kiss a girl's hand much less other parts of her anatomy."[35] Although Lansdale breathed an audible sigh of relief to be out of Vietnam, he had tasted "the magic potion," and, like Graham Greene, he would be drawn back to Vietnam time after time.

While Lansdale returned to Manila, Iron Mike O'Daniel swaggered to Washington to brief the Joint Chiefs of Staff. Like many future American generals in Vietnam, he came away from his trip absurdly over-optimistic. "The French," he wrote, "are in no danger of suffering a major military reverse. On the contrary, they are gaining strength and confidence in their ability to fight the war to a successful military conclusion."[36] At his urging, the administration naïvely embraced the Navarre plan and approved $385 million in extra funding to underwrite French operations.

Desperate to land a decisive blow for the shellacked French army, General Navarre decided to create an "aero-terrestrial" outpost near the border with Laos. He hoped that this fortress, supplied by air, would block the Vietminh from invading Laos and draw them into open battle, where they could be slaughtered by superior French firepower. The place where he chose to situate this base was a valley with a prosaic name that translated as "Big Frontier Administrative Center." Or, in Vietnamese, Dien Bien Phu.[37]

12

A Fortress Falls

I sensed a sort of desperation that I move in fast.

—Edward Lansdale

Operation Castor, as the plan to fortify Dien Bien Phu was known, began in earnest on November 20, 1953, while Edward Lansdale was back in the Philippines advising newly elected President Ramon Magsaysay on how to put together his government. Early that morning, some sixteen hundred French paratroopers were woken up, briefed, and then loaded with their gear aboard a fleet of sixty-five C-47 Dakota transport aircraft at two military airfields in Hanoi. By 9:30, all of the aircraft were airborne and heading west on their 185-mile journey. More than an hour later, as they began to approach the drop zone, the *paras* went through the by now familiar procedures: stand up, hook up to a cable, check the equipment of the man in front. Then doors opened with an "icy blast and deafening noise," followed by the flashing of the green light and the screams of the jump masters: "Go! Go! Go!"[1]

By nightfall, after a six-hour battle against a battalion of Vietminh regulars, these elite troops had secured control of a valley eleven miles long and six miles wide. Within a few months, the French garrison numbered more than ten thousand men and they were spread across a series of eight strongpoints with feminine names—Dominique, Eliane, Beatrice, and so on—each one composed of blockhouses and dugouts protected by sandbags and barbed wire, land mines and inter-locking fields of fire. Ever attuned to the niceties of war, the French even airlifted in two Mobile Field Brothels to keep the troops con-tent in this jungle Verdun.[2] Vo Nguyen Giap, for his part, would assemble fifty thousand carefully camouflaged troops on the forested slopes around Dien Bien Phu. Another fifty thousand or so porters and support troops—a long line of human ants—dragged heavy artil-lery and antiaircraft guns through the jungle. Incredibly enough, the Vietminh would have more than twice as many artillery tubes as the defenders.[3]

The French were blissfully unaware of the extent of Vietminh preparations. Their only concern was that the Vietminh might slink back into the jungle and refuse battle. A young French lieutenant sta-tioned at Dien Bien Phu wrote to his sister on December 26, 1953, in racist prose typical of his comrades, "If they attack, there'll be plenty of yellow meat in the barbed wire."[4]

◆

WHILE THE defenders of Dien Bien Phu in the isolated northwestern corner of Vietnam were still awaiting an enemy assault, Edward Lans-dale left the Philippines on January 20, 1954, to return to the United States and seek his next assignment. No doubt he was sorry to be leav-ing his paramour and confidante once again, but the letter he wrote to her aboard the airplane did not reflect the giddy infatuation that he had exhibited while in limerence almost six years earlier aboard a troopship. In lieu of the ardent expressions of love he had once sent to his "darling Patching," he now addressed his letter "Hi, Pat" and ended with a perfunctory "Love & kisses, Ed"—not so different from the way he wrote to his wife.[5]

Returning home, Ed had to reacquaint himself with his family after nearly three and a half years away. His older son, Ted, was now four-teen years old; Pete was twelve. Both were enrolled at Gordon Junior High School, a public school in northwest Washington, D.C. That fall,

Ted would enter Western High School, followed two years later by Pete. "My kids missed having a father during the days when they'd be going to Boy Scouts, and I missed having them," Ed later said.[6]

Helen, by now fully gray-haired and almost fifty-three years old, had the sole responsibility of raising these "renegade sons," or "hooligans," as Ted referred tongue-in-cheek to himself and his brother many years later.[7] The task was all the harder because she did not know how to drive. Every Sunday, the three of them took a streetcar to attend Christian Science services and Sunday school. "And if worst came to worst," Ted recalled, "Mom would just call a taxi, saying, 'Your father will pay for all of this.'"[8]

Both Pete and Ted, being active teenage boys, rebelled against their mother's attempts to introduce a bit of "refinement" into their lives by taking them to the Army-Navy Junior Cotillion at a posh townhouse in Georgetown, a formal setting where proper boys were expected to dress in suits and dance with girls in dresses and white gloves. "My brother and I hated it," Ted Lansdale recalled. "Absolutely hated it." Bored, the boys wandered over to the window. Looking outside, they spotted a convertible parked downstairs. Close to them stood a punch bowl with a big chunk of ice floating in it. "I wonder what'll happen if that ice chunk hits the ragtop of the convertible?" one of the boys asked. The other answered, "There's only one way to find out!" As it turned out, the ice only caused the ragtop to sag, not to break. Helen was beside herself, lecturing them, in the time-honored tradition of exasperated parents, "You don't appreciate what I do for you!"[9]

No doubt Helen was frustrated, as any mother would be, by the challenges of dealing with these rambunctious boys by herself. She must have felt lonely, too, and resentful that while she was raising the children, Ed was, to her mind, luxuriating in the Philippines with his mistress. "In some ways she had a rough life," Ted reflected. But, to her considerable credit, she never expressed any resentment toward their absent father, nor did she ever mention to them the existence of his mistress, even if, in the manner of most children, they eventually intuited the truth. The impression their mother conveyed, the boys later said, was that their father was a "larger than life" figure, a "great guy" who was away doing very important work for the country, even though he would have preferred to be with them.[10]

In turn, one of Lansdale's closest friends was to state, he never heard Ed say an unkind word about his wife, "even by implication." In spite of his love for Pat Kelly, "Ed was an honorable man with a tremendous sense of duty. After the initial request for a divorce, I think Ed saw it as his duty not to desert Helen and his boys."[11]

On those intermittent occasions when he was with his children—usually a short home leave—Ed would try to make up for lost time by taking them on some fun activity. "Sometimes it was like, 'damn it, we are going to have fun whether you like it or not,'" Pete recalled with a laugh.[12] Their father introduced an earthy, fun-loving element largely absent from their lives with their straitlaced mother, even if she did gamely don a baseball glove to play catch with them and even take them to Redskins football games.[13] One time, for example, Ed taught the boys how to melt snow by peeing on it.[14] Then he was gone again, and it was left to their mother to impose discipline. "She kept us pretty much grounded in what was right and wrong," Ted later said, "and by and large I think we followed that."[15]

Trying to get used to being with his family again—and they with him—while missing Pat Kelly must have made Lansdale's latest homecoming awkward and bittersweet. But his focus lay elsewhere: like many other fathers in the age of those best sellers *The Organization Man* and *The Man in the Gray Flannel Suit*, he was consumed by his work. His reputation was growing along with demands for his service. Just before leaving the Philippines, Ed wrote to Helen, "The French, British, Catholic Church, Nationalist Chinese, Vietnamese, and even South Koreans have all made it known that they want some help from me—apparently since I'm one of the few real optimists left in this gloomy part of the world."[16] But for all the calls on Lansdale, there was little doubt he would wind up focusing on the country that had so enchanted him during his three-week visit the previous summer—a country that increasingly was a source of frustration and concern for American policymakers.

◆

THE DOMESTIC political context played an important role in President Eisenhower's calculations about Vietnam, as it would for all of his next four successors. While Ike liked to play the part of an amiable, apolitical, and dim duffer, he was, in reality, intensely intelligent and keenly attuned to the demands of politics. During his long army career, he had learned the benefits of appearing relaxed and nonchalant: his demeanor inspired confidence. But he could not possibly have accomplished as much as he did—he had rocketed from the rank of colonel in 1941 to become a five-star general in command of the Allied armies that liberated North Africa and Western Europe—if he had actually been the simpleton his detractors imagined. "To those who knew him," writes his biographer Jean Edward Smith, "Ike was a tireless taskmaster who worked with incredible subtlety to move events in the direction he wished them to go."[17]

In his decision-making about Vietnam, Eisenhower was acutely aware of the influence still exerted as the year began by Senator Joseph McCarthy. In the first half of 1954, "Tailgunner Joe" was losing public popularity and credibility, but he remained a force to reckon with in the Senate and the Republican Party. Eisenhower did not want to give him any further ammunition to snipe that the administration was soft on Communism—which McCarthy certainly would have done if Indochina had fallen to Ho Chi Minh. Eisenhower, moreover, had won office with a campaign blasting Truman for having "lost" China, so, even if McCarthy did not exist, he could hardly afford to be seen as "losing" Indochina. But Ike had also won office by promising to extricate the United States from the unpopular war in Korea. He thus could hardly afford to send American troops into another war in Asia either. "This war in Indochina would absorb our troops by divisions!" the president warned, prophetically.[18]

The obvious alternative to sending ground troops was to send more matériel and more advisers to help the French. A decision was reached early in 1954 that Lieutenant General Iron Mike O'Daniel would be sent back to Vietnam in the spring to take over the Military Assistance

Advisory Group even if it meant he would have to voluntarily give up a star to do so. (MAAG was a two-star, not a three-star, command.) But Secretary of Defense Charles Wilson noted at an NSC meeting on February 4, 1954, that "some skepticism existed at the Pentagon as to General O'Daniel's qualifications in the political and psychological field." Vice President Nixon, who had visited Vietnam a few months earlier, added that he was concerned the United States did not have "our first team in the field," and that it was imperative "to have the very best men in the information and propaganda fields" in Vietnam.[19]

The process of sending one of "the very best men" began in the Pentagon on the afternoon of Friday, January 29, 1954. The setting was the office of Deputy Secretary of Defense Roger M. Kyes, a General Motors executive who had been brought to Washington by "Engine Charlie" Wilson, the former CEO of General Motors. Gathered here were Admiral Arthur W. Radford, a strong-willed aviator who was chairman of the Joint Chiefs of Staff; the short-fused under secretary of state, Walter Bedell "Beetle" Smith; and the genially deceptive CIA director, Allen Dulles. After a long discussion of what could be done to help the French, the minutes show, "Mr. Allen Dulles inquired if an unconventional warfare officer, specifically Colonel Lansdale, could not be added to the group of five liaison officers to which General Navarre had agreed." This suggestion won an immediate endorsement from Admiral Radford, although he added that Lansdale's departure should be delayed for a few months until O'Daniel arrived in Saigon. "This was agreeable to Mr. Allen Dulles," the minutes indicate. The reaction of Colonel Lansdale himself was not recorded, but he, too, was very much present at this meeting.[20]

Lansdale was to insist repeatedly in later years that it was *John Foster* Dulles, not *Allen* Dulles, who had sent him to Vietnam—an assertion that has been repeated by numerous writers.[21] In the most complete version of the story, told to two interviewers from the Congressional Research Service in 1982, Lansdale claimed that in January 1954 he attended a meeting about Vietnam at the Pentagon at which John Foster Dulles said, "We're going to send you over there, Ed. . . . We want you to go over there and help the Vietnamese the way you helped the Filipi-

Ed Lansdale (left) in 1914, aged six, with brothers Phil and Ben. (GBPP)

Edward Philips, Lansdale's maternal grandfather, was a larger-than-life character with little tolerance for polite society. He left a large imprint on his grandson's personality. (GBPP)

The Lansdale boys with their parents in Bronxville, 1920. Ed is in the middle rear between mother Sadie and father Harry. (GBPP)

Lansdale as a student at UCLA. He worked as an extra in Hollywood to help pay for college. (GBPP)

Young Lansdale was an aspiring cartoonist. This is one of the cartoons he drew for UCLA's satirical newspaper, *The Claw*. (PCLPP)

Oh! How swordid!

One of the advertisements that Lansdale developed for the Theodore Segall Advertising Agency in San Francisco, 1940. He is at left in the inset photo. (MSFRIC)

Ed and Helen Lansdale around the time of their marriage in New York, 1933. Shared family secrets helped to bring them together amid the misery of the Great Depression. (ECLPP)

Major Lansdale (center) on a "very ratty, dirty and ancient" boat exploring the Ryukyu Islands, 1946. After spending the war years working for the OSS in the United States, this was his initiation to the heady realm of nation building. (HI)

1975
to pat with love
from Ed

Pat Kelly and Lansdale on a beach, Lingayen Gulf in the
Philippines, 1946, shortly after they met. (PYPP)

Huk military leader Luis Taruc.
With Pat Kelly's help, Lansdale tried
repeatedly to meet him and almost
lost his life in the attempt.(Getty)

AP reporter Spencer Davis (left), Lansdale, and Major
Napoleon Valeriano of the Philippine army (right),
with captured Huks, July 18, 1947. (MSFRIC)

Ed and Helen Lansdale
leaving the Philippines
in 1948 with their boys,
Pete and Ted. After
three years, Lansdale
could boast that that he
was known on a first-
name basis by everyone
from the president of
the republic "down
to farmers in [the]
provinces." (ECLPP)

Lansdale's eccentric deputy, Charles T. R. "Bo" Bohannan (left),
and his superior, CIA operations chief Frank Wisner (right),
with Ramon Magsaysay. (HI)

A typical coffee klatsch at Lansdale's bungalow in Manila, December 1950.
He is at the head of the table; *New Yorker* correspondent Robert Shaplen
is at right; Bohannan has his back to camera. The ideas generated at such
informal gatherings catalyzed the anti-Huk campaign. (MSFRIC)

Lansdale (center) and some of his closest associates in the Philippines, December 1960. Left to right: Dario Arellano, Manny Manahan, Johnny Orendain, Oscar Arellano. He used them to help his nation building efforts in Vietnam. (MSFRIC)

Lansdale in Hanoi, June 1953, on his first trip to Indochina. Like Graham Greene and many other Westerners, he was instantly smitten with this alluring country. (MSFRIC)

nos."[22] Lansdale appears to have deliberately twisted the memory of the actual meeting at which John Foster Dulles was *not* present, because he was not yet ready to admit that he had worked for the CIA. Yet even after he admitted in 1984 his CIA association, he still claimed that the secretary of state had sent him to Vietnam;[23] by that point, the fiction may have been too firmly implanted in his memory to be dislodged. Which is not to say that the entire recollection was fictitious: it is likely that Allen Dulles did say to him on January 29 something along the lines of, "Do what you did in the Philippines," even though that comment was not included in the minutes.

Even with top-level support for his mission, however, Lansdale found it hard to get to Saigon. One night, his father, Harry, who was visiting asked him, "Who's that fellow who keeps calling every night?" "Oh," Ed replied, "some guy out in the Philippines."[24] That guy was actually the Guy: Ramon Magsaysay. The president of the Philippines was beseeching Lansdale to return to Manila to help him resolve his difficulties with the Philippine Congress.

Given his success in the Philippines and his affection for its people and for his mistress, Lansdale was torn. He wanted to help Monching, but he also felt he had achieved as much as he could in the Philippines and that he was more urgently needed in Indochina. He tried to get out of another long-term assignment in Manila by recommending to Allen Dulles that "Ambassador Spruance should be loaned the best public relations man possible to carry on."[25] But Magsaysay would brook no substitutes. In late March or early April 1954, Lansdale was informed by his governmental superiors that none other than Magsaysay had just phoned Eisenhower to insist, president to president, on Lansdale's services, and Eisenhower had agreed.[26] There was no escaping an order from the commander in chief.

Before Lansdale could depart for Manila, he received word that his mother, Sarah, had died in Los Angeles on April 6, 1954. She was seventy-two years old. In his memoir, he was to write, "We were a close, affectionate family and the news hit me hard." The latter part of the statement is undoubtedly true. But he was stretching a point to claim that the family was close, given that his father was now living in Detroit with his girlfriend, soon to be his wife, and that Ed had been gone from the country so much that he could go years without seeing his brothers or parents. In Sarah's last years, she had actually been closer to Helen than to Ed, because she had lived with Helen and the boys in California in the 1940s while Ed was away in the Philippines. But Helen's morbid fear of flying meant there was no chance of her going from Washington to California for the Christian Science funeral service. Ed had been planning to stop over in Los Angeles anyway en route to Manila in order to see his mother. Now he would see her buried before proceeding on to Asia "in a deeply somber mood."[27]

His latest stay at home had lasted less than three months.

◆

LANSDALE ARRIVED back in humid, hectic Manila on April 20, 1954, and immediately began spending most of his time at the Malacañang Palace. In the late afternoon, after Magsaysay woke up from a nap after having worked between 5 a.m. and 2 p.m., Lansdale would come to his bedroom for a chat. With Magsaysay in his pajamas, he and the first lady, Luz, would sit down at a table with Lansdale "and talk at length on various and sundry problems."[28] There was continuing good news about the nearly extinct Huk Rebellion—Luis Taruc, the Huk supremo, surrendered on May 17—but Magsaysay was struggling with the challenge of overhauling the government. Pulled once again into the role of "a behind-scenes executive," Lansdale found himself working "long, long hours" on various "national and international problems, including a lot of economics that I had to really study up on."[29]

Lansdale's presence in Manila became widely known and controversial among critics who charged that once again Magsaysay was being manipulated by his American Rasputin. "It became quite a game," Lansdale wrote, "to get things done without notice—just speculative attacks in the scandal sheets and almost completely wrong."[30] Despite the controversy, Magsaysay was eager to have his American friend stay for as long as possible. Lansdale wrote that he was plied with "all sorts of things"—"rooms at *Malacañan*, house in the garden, aircraft, cars, boats to take me any place I wanted to go—etc., etc.," but he turned it all down.[31]

One of his newfound, self-assigned duties was trying to explain the situation in Indochina to Filipinos wondering whether a nearby state was about to fall to Communism. On April 21, 1954, Lansdale was the featured guest at a *Meet the Press* radio broadcast at the Manila Overseas Press Club. He said presciently that the fall of Dien Bien Phu "would not necessarily be fatal from the military point of view" but that it would have a large psychological impact by aiding "the reds in their drive for power."[32] Lansdale learned more about the latest developments in Vietnam during a lightning visit to Saigon three days later to meet with the recently arrived Iron Mike O'Daniel. In Ed's words, it was "eleven hours of flying just to have a couple of hours talk with O'Daniel." The general, along with "almost all of the top Americans there," tried to persuade him to stay. "I sensed a sort of desperation that I move in fast," Ed wrote to Helen. "I stalled them off, but am worried about the atmosphere in Indochina, and my conscience hurts since they feel I can start changing the situation."[33]

◆

As LANSDALE wrote those words, the French garrison at Dien Bien Phu was in its death throes. The Vietminh had methodically overrun strongpoint after strongpoint. The situation became particularly grim after Vietminh artillery fire shut down the lone airstrip in the main camp on March 28. Thereafter all supplies and reinforcements had to be delivered by parachute, and there was no way to evacuate the wounded. In desperation, the French government asked for American intervention. The French and American military staffs had developed a plan for such a contingency, known as Operation Vulture, which called for employing American aircraft to relieve the siege. In one variant, Pentagon planners even contemplated dropping atomic bombs.[34] President Eisenhower tried to win congressional and British support for a military intervention, but when that was not forthcoming he refused to pull the trigger for fear of being drawn into a unilateral and unpopular conflict.[35]

With no American help coming, the bedraggled garrison was doomed. The onset of the monsoon season only added to their agony.

Miserable and wet, soldiers staggered on through sheer exhaustion, surviving on a little rice and canned corned beef of uncertain origin nicknamed "monkey meat."[36] The wounded and the dead piled up in the mud. Flies and rats were everywhere. Gangrene was starting to appear, and the "stink of putrefaction" was in the air.[37] An army lieutenant observed "one-legged soldiers manning machine guns in the blockhouses, being fed ammunition by their one-armed and one-eyed comrades."[38] On May 7, 1954, the French commander, Brigadier General Christian de Castries, concluded that he could hold out no longer. The last message, sent at 5:50 p.m. from the French garrison, was "We're blowing everything up. Adieu."[39] By then, a red-and-gold Vietminh flag was already fluttering over the command post.

General Giap had paid a fearfully high price for his victory—twenty-five thousand of his best troops had been killed or wounded—but he had inflicted on France the worst defeat that any European state had ever suffered at the hands of its colonial subjects. Now the question from the American perspective was, what could be salvaged from the ruins of the French empire in Indochina? Was Ho Chi Minh destined to rule all of Vietnam?

It was natural in this era for the CIA to take the lead in filling this political vacuum—a mission that in another period would have gone to the State Department or the armed forces. There was already a CIA station in Saigon, of course, but the Dulles brothers wanted a political warfare expert on the spot—their very best man, as Nixon had demanded.

Thus, on May 17, 1954, just as Lansdale was "writing detailed plans on how to run a government and build a new social economy" for the Philippines,[40] he received orders from Allen Dulles to report posthaste to Saigon. "The radio message ended with a personal touch that neither the clerks at the message center nor I had seen before in official orders," Lansdale later wrote. "After the string of abbreviations and budget citations normally given in orders, the message closed with 'God bless you'!" (In his memoir, Lansdale attributed this message to John Foster Dulles so as to preserve the fiction that he had not been a CIA operative.)[41]

He would need all the support that he could muster, divine or otherwise, for the nearly impossible task that lay ahead. After having
returned to the United States for an all-too-brief home leave and then
gone back once again to the Philippines, Lansdale had a new mission
that dwarfed anything that he—or anyone else in the postwar world—
had attempted before. The United States had experience creating
new nations such as West Germany and South Korea and transforming existing nations such as Japan and Italy, but those tasks had been
accomplished with hundreds of thousands of American troops—and
even then the going had been hard. Now Lansdale would be charged
with accomplishing an act of state creation armed with little more
than his wits.

After sitting up "practically all night in a last-minute session with
the Philippine gang, helping them plan," Lansdale on May 31, 1954,
was winging his way to Saigon in a U.S. Air Force flying boat. The
Thirty-First Air Sea Rescue Squadron at Clark Air Base had offered
to fly him over, provided he didn't mind spending a few extra hours en
route patrolling the South China Sea. Sitting sleepily in a bucket seat,
his "boxes and other baggage piled up around" him, "shaking gently
with the aircraft's vibrations" and "sipping coffee from a paper cup,"
Lansdale wondered about what he would encounter once he landed. He
knew that "events in Indochina were moving toward a climax and that
the U.S. wanted me on the spot for whatever occurred next," but there
was no way to predict what that would be.[42]

13

"I Am Ngo Dinh Diem"

[Diem] was happiest when cloistered with books or papers in his study.

—EDWARD LANSDALE

L ANSDALE's arrival in the jittery, if outwardly placid, city of Saigon on June 1, 1954, less than a month after the fall of Dien Bien Phu, was as unceremonious as one could imagine. This was entirely fitting for such a self-effacing man who favored an informal approach to dealing with the most important questions of war and peace. He had to wrestle his own luggage off the airplane in the tropical heat and look around for a ride. An American aircraft mechanic offered to take him into town in his jeep. They drove through bustling streets swarming with bicyclists, along with "tiny taxicabs, jeeps, and ancient open touring cars." "The only reminders of a country at war, other than the uniforms worn by so many of the people," Lansdale observed, "were an occasional military truck with an African colonial soldier driver and now and then a French military dispatch rider, helmeted, crouched over his handlebars, zig-zagging through the sluggish traffic on his motorcycle."[1] But even more than in the Manila of 1950, fearful concerns about the future lurked just beneath the patina of normality. No one knew, after all, what fate would befall southern Vietnam and its principal metropolis now that the French empire was effectively finished.

Lansdale's destination was Iron Mike O'Daniel's house in the center of the city. The general offered to share his dinner with the new arrival and to put him up for the night. Lansdale was not long asleep, however, when he was woken up by a "terrific racket." Getting out of bed, he heard "the constant roar of gigantic explosions somewhere not too far away," while "gusts of hot air beat at the wooden shutters . . . setting them dancing and banging."[2] Vietminh sappers had just blown up a French ammunition dump on the outskirts of town—further confirmation, if any were needed, that the situation was "sliding downhill fast, or almost completely sour." Lansdale's challenge was "to start building something positive on our side—if I can discover how."[3]

Lansdale's cover was as assistant air attaché at the U.S. embassy, but he did not find a warm welcome from the thirty-five-year-old Air Force colonel, William L. Tudor, who was serving as air attaché. "The bastard hated my guts," Lansdale recalled. "He could find no place for me to sit in this office, not even a chair. No place to keep any papers, no place to do anything."[4] Nor was the CIA station under Chief of Station Emmett J. McCarthy, a professional intelligence officer who had gotten his start with the OSS in Burma,[5] of any help beyond providing Lansdale with secure communications links back to Washington. In fact, McCarthy was so threatened by the new arrival that he tried to undermine Lansdale at every turn. Eventually Lansdale got so mad that he told McCarthy, "You dirty son of a bitch . . . somebody's got to beat you up and I hereby appoint myself."[6] McCarthy refused to engage in fisticuffs. Instead, he and Lansdale would engage in bureaucratic sniping at each other.

Practically the only American official in Saigon who actively supported Lansdale's presence was Iron Mike O'Daniel, and he provided the newcomer with a temporary apartment. The two men—the short, squat, scar-covered combat veteran and the lean, mustachioed former advertising man—could not have been more unalike, but they developed a mutual respect and admiration. Lansdale lauded O'Daniel as a "good fighting man who clawed his way up despite not going to West

Point" and as "quite a forthright person" who was "fighting a seem-ingly lonely uphill battle to get something done here."[7] O'Daniel, in turn, would tell his officers that Lansdale was "the only guy fighting the enemy in the whole country," thus generating jealousy that the CIA man had to handle as best he could.[8]

The diplomatic scene in Saigon was governed by the same rigid and stuffy rules of protocol as that in Paris with the added necessity—or so it was perceived among Western envoys—of not "losing face" among "Orientals," whom most viewed as not quite their equals. But so lack-ing in resources was Lansdale—only a month earlier a kingpin in the Philippines—that he caused double takes when, amid a long line of black cars discharging self-important occupants, he arrived for his first diplomatic reception at the Gia Long Palace in a rickety three-wheel *cyclo* taxi driven by a Vietnamese man "clad only in a pair of under-shorts." Inside the reception, hosted by the powerless prime minister, Prince Buu Loc, Lansdale was ambushed by "angry American officials" who were furious that he had lowered "the prestige of the United States of America by arriving in such a manner." He replied that if they were so worried about prestige, they should assign him a car. Much amused, O'Daniel overheard the exchange and offered to give Lansdale one of the inexpensive Citroën 2CVs that MAAG had just acquired.

This simple, mass-produced car with only two cylinders "was an ugly little tin can, its seats made from wide rubber bands," Lansdale wrote, but he "loved it."[9] He drove it "French style (although I still do not have a driver license)—gas pedal to the floor and blowing a horn like mad," he said gleefully. "It's a real sport."[10]

In addition to a car, Lansdale acquired in early June a four-room, embassy-owned bungalow at 5 Rue Miche, but he was so low on funds that he spent his first weeks subsisting entirely on fresh rolls from the bakery across the street and big slabs of Roquefort and Swiss cheese that he bought at a French department store. An "overwhelmingly ripe odor" soon permeated the whole house.[11]

The French were even less eager to help Lansdale than his American colleagues were. A Swiss journalist whom Lansdale talked to compared their attitude to that of "a man giving up his mistress": "He knows the affair is over, but he hates it when he sees his mistress ride by in the big car of a rich man she has just met."[12] Yet, even with the end of the affair in sight, the French still exercised enough control in Vietnam— with their officials embedded in all layers of the government, Lansdale noted, "giving advice in tones that sounded strangely like orders"[13]—to stymie the Yankee parvenus. "Am having a little trouble getting out with the Vietnamese Army with the French acting like a suspicious chaperone, suspecting seduction," Ed wrote to Pat Kelly.[14]

Lansdale's task was made harder by his inability to speak not only Vietnamese but French as well. "Am having a real problem with languages here," he admitted, "and will probably become a real expert in charades as I learn to act out all my needs."[15] When he did try to speak rudimentary French, all he got in return was "giggles." This created some practical problems for him. "My housegirl," he wrote three days after his arrival, "took my clothes away a couple of days ago and I suppose sold them to the junk man instead of doing laundry . . . despite my lavish acting out of what I wanted done." Instead of bringing back his clothes, "she just smiles and brings the other housegirls around when I'm taking a shower, at which they all giggle and run away when I yell at them." He was "so blue and mad I cannot even think it great fun, which I would have done at one time." He was down to "wearing khaki shorts and a short-sleeved shirt, with long French khaki stockings," making him look like a "real Boy Scout." "I almost give the scout salute in return when somebody salutes," he joked to his wife, Helen.[16] To his mistress, Pat, he wrote that he was tempted to get up in the morning to "watch the girls below riding by on their bicycles in their black satin pajamas," but "I shouldn't be doing so, because I'm dressed up in the best Boy Scout tradition in my short khakis and tan hose, and we boy scouts have to behave ourselves."[17]

Lansdale's difficulties were compounded by the fact that he was lonely. "Here I am still out 'saving the world' so many thousands of miles away from home at a time when I thought we would all be together again," he lamented to his wife.[18] He told Helen that he had decided against bringing her and the boys to Saigon because of the physical danger and the lack of housing. "The atmosphere is definitely ungood and I shudder to think of you and the boys living with me here," Ed wrote.[19] He might have been suspected of telling a fib to keep his wife back in Washington so that he could spend his time with his Filipino girlfriend except that he was conveying the same message to Pat: "Sure do miss you, but am glad you're not around even though you'd brighten up the gloomy atmosphere—this is no place for a wonderful person."[20] At least Pat would visit Vietnam and also meet Ed in Hong Kong, something that Helen would never do.

The major difference in the letters that Lansdale wrote contemporaneously to Helen and Pat was that his missives to the latter were earthy and to the former, pious. He wrote to Pat, for example, "A popular brand of local cigarettes in a blue package is called 'Bleu Job.' 'Bleu' is pronounced 'blow.' How in heck can I go up and ask the girl at the store counter for a pack of those?"[21] It would have been hard to imagine him making such a jest to his prim, Christian Scientist wife. Instead, he assured her that he was paying attention to his religious studies. "Just going to sit down and read the lesson all the way through as the only way I have of going to church here," he wrote one Sunday.[22]

Lack of administrative support, lack of transportation, lack of language skills, lack of love: all were reasons that Lansdale felt "blue" in his first weeks in Vietnam. "I'm a baffled, frustrated guy at the moment after my first days here," he exclaimed.[23] Years later, he recalled, "My first days in Vietnam were horrible, really."[24]

◆

AND YET most of these difficulties could be addressed more easily than Ed Lansdale's biggest deficiency: his lack of knowledge of Vietnamese society. When he arrived in the Philippines in 1950 to work alongside Ramon Magsaysay, he had previously spent three *years* criss-crossing the country and becoming intimately familiar with its people and its problems—a process aided by his love affair with Pat Kelly and his close friendships with Johnny Orendain and other Filipinos. By contrast, when he arrived in Vietnam, he had previously spent only three *weeks* in the country and had as of yet made no Vietnamese friends.

The challenge of understanding was exacerbated by the fact that, whereas the Philippines was the most Americanized country in Asia, with English as its lingua franca, Vietnam until that point had had little contact with Americans or their language and culture. Its chief foreign influences were China and France. While the Philippines had had decades of experience with democracy and a free press, freedom was an entirely new concept in Indochina. Yet counterinsurgency and state building—the exercises upon which Lansdale was to be engaged—are inherently context-specific: what works in one location may not apply in another.

Lansdale tried to absorb as much about Vietnam as quickly as he could, but he had trouble finding good books in English—a sign of how little attention Anglophone observers had paid to this area up to that point. He was forced to learn "orally through questioning knowledgeable Americans, Vietnamese, and Frenchmen."[25] Journalists were among his best sources of information. Shortly after arriving, he had an all-night session with the veteran reporters John M. Mecklin of Time-Life and Henry R. "Hank" Lieberman of the *New York Times*. The three of them, all friends from the Philippines, wound up going to Lieberman's "favorite eating joint where he could get hot dogs (on French bread) and milk shakes." "While eating," Lansdale wrote, "he told me (and everyone else in the joint) what I should do to win the war."[26]

Such friendly conversations allowed Lansdale to pick up behind-the-scenes scuttlebutt while also shaping media coverage. A small group of American correspondents, including not only Mecklin and Lieberman but also the husband-and-wife team of Tillman and Peggy Durdin of the *New York Times*, Homer Bigart of the *New York Herald Tribune*, and Robert "Pepper" Martin of *U.S. News & World Report*, Lansdale wrote, "joined together and offered to help me out as part of the team, and we used to plan together to get the truth of things out in the world."[27] Such close cooperation between journalists and an intelligence officer would come to be frowned on in later decades, after the setbacks of the Vietnam War and the scandals of Watergate, but in the fifties it was routine.

◆

As HE had done upon first arriving in the Philippines, Lansdale also traveled across Vietnam extensively at a time, June 1954, when the country was poised in a gray zone between war and peace. His most instructive trips were to the rural areas in the south that were the strongholds of two religious sects—the Cao Dai (pronounced *cow-die*) and the Hoa Hao (*wah-how*)—that would assume enormous importance over the next year. The Cao Dai, founded in 1926, claimed to synthesize all of the world's major religions, from Christianity to Taoism, and their eclectic roster of saints included Jesus Christ, Joan of Arc, Shakespeare, Sun Yat-sen and Victor Hugo. Their "Holy See" in Tay Ninh Province was a riotous explosion of colors—yellow, blue, red, pink—with paintings everywhere of the Divine Eye.[28] The Hoa Hao sect, an offshoot of Buddhism, was formed a decade later, in 1939. By 1954, each one had roughly a million adherents as well as armed forces numbering in the tens of thousands, which had received subsidies and training from the French to fight the Vietminh. The power of these sects was limited only by the disunity in their ranks, since their troops were commanded by independent warlords.

Lansdale journeyed to a Hoa Hao stronghold in the Mekong Delta on June 19, 1954, for a graduation ceremony for some Hoa Hao troops. There he met the Hoa Hao general Tran Van Soai, a former bus driver who was so tempestuous that he was nicknamed Nam Lua (Five Fires). Another Hoa Hao general, Le Quang Vinh, earned the nickname Ba Cut (Third Finger Cut) after he chopped off his own middle finger to show his men how committed he was to their cause.[29] Lansdale's conversation with Nam Lua, "a crafty old peasant with big curled up mustaches," was labored: the general spoke in his own Vietnamese dialect, which was translated into French by one interpreter and then from French into English by another. Sensing that this cumbersome translation process was impeding rather than abetting communication, Lansdale said, "I acted impulsively and went over and drew him away from our interpreters with my arm around him, Filipino style . . . at which he gave me a big bear hug. Neither of us could talk to the other. Heck of a thing, huh? But he wound up telling his military to listen to me and the welcome mat would be out always."[30]

Another sect leader Lansdale met, Colonel Jean Leroy, was a Catholic warlord born of a French father and Vietnamese mother who had served as a French army officer. Leroy presided over his home province of Ben Tre like a medieval despot; he "struck," Graham Greene wrote, "with the suddenness and cruelty of a tiger, at the Communists in his region."[31] "Short, wiry, and intense,"[32] Leroy reminded Lansdale of his Philippine army friend Colonel Napoleon Valeriano, who as head of the "Skull Squadron" had also been accused of committing atrocities against Communist forces: "I have to sort of pinch myself now and then," Lansdale wrote, "to realize they are different people."[33] Lansdale got the measure of Leroy when on June 15, 1954, he went to the warlord's house in Saigon, which looked like a fortress "with its barbed wire barriers, the sandbagged machine gun positions in the yard, and heavily armed troops at every vantage point." Leroy had forcibly evicted the previous occupants, and now he "was daring them to start a fight for the house if they had the guts to do so."[34]

Despite the rough tactics employed by Nam Lua, Jean Leroy, and other sect leaders, Lansdale was impressed by their desire to resist the Vietminh and drawn to their resilience, even as many of the French were succumbing to the inevitability of a defeat for the "Free World." "The only people I have found, so far, who have the will to fight are the so-called 'confessional' armies, including the Catholics, and some of the folks up in the Delta," he wrote.[35] The sect armies were asking him to train and fund "fifty commando teams for psy war," but he was "finding excuses" not to, "simply because I don't think they have a chance now, and I hate to slap their fannies and get them out fighting when I know they are going to be deserted by the French and us. It's hard enough on a guy to send men out to die in a good cause, a rotten thing when all the cards are stacked against success."[36]

Lansdale was considerably less impressed by another sect based in Saigon, this one criminal rather than religious. The Binh Xuyen (pronounced *bean-zuyen*) had grown up from pirate bands in the 1920s to take over the underworld of Cholon, Saigon's Chinatown, and its lucrative opium trade. In April 1954, Emperor Bao Dai, desperate for revenue to finance his opulent lifestyle, had sold the position of chief of police of Saigon to the Binh Xuyen general Le Van Vien, known as Bay Vien, for a reported payment of forty-four million piastres ($1.25

million). It was as if Chicago had made Al Capone its police chief.[37] Bay Vien had gotten his start working as a chauffeur for a small-time gangster. Now he had ten thousand men under arms.[38] His holdings included a giant casino known as Le Grand Monde and a giant bordello known as Le Parc aux Buffles. Bay Vien ruled this criminal empire from a fortified villa, where he kept a pet tiger and a giant boa constrictor; "rumor had it," wrote one American diplomat, "that the tiger's diet varied depending on the unexplained, permanent disappearances of the general's enemies."[39]

Lansdale saw for himself the Binh Xuyen's thuggish tactics one sultry evening in June 1954. He was in his second-floor room at the MAAG bachelor officers' quarters, "attempting to read local French newspapers with the aid of a translator's dictionary," when he was interrupted by a phone call from a woman with a Southern accent, demanding to know, "What are all these strange soldiers doing shooting around the house?" The caller turned out to be one of three American embassy secretaries living a few blocks away. They were cowering under their beds, because of the sounds of fighting coming from next door. Lansdale gallantly walked over to rescue them. He found a company of Binh Xuyen troops, distinctive in their green berets, firing into a two-story bungalow next to the secretaries' house. Their submachine-gun bursts were answered with grenades being hurled out of the house, which caused "a wild scramble for safety among the attackers." Employing his "atrocious French," Lansdale talked to the Binh Xuyen commander, who told him he was trying to arrest someone inside the house, a Vietnamese detective who "had been too effective in fighting crime." Barricaded inside his house, the detective shouted that he would surrender only to the Vietnamese National Army. Lansdale persuaded the Binh Xuyen to let him escort the detective to the Vietnamese army headquarters.[40]

From this experience, Lansdale drew a small lesson and a big one. The small, practical lesson: "A man could stay safe behind walls and keep a company of troops at bay with hand grenades tossed through windows or doors. From then on, I kept a supply of grenades in my own living quarters."[41] The larger moral was about how corrupt and deca-

dent southern Vietnam had become—and how divided and dysfunc-
tional. "I am deciding against ever trying to establish our family in the
midst of so much apparent evil," Ed wrote to Helen.[42]

◆

BEYOND LEARNING what he could, there was not much that Lansdale
could do to influence the situation upon his arrival; all seemed in abey-
ance, amid an atmosphere of "deepening gloom,"[43] pending the outcome of an international conference that had convened in Geneva on
April 26, 1954, to broker a deal between the French and the Vietminh.
  Lansdale tried to teach "psywar" techniques to Vietnamese troops,
his curriculum focusing, as in the Philippines, on trying to improve
"the relationship between the troops and the people." He did not have
much success. "Hungry and ill-paid troops still stole chickens, pigs,
and rice during military operations," Lansdale lamented. The French
"found my ideas alien," he wrote, "and suggested laughingly that I take
up smoking opium instead." Lansdale realized that to change the situation would require "some new direction from the top."[44] That new
direction arrived, unexpectedly, on June 25, 1954, in the form of an
"honest mystic,"[45] as he had been dubbed by the CIA, who had just been
named prime minister of the state of Vietnam.

◆

LANSDALE KNEW nothing about Ngo Dinh Diem (pronounced *no-din-
zee'em* in northern Vietnam and *yee'em* in the south). He was surprised
to discover, once he talked to his new Vietnamese acquaintances, that
Diem was "exceptionally well known" and that "people either admired
him or disliked him. Few were neutral. All agreed that he was notably
honest and had a strong character." Most believed that "Diem was a
great patriot, probably the best of all the nationalists still living, with
an outstanding record as a wise and able administrator." "A minority
view," on the other hand, "held that Diem was mulishly stubborn, too
aloof to be a good political leader, and should have obeyed his boyhood
wish to become a monk."[46] This was an early indication of how polarizing a political figure Diem would turn out to be.

Diem had been born in Quang Binh Province, which would become part of North Vietnam, on January 3, 1901, making him a decade younger than Ho Chi Minh and a decade older than Vo Nguyen Giap. His father, Ngo Dinh Kha, was a devout Catholic who took the family to mass every morning, as well as a traditional mandarin who sported two-inch fingernails, a black turban, and a silk robe. He rose to become grand chamberlain and keeper of the eunuchs in the court of Emperor Thanh Thai, but resigned when the French deposed Thanh Thai in 1907 for having demanded more autonomy.[47] From their father, Diem and his eight siblings (five boys and three girls) inherited the three faiths—Confucianism, Catholicism, and nationalism—that would define their lives.

Diem was rigorously educated in Catholic schools, where he learned French, Latin, and classical Chinese. He entered a monastery briefly at age fifteen. But unlike his older brother Ngo Dinh Thuc, who became a bishop, he decided against the priesthood; Thuc said "the Church was too worldly for him."[48] After studying at the same French lycée in Hue that Ho Chi Minh and Vo Nguyen Giap also attended, Diem went to the School of Administration in Hanoi to prepare for a job in the imperial bureaucracy. Here he experienced the only romance of his life with the daughter of one of his instructors, and after she broke off their unconsummated relationship to join a convent, he remained celibate for the rest of his life.

After graduating in 1921, Diem rose quickly, becoming by age twenty-five a province chief with three hundred villages under his supervision. He was police chief and judge, tax collector and public works administrator, all at the same time. "Wearing a conical straw hat and a mandarin robe," a journalist later wrote, "he rode around the countryside on horseback and dealt more closely with the villagers than he ever would again."[49] Despite his budding nationalism, Diem won French favor by cracking down on Communist plots. In 1933, still only thirty years old, he was appointed minister of the interior. Yet he resigned after just two months in office, because the French refused to grant the Vietnamese any power to govern themselves. Thus, like his father, Diem staked out his credentials as a nationalist. Ellen J.

Hammer, an early American scholar of Vietnam who knew Diem personally, was to write, "Nothing he ever did became him better than his decision to resign from that post."[50]

Instead of embracing a life of political intrigue, as Ho Chi Minh had done, Diem retired to the family home in Hue to pursue a quieter life of meditation, study, hobbies (photography, flower raising, horseback riding, hunting), and daily mass attendance in accordance with what Hammer described as "the Confucian tradition that a scholar during a difficult period of history should retire to a tranquil spot and wait for better times in which he might be useful."[51]

Once the Vietminh seized power in August 1945, they began rounding up non-Communist politicians. Diem's brother Ngo Dinh Khoi was arrested and executed along with his son. Diem himself was arrested and detained in a remote jungle camp, where he contracted malaria, dysentery, and influenza. By early 1946, however, Ho Chi Minh was trying to form a government that did not look entirely Communist and saw the potential usefulness of Diem. In their one and only meeting, Ho offered Diem the post of minister of the interior, but Diem refused to accept the job from his brother's killer and reportedly called Ho a criminal to his face.[52] In a rare display of magnanimity, Ho Chi Minh allowed Ngo Dinh Diem to walk free. Four years later, however, the Vietminh pronounced a death sentence on Diem and the French refused to protect him, so he left the country.

Diem moved to the United States, where he lived in two seminaries, in New Jersey and New York, as the guest of Cardinal Francis Spellman of New York. For the next three years, he cultivated not only conservative Catholics but also liberals drawn to the dream of a "third way," neither colonialist nor Communist. The most important patron Diem acquired was the liberal, deeply contrarian Supreme Court justice William O. Douglas. He thought Diem was "the kind of Asian we can live with"[53] and on May 7, 1953, hosted a lunch at the Supreme Court in Diem's honor. The guests included Senator Mike Mansfield of Montana, a former professor of Asian history, and the newly elected senator John F. Kennedy of Massachusetts, recently returned from a trip to Indochina.[54]

The backing that Diem received from prominent Americans was crucial to his appointment as prime minister—not, as widely rumored in Saigon, because the American government pushed for him to get the job, as it had pushed for Ramon Magsaysay to become defense minister and president in the Philippines, but, rather, because after the fall of Dien Bien Phu, Emperor Bao Dai understood that the future of "free" Vietnam depended on American support, and who better to obtain that support than a man who was a personal friend of Cardinal Spellman and Justice Douglas? So despite his well-founded reservations about Diem's "fanaticism and his messianic tendencies,"[55] Bao Dai thrust South Vietnam's future into his hands on June 16, 1954.

◆

DIEM WAS due to arrive back in Saigon, which was still under French control, on June 25. A diplomatic reception was laid on for him at Tan Son Nhut Airport. Lansdale was driving there in his "vacuum cleaner Citroen"[56] when he was struck by the "crowds jamming both sides of the road." "The population of this wartime capital usually was too blasé even to glance at dignitaries in limousines or at the martial passing of troop convoys and tanks," he wrote. "Yet here they were by the thousands, obviously waiting to see just one man." Intrigued, Lansdale parked his car "and joined the massed crowd along the curbstones."

Even though Diem's flight was delayed, Lansdale observed, whole families waited for hours in the hot sunshine as street cart vendors "did a land-office business" selling the sweet juice of freshly crushed sugarcane. Eventually the crowd could hear "a wail of sirens and the pop-popping of motorcycles." People pushed forward to get a look at their new leader. But all they saw was a "big black limousine, Vietnamese flags fluttering from holders on its fenders, windows closed, passengers invisible in its deep interior," Lansdale wrote. "Whoosh! Limousine and entourage were past. The crowds of people looked at one another in disappointment. Was that *him*? Did you see *him*? He didn't even see *us*! They broke up in a disgruntled mood."[57]

Lansdale went back to the embassy and reported to Ambassador Donald Heath that Diem and his advisers were misjudging the "mood of the people." "Diem," he believed, "should have ridden into the city slowly in an open car, or even have walked, to provide a focus for the affection that the people so obviously had been waiting to bestow on him." What Lansdale did not realize was that Diem's younger brother, Ngo Dinh Nhu, had arranged a carefully choreographed welcome reception in the center of the city, where Diem received a "vibrant ovation" from the gathered crowd. A modern scholar, Edward Miller, argues that the success of the downtown reception shows that Diem was not "as hapless and unaware of his political surroundings as Lansdale suggested."[58] That may be true but, as subsequent events (leading eventually to Diem's overthrow and murder) were to show, Lansdale was right to doubt Diem's political acumen. Scholarly and reclusive, long-winded and uncharismatic, Diem fit no one's image of a dynamic leader.

Still, Diem was the best candidate yet for the job, and with his arrival Lansdale finally had a focus for his work. He spent the rest of the day and all night on June 25–26 working on a memorandum offering the new prime minister suggestions on how to govern. He called for integrating all of the sect paramilitary forces into the armed forces, bringing together the nationalist political parties in an anti-Communist coalition, creating public forums around the countryside where government representatives could hear from the people, immediately adopting a Philippine-style constitution, and much else besides.[59] The sun had risen by the time Lansdale finished this paper. He showed it to Ambassador Heath and General O'Daniel. While they approved of its contents, they said the U.S. government could not officially present such a document—it would look too much like meddling in Vietnam's internal affairs. But if the CIA operative wanted to present the paper as a "personal one," he was free to do so. So with George Hellyer, a French-speaking public information officer, in tow as translator, Lansdale marched from the U.S. embassy near the Saigon River to the Gia Long Palace to present his recommendations to Diem.

Symptomatic of the chaos that gripped the whole country in the wake of the French defeat, Lansdale found the palace in a "disorganized state": "There were no guards to challenge our entry, no civil servants to receive visitors." An aide hurrying by with a stack of documents told them the prime minister was upstairs, so up they went. The hallway was empty, but one office door was slightly ajar, so they stuck their heads into a small office where a table was covered in a towering stack of paperwork. "Seated at the table," Lansdale wrote, "was a middle-aged Vietnamese, who looked up at us from a document he was reading as we entered. At first glance, he wasn't very impressive. A roly-poly figure dressed in a white sharkskin, double-breasted suit, his feet were not quite touching the floor. He must be very short-legged, I thought. Intensely black hair, combed strictly, topped a broad face in which the most prominent feature was high rounds of flesh over the cheekbones, as if they had been pushed up there by constant smiling." Hellyer explained they were looking for the prime minister. "I am Ngo Dinh Diem," the man behind the table replied in fluent, if accented, French.

Lansdale introduced himself and handed over his document to Diem. The prime minister, Lansdale noted, "listened intently, asking some searching questions, thanked me for my thoughtfulness, folded up the paper, and put it in his pocket."[60] "Although the plan was not adopted, it laid the foundation for a friendship which has lasted," Lansdale later wrote.[61] The two men would never grow as close as Lansdale and Magsaysay had become; Diem was not a man who entered into close friendships with anyone outside his family, much less with a foreigner. But in spite of their continuing need for a translator, the fun-loving secret agent from Southern California and the ascetic mandarin from central Vietnam gradually developed a relationship of "considerable depth, trust, and candor," as Lansdale wrote.[62]

◆

LANSDALE BECAME the regular CIA liaison to Diem, which, given the power that the CIA then wielded in American foreign policy, made him in effect the chief American interlocutor with the leader of South Vietnam. Lansdale would regularly visit the palace for long talks with Diem, which were typically held in a small alcove off Diem's bedroom—a tiny room very much like a monk's cell, piled floor to ceiling with books and documents.[63] His knees almost touching

Diem's, sweat dripping off his brow, Lansdale would show his trademark patience as the Vietnamese leader chain-smoked cigarettes and drank little cups of tea while expounding for hours on his views. Few other Americans could tolerate Diem's rambling monologues. Among reporters and diplomats in Saigon, a two-hour session was considered a "quickie." Lansdale's friend John Mecklin of Time-Life recounted the experience of one "ashen-faced American newsman" who said that "Diem had kept him for six and one-half hours, from 10 a.m. to 4:30 p.m. with no lunch, and that the last ninety minutes had been spent standing in the doorway after the newsman had gotten up to try to leave."[64]

What made the one-way conversations particularly hard to endure for most Americans was that they had little interest in the political minutiae that fascinated Diem. Lansdale was different. "I never met another Vietnamese that knew as much about those subjects as he did personally," he recalled. "When something would happen he would tell me not only who had been involved but go into a family history, telling me who the man's father was, why he had handled something the way he had, and usually go back about 200 years in history about a particular little place in Vietnam to tell me why the people felt the way they did about things. . . . Amazing detail."[65] Lansdale found that Diem had a "phenomenal memory for details, dates, places, and personal biographies."[66] Unfortunately, Diem's "facts" were not always right. As Mecklin noted, his information "was filtered through such a morass of selfishly motivated bureaucrats that it was often inaccurate, sometimes seriously so."[67]

As he had done with Magsaysay, the soft-spoken American adviser would listen carefully and then summarize what Diem "had said, but in a form stressing the principles involved and enumerating the factors that a man should look at and examine very closely in order to make a decision." "By laying this out for him verbally," Lansdale later explained, "it would help him clarify the issue in his mind, so that he could then make a decision. He apparently found this quite useful. That was the basis for our relationship."[68]

Even some of Lansdale's aides found the prime minister to be "prissy," "authoritarian," and "pompous."[69] Lansdale, however, saw a side of Diem that few others discerned. He later wrote, "True . . . he was happiest when cloistered with books or papers in his study, but he also often had a twinkle in his eyes—eyes that lit up, were full of life, among intimates. He had a wry wit, [and] made zany, teasing comments that were great fun." One time, for example, just when Lansdale was most at odds with the French, Diem gave Lansdale a signed photo of himself. The puckish inscription: "To Ed Lansdale, a great true friend of France and the person who has made all Vietnamese love France."[70] Lansdale found Diem not only unexpectedly humorous but also "courageous, and deeply in love with his country."[71] The chief flaw he detected was that Diem "wasn't a good executive. He tended to want to do most of the work himself, instead of delegating to a member of his personal staff or someone."[72]

Lansdale tried to connect Diem more directly with the problems of the Vietnamese people by pushing the reclusive prime minister to leave his office and go out "into the provinces and streets" to talks with "people from all walks of life."[73] On infrequent occasions, Diem took his advice, but such forays did not change his impulse to rule in an aloof and autocratic fashion. Lansdale had even less success when he tried to humanize Diem by urging him to try to reconnect with, and marry, the girl he had loved in his youth. He suggested that the premier follow the local custom in Hue of taking her for a boat ride on the Perfume River while he serenaded her with a mandolin. Diem subsequently told Lansdale that he went to her house in Hue but lacked the nerve to ring the doorbell, even though he was the leader of the country and could have barged in with a security detail if he had so desired.[74] He was, Lansdale concluded, a "shy, modest sort of person."[75]

As their relationship deepened, Lansdale was invited to Ngo family gatherings—the real nexus of power in South Vietnam. Although Diem as prime minister sat at the head of the table at family meals, his older brother, Bishop Thuc, "usually had the final, positive word on any subject under discussion." Both Thuc and Diem were "trencher-men," Lansdale noted. While they were digging into their food, Diem's handsome younger brother, Ngo Dinh Nhu (pronounced *no-din-new*), who had studied as an archivist in France and "was looked upon as the intellectual in the family," would expound "on his theory of why some current event had happened."[76] Nhu's young and alluring wife, Tran Le Xuan (better known as Madame Nhu), also spoke up forcefully, in contrast to her more reserved sisters-in-law. Diem listened to his family more than to any outsider. That Lansdale was sometimes invited to join them was a mark of high favor.

Lansdale had gotten close to Diem, just as he had intended. But would it do any good? In the summer of 1954, with the truculent French intent on preserving their influence even after the end of their sovereignty, the ascendant Communists eager to claim the entire country as their rightful reward, and the zealous religious sects determined to maintain their hard-won autonomy, few informed observers thought that Diem would last until the summer of 1955. It would be up to Lansdale to help him build a new state out of the ruins of the French empire.

14

The Chopstick Torture

You don't know shit from shinola about what is going on.

—Lou Conein

WHILE Ngo Dinh Diem was still settling into the neoclassical Gia Long Palace, international negotiators half a world away were continuing their efforts to resolve the future of his country. The talks took place in the severe-looking Palais des Nations in Geneva, originally constructed in the 1930s to house the ill-fated League of Nations. Ariana Park, the parcel of land on which it stood, had been donated to the city in 1890 by a prominent Swiss publisher who had demanded, as a condition of his bequest, that peacocks be allowed to freely wander its beautifully manicured grounds. As brightly feathered birds strutted and preened across the lawn, inside the Palais foreign ministers in dark suits strutted and preened before an international audience.

The talks had taken on added urgency with the ascension in Paris of the liberal lawyer and politician Pierre Mendès-France. Taking office as prime minister on June 18, 1954, he dramatically pledged to give up power if the Indochina conflict was not settled by the end of the day on July 20, and in fact the final issues were resolved that very day. The

French and Vietminh representatives agreed to partition Vietnam at the seventeenth parallel, keeping Hue and Da Nang out of Communist hands, much to Ho Chi Minh's consternation. Nationwide elections were to be held no later than July 1956 to decide on a government for the whole country. For the next three hundred days, the population could move freely between North and South, with French forces pledged to leave the North and Vietminh forces the South. Cambodia and Laos would become independent states with non-Communist governments.

Although the Geneva Conference was supposed to create two temporary "withdrawal zones," it actually birthed two new nations: North Vietnam, with thirteen million people, and South Vietnam, with twelve million. In the process, it created a monumental challenge for both Ho Chi Minh and Ngo Dinh Diem—first to consolidate their authority and eventually to reunify the country. Ho Chi Minh, as the leader of a large, victorious army and a powerful political party, had a substantial head start. Diem, by contrast, commanded little beyond the walls of his own palace. The Vietnamese National Army was ineffectual and of dubious loyalty. Much of the countryside was dominated either by the Vietminh or by sect armies. "We didn't think it would last," a twenty-four-year-old aide to Diem recalled, "but we were young and idealistic."[1]

Lansdale was one of the few people who thought "there was still a fighting chance."[2] In top-secret cables to his superiors, he urged that "in order to construct a Free Vietnam which can be an effective bulwark against further Communist aggression in Southeast Asia, the United States must accept a dominant and direct role in aiding the country."[3] It was a role that he was more than happy to take on himself. Pondering the implications of the Geneva Accords, Lansdale concluded "that a number of us in Vietnam had been sentenced to hard labor for the next two years."[4]

◆

To ASSIST him in "saving the world,"[5] as he sardonically and habitually put it, Ed Lansdale asked for assistance from his CIA superiors. He would soon assemble a twelve-man team, eventually growing to twenty, that would be a cross between the Dirty Dozen and the Keystone Kops.

Their highly classified mission: "to undertake paramilitary operations against the enemy and to wage political-psychological warfare."[6]

The first and most colorful arrival was Major Lucien "Lou" Conein, a "stocky" French-born CIA officer with a "leathery face,"[7] "bushy eyebrows,"[8] and limpid blue eyes who had already developed a reputation as a "wild man."[9] Given Conein's boozy proclivity for mythologizing his own life, Great Gatsby style, it was difficult to know where reality ended and the legend began. A superb storyteller, especially if fueled by pear brandy, Conein himself cautioned, "Don't believe anything I tell you; I'm an expert liar."[10]

Some facts, however, appear indisputable. Conein was born in Paris in 1919. When he was five, his father died in a car accident and his penniless mother put him on a ship by himself to the United States, with a tag around his neck attesting to his identity and destination. He was to be raised by his aunt, a French war bride from World War I who had settled in Kansas City. With times hard during the Great Depression, Conein left high school in 1936 to work as a printer and typesetter while also serving in the Kansas National Guard.[11] Once World War II broke out, he traveled back to France to join the regular French army—not the Foreign Legion, as he later boasted. After the fall of France in 1940, he returned to the United States, where he joined the U.S. Army and the OSS.

On August 15, 1944, Conein arrived back in southwestern France as the leader of a Jedburgh team to aid the Allied landing in southern France. "Naturally strong, in excellent shape, and recklessly brave," a journalist friend later wrote, "he liked blowing up things and was good at it."[12] Among the contacts he made were members of the Corsican Brotherhood crime syndicate, which operated an international narcotics network out of Marseille. The gangsters called him Luigi, giving rise to an enduring nickname.

In July 1945, with the war in Europe over, Conein infiltrated Indochina to attack Japanese forces at the head of an OSS squad.[13] He entered Hanoi on August 22, 1945, and met his future foes, Ho Chi Minh, a "fascinating man," and Vo Nguyen Giap, a "brilliant sonofabitch." "Now Ho, the second time I met him," Conein said, "if he'd asked me to join the Party, I would have signed." His only complaint about Ho and Giap: "I was going to die of thirst. Goddamn bastards gave me tea! . . . And I wanted beer!"[14]

Immediately after the war, Conein was dispatched to Germany to run agents behind the Iron Curtain for the OSS's successor organizations. It was during this period that he lost two fingers on his right hand—and not because of some daring commando exploit, as commonly assumed. Conein had been driving with a girlfriend, reportedly "his best friend's wife,"[15] when their car broke down. He opened the hood to figure out the problem. She started the car prematurely, and the motor sliced off two fingers.

As if plucked from the pages of a novel, Lou Conein was an irrepressible character with a fondness for dark deeds and practical jokes. He had a violent temper, a drinking habit, and an eye for the ladies. In Vietnam, where he arrived for the second time at the age of thirty-six in 1954, he would meet and marry his third wife, an exotic young woman of French-Vietnamese ancestry. He was lauded by his colleagues for his loyalty and professionalism, his charm and his direct manner of speaking.

Luigi and Lansdale hit it off, in their own manner. As Conein later said, "Lansdale was a very strange air force colonel, and I was a very strange infantry parachute major."[16] One fellow team member recalled that Conein opened most of their meetings with " 'Godammit, Colonel,' then saying, in effect, 'You don't know shit from shinola about what is going on.' This was usually followed by an equally blustery rejoinder from Lansdale about Conein failing to keep him adequately informed. Then they would get down to business."[17] Bluster aside, each man respected and valued the other—Conein for Lansdale's skills at political and psychological warfare, Lansdale for Conein's commando and agent-running skills. But Ed was under no illusions about his friend Lou. He referred to him privately as "the Thug."[18]

◆

THE GENEVA ACCORDS forbade the dispatch of additional foreign military personnel to Vietnam after August 11, 1954. To beat that deadline, CIA headquarters, flush from its recent successes in Iran, the Philippines, and, most recently, Guatemala (where the leftist president Jacobo Arbenz had been overthrown in June), hastily searched for reinforcements besides Conein who could be sent to abet Lansdale. He had asked for experts in "psywar" and "civic action."[19] Instead, he got "an ideal crew for guerrilla combat, for blowing up things, for jumps behind enemy lines," selected presumably by "personnel officers in Washington who must have had a Korean-style conflict in mind" and who were ignorant "of a Communist 'people's war' such as the Vietminh waged."[20] This was a sign of the rampant confusion in Washington, which was to hinder American operations in Vietnam in the years ahead, about how to counter guerrilla warfare, an activity as dissimilar from *conducting* guerrilla warfare as police work is from robbery. Yet by pure serendipity some of Lansdale's new recruits turned out to be superbly fitted for the task at hand.

Typical of these new arrivals was Rufus Phillips III, a strapping, clean-cut twenty-four-year-old Virginian who had played football at Yale. Bored with law school at the University of Virginia, he decided to drop out and serve his country, exchanging his college tweeds for army fatigues. He was trained as a paratrooper officer by the Army and then was sent by the CIA to South Korea. He was not there long before he was dispatched "on a priority basis" to Saigon, apparently because he spoke some French. "Blinking into the blazing heat of the early afternoon," he stepped off an Air Force C-47 at Tan Son Nhut Airport on August 8, 1954, looking the very embodiment of youthful American vigor and innocence, his uncreased face free of any suggestion of deceit or guile. From there he went to his quarters at the Hotel Majestic on the Saigon waterfront: five stories, yellow stucco, ceiling fans in the lobby, "excruciatingly slow iron-cage elevators," rooms with no air-conditioning but plenty of geckos.[21]

Phillips and nine other recent arrivals spent a week or two hanging around the Majestic until Lansdale came to meet them in a bedroom that had been swept for "bugs"—microphones, not actual insects, which remained plentiful. Lansdale, Phillips saw, "was forty-six years old, of medium height and build, and was dressed in khaki shorts, knee socks, and a short-sleeved uniform shirt with an air force officer's hat worn at a slightly rakish angle. I noticed crew-cut hair, a high forehead, penetrating eyes, a throat with a prominent, slightly swollen Adam's apple, and a brush mustache. He seemed very military yet accessible at the same time."²² "After shaking hands with each of us," Phillips recalled, Lansdale began speaking "quietly in his throaty voice":

> He couldn't tell us what we would be doing yet. He had no office and was operating out of a small house. Soon he would interview us individually to begin making assignments. . . . Our job was to save South Vietnam, but he couldn't tell us exactly how we were going to do that. The present situation was very confused. We had to be patient. With these cryptic statements he gave us a half smile and was gone. I didn't know what to make of him or our situation, and neither did anyone else. I had expected a clear-cut mission; it was a disappointing start. "Save South Vietnam"— how in the world were we going to do that?²³

Eventually the members of what would become known as the Saigon Military Mission would make their way, one by one, to receive their instructions at Lansdale's Rue Miche bungalow. There they would find not only Lansdale but his new housemate, Naval Reserve Lieutenant Joseph P. Redick, who would become his executive assistant and de facto chief of staff. Thirty-eight years old, Joe Redick had a PhD in French literature and linguistics and had served during World War II as a Japanese-language linguist in the Navy. No longer captivated by Molière and Flaubert, he had joined the CIA after the war. He took over translating for Lansdale and dealing with various administrative matters. "A brown-haired man of medium height and build," Redick "had the manner of a schoolmaster, precise and punctilious," a journalist wrote.²⁴ But while "soft-spoken" and "professorial," he was also, Lansdale noted, "the deadliest shot on the team."²⁵

Gradually, in their conversations with Lansdale, the team members began to find a purpose. They would be given assignments and sent to live in various apartments and houses around the capital. Phillips was told to help the G-5 psychological warfare department of the Vietnamese National Army. He objected that he didn't know anything about psychological warfare, so Lansdale gave him a book on the subject and a vague edict "to make friends, see what they were doing, and figure out how to help."[26] Lansdale seldom gave instructions more exact than that; a believer in professional as well as societal freedom, he allowed individual team members free rein to exercise their initiative, and he ran the entire team on an egalitarian basis rare in the military. Phillips saluted Lansdale once in his entire life—when he first showed up at Rue Miche and announced that he was reporting for duty.[27]

The members of Lansdale's team were ostensibly working for the Military Assistance Advisory Group (MAAG), and they often wore military uniforms, albeit French uniforms with shorts and knee-length stockings, because those were more comfortable than the heavier American uniforms in this tropical climate. But there was no real mystery about what they were up to—Lansdale was widely rumored to be, as the *New York Times* put it a few years later, "the chief United States intelligence agent in Saigon."[28] "There are so many secret agents now checking up on me," Lansdale wrote, "that I'm sure real estate values are going up in this neighborhood, as they all try to move in for observation of the front door from across the street and next door. Others are all sorts of people driving cars, motorcycles, bicycles, etc., who dawdle around in front. Think I'll put in parking meters and collect from them."[29]

The situation was no better at a large house with a pool on Rue Taberd where several of his subordinates lived, a few blocks from the Beaux-Arts Norodom Palace, which Diem would take as his residence. "The telephone line was tapped by so many different outfits," Marine Captain Richard W. Smith recalled, "that when you tried to make a call you would hear clicks as everybody picked up and the quality of the transmission went down. More than once I would shout, 'Get the hell off the line. Let me make the call and I will call again and brief you on what was said.' Sometimes they would actually get off the line!"[30] As in the Philippines, Lansdale preferred to hide in plain sight, disdaining the usual conventions of the spy business. His paradoxical modus operandi, he later explained, was "acting covertly in a semi-open manner."[31]

Tall by Vietnamese standards, with a clipped mustache and a military-style haircut, Lansdale cut a distinctive figure tooling around town in his dinky Citroën 2CV, often accompanied by yet another new teammate—a black dog that he had been given by his friend George Hellyer of the U.S. Information Service. Named Pierre, the prickly mutt was "part Kerry blue terrier, part French poodle, and some other unknown breed." Hellyer had to get rid of him because he was biting the servants, but he got along well with Lansdale. Ed wrote to Pat Kelly, "The dog has been in love with me ever since we first met (I think he's slightly queer, the way he gives me hugs and wants to crawl into bed with me). Anyhow he sleeps at the foot of my bed and bites anyone coming close . . . which not only gives me security, but also keeps my virginity intact, dammit."[32]

◆

LANSDALE'S FIRST priority was to make preparations for the evacuation of anyone who wanted to leave North Vietnam, which under the Geneva Accords had to be completed by October 10, 1954. The French were expecting no more than 30,000 people, but by early August 1954 some 120,000 refugees had already streamed into Hanoi and Haiphong, and a seemingly endless flow of refugees kept arriving every day. The populations of entire Catholic villages in the North were leaving en masse, dragging all their belongings with them. The French did not have the resources to transport more than a small fraction, and the American ambassador in Saigon, Donald Heath, was, in the words of a subordinate, "cool to the prospect of saddling the already shaky Diem regime with the logistic and political problems inherent in a major influx from the North."[33]

Lansdale argued that by encouraging migration, the United States could undermine the Vietminh by showing how unpopular their rule was while bolstering South Vietnam with anti-Communist newcomers. On August 5, 1954, at his urging, Heath telegrammed Washington, "It is our considered judgment here that this vitally important mass movement of non-Communist population from North Vietnam will be a failure with political and psychological repercussions that may well be disastrous unless US steps boldly and strongly forward and deals with problem."[34] Lansdale later said he had written the telegram himself, using "'hard sell' tactics to put it over,"[35] while also sending his own personal appeal to Allen Dulles.[36]

Thus was born what became known as Operation Passage to Freedom. The U.S. Navy assembled a flotilla of vessels to ferry refugees south. Lansdale persuaded the French, using American funds, to hire Civil Air Transport to evacuate refugees by air. (CAT was a CIA-run airline that in 1959 would be renamed Air America.) Lansdale was "very mindful of the Palestinian refugees, and how badly that had been handled," with the Palestinians settling after the birth of Israel in squalid refugee camps in neighboring Arab states, where they became ripe for radicalization.[37] Therefore, he insisted, the newcomers should be integrated into South Vietnamese society rather than sent to refugee camps.

The first U.S. Navy ship transporting refugees left Haiphong, a gritty industrial center and railroad hub as well as an important port, on August 17, 1954. Howard Simpson, an American embassy information officer, traveled to Hanoi to accompany one such shipload south. The journey began, he wrote, when "trucks arrived in a din of squeaking brakes, banking tailgates, and authoritative shouting" to discharge eighteen hundred refugees at Haiphong harbor. "Old men and women, their high cheekbones straining at wrinkled flesh, had to be lifted out of the truck by the more able. Bare-bottomed children tottered around the base of the truck, grasping their parents, who were loaded down with household effects, sleeping mats, and fire-blackened pots." Once onboard, they were deloused and "served generous portions of rice from huge stainless-steel vats." Families camped out on the open decks. Children, wearing sailor hats and baseball caps, were given chewing gum and Hershey bars by American sailors. Navy doctors treated tuberculosis and malnutrition. At night a screen was rigged up and "the mesmerized refugees watched the glittering productions of Hollywood, murmuring, clucking their tongues and laughing at the international language of slapstick."

When the refugee ship steamed into Saigon three days later, it was met by a delegation of American embassy and military wives in dresses, hats, and gloves. As if greeting new neighbors next door, they handed out welcome gifts to each family—"several bananas and a large, cellophane-wrapped block of American cheese." The Vietnamese politely took what they were offered, but within twenty-four hours the complaints started coming back—the "American soap . . . didn't produce suds or clean properly." "When the refugees finally discovered they were dealing with cheese," Simpson wrote, "they sold it to middlemen, who in turn sold it to Saigon's street merchants, who sold it back to Americans at an inflated price. For months, toasted cheese hors d'oeuvres were a feature at official American receptions in Saigon."[38]

Though the undertaking had its comical, clash-of-culture aspects, Operation Passage to Freedom was an undoubted success. Some nine hundred thousand refugees moved south, roughly two-thirds of them Catholics, while only thirty thousand people—mostly Vietminh cadres—went north. "By 1956," notes one historian, "the Diocese of Saigon had more Catholics than Paris or Rome."[39] Not only did these Catholics enlarge Ngo Dinh Diem's political base, but their departure from the Communist-dominated North was a propaganda windfall for the "Free World."

◆

NUMEROUS WESTERN publications exuberantly covered the exodus from the North. Most influential of all was a best-selling memoir, *Deliver Us from Evil*, written by a young U.S. Navy doctor named Thomas Dooley who had provided medical care for northerners. He recounted not only the altruism of American sailors taking care of woebegone refugees but also the supposedly fiendish "Oriental tortures" being perpetuated behind the "Bamboo Curtain" that were causing so many people to flee. One of his most lurid anecdotes concerned the fate suffered by students who had attended a Catholic class: Vietminh soldiers jammed wooden chopsticks into their ears, piercing their eardrums, to ensure they could never hear any religious teaching again. "The shrieking of the children could be heard all over the village," Dooley wrote.[40]

First appearing in April 1956 in *Reader's Digest*, at the time the world's best-selling magazine with twenty million subscribers, and then published as a book in its own right, *Deliver Us from Evil* became the very first best seller to come out of Vietnam. It influenced how a whole generation of Americans thought about the country. By 1960, the book's young, handsome, Catholic author had become one of the ten most-admired people in the United States—right up there with Albert Schweitzer and Winston Churchill. Many called him Dr. America, as if he were a superhero like Captain America.[41]

But there was more to the story than most readers realized. In the first place, Dr. Dooley was not the paragon of Catholic rectitude that he was made out to be. He was a homosexual who was forced to resign from the Navy for his sexual behavior in 1956. Given that homosexuality was still a crime under the Uniform Code of Military Justice, Dooley might have been court-martialed had he not been so useful in publicizing the Navy's success in Operation Passage to Freedom. According to many of those who worked with him, Dooley was also a consummate "bullshit artist"[42] who exaggerated his own role in helping Vietnamese refugees and simply made up many of the atrocity stories about the Vietminh. His book was written with the help of Captain William Lederer, a Navy public affairs officer and a friend of Lansdale's, yet even Lederer was to say, "The atrocities he described . . . either never took place or were committed by the French."[43]

Did Dooley concoct these horrors from whole cloth, or was he merely passing along rumors that he had heard? Some light is shed on this question by the embassy information officer Howard Simpson. He recalled having an argument in 1954 with none other than Edward Lansdale "over a propaganda story" he had heard while visiting the North "about village children whose eardrums had been ruptured by the insertion of chopsticks during a Vietminh torture session." Simpson was as anti-Communist as the next American, but he had been in Vietnam since 1952 and "there was something about the account that didn't ring true. I had seen and heard enough of torture by both sides during my time in the field. Chopsticks had never featured as a preferred instrument. There were many more direct, simple, and horrifying methods." When questioned, however, "Lansdale only flashed his all-knowing smile and changed the subject."[44]

The implication is that Lansdale and his team spread the chopstick story and that it was then picked up by Dooley. This is plausible, even probable, because Lansdale was using every psywar technique in his repertoire to encourage emigration to the South and many of them were even more fanciful and lurid than the chopstick torture.

◆

ONE "BLACK psywar strike in Hanoi" of which Lansdale was particularly proud involved leaflets purportedly "signed by the Vietminh instructing Tonkinese [northern Vietnamese] on how to behave for the Vietminh takeover of the Hanoi region"—including instructions to make an inventory of their personal property so that the Vietminh would know how much to confiscate. Lansdale bragged that "the day following the distribution of these leaflets, refugee registration tripled. Two days later Vietminh currency was worth half the value prior to the leaflets."[45] In a midcentury forerunner of "fake news," another handbill showed a picture of Hanoi with three circles of nuclear annihilation superimposed on it, implying that it was about to be atomic-bombed by the United States. Other fliers claimed "Christ Has Gone to the South" and "The Virgin Mary Has Departed from the North."

When Polish and Russian ships arrived in the South to transport Vietminh sympathizers to the North, a pamphlet, attributed to a non-existent Vietminh Resistance Committee, reassured "the Vietminh they would be kept safe below decks from imperialist air and submarine attacks, and requested that warm clothing be brought." This was accompanied by a "rumor campaign that the Vietminh were being sent into China as railroad laborers."[46] Because this propaganda painted such a "scary picture" of life in the North, Lansdale claimed, "there was a really significant refusal to go North"[47]—not on the part of hardened Vietminh operatives, many of whom were ordered to remain behind in any case, but, rather, among the impressionable teenagers whom Hanoi hoped to lure north for insurgent training and subsequent infiltration back into the South.

To bolster morale in the South, Lansdale's team had a Vietnamese agent, a refugee journalist from the North, prepare a series of "Thomas Paine type" essays "on Vietnamese patriotism" that appeared in a newspaper owned by a Vietnamese woman who was "the mistress of an anti-American French civilian." "Despite anti-American remarks by her boy friend," Lansdale wrote, "we had helped her keep her paper from being closed by the government . . . and she found it profitable to heed our advice on the editorial content of her paper."[48] The Saigon Military Mission even hired a soothsayer to produce an almanac that predicted good fortune for the South and calamitous tidings for the North. So popular did this eight-page publication become that the CIA made a profit on it that was used to fund refugee resettlement.[49]

Many of these propaganda products were distributed in the South by Vietnamese soldiers in plain clothes; others were infiltrated into the North and distributed by North Vietnamese agents. One of these local agents, who happened to be the chief of police in Hanoi, was arrested by French police after an early-morning car chase through the city; the phony "Vietminh" posters that he was distributing were so convincing that he was held as a suspected Vietminh operative.[50] Lansdale had to ask Diem, who thought the police chief was a "traitor," to intercede with the French to get him released.[51]

The French were not the only ones fooled by Lansdale's black propaganda. In the summer of 1954, Lansdale received orders from CIA headquarters in Washington to investigate intelligence "that three Chinese Communist divisions had crossed the border into North Vietnam." He found that the reports originated with a rumor campaign that had been started by the South Vietnamese army's G-5, at his suggestion, to create the impression that the Vietminh were tools of Chinese imperialists. "Officials in Washington let it be known subsequently," Lansdale said, "that they did not appreciate the joke."[52]

Lansdale was later to deny that his propaganda efforts were responsible for the exodus of refugees from North to South Vietnam. "People don't leave ancestral homes that they care a lot about without a very good reason, particularly in Asia," he said. "So it took tremendous personal fear to get them to leave, and when a million of them did it, it wasn't just words and propaganda making them do it."[53] But Lansdale's propaganda unquestionably did help—as did his efforts to facilitate their movement. Bernard Fall, a leading authority on Vietnam, would write, "Although there is no doubt that hundreds of thousands of Vietnamese would have fled Communist domination in any case, the mass flight was admittedly the result of an extremely intensive, well-conducted, and, in terms of its objective, very successful American psychological warfare operation."[54]

Lansdale followed up this initial success by publicizing the fact that Vietnamese were voting with their feet against Communism, a "propaganda job" assisted by other CIA stations around the Far East.[55] There is no evidence that Tom Dooley ever became a CIA "asset," but even if he was not on the payroll, Lansdale helped to spread his story far and wide. This included persuading Diem to award a medal to Dooley along with other Americans who participated in the sealift. Lansdale typed up the proclamation himself.[56] Unfortunately, "Dr. America" did not have long to enjoy his fame; he was to die of cancer in 1961, at age thirty-four.

◆

THERE WAS yet another aspect of the exodus story, of which few were aware until the publication of the Pentagon Papers seventeen years later (leaked, ironically, by a Lansdale protégé): Lansdale had used Operation Passage to Freedom as a cover to infiltrate his own covert-warfare team, led by Lou Conein, into the North. While this paramilitary operation was arguably a violation of the Geneva Accords, as critics later charged, it was the mirror image, on a much smaller scale, of what the Vietminh were doing in leaving an estimated ten thousand cadres in the South.[57]

As the deadline approached for the French pullout on October 10, 1954, Hanoi became, in the words of the U.S. consul general, "a city of 'hello' and 'goodbye' as old guard takes leave and new teams arrive to continue the show." Houses and offices were stripped of furniture and boarded up.[58] The French even took with them the radium from the X-ray machines in the city's hospitals.[59] Conein and his operatives exploited the chaos to move into the abandoned residence of the French governor-general. They hot-wired half a dozen large Citroëns, left by their owners on the streets, and transported them back to Saigon by ship. The cars subsequently were adorned with yellow diplomatic license plates and used by the Saigon Military Mission; one of them replaced the dinky 2CV as Lansdale's personal vehicle.[60]

Conein's attempts at sabotage were less successful. One of his Vietnamese agents tried to destroy the largest and most modern printing presses in the North, Lansdale reported, but "Vietminh security agents already had moved into the plant and frustrated the attempt."[61] Taking matters into their own hands, Conein and Marine Captain Arthur "Nick" Arundel, a wealthy, "intense," and very youthful-looking graduate of Harvard,[62] sneaked explosives disguised as lumps of coal into the Hanoi railroad yard and broke into the bus depot to contaminate its oil supply[63]—actions that critics would later denounce, during the heyday of the anti–Vietnam War movement in the early 1970s, as "little more than terrorist acts."[64] If he noticed such criticisms, Conein did not care. But he did become indignant when David Halberstam wrote in *The Best and the Brightest* (1972) that the "Lansdale group" had put "sugar in the gas tanks of Vietminh trucks."[65] "Sugar?" Conein fumed. "That was a high-school trick, something a goddamn amateur might do, not a professional."[66] A professional like him used corrosive acid. The fumes from the acid canister nearly made Conein and Arundel pass out. Dizzy and weak-kneed, they had to mask their faces with handkerchiefs to finish the job.[67]

With a typical commando's love for blowing things up, Conein hoped to do more damage by igniting the giant oil tanks in Haiphong belonging to Standard Oil and Shell. But he was ordered to stand down by the embassy in Saigon. Lansdale explained that this was due to "U.S. adherence to the Geneva Agreement."[68] But it was just as likely that the U.S. government did not want to harm two giant Western oil companies and feared that if too much damage was traceable to the CIA, the Vietminh could retaliate against the U.S. consulate in Haiphong, which would remain open until that city was handed over in May 1955.

In addition to sabotaging the North, Conein established two "stay behind" networks. Nearly forty agents were recruited from two of the most prominent anti-Communist political parties—the Dai Viet and the Vietnam Nationalist Party (VNQDD). Both groups were transported separately in the summer of 1954 to a secret CIA training facility on the island of Saipan, where they received instruction in espionage along with "weapons, demolitions, and sabotage." In March 1955, twelve agents from the Dai Viet were brought back to Haiphong from Saipan. Conein briefed them, gave them forged papers with their cover identities (most were pretending to be fishermen), and sent them to various locations around the North. The following month, it was the turn of the VNQDD group. As more agents were recruited and trained, Conein continued to infiltrate them into the North as late as 1956, employing either motorized junks or parachute jumps from Civil Air Transport (CAT) aircraft.[69]

To supply these agents, the Lansdale team used CAT flights and Navy ships to bring in tons of supplies: radios, explosives, guns, ammunition, gold. A lot of the matériel was hidden in building basements covered with concrete to create a phony foundation. Some, almost sitcom style, was buried in coffins during phony funeral proceedings. The VNQDD group alone received fourteen radios, three hundred carbines, fifty pistols, a hundred thousand rounds of ammunition, and three hundred pounds of explosives.[70] This may have seemed a considerable armory, but it was only a pittance compared with what Lansdale described as the "huge quantities of weapons, ammunition, mines, grenades, and other materiel . . . being buried secretly by the Vietminh [in South Vietnam] before they withdrew."[71]

Dick Smith, who served as logistician for the Saigon Military Mission, recalled that at the "pool house" in Saigon, team members assembled crates of equipment and used a blowtorch to remove the MAAG insignia from the boxes. Then he would fly to the North with the crates. A DC-9 aircraft would swoop down to land on a remote jungle airstrip and Smith would hop out, meet a local Vietnamese contact with a truck, hand over his cargo, and take off again. Such missions were particularly incongruous because the CAT pilots, in keeping with their cover story of working for a commercial airline, wore the same kind of uniforms that Pan Am pilots might be expected to wear on a route from Los Angeles to New York. But instead of informing him to keep his seat in the full upright position for takeoff, CAT's pilots would ask Smith, "If we have to land in Indian country, which of these boxes should we get rid of before landing?"[72]

◆

LOU CONEIN had accomplished his mission, but his resistance networks failed to accomplish much. The efficient North Vietnamese security service penetrated the Dai Viet network and ran some of its personnel as double agents before arresting all of them in 1958. The next year they were given a show trial in Hanoi, at which the regime displayed some of the spy gear supplied by the Lansdale team—in the words of the historians Kenneth Conboy and Dale Andrade, "silenced submachine guns, explosives, small spring-loaded pistols hidden inside toothpaste tubes, and radio sets." Working in an atmosphere of haste and improvisation, Smith and other team members had not been as thorough as they should have been in "sanitizing" the equipment: while the weapons were untraceable, "the radios were clearly marked with U.S. Army Signal Corps plates." Most of these agents received long prison sentences; their leader was executed by firing squad. The VNQDD network lasted longer. Ten of its agents were uncovered in 1964 and put on trial the following year; two were executed and the rest sent to prison. Eleven other agents remained operational until 1974—that is, almost until the end of the South Vietnamese state and nearly twenty years after beginning their assignments.[73] But they did not carry out any substantial sabotage operations, and Donald Gregg, who served as CIA desk officer for Vietnam from 1962 to 1964, does not recall any important intelligence produced by Lansdale's agents or any others in the North.[74]

Left unanswered is the question of how these networks were ultimately exposed. The North Vietnamese claimed to have run across them by accident—for example, a lump of explosive "coal" was discovered in Hanoi during a police crackdown on black-market coal sales and traced back to its source. This may well have been true, or it could have been a cover story put out by a savvy intelligence service to protect its true source of information inside the South Vietnamese government.

One of the most successful North Vietnamese deep-cover agents in South Vietnam was, in fact, close to Lansdale and his team. Pham Xuan An became a well-known correspondent in Saigon, working for the *New York Herald Tribune*, Reuters, and *Time* magazine. He befriended prominent American correspondents such as David Halberstam and Morley Safer, all the while secretly sending intelligence reports to Hanoi. After the fall of South Vietnam in 1975, he was revealed to be a general in the North Vietnamese army. An had gotten his start as a Vietminh agent in 1954 while working for his cousin, Captain Pham Xuan Giai, in the South Vietnamese army's psychological warfare directorate, G-5, at a time when it was closely cooperating with the Saigon Military Mission. An said that his training in psychological operations came from Lansdale himself. Lansdale joked with him, because An seemed so artless, "An, you would make a terrible spy."[75] Lansdale even arranged for the Asia Foundation, a CIA front group, to send An to college in California.[76] An so admired the American operative—"Lansdale was excellent, really excellent," he later said—that he went so far as to imitate his mentor's habit of going everywhere with a dog, in his case a German shepherd. He was also close to Lou Conein (a "very good friend") and Rufus Phillips (a "close friend").[77]

Given An's proximity to the Saigon Military Mission, it is possible he played a role in exposing its operations in the North even if Lansdale did not intend to share any secrets with him. If An was not the culprit, there were plenty of other possible suspects; the South Vietnamese government was full of Communist moles.

Ultimately, the failure of Lansdale's sabotage and intelligence operations in North Vietnam—which stood in marked contrast to his success at resettling refugees in the South—was hardly surprising. The same fate befell other CIA operations in the early Cold War years to infiltrate agents into Communist countries. All ended, without exception, in tragedy, with agents swiftly captured and either imprisoned or killed. One of Rufus Phillips's Yale fraternity brothers, John "Jack" Downey, was shot down on such a mission over Chinese airspace in

1952; he would spend the next twenty years in a Chinese prison. Communist police states were simply too effective at internal surveillance and Western intelligence services were too riddled with Communist spies for such missions to have much chance of success.

This was a bitter lesson that Lansdale would learn anew when he was tasked nearly a decade later with penetrating Fidel Castro's Cuba.

15

Pacification

I guess there's nobody here as the personal representative of the
people of the United States. . . . So, I hereby appoint myself as
their representative—and we're walking out on you.
—EDWARD LANSDALE TO LIGHTNING JOE COLLINS

THE creation of modern nation-states in Europe was a protracted and bloody business. In the Middle Ages, the continent was divided into roughly a thousand political entities—duchies, free cities, kingdoms, republics, and the like. By 1789, there remained only 350 and by 1900 a mere 25.[1] Countless conflicts such as the War of the Roses, the Thirty Years' War, and the Wars of German Unification had to be fought before the map of Europe could assume its modern shape. The whole process took hundreds of years.

In South Vietnam, the nation-building experience began in earnest in mid-1954, and its first stages had to be completed before mid-1956, when a national reunification election was scheduled. Actually there was even less time than that. Ngo Dinh Diem's authority at first was so tenuous that, if he did not show immediate success, he would lose the support not only of local power brokers but also of his primary outside sponsors, France and the United States, which somehow expected

South Vietnam to develop virtually overnight the kind of strong and responsive central government that had taken centuries to emerge elsewhere. Even as he was supervising the movement of refugees from North Vietnam and trying to subvert the Hanoi regime, Edward Lansdale took on the herculean challenge of trying to consolidate Diem's power. He would have to figure out how to fill the power vacuum in the countryside that would be left by departing Vietminh cadres. But first he had to make sure that Diem wasn't toppled in a coup d'état.

◆

THE MOST immediate threat came from the armed forces chief of staff, General Nguyen Van Hinh, a career French officer. When Diem tried to give Hinh orders, the general replied that he answered only to Emperor Bao Dai. When Diem threatened to dismiss him, Hinh replied, in effect, that he would get rid of Diem first. Hinh dropped a broad hint to Lansdale of what he was up to by brandishing a silver cigarette box given to him by President Muhammad Naguib of Egypt, the leader along with Gamal Abdel Nasser of a military coup two years earlier.[2]

Behind the scenes, the army chief and the prime minister carried out what Lansdale described as a "dirty, gangster-type of warfare of tommy-gun fire from moving vehicles, grenades thrown into houses, kidnappings and torture."[3] Lansdale saw for himself the depth of enmity between Diem and Hinh on September 8, 1954, when he walked into the Defense Ministry to find the five-foot-tall defense minister Le Ngoc Chan in an armed confrontation with two of Hinh's men, Lieutenant Colonel Tranh Dinh Lan and Captain Pham Xuan Giai. They were pointing submachine guns at Chan, telling him they had orders to arrest him; Chan was holding a revolver, saying he was going to arrest *them*.[4] Lansdale defused this standoff, but the next week the rift became public knowledge when Hinh sent an armored platoon to "guard"—really, to seize—the South Vietnamese army radio station. Before long, the station was broadcasting vitriolic anti-Diem propaganda.

Lansdale knew that Lieutenant Nguyen Van Minh, the officer

in charge of the radio station, and his supervisor, Captain Giai, had attended the U.S. Army's Psychological Warfare School at Fort Bragg, North Carolina. He asked the Pentagon to find out whether there were any American officers who knew them. Word came back that Navy Lieutenant Lawrence Sharpe, currently helping to transport refugees from the North, had not only gone to school with Minh and Giai but had "housed them in his personal quarters at Fort Bragg."[5] Orders were immediately cut to send Sharpe to Saigon and assign him to the Saigon Military Mission.

As soon as Sharpe showed up, Lansdale drove him to the radio station. They arrived to find a tank swiveling its gun at Lansdale's Citroën. Undeterred, Lansdale banged on the radio-station door and demanded to see Lieutenant Minh. When Minh poked his head out, Lansdale told him, "I've got an old friend of yours here. Tell your goddamn tank to point his cannon some other direction so I can bring him in and we can talk to you."[6] Lansdale persuaded Minh to accept Sharpe as his "technical adviser," and Sharpe worked behind the scenes to change the station's message in stages. "Switch from character assassination of Diem," Lansdale instructed him, "to attacking him for not taking action against Communist subversion in the south, and then again switch from that to a plain attack against the Communists for their subversive work." It was a clever approach, even if Lansdale had to admit that it met with only "partial success."[7]

When Lansdale visited General Nguyen Van Hinh's home for dinner, he found "a beehive of activity, staff officers shouting into telephones, motorcycle messengers coming and going, and several unit commanders poring over maps of the Saigon metropolitan area."[8] Hinh dropped hints that he had selected October 26, 1954, as the date for his uprising. Lansdale thought fast about how he could avert the coup. He announced that "an opportunity had come up to take Hinh and his staff officers for a brief visit to the Philippines."[9] Hinh said regretfully that he was too busy to join the trip, notwithstanding his fond memories of the fleshpots of Manila, but he agreed that his key lieutenants—Lieutenant Colonel Tranh Dinh Lan, Captain Pham Xuan Giai, and Lieutenant Nguyen Van Minh—could go. So on the evening of October 25, 1954, Lansdale found himself winging his way over the South China Sea in a C-47 transport aircraft along with the three Vietnamese officers.[10] After a few days in Manila, Lansdale returned to Saigon to find that no coup had occurred. At the end of November, General Hinh finally agreed to step down and leave the country. He moved to France, where he eventually rose to become deputy chief of staff of the French air force.

In his memoir, Lansdale claimed that Hinh had called off his coup because he "had forgotten that he needed his chief lieutenants for key roles in the coup and couldn't proceed while they were out of the country with me."[11] That claim has been credulously repeated in most historical accounts, including the Pentagon Papers.[12] It seems unlikely, however, that Hinh, who was far from a half-wit, could have "forgotten" something so important. Rather, the whole episode suggests that the general was not as serious about staging a mutiny as he pretended to be. "In retrospect," the CIA's official historian concludes, "General Hinh's anti-Diem posturing looks like a French ploy to intimidate Diem into either cooperating or resigning, and Hinh's departure for exile in Paris in November suggests French acknowledgement of failure."[13] The French held Hinh back from launching a coup in no small part because President Eisenhower threatened to cut off aid to South Vietnam if Diem were overthrown.[14] But even if Lansdale's ploy was not as pivotal as he later pretended, it was, along with his suborning of the radio station, nevertheless a good example of his subtle and indirect approach to dealing with the most difficult political problems.

◆

IN THE Philippines, Lansdale had had to fight a two-front war, not only against Communist insurgents but also against adversaries within the U.S. government. Vietnam was no different. But whereas in his earlier posting the retired admiral Raymond Spruance had been a staunch supporter, here Lansdale could not always count on the backing of the U.S. ambassador.

Lansdale got along reasonably well with the "calm, low-key"[15] Donald Heath—"a very likeable person," he later said[16]—but Diem saw Heath as too pro-French, and he gave Lansdale a long message for transmittal to Washington asking that the ambassador be relieved. On October 18, 1954, Lansdale sent the cable straight to Allen Dulles, telling him that, in his own view, it would be "constructive [to] replace Heath soonest," provided that his replacement was "out of the top drawer."[17] Dulles shared the message with his brother the secretary of state, and Heath was replaced shortly thereafter, suffering the same fate that had already befallen General Albert Pierson, the Joint U.S. Military Advisory Group commander in the Philippines who had also run afoul of Lansdale at a time when he had the support of the powerful Dulles duo. But in this instance Lansdale's scheming backfired, which may be why he omitted any mention of it in his memoir.

President Eisenhower decided to replace Heath with General J. Lawton Collins, who had served under his command in Europe during World War II and later as deputy chief of staff when Ike was Army chief of staff. Subsequently, from 1949 to 1953, Collins had served as chief of staff in his own right, before becoming the U.S. representative to NATO's Military Committee. On November 8, 1954, he arrived in Saigon with a small entourage of military aides. Lansdale scrambled to learn what he could about the new ambassador with the gray hair, steely eyes, boyish face, and Southern accent. A West Point graduate from a large Irish Catholic family in New Orleans, the fifty-eight-year-old Collins had compiled a sterling record in World War II. A mere major in 1940, he had risen by 1942 to become the two-star commander of the Twenty-Fifth Infantry Division, leading it into combat on Guadalcanal and the Solomon Islands. The "Tropic Lightning" division's lightning bolt insignia accounted for his nickname, Lightning Joe. One of the few U.S. generals to see action in both the Pacific and the European theaters, Collins led the breakout from Normandy after D-Day and won praise from General Omar Bradley as "one of the outstanding field commanders in Europe."[18]

Lightning Joe was renowned as a "GI's general" who went wherever the fighting was the worst; in the Solomon Islands, he personally dueled with Japanese snipers.[19] He was also a skilled battlefield orator who always knew the right words to inspire his men. However, like a long line of American generals culminating in William West-moreland, he would turn out to be unsuited for the complexities and difficulties of Vietnam, where the threat did not come from enemy tanks rolling over the border. "Saigon," a veteran American diplomat noted, "was a confused, chaotic political environment where yes often meant no and the best staff work in the world could become meaning-less overnight."[20]

Lansdale would have cause to regret his role in Don Heath's recall as soon as he attended the first "country team" meeting that Collins convened at the U.S. embassy, at 39 Hàm Nghi Boulevard, a trian-gular office building near the Saigon River that did not yet have the fortress-like aspect that newly built American embassies around the world would acquire in the years ahead. Under Heath, meetings of the senior staff had been "friendly gatherings with much open discussion," Lansdale wrote. By contrast, Collins "insisted upon a more disciplined format, calling for brief oral reports from each member, after which we would all shut up and sit there while he told us what the situation *really* was like and what each of us was to do about it until the next weekly meeting. He was very much the boss, to whom we were to respond with a yes sir or a no sir, period."[21]

At that initial meeting, Collins outlined his priorities, which included paring back the costly South Vietnamese armed forces that U.S. taxpayers were funding, from 170,000 troops to 88,000.[22] Lans-dale spoke up to say that the general had ignored the need for the army to take control of rural areas being vacated by the Vietminh and to integrate sect militaries. Cutting back army ranks would be antitheti-cal to both goals. "You're out of order!" Collins barked. He explained in staccato tones that he was the personal representative of the presi-dent of the United States, that he set the priorities, and that there was no need to discuss them.

"Do you understand?" he asked icily.

Lansdale pushed his chair back and rose to his feet. "Yes sir, I understand," he said in his deceptively soft-spoken way. "I guess there's nobody here as the personal representative of the people of the United States. The American people would want us to discuss these priorities.

So, I hereby appoint myself as their representative—and we're walking out on you."

And out he walked. Or so he later told the story.[23]

Even Lansdale realized he might have gone too far. Years later he was to say, with a chuckle, "If I had been ambassador, I would have kicked me out of the country immediately."[24] But Lansdale was not as naïve or impetuous as he appeared. He had taken a risk in challenging the incoming ambassador, but even a four-star general would be reluctant, as his first act in office, to fire a man who was the personal representative *not* of the American people but of the CIA director—a director who happened to be the brother of his own boss, the secretary of state.

Instead of exiling Lansdale, Collins summoned him to his office for a "more in sorrow than in anger" upbraiding. "Gee, you're sure a hot-head aren't you?" Collins began.[25] Collins then lectured him in a fatherly tone, telling him that his behavior had been "sadly disappointing." As a military man, surely Colonel Lansdale "understood that there could be only one commander giving the orders." Lansdale agreed, but he pointed out that in this "highly complex" situation, Collins could not succeed if he were "to wear blinders and gags." Collins relented enough to let Lansdale brief him while he was lying down for a post-lunch rest. Lansdale spent hours sharing his ideas with Collins before he noticed that the jet-lagged ambassador was falling asleep. He apologized for taking up so much time and beat a "hasty retreat."[26]

This was symptomatic of how out of sync Collins and Lansdale were, and would remain. Lansdale later felt as if they were living "in two wholly separate worlds."[27] Locked into a rigid, conventional-war mindset, Collins would remain largely impervious to Lansdale's unconventional insights. In fairness, Lansdale's sometimes abrupt manner would impede his efforts to win over his skeptics. Lansdale seldom extended the same patience and understanding to his own superiors that he routinely gave to foreign leaders such as Ramon Magsaysay and Ngo Dinh Diem.

◆

GIVEN THE pressure he was under, Edward Lansdale reported to Pat Kelly, "Everyone says I'm losing weight and look like Hell."[28] A few days later, he told her, "I'm punch-drunk from no sleep and too much work."[29] Lansdale's spirits briefly lifted in early September 1954 when he was able to leave behind the small, cramped house on Rue Miche. He and Joe Redick moved into a more spacious, two-story house at 260 Rue Legrand de la Liraye. Not only did it have air-conditioned bedrooms and a large garage, but it also offered better protection from attack because it was set back farther from the street.[30] To make his meals, Lansdale hired a "grandmotherly" cook named Ti Bah. "She's doing her best to fatten me up," Ed wrote to Pat, "except that I still miss out on meals with so much running around."[31]

Ed bragged to Pat about the "20-foot-wide bed" in his bedroom but lamented, "What the hell is the good of an air-conditioned bedroom when I seldom get to use it, and at those times just go to bed with myself, of all people. You get seduced in my dreams, and quite thoroughly, but then I have to wake up from them." He lasciviously urged Pat to come to Saigon to "enjoy the air-conditioned bedroom." Pat sent back a typically peppery response—one of the few that survives among their correspondence: "I noticed that you have repeatedly commented on how intact your virginity is. Is this merely a ruse to get me talking about mine? I am not biting. I am awfully interested in the 20-foot bed you claim to have in your abandoned mansion. I sure can use a wide bed to get [out] the tiredness in my bones."[32]

To inaugurate the new house, Lansdale decided to throw a big party, his first one in Vietnam, even though he did not yet have enough glasses for a horde of guests. "You are cordially invited to bring your own glasses and an urge to make merry," read the invitation from Lansdale and Redick, who styled themselves "the fun-loving Boy Scouts."[33] A gaggle of more than two hundred people, a mixture of Vietnamese and Americans, accepted the invitation on the night of September 11, 1954. A Filipino nightclub band came over to offer entertainment and before long the guests were doing the tinikling, a traditional Philippine dance in which dancers step over and between bamboo poles—in this case, two of Lansdale's brooms. Lansdale claimed credit for introducing the dance into Vietnam, and would use it thereafter "as a real ice-breaker for parties."[34]

He would host many such gatherings in the years ahead in an attempt to break down political and social barriers among Vietnamese and Americans and to foster a spirit of friendship—as well as simply to have some fun in a high-pressure environment. An American reporter who worked in Saigon during this period called Lansdale's house "the place to be . . . it was where the action was."[35]

◆

ON DECEMBER 23, 1954, Lansdale departed Vietnam to spend Christmas in Manila, taking with him two of his young team members, Lieutenants Rufus Phillips and Frank "Zsa Zsa" Garber. In his typical manner, Lansdale went straight to the Malacañang Palace and wandered into a conference that President Ramon Magsaysay was having with Admiral Arthur Radford, chairman of the U.S. Joint Chiefs of Staff. By way of greeting, he asked Magsaysay whether the coffee was any good that morning. Radford turned around grinning and "said there was only one guy that informal in this part of the world."[36]

Much against Lansdale's will, Magsaysay dragged him that night to a state dinner; because Lansdale had nothing else to wear, Magsaysay lent him the very *barong Tagalog* shirt that he had worn at his inauguration. After being spurned by the chief American envoy in Saigon, Lansdale could now spend Christmas morning with a head of state and his family. Lansdale found Monching "moody, saying he was fed up with being president and with all the politicians." But Magsaysay "brightened up, and I guess stayed happy," Lansdale wrote, "because he told me later on that he changed into a more relaxed person with me close by."[37] Lansdale, too, turned into a more relaxed person in the Philippines, because he got to spend the rest of Christmas with his beloved Patching.[38]

Quickly going to work, Lansdale also had plenty of business to conduct in Manila. He wanted to avoid insinuations that American "imperialists" were arriving to replace the French—a standard trope of Vietminh propaganda—by putting a Philippine face on aid to Saigon.[39] Ever the hard-bitten commando, Lou Conein cynically grumbled that Lansdale's idea was that "all the little brown brothers in Asia should become one big happy family and help one another."[40]

Lansdale had already set up with his Filipino friend Oscar Arellano, "balloon-shaped, energetic, an architect by profession,"[41] an organization known as Operation Brotherhood (OB) to bring Filipino doctors and nurses to South Vietnam to provide free medical services. Arellano had also been involved in an earlier Lansdale effort to safeguard the 1953 Philippine presidential election. Once again the CIA was secretly footing the bill. By the spring of 1955, more than a hundred OB doctors and nurses would be treating two thousand patients a day at ten clinics, their efforts focused not only on newly arrived refugees but also on rural residents in districts newly freed from Vietminh control.[42]

To complement OB's efforts, Lansdale created Freedom Company, another CIA-funded organization run by another Filipino friend who had been a leader in the CIA-supported National Movement for Free Elections (NAMFREL). Frisco "Johnny" San Juan was a thirty-two-year-old former anti-Japanese guerrilla who had been commander of the Philippine Veterans Legion. Lansdale called him "a hard-working idealist with executive ability."[43] San Juan brought over fellow Philippine army veterans to teach the South Vietnamese how to handle weapons and maintain military equipment. "I knew we were being helped surreptitiously by the U.S. government, but I believed in what we were doing—I believed in the fight against Communism," Frisco San Juan explained sixty years later, by then a small, frail, wizened man of ninety-two sitting on the patio of his Manila house, a walker next to his chair, as the wind whistled through the palm trees. "Why should I feel guilty about getting the U.S. government's help? I wasn't betraying my country."[44]

When Lansdale first broached the idea of importing experts from the Philippines, Diem scoffed that "the Vietnamese didn't need the help of a bunch of orators and nightclub musicians," a reference to the fact that "most of the dance bands in Asia at the time were made up of Filipinos."[45] But when Diem actually met San Juan and other Filipinos who had been active in putting down the Huk Rebellion, he was won over and agreed to sign a contract with Freedom Company. The funds, of course, came covertly from the CIA.

Diem may have been swayed because one of the very first experts that Freedom Company sent to Saigon was there to protect him. Lansdale persuaded Magsaysay to dispatch Colonel Napoleon "Poling" Valeriano, who was serving as commander of the Presidential Guard Battalion, to reorganize Diem's bodyguards.[46] Freedom Company would also provide bodyguards for Lansdale himself in the form of a couple of Philippine army veterans, Proculo L. Mojica and Amador T. Maik. Mojica later recalled that when Lansdale walked through a marketplace in Saigon he would tell him, "Open your eyes wide, Proc. Don't hesitate to pull that trigger if you see anything funny." Fingering his hidden pistol, he recalled, "There were times that I felt I was in Jap-occupied Manila during the Pacific War."[47]

Employing Filipino instructors, Freedom Company also undertook covert training in the Philippines to teach anti-Communist Vietnamese the art of guerrilla warfare; if the Vietminh ever overran South Vietnam, they were supposed to serve as the nucleus of a resistance network. This effort was soon expanded to train South Vietnamese soldiers in Lansdale-style counterinsurgency in order, as Lansdale explained, to get the Vietnamese "gently 'brain-washed' by the Filipinos."[48]

◆

HAVING FINISHED his business in the Philippines, Lansdale winged his way back to Saigon on December 27, 1954. He wrote to Pat Kelly, "Felt blue as hell New Year's Eve without you—sure as hell a contrast to Christmas, which you made so happy for me."[49] But Pat did visit Vietnam early in the new year. She and Ed got a chance for some oceanside relaxation, and she taught Iron Mike O'Daniel to mix martinis the way she liked them and to dance the tinikling. He was so smitten that he took to calling her "Colonel Kelly."[50] This was the first of several trips to Vietnam that Pat would make as her relationship with Ed became increasingly common knowledge among his colleagues.

Meanwhile, Ed was reassuring his wife that he had tried to contact her on the telephone "all the time I was in the Philippines—even to getting Magsaysay to try it himself—but either the circuits were out or you were." He concluded with a plea for Helen to let him "know all about Christmas at home." "It's awful being so far away and under pressures of our peculiar combat and to miss all the things we are fighting for, without even being able to explain what's going on."[51]

In truth, by now the tropical capitals, Manila and Saigon, felt more like home than did wintry Washington. As Ed later wrote to Helen, "It's a sad commentary on the way I've had to live, but I know the streets of Saigon and Manila far better than Washington which is now supposed to be my hometown."[52] He knew that Helen did not like how deeply he was becoming immersed in Vietnamese life, just as he had previously immersed himself in Filipino life. "Helen won't like this," he wrote to his family, "because it sounds like Magsaysay, but a group of Tonkinese brought in some food and claim that I now belong to Vietnam. The same folks who fed me a colorless liquid which turned out to be essence of cockroach. Honest injun. A Central Vietnam delicacy. I should pick my countries better, huh. At a staff meeting at the Ministry of Defense here, the Secretary of State for Morale Action explained to the staff that I really wasn't an American, but had been loaned to Vietnam by the Philippines. Nuts."[53] Helen's groan upon reading this would have been loud enough to carry the whole length of the Pacific.

Essentially abandoned by her swashbuckling husband, Helen Lansdale was feeling miserable, as Ed's friend, Wesley R. Fishel of Michigan State University, found when he saw her a few months later. "She apparently thinks you're one hell of a lug, since, among other things, you forgot her birthday (or was it your anniversary?)," Fishel wrote to Ed. "She sounded very lonely, and had I not been such a gentleman, I would have taken her out to dinner."[54] It was her birthday that Lansdale had forgotten; Helen turned fifty-four in 1955. But, for good measure, he forgot their twenty-second wedding anniversary, too.[55]

◆

THE YEAR 1955 brought additional duties for Lansdale. He and his team were writing what was in effect a counterinsurgency blueprint for South Vietnam, even if the word "counterinsurgency" did not yet exist. The preferred term was "pacification." Ngo Dinh Diem did not like this word, however, because he associated it with the French. So in deference to his sensibilities Lansdale dubbed his agenda "national secu-rity action." Implementing this agenda was an urgent priority because the Vietminh were due to pull out of South Vietnam by April 1955, leaving large areas bereft of any authority. South Vietnam had few trained civil servants, and few members of this privileged caste had any desire to live among the peasants—most had joined the civil service precisely to escape such a fate. Lansdale urged that the army be given the lead role in delivering government services to the most dangerous areas.[56] His memorandum on "National Security Action (Pacification)" was issued virtually unchanged by Diem on December 31, 1954.[57]

A few days later Lansdale laid out his pacification ideas in a long memorandum for Lightning Joe Collins, essentially echoing what he had written to Diem. He began portentously: "We have no other choice but to win here or face an increasingly grim future, a heritage which none of us want to pass along to our offspring." And what would it take to win? Lansdale, with Cassandra-like clarity, listed three imperatives whose historical significance could not be underestimated. First, elimi-nate "dangerous frictions existing among key members of the U.S. team here." (Oblivious to the rivalries playing out around him, Collins scrib-bled dismissively in the margin, "Rumors from newspapermen based on cocktail stories.") Second, implement an "operating philosophy of helping the Vietnamese to help themselves" so as not to "merely make them more dependent on us." And third: "We must then set about con-vincing, and accomplishment is most convincing, the people that their own future (and that of their children and children's children) will be more rewarding under our system than under Communism—more rewarding politically or socially, economically, and spiritually."

Having outlined what needed to be done, Lansdale concluded with a suggestion for who could do it. He proposed that the ambassador appoint *him* to "bring about a coordination of the efforts of our entire team, starting with the U.S. team and, through them, the Vietnamese and French." Collins might have had his differences with Lansdale, but he could see a good idea when it was presented to him. On the margin he scrawled, "Designated Lansdale to coordinate our phases of pro-gram under Gen. O'Daniel's direction."[58] Thanks to a virtuoso display of bureaucratic maneuvering—a rarity in his career—Lansdale had become the first American charged with overseeing counterinsurgency in Vietnam, a responsibility that in years to come would be exercised by a vast, ponderous bureaucracy.

To go along with his new responsibilities as "half soldier and half diplomat,"[59] Lansdale received a new position. In December 1954, Collins worked out an agreement with General Paul Ely, the French commander, to transfer responsibility for training South Vietnamese troops to American advisers by July 1, 1955. To take charge of training during the transition, they agreed to create a joint Franco-American organization named TRIM (Training Relations and Instruction Mission)—"one of those screwy military names coined to get some nice initials," Lansdale explained.[60] The French assigned 200 officers to its staff; the Americans 68, a figure that grew by summer 1955 to 120.[61] There were four divisions at TRIM, for the Army, Navy, Air Force, and "national security" (i.e., pacification). Colonel Lansdale was designated the first head of the National Security Division, the only one of the four advising the Vietnamese on ongoing operations. It was a title designed, he joked to Pat Kelly, "to keep a fellow working 22 hours a day and happy."[62]

Iron Mike O'Daniel gave him typically concise marching orders: "Sky's the limit, keep peace in the family (meaning MAAG, the French etc.), and get going dammit."[63]

◆

"I HAVE now moved to [TRIM]," Ed wrote to Pat at the end of January 1955, "where I can save the world except for Wednesday afternoons off, and Saturday afternoons off, and Sundays off, it says in the big mimeographed print here."[64] His new office was a shed with duckboards over its dirt floor, two bare lightbulbs dangling from their cords, and, for furniture, folding chairs, field tables, and open crates to hold files.[65]

Both Lansdale's immediate superior at TRIM and his deputy were French. He got along well with his deputy, Lieutenant Colonel Jacques Romain-Desfossés, a "tough" and "tanned" paratrooper who sported a red beret and a monocle.[66] Destined to go to Algeria soon to fight in another dirty war, he was an old Indochina hand, and he seemed to have the best interests of the Vietnamese at heart, thereby endearing himself to Lansdale. Lansdale did not get along as well with his boss, Colonel Jean Carbonel, who was TRIM's chief of staff. Lansdale viewed Carbonel as an unrepentant colonialist; Carbonel viewed Lansdale as a naïve meddler in France's traditional sphere of influence. Their feud was straight out of an *opéra bouffe*. Carbonel turned his back on Lansdale at parties and refused to speak to him directly. Instead, while looking straight at Lansdale, the English-speaking Carbonel would relay messages to him through his adjutant, who was standing nearby. After Lansdale replied, Carbonel would ask the adjutant, "What did he say?" forcing him to repeat Lansdale's words.

Lansdale would get his revenge at receptions by putting his arm around Carbonel's shoulders and, in the most "grating American manner," loudly exclaim, "This guy is my buddy. You treat him right, you hear?" This would make Carbonel "explode," angrily shaking Lansdale's arm off his shoulder.[67]

Lansdale suspected the French officers at TRIM of reporting about him to one of the French intelligence services. "Once in a while," Lansdale said, these officers "would have the grace to blush when I came upon them as they were busy writing reports of my daily activities, presumably for a parent service."[68] Once-secret documents from the French archives reveal that their operatives watched his house and movements as well.[69]

Lansdale blamed the French for their strained relations, but he contributed to the tension with his own prejudice—as symbolized by his refusal to ever visit France. One of his team members, Joe Baker, was later puzzled why Lansdale had "such a great dislike or hatred of the French"[70]—an attitude not shared either by Baker or by Joe Redick, who said, "I liked the French that we worked with very much, except for maybe one or two who were very anti-American."[71] By contrast, Lansdale's letters positively bristled with anti-French animus, a sentiment fully shared by his protégé Ngo Dinh Diem. "My facetious recommendation to the ambassador," he wrote home, "was that we bring in American advisers throughout and pay the French to send all their advisors to Moscow where they can teach the Russians how to make a really complex bureaucracy."[72]

Lansdale's anti-French bias was prevalent among Americans in Vietnam. They thought they had little to learn from the French, who had failed to win their war against the Vietminh. Little did they suspect that they would soon repeat and even exceed most of their forerunners' mistakes.

◆

DESPITE THE mutual distrust among the South Vietnamese, French, and Americans, they were all supposed to work together to pull off the first big test of their nation-building prowess: Operation Liberty to reoccupy the Ca Mau Peninsula, jutting out into the South China Sea at the very tip of South Vietnam. It was due to be evacuated by the Vietminh in February 1955. When a group of French and American officers gathered for a briefing on the Ca Mau plans, the Vietnamese commander of the operation, Lieutenant Colonel Duong Van Duc, gave such an uninspired presentation that Iron Mike O'Daniel started asking some tough questions—until Lansdale pulled him aside and explained that Duc was not briefing the *real* plan. He was making one up on the spot because he was afraid that if he briefed the real operation the French would sabotage it.[73]

While the Vietnamese were willing to tell the Americans what they were up to, they were eager to run Operation Liberty all by themselves. It took all of Lansdale's persuasive powers to win permission for two members of his staff, Lieutenant Rufus Phillips and Lieutenant Colonel Samuel Karrick, to observe the operation. The soft-spoken Karrick would supervise logistics from the Vietnamese army command post at Soc Trang, a town in the Mekong Delta just north of Ca Mau, while the good-natured Phillips, pretending to be a foreign reporter, would go in with the troops. At more than six feet tall and 220 pounds, with the build of the Yale defensive tackle he had once been (albeit at a time when linemen were not as jumbo-sized as they would subsequently become) and with a fair complexion, Rufe would cut a conspicuous figure among the shorter and darker Vietnamese, giving rise to a new nickname: *le monstre aimable* (the likeable monster).[74] Also going along would be Colonel Joe Banzon, a Philippine army officer who was Ramon Magsaysay's informal envoy to South Vietnam. While getting the South Vietnamese to accept even Phillips was a major struggle, Lightning Joe Collins was dismayed to hear that only one very junior officer was going on such an important mission. Why weren't more senior advisers involved, he demanded? Iron Mike O'Daniel replied that Phillips was "one of Ed's people." Collins was satisfied. He probably thought that Phillips's lowly rank was just a cover.[75]

Colonel Duc was as resistant to letting Filipino doctors and nurses accompany him as he was to American advisers, even though he had only one army doctor of his own—hardly sufficient for his own troops, much less for the civilians of Ca Mau. Lansdale overcame this obstacle by rounding up "several of the prettiest nurses" from Operation Brotherhood and flying out to meet Colonel Duc and his staff at their headquarters in Soc Trang. At lunch, he made sure that the best-looking Filipinas were seated next to Duc and his senior officers. "Lunch had hardly started," Lansdale later wrote, "before the Vietnamese had decided that Philippine medical teams simply must accompany them into Camau."[76]

Prior to the start of Operation Liberty, Rufe Phillips had launched a training program to teach the troops how to interact with the populace. A courteous driving class stressed "the importance of not alienating the population by killing their chickens or running people off the road," with prizes for the best drivers. The psychological-warfare unit of the South Vietnamese army put on plays to hammer the point home for illiterate soldiers. In one version, Lansdale wrote, "the Good Soldier would pay the villagers for a chicken, while the Bad Soldier would steal one over the Villagers' protests; afterward the Villagers would talk about the soldiers, with friendly words for the Good Soldier's unit but with Villagers going to help the local guerrillas attack the other unit, the Bad Soldier's unit."[77] The classes and plays were well received, but after one good-driving class, Phillips noted, the soldiers got right back into their trucks "and barreled off in various directions to their units, scattering chickens, pigs, and people right and left." "A single lecture was not going to change ingrained habits."[78]

The operation began on February 8, 1954. Phillips, wearing civilian clothes with a Beretta automatic concealed in the small of his back, rode along with Colonel Duc in his jeep. They made slow progress down a dilapidated dirt road zigzagged by Vietminh trenches designed to impede French army movements. They saw many banana, mango, and palm trees but few people. The inhabitants were hiding, because they had been warned by the Vietminh that they would be raped and robbed by the invading troops. Around noon, they reached Ca Mau Town, where they found ramshackle buildings still pockmarked with bullet holes. In the middle of the square was a monument to the brave fighters of the Vietminh; hardly anyone was visible.

The population's wariness began to recede the next day when an Operation Brotherhood medical team set up shop with a sign out front: "Free Medical Clinic, All Are Welcome." By midmorning, more than fifty people were waiting to be treated, and the doctors and nurses worked without stopping until nightfall. The troops also distributed blankets and mosquito nets and fixed roads and bridges. Psychological-warfare soldiers drove around with loudspeakers proclaiming, "We are different from the Vietminh who left you in poverty and disease. We will help you."[79] Before long, the people demonstrated their growing trust by alerting troops to secret arms caches and cadres left behind by the Vietminh.

A major failing, however, was that the troops did not penetrate the U Minh forest, notorious as both a Vietminh stronghold and a breeding ground for cerebral malaria and other deadly diseases. Lansdale figured that eventually the Vietminh would leave this uncongenial environment on their own. He was wrong; the forest would remain a Communist stronghold throughout America's subsequent war in Vietnam.[80] But, on the whole, Operation Liberty had gone as well as anyone could have expected—and with far less American involvement than in the years ahead.

◆

THE NEXT major effort to reclaim an area from the Vietminh was Operation Giai Phong (Breaking Chains). It was focused on southern

Quang Ngai and northern Binh Dinh Provinces in central Vietnam, an area twice as large as Ca Mau with a population of a million and a half people. The South Vietnamese commander here was Colonel Le Van Kim, who had been born in a village in Binh Dinh and was one of the few Vietnamese to graduate from the French General Staff College. To assist him, Lansdale had the Saigon Military Mission prepare an "after-action" report on the Ca Mau operation, along with a plan for Breaking Chains, both of which Kim was then allowed to present to the Vietnamese high command as his own handiwork. This was the kind of "under the table" help that Lansdale favored, so as to allow his local partners to gain "face."[81] All of Kim's troops received a Lansdalian code of conduct printed on pocket-size cards. Its theme: "Every soldier a civic action agent."

This operation began on April 22, 1954, and, like Operation Liberty, encountered no resistance—just wary villagers uncertain of what these heavily armed men were up to. Once again Rufe Phillips, who was winning Lansdale's admiration as an "outstanding psychological warrior,"[82] was the only foreign adviser allowed to go along, and once again Operation Brotherhood worked to win over the public with free medical care. Repeating the experience of Operation Liberty, as the people became used to the troops' presence they began to point out hidden Vietminh weapons caches and to identify stay-behind Vietminh cadres.[83] To discredit the Vietminh cadres as they were leaving, Lansdale sent word in the name of the Vietminh to the people of Binh Dinh, asking them to redeem their Vietminh currency for Bank of Indochina piastres at the Vietminh's official evacuation point. "Thousands traveled to Qui Nhon," Lansdale boasted, "where red-faced Vietminh lamely explained that they had no money."[84]

Despite such coups, there was a fundamental problem common to both this operation and its predecessor: there was no capable and honest civilian governance team ready to come in and take over from the army once it departed. Lansdale had tried to address this deficiency by persuading Diem to create a Civic Action Commission under a dynamic former Vietminh officer named Kieu Cong Cung. He trained students who had arrived in the South as refugees from the North to don black pajamas and bring a semblance of governance to the villages in accord with a "Three Withs" mantra: "eat with, sleep with, and work with the people." By October 1955, forty-six civic-action teams would be deployed in twenty-five provinces.[85] Other efforts to train administrators were launched by a team from Michigan State University, led by Wesley Fishel and funded in part by the CIA.[86] But even the best-trained administrators would be undermined by the corruption and lethargy of the Saigon government, the villagers' xenophobic resistance to outsiders, and growing attacks from reconstituted Communist insurgents. The lack of effective civilian follow-up would render Lansdale's 1955 pacification successes as transitory as the "surge" in Iraq from 2007 to 2008.

That problem was not, however, at first evident. Operation Breaking Chains appeared to be so successful that Lansdale urged Diem, who was normally loath to leave his palace, to travel to the scene to claim credit. The premier wanted Lansdale to go with him, but Lansdale refused—he did not want to be seen as the kingmaker. He urged Diem to take only a few French officials and correspondents.[87]

On the morning of May 26, 1955, Diem's C-47 landed in a cloud of dust on a dirt airstrip outside Qui Nhon, the coastal city that was the capital of Binh Dinh Province. A large crowd of Vietnamese villagers "dressed in traditional black pajamas and conical hats" was waiting along with Colonel Kim and Lieutenant Rufus Phillips. Kim drove the prime minister into town in his open jeep, Diem standing and ceremoniously waving as if he were the Queen of England. The entire route was lined five and ten deep. Suddenly the jeep stopped and Diem plunged into the spectators. Phillips, who was in the next jeep, observed the crowd go wild: "all the traditional Vietnamese restraint was gone." He was struck by the "remarkable response" Diem had received in an "area completely controlled by the Vietminh for nine years"—a reaction that was "too genuine and spontaneous" to have been "coerced."[88]

Lansdale had done a virtuoso job of orchestrating the pacification program. But all of his initiatives would be for naught if Diem could not hold on to power in Saigon. Yet even as pacification was occurring in the countryside, the prime minister was being forced to battle for his survival in the capital. Lansdale cleverly had helped to defuse General Nguyen Van Hinh's coup, but other plotters would not be so easily deterred. The resulting battles would offer the supreme test of Diem's survival skills and Lansdale's advisory skills.

16

The Viper's Nest

There was a sudden madness that nearly tore Vietnam apart at the seams.

—EDWARD LANSDALE

"ONE man's terrorist is another man's freedom fighter." Never has this hoary adage been more applicable than in the case of Trinh Minh Thé (pronounced *tay*), a warlord who was reviled by the French as a mass murderer and revered by many Vietnamese as a hero. Both sides could agree on one thing: he would play a paramount role in determining whether the Ngo Dinh Diem regime would live or die. In fact, the chief challenge to Diem's rule in 1954–55 did not come from Hanoi. Ho Chi Minh at that point was too focused on consolidating his own authority in North Vietnam to actively challenge Diem's nation-building aspirations. The primary obstacles were the three sects—the Cao Dai, the Hoa Hao, and the Binh Xuyen—which fielded their own armies. And no sect general was more prominent or mercurial than Trinh Minh Thé.

Trinh Minh Thé would become notorious in the English-speaking world following the publication in late 1955 of Graham Greene's *The Quiet American*. The novel features a series of terrorist explosions in

Saigon that are blamed on Thé and indirectly on Alden Pyle, a naïve young CIA officer who is revealed to be helping him. In January 1952, there was, in fact, a series of bombings in Saigon. Thé, who hated the Communists and the colonialists with equal fervor, was responsible, but at that stage he did not have American support; the United States was still backing the French war effort. Norman Sherry, Greene's biographer, quotes an unnamed CIA officer: "To my knowledge no single agency official was—at that time—in contact with Colonel Thé. And I would know."[1] Yet the French blamed the Americans for assisting in the killing of their countrymen, and it was from them that Greene picked up the story. The French already hated Thé for dispatching a grenade thrower who in 1951 had assassinated the French commander in Cochin China. Thus it is not surprising that when Lansdale became involved with Thé, French hostility toward him became venomous.

In real life rather than fiction, Lansdale's relationship with Trinh Minh Thé began in September 1954, more than two and a half years after the Saigon terrorist bombings. At a time when Lansdale already was preoccupied heading off coups, undermining North Vietnam and moving refugees from the North, Diem asked him to take on another task: to persuade Thé to integrate his men into the national army. Unknown to Lansdale, Diem's brother Ngo Dinh Nhu was carrying on his own negotiations to achieve the same result.[2] But Lansdale, as the representative of the United States, had prestige and resources that Nhu could not match.

Thé was only thirty-two years old but already, in Lansdale's words, a "legendary rebel guerrilla chief"[3] who had been described by one correspondent as "the most charming cut-throat [he] had met."[4] Originally trained along with other Cao Dai militiamen by the Japanese during World War II, Thé had at first fought alongside the Vietminh before turning, along with the rest of the Cao Dai, against Ho Chi Minh. With French help, the Cao Dai formed a militia to protect themselves against Communist encroachments. Thé became its chief of staff. In 1951, however, he broke off from the mainstream Cao Dai and began to fight both the Vietminh and the French in the hope of creating an independent, non-Communist state. By 1954, he was in command of twenty-five hundred battle-hardened fighters operating out of Nui Ba Den (Black Virgin) Mountain, an extinct volcano more than three thousand feet high located sixty miles northeast of Saigon.

Ed Lansdale and Joe Redick set off in a car with several other teammates to find this mysterious warlord on September 15, 1954, wearing casual clothes as though out for a picnic, with guns carefully tucked away. They cruised down the highway past "lonely watch-towers and little roadside forts siting in the rice paddies" and then rattled along a "rutted dirt road" until they were surprised by a group of guerrillas who emerged silently from the jungle. In the lead, Lansdale noted, was a youth "no more than five feet tall and maybe weighing ninety pounds dripping wet. . . . Wearing a faded khaki shirt and trousers, tennis shoes on his feet, weaponless, hatless, he looked as if he might be a guide sent to take me to his leader." Lansdale was astonished to learn that "*this* wiry youngster was the villainous guerrilla hated by the French!"[5]

Lansdale and Redick hid their car in the jungle and hiked with Thé up the mountain. Eventually they reached a small shelter in the jungle that served as Thé's headquarters. Their conversation required two translators—one of Thé's aides translated from Vietnamese into French and Redick from French into English—supplemented by facial expressions and gestures. But then, Lansdale had found in the Philippines that even a complete absence of any common tongue did not impede his efforts to communicate with Negrito tribesmen. Lansdale found himself liking Thé "instinctively," and Thé, in turn, took a liking to Lansdale. Lansdale stressed that Americans were dedicated to principles of liberty. "That's what we fight for!" Thé replied. Lansdale urged him to join the South Vietnamese army. Thé said that this would be a good idea in principle, but there were too many "bad elements" in the army—too many "French officers" such as General Nguyen Van Hinh. He did promise to take care of Diem in case he was overthrown by Hinh and in principle confirmed his support for the Diem government. He also promised to release three French prisoners he was holding.[6]

The rest of the visit was spent with Thé taking Lansdale around to see his guerrillas—"platoon after platoon of barefooted men dressed in the *calicot noir* pajamas of the southern farmers." Thé's men were so impoverished that every time Lansdale went from one platoon to another a runner went ahead of him carrying to the next platoon commander the only "French officer's shoulder insignia" in the entire camp. But their weapons were immaculately clean, and more munitions were being manufactured in makeshift jungle workshops run by anti-Communist Chinese expatriates. "Outside of the Foreign Legion troops, for whom I have real respect as fighting men, I feel that these troops are the toughest in the country," Lansdale wrote.[7]

A few weeks later, Lansdale received word that Trinh Minh Thé was going to see him at his house in Saigon. When Lansdale stepped outside, he found cars full of French troops who had heard that Thé was coming and were ready to shoot the guerrilla chief on the spot. Suddenly a small sedan turned the corner and began heading toward Lansdale's bungalow. All eyes examined the car's occupants, the tension mounting with every yard that it advanced. "The driver was a small man, wearing nondescript khakis, an old hat pulled down over his eyes," Lansdale noted. "The passenger on the back seat was a fat and prosperous-looking Vietnamese, dressed in a white sharkskin suit, fanning himself with a panama hat." As the driver sprang out to open the back door, Lansdale saw that it was none other than Trinh Minh Thé. Lansdale escorted the fat passenger, who turned out to be Thé's interpreter, into the house, while loudly telling the "chauffeur" to go around to the kitchen "where there would be refreshment for him." Thé had come seeking Lansdale's help to arrange a truce between his own forces and those of the Hoa Hao general Ba Cut. Lansdale had to explain that he had no influence with Ba Cut. So the fighting resumed. Thé badly wounded Ba Cut; his life was saved only because the French evacuated him to a hospital.[8]

A few months later, after more behind-the-scenes negotiations involving Ngo Dinh Nhu as well as Lansdale, the renegade warlord finally agreed to join the national army. On February 13, 1955, Thé and his twenty-five hundred men marched through Saigon toward a reviewing stand where the prime minister and other notables were gathered. The troops wore their black pajamas, faded to a "rusty gray."

The outer ranks wore sneakers, the inner ranks no shoes at all. "The absence of heavy boots made the march seem almost ghostly," Lansdale wrote, although their weapons remained in excellent shape, clean and ready to be used. A French officer sneered, "Look at what Lansdale calls soldiers!" Lansdale turned around and shot back, in a retort that won him no French friends, "Hold it! You French types were never able to beat them!"[9]

Lansdale was feeling triumphal that day as Thé's men gave him "big grins" and "extra salutes." Thé's decision to join forces with Diem was the first "public moment of real fun" he had had since Ramon Magsaysay's presidential inauguration fourteen months earlier.[10]

◆

NUMEROUS OBSERVERS would claim that Lansdale had bribed Thé and other warlords to join Diem's side. Lansdale always denied it, even if he did occasionally slip up and refer to "payoffs" himself.[11] "I know of no bribery of the sect leadership by Ngo Dinh Diem, by France, or by the U.S.," he said.[12] Lansdale insisted that "the most I ever 'paid' him was a cup of coffee or a meal when he visited me,"[13] and that Thé more than repaid the favor by giving him a pair of mongooses, which his poodle, Pierre, forced to live under the refrigerator, where they took "turns hissing and growling at him."[14] Instead of bribing Thé, Lansdale claimed to have enticed him with a vision of "something he had wanted all his life, a free united country."[15]

The controversy over Lansdale's relations with the sect leaders was not dissimilar to that involving T. E. Lawrence, a figure to whom Lansdale was now being compared. (The French had taken to calling him "Lawrence of Asia," which in their minds was hardly a compliment, given how Lawrence had schemed to stymie their colonial designs in the Middle East.) Lawrence had been accused of buying the loyalty of Arab tribal leaders, but a British officer who worked alongside him said, "Lawrence could certainly not have done what he did without the gold, but no one else could have done it with ten times the amount." In truth, Lawrence was so successful because he had "established himself by sheer force of personality" among the Bedouin tribes.[16] In Lansdale's case, his offers of friendship and his appeals to the patriotism of men such as Thé were not insignificant; previously Thé had refused to take money from the French. But, contrary to Lansdale's denials, his idealistic appeals were combined with more tangible inducements to "rally" to Diem.

The entire dispute over whether Lansdale "bribed" Thé and other sect chieftains seems to be more semantic than anything else because Lansdale, at least in private, did not deny providing funds. His own CIA report was to say, "At Ambassador Heath's request, the U.S. secretly furnished Diem with funds for Thé, through the SMM [Saigon Military Mission]."[17] Whether this constituted pay, as Lansdale preferred to describe it, or bribes, the word generally used by others (including his CIA colleagues), is a matter of taste. Published estimates of the total spent by the CIA to win over the sect leaders are in the range of twelve million dollars, equal to a whopping hundred million dollars in today's currency.[18] The CIA's in-house history says there is "no basis" for this immense figure, an assertion echoed by Lansdale without, however, providing an alternative accounting.[19]

Lansdale was willing to spend money not only to win over the sect leaders but even to kill them if necessary. In a section of the Saigon Military Mission report not declassified until 2014, he admitted furnishing two million piastres ($57,000) in a "large suitcase" to Diem to pay a former Vietminh activist who had vowed "to get rid of" Ba Cut "through Vietminh who are close to this Hoa Hao rebel." The scheme never came to anything, and Diem, "somewhat embarrassed," returned the money, but Lansdale's willingness to back the operation exposed a ruthless streak that would surface once again a few years later when he was asked by the Kennedy administration to "get rid of" Fidel Castro.[20]

Lansdale was enough of a realist to provide the necessary cash to achieve his objectives, even if it required a murder for hire, but he was so eager to protect his image as an idealist that he was deeply reluctant to admit what he was up to, not least to himself. He was not as naïve and unworldly as he pretended to be, even if he had a powerful ability, which might be traced back to his upbringing in Christian Science, to repress unseemly aspects of reality that he preferred not to acknowledge.

—

WHATEVER THE exact amount, the CIA payoffs to the sects were insufficient to avert an uprising against Ngo Dinh Diem. The prime minister had alienated the Binh Xuyen, whom he considered to be "gangsters of the worst sort,"[21] by revoking their license in January 1955 to operate the Grand Monde casino, a major source of revenue. He also threatened to end Binh Xuyen control of the Saigon-Cholon police. The Binh Xuyen leader Bay Vien responded on March 3, 1955, by forming a United Front of Nationalist Forces with the Cao Dai and the Hoa Hao to oppose Diem. But while the sects were united in their opposition to Diem, they had no consensus candidate to replace him. If he had been overthrown, the most likely consequence would have been unstable rule by an ever-shifting junta lacking popular legitimacy—what, in fact, transpired when Diem was finally assassinated in 1963. Little wonder that a local newspaper referred to the political situation as *un panier de crabes* (literally a "basket of crabs," but really meaning "a nest of vipers"), a description that Lansdale heartily endorsed.[22] As he later wrote, Vietnam was in the grip of a "sudden madness" that nearly tore the country "apart at the seams."[23]

Much to Lansdale's dismay, Trinh Minh Thé and another sect general he had wooed, Nguyen Thanh Phuong, were part of the United Front. Lansdale took it upon himself to try to bring them back to Diem's side. Since Phuong's chief complaint was that Diem had not fully delivered on his American-financed promise to pay him and his men six million piastres ($171,400) a month,[24] Lansdale's arguments were undoubtedly buttressed by further offers of aid along with his trademark empathy and understanding. Having finally succeeded in once again winning over the two Cao Dai leaders in an all-night parley, Lansdale drove them over to the American ambassador's residence on the morning of March 22 for what he assumed would be "just a brief and friendly call." He was surprised to see that J. Lawton Collins had assembled a phalanx of aides armed with notepads, and even more surprised that instead of welcoming the two wayward warlords back into the fold, Collins began castigating them for their disloyalty. Lansdale cut off Joe Redick before he could translate Collins's words and abruptly ushered the Vietnamese out the door on the pretext of feeding them breakfast.[25]

In a subsequent cable to the State Department, the ambassador petulantly complained that talking with Thé and Phuong "was like trying to reason with two stubborn four-year-old children": "They were either lying very ineptly or they were alarmingly stupid considering the influence and power they wield. In most instances their accusations were without foundation and their arguments without logic. Trying to determine from them exactly what they wanted was completely futile."[26] In reality, both Thé and Phuong were savvy survivors who were maneuvering for maximum advantage in a Byzantine world of Vietnamese politics that Collins did not understand. The ambassador's *cri de coeur*, full of stereotyped insults, was typical of the condescending mindset that had afflicted many American representatives in their dealings with Asians in the past and would do so again in the future as a colonial imbroglio escalated into a larger war. Much of Lansdale's effectiveness derived from the fact that he did not share Collins's prejudices: he knew that the Vietnamese leaders, however duplicitous, were rational and that it was imperative to win them over rather than dismiss them with befuddlement and belittlement.

That Lansdale was able to win back these two Cao Dai warlords was a considerable coup for Diem, but the prime minister still faced a formidable array of foes. By Lansdale's estimate, the Binh Xuyen had as many as 10,000 troops, the Cao Dai 30,000, the Hoa Hao 50,000. (Other estimates were considerably lower.)[27] The sects' military might became clear when Binh Xuyen troopers in green berets set up checkpoints and sandbagged positions across Saigon. They soon had control of all food supplies moving into the city and had placed mortars within range of the presidential palace. They even had gunboats on the Saigon River.[28]

Diem had 151,000 troops of his own, but only 10,000 of them were deployed around the capital, and he could not be sure of their loyalty. Before fleeing to Paris at the end of November 1954, the mutinous General Nguyen Van Hinh had handed over command to General

Nguyen Van Vy, another pro-French Bao Dai loyalist. Bao Dai, the chief of state who was widely seen as a French puppet, was collaborating with the sect leaders.

Lansdale found Diem in his office on Monday, March 29, 1955, poring over large-scale maps of the metropolitan area, pointing out locations where Binh Xuyen mortars had been spotted. There were disquieting reports that the Binh Xuyen had acquired heavy 81-mm mortars that could rip apart the Norodom Palace as if it were a Lego set. Yet Lansdale saw no sign of panic in either Diem or the army troops fortifying the palace grounds. A few days earlier, Lansdale had worried about Diem's passivity—his tendency to cry on Lansdale's shoulder rather than to take charge.[29] But the crisis brought out the best in the prime minister. "I was struck by his calm," Lansdale wrote. "This was a man in control of himself."[30]

◆

ON THE night of March 29–30, only a few hours after visiting Diem, Lansdale was awakened at his spacious new home at 65 Rue Duy Tan, eight blocks from the presidential palace, by the sounds of explosions and the "stutter of machine guns and the popping of rifles." His poodle, Pierre, took refuge in a narrow space under the bed, leaving only "two big eyes" visible. Joe Redick telephoned Diem to see whether he was all right. An aide reported that the premier was checking the troops on the front lawn while still in his pajamas and slippers.[31] There had been shelling of the palace but no ground assault. The infantry combat, which Lansdale could hear in the distance, was going on in Cholon, where the Vietnamese National Army was driving back Binh Xuyen assaults. Lansdale called Ambassador Collins to share this information and, at Collins's request, set out for his residence to help manage this crisis.

Driving through the streets of Saigon in the predawn darkness, Lansdale saw that "each tree trunk, shrub, alley and fence" sheltered troops whose "weapons and eyes" followed his car as he drove past. At one intersection, he came upon a column of Vietnamese army troops blocked by French tanks. (The French still had thirty thousand troops in and around Saigon.) The Vietnamese commander was loudly remonstrating with the French officers to let his men through, but to no avail. "I could only conclude," Lansdale wrote, "that the French military wanted the Binh Xuyen to win, inflicting defeat not only on the national army but on Diem and his government."[32]

Collins told Lansdale that, in order to stop the shedding of innocent blood, he had agreed to a French proposal for a cease-fire. Lansdale argued that a "cease-fire now merely put off the day of reckoning for which each side would prepare more thoroughly." But once again the CIA operative and the four-star ambassador were talking past each other. Lansdale had little choice but to trudge home in the early morning hours as the cease-fire was taking effect. He found both government and gangster forces in combat positions on his block, watching each other warily in the evanescent early-morning darkness. As soon as Lansdale opened the door, Pierre bolted into the street. While Lansdale frantically tried to catch his dog, he heard "subdued laughter" from the soldiers on both sides crouched around the house.[33]

◆

FOLLOWING THIS brief outbreak of fighting in late March 1955, an uneasy peace descended on Saigon. Jeeploads of men raced through the streets of Cholon firing submachine guns. "Both sides want to show me pictures," Lansdale wrote, "of their lads who've been fished out of the river with their throats cut."[34]

The French hand in the unrest was obvious to Howard Simpson, an American information officer who drove past roadblocks manned by gangsters to visit the Binh Xuyen headquarters in Cholon; he was particularly struck by one "long-haired officer" in a red sport shirt and camouflage pants, his "gold-capped teeth" clamped around an "ivory cigarette holder," a cocked revolver in his hand and a holstered automatic on his hip. As Simpson sat talking with his Binh Xuyen interlocutors, he noticed French army motorcycle dispatch riders roaring in and out. A French captain in his shirtsleeves wandered out of the radio room before quickly scuttling away when he saw Simpson. "The French are running the goddamn show," Simpson muttered,[35] a conclusion shared by Lansdale but denied by Lightning Joe Collins.

Rather than blame the French and the sects for fomenting insta-bility, Collins had joined the French in concluding that Diem was the culprit. The ambassador had never much cared for the prime minister; he viewed Diem as a "small, shy, diffident man with almost no personal magnetism," hobbled by an "inherent distaste for decisive action."[36] Lansdale thought Collins talked to Diem as if he were a "country squire looking down his aristocratic nose at a bumpkin, and a non-too-clean bumpkin at that."[37] Ironically, now that Diem was moving against the sects, Collins was not crediting him for taking "decisive action" but rather blaming him for "operating practically a one-man government." On March 31, the day after the inconclusive skirmishes in Saigon, Col-lins cabled the State Department, "I seriously doubt this can last long." He argued that "it is, therefore, essential to consider possible alterna-tives to present situation," proceeding to list several political figures who could replace Diem.[38]

John Foster Dulles told his brother, Allen, that "it looks like the rug is coming out from under" Diem.[39] On April 11, 1955, the secretary of state sent Collins a momentous cable, revised personally by President Eisenhower. "In light of your reiterated conviction that Diem cannot gain adequate Vietnam support to establish an effective government and that other men are available whose designation as Premier would improve the existing status," it said, "you are authorized to acquiesce in the plans for Diem's replacement."[40] Dulles then summoned Collins to Washington to work out "a program for replacing Diem."[41] Given the CIA's recent record of toppling Mohammad Mossadeq in Iran in 1953 and Jacobo Arbenz in Guatemala in 1954, that was no idle threat: this was one administration that did not hesitate to remove foreign leaders if it felt that doing so was in America's interest.

Before Collins departed, on April 20, 1955, Lansdale asked him what he should say if Diem wanted to know whether U.S. support for him was wavering. Lightning Joe disingenuously replied that Lansdale might "hear all sorts of rumors of other things, even stories that the U.S. wouldn't support Diem." But Lansdale was to "disregard such tales" in the assurance "that the U.S. would continue to support Diem."[42] And then Collins flew off to conclude the process of dumping Diem.

◆

IN WASHINGTON, Collins persuaded the president and secretary of state to go along with a scheme to kick Diem upstairs into a largely ceremonial office of president while delegating real authority to a new premier. At 6:10–6:11 p.m. on Wednesday, April 27, 1955 (7:10–7:11 a.m., April 28, in Saigon), Dulles sent out cables to the U.S. embassies in Saigon and Paris announcing the new policy,[43] yet less than six hours later, he sent out another cable retracting his earlier decision and warning the embassies to "take no action whatsoever . . . until further instruction."[44]

What happened during those six critical hours to make Dulles change his mind? Edward Lansdale had learned what was in the offing and had acted to stop it. At 8:48 a.m., Wednesday, Saigon time (7:48 p.m., Tuesday, in Washington), Lansdale sent a telegram to CIA headquarters arguing "that the Diem government represented a better chance for success than any non-Vietminh government it would be possible to form in South Vietnam. Failure to support Diem would cause great damage to American prestige and would doom any successor government to Diem's to failure. The only winners would be the Viet Minh."[45] Lansdale's messages prompted the "stay order" from Dulles, along with a request for Lansdale to provide a full report that could be discussed at a National Security Council meeting on the morning of Wednesday, April 28, Washington time. With this insubordinate intervention, Lansdale had won Diem a stay of execution— much to Collins's consternation.

◆

WHILE POLICYMAKERS in Washington were going to bed on the evening of April 27, events in Saigon were moving at tsunami speed. In his memoir, Lansdale recounted getting a phone call from Diem at his Cholon office at noon on Wednesday, April 28, asking him to come to the Norodom Palace. He and Joe Redick set out immediately in Lansdale's new car, a big, black Citroën sedan that had been smuggled out of Haiphong by Lou Conein.[46] As they were approaching Place Khai-

Dinh, they saw bicyclists falling in the street while cars were stopping and their occupants were sprawling on the pavement. At first it looked like a "massive slapstick scene," but then they heard the sound of machine-gun fire, which had previously been muffled by surrounding buildings. A number of the bicyclists had just been killed. Lansdale and Redick stopped their own car and joined the others lying flat on the pavement. A few minutes later the firing died away, and they resumed their journey.[47] The war between the government and the Binh Xuyen, which had started and stopped a month before, had just resumed.

Lansdale and Redick found Diem on the porch of the palace. According to Lansdale's memoir, Diem had heard that "Ambassador Collins had obtained President Eisenhower's approval for a change of U.S. policy toward Vietnam." Diem wanted to know whether it was true that he was being "dumped." Lansdale supposedly responded that he didn't believe this report and asked Diem where he got his information. This account makes no sense, given that just a few hours earlier Lansdale had been sending cables to stop Diem from being dumped. He was dissembling when he claimed in his memoir, "None of these high-level deliberations in Washington were known to me in Saigon at the time,"[48] probably to protect his CIA sources, possibly even Allen Dulles himself. As for how Diem found out about the decisions being made in Washington, that information was either shared by Lansdale himself or by the prime minister's American friend Wesley Fishel, who was back in the United States.

Just as Lansdale and Redick were returning from the Norodom Palace at 1:30 p.m., they heard a "series of loud explosions from the direction of the palace." Binh Xuyen mortars had opened up on the prime minister's residence.

Who fired the first shots? The French blamed Diem, and the most careful reconstruction of events, by the historian David L. Anderson, supports that conclusion.[49] On April 26, 1955, Diem had resumed his efforts to replace the Binh Xuyen–appointed chief of police with his own man, knowing that the Binh Xuyen would resist by force. Not waiting for the gangsters to strike, Vietnamese army troops had gone by truck to Cholon on April 28 and gotten into a firefight with the Binh

Xuyen. The mortar attack on the presidential palace was a response. The French were convinced that this armed confrontation was all Lansdale's fault for encouraging Diem to "take armed action."[50] In reality, having told Diem how close he was to losing U.S. support, Lansdale did not need to do much to spur him into action. Diem must have realized that he had nothing to lose by launching an attack against the Binh Xuyen. If the offensive succeeded, Diem would give the Eisenhower administration no choice but to support him. And if it failed, he would lose power and possibly his life. But he would lose power anyway if he did nothing and waited for Washington to oust him. The time for action was all the more propitious given that Collins was in transit from Washington and therefore unable to intervene, as he had done a month earlier.

◆

LANSDALE TAPPED into his wide network of friends to keep track of the fighting. Early on the afternoon of Wednesday, April 28, for example, shortly after his return from the palace, Lansdale received a call from the Time-Life correspondent John Mecklin. He and a photographer were in a police station where a company of Vietnamese National Army troops was being besieged by a Binh Xuyen battalion. Mecklin was worried that they would all be killed. But then the army troops counterattacked and put the Binh Xuyen to flight. The gangsters were running away as fast as they could, shedding their uniforms as they ran. "Who said these army guys wouldn't fight!" Mecklin shouted before hanging up.[51]

Lansdale set out for the embassy to share his information. He was astonished to discover that the diplomats "were debating which adjectives to use to describe the low morale of the Vietnamese Army troops who now had to stand up to the high-spirited Binh Xuyen."[52] They were getting their reports from the French, and they did not believe Lansdale's more optimistic assessment. Lansdale seethed about desk-bound diplomats—"the precious lads who sit in offices or make the cocktail circuit and know the surface of a country so brilliantly."[53] But he knew that if the president accepted the State Department's gloomy estimate, Diem was done.

Urban warfare has always been a grim, confused, ugly business. From the fighting in Jerusalem in AD 70 between Jews and Romans to the Warsaw Uprising in 1944, close-quarters combat in cities has always led to extensive casualties and property damage. The Battle of Saigon in the spring of 1955 would be no different. As Lansdale drove around on Wednesday afternoon, he could see "dense clouds of smoke" darkening the skies above Cholon. A large section of the city was on fire, with both sides blaming the other for starting it. Because fire trucks could not get through the front lines, at least a hundred people died in the blaze and many more were injured or rendered homeless. In front of his team's "pool house" on Rue Taberd, Lansdale found "burned-out and shell-shattered vehicles," which gave "the street outside a junkyard look." Even the hard-bitten Lou Conein had been shaken when he saw a mortar shell fall right on a Renault taxicab, killing a family inside, including three children.[54]

Given that the "pool house" was packed with explosives due to be shipped to agents in the North, a hit from a mortar shell would have been a catastrophe, setting off secondary explosions that would have killed everyone inside. The possibility of the house being taken in a Binh Xuyen ground assault could not be dismissed either. Some of the team members asked for permission to abandon the building. Lansdale refused. He thought the house was defensible, with walls thick enough to withstand an 81-mm mortar round. Inside, Lansdale noted approvingly, "all files were fixed for instant destruction, automatic weapons and hand grenades distributed to all personnel."[55]

Once Lansdale had determined that all his men were safe, or at least as safe as they could be under the circumstances, he returned to his own house and sat down at a typewriter to produce the report for the NSC meeting that John Foster Dulles had requested. Rufus Phillips marveled at how Lansdale was able to bang out a single-spaced, twenty-page cable in a single sitting "without pause and without changing a single word."[56] (Another team member noted that Lansdale was "one of the best typists in Saigon.")[57] Lansdale's cable gave a firsthand account of what he had seen, namely, that the army was winning, and concluded with a warning that "no nationalist aspirant for power in Vietnam had as much to offer as Diem and no pro-French leader could succeed against the Viet Minh."[58] This report reached Washington at 7:44 a.m. on Wednesday, just in time for the NSC meeting. It was nighttime in Saigon, and Lansdale was so exhausted that he went to bed, not knowing whether he had saved Ngo Dinh Diem or not.[59]

At the NSC meeting in the Cabinet Room, Lightning Joe Collins reiterated his conviction that "Diem's number was up." For the first time, however, President Eisenhower was beginning to question the judgment of his "personal representative." He "commented that it was an absolute sine qua non of success that the Vietnamese National Army destroy the power of the Binh Xuyen." When the meeting broke up, the participants had tacitly moved away from Collins's plan to get rid of Diem. Lansdale had succeeding in buying Diem yet another reprieve. Now much would turn on how the fighting went. As John Foster Dulles told his fellow NSC members, "The developments of last night could either lead to Diem's utter overthrow, or his emergence from the disorder as a major hero. Accordingly we are pausing to await the results."[60]

◆

THE NEXT morning, Thursday, April 29, Lansdale got an angry reception from French officers at TRIM headquarters. One of them was holding a Vietnamese girl who had suffered a shrapnel wound. "Look what Lansdale has done," he declared dramatically. "He makes war on children!" Unfazed, Lansdale handed the girl to another American officer and left for MAAG headquarters with Rufus Phillips and Colonel Le Van Kim. They were in town to request additional support for the pacification campaign in central Vietnam, Operation Breaking Chains, which had started a week earlier. Thus Lansdale had to simultaneously manage both pacification in the countryside and an urban battle in Saigon—challenges that dwarfed anything he had experienced in the Philippines. He wrote to Pat Kelly, "While it has been an extremely trying time, I've got about a thousand tigers by the tail and I'm afraid to let go of any single one of them right now or there will be a big snarling mass of tigers gobbling me up—which I understand a number of people would enjoy but am still doubtful that I would."[61]

The carnage of conflict was apparent everywhere. The road through Cholon, Rufus Phillips noted, "was littered with burned out buildings and cars," as well as a few corpses.[62] Just as they were sitting down with Iron Mike O'Daniel in his office, a battle broke out around the MAAG building. The officers had trouble making themselves heard "over the din of machine gun fire and exploding grenades."[63] When Lansdale excused himself for a bathroom break, he could see through a window above the urinal Binh Xuyen troops on a nearby rooftop firing at army forces. By the time they walked out of their conference with O'Daniel, however, the Binh Xuyen were gone, their green berets strewn on the sidewalk. This was another sign that low morale was more of a problem for the gangsters than for their government adversaries.

The situation was fraught with peril. Back home on Rue Duy Tan, Lansdale got an unexpected visitor: his old acquaintance Jean Leroy, the half-French, half-Vietnamese Catholic warlord who was now allied with the Binh Xuyen. He arrived with a heavily armed squad of troops to escort Lansdale to "meet" the Binh Xuyen leader, Bay Vien. As the Binh Xuyen were broadcasting grisly threats to disembowel him, Lansdale declined the invitation. Lansdale's Filipino bodyguard, Proc Mojica, was asleep after having stayed up on guard duty the entire night, so Lansdale's hand was edging toward a hand grenade he had hidden nearby. The situation was saved only by the unexpected arrival of Charles "Bo" Bohannan and another Saigon Military Mission officer. Bohannan, visiting from Manila, teased Lansdale about all the troops lounging in front of the house, saying he didn't really need that many bodyguards. Ed introduced Jean Leroy and told Bo that he was just leaving. Seeing that they could not take Lansdale without a fight, Leroy and his gunmen roared off. "You couldn't have picked a better time to come," a grateful Ed told Bo.[64]

No venue was immune to the disfiguring toll of war. Late that afternoon, Diem summoned Lansdale to the Norodom Palace. He found "shell holes and martial litter in the gardens, walks, and driveways and great gouges cut in the palace walls. Windows were shuttered, sandbagged defense positions could be seen throughout the palace grounds, and heavily armed troops were very much in evidence." Diem was showing the strain of the crisis as much as his residence was. He had gone without sleep the night before, and now his body slumped, there were "strain lines" around his eyes and mouth, and his speech was slower than normal.[65] The prime minister was cheered by the progress his troops were making against the Binh Xuyen, but he was upset about a telegram he had just received from Bao Dai. After accusing Diem of plunging the Vietnamese people into "the horrors of a fratricidal conflict," Bao Dai demanded that Diem leave for France immediately and turn over the government to General Nguyen Van Vy, the pro-French army commander.

Diem asked Lansdale what he should do, although in truth there was not much doubt that he was going to ignore this appeal from a man that most patriotic Vietnamese viewed as a French puppet; his brother Ngo Dinh Nhu had already said as much to his own CIA contact, Paul Harwood.[66] Diem was more interested in hearing from Lansdale what stance the U.S. government would take. A professional diplomat would have cabled back to Washington for instructions. But like Wild Bill Donovan and other OSS veterans, Lansdale did not believe in awaiting orders from headquarters. He told Diem that Washington would "accept a legal action" to remove him as prime minister, but the telegram from Bao Dai was not a "legal proceeding." Then Lansdale told Diem to do as his conscience dictated, knowing that there was no way Diem was going to leave the country. [67]

That night, back at home, Lansdale had one more meeting. His friend Trinh Minh Thé stopped by to say that he had slipped into town with thirteen hundred of his guerrillas to support the army in its assault on the Binh Xuyen. Thé was, in fact, emerging as one of Diem's staunchest defenders.

The following day, Friday, April 30, American diplomats and reporters witnessed an extraordinary scene at the presidential palace. General Nguyen Van Vy, the army commander, was standing in the center of the room holding in his hands a statement repudiating Bao Dai and supporting Diem. In front of him was a microphone and a tape recorder. Next to him was Trinh Minh Thé. Vy was perspiring profusely and his hands were trembling. He was stalling for time, refusing to read the statement. Finally Thé lost his temper, whipped out a Colt .45 pistol, and put the muzzle to Vy's temple. Time seemed to stand still as everyone waited for the hammer to drop. Ashen and sweating, Vy finally read the statement. Thé demanded that he speak up. Only when he was done did Thé put the automatic away.[68] With Vy's coerced blessing, the Vietnamese army was now free to press its assault on the Binh Xuyen.

The heavy fighting continued into the new month. Lansdale saw Thé for the last time three days later, on Monday, May 3. Blood dripping from a flesh wound on his hand, Thé arrived at 5 p.m. to tell Lansdale that his troops were pinned down at the Tan Thuan bridge by Binh Xuyen gunboats. His men were taking heavy casualties and could not cross the bridge, because they had no artillery with which to fight back.[69] As soon as he heard this, Lansdale sped over to the Norodom Palace. He found Diem in a conference with several officers. They were jubilant because the army had put the Binh Xuyen to flight. Lansdale was furious that they were celebrating while Trinh Minh Thé's men were getting slaughtered. He demanded they do something to help the diminutive guerrilla—an indication of how freely he was willing to involve himself in what other American officials would have viewed as internal Vietnamese affairs. Shamefaced, Diem told a colonel to get some artillery over to Thé.

The officers then left while Diem, as was his wont, delivered a two-hour exposition to Lansdale on Vietnamese politics. He included some derisory comments about Thé, who "he pointed out was only a peasant and presumably not as worthy as present company," Lansdale recalled. Ed was "pretty sharp" in his retort. Their colloquy was interrupted at 8 p.m. by Ngo Dinh Nhu, who walked in to announce that Trinh Minh Thé had just been killed. Both Diem and Lansdale were shocked and grief-stricken. Diem asked Lansdale "to forgive what he had just said" and began crying. Lansdale held him in his arms as great sobs racked his body—the only time Lansdale ever saw him cry.[70]

Thé had been shot in the back of the head. The culprit could have been French, Binh Xuyen, one of Thé's own men, or even an agent sent by Ngo Dinh Nhu to eliminate a potential challenger to his brother.[71] The mystery would never be solved. Lansdale grieved over the loss, describing Thé in a letter as "a little guy who was becoming a very close friend."[72] As if sensing a shift following Thé's death, Lansdale's poodle, Pierre, chased away the two mongooses that Thé had given his master.[73]

Thé was far from the only casualty; the Battle of Saigon left five hundred dead and two thousand wounded. In the process, however, the sect forces had been routed.[74] Bay Vien and his remaining followers fled Saigon to seek refuge in the swamps and canals where they had gotten their start decades earlier. Before long, Bay Vien would retire to Paris. The Cao Dai pope fled to Cambodia. Most of the Hoa Hao leaders were either captured or surrendered. One of the last holdouts was Ba Cut, the Hoa Hao general whom Lansdale and Diem had once plotted to kill. He was finally arrested in the spring of 1956 and, despite Lansdale's entreaties for mercy, executed by guillotine a few months later.[75]

The American information officer Howard Simpson joined Vietnamese troops to search Bay Vien's deserted and once luxurious villa, now a wreck wreathed in the smell of putrefaction. Opium-packaging equipment and Binh Xuyen identity cards were strewn on the floors. The stench came from the "rotting, fly-covered" carcasses of Bay Vien's exotic zoo animals. "His tiger looks like an outsize deflated child's toy; and the python, its coils ripped and torn by shrapnel, resembles a thick, discarded electrical conduit," Simpson noted. "In one cage a black monkey, stiff with rigor mortis, lies on its back, its two long arms extended."[76]

◆

DIEM HAD won a resounding victory—not only in the noisome and cacophonous streets of Saigon but also in the hushed corridors of power in Washington. On May 1, 1955, John Foster Dulles sent a telegram to the U.S. embassy in Saigon saying that it was impossible to stop supporting Diem at a time when, "rightly or wrongly," he was "becoming [a] symbol of Vietnamese nationalism struggling against French colonialism and corrupt backward elements." The U.S. government would continue "supporting Diem Government to maintain its authority and to restore law and order."[77]

By the time Lightning Joe Collins arrived back in Saigon the next day, he was confronted, much to his frustration, with a fait accompli. The ambassador was left to reflect that when "word of Diem's bold action and the army's initial success reached Washington, whatever influence I might have had . . . was quickly dissipated."[78] Collins was summarily informed that he would be replaced by a new ambassador, the career diplomat G. Frederick Reinhardt, who arrived in Saigon on May 10. He would take a more conciliatory stance toward Diem, as advocated by Lansdale.

Collins had defeated Japanese and German armies, but in South Vietnam he had been bested by a former advertising man with a colonel's wings on his collar. Privately smarting at what he viewed as Lansdale's insubordination (he later griped that it was a "big mistake" to have "two people supposedly representing the United States government" in Saigon),[79] Collins planted his tongue firmly in his cheek when he thanked Lansdale in a farewell letter for his "splendid help during the past six months."[80] Also leaving was Emmett McCarthy, the chief of the regular CIA station in Saigon who was constantly at odds with Lansdale.[81]

Amid all these departures, the French, Lansdale noted, "were asking me pointedly when in hell I was leaving." He jested that he "was being traded for two French generals and a second baseman," but the joke fell flat, and not only because the Europeans were unfamiliar with America's national pastime; "these local French are now so sour on life that they just glared at me."[82] While the French sulked, Lansdale and his team exulted. For one bright, shining moment in the glorious spring of 1955, Ngo Dinh Diem and Edward G. Lansdale—the premier and his premier supporter—reigned supreme in Saigon.

◆

LANSDALE DID not, of course, single-handedly determine the outcome of the 1955 sects crisis, any more than he had done with the 1953 Philippine presidential election. Diem, like Ramon Magsaysay, was ultimately master of his own fate. Bernard Fall was right to call Diem's handling of the Battle of Saigon his "finest hour."[83] But it was Lansdale's finest hour, too. His wooing of sect leaders such as Trinh Minh Thé had swung the balance of power in Diem's favor and given Diem the confidence to fight and defeat the Binh Xuyen. Most importantly, he had persuaded the Eisenhower administration to reverse its decision to topple Diem. The CIA's official history, which is generally hostile to Lansdale because he was so often at odds with career CIA officers, nevertheless concludes that he was "the largest single influence on deliberations in Washington at the most critical point of Diem's tenure before 1963."[84] The history goes on to assert that the CIA's role in helping Diem to consolidate power was the biggest achievement of its entire involvement in Vietnam, which was to last twenty more years.

Lansdale's pro-Diem cables would not prove as important as George F. Kennan's Long Telegram, sent from Moscow in 1946, which laid out the policy of containment. But they surely rank among the more influential diplomatic dispatches of the postwar period. And just as Kennan's telegram was influential because it gave expression to an already existing disposition to oppose Soviet expansionism, so too Lansdale's cables were influential because they also crystalized an already existing policy, albeit one that was in momentary danger of being abandoned— a policy of backing Diem as an anti-Communist bulwark in Southeast Asia. It became known as "sink or swim with Ngo Dinh Diem," and its author was the buoyant chief of the Saigon Military Mission. William Conrad Gibbons, a leading historian of the American war effort, was later to say, "If it hadn't been for Lansdale, Diem would have been out in April of 1955. . . . He was the mastermind of the whole thing."[85]

Eight years later, a different set of policymakers in Washington would decide to topple Diem, with calamitous consequences. That mistake was narrowly avoided in the spring of 1955 largely because of Lansdale's intervention. Some might argue, given the problems subsequently encountered by Diem, that it might have been better to remove him early on, but the coup plotters in 1955 were as unlikely as the ones in 1963 to form a government that could have been successful in mobilizing popular support. Indeed, the 1955 plotters would have been even harder put to assert any legitimacy because of their French colonial connections. By saving Diem from his enemies in Saigon and Washington, Lansdale had made a powerful and on balance positive impact on the course of Vietnamese history. Although he did not know it at the time, he had reached the apogee of his power and influence.

17

"Stop Calling Me *Papa*!"

I like the guy, but won't buy fascism.

—EDWARD LANSDALE

THE Battle of Saigon, waged across the metropolis in the spring of 1955, had made Edward Lansdale the object of violent antipathy on the part of the French and the rebellious sects because of the pivotal role he played in keeping the Ngo Dinh Diem regime alive. "The Binh Xuyen, the Hoa Hao, the French, and the Vietminh are still keeping me on their old s——t lists as public enemy number one," Ed wrote to Pat Kelly.[1] Even after the outcome of the battle was clear, some of the French "soreheads" came gunning for him and his team members in a subterranean spy-versus-spy war that raged for months.[2]

One day in 1955, Richard "Dick" Smith, the Marine captain who handled logistics for the Saigon Military Mission, came out of the "pool house" on Rue Taberd and saw a French army jeep that had been parked down the street accelerating toward him. As the car sped past, a soldier in the rear seat leaned out and opened fire at him with a pistol through a side curtain. Because it was an awkward angle and the jeep was going too fast, the rounds went into the curb and the wall. Just as Smith was reaching for the .38 pistol he normally carried in his pocket

278 | THE ROAD NOT TAKEN

to return fire, he realized that he had left it in the house. He could do nothing but watch in frustration as the jeep sped away.

And one night, while Army Captain Russell "Mike" Moriarty, the Saigon Military Mission's "tough, funny, very Irish" man in Haiphong, was sleeping in his apartment, he woke up to see assassins in his room. He opened fire with the pistol he kept by his bed. Once he was fully awake he realized that he had been shooting at his own clothes hanging on wooden valet stands; in the dark the suits and hats resembled men. He subsequently showed Dick Smith the bullet holes in some of his jackets—a sign of how paranoid he was becoming, and not without reason.[3]

Such attacks, previously isolated incidents, became endemic in the summer of 1955. Lansdale's men received an anonymous mimeographed note from a hitherto unknown group calling itself the Front for National Unity and against American Domination, warning them that if they did not leave the country immediately their safety could not be assured. Explosions shattered the plate glass window of the U.S. Information Service Library in Saigon, cars belonging to Americans were blown up, and grenades were tossed into the yards of houses where Americans lived. Rufus Phillips, now driving Lansdale's old 2CV, checked it regularly for bombs every morning before starting the ignition.[4]

That June, a Frenchman with a mustache similar to Lansdale's parked a black Citroën nearly identical to Lansdale's on his block and spent the night in a house across the street. In the morning, as the Frenchman was driving away, a jeep filled with men with automatic weapons pulled alongside his car and riddled him with bullets. The police detectives investigating the murder told Lansdale that the gunmen had been after him. "Now the French with mustaches like mine will be shaving them off," Ed joked to Pat Kelly. "I'd shave mine off only you say I look like hell without it. So I'll just keep ducking."[5]

When Lansdale complained to French security officials, they blamed such attacks on the Vietminh. But Lou Conein heard that Colonel Jean Carbonel, Lansdale's boss at TRIM, was responsible. Lansdale confronted Carbonel. Speaking as usual through the adjutant, Lansdale told Carbonel that, with the death of the mustachioed Frenchman, this "cruel farce" had gone too far. He added melodramatically, "I hereby inform you that I am withdrawing my protection from the French Expeditionary Corps. Don't forget you are ten thousand miles from Metropolitan France. Whatever happens to you from now is on your own heads."

This earned Lansdale an upbraiding the following morning at the American embassy. The new ambassador, the veteran diplomat G. Frederick Reinhardt, told him that his words were at odds with the spirit of Franco-American friendship. Lansdale defiantly replied that as long as junior French military personnel continued to terrorize Americans in Saigon, he and his small staff of a dozen men were certainly not going to "protect" the French Far East Expeditionary Corps of eighty thousand troops[6]—thus bringing himself into conflict with yet another American envoy.

Soon thereafter Rufus Phillips stopped by the "pool house" to find Lou Conein in the kitchen. In front of him, on an enameled kitchen table, were "bars of C-3 plastic explosives, orange-colored primacord, a roll of fuses, a box of caps, and rolls of friction tape." Conein was assembling plastic bombs while uttering a string of curses in English and French—"*salauds, espece de con*, bastards, goddam sons of bitches, assholes." Phillips asked what was going on. Conein replied, "None of your goddam business. What the hell does it look like?"

Phillips offered to help. Conein gave him a kitchen knife and asked him "to cut up the rest of the C-3 into five-inch lengths and tape primacord to the sections, just like the others." When Phillips was finished, he asked Conein whether he needed any more assistance. "No, goddammit," Conein muttered. "You didn't see any of this. Get out of here!"

After midnight, Conein set off for a little drive through Saigon along with his fiancée, a woman of mixed French and Vietnamese ancestry named Elyette Brochot. She was cradling the bombs in her lap, handing them to Conein as they drove by the homes of Colonel Carbonel and other Frenchmen. Conein lit the fuses with his cigarette lighter and tossed the bombs into the yards of the houses. The final bomb went into the garden of the French ambassador.

The French naturally complained about this attack, even though no one had been hurt, but they had little more to say when some junior French officers were arrested by Vietnamese police. In their possession were explosives and a list of American targets. With French complicity exposed, the attacks on Americans finally ended.[7]

◆

As THE summer of 1955 progressed, South Vietnam became more peaceful than it had been at any time since the 1930s—or that it would be again until the 1980s. The French war was over; the American war had not yet begun. The Communist regime in Hanoi was in the midst of a brutal collectivization and land redistribution program that would result by mid-1956 in the deaths of an estimated fifteen thousand "landlords" and "traitors" in a process that even Ho Chi Minh later admitted had gotten out of control.[8] The sects in South Vietnam were in disarray. French forces were finally leaving after nearly a century of colonial occupation. The Vietnamese army was regaining control of areas vacated by the Vietminh. "Diem was pretty well consolidated at this time . . . so these were fairly tranquil days for Vietnam," recalled an American reporter.[9]

Under the Geneva Accords, an election was supposed to be held by July 1956 to unify the country. But neither South Vietnam nor the United States had signed the treaty, and neither Diem nor Eisenhower had any interest in holding a vote that they were sure would be won by Ho Chi Minh—not just because of his popularity but also because of the police-state control he exerted over the North. For the foreseeable future, Vietnam would be divided into two nations. North Vietnam was already a Communist dictatorship. What kind of nation would South Vietnam become?

The debate over this question, in both Saigon and Washington, would echo similar debates that recurred during the Cold War. The United States would find itself allied with numerous undemocratic regimes such as Fulgencio Batista's Cuba, Anastasio Somoza's Nicaragua, Mobutu Sese Seko's Zaire, Chiang Kai-shek's Taiwan, and the Shah's Iran. There was considerable discussion over the years about whether and how the United States should push its allies to democratize, but with a few exceptions, including the Philippines, South Korea, Taiwan, and Chile in the 1980s and Iraq and Afghanistan in the 2000s, both Republican and Democratic administrations were generally content to ignore the illiberal practices of allied regimes as long as they contributed to stability and security. The credo of this realpolitik policy came from President Franklin Roosevelt's apocryphal comment about Somoza: "He's a sonofabitch, but he's our sonofabitch."

This was not a view that Lansdale shared. In both the Philippines and South Vietnam, he was convinced that fostering representative government was not only morally right but strategically smart. In June 1955, he wrote of his "strong feelings about how to fight Communism: by giving the guy in the street or the rice paddy something he can believe in so strongly that he will defend it with everything he has, whether or not anybody asks him to do so. It's old-fashioned Americanism, representative government, an armed force which protects the people as brothers, all men created equal."[10]

In long conversations during the summer of 1955 with Ngo Dinh Diem, accompanied as usual by small cups of tea and endless cigarettes, Ed Lansdale explained the drafting of the American Constitution and urged Diem to replicate the division of powers created by the Founding Fathers. Above all, he extolled the example of George Washington, the aristocratic Virginian who had put himself above party politics and had left office after two terms, making himself the beloved "father" of his country. Diem was unconvinced. An old-fashioned mandarin, he believed in the rule of the scholarly and virtuous elite—men like himself—and did not think that South Vietnam could risk the messiness of French-style democracy, with governments rising and falling on an annual basis, while confronting Communist subversion. Given his own philosophy of "benevolent authoritarianism,"[11] Diem became annoyed when Lansdale tried to upbraid him for undemocratic moves such as closing opposition newspapers. Lansdale would ask him, "Do you think that's the right thing for 'the father of his country' to do?" Diem would snap, "Stop calling me *papa!*"[12]

Lansdale's advice was being eclipsed by the influence of Diem's brother Ngo Dinh Nhu and his sister-in-law, the tart-tongued Madame

Nhu, known for her intemperate opinions and form-fitting *ao dai* dresses. Having studied in France, Ngo Dinh Nhu was in thrall to the abstruse French Catholic philosophy known as personalism, which claimed to be a communitarian, split-the-difference alternative to both "liberal individualism and Marxist collectivism."[13] In Nhu's hands, this became the justification for an increasingly powerful state designed to buttress his brother's authority at all costs. Lansdale thought that Nhu was a "Mussolini-type character" who was attempting to "evolve a Fascist type state."[14] But he was powerless to block Nhu, who had moved into the presidential palace with his family, with Madame Nhu now serving as first lady to her bachelor brother-in-law.

Not only did Nhu have the trust of Diem; he also had the CIA and State Department behind him. Having established a covert relationship with the CIA in 1952, Nhu had his own CIA liaison officer, Paul Harwood, who was working at cross-purposes with Lansdale.[15] A bespectacled and buttoned-down intelligence officer with a degree in Asian studies and a "modest, reflective" air that was far removed from the "macho covert action type" of legend, Harwood became as close to Nhu as Lansdale did to Diem—he served as confirmation sponsor for the Nhus' daughter.[16]

Ambassador Frederick Reinhardt and the new CIA station chief, John Anderton, backed Nhu and Harwood over Lansdale. Lansdale tried appealing to his patrons, the Dulles brothers, but they were not sympathetic. John Foster Dulles argued at an NSC meeting on May 19, 1955, "In the Orient, it was necessary to work through a single head of government rather than through a coalition in which various personal interests had to be submerged in a common loyalty." Dulles cited approvingly the examples of Syngman Rhee and Ho Chi Minh. His only quarrel with Ho, it seemed, was that he was on the other side.[17]

With Washington's support, Diem, in the manner of a Southeast Asian Franco or Perón, set about creating a one-party state built around his own, CIA-funded political party, the National Revolutionary Movement (NRM).[18] It would assume a prominent role in organizing pro-government rallies and parades and in crusading against what the puritanical Diem called the "four social evils": alcohol, prostitution, opium, and gambling.[19] Not content with creating a public political party, Nhu set up a secret party, too, known as the Can Lao (the Personalist Labor Revolutionary Party). Like the Communist Party, it was organized into covert cells. New members reportedly had to kiss a picture of Ngo Dinh Diem and to swear loyalty to him. Membership in either the NRM or the Can Lao became a prerequisite for career advancement in the government, whereas Vietnamese who belonged to older political parties such as the Dai Viet and the Vietnam Nationalist Party (VNQDD) were discriminated against or worse. A secret police organization with the deceptively innocuous name Service for Political and Social Study (known as SEPES after its French initials) monitored anyone who could pose a threat to Diem's rule, whether pro- or anti-Communist.

While building up their own political base, Nhu and Diem were determined to eradicate the remaining Vietminh infrastructure in the South. In July 1955, they launched a "Denounce the Communists" campaign and in January 1956 issued the notorious Ordinance No. 6, permitting the authorities to lock up for two years anyone considered a danger "to the defense of the state and order." A year later, Lansdale passed along a report that seven thousand political prisoners were being held at one Saigon prison alone.[20]

Many of the detainees were held on nebulous or unconvincing evidence and, where possible, Lansdale exerted his influence to free them. But he found it hard to "come to grips" with Diem's growing authoritarianism, which was far removed from Ramon Magsaysay's more democratic practices in the Philippines. "Every time I charge in when folks are arrested for 'political crimes,'" Lansdale complained, "I discover no charges, and nobody who ordered the police to arrest, and everyone is released. Next thing, everyone disappears, and then comes the baffling deal of trying to find out if they were kidnapped and bumped off, or are in hiding, or have run out of the country."[21]

Vietnamese Communist historians later said the years from 1955 to 1959 were "the darkest period" in the party's history, with membership in the South declining by two-thirds, but, as Lansdale suspected at the time and as became obvious in retrospect, the cost of such repression was high. Diem needlessly alienated individuals who were not Communist true believers and hounded some of them into the arms of the insurgents. The Hanoi regime, while still bent on using "peaceful means" to reunify the country, authorized its southern cadres to use limited force to defend themselves. Acts of terrorism began to reappear in the countryside in the late 1950s.

◆

THE TERM "workaholic" had not yet been coined—it would not be added to the lexicon until 1971[22]—but Edward Lansdale was an exemplar of the phenomenon *avant la lettre*. His days immersed in tension-filled intrigue on the front lines of the Cold War were taking a personal toll, all the more so because he was finding himself in an increasingly painful conflict with the man he was supposed to be mentoring, Ngo Dinh Diem. In a letter home, he explained, "Work goes on from the moment I roll groaning out of the sack in the early morning until late night; some of the gang talk to me while I shave; I write orders while sitting on the bathroom throne; and keep moving all the time; in just one phase of my work (the joint French-US one) I have to keep 23 big projects moving; there's just no time for personal life."[23]

Seeking to escape from the Saigon pressure cooker in the summer of 1955, Lansdale floated the idea of returning to the Philippines to become Ramon Magsaysay's CIA liaison, a job now occupied by his old deputy Charles "Bo" Bohannan. John Foster Dulles, however, was reluctant to grant this request because, as he told Eisenhower, "Lansdale was now in a position of special responsibility in relation to Premier Diem."[24] But the Dulles brothers let Lansdale take a holiday in the Philippines to see whether it made sense to send him back permanently.

Returning to Manila, Lansdale enjoyed his chance to relax "sitting in the sun under some coconut trees"[25] as well as to spend time with Pat Kelly; when he came back to Saigon at the end of July, he wrote that he was "deeply grateful" to her "for a wonderful leave."[26] But his appearance in Manila also prompted a resurgence of the old accusation that he was Magsaysay's Rasputin. That charge resonated because his visit coincided with Magsaysay's decision on July 12, 1955, to grant formal recognition to Diem's regime following a propaganda campaign covertly orchestrated by Bohannan.[27] Senator Claro Recto, the Nacionalista leader who had supported Magsaysay in 1953 but had now turned against him, charged that Lansdale had given Magsaysay two hundred thousand dollars to secure the presidency. "The rumors in 1953 were that I'd given him 3 million dollars," Lansdale wrote to his family, "and I'm disappointed that Recto thinks I'm such a cheapskate."[28]

The CIA operative's reputation as a kingmaker in Manila ensured the hostility not only of Recto and his allies but also of Homer Ferguson, a former Republican senator from Michigan who had been given the post of ambassador as a sinecure after losing his reelection campaign in 1954. New to his job and ignorant of Asia, Ferguson did not want to risk being upstaged by a well-connected competitor. All of this opposition led John Foster Dulles to conclude that Lansdale's visit "had been counterproductive."[29]

Lansdale had to write sheepishly to Magsaysay, expressing the "hope that the use of my name to attack you hasn't hurt you. It sure hasn't helped me any. But, neither of us bruises too easily."[30] He was left to reflect that he had become a victim "of so much publicity, and so much of it unfavorable" that he felt "a little like Lenin who had to be sent through Germany in a sealed car. No fun in being notorious."[31]

◆

BACK IN Saigon, Lansdale at least had the consolation of being moved out of TRIM to work at the Military Assistance Advisory Group (MAAG) directly under his friend Iron Mike O'Daniel. "Means I won't have disgruntled French working alongside me all day long," he noted merrily.[32] His relief was short-lived, however, for in November 1955 Iron Mike was replaced by another officer with a colorful nickname—Lieutenant General Samuel T. Williams, better known as Hanging Sam.

MAAG's new commander had gotten his start as a private in the Texas National Guard chasing the Mexican revolutionary-cum-bandit Francisco "Pancho" Villa in 1916. Subsequently commissioned an officer, he was wounded and decorated for heroism in France in 1918. His nickname derived from his days in 1943 commanding an infantry regiment in Texas. He sat as a judge in the court-martial of a soldier accused of raping and killing a ten-year-old girl. When the defense tried to present psychiatric testimony to show that the defendant was insane, he snapped, "I've heard enough! Let's hang the sonofabitch!" During the Normandy campaign, Hanging Sam was relieved of his job as an assistant division commander and busted down to colonel after berating his incompetent division commander for "goddam stupidness," but he made a comeback to become a well-respected division commander during the Korean War. [33]

Arriving in Saigon, he was dismayed by what he found at MAAG—"it was an enormous mess," he fumed, a situation that he blamed on his predecessor Iron Mike, who "was an aggressive fighter" but "knew no more about running an office than the man in the moon."[34] The fastidious Williams was disgusted one morning when he saw coming up the stairs of MAAG an unshaven American, "dirty as hell," who left his "very dilapidated automobile" parked where it wasn't supposed to be. He asked the first officer he saw, "Who is that character?" The answer: "He's one of Lansdale's people."[35]

Hanging Sam immediately summoned to his office Colonel Lansdale, who arrived just as a brigadier general was leaving, "his face bloodless and stunned," warning Lansdale, "God help you." Williams launched into a diatribe about the slovenly appearance of Lansdale's men. "You run them like a band of gypsies!" he thundered. "What have you got to say for yourself?" In truth the "dirty as hell" officer was just back from an arduous trip to meet with Vietnamese mountain tribes that Lansdale was trying to bring over to the government side. But instead of explaining this, Lansdale insouciantly replied, "I like gypsies, sir." This set off another explosion from Williams—an upbraiding, Lansdale wrote, meant "not only for my own ears but for every living creature in the entire metropolitan area and maybe even the ships at sea."[36] On another occasion, Williams exploded when he spotted one of Lansdale's officers using an umbrella in the rain, a breach of army etiquette. "What kind of candy-assed, sissified bunch have you got in that outfit of yours?" he demanded.[37]

Such outbursts might have made Lansdale hate Williams, but they did not. They reminded him of his exuberant and combative grandfather Edward Philips. Lansdale invited Williams to dinner and struck up a friendship with him. By February 1956, he was reporting that the general "has started taking me into his confidence quite a bit, and we're starting to team up the way I did with O'Daniel."[38]

In spite of their budding friendship, the two men would disagree over how the Vietnamese army should be trained. A veteran of the Korean War, Williams worried primarily about a conventional invasion across the DMZ. During the five years (1955–60) he spent in charge of MAAG, he removed the Vietnamese army from the civic-action role Lansdale had emphasized, sending troops back to their barracks to train for a conventional war. The army that he was building was ill equipped to handle the guerrilla threat that South Vietnam would soon face. Lansdale tried to warn against this ill-fated military transformation, but, just as he had been overruled on the nature of the political system in South Vietnam, he was overruled on the nature of the South Vietnamese military, too—another mistake with severe repercussions that would become obvious in the years ahead.

◆

GENERAL TRAN VAN DON, the new Vietnamese army chief of staff, noted Lansdale's diminished status after the sects had been defeated. Initially, he wrote, Diem "relied heavily on Lansdale, so much so that members of his staff had orders to always put him through to Diem, night or day, whatever he was doing." But Lansdale "went a little far when he tried to have Diem copy Magsaysay" by creating a Philippine-style democracy. By the end of 1955, Tran Van Don was not seeing Lansdale at Diem's side as regularly as before and asked Diem why not. The prime minister answered, "Lansdale is too CIA and is an encumbrance. In politics there is no room for sentiment."[39]

Lansdale was getting his own intimations of Diem's displeasure. "I hear by the bamboo telegraph," he wrote on March 31, 1956, "that Diem has decided I'm too tricky a person and doesn't trust me any more." The two men had just disagreed about "the sovereignty of the people," a rather large issue, with Diem claiming that it was "an out-moded idea." In support of his position, Diem cited "Austrian and German jurists." Lansdale replied heatedly that this "Hegelian non-sense had brought on a disastrous world war and was a really dangerous philosophy for a state. And as for sovereignty of the people, this was still the U.S. idea, and the most powerful nation in the world still found it practical in all of today's complex situations." Lansdale's attitude was: "Somebody has to talk straight to him, and if he wants me muzzled, I'll leave. I like the guy, but won't buy fascism."[40]

As this exchange made clear, Lansdale was intent on implanting representative government in South Vietnam, as he had done in the Philippines, but Diem, far from being an American puppet, had his own ideas. In a series of state-building steps from 1955 to 1956, the South Vietnamese leader consistently opted to define his government in autocratic, rather than democratic, terms.

Diem, then only the prime minister, took no chances when he called a referendum for October 23, 1955, on whether the former emperor Bao Dai should remain as head of state or whether the position should go to Diem himself. Lansdale cautioned that the most Diem should do to influence the outcome would be to print the pro-Diem ballots in a propitious color—"the cheerful red of Asian weddings"—while print-ing the pro–Bao Dai ballots in an unlucky hue—"an uninspired shade of green."[41] But Diem did not stop there, mounting a propaganda cam-paign to revile Bao Dai as an "evil king" with a weakness for "gam-bling, women, wine, milk and butter" and as a "dung beetle who sold his country for personal glory." No campaigning in favor of the erst-while emperor was allowed.[42] Ignoring Lansdale's imprecations against voter fraud, Diem then announced that he had won 98.2 percent of the 5.8 million ballots cast, a "totally unbelievable" figure that Howard Simpson of the USIA said "would have made a Tammany Hall boss blush."[43] Armed with these dubious election results, Diem proclaimed himself president of the Republic of Vietnam.

Diem also made sure that the outcome of elections for a new Con-stituent Assembly on March 4, 1956, would be to his liking, with his supporters winning two-thirds of the seats. Lansdale subsequently defended the vote in his memoir, but at the time he was not impressed, writing home that "such rigging is just as bad as what the Commies do, and how can the average guy feel that the government is his own . . . which is the only way to really lick Communism any place."[44]

The newly chosen assembly's first task was to craft a new constitution, with the assistance of Lansdale's old friend the Filipino lawyer Johnny Orendain. With Lansdale's protests ignored by Washington, however, the National Assembly promulgated a constitution that gave Diem, at his insistence, virtually unlimited authority.[45]

Diem further enhanced his power by ending the old practice of letting villages select their own leaders. From now on, village, district, and province chiefs would be appointed by Saigon. Lansdale did not find out about this move until after he had left Vietnam. He called this a "disastrous" decision because it "transgressed the ancient Vietnamese edict that 'the Emperor's rule ends at the village wall,' and gave Communist agitprop cadre a highly effective argument to turn villagers against the Diem regime; everything that went wrong in a village could be blamed upon the Diem-appointed officials, whether they were responsible for it or not."[46]

Lansdale felt betrayed by the failure of his American colleagues to back his pro-democracy push. He complained about getting enough "knives in the back from Americans and allies" to make him "sound like a clanking hardware store when I try to get things done." He was, of course, used to dealing with opposition from other Americans, but by the fall of 1955, even with Lightning Joe Collins gone, it was "worse than at any time I can remember."[47]

So upset was Lansdale by the U.S. government's support for the Ngos' repressive moves that he flew back to Washington in January 1956 to protest personally to the Dulles brothers as well as to get treatment for a nagging toothache.[48] The CIA director and secretary of state were not won over by his argument that "this was one of the times when principled idealism was the most pragmatic and realistic course." They thought, Lansdale wrote, that he was being "too visionary and idealistic" and advised him to "disengage" from providing any further "guidance to political parties in Vietnam."[49]

Yet even as Lansdale's influence was slipping in Saigon, his reputation in the wider world was still swelling.

◆

THE LEGEND of "Lawrence of Arabia" was concocted single-handedly by the American impresario Lowell Thomas, who in 1919 premiered a lecture and slide show on Colonel Lawrence's exploits that played to packed houses in New York and London and beyond. The legend of Edward Lansdale had more authors, but one of the most important—and inadvertent—was Graham Greene.

In December 1955, the eminent English writer published *The Quiet American*, a novel featuring a character named Alden Pyle, the "quiet American" of the title, who was an undercover intelligence operative, a supporter of Trinh Minh Thé's, the owner of a black dog, and an enthusiast for promoting a "third force"—that is, a democratic alternative to communism and colonialism. For understandable reasons, the widespread assumption, held not least by Lansdale himself, was that he was the model for the protagonist, who was hardly painted in flattering hues: Graham depicted Pyle as a naïve young interloper who supplied Trinh Minh Thé with explosives that maimed innocent Vietnamese. "I never knew a man who had better motives for all the trouble he caused," sighed Thomas Fowler, the world-weary English correspondent who is the novel's narrator. In retribution, he would arrange for Pyle to be murdered by the Vietminh.[50]

Lansdale first heard of the new book at a diplomatic party early in 1956. As he reported to his wife,

At the reception, the Embassy staff were teasing me about my love life. Seems that Graham Greene has written a new novel, supposedly based upon me. Called the "Quiet Man" or maybe it's the "Quiet American." Anyhow, a naïve American, me, makes friends with a murderous Vietnamese called General The (Trinh Minh The, I suppose) who fools him and leads him astray, but the American finally wakes up and finds he has been sucked in by a very despicable guy. Meanwhile the story says he has had a wild love life, I presume due to General The. Sounds as though the French propagandists are really able to sell a bill of goods to the British, since the French peddled stories that I was very naïve and The sold me a bill.[51]

By mid-February, Lansdale had managed to get his hands on a copy and decided that "the book has about everything wrong politically." It was also wrong in details such as Greene's inaccurate description of plastic explosives. "However," he continued, "I like the way the fellow writes. . . . Trouble is, it will fill a lot of Americans with quite a false picture of things here, and follows the French propaganda line quite faithfully, despite its being critical of the French."[52]

Lansdale remembered seeing the English novelist only once, in 1954, when Greene was sitting on the terrace of the colonial-era Continental Hotel, a favorite haunt of expatriates in Saigon, along with a large number of French officers who began to boo Lansdale when they saw him. Lansdale was with two of his friends, the husband-and-wife *New York Times* correspondents F. Tillman Durdin and Peggy Durdin. Peg stuck her tongue out at the crowd on the terrace and said, "But we love him," and turned around and gave Lansdale "a big hug and kiss." In an anecdote a bit too good to be true, Lansdale recalled saying, "Well, I'm going to get written up someplace as a dirty dog. Thanks a lot!"[53]

In truth, Greene always denied that he modeled Pyle on Lansdale. "Pyle was a younger, more innocent, and more idealistic member of the CIA," he wrote. "I would never have chosen Colonel Lansdale, as he then was, to represent the danger of innocence."[54] The novelist claimed that his inspiration was Leo Hochstetter, a young American economic aid official with whom he had shared a room one night while visiting Colonel Jean Leroy, the Catholic warlord. According to Greene, Hochstetter, who was assumed by the French "to belong to the CIA," lectured him on the "long drive back to Saigon on the necessity of finding a 'third force in Vietnam.' "[55] Greene's denials are buttressed by the fact that, while he worked on *The Quiet American* between March 1952 and June 1955, he completed a draft before Lansdale arrived in Vietnam for good in June 1954.[56] That makes it unlikely that Lansdale was the model for Alden Pyle, as generations of writers have assumed,[57] but *The Quiet American*'s success only added to Lansdale's luster by association.

If *The Quiet American*, the novel, was anti-American, the movie version, which came out in 1958, was very different. In the movie, Trinh Minh Thé is not really responsible for the terrorist bombings in Saigon—the Vietminh are. Thé, along with the Alden Pyle character (played rather woodenly by war hero Audie Murphy), is framed by the Communists. Thomas Fowler (the veteran English actor Michael Redgrave) sets up Pyle to be killed by the Vietminh not because of his revulsion at Pyle's complicity in terrorism but because he is a Communist dupe who is intensely jealous of Pyle for stealing his Vietnamese girlfriend, Phuong—played, bizarrely, by the Italian actress Giorgia Moll. The cinematic version ends with Inspector Vigot (Claude Dauphin), the detective investigating Pyle's murder, telling Fowler that he has been "used" and "childishly manipulated" by the Communists: "If you will pardon my attempt at colloquial English, Mr. Fowler, they have made a bloody fool of you."

This was a neat inversion of Greene's plot, one that infuriated the author, who later decried the "treachery" of the film's writer and director, Joseph L. Mankiewicz.[58] (The second movie version of *The Quiet American*, starring Michael Caine and Brendan Fraser, would be more faithful to the novel, but Greene would not live to see its release in 2002.) What Greene may not have realized was that Edward Lansdale had taken a considerable hand in altering the movie's political message to make it pro-American.

Lansdale met Joseph Mankiewicz when the filmmaker arrived in Saigon at the end of January 1956 to research the script. The product of a leading Hollywood family (his older brother, Herman, was the screenwriter of *Citizen Kane*), Mankiewicz had won Oscars as the director and writer of *A Letter to Three Wives* (1949) and *All About Eve* (1950). More recently he had directed Marlon Brando in *Julius Caesar* (1953) and Humphrey Bogart and Ava Gardner in *The Barefoot Contessa* (1954). Richard Burton, who later worked with him on *Cleopatra* (1963), wrote that Mankiewicz was himself a quiet American—an "Oxford don manqué," with an "ever-present pipe" and a "way of making considered statements with his twinkling eyes peering through a miasma of tobacco smoke."[59]

With a talent for witty, ribald tales, Mankiewicz was just the sort of person who would have gotten along well with a CIA operative who had once dreamed of becoming a *New Yorker* cartoonist. Over dinner at Lansdale's Rue Duy Tan house, Mankiewicz said he had bought film rights to *The Quiet American* "to prevent the British or French from making an anti-U.S. movie."[60] Lansdale helped him craft an alternative storyline. A few weeks later, Ed wrote to Helen, "Seems that Mankiewicz liked the plot twist for 'The Quiet American' that we discussed. . . . Quite a change in the French propaganda!"[61] A month later, Lansdale sent Mankiewicz a follow-up letter urging him to "go right ahead and let it be finally revealed that the Communists did it after all."[62]

A liberal anti-Communist, Mankiewicz took Lansdale's advice and produced a film that Graham Greene did not recognize. He was able to win permission from Diem to film in Vietnam—the first Western moviemaker granted that privilege—thanks to Lansdale's intervention.[63] In October 1957, when the film was ready for viewing, Lansdale wrote to Diem that "Mr. Mankiewicz's 'treatment' of the story" was "an excellent change from Mr. Greene's novel of despair"—"I feel that it will help win more friends for you and Vietnam in many places in the world where it is shown."[64] Lansdale arranged a screening of the film in Washington, inviting representatives from "practically all [U.S. government] departments, agencies, and services concerned with psychological, political, and security affairs." "They all seemed to enjoy it as much as I did," Lansdale wrote to his old friend Iron Mike O'Daniel, now retired from the Army and chairman of a new lobby group, the American Friends of Vietnam, which had been formed to support the Diem regime.[65] On January 22, 1958, the American Friends of Vietnam, whose ranks came to include prominent politicians, academics, and journalists, sponsored a "world premiere" screening of *The Quiet American* in Washington. *Tout le monde* of "Washington's society" turned out "in all its glitter," wrote the pro-Diem *Times of Viet Nam*.[66]

Lansdale may have been losing influence in Washington and Saigon, but he had not lost his touch for psychological warfare. His handling of *The Quiet American* was as deft a propaganda coup as all of the rumors he had spread to encourage emigration from North Vietnam in 1954–55 or the anti-Huk rumors he had spread in the Philippines a few years earlier. He was shaping Western public perceptions so as to bolster the new Republic of Vietnam even as he was experiencing an erosion of his preeminent position of influence in Saigon.

◆

ONE OF the final projects that Lansdale undertook in 1956, his last year in Vietnam, was to improve the quality of Ngo Dinh Diem's vacations. This was not as trivial as it sounds: Lansdale was convinced that well-rested leaders make better decisions. Diem had an official vacation home at Dalat, a town in the Central Highlands, but it was so quiet there that he was restless. He returned to Saigon after brief stays in Dalat, Lansdale noticed, looking "haggard" and confessing that he had been unable to sleep.

After much importuning, Diem agreed to spend a couple of days at a beach cottage at Vung Tau, on the coast of the South China Sea about an hour's drive from Saigon, along with his brother and sister-in-law. Lansdale and Pat Kelly came too. Pictures snapped during this idyll show Pat in a white one-piece swimsuit and the always soignée Madame Nhu in a black one-piece number happily cavorting in the waves. Lansdale had brought swim trunks for Diem, but the president insisted on jumping into the surf in his underwear—to Lansdale's amazement, he wore "old fashioned long johns." Lansdale played Scrabble with the cerebral Nhu and lost steadily as long as the game was in French. When they agreed to play in both French and English, Lansdale won and Nhu immediately stopped playing. "He doesn't like to lose," Madame Nhu explained. Diem was still prone to deliver long lectures on Vietnamese politics but "with the steady sound of the surf and the wind through the pines," his eyelids would begin to droop in mid-monologue and Lansdale would quietly steal away to let him get some much-needed rest.

When they returned to Saigon, Diem said he had never felt so refreshed. Yet after Lansdale left Vietnam, the president returned to his habit of short, fitful getaways at Dalat. When Lansdale wrote to remonstrate with him, Diem explained that Vung Tau was becoming infested with Communist guerrillas and that he didn't want to risk his soldiers' lives to safeguard a vacation. Even in matters of holidaying, Lansdale's influence on Diem was hardly unlimited.[67]

Despite the negativity that now swirled around Lansdale, Diem still wanted him to remain where he was. In mid-1956, Diem asked Washington to keep his adviser in Saigon for two more years and to place him in charge of U.S. political strategy for all of Southeast Asia.[68] Diem told a mutual friend, Lansdale reported, "that his reason for suggesting this was that the U.S. doesn't send out ambassadors or economists who understand the problems or peoples of the area, and Asia trusts me."[69] Lansdale was humbled by the praise ("Wow!"), but he was exhausted and ready to leave. By the fall of 1956, he was making arrangements to return to the United States before Christmas, confident that the secret mission he had been given by Allen Dulles—to build a viable South Vietnamese state as an anti-Communist bulwark in Southeast Asia— had been accomplished.

◆

IN THE fall of 1956, the Eisenhower administration had to deal with two simultaneous foreign crises. Israeli forces attacked Egypt on October 29 in a coordinated offensive with the British and French, who were alarmed by the nationalization of the Anglo-French Suez Canal Company. Eisenhower feared that their actions would drive Egypt's strongman, Gamal Abdel Nasser, into the arms of the Soviets. A week later, on November 4, the Red Army invaded Hungary to put down a revolt against Soviet rule. By comparison with these dispiriting developments, South Vietnam stood out as an improbable success story—a ray of sunshine amid diplomatic troubles around the globe.

South Vietnam had come a long way from the disorderly days of June 1954, when, just after the fall of Dien Bien Phu, Edward Lansdale had first arrived, so bereft of resources that he had no car or home, to find no state worthy of the name and no statesman worth supporting. When, a few weeks later, Ngo Dinh Diem was appointed premier, few expected his ramshackle regime to last two and a half months, much less two and a half years. Lansdale had labored indefatigably and, on the whole, successfully to construct a stable government against daunting odds.

During that period of the mid-1950s, the Quiet American, as he was becoming known, had helped arrange for nearly a million refugees to escape North Vietnam and resettle in the South. He had, in addition, initiated the pacification of the South Vietnamese countryside, while employing his psywar skills to buttress South Vietnam and undermine the North with propaganda coups, such as the almanac predicting ill fortune for the North and the film version of *The Quiet American*. Most significantly, he had helped Diem prevail against foes both in Saigon and in Washington during the Battle of the Sects. His failures—especially his inability to prevent the South Vietnamese army from being restructured to fight conventional adversaries and to restrain Diem's authoritarian instincts—would loom larger in the future, when they would be seen as critical weaknesses in the fight against a resurgent Communist threat, but for the time being these shortcomings seemed to pale in comparison with his achievements. For Lansdale's service in Vietnam, to go along with the National Security Medal he had received in the Philippines, he would get a Distinguished Service Medal, the highest decoration the Department of Defense can award for "exceptionally meritorious and distinguished service" outside of combat.[70]

"When I left at the end of 1956," Lansdale later said, "I left a very popular Vietnamese leader running things, a man who was being very responsive to the needs of the people. I thought the show was on the road when I left."[71] In his optimism, he perfectly reflected the buoyant mood of America. In the spring of 1957, Diem would undertake a triumphal tour of the United States that would include an address to a joint session of Congress and a ticker-tape parade in New York. The press, public, and policymakers hailed him as, in the words of *Life* magazine, "The Tough Miracle Man of Vietnam," a leader who "has roused his country and routed the Reds."[72] Americans were ecstatic that his unexpected success had made it unnecessary, at least for the time being, to commit their own troops to prevent another "domino" from falling to Communist designs.

Yet Diem's achievement would prove more transitory than those of such contemporary nation builders as David Ben-Gurion, Sukarno, Syngman Rhee, and Lee Kuan Yew. The reasons for his ultimate failure can be ascribed primarily to a combination of geography—i.e., the proximity of a hostile and heavily militarized North Vietnam—and personality—i.e., the diffident and autocratic traits that disfigured Diem's rule. But the downfall of Diem and the country that he had created can also be ascribed in no small measure to the unwise influence exercised by his patrons in Washington. The problems would reach crisis proportions in 1963, leading to Diem's assassination and the subsequent Americanization of the conflict, with tragic consequences for all concerned. But already long before then, the bitter seeds of despair were being planted in 1956 as Edward Lansdale was returning home.

For Washington made no attempt to replace his constructive, if not always decisive, position of influence, thus setting South Vietnam on the road that would, within less than a decade, render it a failing state kept alive only with heavy infusions of American blood. How different history might have been if Lansdale or a Lansdale-like figure had remained close enough to Diem to exercise a benign influence and offset the paranoid counsel of his brother Ngo Dinh Nhu, who would push the regime into a fatal and far from inevitable confrontation with the Kennedy administration. Perhaps Lansdale's achievements could not have lasted in any case—perhaps Diem would have fallen and Hanoi would have prevailed no matter what—but the course on which Washington had now embarked made failure far more likely and at far higher cost.

The first intimations of how things were about to change, and not for the better, came shortly after Lansdale's departure, when the new chief of the CIA's Far East Division, Al Ulmer, visited Saigon to announce "that the era of free-wheeling improvisation was over, and that the CIA in Saigon would begin operating like a normal station, with more emphasis on intelligence collection."[73] The next CIA chief of station, Nicholas Natsios, who took over in the spring of 1957, concentrated, as an in-house history puts it, "more on illuminating the workings of the regime than on helping it against its adversaries."[74] For the CIA station, "normal" intelligence gathering meant recruiting a member of Diem's housekeeping staff to steal trash from his wastebaskets. By contrast, when Lansdale wanted to know something, he went straight to Diem or another official and asked—and more often than not he learned more than traditional spies, with their elaborate tradecraft, ever did.[75]

With Lansdale departing after two and a half turbulent and momentous years, the bureaucracy was returning to its comfort zone, as if Saigon had suddenly become Stockholm—the capital of a stable and prosperous state where the only tasks expected of the pinstriped American representatives were to attend dull banquets and convey routine démarches. Neither the State Department nor the Pentagon nor any other institution was prepared to fill the resulting vacuum by providing Diem with the kind of guidance that Lansdale once had offered.

As the CIA's official history notes, Lansdale's departure marked the end of an era—"When Lansdale left Saigon in December 1956, he took with him whatever modest capacity the United States had to persuade Ngo Dinh Diem of the need to win the consent of the governed."[76] Maybe it was simply a coincidence, but the post-Lansdale epoch would turn out to be far more sanguinary and far less successful.

PART FOUR

WASHINGTON WARRIOR

(1957–1963)

Brigadier General Lansdale addresses a graduating class at the U.S.
Army Civil Affairs School at Fort Gordon, Georgia, November 1,
1960. He was a frequent speaker on counterinsurgency in the years
between his two tours in Vietnam. (HI)

18

Heartbreak Hotel

I can't go on the same old way and still retain respect for either of us.

—PAT KELLY

THE Washington, D.C., world to which Edward Lansdale returned just before Christmas 1956 bore little resemblance to the one that he had left in September 1950. Back then, President Harry Truman was building up America's military strength for a costly conflict on the Korean Peninsula while dealing with a "Red Scare" stoked not only by the McCarthy political witch hunts but by the Communists' appropriation of China and by the Soviet Union's acquisition of "the Bomb." President Dwight Eisenhower, who had just been elected to a second term in November 1956, was now presiding over a far more placid international scene, notwithstanding the short-lived Suez Crisis and the tragic Hungarian Uprising. The nation seemed at long last to be at peace and enjoying the growing fruits of prosperity, symbolized by the stock market's reaching in 1954 a peak not seen since just before the Wall Street crash of 1929. A new, mass-produced entertainment aesthetic was transforming America and soon much of the world, exemplified by the opening in 1955 of Disneyland in Anaheim, California, and of Ray Kroc's first McDonald's franchise in a suburb of Chicago.

Lansdale's home with Helen and their two sons, Ted and Pete, was sagging, however, under the emotional weight of a father and a husband who had been largely absent for more than a decade, making a mockery of the *Ozzie and Harriet* nuclear-family ideal promulgated on TV. But to a casual observer, their household in the Palisades neighborhood appeared like any other mid-1950s suburban domicile, replete with juvenile excitement over Slinkys and Frisbees. Nationally, the teenage world was being "all shook up" by the appearance of a twenty-one-year-old singing sensation from Memphis. Helped by three transformational appearances on *The Ed Sullivan Show*, Elvis Presley would dominate the charts with hits such as "Heartbreak Hotel" and "Hound Dog." As if embodying the Presley lyrics, Lansdale himself would soon be engulfed in his own "heartbreak"—indeed, multiple heartbreaks.

◆

AMONG THOSE Lansdale had left behind in Saigon was his beloved dog Pierre. In practically every letter that he wrote to Helen Lansdale or Pat Kelly between 1954 and 1956, he gave lengthy updates on the poodle's doings. A typical example of his canine obsession: "Pierre has had a haircut for the hot weather, which is very much with us and tried to fight a fight to the death with a big black mutt next door."[1] It is questionable whether Ed's family was that interested in reading so much about a dog they had never met, but the lengthy accounts of Pierre's activities were a sign of how much, in lieu of a real family, the animal meant to him. (The dog also gave him a safe subject to write about, avoiding both government secrets and personal secrets concerning his relationship with Pat Kelly.) "See, he's rapidly becoming a member of the family," Lansdale said.[2]

In May 1956, however, Pierre ran out of the yard and into the street, never to return. This was Lansdale's first heartbreak, one that he tried to assuage by immediately acquiring a "blue-eyed, brown-haired poodle pup" called Koko who was an "expert at gnawing off shoe-laces and refusing to be house-broken."[3] Koko accompanied Ed back to

Washington, where he was glad to discover that the puppy had "given up chewing my gloves and pissing on the floor."[4]

—◆—

AND WHAT of Lansdale's other friends—his human friends? No one was more important to him than his darling Patching. He had not, of course, seen as much of Pat Kelly once he moved to Saigon as he had in the days—1945 to 1948, 1950 to 1954—when he lived in Manila, but still he had visited the Philippines and she South Vietnam. Their affair was well known to Lansdale's associates in both Vietnam and the Philippines. Charles "Bo" Bohannan told Frisco San Juan, the head of Freedom Company, that "if and when Ed will be free, he will take Pat as his life partner."[5]

Whenever Pat was away from him, Ed wrote plaintive letters about how much he missed her. On January 29, 1955, for example, just a few weeks after getting back to Saigon after spending Christmas with Pat and the Magsaysays in Manila, he wrote, "I love you. With this simple, straightforward sentence, about love, not resolutions, we move into a letter in which someone who misses you very much, loves you very much, and is out to save the world with one box top ripped from a carton of Chesterfields, is trying to say how much he misses you, at 3:30 in the morning while punch drunk from work, and at 7:30 in the morning and at 17:00 and all through the day in this place."[6] More than a year later, on April 13, 1956, after one of the big parties that he regularly hosted in his villa, Ed wrote, "Darling, I am drunk and sitting here all alone to write to you, after getting rid of all the people having fun and reminding me that I need you for real happiness. . . . I love you, honey chile."[7]

Obviously the ardor between Ed and Pat had cooled a bit, but real passion still remained in a romance that had commenced ten years earlier, in 1946, when he had spotted a good-looking war widow in a white dress sitting in Johnny Orendain's car. Back then, Ed was thirty-eight years old and Pat thirty-one; now he was forty-eight and she forty-one. Their relationship had been intellectually as well as emotionally fulfilling; the canny Filipina had played a critical role in helping her

American lover to better understand the dynamics of Southeast Asian societies. But with Ed leaving Asia and heading back to Washington, while still refusing to divorce his wife, their relationship had reached a critical turning point.

Already Pat had let Ed know that she was dating other men, news that earned her a jealous rebuke from a boyfriend who, to judge by the extant evidence, did not dally with other women, his wife of course excepted. "OK, so you wanted to hurt me," Ed wrote to her. "It hurts. Why? The guy isn't worth even the little finger of someone like you, even if he is a good dancer. . . . What in hell is amusing about seeing someone you are in love with following anything new in pants? And people who are poseurs?"[8] Ed continued to tell Pat that he needed "his *real* woman, you."[9]

Then, on September 7, 1956, knowing that Ed was about to return to his family in Washington, Pat sat down at her typewriter and wrote him a letter full of pain and longing that deserves to be quoted at length for the light it sheds on the state of their relationship:

> I am having an extremely difficult time trying to say the right things. What does one write when one wants to terminate 10 years of a wonderful association? Does one merely scribble "finis" and let it go at that? Or does one merely keep silent and thus let it be understood that everything is all over. This would have been the easiest thing to do . . . just like running away and hiding and refusing to face facts. It would have been very cowardly too.
>
> I think what we have or had, deserves something better than that. It is so hard to give you up without a struggle which I suspect you are ready to do.
>
> The years go by, people change and the things they want are different. I wish I could just keep on feeling the same old way, happy to compromise, blind to almost everything except to be with you, to love you and have you love me, to be content after some fashion. But things have changed. I feel I must keep faith with myself. I have reached a bridge and it has to be crossed.

I am no longer contented with just knowing you love me and being with you now and then. I want more. I want to have the right to be with you for always, to have security and peace and happiness. You need me too. You will be needing more as time goes on, when there will be no more countries to save, no more wars to be won, no more troubles to shoot. Without us together, your life will just be one long, continuous work—empty in the end. There won't be anyone to nag you or tease you or jump you or tell you what a stinker you are getting to be.

My fight isn't against your work or your devotion to it. (I remember, though, that one of your real friends did say that you put so much in your work because you have nothing else in this world to look forward to. I remember too how this saddens me.) My fight is against what you think is your moral obligations to your wife and children. You seem to have forgotten a moral obligation to yourself too, and to both of us.

Years ago, there was no doubt your family had first claim on you. But things are changed now. You have given your family (people who see you once or maybe twice a year) all that is due them—the prestige and protection of your name, a social standing in the community due to your position, and all the material comforts they need. They have enjoyed all these things while you were thousands of miles away from them, not just for a few days but for a number of years! Obviously they can get along fine without you. They can't miss you very much anymore.

So why should you feel you should still belong to them? So why should you feel they need you except for the things you have afforded them? Which you can keep on giving them for the rest of your life! . . .

Also, we . . . Asian women are coming into our own. We want our rightful position which the democratic world has promised us. Years and years ago, a mixed marriage would have demean[ed] both parties but with the world as it is today it would not only be morally right but also politically and psychologically. . . .

You aren't putting in practice the principle of being fair, which I am told is the American standard of life. . . .

Anyway let's save us both some face and start life anew in our separate way. I can't go on the same old way and still retain respect for either of us.

It has been a wonderful ten years, and if I had a choice, I won't change any little bit of it. It has been wonderful knowing you and I hope we will continue to be friends after a while. Right now, I hope you will keep away from me and stop writing. (Did I ever tell you you write the most wonderful drunken letters?)

So long.

This letter is still painful, even for a biographer, to read, after all those years; it must have been unimaginably difficult to digest for its intended recipient, a man still very much in love with his Patching.

In fact, Ed and Pat would not sever all contact. They would continue to correspond infrequently. Their meetings became more infrequent still—once every few years. But the most intense relationship of Lansdale's life was, for the time being, over, along with the central purpose of his life—to fight for freedom on the ground in Asia. In the immortal words of Elvis, since Ed's "baby left" him, he was taking "a walk down lonely street to Heartbreak Hotel."[10] Now he would have to find what solace he could in the bosom of a family that, as Pat noted, he had barely seen during the past decade.

◆

PAT KELLY was not the only close friend in the Philippines from whom Lansdale was now separated.

Since his inauguration, Ramon Magsaysay had lived up to the hopes of Lansdale and his other American backers by becoming a staunch supporter of American foreign policy in Asia. Once Lansdale left the Philippines in 1954, however, Magsaysay fell under the influence of established politicos and failed to enact reforms to clean up Philippine politics or to correct the economic inequities that generated so much

resentment. While Magsaysay maintained his own reputation for pro-
bity, he "became lazy and was manipulated,"[11] Lansdale later acknowledged, and Lansdale's periodic trips to Manila between 1954 and 1956
were not enough to get him back on track. When he did see Lansdale,
Magsaysay complained, in Ed's words, that "he didn't have any Americans he could trust anymore."[12]

By early 1957, as Lansdale was adjusting to life back in America,
Magsaysay was gearing up for a reelection campaign in which, despite
the disappointments of his first term, he would be the prohibitive
favorite. On March 16, 1957, he flew to Cebu, one of the most densely
populated islands in the archipelago and one of considerable historical
importance as the place where in 1521 Magellan had converted the first
Filipinos to Christianity. Arriving at 4 p.m., he was greeted by a rapturous throng at the airport and proceeded through a long afternoon
and evening of speeches and meetings. By the time he finally reached
Lahug Airport again, located in a hilly section of Cebu City not far
from downtown, it was past midnight. The former president Sergio
Osmena Sr., who had waded ashore alongside Douglas MacArthur at
Leyte Gulf in 1944, was waiting to see him off, despite his advanced
age (he was nearly eighty years old). He urged Magsaysay to spend the
night at his house and fly back to Manila in the daylight. But the president said he had too much to do. Finally, at 1:15 a.m. on March 17, the
presidential airplane, a twin-motor C-47, dubbed *Mount Pinatubo* after
a volcanic mountain where the president had hidden in his guerrilla
days, took off in the early morning moonlight. At the controls for the
three-hour flight back to Manila was the Philippine air force chief of
staff, Brigadier General Benito Ebuen. Ten minutes after takeoff, he
radioed "ceiling unlimited." Then there was only silence, a silence that
grew increasingly ominous with the passage of time.

As morning dawned in Manila, wild rumors circulated. Some said
Magsaysay had made an unscheduled stop. Others said that the plane
had crashed but the president had survived. An all-out search by air and
sea was mounted, with U.S. ships and aircraft joining in. The plane's
wreckage was finally found late in the day on March 17 amid the dense
jungles of Mount Manunggal, a six-thousand-foot peak located twenty-

two miles north of Cebu City. There was only one survivor—a Filipino newsman who had not been wearing his seatbelt and was thrown clear of the crash with severe burns. He said that the plane had exploded just twenty minutes after takeoff. Sabotage was initially suspected, but responsibility was later affixed on pilot error aggravated by a failure of the lighting system. In the dark, General Ebuen, whose flight experience was in fighters not passenger aircraft, failed to clear the top of the mountain. Twenty-five bodies were found, most of them charred beyond recognition. One of the president's brothers had to identify his blackened corpse from a wristwatch.[13]

When the president's family heard the devastating news, his oldest daughter threw her rosary across the room—a shocking act in a devoutly Catholic family—and exclaimed, "There is no God!"[14] A radio announcer sobbed when he broke the news of the death of this young and vibrant leader, not yet fifty years old, whose passing was as much of a shock to Filipinos as the assassination of John F. Kennedy would be to Americans nearly seven years later. His funeral proceedings in Manila five days later would last seven hours and be mobbed by hundreds of thousands of weeping and screaming men, women, and children.[15]

Lansdale got the news in Washington in a phone call from one of Magsaysay's aides, "his voice so choked with tears that I barely understood his words." This was Lansdale's third successive heartbreak. He passed along the news to Carlos Romulo, the prominent soldier, politician, and journalist who was serving as Philippine ambassador to Washington, and the two men "sat together for hours trying to console each other."[16] A few days later, Lansdale noted, "The RM business really hurt. Still am not used to losing such friends."[17]

In tribute to Monching's memory, Lansdale persuaded two of the Rockefeller brothers—Nelson Rockefeller, who was about to embark on a campaign for governor of New York, and his older brother, John D. Rockefeller III, founder of the Asia Society among other philanthropic endeavors—to fund a Magsaysay Award Foundation, which would give out prizes for "public-spirited government service" in Asia. (Lansdale also mentioned the good work being done by Operation Brotherhood in Laos; Nelson wrote a check for $15,000 on the spot.)[18]

Nearly sixty years later, the Magsaysay Award Foundation still hands out beneficial awards.

Lansdale had less success in persuading the CIA to back a successor in Magsaysay's mold. He "quietly" pushed for the CIA to support Manuel Manahan in the 1957 election.[19] Manny was a former newspaper publisher who had worked closely with Lansdale to elect Magsaysay and had subsequently served as head of the Presidential Complaints and Action Commission and as commissioner of customs. In the latter position, he had cleaned up a notoriously corrupt government agency. But Lansdale's old nemesis George Aurell, now CIA station chief in Manila, refused to throw CIA resources behind Manahan, who was running on the Progressive Party ticket. Aurell preferred the Liberal Party, because he had a "deep-cover agent" close to its vice presidential candidate,[20] thus putting the imperatives of American intelligence gathering over the dictates of good government in the Philippines. While the CIA sat on the sidelines, the Progressive and Liberal candidates split enough votes between them to allow the election to be won by Magsaysay's vice president, Carlos Garcia, a Nacionalista ward heeler who had been given the job as part of their price for supporting Magsaysay. "Garcia hadn't been in office six months," a CIA officer stationed in Manila later wrote, "before false bills of lading became standard at the Manila harbor, copra was being smuggled out of the southern islands in huge amounts, and a payoff system was put into effect for conducting any sort of transaction with the government."[21]

Everything that Lansdale and Magsaysay had strived to achieve by making the government more honest and accountable was unraveling. In 1962, five years after Magsaysay's death, Lansdale lamented that "the end result of corruption and mal-administration has been the frittering away of the Philippine military establishment to a hollow shell . . . , the lowering of public morale to a point where there is little of political value worth a Filipino's life to defend, and an increase of vulnerabilities inviting illegal overthrow of the government."[22] Just three years after he wrote those words, Ferdinand Marcos would be inaugurated as president.

The post-1953 tribulations of the Philippines showed how difficult it was to fundamentally transform a country, any country, whose social and political contours had been shaped by myriad factors over the course of a long history, like rocks formed by the accumulation of sediment over the millennia. Lansdale could accelerate and guide political change in the short term. Making that change last was a much more difficult proposition, mainly because of indigenous resistance but also because of resistance within the U.S. government. Before long Lansdale would have cause to learn that lesson anew in Vietnam.

19

Guerrilla Guru

The strongest control is one that is self-imposed; it is based on mutual trust and the awakening of unselfish patriotism on ideals or principles we ourselves cherish.

—EDWARD LANSDALE

B Y the time that Edward Lansdale returned home to Eisenhower's America at the end of 1956, he had a firmly established reputation inside the U.S. government not only as the country's most successful political warrior but also as an inveterate maverick at odds with whichever bureaucracy he happened to find himself in. Lansdale had been fighting with his bosses since his days in San Francisco advertising. He operated best on his own, or at most leading a small team, and he constantly vented his frustrations with the workings of the U.S. government. Referring to visiting "American psywar people," he wrote in 1956, "One of the really amazing things is some of them actually talk Washington gobbledygook as normal conversational language! It surprised some of my gang, so I told them that such people were not too certain of themselves and so covered up their lack of certainty or depth by talking in a way that sounds profound but is impossible to analyze."[1] Given his contempt for bureaucrats, it was not easy for Lansdale, once he left Vietnam, to find a niche in what he referred to as "the Washington jungle"[2] or, alternatively, "the squirrel cage of Washington."[3]

Senior executives at the CIA, from Allen Dulles on down, told Lansdale that he was welcome to work in their headquarters, still located in temporary buildings along the Washington Mall.[4] There was some talk of sending Lansdale to Egypt to work with Gamal Abdel Nasser, but Lansdale put a stop to that by pointing out "how the Quai d'Orsay [the French Foreign Ministry] would react," given his feuding with the French in Indochina.[5] No other job was forthcoming from the CIA. "My present shop simply didn't come through with anything concrete, except that they loved me," Lansdale wrote to his old deputy, Charles "Bo" Bohannan. "I told them I loved them too, and let it go at that."[6]

Protestations of mutual affection notwithstanding, it was hardly a surprise that the CIA was not all that eager to find headquarters employment for Lansdale and that he was not that eager to press for a job there. Lansdale had had heated and continuing clashes with many of the career intelligence officers at the CIA, most recently over whether the agency would support Ngo Dinh Nhu's pro-government political parties. Ed wrote in 1957 to Bohannan that George Aurell ("Big George"), the CIA station chief in Manila, regarded both of them "with undying hatred," and was reportedly "getting drunk at cocktail parties, receptions, etc.," naming them "as Company," and "sounding off to all and sundry that there is [a] new era now, without the bribery that we did."[7]

This was not just a clash of personalities but also a difference of ideas about how the CIA should operate. The mainstream view at the spy agency held then, and still does, that the job of a case officer is to create "formal, controlled agent relationships"—that is, to pay or blackmail foreigners into spying on their countries.[8] Lansdale was willing to give funding to his friends in the Philippines or Vietnam to help them accomplish certain tasks, whether to publish a pro-Magsaysay newspaper or to lure sect troops over to Diem's side, but he did not believe in creating formal reporting relationships with agents. In his Saigon Military Mission report, Lansdale went out of his way to express his dissent from CIA orthodoxy: "There is a lesson here for everyone concerned with 'control' of foreign persons and groups. The strongest control is one that is self-imposed; it is based on mutual trust and the awakening of unselfish patriotism on ideals or principles we ourselves cherish. Once established, the foreign person or groups serve our own best national interests by serving their own national interests, which coincide with ours."⁹ This view was anathema at the CIA, where cynical intelligence officers viewed it as hopelessly naïve.

Lansdale was hardly the first or last covert operative to run up against this prejudice. So did, among others, Robert Ames, the CIA's premier Middle East case officer in the 1970s and 1980s. Ames established an invaluable friendship with the Palestine Liberation Organization's Ali Hassan Salameh, who served as an informal American conduit to the PLO leader Yasser Arafat. Yet, as the historian Kai Bird has shown, CIA colleagues repeatedly sabotaged the relationship and almost drove Salameh away by demanding, over Ames's protests, that he sign a contract to become a controlled agency asset—something that he refused to do.¹⁰

Not finding a niche in the intelligence bureaucracy, Lansdale in 1957 severed his relationship with the CIA, which had begun in 1950 when he had gone to work for its forerunner, the Office of Policy Coordination. His most productive and influential years had been spent as a CIA officer, and his legend would forever be intertwined with the history of the spy agency, but now he was hanging up his cloak and dagger, choosing instead to join the staff of the Air Force in the world's biggest and possibly most depressing office building.

◆

THE PENTAGON had been erected hurriedly during World War II by fifteen thousand workers laboring around the clock for sixteen months to create a new home for the fast-expanding Army bureaucracy. (The other services moved in after the war.) The five-story, five-sided design was meant to minimize the use of steel, which was in short supply in wartime, so it featured concrete ramps rather than steel elevators. "The Building," as it came to be known, had five rings of drab offices housing twenty-seven thousand functionaries, more than seventeen miles of gray corridors, seventy-seven hundred no-frills, institutional windows, eighty-five thousand fluorescent light fixtures, and six and a half million square feet of floor space, three times more than the Empire State Building.[11] Even General Dwight D. Eisenhower got lost in the building when he became Army chief of staff at the end of 1945. "One had to give the building his grudging admiration; it had apparently been designed to confuse any enemy who might infiltrate it," Ike wrote.[12] The future president was inaugurating a long tradition of Pentagon employees joking about the place where they worked—a sign of how unhappy most officers were to find themselves confined within its walls, far from the work with soldiers in the field that had drawn them into military service.

If Lansdale was an odd fit within the Pentagon, he was even more of an anomaly in the Air Force, a service then focused on waging nuclear war against the Soviet Union, not on fighting guerrillas. After just three months as Far East action officer for the Air Force's deputy chief of staff for operations, Lansdale found a more congenial niche in the Pentagon. He became deputy director of the secretary of defense's Office of Special Operations—"one of those awful Washington titles," he wrote, "which I'm sure must puzzle the Communists as much as it does me. It merely means that I have an 'In' basket with problems that nobody else is damfool enough to want to tackle, so they pass them along."[13]

Lansdale's new boss was the retired Marine general Graves B. Erskine, yet another fighting man—like Iron Mike O'Donnell, Hanging Sam Williams, and Ray Spruance—with whom he would establish a close rapport. "Big E" was a native of Louisiana who had started his military service as a National Guardsman chasing Pancho Villa in 1916. Thereafter he had joined the Marine Corps and earned a Silver Star while fighting in France in World War I. In the interwar years, he served in the Marines' "small wars" in Haiti, the Dominican Republic, and Nicaragua, where he experienced guerrilla war firsthand. In 1945, as commander of the Third Marine Division, he spearheaded the bloody invasion of Iwo Jima. He was a four-star general in 1953 when he retired from the Marine Corps to become assistant to the secretary of defense for special operations and director of the Office of Special Operations.[14]

Not long after Lansdale's arrival in June 1957, Erskine suffered a heart attack and was admitted to Bethesda Naval Hospital. He would spend much of the next two years on convalescent leave, giving Lansdale the opportunity to run the office in his absence. Some bureaucratic rivals tried to use Big E's ill-health as an excuse to ease him into retirement, but the loyal Lansdale would have none of it. He notified the White House, expecting that President Eisenhower, himself a heart-attack victim, would be sympathetic. The president handwrote a nice "get well" note to "Gravestone" (a macabre pun on his first name), expressing the hope that he would return to work soon. Before taking the note to Erskine's hospital bed, Lansdale read it to a senior staff meeting at the Pentagon, thereby making clear that his boss had the president's full support. That "stopped all the sniping," Lansdale recalled, "and so Erskine and I became very close after that."[15]

Headquartered in Room 3E-114 of the Pentagon (an office that, following post-9/11 remodeling, no longer exists), the Office of Special Operations (OSO), which Lansdale ran in Erskine's absence, was utterly obscure but also quietly powerful, as is so often the case in Washington. Its head was expected to serve as the senior adviser to the defense secretary on special operations, psychological warfare, guerrilla warfare, counterguerrilla warfare, intelligence, and civic action, and with Lansdale installed, it became the primary Pentagon office for dealing with Vietnam issues as well. The CIA often needed military support for its operations in the form of weapons, aircraft, personnel, and other necessities. All such requests were funneled through OSO, meaning that Erskine or, in his absence, Lansdale had to approve the plans. In addition, the head of OSO was a member of important interagency committees that supervised the entire U.S. intelligence bureaucracy. Still only a colonel, albeit no longer as young as when he had first pinned on his wings in 1952 (he turned fifty in 1958), Lansdale was expected to hold his own in interagency meetings with two- and three-star generals as well as senior executives from the civilian intelligence agencies. To make the disparity in their ranks less glaring, Lansdale usually left his uniform at home and wore a civilian suit, "because it was embarrassing really to be junior to them and try to give them guidance."[16]

Despite his newfound power, being in the "Washington bureaucracy was a horrible experience" for Lansdale, his aide Jerry French recalled.[17] Ed complained in his letters to Pat Kelly that his Pentagon superiors had more "uninspired drudgery for me than any guy should be expected to do."[18] He spent a lot of time looking wistfully out his Pentagon window at the airplanes taking off and landing at National Airport. In the fall of 1957, he wrote to Pat, "Rumors reach me that I've been in Manila (also Saigon). Only wish they were true. Unfortunately I'm stuck in a Pentagon job with a view of the airport—and keep wishing I was aboard one of the flights west which seem to take off about every five minutes."[19]

In spite of Lansdale's obligatory complaints about the arid bureaucratic routine, his subordinates discovered that he would often stay in the office late into the night—an indication not only of how devoted he was to his work but also of how little desire he had to go home to a family he barely knew. While Lansdale was as unmindful of his family and as consumed with his work as many other "organization men" of the fifties, he was not a self-serving schemer striving to advance his own interest at the expense of his colleagues. He showed unusual empathy for those around him. French recalled that one day he got word that his brother, a Detroit police officer, had been involved in a serious accident. He immediately left for National Airport to catch a flight to Detroit, and was surprised to find Lansdale in the airport's waiting area. "He had taken the trouble to leave the office and see me and talk to me at the airport before I took off," French said. "This meant a lot to me, that a guy who was several ranks above me would do that."[20]

While the usual Washington pattern is "kiss up, kick down," Lansdale, in fact, did the opposite—to the long-term detriment of his career.

❖

FAR AHEAD of most of his contemporaries, Lansdale apprehended in the 1950s that in the post–World War II era the United States would be involved more often in conflicts against shadowy guerrillas than in battles against uniformed foes such as the Wehrmacht or the Imperial Japanese Navy. To his new job, he brought a passion for developing capabilities that would better enable the United States to compete with the Communists in the kind of unconventional combat that he had waged in the Philippines and Vietnam. "Since the cease-fire in World War II, the communist enemy has conquered some 550 million people living on over 4 million square miles of territory," he wrote in September 1957, attributing the Communist successes to their ability to perfect "unconventional warfare techniques," while "our Armed Forces . . . are still too dependent upon mechanical means of warfare," which "tends to make us conventional—even when we are engaged in unconventional warfare."[21]

With machine-gun rapidity, Lansdale sprayed out ideas to rectify these shortcomings. In one secret memorandum, titled "A Cold War Program for Defense," he called for "proper indoctrination" of American personnel sent abroad so that "they will want and know how to make friends among the people," "a global program of bringing U.S. personnel and foreigners together on a favorable basis," assigning "trained counter-guerrilla advisers to MAAGs [Military Assistance Advisory Groups] where required," and stimulating "U.S. thinking on unconventional warfare through seminars conducted by outstanding, experienced persons."[22] In short, he was proposing to train thousands of Edward Lansdales—soldiers who would interact on a sympathetic basis with embattled societies and spread the gospel of freedom.

Lansdale might be accused of an excess of idealism, but he was not naïve—he knew from personal experience how far most Americans fell short of his ideals. And if he needed any reminding, Pat Kelly wrote to him about the way the U.S. embassy in Manila, where she worked for the U.S. Information Agency, was being run: "As of a few weeks ago, the snack bar here is only for American employees and their guests, and Filipino employees may only use it as a special concession or condescension as the gossip goes. The gossip further says that the real joke, brittle and bitter, is that this privilege was given to the Filipinos so that the American in the office can have his coffee bought and brought in by his Filipino clerk while he is busy talking to his wife over the telephone about the cocktail party the night before."[23] This was exactly the kind of racist attitude that, in Lansdale's view, undermined the American position in the Cold War. In one of his speeches, he said that Filipinos bristled at foreigners with "hidden attitudes of superiority" who treated them as if they were children. "The Filipino is adept at what some call 'the deep freeze'—a surface compliance or agreeableness hiding their true feelings."[24]

Other Lansdale ideas that promoted a philosophy of "soft power," decades before that term was coined, included plans to give "foreign military personnel . . . training that would allow them to assist in certain situations of a basically civilian nature, e.g., critical road building, flood control, etc.";[25] to send retired American military personnel "as civilian instructors in African educational institutions";[26] and to assign American military advisers to create "a national ideal for the [local] troops to admire and aspire to emulate" by promoting national heroes such as Ramon Magsaysay in the Philippines or, in Vietnam, "the fabulous Trung sisters who led Vietnamese armies to battle the invading Chinese in olden days."[27] In a more hard-power vein, Lansdale proposed to take Freedom Company global, utilizing an ostensibly private entity secretly supported by the U.S. government to dispatch military personnel from nations such as South Vietnam, Pakistan, Taiwan, and South Korea to battle Communist advances. He suggested calling the new entity, which anticipated the rise of military contractors decades later, Freedom Inc. and said that "it may be concerned with sending of a single infantry battalion or possibly a force as large as two divisions."[28]

Like many visionaries before him, Lansdale was better at generating ideas than at implementing them. Few of his brainstorms were enacted. His lack of skill in manipulating a giant bureaucracy was becoming a bigger problem in Washington than it had been in Manila or Saigon, where he had thrived in a more freewheeling, chaotic culture amid a far smaller American presence.

◆

CHARACTERISTICALLY, LANSDALE did not confine his advocacy to the inner councils of power. In fact, no sooner had he returned from

Vietnam at the end of 1956 than he became an active speaker before military, intelligence, and Foreign Service audiences, proselytizing for his version of "counterguerrilla" warfare, as counterinsurgency was then known.

A representative talk was the one that he gave at the Army War College in Carlisle, Pennsylvania, on December 1, 1958. He began by addressing the audience as "Gentlemen and Gremlins," the latter a word coined in the 1940s for an "imaginary mischievous sprite"; it had become a favorite term of his to refer to those who might share his unconventional ideas. His focus was on Southeast Asia, "one of the major battlegrounds of today's death struggle," with one-fourth of the world's population up for grabs. He warned, "We don't want to be like the French, who went marching out of Hanoi in defeat in 1954, with millions and millions of dollars' worth of modern U.S. equipment— brave men whose heroism and weapons and numbers were not enough— licked by a local army wearing tennis shoes and pajamas." To counter the Communists, Lansdale advocated that armies in the region "under- take missions of public works, welfare, health, and education, as well as national security." "As the soldier becomes the true brother of the people, the enemy and his weapons become identified, with the help of the people, and the enemy when so identified can be defeated."[29]

From the perspective of the twenty-first century, much of this might seem to be conventional wisdom—counterinsurgency 101, as codified in the 2006 Army-Marine Field Manual on Counterinsurgency, which preached the importance of winning over the populace rather than simply killing insurgents. But in the aftermath of the greatest war in history—one decided in such epic battles as Midway, El Alamein, Stal- ingrad, and D-Day—there was nothing remotely conventional about Lansdale's wisdom. He was part of the first generation of postwar counterinsurgents, men such as the British officer Gerald Templer and the French officer David Galula, who were articulating a new doctrine to deal with "wars of national liberation" across the Third World.

The folksy way in which Lansdale delivered his homilies, blending in his own experiences while eschewing hard-to-follow jargon, made an indelible impact on listeners. After a talk that Lansdale delivered at the Army War College in February 1957, lasting from 8:30 p.m. until midnight, two infantry captains were so interested by what he had to say that they stayed up talking with him until 4:30 in the morning.[30]

Then-Major Samuel V. Wilson, an army officer on loan to the CIA, remembered that in 1957 one of his colleagues went to hear a lecture at the Pentagon. The CIA man returned and said, "Sir, I have just just listened to the most remarkable individual that I have ever heard. When he began talking, he was dry, had a monotonous voice, and I thought I'm not sure that I was wise in coming here. But as he kept talking I was mesmerized by what he had to say." Wilson had never heard of the speaker. What did you say his name was? he asked. "Ed Lansdale," his colleague replied. "They call him 'Landslide' Lansdale for his exploits in the Philippines, and he's just come back from Vietnam."[31]

◆

SAM WILSON would come to know Landslide Lansdale the following year. Having left the CIA in March 1958, he had some free time before he started attending classes at the Army Command and General Staff College at Fort Leavenworth in August and spent that interregnum by "snowbirding" (army slang for a short-term assignment) in the Office of Special Operations. Later, he would return to the Pentagon to become Lansdale's deputy.

A veteran of Merrill's Marauders, a U.S. Army unit that had fought behind Japanese lines in Burma, Wilson was a highly decorated combat soldier who looked as if he could have stepped out of an Army recruiting poster; the columnist Jimmy Breslin later described him as "six-foot-two, 195 pounds, with blue eyes and light wavy hair and the outdoors on his face and big hands."[32] But he was entranced by this offbeat Air Force colonel with the movie-star mustache who had never fired a gun at the enemy. More than half a century later, looking back on those distant days from his farm in rural Virginia, where he settled after retiring as a three-star general, the elderly Wilson, by then white-haired and infirm, recalled in his soft Southern accent that Lansdale was a "guru" to him: "To me he was a bit of a mystic. He had dark, soulful brooding eyes. He spoke softly and in order sometimes to understand him clearly, you had to lean forward. It took me some time to realize that was really a technique of his. If he spoke softly and you had to lean forward to hear him, he already had placed himself in the position that he wanted to be in. It was subtle but effective."

Every night after the Pentagon shut down, "Lansdale would stand there leaning against the doorjamb of his office, and I'd put my backside on the desk of the secretary who had long ago gone home," Wilson recalled. "He'd start almost in midsentence from something he had been talking about a week ago, as though it had just occurred, and spin some sort of yarn. I loved it, I absolutely loved it. I thought, 'This fella has found the golden fleece. He understands how warfare has changed, and he knows what the dynamics are.' I felt I had better listen to him and learn all I could. I was kind of like a lamprey eel, sucking on him." After getting "a good dose of the Lansdale philosophy," Wilson pronounced himself a "complete convert."[33]

After his year at Leavenworth, Wilson, by now a lieutenant colonel, was assigned as director of instruction at the Army Special Warfare School at Fort Bragg, North Carolina. The Army Special Forces, not yet known as the Green Berets, had been formed in 1952. Numbering 2,300 men, they were initially envisioned primarily as guerrillas operating behind enemy lines, just like Merrill's Marauders. By the late fifties, it was dawning on Special Forces officers that, on the "it takes a thief to catch a thief" principle, they were well positioned to become the country's premier counterguerrilla force.

In 1959, one year after Sam Wilson first met Lansdale, Colonel George M. Jones, the commander of the Special Warfare School, assigned him to put together the school's first course on fighting guerrillas. Wilson, however, struggled for a name. He recalled thinking that " 'counterguerrilla operations' was too narrow because it did not embrace those nonmilitary factors that so often dominate the scene in this conflict arena. 'Counterresistance' was a bad choice because we had identified ourselves so many times in our history with resistance forces that were trying to pursue worthy causes, to include our own revolution. To call it 'counterrevolutionary' played right into the hands of Soviet dogma." Wilson and his colleagues were stumped until he wrote on a chalkboard a new word that they all liked: "Counter-Insurgency." *Eureka*. By then it was two in the morning, and a major said, "Let's go home."[34] They had come up with their term.

By the fall of 1961, the title of the course had been changed to "Counter Insurgency Operations."[35] And soon thereafter "counterinsurgency" would become a familiar military term, first abbreviated as CI and later as COIN. Sam Wilson was not alone in claiming credit for this coinage, but his claim is superior to the *Oxford English Dictionary*'s attribution of the term to the *Times* of London in 1962.

As Wilson continued to formulate the course, he recalled, "I would get on the phone and call Lansdale and ask him questions. Lansdale's theses and little homilies and so on were sprinkled throughout the curriculum." The regular army, Wilson said, "thought we were crazy. Indeed, they thought we were dangerous. They accused us of trying to think like political commissars by introducing politics to the field of battle."[36] At first, Wilson could not even get regular officers to take the course. His initial groups of students, in early 1961, were CIA operatives and foreign military officers. Gradually more American officers enrolled. Lansdale supported Wilson from his perch at the Pentagon, helping to overcome opposition from more conventionally minded soldiers. He applied similar pressure on the Air Force, leading to the creation in 1961 of the 4400th Combat Crew Training Squadron (code-named Jungle Jim) to advise foreign air forces, and on the Navy, leading to the creation in 1962 of the first SEAL (Sea, Air, Land) teams to serve as naval commandos. All of these newfangled Special Operations Forces were soon heading to Vietnam. Colonel Jones, for one, was grateful for Lansdale's help. "Things certainly seem to be moving now in the Special Warfare field," he wrote to Lansdale in May 1961, "and I attribute most of this to you personally."[37]

The growth of Special Operation Forces is usually associated with President John F. Kennedy, who authorized the Army Special Forces to wear their distinctive green beret. JFK was indeed an avid supporter of these specialized troops, but they were already beginning to expand their capabilities before he came into office. Lansdale had no minor role in this process; in fact, he would help to spark the young president's interest in the subject of "brushfire wars."[38] That made Lansdale one of the godfathers of counterinsurgency in the postwar American military establishment—one of his more significant, if lesser-known, legacies.

◆

ED LANSDALE was hardly the only American official of the late fifties who was frustrated by the failure of the U.S. government to do more to adapt itself to the demands of unconventional warfare. His old friend Navy Captain William J. Lederer, whose first wife, not insignificantly, was a Filipina and who had traveled widely in Asia, had reached similar conclusions. On December 3, 1957, he wrote to Lansdale,

> I feel so strongly on this general subject that I have concluded it is impossible to accomplish what you have in mind (not only for the military but for all agencies) unless public indignation is aroused. There is nothing wrong with our foreign policy, the weak link is in its diluted implementation—particularly along the "Lansdale lines." I am taking a stab at arousing this public indignation. Eugene Burdick and I are writing a book on it which will be published in the Spring; and if you want more information on it, I'll be glad to send it.[39]

Lederer had been writing since 1947 for magazines such as *Reader's Digest*, but for his latest project he wanted authorial help to get the tone exactly right ("the book had to be written in flawless, relaxed, un-mad perspective," he noted), and he got it from another Navy veteran he had met in 1948 at the prestigious Bread Loaf Writers' Conference in Vermont.[40] Eugene "Bud" Burdick was a professor of political science at the University of California at Berkeley, who had already written one successful novel (*The Ninth Wave*, about a California surfer turned political consultant) and would later coauthor the popular potboiler *Fail-Safe*, about a nuclear crisis.

Together Lederer and Burdick set out to write a series of essays expressing their outrage over the steady deterioration in "the American position in Southeast Asia," which they attributed to "the way many

Americans overseas were recklessly doing the wrong thing, or doing the right thing in the wrong way, or just doing nothing."[41] Eric P. Swenson, an editor at W. W. Norton & Company who was himself a Navy veteran, suggested turning their critique into a novel. And that is just what they did. They brainstormed titles, including "A Handful of Seeds," "The Mysterious American," "The Noisy American," "The Ugly Engineer," and "The Stumbling American," before Swenson decided to call it "The Ugly American."[42]

The Ugly American appeared in the fall of 1958 shortly after Lederer retired from the Navy. It began with an unflattering depiction of the U.S. ambassador to the fictional nation of Sarkhan—"a small country out toward Burma and Thailand" that resembled Vietnam. Much like Homer Ferguson, the ambassador to Manila from 1955 to 1956 who did not want Lansdale intruding on his turf, Louis Sears is another former senator who is eager to become a federal judge and only slumming in Sarkhan while his appointment comes through. He has nothing but contempt for the locals (he refers to them as "strange little monkeys"),[43] and neither he nor any of his staff can read the local language or be bothered to spend time with ordinary people. There is an equally scathing portrait of a secretary in the legation who writes home boasting about all the amenities she and the other Americans enjoy ("There are built-in servants! . . . Liquor over here in the government liquor store is dirt cheap"), while commenting favorably on how little interaction they have with the locals.[44] These negative portraits are contrasted with positive depictions of a few Americans who are doing things right, including the "Ugly American" of the title: Homer Atkins is a homely engineer who isn't afraid to get his hands dirty helping the people of Sarkhan.

Another of the book's heroes is Colonel Edwin Barnum Hillandale, a U.S. Air Force officer who in 1952 "was sent to Manila as liaison officer to something or other." He is so fascinated by the Filipino people that he "ate his meals in little Filipino restaurants, washing down huge quantities of *adobo* and *pancit* and rice with a brand of Filipino rum which cost two pesos a pint." He regularly ventures out to the rural areas on a motorcycle and, once there, plays his harmonica to enchant the children. He "even attended the University in his spare hours to study Tagalog." The Filipino musicians with whom he jams on his harmonica call him "the Ragtime Kid." A diplomat at the U.S. embassy calls him "that crazy bastard." Yet, Lederer and Burdick wrote, "within six months the crazy bastard was eating breakfast with Magsaysay, and he soon became Magsaysay's unofficial adviser." (The by then deceased Magsaysay is the only character to appear under his real name.) The chapter goes on to recount how Hillandale, by repeatedly visiting a province north of Manila that is hostile to Magsaysay, persuades 95 percent of its inhabitants to support him in the 1953 presidential election.[45] Later in the narrative, Hillandale takes a break from the Philippines to visit Sarkhan, where he uses his knowledge of astrology to win over local officials. He explains to a skeptical U.S. diplomat, "Every person and every nation has a key which will open their hearts. If you use the right key, you can maneuver any person or any nation any way you want. The key to Sarkhan—and to several other nations in Southeast Asia—is palmistry and astrology."[46]

The resemblances to Lansdale are uncanny, even if the real-life Lansdale never mastered Tagalog or owned a motorcycle. "Tragically," Lansdale wrote, "later Americans in the U.S. advisory days in Vietnam tried to pattern their activities on the fictional Hillandale—and rode motorcycles around, played the harmonica, etc. without getting much else done—except to wind up dead or captured by the enemy. Yes, I used to play the harmonica at times when visiting the provinces, to take up the tedium of long waits alone or to entertain children when they'd gather around and start asking me a lot of questions. But I always had some other purpose for being there."[47]

Lederer privately acknowledged that the "first Colonel Hillandale story in *The Ugly American* is sort of based on Ed." (He later told Lansdale that the character was a composite of the two of them.)[48] Lederer went on to make clear his admiration for Lansdale: "The way Ed operates requires a frightful amount of patriotism, discipline, energy, and skill. He takes some little job in the area; and then proceeds to become the confidential adviser of the man he is trying to help. Everything is done hush hush and Ed sees that everyone but himself gets the credit.

His mind is alert. He can dissemble and camouflage as easily as a ballerina can change her costume. He has limitless courage and patience."[49]

In spite of its pedestrian writing style, *The Ugly American* spent seventy-eight weeks on the best-seller lists and sold millions of copies,[50] thus winning more converts to Lansdale's views than a lifetime of his speeches and memoranda could possibly have accomplished. Senator John F. Kennedy sent a copy of the book to every member of the U.S. Senate and later used it as inspiration to create the Peace Corps. In turn, many young Americans volunteered for the Peace Corps after reading *The Ugly American*.[51]

In 1963, *The Ugly American* was made into a movie starring Marlon Brando as Harrison Carter MacWhite, an idealistic American ambassador to Sarkhan. Pat Kelly approved of the casting. Perhaps not the best person to objectively assess Lansdale's resemblance to the great movie star, she told Ed, "Marlon Brando looked so much like you, especially his mustache, but not his voice which is bad compared to yours."[52] Although the film had almost nothing in common with the book beyond its title and setting, it did have some (probably coincidental) resonance with Lansdale's real-life story. In the first place, the movie's suave hero, Ambassador MacWhite, who is a composite of the admirable characters from the book, including Colonel Hillandale, favors driving a "Freedom Road," built with American aid, into Communist territory in Sarkhan. He sees the road as a weapon to foster military mobility as well as economic development and thus to battle Communism. Lansdale likewise advocated building roads as a counterinsurgency tactic. In 1959, for example, he wrote a Defense Department memorandum proposing that funds be allocated "to complete an all-weather road between Pakse in southern Laos and Kontum in [the Central Highlands of] Vietnam."[53] This project later received a name that could have come straight out of the movie—the Peace Highway.[54]

The film version of *The Ugly American* ends with Ambassador MacWhite telling a group of reporters in Sarkhan, "We can't hope to win the Cold War unless we remember what we are for as well as what we are against. . . . I've learned that the only time we're hated is when we stop trying to be what we started to be 200 years ago. Now I'm not blaming my country. I'm blaming the indifference that some of us show toward its promises." As he continues talking in a Lansdalian vein, the scene shifts to a suburban home in America where MacWhite is seen speaking on a television set. While he drones on, a distracted man turns off the TV, cutting off MacWhite in midsentence. This is an uncannily accurate depiction of the indifference with which Lansdale's views ultimately would be received by both policymakers and the general public.[55] Despite its cautionary ending, however, the film of *The Ugly American* further burnished the book's fame—and indirectly Lansdale's as well. When Robert F. Kennedy first met Lansdale in 1961, he referred to him in his diary as "the Ugly American."[56]

As Lansdale had already discovered after the publication of *The Quiet American*, his outsize reputation enabled him to get a wider hearing for his views but increasingly rankled many bureaucrats and created animosities that made his job harder. In 1963, the year that the Marlon Brando movie came out, Ed wrote to a friend, "I've ducked publicity very hard since it slows down the effectiveness of my activities."[57] If he was ducking publicity, he wasn't doing so very effectively.

◆

As FAR as Ed Lansdale was concerned, the most immediate consequence of *The Ugly American*'s publication was that it served as his ticket back to Vietnam, if only briefly. Inspired in part by the controversy created by the novel, President Eisenhower on November 24, 1958, appointed a committee of gray eminences to undertake a "completely independent, objective, and non-partisan analysis" of U.S. military assistance programs in some forty nations.[58] It became known as the Draper Committee, after its chairman, William Henry Draper Jr., a former Army general and Wall Street banker who had been the first U.S. ambassador to NATO.

Lansdale was asked to serve on the Southeast Asia subcommittee chaired by Dillon Anderson, the former national security assistant to Eisenhower and a prominent lawyer in Houston. His fellow subcommittee members were the retired general J. Lawton Collins and a young government economist named Charles Wolf Jr. Together they were slated to undertake a monthlong tour of Southeast Asian nations beginning in mid-January 1959. Lansdale was nervous about clashes with the imperious General Collins, but, Wolf recalled, the "good-humored" and "savvy" Anderson made sure they all got along. Between stops, the four subcommittee members peaceably played gin rummy together on their airplane, an Air Force C-47.[59]

The group reached its first foreign capital, Manila, on January 30, 1959, to find a city that had recovered from wartime damage and had not yet become as overbuilt and polluted as it would later become. This gave Ed a chance to see Pat Kelly for the first time since their breakup in 1956. Since then their communications had been limited to infrequent letters—and to small gifts such as stockings and lipstick that Ed conveyed via friends and colleagues passing through Manila. This earned him a semiserious upbraiding from Pat: "Why do you have to send emissaries and packages? I really don't mind the former but I wish you would stop the latter. Why don't you just drop me a line now and then? Or send me cards or just keep in touch little notes, just to let your friends know you are not spending all your time saving this world?"[60] We can only speculate how uncomfortable the lovers' reunion was; no epistolary record is extant. The most wrenching part of the trip was a visit to Magsaysay's relatively modest, white marble tomb in the Manila North Cemetery, which Ed found "a bit rough emotionally,"[61] all the more so because he had just received news that his father, Harry Lansdale, had died in Detroit. He stood alone in front of the Magsaysay memorial, he later recalled, in an "infinitely sad communion" with "both men who had been so close to me."[62]

By February 3, the Anderson subcommittee was winging its way over the South China Sea toward a still-peaceful Saigon. The highlight of their visit was meeting with the shy and cerebral president, who was continuing to expand his authority at the expense of his opponents. Lansdale had contacted Ngo Dinh Diem beforehand, asking, "Would you like to 'play hookey' from your work and go swimming at Long Hai with me? I'm sure you are working too hard, as usual, and could stand a day's vacation."[63] In Hawaii, Ed had even bought a pair of red swim trunks for the portly president.[64] Diem did not go to the beach, but he did treat the group to one of his trademark two-and-a-half-hour brief-ings as well as a private dinner at the palace. His theme "boiled down to a strong plea to maintain [South Vietnamese military] force levels and economic aid at present levels."[65] The subcommittee members came away impressed, Charles Wolf said, with "Diem's concentration and focus," his "intelligence and mastery." They concluded that "Diem was a good bet and we should support him,"[66] precisely the conclusion that Lansdale wanted them to reach. "The President is very pleased . . . ," the American agronomist Wolf Ladejinsky, an aide to Diem, wrote to Lansdale. "He credits you, as he should, with these developments, and he wants you to know this."[67]

After leaving South Vietnam on February 6, 1959, the group headed to Thailand, Cambodia, and Indonesia. While they were in Phnom Penh, a riverside city full of elegant French colonial buildings that had been dubbed the Pearl of the Orient, on February 10–12, a mili-tary coup against the modernizing prime minister, Prince Norodom Sihanouk, was getting under way. Sihanouk had angered Thailand and South Vietnam, as well as some of his more anti-Communist mil-itary officers, by recognizing the Communist regime in China. A wily survivor, Sihanouk crushed the military mutiny, led by General Dap Chhuon, who was "shot while attempting to escape." Sihanouk blamed the CIA in general and Lansdale in particular for this abortive upris-ing. His evidence? That Lansdale, "the renowned CIA specialist in cloak and dagger operations," had signed the guestbook at the ancient temple of Angkor Wat, Cambodia's most famous tourist attraction, which was located in a province run by General Chhuon.[68] In 1969, Sihanouk got his revenge when he produced, directed, and starred in a movie called *Shadow over Angkor*, in which he battled and killed a villainous CIA agent named Lansdale.[69] "Evidently he loved fantasy,"[70] Lansdale chuckled, describing the story as "a complete fabrication."[71]

In point of fact, the CIA did have a radio operator with the coup plotters, and when the coup collapsed he was captured by Sihanouk's troops. CIA officials later claimed that the radioman was there merely to monitor events.[72] It is possible that the CIA involvement went deeper—in 1970, the CIA would sanction a successful coup against

Sihanouk led by another general—but it is unlikely that Lansdale was involved. He was no longer a CIA operative, and even for a man of his talents it would have been a stretch to imagine that he could have organized a coup during a three-day visit to a country where he had no prior connections. But, given Lansdale's outsize reputation, few would believe his denials—not even State Department officials on the scene. "The embassy here is quite touchy about my presence," Lansdale wrote, complaining that "our official family are the usual weak-kneed lot, so I am boiling mad by tonight by their over-sensitivity to my presence."[73]

The blue-chip Draper Committee concluded its work with a recommendation that U.S. foreign military aid, then at $1.6 billion, be boosted by another $400 million. President Eisenhower supported this recommendation in principle but held off in practice for fear of blowing a hole in the budget.[74] The canny president's real goal in appointing the committee had been to make the case to Congress and the public for why foreign aid, never popular to begin with and now under heavy attack after the publication of *The Ugly American*, was in the country's interest. That the committee had done.

◆

THE TRIP with the Anderson subcommittee reminded Edward Lansdale of what he viewed as his true calling. Although he had grown exhausted in Vietnam by the end of 1956, now, after more than two years in Washington and a short visit to Saigon, he was eager to return. His brief reunion with Pat Kelly further reminded him of how much he was missing on a personal level while living in Washington. But the trip had also revealed how difficult it would be to get a return ticket to South Vietnam. If State Department officials were wary of Lansdale's spending three days in Cambodia, how much more resistant would they be to letting him spend a longer period in Vietnam? Overriding their objections would be all the harder now that one of Lansdale's primary patrons was no longer around: suffering from colon cancer whose spread could not be arrested by radiation therapy, John Foster Dulles resigned as secretary of state on April 15, 1959, and died in his sleep the following month at Walter Reed Army Hospital.

A few weeks after returning home from his Asia swing in the spring of 1959, Ed wrote to Pat, "I'm fighting all the brass to get on back to Asia again. . . . I'll outflank them yet—because that last visit showed me how very much I have been missing in my life."[75] Lansdale would learn that outflanking the bureaucracy was not easy to do, even if the case for his presence in Vietnam was becoming ever more urgent.

20

A New War Begins

In a people's war, you never make war against your own people.
—EDWARD LANSDALE

THE Vietnamese Workers' Party, as the Communist Party was known, always had a collective leadership. But some leaders were more equal than others. The First Vietnam War—the French war—had been largely directed by Ho Chi Minh in consultation with Vo Nguyen Giap and, after 1949, Chinese advisers. But by the late 1950s, "Uncle Ho" was in his late sixties and was increasingly being pushed by his Politburo colleagues into a largely symbolic role. The Second Vietnam War—the American war—would be instigated and directed primarily by his ruthless and single-minded successor as secretary general: Le Duan. Of diminutive stature, with "perennially sad eyes and protruding ears,"[1] Le Duan did not project the warmth and charisma of Ho Chi Minh or the intellectual sophistication of Vo Nguyen Giap. In political maneuvering, however, he would turn out to be their superior.

Le Duan came from Quang Tri Province, just below the DMZ. No urbane intellectual like so many of his senior party comrades, Le Van Nhuan (his real name) was the son of a carpenter who had gone to work after high school as a railway attendant. One of the founding members of the Indochinese Communist Party, Le Duan was locked up as a political prisoner by French authorities in a series of brutal colonial gulags from 1931 to 1936 and again from 1940 to 1945. Like countless prisoners, from Michael Collins, Joseph Stalin, and Fidel Castro to Ayman al-Zawahiri and Abu Bakr al-Baghdadi, he left prison more militant than he arrived—and better educated in revolutionary methods. After war broke out against the French, Le Duan rose to a dominant position among Vietminh cadres in southern Vietnam.

Already married but separated from his wife and family, who remained in the North, Le Duan fell in love with another woman while he was in the South—a party comrade named Nguyen Thuy Nga. He met her when she was assigned to bring him his breakfast, a relatively sumptuous meal of rice congee and two boiled eggs. He offered to share one of his eggs with her, and soon took her as his wife, even though he was not divorced. This would cause him considerable personal difficulties, for his first wife and children refused to acknowledge his second family, and the party forbade taking more than one wife. But as a member of the Politburo from 1951 on, he was, as Lien-Hang T. Nguyen makes clear in her groundbreaking narrative, *Hanoi's War*, effectively above the law.

Le Duan refused to go north along with other cadres after the Geneva Accords, preferring to stay behind in the South to organize a covert Communist network. He did not return to Hanoi until 1957, and then in 1958 he undertook another secret trip to the South to assess conditions there. He found rising discontent among southern cadres about Ngo Dinh Diem's repressive policies. Le Duan returned to Hanoi determined to wage war on Saigon—a stance that placed him at odds with more cautious leaders such as Ho Chi Minh and Vo Nguyen Giap, who favored building communism in the North first. After a heated debate, Le Duan and the "South first" faction won the argument in January 1959 at the Fifteenth Plenary Session of the Party Central Committee, which approved a resolution "to liberate South Vietnam from the yoke of oppression imposed by the imperialists and the feudalists."[2]

To implement the party's decision, the People's Army of Vietnam began training a new unit, the 338th Division, composed of "Southern regroupees," that is, cadres who had gone north after the Geneva Accords and who would now be sent back to infiltrate the South. In contrast to American soldiers, who were, to Lansdale's consternation, trained only in technical tasks, these future guerrillas were schooled first and foremost in politics. As the French journalist and novelist Jean Larteguy was to note, Hanoi had "created a remarkable type of army, a total army, in which every soldier is at one and the same time a propagandist, a schoolmaster, and a policeman, every officer an administrator, a priest, and an agronomist."[3] In the U.S. and South Vietnamese armies, by contrast, soldiers were simply soldiers.

Alongside the 338th Division, another new military unit was activated: Military Transportation Group 559. Its duty was to create a covert supply route to move weapons and fighters south, expanding trails that had been used by the Vietminh during the French Indochina War. Initially its men traveled on foot and by bicycle; eventually roads would be hacked through the jungle big enough to accommodate trucks. By the end of 1959, 543 cadres and soldiers had been smuggled into South Vietnam along with "1,667 infantry weapons, 788 knives, 188 kilograms of explosives, and a number of military maps, compasses, and binoculars."[4] It was a modest start to a supply route, snaking through the jungles of Cambodia and Laos to penetrate deep into South Vietnam, that would later become legendary as the Ho Chi Minh Trail.

At the end of 1960, Hanoi created the Liberation Armed Forces of South Vietnam to wage war in the South, along with the National Front for the Liberation of South Vietnam (NLF) to serve as an umbrella organization for opposition political parties. The NLF was designed to foster the illusion that the war breaking out was a spontaneous, non-Communist uprising against the hated *My-Diem* (American-Diem) regime and its "lackey ruling clique of U.S. imperialists."[5] In reality, the NLF was as wholly controlled by the Communist Party as its predecessor, the Vietminh, had been. All of the insurgents soon became known generically as the Vietcong (Vietnamese Communists)—a pejorative label coined in Saigon that represented one of the few propaganda victories won by South Vietnam and its American allies in this new war.

Later, the people of Vietnam would look back on the years from 1954

Lansdale with Ngo Dinh Diem, the shy, bookish nationalist politician who was appointed prime minister in 1954. Together they created the state of South Vietnam. (HI)

Filipino doctors and nurses treating Vietnamese civilians. Lansdale created Operation Brotherhood with covert CIA funding as one of his signature civic-action initiatives. (HI)

Trinh Minh Thé, the controversial Cao Dai warlord whom the French reviled as a terrorist and many Vietnamese saw as a freedom fighter. Lansdale became so close to him that he stood in for him when his son was married years after his death. (Image Works)

General J. Lawton "Lightning Joe" Collins, a former U.S. Army chief of staff who clashed with Lansdale during his tenure as ambassador to South Vietnam, 1954–55. (Getty)

South Vietnamese troops advancing during the battle of Saigon, April 1955, pitting Diem's forces against three French-backed sects—the Cao Dai, the Hoa Hao, and the Binh Xuyen. (HI)

General John W. "Iron Mike" O'Daniel, the commander of the U.S. Military Assistance Advisory Group (left), Ambassador G. Frederick Reinhardt (center), Diem (right), and Lansdale (behind Reinhardt). (MSFRIC)

Three members of Lansdale's Saigon Military Mission. Left to right: CIA officers David Smith, Lou Conein, and Rufus Phillips. Conein would later become infamous as the architect of the 1963 anti-Diem coup. (RPPP)

A regular party-giver, Lansdale used the tinikling, a Philippine pole dance, to break down social barriers. This party was in 1956 at his Rue Duy Tan villa in Saigon. (HI)

Pat Kelly (right) visited Lansdale in Vietnam and, in 1956, went swimming with Madame Nhu (left). (HI)

Ngo Dinh Diem's conspiratorial brother, Ngo Dinh Nhu, and his wife, Madame Nhu, who served as first lady for the bachelor president. After Lansdale left Vietnam at the end of 1956, their hold on Diem increased—and conflict with Washington grew. (Image Works)

TEN THOUSAND MYSTERIES SWIRLED AROUND THEM — VIOLENCE EXPLODED IN THEIR FOOTSTEPS!

Three caught in the shadow-world of the seething Orient...and now one of them carried the other back from hell — so that the Saigon goddess could take her choice!

FIGARO, INC. presents JOSEPH L. MANKIEWICZ' production of

THE QUIET AMERICAN

starring AUDIE MURPHY · MICHAEL REDGRAVE · CLAUDE DAUPHIN · GIORGIA MOLL

One of Lansdale's greatest propaganda coups was turning Graham Greene's anti-American novel *The Quiet American* into a pro-American movie. He was often identified, wrongly, as the model for the naïve protagonist, Alden Pyle. (Image Works)

Vice President Nixon awards Colonel Lansdale a medal (possibly the National Security Medal for intelligence work) in the mid-1950s as Helen Lansdale looks on. Nixon championed Lansdale's work as vice president but not as president. (MSFRIC)

Lansdale with, left to right, CIA director Allen Dulles, the CIA's deputy director, Lieutenant General Charles Cabell, and the Air Force vice chief of staff, General Nathan Twining. Allen and his brother, Secretary of State John Foster Dulles, were Lansdale's greatest supporters in Washington. (MSFRIC)

Lansdale at home in Washington with his poodle, Koko, late 1950s. (ECLPP)

Lansdale in early 1961 visiting the remote village of Binh Hung, defended by the Sea Swallows militia led by the "fighting priest," Father Nguyen Loc Hoa (in glasses and dark uniform). (MSFRIC)

The leaders of North Vietnam, left to right: Vo Nguyen Giap, Truong Chinh, Le Duan, and Ho Chi Minh. The little-known Le Duan was the driving force behind the North's war on South Vietnam. (AP)

to 1960 as a golden age. "The six years of peace," they would call it.[6] Now the interlude between wars was over and a new struggle was beginning, one that would eclipse the French Indochina War in its inhumanity.

◆

Ngo Dinh Diem responded to the Communist threat in the summer of 1959 with a new program to move residents of the Mekong Delta out of their isolated villages into "agricultural towns," eventually known as agrovilles, where they would be provided with amenities such as electricity, markets, clinics, schools—and, above all, security. This was not, at least in theory, a bad idea: similar population resettlement plans had been implemented in campaigns against guerrillas from turn-of-the-century South Africa and the Philippines to, more recently, Malaya and Algeria. But the implementation of the agroville plan was badly flubbed. Local government officials coerced peasants into building the new settlements for no pay, and then coerced them again to move their families there. As the agrovilles' unpopularity became clear, Diem throttled back ambitious expansion plans. While his initial goal had been to resettle half a million farmers, the actual number never exceeded fifty thousand.[7]

Meanwhile, dissatisfaction with Diem was rising in the South. On April 19, 1960, a group of eighteen political figures from opposition parties gathered in the Caravelle Hotel, the newest and most luxurious hostelry in Saigon, to produce a manifesto denouncing the lack of freedom: "You should, Mr. President, liberalize the regime, promote democracy, guarantee minimum civil rights, recognize the opposition so as to permit the citizens to express themselves without fear, thus removing grievances and resentments." The apparent arrogance with which Diem dismissed their concerns further contributed to the image of an increasingly autocratic and out-of-touch leader, especially among U.S. diplomats who were in close contact with the Caravelle group.[8]

Harder to ignore, even for Diem, were the events of November 11, 1960. The CIA station chief in Saigon, William E. Colby, was awakened at his house around three o'clock in the morning by a "series of sharp noises." It was not "the usual thunderstorms." Rather, it was the sound of tracer bullets arcing across the night sky and thudding into his house.[9] The bullets were meant not for him but for President Diem, who lived nearby. This was the beginning of what became known as the paratroopers' coup. A tense standoff ensued between the mutinous airborne units and the presidential guard. To gain time, Diem entered into negotiations with the coup plotters while secretly radioing for help from army units based in the Mekong Delta. By the following day, November 12, armor and infantry units loyal to the president had streamed into the capital to surround the paratroopers. The rebellious troops surrendered and their leaders fled the country.

The failed coup exacerbated tensions between Diem and the U.S. government. The U.S. ambassador, a "combative and peppery"[10] career diplomat with the ambassadorial-sounding name of Elbridge Durbrow, had alienated Diem in various ways since his arrival in 1957. In September 1960, Durbrow had demanded that Diem make drastic changes in the government, including shipping his younger brother, Ngo Dinh Nhu, abroad as an ambassador, removing his trusted intelligence chief, adding opposition politicians to the cabinet, forcing all officeholders to publicly declare their finances, and lifting restrictions on the press. Even Durbrow had to concede that "some measures I am recommending are drastic and would be most impolitic for an ambassador to make under normal circumstances. But," he insisted, "conditions here are by no means normal. Diem government is in quite serious danger."[11]

Two months later, when Diem's presidency and even his life were in danger during the paratroopers' coup, Durbrow adopted a neutral tone. The only U.S. interest, the upper-class diplomat lectured the president and the paratroopers, was in fostering unity against the Communists and preventing further bloodshed. Beyond that, they were welcome to settle their differences among themselves.[12] This was a long way removed from the kind of wholehearted assistance that Lansdale had given to Diem. Durbrow's "no bloodshed" mantra, was, in fact, the same one that Diem had heard from Lightning Joe Collins during the sect uprising in 1955, and it convinced him that the U.S. embassy was once again conniving in his overthrow.

From the Pentagon, Edward Lansdale protested, "The actions of the U.S. ambassador undoubtedly have deepened President Diem's suspicions of his motivations."¹³ Lansdale was no fan of the devious Ngo Dinh Nhu, but he was skeptical of Durbrow's proposal "to transfer Mr. and Mrs. Nhu" out of the country. This "involves the traumatic surgery of removing President Diem's 'right arm' . . . ," he wrote. "*What is proposed as a substitute?.* . . Would an American be used to fill this vacancy, partially? . . . Would another brother be used to fill the vacancy? . . . Would someone outside the family move in?"¹⁴ There was, of course, no substitute proposed—only a series of nonnegotiable demands.

That Durbrow and Lansdale would advocate such different policies was hardly surprising. Although both were Californians, "Durbie," as his friends called him, came from a privileged milieu in San Francisco far removed from Lansdale's middle-class background in Los Angeles. His family's largesse had made it possible for him to attend an almost comically long list of elite educational institutions, beginning with undergraduate studies at Yale, followed by graduate work at Stanford, the University of Dijon, The Hague Academy of International Law, Sciences Po in Paris, and the University of Chicago,¹⁵ before joining the Foreign Service, another elite institution dominated in those days by WASPs from "good" families. While working at the State Department during World War II, he had been instrumental in burying evidence that Hitler was carrying out a genocide against the Jews—a subject that he believed had nothing to do with "American interests," properly understood.¹⁶ Having previously served only in Europe, Durbrow had scant patience with the difficulties of running a government in a newly independent Third World country while under incessant insurgent assault.

Ngo Dinh Diem had had his differences with Lansdale in 1956 when the "Ugly American" had urged him to create a more democratic political system, but he also knew that Lansdale was one of the few friends he possessed in Washington. Whether to counter Ambassador Durbrow's hostility or simply to provide guidance in difficult times, Diem officially requested in April 1960 that the Eisenhower administration send Lansdale back to Saigon to help deal "with intensified Communist guerrilla activity."¹⁷ Lansdale professed himself to be "damn tired and worn out," but his reaction was that "if Diem really wants me, I'll come."¹⁸

By now Lansdale was a brigadier general.[19] His first star, even more than his National Security Medal and Distinguished Service Medal, was a welcome validation of his efforts to fight the Cold War in Asia. That he was being promoted within the Air Force was all the more remarkable given how little he had to do with its operations. As neither a pilot nor a navigator nor even a conventional public affairs officer or intelligence officer, he was one of the more unlikely generals in the history of the aerial service—or any other military service, for that matter. Lansdale would later write, "It takes a Service mighty big of spirit to care for a bastard child—and this bastard child returns the affection."[20]

Yet Lansdale found that his new rank did not lessen internal opposition to sending him back to Vietnam. His proposed trip would become the subject of months of behind-the-scenes acrimony between the State and Defense Departments, with the diplomats complaining that "it was extremely difficult for Lansdale to work on a team."[21] The State Department finally relented when it realized that it could not move Diem with blunt-force methods. On November 27, 1960, Durbrow conceded, through gritted teeth, that a "Lansdale visit may be useful . . . if he follows Department's instructions and cooperates fully and openly with me, including reporting accurately to me on talks with and advice given Diem and other top Vietnamese."[22] Admiral Harry Felt, commander in chief Pacific Command, also backed a Lansdale visit but lectured him that he was only to further "the objectives" that had already been agreed to by the Departments of State and Defense.[23] He was forbidden to exercise his independent judgment and initiative.

Lansdale had no choice but to accept these straitened conditions. "While I resent being treated as a second-class citizen, I think it wise to get on out there," he wrote to Hanging Sam Williams, who had retired from the Army. "Diem and the Vietnamese need a friend present right now."[24]

◆

LANSDALE LEFT Washington on December 29, 1960, at the end of a fraught year during which an ill-fated American U-2 spy plane had been shot down over the Soviet Union and the truculent Soviet leader,

Nikita Khrushchev, had banged his shoe to make a point at the United Nations. His itinerary took him on "smooth as cream" Pan Am flights to Saigon via stops in San Francisco, Honolulu, Tokyo, and Manila. Along the way he picked up his trusty translator Joe Redick, who was again lent to him by the CIA, this time from his post in Laos. The layover in Manila was only about an hour, but many of his old friends, including Johnny Orendain, Manual Manahan, Oscar Arellano, and, of course, Pat Kelly, heard that he was on Philippine soil for the first time since 1959 and flocked to the airport to meet him. (Although he denied it, Lansdale probably tipped them off himself.) Some friends in the Philippine customs service even allowed Lansdale to leave the transit area and have coffee with his visitors in an airport office.

"That hour in the airport was a darn frustrating thing to everyone," Pat wrote to Ed a few weeks later. She had thought of following him to Saigon, "but I sobered up in time with the thought that it had been a couple of years since I had seen you, with only a note or two in between." In truth, as subsequent events were to show, she remained very much in love with this married man. "If you ever come this way again, don't time it with our election year, so there won't be too much fuss about your staying overnight," she implored him, "though I suppose there will always be much-ado about you."[25]

Any hopes that Lansdale might have had of keeping his brief stopover in Manila private were lost because a fellow passenger aboard the flight was the publisher of the *Manila Bulletin*. The next day, the newspaper ran a fanciful story beginning, "United States intelligence man Edward Lansdale, a former ranking official at the American embassy here, slipped quietly into town yesterday on a secret mission which apparently has something to do with the uneasy situation in the strife-torn Laos."[26] This article was picked up in other newspapers around the region, getting "the boy diplomats highly exercised,"[27] in Lansdale's phrase. Already the other U.S. ambassadors in the region, fearing his insubordinate tendencies and his reputation for "dirty tricks," had demanded that he stay out of their countries, and this incident seemed to confirm their concerns. Ambassador William C. Trimble in Phnom Penh wrote to Washington, "Department will recall this treatment of

Lansdale's trip was predicted (reference telegram). Under present circumstances feel impelled urge once again in strongest terms that Lansdale not visit Cambodia."[28]

This was the price that Lansdale paid for his growing fame. His very appearance in any country, even for an hour, was treated with panic, as if he were a modern-day Pied Piper capable of magically making governments rise and fall with a few catchy notes from his harmonica. Writing of the powers imputed to him by critics, including so many serving ambassadors, Lansdale cracked, "If I could only figure out what it is they think I'm doing, I'd go do it."[29]

◆

SAIGON WAS the city, after Manila, closest to Lansdale's heart—the scene of earlier triumphs mixed with inevitable frustrations, of song-filled soirees and close brushes with death, of friendships forged and dear friends lost. Now he was returning to this bustling metropolis, which still retained its colonial charm, on January 2, 1961, for the first time in nearly two years,[30] at a pivotal moment in the history not only of Vietnam but of the United States as well. Less than two months before, Senator John F. Kennedy of Massachusetts, young, handsome, and charismatic, had defeated the dour vice president, Richard M. Nixon of California, in a bruising presidential contest decided by the slimmest of margins. The primary national security issue was a "missile gap" with the Soviet Union that Kennedy sincerely, if erroneously, claimed had been created by the Eisenhower administration's restrained defense spending. Vietnam was almost entirely absent from the election in spite of Kennedy's long-standing interest in that country. He had visited Vietnam in 1951 and had come back presciently skeptical that the French war effort could succeed without addressing Vietnamese desires for independence. After the Geneva Accords were signed, as noted by the historian Fredrik Logevall, he had become a staunch supporter of Ngo Dinh Diem and echoed Eisenhower's warnings that the fall of South Vietnam could send "dominoes" toppling across the region.[31]

No one knew how the untested president-elect would react to the new Vietcong offensive. Would he send more American advisers or even combat troops? Would he support Diem or jettison him? Would he press for liberal reforms or conclude that authoritarianism was the best option? Or would he abandon South Vietnam altogether if it was deemed incapable of defending itself? Neither Kennedy's campaign nor his transition team had focused on the problem of Vietnam; Laos, which appeared to be in imminent danger of falling to the Communist Pathet Lao, had gotten more attention. Thus the Kennedy administration's Vietnam policy remained to be defined as Lansdale stepped onto the tarmac at Tan Son Nhut Airport to be greeted by the familiar tropical heat and smell of rotting vegetation.

Lansdale was surprised to find that, after opposing his trip, the U.S. embassy "killed me with kindness."[32] The reason was that, as CIA station chief Bill Colby, a daring wartime commando with a deceptively nondescript appearance, later wrote, "There were rumors that Kennedy was considering naming Lansdale as his Ambassador to Vietnam."[33] Colby thought that Lansdale was "very suspicious of the CIA station" initially, which was to be expected in light of Lansdale's clashes with Colby's predecessors, but eventually the CIA man won him over, and the two became friends. Colby, a future CIA director, was later to say that he had "great respect" for Lansdale and felt "very warm and friendly and very supportive of him," feelings that Lansdale fully reciprocated.[34] Predictably, Lansdale was less impressed with Ambassador Durbrow, whom he found to be worn-out, ill, and ineffectual.[35]

Among the many other people Lansdale saw were the arch-schemer Ngo Dinh Nhu and his wife, the caustic and comely Madame Nhu, a power couple that was becoming even more important in the councils of government than when he had left in 1956. She asked about "that beautiful girl who was at Long Hai [beach]," recalling his waning days in Vietnam, when he had prevailed on Diem and his family to take a seaside vacation. Lansdale wistfully had to admit that he hadn't seen much of Pat Kelly for the past two years "and was even more curious than she about that beautiful girl."[36]

Seeking to reestablish his old relationship of trust with Ngo Dinh Diem, Lansdale found that at first the president "was a bit cautious with me. I suspected that he was waiting for me to drop Washington's other shoe as a follow-up to the Ambassador's demands that he reform his ways." Lansdale sought to dispel Diem's wariness: "I reminisced on what we had gone through together in the past and he joined in, adding the story of the 11 November [1960] coup as he saw it." His reserve starting to melt, Diem gave Lansdale a tour of his bedroom, not something he would have done with an outsider, to show the damage inflicted by the paratroopers' .50-caliber machine-gun fire. "Our meetings from then on became more like the old days, with plenty of give and take . . . ," Lansdale wrote, "but only after I convinced him that I still had affection for the Vietnamese people and was trying to understand their problems before sounding off."[37]

Diem's primary complaint was not with the United States but rather with his aides, who were lacking in "strong executive capability." The president was feeling overworked because he felt there were so few others he could trust.[38] Of course, part of the problem was self-inflicted: Diem was by nature a micromanager and an introvert who found it hard to reach out to others. Aware of Diem's shortcomings, Lansdale closely questioned him about how often he met with his vice president, Nguyen Ngoc Tho, who was also the economics minister. Diem assured him that he saw Tho "all the time."

Lansdale asked, "When's the last time you had him over for dinner?"

Diem replied, "Oh, a short time ago. I don't know exactly when."

Lansdale then went over to the Economic Ministry and talked to Tho, who told him that he hadn't had dinner with Diem in a year or two. Asked whether he would like to have dinner with the president, Tho replied that he would love to.

Lansdale went back to see Diem and told him, "Tho hasn't seen you for a year for dinner. Why don't you call him right now and invite him tonight for dinner?" Diem did just that, and relations between the two men briefly improved.[39]

The rapprochement between Diem and Tho was but one example of the kind of political action that Lansdale favored and that was largely neglected in his absence. Unsurprisingly, the relationship between Diem and Tho would go sour once again after Lansdale left Saigon, and Tho would join the cabal plotting a coup against Diem a few years later.

◆

LANSDALE FOUND that in Saigon, amid the cyclos and the cafés, the cocktails and the sumptuous banquets, the "guerrilla fighting in the countryside . . . seems far, far away."⁴⁰ There were "crowds of people" on the streets and shops full of goods but, just as in Manila in 1950, the atmosphere of frenetic gaiety was permeated by "suspicion and fear." He was disgusted by infighting and plotting among "the intellectuals and Americans in Saigon." "They don't know how hard the Communists have hit them yet," he wrote. Many of his acquaintances were "in jail or in exile. Others are sitting around griping." He felt besieged by "so damn many kibitzers." "It was almost as bad as Washington," he wrote to Pat Kelly. "The Americans and Vietnamese sit around writing papers all the time, in triplicate." "What a place," he lamented. "It got me down."⁴¹

To get away from "the protocol" and get a taste of the real war, he asked Diem to borrow a helicopter and a member of his staff to tour the provinces. Diem wanted to know where he was going. Lansdale refused to say. "I'll tell your pilot that; I don't want to tell you," he replied, because he didn't want to give the president time to construct a Potemkin village for his inspection. Diem played along, assigning his secretary of defense, Nguyen Dinh Thuan, to accompany Lansdale, and even providing some sandwiches for them to munch en route.⁴²

Early on the morning of January 10, 1961, only ten days before John F. Kennedy's inauguration, Lansdale, along with Joe Redick and Thuan, took off in a South Vietnamese C-47 transport aircraft from Saigon bound for Soc Trang, a provincial capital with a South Vietnamese army base set amid one of the world's lushest rice-growing regions, the Mekong Delta. Amid the watery rice paddies, worked in the age-old manner by water buffalo and farmers in black pajamas and conical bamboo hats, Lansdale discovered a disturbing development: "Vietnamese artillery firing on villages down in the Delta." "That shocked me more than almost anything else," he said. "That's something you don't do in a guerrilla war, you know. In a people's war, you never make war against your own people." Lansdale demanded that the battery commander cease firing, which made the officer so angry that for a minute Lansdale thought he was going to get shot. Fortunately the defense minister "talked him out of it."[43]

Amid the Vietcong resurgence in the Mekong Delta, Lansdale managed to find one good-news story—the village of Binh Hung on the Ca Mau Peninsula. Its unusual and inspirational leader was known as "the fighting priest." Father Nguyen Loc Hoa was a Catholic cleric who had once been a colonel in the Chinese Nationalist Army (he had adopted a Vietnamese name after moving to Vietnam). After Chiang Kai-shek's defeat, Father Hoa (pronounced *wah*) had fled with his parishioners. Eventually Diem allowed them to settle in one of the least promising parts of South Vietnam—an area of swamps and forests that resembles the Florida Everglades. They had to build their own village out of mud dragged out of the water.

Lansdale had met Father Hoa in Saigon and been impressed by this almost six-foot-tall figure with, in a journalist's words, wire-rim spectacles, a placid countenance, and a "wide smooth face with gently slanted gray eyes."[44] Father Hoa, who spoke fluent Chinese, Vietnamese, French, and English and typically wore a .45-caliber pistol on his hip, regaled him with tales of how he had organized his own 300-man militia, named the Sea Swallows after a local bird. When the Vietcong first struck, the Sea Swallows had nothing to fight with save staves and knives. But by counterattacking swiftly, Hoa's men seized M-1 rifles and Browning Automatic Rifles from the enemy. After appealing for support from Saigon, Father Hoa was given some outdated weapons captured from the Binh Xuyen along with a pittance to pay his fighters. Gradually, his community, which had started with 375 Chinese Catholic refugees, grew with the addition of Vietnamese farmers. By early 1961, there were 1,200 people living in Binh Hung.

Lansdale and his party alighted from their helicopter on "a small landing pad in the midst of deep mud just outside the village." As soon as they got off, three of Father Hoa's men, who had been wounded in combat, were put aboard the helicopter for transport to a hospital in

Soc Trang. "Some of these tough guerrilla troops gave me the only salute they knew, the three-fingered Boy Scout hand salute," Lansdale wrote. Father Hoa's followers reported that they had lost seventeen men in one recent battle while killing thirty to sixty Vietcong.

Much of the combat in this "dirty war" was not waged with guns. "The majority of casualties," Lansdale found, "are foot wounds, caused by the most common weapon: a long iron nail." The Vietcong would drive six-inch nails into thin boards and hide them in the mud where, in an omen of things to come for American soldiers, the booby trap would perforate the foot of any unsuspecting Sea Swallow who stepped on it. Sea Swallows were thus forced to advance "with a sliding motion that looked as though they were ice-skating." Because they had nothing to wear but basketball shoes bought in Saigon, they took to adding inner soles made of iron sheeting.

While Lansdale was visiting Binh Hung, the imperturbable Father Hoa received a report of Vietcong movements to the north. He wanted to check it out and invited Lansdale, Redick, and the minister of defense to accompany him. They all climbed aboard a motor launch "and went chugging northerly up a canal," while a company of Sea Swallows shadowed them on foot. The "tall grass and mangrove swamp along the canal showed how easily ambushes could be laid," Lansdale wrote. Eventually they reached the tiny village of Cai Doi, where, Lansdale wrote, "Secretary Thuan and Father Hoa shook hands with many of the villagers, talking about rice, fish, and the Viet Cong."

And then it was time to return to the isolated, mud-brick redoubt of Binh Hung. This was a moment of maximal danger, for, as Father Hoa explained, "A favorite VC tactic is to let a group through on an outward march and then to ambush them on the return. The group becomes unalert when a patrol seems to have been uneventful." Father Hoa and his party were accompanied on the return trip by a second company of troops and another boat. The journey was uneventful, but Lansdale told Pat Kelly that he "broke all the rules" in order to go out "with a small patrol of local villagers" in terrain where "not even the French ever dared to go, nor the Vietnamese Army."

Even though he had seen for himself that the Vietcong were gaining ground, Lansdale returned to Saigon buoyed by this foray into the increasingly embattled Mekong Delta. "The morale of Vietnamese officials and people in the 5th Military Region was quite refreshing to encounter after visiting people in Saigon–Cholon, which is full of defeatist rumors," he wrote, echoing an observation often made by visitors to war zones, who find, paradoxically, morale soaring on the dangerous front lines and sagging in the safer rear areas.[45]

◆

LANSDALE'S GOOD feelings had dissipated somewhat by the time he left Vietnam on January 14, 1961, after additional exposure to the hothouse atmosphere of Saigon, where political intrigue was an art form not infrequently practiced for its own sake. The self-serving politicos in the capital were far removed, geographically and ethically, from Father Hoa's stout Sea Swallows, and their entreaties and imprecations depressed him. "Everyone wanted me to do some sort of miracle," he wrote to Pat Kelly the day of his departure, "and did their level best to make sure I wouldn't have a chance. . . . It's heart-breaking to see what a bunch of self-centered people have done to ruin the dreams in the Philippines, Vietnam + Laos. . . . Whatever happened to people with guts like Spruance and O'Daniel?"[46]

In that melancholy mood, Lansdale flew to Hawaii to write a lengthy report on the trip amid crashing waves and gently swaying palm trees. He returned to Washington via Los Angeles, Tucson, and Chicago, arriving home during an unwelcome cold snap on the afternoon of January 18, 1961.[47] Two days later, a new president a decade younger than the fifty-three-year-old "Ugly American" would take office, uncertain of what to do about the growing Communist challenge in Indochina. One of the very first documents he would find on his Oval Office desk would be a report on Lansdale's trip.

21

The Ambassador
Who Never Was

*I don't know which has the worst jungle, Vietnam or
Washington.*

—EDWARD LANSDALE

THE snow began to fall at noon on Thursday, January 19, 1961, the
day after Edward Lansdale's return, and continued deep into the
night, inch after inch compounding the capital's misery. Washington,
essentially a Southern city, was notorious for its inability to cope with
snow, and the situation was now exacerbated by overcrowding. The city
was so jammed with inauguration-goers that one national magazine
was reporting that "by midweek it seemed easier to get a Cabinet job
than a bed."[1] Thousands of cars were abandoned in the snowdrifts, and
airplanes were diverted from National Airport. Many guests could not
reach the inaugural-eve parties.

By the time Washington awoke on Friday morning, the snow had
finally stopped. An army of three thousand workers, using seven hundred trucks and snowplows, cleared the streets, while soldiers wielded
flamethrowers to melt the snowbanks that had accumulated on the
inauguration grandstands in front of the freshly painted Capitol build-

ing.[2] The ceremony began at noon under a winter sun and a brilliant blue sky. Despite what seemed to locals to be an Arctic chill, John F. Kennedy left his overcoat and silk top hat behind when he strode to the podium in his formal morning dress to take the oath of office. Seemingly impervious to the weather, he stayed outside for hours, sitting in the open air on a reviewing stand in front of the White House to watch the inaugural parade go by. The *New York Times* was to write, "Bronzed by the Florida sun during his pre-inauguration holiday, with his brown hair neatly brushed, he looked the picture of health as he tackled the White House job."[3]

We now know that appearances were deceiving. Far from being in rude health, Kennedy, like Franklin D. Roosevelt, suffered from an astonishing variety of ailments, in his case including Addison's disease, inflammations of the prostate and colon, and compression fractures of the spine. He had nearly died in 1954 during a back operation designed to relieve his almost unbearable suffering. Simply to keep functioning and stay off crutches he had to take numerous hot baths daily, sit in a rocking chair (which put less pressure on his lower back than a conventional chair), and allow himself to be injected with painkillers and amphetamines by a physician with the apposite moniker of "Dr. Feelgood."[4] That Kennedy was in so much pain throughout his life makes his considerable accomplishments—including his wartime heroism aboard a small patrol-torpedo boat that bucked like a bronco—appear all the more impressive in retrospect.[5] But Kennedy did not want the truth revealed at the time, because it would have left him open to charges that he could not withstand the physical rigors of the presidency.

Kennedy's medical condition was not the only secret to emerge after his death. We now know, too, about his incessant womanizing, which hardly slowed after he married the ravishing and perspicacious Jacqueline Bouvier in 1953. Historians have speculated that his insatiable, nearly pathological quest for fresh sexual conquests was driven in part by a sense of mortality—"an existential pinch on the arm to prove that he was there," in the words of his biographer Robert Dallek—and in part by his "deep difficulty with intimacy."[6] Whatever the case, his indiscreet private life left him exposed to the potential of blackmail, venereal disease, and sheer embarrassment.

In the more wide-open, anything-goes media culture of the twenty-first century, JFK's health woes and skirt chasing might well have doomed his presidency, but in the more repressed climate of the early sixties reporters either did not know the facts or did not consider them fit to print. Most Americans had a largely unvarnished portrait of their young president, a handsome war hero with a winsome family, a ready wit, and charisma to burn. The doubts about him concerned not his moral or physical capacity for the job but his sheer inexperience. Some feared that at only forty-three, and having accomplished little in the Senate, this rich man's son was a lightweight who was not ready to shoulder the demands of the nation's highest office.

But his masterful inauguration address, one of the greatest ever delivered, impressed even his critics. Its catchphrases, drafted by the speechwriter Theodore Sorenson and refined by Kennedy himself, still resonate more than half a century later: "Let every nation know, whether it wishes us well or ill, that we shall pay any price, bear any burden, meet any hardship, support any friend, oppose any foe to assure the survival and the success of liberty. . . . Let us never negotiate out of fear. But let us never fear to negotiate. . . . And so, my fellow Americans: ask not what your country can do for you—ask what you can do for your country."[7]

As a Cold Warrior himself, as someone who had dedicated his life to fighting Communist insurgents in order to ensure the survival and success of liberty, Edward Lansdale could not help being impressed by the new president's stirring call to action. Less than a week before the inauguration, Ed had written to Pat Kelly, "I'd gotten to know Nixon well enough so that I'd have had a real go if he'd won." Now, "it's going to take time to let the new bunch make their mistakes, learn a little, maybe, and then perhaps be ready to get away from the bureaucrats who really run our government."[8] Little did Lansdale suspect that the report he wrote on his trip to Vietnam would serve as a significant part of the "new bunch's" learning process.

◆

LANSDALE'S REPORT began, "1961 promises to be a fateful year for Vietnam. The Communist Viet Cong hope to win back Vietnam south of the 17th Parallel this year, if at all possible, and are much further along towards accomplishing this objective than I had realized from reading the reports received in Washington." He found that the "Viet Cong have the initiative and most of the control over the region from the jungled foothills of the High Plateau north of Saigon all the way south down to the Gulf of Siam, excluding the big city area of Saigon–Cholon." If "Free Vietnam" falls, he warned, "the remainder of Southeast Asia will be easy pickings for our enemy, because the toughest local force on our side will be gone."

Lansdale argued, as he had done since 1954, that the key to saving South Vietnam lay in backing Ngo Dinh Diem, "still the only Vietnamese with executive ability and the required determination to be an effective President." Rather than replace Diem, he continued, it was time to replace the U.S. ambassador, Elbridge Durbrow: "Correctly or not, the recognized government of Vietnam does not look upon him as a friend, believing that he sympathized strongly with the coup leaders of 11 November [1960]." In place of Durbrow, Lansdale recommended the appointment of an ambassador "with marked leadership talents who can make the Country Team function harmoniously and spiritually, who can influence Asians through understanding them sympathetically, and who is alert to the power of the Mao Tse Tung tactics now being employed to capture Vietnam and who is dedicated to feasible and practical democratic means to defeat these Communist tactics."

To a casual reader—including, as it would turn out, the new president—it might have sounded as if Lansdale were promoting himself as the next ambassador. Numerous authors have stated as a fact that Lansdale's "ulterior motive" in writing the report was to claim Durbrow's job for himself.[9] But, recognizing his own limitations, Lansdale told his friend Rufus Phillips that he had no desire to deal with all of the ceremonial and managerial tasks of being an ambassador. With his aversion to pomp and protocol, Lansdale was later to say, "I didn't want to be an ambassador. Jesus. . . . That's one of the world's worst jobs."[10] According to Phillips, Lansdale preferred that the appointment go to one of his State Department friends—Kenneth Young, who had handled Southeast Asia issues during the Eisenhower administration—in the expectation that he could work as closely with Young as he had with other ambassadors such as Raymond Spruance and Donald Heath.[11]

That Lansdale did not have the ambassadorship in mind for himself was clear from his recommendation, within his trip report, that "a mature American, with much the same qualifications as those given above for the selection of the next Ambassador, should be assigned to Vietnam for political operations which will start creating a Vietnamese-style foundation for more democratic government without weakening the strong leadership required to bring about the defeat of the Communists." Rather than the "Ugly American" or the "Quiet American," the sobriquets bestowed on him by others, Lansdale saw himself as this "mature American": an influential, behind-the-scenes political operator assisted by a small, handpicked team of loyalists—in other words, the role he had previously played in the Philippines and South Vietnam. "If the next American official to talk to President Diem would have the good sense to see him as a human being who has been through a lot of hell for years—and not as an opponent to be beaten to his knees—we would start regaining our influence with him in a healthy way . . . ," he wrote. "If we don't like the heavy influence of Brother Nhu, then let's move someone of ours in close. This someone, however, must be able to look at problems with understanding, suggest better solutions than does Nhu, earn a position of influence."

Lansdale envisioned that the American envoys to Saigon would also "be given the task of creating an opposition party which would coalesce the majority of the opposition into one organization." How it would be possible to work at the same time with both Diem and the opposition he did not explain. But if Lansdale's prescription for solving Vietnam's most pressing political problem was overly ambitious, his description of what would happen if something did not change rang all too true, all the more so when viewed in hindsight, with full knowledge of what was to come in 1963. He warned, "Unless the energies of the malcontents, the frustrated, the patriots on the outs are quickly channeled into constructive political works, they are going to explode into destructive political work. The opposition situation in Saigon–Cholon is at the bursting point, and there is no safety valve. When it next blows, and if Diem cannot cope with it, the Saigon political scene has all the makings of turning into anarchy. It can happen, and soon." Just as prophetic was Lansdale's warning of the cost of abandoning Diem: "If the 11 November coup had been successful, I believe that a number of highly selfish and mediocre people would be squabbling among themselves for power while the Communists took over."[12]

In addition to this Cassandra-like twelve-page report, Lansdale penned a separate thirteen-page memorandum on his experiences with Father Hoa.[13] His intent was to balance out the more negative tone of his main report by holding out hope that successful resistance to the Vietcong was still possible if the Sea Swallows' example was emulated elsewhere. Yet his case study did not address the main reason why the experience of Binh Hung was not readily applicable in other parts of South Vietnam: much of Father Hoa's community was made up of Catholics, who were ideologically distinct from the mainstream Vietnamese population and largely impervious to appeals from atheist insurgents. Lansdale later argued that there were other "free villages" out there—"Catholic villages, Hoa Hao villages etc."—that could be pillars of a successful counterinsurgency strategy.[14] But keeping the Vietcong out of ordinary Vietnamese villages without a distinctive religious identity would prove much tougher.

◆

GENERAL ANDREW GOODPASTER, one of Eisenhower's most trusted aides, gave Lansdale's trip report to Walt Whitman Rostow, an economist from the Massachusetts Institute of Technology who was Kennedy's new deputy national security adviser, telling him, "I think President Kennedy ought to see this." Rostow read it and concluded that Goodpaster was right—"it was an ominous draft." He took it into the Oval Office, saying, "Mr. President, I think you ought to read this."

Kennedy was feeling rushed. "I've only got half an hour today," he said. "Can you summarize it?"

"No sir," Rostow replied. "I think you must read it."

"I may have no time for anything else," Kennedy warned. "Must I read it?"

"Yes, sir," Rostow insisted.

Kennedy put on the horn-rimmed glasses that he used for reading and that the public did not realize he wore,[15] and read it all. When he was done, he looked up and said, "That's the worst one we've got, isn't it? I'll tell you something. President Eisenhower never mentioned it. He talked at length about Laos, but never uttered the word Vietnam."

So impressed was Kennedy by the importance of this looming problem that he instructed Rostow "to go deeply into the problem of Vietnam and get him some materials to read about guerrilla warfare in general." Thus Lansdale's report directly sparked Kennedy's interest both in the Vietnam War and in guerrilla warfare more broadly, two of the defining themes of his administration.[16]

◆

BECAUSE OF Kennedy's "keen interest in General Lansdale's recent report and his awareness of the high importance" of Vietnam, the new national security adviser, McGeorge Bundy, decided that a White House meeting on January 28, 1961—the second Saturday after the inauguration—would be broadened to include a discussion of Vietnam.[17] The new defense secretary, Robert S. McNamara, asked Lansdale to join him at the White House that chilly morning without telling him whom he would brief. Lansdale was surprised when he was ushered into the Oval Office—the most famous room in the world—to find himself at a meeting not only with McNamara but also with President Kennedy, Vice President Lyndon Johnson, Secretary of State Dean Rusk, General Lyman Lemnitzer, the chairman of the Joint Chiefs of Staff, Assistant Secretary of State Paul Nitze, Deputy National Security Adviser Walt Rostow, and his old mentor, CIA Director Allen Dulles.

Kennedy, as was his habit, must have been sitting in his favorite rocking chair, the rattan-and-oak Carolina Rocker, wearing a two-button, single-breasted, narrow-lapel suit, and radiating what an aide called "a contained energy, electric in its intensity." When he became impatient with the discussion, Arthur Schlesinger Jr. noted, Kennedy's fingers would begin "drumming the table, tapping his teeth, slashing patient pencil lines on a pad, jabbing the air to underscore a point."[18] The blue-green rug, inherited from the office's previous occupant, still bore visible golf-cleat indentations, but the new president had added some personal touches of his own. Scattered around were naval bric-a-brac—a coconut paperweight (a memento of the sinking of PT-109), paintings of the sailing ships USS *Constitution* and USS *Bonhomme Richard*, models of the Coast Guard cutter *Danmark* and the China clipper ship *The Sea Witch*—which served as reminders of his heroic wartime service in the Navy as well as his long-standing love of the sea nurtured by summers at Hyannis Port. Winter sunlight streamed through the three majestic windows, each more than eleven feet tall, located behind the president's massive desk. The White House Rose Garden, bare and brown at this time of year, could be glimpsed through the French doors.[19]

The assembled policymakers had already been discussing the CIA's plans for the Bay of Pigs for forty-five minutes when Lansdale joined the meeting at 10:45 a.m. along with J. Graham "Jeff" Parsons, the assistant secretary of state for Far Eastern affairs. President Kennedy thanked Lansdale for his memorandum and said that "it, for the first time, gave him a sense of the danger and urgency of the problem in Viet-Nam."[20] The group then turned to Parsons to hear a presentation on the existing counterinsurgency plan for Vietnam, which called for greater U.S. funding to increase the size of the South Vietnamese army by twenty thousand men in return for a promise from Diem to institute political reforms. Kennedy interrupted this presentation to express skepticism that such a military increase would appreciably change the balance of power on the ground. Showing that he had digested Lansdale's report, Kennedy wanted to know "whether the situation was not basically one of politics and morale." He then opened the floor to Lansdale.

"The essentials," Lansdale said, "were three: first, the Americans in

Viet-Nam must themselves be infused with high morale and a will to win, and they must get close to the Vietnamese; secondly, the Vietnamese must, in this setting, be moved to act with vigor and confidence; third, Diem must be persuaded to let the opposition coalesce in some legitimate form rather than concentrate on the task of killing him."

In response to a question from Kennedy about Durbrow's job performance, Lansdale did not hold back. "Well, I'm a little hesitant, but you're the President and you need the truth, so I'll tell you right now, I think he's a very ill man. His judgment's impaired by his physical condition. He's a fine professional Foreign Service officer and could be used in some place, but don't keep him on in Vietnam anymore."[21] Secretary of State Rusk did not bother to defend the ambassador he had inherited from the Eisenhower administration, conceding that "it was now time for a change and he should be relieved in the near future." Thus Lansdale effectively claimed the scalp of yet another ambassador in Saigon, having previously helped force out Donald Heath and J. Lawton Collins.

The question now was who would succeed Durbrow. Walt Rostow's minutes note, "The question of whether General Lansdale or Mr. Kenneth Young should go to Viet-Nam as the new ambassador was considered." Lansdale's own recollection was that the president, who was sitting directly across from him, said to him, "Did Dean [Rusk] tell you I want you to be ambassador to Vietnam?" "No, he didn't," a startled Lansdale replied. There followed a "long, painful silence" as he tried to figure out how to respond.[22] His hesitation adds further credence to the notion that he was not lobbying for the job, but it must have puzzled Kennedy, because that was the impression the president undoubtedly had received from Lansdale's own memorandum. Kennedy liked men of action; he would not have appreciated this sudden indecisiveness.

Lansdale's recollections of what happened when he finally spoke varied, and no transcript of the meeting was made. In a 1984 interview, Lansdale remembered stammering, "Thank you very much, but I'm a regular military officer and I don't think my place is in diplomacy."[23] On two other occasions, including a 1970 interview, Lansdale recalled saying, after a considerable pause, "It would be a great honor."[24] Whatever he said, he had not enthusiastically and immediately embraced a job offer that engendered predictable opposition within the State Department. Later Lansdale was to hear from one of Rusk's aides that the normally passive and deferential secretary of state, a gracious product of rural Georgia and Oxford University, had threatened to resign if Lansdale were selected. Rusk apparently felt so strongly not just because he viewed Lansdale as a "lone wolf" but also because Lansdale was an active-duty military officer as well as a former CIA officer, and Rusk, a stickler for diplomatic protocol, did not want either military or intelligence officers as ambassadors.[25]

The ambassador's job went instead to a career Foreign Service officer, Frederick "Fritz" Nolting Jr., a handsome and courtly Virginian with a PhD in philosophy who spoke fluent French and was serving as an envoy to NATO. Lacking the kind of personal history with Diem that Lansdale possessed, Nolting would find himself hard-put to influence the stubborn president even though he tried to adopt the conciliatory approach that Lansdale advocated. Only Lansdale, of all the Americans who might have been sent to Saigon, had any chance, however remote, of persuading Diem to peacefully reform and thus to avert his own overthrow two and a half years later. The failure to appoint Lansdale as ambassador, in the judgment of the New Yorker correspondent (and Lansdale friend) Robert Shaplen, "was another vital turning point in the long and tortuous history of America's Vietnamese involvement." If this episode had turned out differently, Shaplen was to write five years later, it "might have made all the difference in the world in our relations with Vietnam and in the prosecution of the war."[26]

Having failed to appoint Lansdale as ambassador, Kennedy considered promoting him to three-star rank and sending him to Saigon as head of the Military Assistance Advisory Group. This appointment also could have changed the course of American–Vietnamese history, but it aroused as much opposition from the Joint Chiefs of Staff as his potential ambassadorship had aroused from the State Department. The chiefs did not view Lansdale as a "real" soldier, and they scolded him for putting Kennedy up to the job offer—something he insisted that he had not done.[27]

◆

A FEW days after the January 28 Oval Office meeting, Lansdale got a call on his office telephone. Picking up the receiver, he heard a man with a familiar Boston accent identify himself as "President Kennedy." The caller proceeded to tell Lansdale how much he had enjoyed reading his case study on Binh Hung and urged him to publish it in a magazine such as the *Saturday Evening Post* so that it would become more widely known. The whole time Lansdale was wondering to himself, "Which of my friends is trying to imitate the new president?" As soon as he hung up, he called the White House and spoke to one of the president's military aides, who assured him that it had indeed been President Kennedy on the line.[28] His next call was to the editor of the *Saturday Evening Post*.

On May 20, 1961, the *Post* published Lansdale's case study, along with Joe Redick's photos, under the headline "The Report the President Wanted Published." The byline read simply, "By an American Officer." The editors appended a note of explanation:

> When it came to the President's desk, the report was classified. But behind the official language of the report, the President saw a story of human valor and dedication to freedom, a reminder that Communism is *not* the wave of the future. It was a story, he felt, that many people ought to read, and he wrote a memorandum suggesting that the report would make "an excellent article for a magazine like The Saturday Evening Post. I would like to see this type of material have good distribution, as it shows what can be done." The substance of the report is published herewith.

After this publicity, Father Hoa received not only thousands of weapons from the CIA but also assistance from U.S. and Taiwanese Special Forces teams.[29]

"We can put this down as having struck a blow for liberty," Lansdale wrote to Redick. "A magazine writer changed a few words; otherwise think you'll recognize this. At least you can read the ads to see what's doing in the land of milk and honey."[30] For those in the know within the U.S. government, the publication of the Binh Hung case study, along with this flattering editor's note spelling out the president's endorsement, was a powerful blow not so much for liberty as for Lansdale's reputation. And this was far from the last boost that Lansdale would receive from the Kennedy administration.

◆

WHEN GRAVES ERSKINE finally retired, in February 1961, Lansdale replaced him as assistant to the secretary of defense for special operations. He did not inherit the other part of Big E's responsibility, running the Office of Special Operations; it was abolished and its intelligence-oversight functions were folded into the newly created Defense Intelligence Agency.[31] But this was still a big promotion for Lansdale, who was now performing duties equivalent to those of an assistant secretary of defense. He broke the news to South Vietnam's minister of defense, Nguyen Dinh Thuan, in a typically lighthearted manner. "My penalty for visiting Vietnam and having an outing with you to the Fifth Military Region was a new job," he wrote. "I pay for the fun now with a lot more papers and problems."[32] Nguyen extended congratulations not only from himself but from Diem, who was "jubilant" about the news, adding, "The President would like to get you here once more—Is it feasible?"[33] General Lionel McGarr, Hanging Sam Williams's replacement at MAAG, reiterated that message, telling a senior meeting that Diem would like to see Lansdale "stay in Viet-Nam as long as possible."[34]

Walt Rostow, who was emerging as one of the administration hardliners on Vietnam, was supportive of sending Lansdale. He later said, "I've met a handful of people in my life who have this particular genius for dealing with human beings in ways that make them feel dignified." Ed Lansdale was one such man—"an extraordinary man," a "first-class man."[35] Rostow told the president, "We must find a way to send Lansdale for a visit to Viet Nam soon in a way that will strengthen Nolting's hand—not weaken it. This is wholly possible."[36] The job Rostow had in mind for Lansdale was to act, he wrote the president on April 13, 1961, as a "full-time, first-rate, back-stop man in Washington."[37]

At Rostow's urging, Lansdale drafted a memorandum laying out the role he could play in Vietnam policy.[38] Lansdale's unsigned memorandum, dated April 19, 1961, proposed that the president should "establish a Washington task force" that not only would come up with "an approved plan of action prior to sending a new U.S. ambassador to Vietnam" but would "then supervise and coordinate" the implementation of that plan. Writing of himself in the third person, he argued, "Fullest use should be made of the existing position of personal confidence and understanding which General Lansdale holds with President Diem and other key Vietnamese. In addition to giving a major assist to the new Presidential Task Force for Vietnam in Washington, General Lansdale should accompany the new U.S. Ambassador to Saigon to facilitate good working relations with the Vietnamese Government from the earliest moment and to be in command of the initial implementation of President Kennedy's Task Force Plan for Vietnam." "While in Vietnam," Lansdale continued, he "could obtain President Diem's permission and then call non-Communist political opposition leaders together and encourage them to rely on legal means of opposition, to help in the fight against the Communist Viet Cong, and to cease scheming coup d'etats."

In addition to promoting political unity, he advocated what could be seen as his Greatest Hits: create "a Presidential Complaints and Action Commission" to make the government more accountable; set up an Economic Development Corps (EDCOR) to offer free land to Vietcong prisoners who could be induced to defect; improve public administration across South Vietnam using American and Filipino volunteers; step up psychological operations against North Vietnam; and implement a plan to eventually overthrow the Hanoi regime, beginning with "initial actions against symbols of Communist power; the railroad, the cement plant, and the larger modern printing plan[t] in Hanoi"—in other words, the targets that Lou Conein had not been permitted to blow up in 1954. He did not call for sending U.S. combat troops to South Vietnam, but he did advocate increasing the number of military advisers and for easing the prohibition that forbade them to participate in combat alongside South Vietnamese forces. Lansdale summed up his ambitious agenda as follows: "1. Pacification—to end the internal Communist threat in South Vietnam. 2. Stabilization—to promote the growth of healthy democracy in South Vietnam. 3. Unification—to provide a favorable climate for a free choice by the Vietnamese to unify their country."[39] The implementation of this program would, of course, be overseen by the memorandum's author and his trusted associates. To buttress his case, Lansdale sent a copy of his top-secret 1955 Saigon Military Mission report to senior Kennedy officials under the title "A Cold War Win" to show them what he had done in the past—and implicitly what he could do in the future.[40]

Lansdale's proposal for a new Presidential Task Force on Vietnam was adopted by John F. Kennedy on April 20, 1961, the very day that the Bay of Pigs invasion reached its catastrophic denouement. Having failed to topple Fidel Castro, the president was determined to stop the advance of Communism in Southeast Asia.[41] The head of the task force was Deputy Defense Secretary Roswell Gilpatric. A product of the Hotchkiss School and Yale University, Gilpatric had been a prominent corporate lawyer in New York and was a well-known ladies' man; he would be married five times and romantically linked to Jacqueline Kennedy after she became a widow. Like Rusk, he viewed Lansdale as a "solo operator" and an "unusual military type" who "didn't go along with the usual channels and guidelines," but, unlike Rusk, he found him to be "very useful," "knowledgeable," and "very able." "Lansdale was not in favor . . . with either the military or with the State Department," Gilpatric said. "And I was convinced they were wrong. I was convinced he was not a wheeler dealer; he was not an irresponsible swashbuckler."[42] "To the best of my knowledge," Gilpatric wrote in early 1961, "General Lansdale is the most highly qualified officer on active duty today serving in the area of counter-insurgency affairs."[43] With Gilpatric's endorsement, Kennedy designated Lansdale as "operations officer" of the task force.

The Vietnam Task Force met for the first time on Monday, April 24, four days after receiving its mandate from the president. Notwithstanding the mutual antipathy between Lansdale and the State Department representatives—similar to the poisonous relations that had existed between him and the French in Vietnam in the mid-1950s— the task force produced a draft plan just a few days after the initial meeting. As the Pentagon Papers were later to note, this first draft was "very much a Gilpatric–Lansdale show," incorporating many of Lansdale's suggestions. In a covering memorandum to the president, Gilpatric wrote that Lansdale "will proceed to Vietnam immediately after the program receives Presidential approval." Lansdale sent off letters to various individuals from his old team, asking them to meet him in Saigon on May 5, 1961, in the expectation that he would resume his old position of prominence. "This appears to have been the high point of Lansdale's role in Vietnam policy," the Pentagon Papers concluded. Lansdale's downfall was as swift and unexpected as his ascent. On Robert McNamara's copy of the memorandum, he crossed out the words "will proceed to Vietnam immediately" and scrawled instead "will proceed to Vietnam when requested by the Ambassador"[44]— a request that, as McNamara knew, was not likely to come until the Mekong Delta froze over.

By the time the interagency process had finished rewriting the task force report, Lansdale's role had been all but eliminated.[45] The leadership of the task force passed to the State Department, where it faded into insignificance. Most of Lansdale's specific recommendations were replaced with meaningless gobbledygook—for example, "the Ambassador should also consider such special arrangements within the field organization as he may deem required to assure a capability for rapid County Team response to evolving problems."[46] The only real victory Lansdale won was the task force's recommendation, as the Pentagon Papers put it, "to take a crack at the Lansdale approach of trying to win Diem over with a strong display of personal confidence in him."[47] After reading the final Vietnam Task Force report in dismay, Lansdale "strongly" recommended to McNamara and Gilpatric that the Pentagon stay out of the task force altogether: "Having a Defense officer,

myself or someone else, placed in a position of only partial influence . . .
would be only to provide State with a scapegoat to share the blame
when we have a flop."[48]

◆

LANSDALE HAD tried but failed to take control of the Kennedy administration's policy toward Vietnam. He had won the president's favor
before being just as swiftly marginalized. Lansdale was to say that "by
the summer of 1961, I was practically without voice on the number one
problem area for CI [counterinsurgency], Viet Nam."[49]

He believed that his influence "had been severely damaged" by Kennedy's suggestions that he be appointed either ambassador or MAAG
chief. Those rumored promotions stirred jealousy and animosity that
Lansdale did nothing to dissipate. Once again, he had been outma-
neuvered by his bureaucratic adversaries. "I don't know which has the
worst jungle, Vietnam or Washington," he complained.[50] He was certainly not proving as sure-footed in navigating the latter as he had been
in the former. He had erred, in particular, by making an enemy at the
very top of his own department.

22

"The X Factor"

Your list is incomplete. You've left out the most important factor of all.

—EDWARD LANSDALE TO ROBERT MCNAMARA

BEING secretary of defense was, from the start, an almost impossible job. Although the National Security Act of 1947 had created this post to preside over the Army, Air Force, Navy, and Marine Corps, it gave the officeholder scant power. The first secretary of defense, the Wall Street banker and former Navy secretary James Forrestal, spent his tenure locked in internecine battles with the military services over their funding and missions. He left office in 1949 a broken man, suffering from what psychiatrists diagnosed as the equivalent of combat fatigue. Just two months later, he jumped to his death from the window of the naval hospital where he was receiving psychiatric treatment.[1]

After Forrestal's tragic exit, a revolving door was in effect, with none of Harry Truman's remaining secretaries of defense serving longer than a year and a half. Eisenhower's first secretary of defense, Charlie Wilson, was in office much longer—nearly five years—but he was widely regarded as a figurehead; the five-star president was, in many ways, his own defense secretary. A former automobile executive,

Wilson would be remembered primarily for saying that "what was good for the country was good for General Motors and vice versa." The first secretary of defense who would exercise real, indeed nearly absolute, authority was John F. Kennedy's choice: Robert Strange McNamara. This would be good news for those who believed that the Pentagon's unruly bureaucracy needed a firm hand at the top. It would be bad news, however, for Edward Lansdale and his hopes of influencing the nation's Vietnam policy.

Lansdale got his first intimation of what McNamara was like in the early days of 1961 when he was summoned to the Pentagon's inner sanctum, Room 3E-880, to give the new defense secretary a ten-minute briefing—and not a second more—on his Vietnam trip. He knew that McNamara, who had come to the Pentagon, like Charlie Wilson, from a car company, in his case the Ford Motor Company, had no background whatsoever in guerrilla warfare in general or Vietnam in particular. McNamara later admitted as much, conceding, "I had never visited Indochina, nor did I understand its history, language, culture, or values."[2] Lansdale sought to begin McNamara's education by bringing with him a collection of Vietcong weapons, including "handmade pistols and knives, old French rifles, and bamboo punji sticks,"[3] that he intended to donate to the Special Forces headquarters at Fort Bragg.

Lansdale found the defense secretary wearing, as always, a dark suit, his thick brown hair slicked back on his head and parted in the middle, old-fashioned wire-rim spectacles framing his mirthless eyes, his jaw clenched tight, a severe expression on his face, looking very much like the Presbyterian elder that he was. He was ensconced behind his nine-foot-long mahogany desk, which was polished to a mirrorlike shine and adorned, as a reporter noted, "with half a dozen in-and-out baskets brimming with problems of peace and war."[4] Behind him was a portrait of his tightly wound predecessor James Forrestal. It was a fitting if unconscious warning of the way that McNamara himself would crack under the pressure of the Vietnam War.

Lansdale unceremoniously dumped his cargo of dirty weapons, caked with mud and blood, on the secretary's immaculate desk with a "great clatter." He recalled telling McNamara,

The enemy in Vietnam uses these weapons—and they were just using them just a little bit ago before I got them. Many of them are barefoot or wear sandals. They wear black pajamas, usually, with tatters or holes in them. I don't think you'd recognize any of them as soldiers, but they think of themselves that way. The people that are fighting there, on our side, are being supplied with our weapons and uniforms and shoes and all of the best that we have; and we're training them. Yet, the enemy is licking our side. Always keep in mind about Vietnam, that the struggle goes far beyond the material things of life. It doesn't take weapons and uniforms and lots of food to win. It takes something else, ideas and ideals, and these guys are using that something else. Let's at least learn that lesson.[5]

"Watching his face as I talked," Lansdale was to say, "I got the feeling that he didn't understand me. Too unconventional. Somehow I found him very hard to talk to."[6] That was because Lansdale did not speak McNamara's language—the language of numbers.

Ever since he was a schoolboy, Robert S. McNamara had been entranced by the seductive logic of mathematics. As an undergraduate at the University of California at Berkeley, in the 1930s, he began, he later said, "to talk and think in numbers."[7] That tendency became even more pronounced during his postgraduate studies at Harvard Business School, where he became convinced that a mastery of financial data was the key to business success. Cold, unemotional, aloof, and intolerant of those less brilliant than him, Bob McNamara began to cultivate a reputation as a human computer—an "IBM machine with legs."[8] During World War II, he became a statistician in uniform, helping the Army Air Forces to maximize the effectiveness of their bombing campaign against Japan. In a sign of what was to come in Vietnam, his number crunching helped kill hundreds of thousands of civilians, but he remained seemingly impervious to the human cost of his work. After the war, he and his fellow Air Force statisticians, dubbed the Whiz Kids, moved en masse to the Ford Motor Company, where they engineered a turnaround employing quantitative methods, much to the chagrin of automobile enthusiasts such as Lee Iacocca. McNamara's incisive biographer Deborah Shapley was to write that he became "the epitome of a bean-counting manager who understood nothing about engineering cars."[9] By the end of 1960, he had risen to become president of Ford, the first nonfamily member ever to hold that post.

The president-elect had said that he wanted a Republican or two in the cabinet, and McNamara seemed to fit the bill. "That a young Republican businessman could also be well thought of by labor, be Harvard-trained, support the ACLU, and read Teilhard de Chardin were all bonuses," Shapley wrote.[10] (Pierre Teilhard de Chardin was a trendy French philosopher.) Jack Kennedy instructed his aides, sight unseen, to offer McNamara his choice of cabinet posts, either Treasury or Defense. McNamara chose Defense, and began, with the help of his Whiz Kids, to apply his number-crunching philosophy to the armed forces.

"You can't substitute emotions for reason," he often said.[11] He honestly believed that if only you got the inputs right, his mathematical models would unerringly spit out the right answers to such complicated questions as: How big should America's nuclear arsenal be? What kind of next-generation fighter airplane should the Air Force and Navy buy? And how should the United States respond to Vietcong attacks? Anyone like Lansdale who tried to challenge McNamara's "systems analysis" was given short shrift by the imperious secretary.

A year later, in early 1962, Lansdale was called in again to McNamara's office to help him "computerize" the war in Vietnam. McNamara presented him with a long list of entries, written out with a pencil on graph paper, including factors such as the number of Vietcong killed—the "body count" of later infamy.

"Your list is incomplete," Lansdale said. "You've left out the most important factor of all."

"What is it?" McNamara demanded.

"Well, it's the human factor," Lansdale said. "You can put it down as the X factor."

McNamara duly wrote down in pencil, "X factor." "What does it consist of?"

"What the people out on the battlefield really feel; which side they want to see win and which side they're for at the moment. That's the only way you're going to ever have this war decided."

"Tell me how to put it in," McNamara said.

"I don't think any Americans out there at the moment can report this to you," Lansdale replied.

McNamara then took out an eraser and began to erase the "X factor." "No, leave it in there," Lansdale said.

He then spent a week trying to figure out how to provide the numbers that McNamara wanted. He suggested that U.S. troops working with Vietnamese forces in the field answer questions such as "What was the villages' attitude towards the Vietnamese troops?"; "What is attitude of Vietnamese troops towards civilians at check points on the highway?"; and "What are the feelings of [Vietnamese] troops at being in military service? Proud to be in uniform? Indifferent? . . . Homesick?"[12] His work ultimately led to the Hamlet Evaluation System, a systematic way to judge whether each Vietnamese village was dominated by the government or by the Vietcong. But Lansdale knew all too well that such figures were inherently subjective and prone to manipulation. He pleaded with McNamara: "You're going to fool yourself if you get all of these figures added up, because they won't tell you how we're doing in this war."

Lansdale's deputy, Lieutenant Colonel Samuel V. Wilson, recalled seeing McNamara's eyes "glaze over" as Lansdale kept lecturing him about the X Factor. Wilson tried to get Lansdale's attention by nudging him with a knee but Lansdale "just kept going strong," uncharacteristically oblivious to the impression he was making. "He was turning McNamara off," Wilson said, "but waxing more and more enthusiastic, speaking more rapidly."[13]

From then on, McNamara had little time for Lansdale. With a bitter laugh, Lansdale later remembered McNamara's reaction to his contributions: "He asked me to please not bother him anymore. He used to say, 'Thank you, I've got something else to do now.'"[14] When McNamara needed something from Lansdale's office, he would call Sam Wilson. "Things were simply broken between Lansdale and McNamara," Wilson said.[15]

McNamara was later to lament that no one in the administration knew much about Vietnam—"we found ourselves setting policy for a region that was terra incognita. Worse, our government lacked experts for us to consult to compensate for our ignorance." Lansdale was, he grudgingly admitted, the only "Pentagon officer with counterinsurgency experience in the region," but McNamara denigrated him as hardly comparable to Soviet experts such as Charles "Chip" Bohlen and George Kennan. "Lansdale," he sniffed, "was relatively junior and lacked broad geopolitical experience."[16] Actually Lansdale was eight years older than McNamara himself, who was forty-four in 1961, and he had been working in Asia since 1945.

One suspects that McNamara's problem with Lansdale was not that he lacked broad experience but that he lacked McNamara's own misguided passion for reducing the complex problems of war and peace into easily solvable and greatly deceptive mathematical equations. Lansdale's mishandling of the prickly secretary of defense—his tendency to drone on a little too long and a little too stridently—compounded the problem. In his attempts to influence American leaders, Lansdale lacked the deft touch he displayed in dealing with foreign leaders.

That would turn out to be an increasingly serious stumbling block for Lansdale because McNamara was fast becoming the most forceful and powerful member of the Kennedy cabinet, next to Attorney General Robert Kennedy himself. McNamara's influence, as much as Dean Rusk's, led to Lansdale's precipitous fall from grace in the first half of 1961: he went from being the president's favorite counterinsurgency expert and the front-runner to become the next ambassador to South Vietnam to being "practically without voice" as the situation continued to worsen.

◆

BY SEPTEMBER 1961, the number of Vietcong attacks had nearly tripled, to 450 a month from 150 a month earlier in the year. In the early morning hours of September 18, insurgents overran Phuoc Thanh, a provincial capital only fifty-five miles from Saigon, beheaded the provincial governor, and slipped away into the jungle before government troops arrived.[17] In response, Ngo Dinh Diem asked that the United States not only support a further buildup of the South Vietnamese army but also sign a bilateral defense treaty committing the United States to South Vietnam's defense. Robert McNamara and the Joint Chiefs circulated plans, over the opposition of the State Department, to insert U.S. combat troops primarily to protect South Vietnam's borders against Communist incursions.

President Kennedy was not sure what to do, and he could not devote his full attention to Vietnam. East German and Soviet forces had begun erecting the Berlin Wall in the early morning hours of August 13, 1961, to stop the hemorrhaging of refugees to the West. The Communists were threatening to force American troops out of the city altogether— a threat that Kennedy vowed to resist with force if necessary. While World War III was looming in Berlin, Kennedy decided on October 11 to send a team of trusted advisers to Saigon to recommend a way forward in Vietnam. The mission would include Edward Lansdale, and it would be led by two of the president's favorites—Maxwell Taylor and Walt Whitman Rostow.

Kennedy had summoned Taylor, a former Army chief of staff, out of retirement in April 1961 to study the disastrous Bay of Pigs operation and had kept him in the White House as an all-purpose troubleshooter. Described by a fawning journalist as "an aloof, handsome man with cool china blue eyes, a knack for sketching a problem in broad perspective, and a talent for hammering out explicit courses of action,"[18] Taylor was not only a decorated combat veteran who had jumped into France at the head of the 101st Airborne Division on the eve of D-Day; he was also fluent in four foreign languages and capable of citing Virgil, Polybius, Caesar, or Clausewitz in casual conversation.[19] He was, in short, JFK's kind of general. But he was not as attuned to the demands of counterinsurgency as the president might have imagined. Taylor had written a book called *The Uncertain Trumpet* to argue that the military had to prepare for "limited wars" rather than only World War III, but, as Lansdale had discovered during his battles with the Army in the late 1950s over giving the counterinsurgency mission to the Special Forces, Taylor did not advocate civic action and psychological warfare as Lans-

dale did. Instead, he seemed to believe that guerrillas could be defeated
with the same kind of fire-and-maneuver tactics that his paratroopers
had employed in the liberation of Europe.

A former professor of economic history at the Massachusetts Institute of Technology, Rostow was more attuned to the softer side of
counterinsurgency. His 1960 magnum opus, *The Stages of Economic
Growth: A Non-Communist Manifesto*, argued that economic growth
was ineluctably leading the world in a liberal democratic, rather than
a Marxist, direction and that it was in America's interest to help developing nations reach the "takeoff" stage. He was already working with
Lansdale on a small National Security Council task force to formulate a "U.S. Strategy To Deal With 'Wars of National Liberation'";
their work would soon lead to, among other things, the creation of a
high-level committee called the Special Group (Counterinsurgency),
chaired by General Taylor and designed to focus bureaucratic attention on the "deterrence and countering of guerrilla warfare."[20] But,
while he advocated Lansdale-style civic action, Rostow was also a firm
believer in the efficacy of airpower. As an OSS officer in London, he
had helped pick targets for the U.S. bombing campaign against Germany, and he would later be nicknamed Air Marshal Rostow for the
enthusiasm with which he recommended bombing North Vietnam.[21]
He would never be mistaken, however, for a cigar-chomping milita-
rist in the mold of General Curtis LeMay. Even those who disagreed
with Rostow had to admit that he was a "warm human being."[22] A veteran of the Johnson administration was to call him "a sheep in wolf's
clothing."[23]

By contrast, Taylor was more of a "loner" and "not a conciliator."[24]
Lansdale got along well with the amiable Rostow but not with Taylor,
who reminded him of his old nemesis Lightning Joe Collins—"the two
of them were remarkably alike in their mastery of the fleeting smile,
their pose of clean-cut all-American boy with graying hair, gentlemanly
diction, and cold-blooded arrogance with subordinates in private."[25]

The Taylor-Rostow mission took off on an Air Force executive jet,
a Boeing 707, from Andrews Air Force Base outside Washington on
October 15, 1961. Taylor, dressed in a yellow shirt and blue sweater,

and Rostow, in gray sweater and open collar, called the eighteen group members up to the front cabin.[26] Taylor then drew a line under the first four names and announced that everyone above the line would be going on protocol visits to meet Ngo Dinh Diem and other senior officials, while everyone below the line would not. Brigadier General Lansdale's name was just below this line.[27]

While the group was flying to Vietnam, Taylor demanded that everyone write out "a list of the things you think you're qualified to look into." Lansdale gave him a long list of his interests and his contacts in Vietnam. Taylor ignored what he had written and assigned him to come up with a detailed plan to erect a high-tech barrier—a fence with electronic sensors—to prevent Communist infiltration of South Vietnam from Laos and Cambodia. "That's not my subject," Lansdale protested. "I'm not good at that." Taylor wasn't listening.[28] When the delegation arrived in Saigon on October 18, 1961, Lansdale went over to the Military Advisory Assistance Group and told them, "You guys are good at figuring it out. This is going to cost us several billion dollars. Tell me how many billions and I'll report it in."[29] (MAAG duly came up with a proposal, the first stage of which involved defoliating more than eight hundred miles of jungle at a cost of $3.5 million.)[30]

As soon as he heard that Lansdale was back, Diem sent an aide to bring him to the presidential palace for a talk—the last one the two men would ever have. Taylor was busy briefing the press, so Lansdale told Rostow that he was going to the palace "to see an old friend." The big question on Diem's mind was whether he should request U.S. troops. Lansdale recalled asking him, "Have you reached that point in your affairs now that you're going to need that to stay alive?"

"So you think I shouldn't ask?" Diem asked.

No, Lansdale said, just tell the truth—do you need troops or not? Diem couldn't make up his mind. Ngo Dinh Nhu was sitting in on this meeting, and when Lansdale tried to press the issue he broke in to answer.

"I'm asking your brother these questions, not you," Lansdale snapped. He was dismayed to see the extent to which Diem now deferred to Nhu on pivotal decisions.

Finally the brothers decided they didn't need U.S. troops. "Well stay with that then," Lansdale advised.[31]

While the world was transfixed by the continuing standoff between the superpowers in Berlin, the White House group spent seven whirlwind days in Vietnam—"a maelstrom of official calls, briefings, discussions, and visits to the field," Taylor was to write.[32] One day was spent visiting the DMZ, another day overflying the Mekong Delta to see the effects of recent flooding, the worst in decades, which had destroyed crops, left hundreds of thousands homeless, and exacerbated "a collapse of national morale."[33] The group left Saigon on October 25, 1961, and retreated to Baguio, the summer capital of the Philippines, to write their report amid the cool mountain breezes.

Taylor was to explain, "Personally, I had no enthusiasm for the thought of using U.S. Army forces in ground combat in this guerrilla war. . . . On the other hand, there was a pressing need to do something to restore Vietnamese morale and to shore up confidence in the United States."[34] As a compromise, Taylor and Rostow proposed the introduction of six thousand to eight thousand U.S. combat troops under the guise of flood relief.[35] While Taylor did not envision U.S. troops clearing "the jungles and forests of Viet Cong guerrillas," he did foresee the possibility of their being thrown into action "against large, formed guerrilla bands which have abandoned the forests for attacks on major targets." And if this was insufficient to save South Vietnam, Taylor noted, in a separate "eyes only" cable to the president, bombing North Vietnam was always an option; he claimed that Hanoi "is extremely vulnerable to conventional bombing."[36]

Lansdale was not entirely averse to the introduction of more American troops per se—certainly not as averse as he later said he was. He was willing to send a " 'hard core' of combat forces" to buttress military units focused on civic action missions such as building roads and improving public health.[37] But Lansdale never advocated bombing the North, nor did he envision U.S. troops fighting North Vietnamese formations as directly as Taylor did. In his report, Lansdale warned that "just adding more of many things, as we are doing at present, doesn't appear to provide the answer we are seeking." To "spark a complete psychological change in Vietnam's situation, give the Vietnamese the hope of winning, and take the initiative away from the Communists," he advocated sending more American advisers "as helpers, not as orderers."[38]

The members of the Taylor-Rostow mission presented their findings to the president at the White House on November 3, 1961, as the Berlin Crisis was approaching a peaceful end.[39] Kennedy turned down the proposal to send troops to Vietnam under the guise of flood relief. He told Arthur Schlesinger Jr., "The troops will march in; the bands will play; the crowds will cheer; and in four days everyone will have forgotten. Then we will be told we have to send more troops. It's like taking a drink. The effect wears off, and you have to take another."[40] But Kennedy did approve a substantial enlargement of the advisory effort, as recommended by Taylor and Rostow. By the end of 1963, there would be sixteen thousand U.S. advisers in South Vietnam, up from only 685 when he assumed office. In February 1962, the lower-level Military Assistance Advisory Group would be expanded into the U.S. Military Assistance Command—Vietnam (MACV), led by a four-star general, initially Paul Harkins, a protégé of George S. Patton's. American advisers would now be embedded with all South Vietnamese army units down to battalion level, while American-flown aircraft would provide air support to the South Vietnamese army.

Lansdale had argued in favor of letting military advisers participate in combat. "It would make all the difference in the effectiveness of their relationship to the Vietnamese," he argued; "comrades are listened to, when they share the risk."[41] His advice was taken, and before long U.S. Air Force crews were flying attack missions in the guise of training Vietnamese crewmen who were simply along for the ride—not quite what Lansdale envisioned, but the natural consequence of allowing gung-ho Americans eager for combat to get into the thick of the action.[42] The Taylor-Rostow mission subsequently would be seen as a major step toward the American armed forces' entering the Vietnam War as a full-fledged combatant.

THE TAYLOR-ROSTOW task force put forward one additional idea that the president did not implement: a recommendation that Edward Lansdale be sent to Saigon as an adviser to Diem. South Vietnam's president had personally made this request to Maxwell Taylor. On the cable sent back to Washington reporting the request, some unidentified State Department official wrote in the margin, "No. No. NO!"[43]

The diplomats did soften their opposition a bit a few weeks afterward, in late November 1961, when they found Diem still reluctant to implement the governmental changes they advocated, including giving the United States a significant say in South Vietnamese decision-making. Diem saw that as a return to colonialism, this time under the Americans rather than the French.[44] At that point, State suggested, just as Elbridge Durbrow had done in 1960, that Lansdale go to Saigon "and, presumably, clobber [Diem] from up close."[45] At least that was how Lansdale interpreted the request, which he adamantly rejected.

"Rather than just 'hold Diem's hand,' apparently they want me to accept the hospitality of a friend whom I respect and then follow orders to threaten him with penalties from that close-in position, simply because he doesn't comply with every wish of some Americans who remain foreign to the scene," he wrote angrily to McNamara and Gilpatric. "The Communists in Vietnam can be defeated, but this isn't the way to do it."[46]

In his own eyes, and those of his friends, Lansdale was taking a stand on principle in a way that few other government officials would ever dare to do. In the eyes of Lansdale's many internal critics, his position—go on his terms or not at all—was simply more evidence that he was an uncontrollable prima donna.

Walt Rostow, who at the end of 1961 was moving to the State Department to take over policy planning, tried one last time before he left the White House to persuade the president to post Lansdale to Saigon. It is "crucial," he wrote to Kennedy on December 6, 1961, "that we free Ed Lansdale from his present assignment and get him out to the field in an appropriate position. He is a unique national asset in the Saigon setting."[47] Once again, however, Kennedy did not act. McGeorge Bundy later explained that the president "was relatively sympathetic to Lansdale. Lansdale was temperamentally somewhat his kind of person. I don't think, on the other hand, that he felt so strongly about it that he wanted to push it against strong opposition from either the military or the diplomatic bureaucracy."[48]

In his memoir, published a decade later, after tens of thousands of bodybags had come home, Rostow was to lament the failure to find a role for Lansdale in Saigon: "It is by no means certain Lansdale could have altered the tragic course on which Diem was launched; but he represented a kind of last chance."[49] With that chance lost, the abyss was looming nearer.

23

"Worms of the World Unite"

Let's get the hell on with it. The President wants some action, right now.

—ROBERT F. KENNEDY

THE origins of Edward Lansdale's next assignment could be found in the calamitous events of April 17, 1961. In the early morning hours, an armada of six cargo ships appeared off the southern coast of Cuba. They had been chartered by the CIA and filled with fourteen hundred Cuban exiles trained and armed by the CIA. (The trainers had included one of Lansdale's old friends, the former Philippine army officer Napoleon Valeriano.) The mission of Brigade 2506 was nothing less than to overthrow the regime of Fidel Castro, the strongman who had seized power on January 1, 1959, and had steadily moved closer to the Soviet bloc. The liberation of Cuba was supposed to begin with a landing at the Bahia de Cochinos—in English, the Bay of Pigs—a scenic site of turquoise waters, white sand beaches, and mangroves that Castro was hoping to develop into a tourist destination.

Lansdale had been among a minority of officials who opposed the invasion plans. In November 1960, in the waning days of the Eisenhower administration, Allen Dulles had presented the CIA's proposal for Operation Zapata to the senior interagency group charged with approving all covert actions. After analyzing the proposal, Lansdale later said, he concluded that "too little attention was being paid to the political preparation in Cuba and that too small a force was being utilized for what had turned into an over-the-beach invasion." "We are going to get clobbered," he warned, much to Dulles's consternation. Lansdale even tried and failed to block the assignment of two dozen army sergeants to work as trainers for Brigade 2506.[1]

When the operation went ahead anyway, it would amply vindicate Lansdale's warnings. The plan had been for brigade B-26 bombers flying out of Nicaragua to destroy Castro's air force on the ground. But at the last minute President Kennedy became worried about exposing American complicity and ordered three-quarters of the initial air strikes canceled. Lacking air cover, the invaders were trapped in the open on a beach where, as Lansdale had predicted, they were "clobbered" by twenty thousand Cuban troops equipped with tanks, machine guns, artillery, and aircraft. On April 17, Kennedy relented and allowed the B-26s to fly again, but many of these slow, propeller-driven aircraft were blasted out of the sky by Castro's T-33 jet trainers, which, unbeknownst to the Americans, had been equipped with 20-mm cannons. On April 19, after the invaders had already suffered a shellacking, Kennedy reluctantly authorized six unmarked Navy jets to spend exactly one hour over the beachhead without, however, giving them authorization to shoot down Cuban aircraft.

By April 20, it was all over. Only a few of the exiles escaped to sea to be rescued by the U.S. Navy; 114 men were killed, and almost all of the rest (1,189) captured. That Castro's forces suffered heavier casualties was no consolation. It was, as the historian Theodore Draper wrote a few weeks later, "one of those rare politico-military events—a perfect failure."[2]

◆

JUST TWO days after Operation Zapata's failure, a National Security Council meeting convened on April 22, 1961, to consider next steps. Under Secretary of State Chester Bowles read aloud a State Department paper concluding—correctly, as it turned out—that Castro was secure absent an American invasion. As soon as Bowles finished, Attorney General Robert F. Kennedy exploded, "That's the most meaningless, worthless thing I've ever heard. You people are so anxious to protect your own asses that you're afraid to do anything. All you want to do is to dump the whole thing on the president. We'd be better off if you just quit and left foreign policy to someone else."

A twenty-nine-year-old White House aide named Richard Goodwin noted that, "as the embarrassing tirade continued, the president sat calmly, outwardly relaxed, only the faint click from the metallic pencil cap he was tapping against his almost incandescently white, evenly spaced teeth disrupting his silence—a characteristic revelation that some inner tension was being suppressed." Gradually it dawned on Goodwin "that Bobby's harsh polemic reflected the president's own concealed emotions, privately communicated in some earlier, intimate conversation." When Robert Kennedy was done, "the group sat silently, stunned by the ferocity of his assault." Then the president calmly appointed a task force to take charge of Cuba policy from which the State Department "was pointedly omitted."[3] Bowles left the meeting lamenting that the "fire eaters" were in charge.[4]

Far from dissuading the Kennedys from further plots, the Bay of Pigs operation had only made them more determined to oust Castro. In the judgment of the CIA's deputy director for operations, Richard Bissell, who was soon forced into retirement along with Allen Dulles, the Kennedys developed an "obsession with Cuba": "From their perspective, Castro won the first round at the Bay of Pigs. He had defeated the Kennedy team; they were bitter and they could not tolerate his getting away with it. The president and his brother were ready to avenge their personal embarrassment by overthrowing their enemy at any cost."[5]

Not only was this Caribbean island emerging, improbably enough, as the administration's "highest priority project" (in Robert Kennedy's words),[6] but, just as improbably, Robert Kennedy was emerging as the administration's point man on this issue. It was not a role that might have been expected for the attorney general but one that made perfect sense, given his long-standing role as his older brother's keeper and protector.

Robert Francis Kennedy had been, in his father's description, the "runt" of the litter.[7] He was a mediocre student and too young to see combat in World War II as his older brothers Jack and Joe Jr. did (Joe Jr. was killed on a bombing mission in 1944). Bobby made up for his perceived shortcomings with obnoxious aggressiveness in defense of his family. "Desperate to win his father's attention and respect," the biographer Evan Thomas wrote, "Kennedy became a hard man for a long while, covering over his sensitivity and capacity for empathy with a carapace of arrogance."[8]

Eventually another side of RFK would be revealed; as the sixties progressed, many would come to see him, in Thomas's words, as "the gentle, child-loving, poetry-reading, soulful herald of a new age."[9] But in 1961 few could have imagined the transformation that would occur in Bobby's image. At the dawn of Camelot, RFK was known, as he had been since he was a schoolboy, for having "a chip on his shoulder" and "a short fuse."[10] He showed his pugnacity when he served as campaign manager during his brother Jack's Senate campaign in Massachusetts in 1952. JFK, eight years older, was cool, elegant, and above the fray. His younger brother played the heavy to make sure that crucial tasks were accomplished.[11]

Bobby's reputation as a bully grew in 1953 when he joined the staff of soon-to-be-disgraced Senator Joe McCarthy. He did not last long in that job—not because he disapproved of "Tailgunner Joe's" Red-baiting tactics but because he did not get a promotion he was seeking. Two years later, with Democrats in control of the Senate, he became chief counsel of the Senate Permanent Subcommittee on Investigations. In charge of a staff of a hundred investigators, Kennedy sought to uncover links between mobsters and labor leaders. That, in turn, led him to pursue a relentless vendetta against the Teamsters boss Jimmy Hoffa, whose "absolute evilness" he was determined to expose by any methods necessary.[12] To Bobby's fury, Hoffa beat all the charges until finally, in 1964, he was convicted of jury tampering. "For him," Bobby's wife,

Ethel, said, "the world is divided into black and white hats. Bobby can only distinguish good men and bad."[13] Fidel Castro was a bad man, and Bobby, a latter-day Torquemada,[14] was determined to go after him as he had previously gone after Hoffa: all-out, no holds barred.

◆

AT NOON on November 3, 1961, just a few hours before the Taylor-Rostow group was to deliver its report on Vietnam, the president convened a White House meeting to consider Cuba. The only record of what was said is a handwritten note from Bobby Kennedy. "My idea," he wrote, "is stir things up on island with espionage, sabotage, general disorder, run & operated by Cubans themselves with every group but Batistaites & Communists. Do not know if we will be successful in overthrowing Castro but we have nothing to lose in my estimate." (His breezy assurance that there was "nothing to lose" would be proven disastrously wrong less than twelve months later.) To "stir things up," Bobby continued, McNamara had agreed to make Edward Lansdale, who was sitting in the back, "available for me—I assigned him to make survey of situation in Cuba—the problem and our assets."[15]

It was not hard to see why Lansdale was chosen, even if, in hindsight, the reasons do not look like good ones. "Lansdale had a great reputation because of his work in Southeast Asia," Dick Goodwin recalled. "If you were going to mount a covert campaign against Cuba, he seemed the logical choice."[16] The very fact that Lansdale had not previously worked on Cuba policy was seen as a plus: he was not tainted by the Bay of Pigs. No one was daunted that, while Lansdale had enjoyed considerable success with counterinsurgency and nation-building operations in the Philippines and South Vietnam, he had not notched any comparable achievement in his efforts to undermine North Vietnam and that, moreover, he had no personal acquaintance with the people of Cuba. The aura of the "Ugly American" was strong enough to override any objections.

Lansdale thus became chief of operations of the Caribbean Survey Group. Soon it would be dubbed Operation Mongoose. This was an arbitrary cryptonym generated by the CIA to fool those without the proper clearances into thinking that it designated an operation in Thailand. (The "MO" diagraph was used to denote Thailand; "AM" was the designation for Cuba. Thus Castro's cryptonym was AMTHUG and Che Guevara, a physician, was AMQUACK.)[17] Although picked randomly, the name seemed appropriate: not only had Lansdale once kept pet mongooses in Saigon—his gift from Trinh Minh Thé—but mongooses were known for killing venomous snakes. That is exactly how U.S. officials viewed Castro, as a serpent that had to be exterminated for the good of the entire neighborhood.

Lansdale answered to a high-level interagency committee called Special Group (Augmented). Maxwell Taylor was designated chairman, but there was no doubt who the real boss was. The attorney general was, as Arthur Schlesinger Jr. noted, "wildly busy in 1962," with an around-the-world trip in February, a fight in April with the steel companies over alleged price fixing, a battle in September to desegregate the University of Mississippi, constant pressure against Jimmy Hoffa, and incessant feuding with Lyndon Johnson and J. Edgar Hoover about various matters. Yet he still found time to check in on Mongoose regularly in order "to needle the bureaucracy."[18] At meeting after meeting, the attorney general stressed that there had to be "maximum effort" and that "there will be no acceptable alibi" for failure.[19] "Let's get the hell on with it," he would say. "The President wants some action, right now."[20] His performance at Mongoose meetings reminded the CIA's deputy director, Marshall Carter, of "the gnawing of an enraged rat terrier."[21]

The full weight of all that pressure fell directly on Edward Lansdale. When he first saw the attorney general at a meeting, Lansdale recalled, he "wondered what the youngster was doing sitting in the meeting talking so much." He didn't connect the man before him "with the pictures of him on TV." The mistake was understandable, given that Robert Kennedy was still only thirty-seven years old (to Lansdale's fifty-three). As Evan Thomas noted, "With his buck teeth and floppy hair and shy gawkiness, he sometimes came across like an awkward teenager."[22] But there was nothing diffident about the way Bobby threw his influence around in meetings. Bobby, Lansdale said, "was the most interested of anyone in the room of what I would say on things and would plague me with many questions."[23] It was hardly surprising that Lansdale chafed under this constant harassment. His friend Rufus Phillips recalled, "While Ed respected the president, he didn't like Bobby worth a damn."24

◆

LANSDALE WAS under no illusion about the enormity of his task as chief of operations for Operation Mongoose. After a week on the job, while Lansdale was sitting in Dick Goodwin's office at the White House, he turned and said, "You know, Dick, it's impossible."

"What's impossible?" Goodwin asked.

"There is no way you can overthrow Castro without a strong, indigenous political opposition. And there is no such opposition, either in Cuba or outside it."25

Despite his doubts, Lansdale threw himself into his new assignment. Why did he so eagerly embark on such a dubious project under such a disagreeable taskmaster? In the recent past, he had turned down assignments that he did not believe in, such as the mission to pressure Diem. Like most other government officials, however, he was susceptible to the lure of high-level access, of working directly for the president and his brother on a high-priority project. Much as he might pretend otherwise, Lansdale was not free of ego or ambition. "He was proud," Sam Wilson recalled, "that he was talking to the president and Robert Kennedy."26 Lansdale would later regale his sons with tales of how he would discuss top-secret plans at Bobby's Hickory Hill mansion in McLean, Virginia, while Bobby's small children played "choo-choo" and other games around them.27

Beyond the dictates of duty and the desire for enhanced status, Lansdale also had a more practical reason for embracing his new assignment. He was determined to give the Kennedys what they most wanted—a plan to overthrow Castro—in the hope that in return they would give him what he most wanted: a return ticket to Saigon.28

◆

TO ACCOMPLISH his objective, Lansdale had to rely on liaison officers from the State Department, the CIA, the U.S. Information Agency, and other government agencies that were supposed to voluntarily cooperate with him. That ideal was not easy to achieve in practice, given the level of skepticism especially within the CIA toward the project in general and to Lansdale in particular. "The notion that the various agencies were simply to detail men, money, and material to Lansdale was dead on arrival," said Richard Helms, the CIA's deputy director for plans.[29]

"It was the most frustrating damn thing I've ever tackled," Lansdale wrote two years later. "I was given full responsibility for a US effort, but had no say on disciplining or giving orders to US personnel working in this effort. Most of these were State and CIA folks who made it plain to me that they hated my guts. So about once a week I would formally request relief from this duty, and be told that this was unacceptable."[30]

The more that other agencies resisted Lansdale's dictates, the more he blustered to get his authority respected—and the less respect he commanded. In an uncharacteristically pompous memorandum referring to himself in the third person, he demanded "that *all* plans and actions with operational aspects hereafter be made known to the Chief of Operations at the very earliest time feasible."[31] Such diktats led CIA operatives to mock him behind his back as "the FM," short for field marshal.[32]

Lansdale was annoyed by the CIA's tendency not only to ignore his authority but also to focus on covert actions such as "smash and grab raids." He believed, as he informed the Special Group (Augmented) on December 7, 1961, that the CIA had to be reoriented "180 degrees," relegating "militant (sabotage, etc.) actions" to a secondary role in support of building up a "genuine internal popular movement."[33] "I remember thinking at the time," he was to say years later, "I have to start back in kindergarten with these people and start teaching them."[34] Lansdale's condescending attitude toward his CIA colleagues—similar to his attitude toward his French colleagues in Vietnam—did not help to win them over.

◆

BY JANUARY 18, 1962, less than three months after his appointment, Lansdale had come up with a preliminary "concept of operation" to

"bring about the revolt of the Cuban people." This required the creation of a "political action organization . . . in key localities inside
Cuba, with its own means for internal communication, its own voice
for psychological operations, and its own action arm (small guerrilla
bands, sabotage squads, etc.)." This organization would have to gain,
Vietminh-style, "the sympathetic support of the majority of the Cuban
people." The "climactic moment of revolt," he predicted, "will come
from an angry reaction of the people to a government action (sparked
by an incident), or from a fracturing of the leadership cadre within
the regime, or both." The task of Mongoose would be to "bring this
about." Once a popular revolt had broken out, it could ask for international assistance, and the U.S. could then provide open support,
including "military force, as necessary." Lansdale recognized that
American military intervention would be needed to push Castro out;
the job of the internal resistance movement was merely to legitimate
such an intervention.

To bring about the Cuban people's revolt, Lansdale assigned thirty-
two operational tasks to various government agencies. The first priority was to increase intelligence collection in Cuba. Under "political
tasks," the CIA was to submit a plan "for defection of top Cuban government officials, to fracture the regime from within"; a "name defec-
tor" would be "worth at least a million U.S. dollars"—an indication
that money was no object for Mongoose. The U.S. Information Agency
and CIA jointly were assigned psychological warfare tasks "toward
the end result of awakening world sympathy for the Cuban people (as
a David) battling against the Communist regime (as a Goliath) and
towards stimulating Cubans inside Cuba to join 'the cause.'" The Pentagon was "to submit contingency plans for use of U.S. military force
to support the Cuban popular movement." The "economic" provisions
included various ways to disrupt Cuban trade, including a requirement
that the CIA "submit plan by 15 February for inducing failure in food
crops in Cuba."[35] The next day, Lansdale sent around another memorandum shedding light on how he hoped to induce failure in food
crops: it called for developing "a plan for incapacitating large segments
of the sugar workers by the covert use of BW [biological warfare] or

CW [chemical warfare] agents." The idea was to employ some kind of bug or chemical that would make the sugar workers sick enough to stay home from work but that would not cause any lasting damage.[36]

No such capacity was ever developed. This was typical of what the CIA's Richard Helms described as "very nutty schemes [that] were born of the intensity of the pressure" applied by the Kennedys to produce results.[37] "We were hysterical about Castro at the time of the Bay of Pigs and thereafter," Robert McNamara was later to say.[38]

◆

THESE "NUTTY schemes" were exposed publicly for the first time thirteen years later by the Church Committee—the Senate Select Committee to Study Government Operations with Respect to Intelligence Activities, chaired by Senator Frank Church, Democrat of Idaho. Its hearings in 1975 would do irrevocable damage to Lansdale's reputation.

Especially damning was an "example of Lansdale's perspicacity" sarcastically cited by the CIA veteran Thomas Parrott. He related to incredulous committee members a plan Lansdale had developed for a U.S. submarine to surface near the Cuban coast and fire star shells into the sky in order to convince Cubans "that the Second Coming of Christ was imminent and that Christ was against Castro." Parrott said that "by this time Lansdale was something of a joke in many quarters and somebody dubbed this Elimination by Illumination," a catchy nickname that stuck to Lansdale thereafter like a tropical rash.[39] In response, Lansdale indignantly wrote to Senator Church, "I assure you that this is absolutely untrue. I never had such a plan nor proposed such a plan."[40] In private, he called Parrott a "jerk" and a "real psycho case" for spreading this "weirdo" tale.[41]

However, a document declassified long after Lansdale's death and not previously cited by any other author makes clear that, notwithstanding Lansdale's protestations, this story was mostly true. On October 15, 1962, Lansdale wrote a memorandum on "Illumination by Submarine." It proposed firing "star shells from a submarine to illuminate the Havana area" after dark on November 2, All Souls' Day, in order "to gain extra impact from Cuban superstitions." The memo did not mention the Second Coming, but it did suggest that the star shells could be coupled with a CIA-generated "rumor inside Cuba, about portents signifying the downfall of the regime and the growing strength of the resistance."[42]

By the time this and other Cold War schemes were exposed in the 1970s, at a time of détente with the Soviet Union and an opening to China, they seemed ludicrous and inexplicable. How could grown men seriously have considered such puerile ideas? The answer can be found in the history of the OSS, which gave Lansdale his start in intelligence work. The ethos of the OSS, as we have seen, was "Woe to the officer who turned down a project because, on its face, it seemed ridiculous," and that was Lansdale's motto too. His deputy Sam Wilson recalled that Lansdale "was always coming up with outlandish ideas. He would release them like clay pigeons, and they'd systematically get shot down. One of them would sprout wings and fly away and be a real pigeon."[43] But while Lansdale dreamed up a few madcap schemes for Mongoose, he was hardly the only or even the main culprit.

Long before Lansdale was assigned to work on Cuba, CIA officers in 1960 had come up with brainstorms such as slipping Castro a box of cigars contaminated "with some sort of chemical" that would lead him to "make a public spectacle of himself" or feeding him a depilatory drug to make his beard—supposedly a source of his power—fall out.[44] It was almost as if the Marx Brothers had been put in charge of America's premier intelligence agency. Once Mongoose got under way, the flow of far-fetched ideas turned into a deluge. Among the discarded ideas was a plan submitted on January 30, 1962, by Brigadier General William H. Craig, the Defense Department representative to Mongoose, for Operation Bounty, "a system of financial rewards commensurate with position and stature, for killing or delivering alive known Communists." The proposed bounty system was $100,000 for Cuban government officials, $97,950 for foreign Communists, $45,000 for block leaders, and so on down the line, culminating in an offer of a mere two-centavo reward "for the delivery of Castro." This was not a serious assassination or kidnapping plan but rather a propaganda ploy to indicate how worthless the Maximum Leader was.[45] "I tabled it,"

Lansdale later said. "I did not think that was something that should be seriously undertaken."[46]

Undeterred by Lansdale's failure to embrace Operation Bounty, General Craig submitted numerous other brainstorms, each complete with its own catchy code name. Operation Free Ride: "Create unrest and dissension among the Cuban people . . . by airdropping valid Pan American or KLM one-way airline tickets good for passage to Mexico City, Caracas, etc." Operation Good Times: "To disillusion the Cuban population with Castro image by distribution of fake photographic material . . . such as an obese Castro with two beauties in any situation desired, ostensibly within a room in the Castro residence, lavishly furnished, and a table brimming over with the most delectable Cuban food with an underlying caption (appropriately Cuban) such as 'My ration is different.' "[47] An Air Force lieutenant colonel assigned to work with the CIA in Miami came up with an even more outlandish idea in response to news that there was a shortage of toilet paper and sanitary napkins in Cuba. He suggested that the CIA air-drop toilet paper into Cuba with pictures on alternate sheets of Fidel Castro and Nikita Khrushchev to "drive Castro mad."[48]

A more sinister plot, known as Operation Northwoods, was submitted by General Lyman Lemnitzer on behalf of the Joint Chiefs of Staff. It laid out a host of "pretexts which would provide justification for US military intervention in Cuba," such as having friendly Cubans in Cuban army uniforms attack the U.S. base at Guantánamo Bay, Cuba; sabotaging an empty U.S. ship in the harbor and blaming Cuba in a " 'Remember the Maine' incident" (the United States had declared war on Spain in 1898 after a naval ship called the *Maine* mysteriously exploded in Havana harbor); or carrying out "a terror campaign in the Miami area, in other Florida cities and even in Washington" that could be blamed on Castro. The U.S. armed forces could respond to such provocations, the chiefs gleefully recommended, by commencing "large scale United States military operations."[49] It is hard to imagine a more outlandish or distasteful document, redolent of the ruse that Hitler used on August 31, 1939, to start World War II: Wehrmacht soldiers in Polish uniforms attacked a German radio station on the border with Poland. That the Joint Chiefs would seriously offer these suggestions shows that Lansdale was neither the only one to fall victim to the fevered atmosphere of the day nor even the worst sufferer.

◆

AFTER HAVING sifted through various ideas to topple Castro, Lansdale on February 20, 1962, produced a detailed, if delusional, plan.[50] The operation was supposed to start in March and culminate in October with what Lansdale described as the "touchdown play":[51] Castro's overthrow. How on earth could Lansdale expect the weak and divided opposition to prevail within less than a year? He prided himself on being unafraid to tell unpleasant truths "point blank" to his superiors,[52] and he often had in Vietnam, but when it came to Cuba he succumbed to the temptation to tell his superiors what they wanted to hear. In his own defense, the best that Lansdale could say was: "I was hopeful and I put it down as a date without believing myself that it was a firm date—it was a prospective date of the early fall of 1962."[53]

The only realistic way that Castro could have been toppled that fast was through an American military intervention. That is why Lansdale demanded an "early policy decision" on the fundamental question: "If conditions and assets permitting a revolt are achieved in Cuba, and if U.S. help is required to sustain this condition, will the U.S. respond promptly with military force to aid the Cuban revolt?"[54] The answer was that President Kennedy was no more willing in early 1962 than he had been a year earlier, during the Bay of Pigs invasion, to wage open war against Castro. Therefore the Special Group (Augmented) directed that Lansdale scale back his plans, putting the focus for the time being on "the acquisition of intelligence."[55]

Assigned to take charge of intelligence gathering was one of the CIA's oddest officers: William King Harvey.

◆

PRESIDENT KENNEDY had teased Ed Lansdale about being in the mold of James Bond. Lansdale told the president that he was no James Bond, but he had the "American 007" available if the president wanted to meet him. Not surprisingly, JFK did. So Lansdale brought Bill Harvey to the White House. Just as they were about to enter the Oval Office, Lansdale remembered that Harvey always went about heavily armed. "Are you carrying a gun?" he asked. Harvey said he was. Lansdale told him not to pull it out; he was liable to be shot by the Secret Service. Lansdale discreetly went over to a Secret Service agent and told him about the situation. Harvey then slowly pulled his pistol out of a shoulder holster and handed it to the Secret Service man. "Wait!" Lansdale said. "Don't you usually carry another gun too?" Harvey thereupon pulled out an automatic that had been tucked into his waistband in the small of his back.

When Harvey finally entered the Oval Office, JFK must have wondered whether there had been some mistake. Was it possible that, as the journalist David Martin wrote, "this red-faced, pop-eyed, bullet-headed, pear-shaped man advancing on him with a ducklike strut that was part waddle and part swagger" was really the "American 007"?[56] The disparity with the British super-agent, who was portrayed on the screen for the first time that year by the suave Scottish actor Sean Connery, was striking. But there was a deeper similarity that even Kennedy might not have recognized. And it was not just that Harvey, like Bond, was a prodigious drinker and womanizer—he liked to brag that he never went a day without "having" a woman.[57] Like 007, Bill Harvey also had a "license to kill," granted to him, perhaps unwittingly, by the president himself.

Harvey was a small-town lawyer from Indiana and a former FBI agent. The trim and elegant Ivy Leaguers who dominated the CIA looked down upon him as an ignorant and uncultured gumshoe.[58] But his police skills came in handy when he uncovered the British double agent Kim Philby, precisely the sort of upper-class snob whom he resented.[59] On the strength of this achievement, he was transferred in 1952 to become chief of the CIA's base in West Berlin, on the front lines of the Cold War. He didn't speak a word of German and drank so heavily that he served martinis in water goblets, but he pulled off one of the CIA's most celebrated intelligence coups when he supervised the construction of a secret tunnel into East Berlin designed to

390 | THE ROAD NOT TAKEN

tap into Soviet communications. Operation Gold operated for eleven months in 1955–56, producing warehouses full of intercepts. Only later did the CIA learn that the KGB, because of a mole in MI6, knew about the operation the whole time, raising the disquieting suspicion that the tunnel had been used to feed the CIA disinformation. But even if the Berlin tunnel, known internally as "Harvey's hole," was not quite the success it had seemed at first blush, its inglorious end did not hurt Harvey's career. He returned to Washington in 1959 to become head of the CIA's Division D, charged with breaking into foreign embassies to steal secret codes.[60]

Early in 1961, Harvey was approached by Dick Bissell, the CIA's operations chief, and told to develop "Executive Action capability," a euphemism for assassination. Bissell made clear that this request came from the top. Harvey knew better than to inquire too closely. (Years later, Bissell testified that his orders had come from McGeorge Bundy and Walt Rostow and that they "would not have given such encouragement unless they were confident it would meet with the president's approval.")[61] Harvey duly developed a program known as ZRRIFLE to give the White House what it wanted. In the process, he inherited an ongoing plot to use mobsters with Cuban business interests—specifically Johnny Rosselli of Las Vegas and Salvatore "Sam" Giancana of Chicago—to bump off Castro. To make the situation even more bizarre, Giancana shared a mistress with the president, Judith Campbell Exner, until J. Edgar Hoover found out and made Kennedy end the relationship.[62]

Harvey ran this troubled, and troubling, operation once he became the CIA's representative to Mongoose and the head of the CIA's Task Force W, charged with overthrowing Castro. (The W—Harvey's choice—was in honor of William Walker, an American adventurer who had ruled Nicaragua in 1856–57.)[63] But Harvey did not tell Lansdale what he was up to. Everything was on a strictly "need to know" basis, and Harvey did not think that Lansdale, as an outsider, needed to know. When Lansdale tried to get information, the CIA man turned "monosyllabic"—"I got yes and no types of answers and very brief ones," Lansdale said.[64] All Harvey would tell him was "Everything's under control." In frustration, Lansdale would say to Harvey, "I'm not the enemy. You can talk to me." Once, when Lansdale was talking with Harvey and a phone call came in, Harvey began talking on the phone in code. "After a while I caught on and realized he was talking about me," Lansdale said. "The son of a bitch."[65]

Such was the cult of secrecy that Harvey was mortified when Lansdale sent around a Mongoose policy paper that, among other options, listed the "liquidation of leaders." This was done in response to a suggestion made at an August 10, 1962, Special Group (Augmented) meeting by Robert McNamara, who subsequently was to deny knowledge of any assassination plots.[66] As soon as he saw the memo, Harvey immediately called Lansdale's office and lectured a CIA liaison officer on "the inadmissibility and stupidity of putting this type of comment in writing in such a document." Shortly thereafter Lansdale sent around a revised copy of the memo that excluded the offending words.[67] Needless to say, Harvey objected not to assassinating Castro but rather to mentioning the operation in print.

This episode confirms what earlier experience in Vietnam, where Lansdale had delivered $57,000 to Diem to "get rid of" the sect leader Ba Cut, had already indicated: Lansdale was not averse, if necessary, to assassination as a tool of foreign policy. But in this case he did not know that an assassination plot was already under way and was dubious about its utility; he feared that if Fidel were killed, he would be replaced by Raúl Castro or Che Guevara, both doctrinaire Marxists, and "we might very well [wind up] in something much worse."[68] Years later, Lansdale was to write, probably truthfully, to one of his brothers, "On the Castro assassination thing, my conscience was very clean."[69]

The obsession with "deniability" ensured that there was never anything in writing tying the Kennedys to the planned assassination of Castro, but all of the CIA officers involved were convinced that they were carrying out the White House's sotto voce desire. Richard Helms said, "I believe it was the policy at the time to get rid of Castro and if killing him was one of the things that was to be done in this connection, that was within what was expected. . . . No member of the Kennedy administration, as I recall it, ever told me that it was proscribed."[70]

In the climate of the early 1960s, at the height of the Cold War, that which was not expressly prohibited was implicitly permitted.

◆

THE CIA's Miami station, JMWAVE, became in short order its second-largest outpost in the entire world, behind only the new headquarters in Langley, Virginia, which had opened in the fall of 1961. Housed on the University of Miami's sprawling South Campus, under the cover name of Zenith Technical Enterprises, JMWAVE grew to as many as six hundred personnel headed by the "blond ghost," as the young and dashing station chief, Ted Shackley, would be nicknamed. Another two hundred or so CIA employees toiled for Task Force W at Langley.[71]

JMWAVE had more than a hundred cars under lease and so many boats, used to ferry agents and supplies to Cuba, that it controlled the third largest navy in the Caribbean, after the United States and Cuba. It operated an archipelago of safe houses and training sites across south Florida. Some fifteen thousand Cubans were connected with JMWAVE.[72] Dozens of Cuban exile groups were setting up shop in the Miami area, many with CIA backing. Miami came to resemble "wartime Casablanca," in the words of two reporters, who noted that it "swarmed with spies, counterspies, exiled dictators, Mafia executives, refugees, entertainers, countesses, smugglers, gamblers, fortune-tellers, gun runners, soldiers of fortune, fugitives, and loudly dressed tourists—many pursuing possibly criminal ends against the garish backdrop of Miami Beach."[73]

Lansdale was impressed by the CIA's operations when he visited Miami in June 1962. He called it "a splendid effort . . . within present guidelines."[74] But while Mongoose was generating considerable activity, its operational results were more meager.

◆

AT THE end of July 1962, Lansdale took stock of Phase I. William Harvey reported that the CIA had met its intelligence targets by establishing "inside Cuba 59 controlled Cuban agents and 31 third country controlled agents." In addition, 169 lower-quality agents were "producing intermittent intelligence reports," and an interrogation center set up in Opa-Locka to debrief Cuban refugees was generating eight hundred reports a month. No sabotage had taken place to date, but the CIA had infiltrated eleven sabotage teams into Cuba.[75] The Defense Department, for its part, had completed detailed contingency planning for a military intervention that would involve a quarter of a million troops.[76]

Under Lansdale's prodding, the CIA had come up with a symbol for the Cuban resistance: *Gusano Libre* (Free Worm). Castro had denigrated his enemies as "worms"; the CIA hoped to turn a term of derision into "a symbol of resistance and pride." Cartoons were commissioned and mailed to Cuban households showing a smirking worm cutting electrical wires and spilling tacks in front of a jeep carrying Castro's troops.[77] Soon to come were "Gusano Libre pins, armbands, seals, pencils, balloons, etc.," which could be delivered to Cuba via helium-filled balloons launched from a chartered ship in international waters.[78] A State Department official expressed well-justified skepticism about "whether 'worms of the world unite' will cause people to revolt," but such doubts were ignored in the heat of the moment.[79]

Bill Harvey concluded that, based on what the CIA now knew, it would be feasible to incite a revolt by late 1963, a year behind Lansdale's original schedule, "provided the Cubans could be assured . . . their revolt would be supported by U.S. intervention."[80] But there was still no sign that the Kennedy administration would make such a commitment. In planning for Phase II of Operation Mongoose, the Special Group (Augmented) ruled out options that "would commit us to deliberate military intervention," while acknowledging that absent such intervention "we perceive no likelihood of an overthrow of the government by internal means." "For the time being," Maxwell Taylor wrote, "we favor a somewhat more aggressive program than the one carried out in Phase I, wherein we continue to press for intelligence, attempt to hurt the local regime as much as possible on the economic front and work further to discredit the regime locally and abroad." "Higher authority," meaning President Kennedy, approved these guidelines on August 20, 1962.[81]

As Mongoose failed to achieve a breakthrough, tempers flared and relations frayed among everyone involved. Bill Harvey was drinking more and becoming steadily more obstreperous. At meetings, Harvey would "lift his ass and fart and pare his nails with a sheath knife." During one gathering at the Pentagon, he "took his gun from his pocket, emptied all the ammunition on the table, and began playing with the bullets in an elaborate show of boredom." Harvey was no more respectful to Robert Kennedy, whom he privately referred to as "that fucker." As far as Harvey was concerned, the Kennedys were "fags" for not having the guts to take on Castro directly; the CIA wouldn't be in this mess, he crudely claimed, if the president had displayed some "balls" during the Bay of Pigs.[82]

The relationship between Bill Harvey and Bobby Kennedy, a CIA officer recalled, was "bad from the beginning, and then it deteriorated steadily."[83] At Langley, a story was making the rounds that when Kennedy demanded to know why a team of exiles had not yet been infiltrated into Cuba, Harvey replied they had to be trained first. "I'll take them out to Hickory Hill and train them myself," Kennedy snorted. "What will you teach them, sir?" Harvey shot back. "Baby-sitting?"[84] During a meeting where the attorney general said he had ten minutes to hear the CIA's plan, Harvey droned on and on. He was still not finished when, after ten minutes, Kennedy abruptly got up and left.[85] "Your friend Mr. Harvey does not inspire confidence," McGeorge Bundy drily told Thomas Parrott, a CIA liaison officer working for Maxwell Taylor.[86]

It became apparent that confidence was also faltering in Lansdale. By the fall of 1962, Parrott recalled, "all the members of the [Special] Group were quite disaffected with both Lansdale and with Harvey."[87] In a contemporaneous memorandum, another CIA officer wrote, "Practically everyone at the operating level agrees that Lansdale has lost his value. Bundy and Taylor are not impressed with him."[88] It was hardly Lansdale and Harvey's fault that they had not been able to achieve the impossible results demanded of them, but they were set to become the fall guys.

▾

ROBERT F. KENNEDY's office at the Justice Department was so big that sometimes he tossed a football in there with Deputy Attorney General Byron "Whizzer" White, the former Rhodes Scholar and professional football player and future Supreme Court justice.[89] It was, in Arthur Schlesinger's description, "a vast, somber, walnut-paneled chamber" enlivened with, inter alia, "a varnished sailfish over the mantelpiece," "a stuffed tiger standing near the fireplace," and, affixed to the walls by Scotch tape, "an ever-changing montage of children's drawings." Amid this "genial clutter," the attorney general could be found leaning back casually in his armchair, "foot propped on an open drawer, jacket off, tie yanked aside, trousers rumpled, hair uncombed," often with his "large and ill-tempered" Labrador, Brumus, lounging at his feet.[90]

At 2:30 p.m. on October 16, 1962, an unseasonably warm autumn day, the attorney general's cavernous office was the setting for yet another Mongoose meeting. Present along with Robert Kennedy were Edward Lansdale, Richard Helms, and four staff members. Kennedy opened the meeting by expressing the "general dissatisfaction of the president" with the state of anti-Castro plotting. He lamented that Mongoose "had failed to influence significantly the course of events in Cuba" and vowed to give the operation even more of his "personal attention." Helms and Lansdale could barely pay attention to the by now familiar hectoring. They knew before the meeting had convened that the situation in Cuba was about to change in ways that would have the most far-reaching consequences, not just for Operation Mongoose but for all of mankind.[91]

For some time, the CIA had been receiving reports about the installation of Soviet medium-range and intermediate-range ballistic missiles in Cuba. This was part of the intelligence haul generated by Mongoose, even if it was not initially believed by CIA analysts in Washington. These reports were finally confirmed on October 14 by a U-2 overflight that photographed three ballistic-missile sites near San Cristóbal. Two more U-2 missions on October 15 revealed three more missile sites. When Richard Helms broke the news to Robert Kennedy on the morning of October 16, 1962, the attorney general stared for a minute out the window and then, "raising both fists to his chest as if he were about to begin shadow boxing," exclaimed, "Shit! Damn it all to hell and back." "Those were my sentiments exactly," Helms drily noted. Although Kennedy proceeded with the previously scheduled Mongoose meeting that afternoon, it was obvious that Lansdale's project would have to wait while the president and his advisers tried to figure out how to avert Armageddon.[92]

◆

JOHN F. KENNEDY has been applauded by historians for his coolness under pressure during what became known as the Cuban Missile Crisis. The president wisely rejected advice from the Joint Chiefs of Staff and his more hard-line civilian advisers in the NSC's ExComm (Executive Committee), including Robert McNamara and Robert Kennedy, to undertake military action against Cuba. The president rightly called this option "one hell of a gamble."[93] Unbeknownst to the CIA, the Soviets had already shipped tactical nuclear weapons to Cuba, along with 42,000 Red Army troops, and given their commanders authority to launch the weapons in the event of an American assault.[94] An American attack on Cuba could have precipitated World War III, which is why the attorney general and the defense secretary later adjusted their recollections to excise their hawkish proposals.

As an anxious nation held its breath, Kennedy opted for a more prudent response. He declared an air and naval "quarantine" of Cuba to prevent Soviet ships from delivering more weapons, while pursuing a secret diplomatic channel to Moscow. Eventually, Kennedy quietly reached a deal with Nikita Khrushchev to remove the Soviet missiles from Cuba in return for an American pledge not to invade Cuba and to remove obsolescent Jupiter missiles from Turkey.[95] On October 28, 1962, Khrushchev announced he was withdrawing the Soviet missiles from Cuba. The world exhaled. A nuclear war had been averted.

But while President Kennedy deserves considerable credit for walking away from the precipice of thermonuclear conflict, he can also be blamed for helping to cause the crisis in the first place by trying to topple Castro. Castro later said, "Six months before these missiles were installed in Cuba, we had received an accumulation of information that a new invasion was being prepared under the sponsorship of the Central Intelligence Agency."[96] "It was clear to me," Khrushchev said, "that we might very well lose Cuba if we didn't take some decisive steps in her defense."[97] Although Mongoose helped to precipitate the Cuban Missile Crisis, it also made possible its peaceful resolution by providing the intelligence that allowed Kennedy to act before the Soviet missiles were operational. "That's the only decent thing Mongoose ever did . . . because we turned it into a decent collection operation," concluded the CIA officer Sam Halpern.[98]

◆

OPERATION MONGOOSE was not revived after the end of the crisis. On January 4, 1963, McGeorge Bundy wrote to President Kennedy, "There is well-nigh universal agreement that Mongoose is at a dead end."[99] Efforts to overthrow Castro resumed shortly thereafter, with Bobby Kennedy as eager as ever to topple the Cuban strongman, but Lansdale was no longer in charge. A new Cuba Coordinating Committee, headed by Sterling J. Cottrell, a deputy assistant secretary of state, replaced the Caribbean Survey Group.[100]

Among the ideas explored in 1963, after Lansdale's removal from the project, was a plan to give Castro a skin-diving suit contaminated with "a fungus that would produce a disabling and chronic skin condition" and another one to plant an "explosives-rigged sea shell" in an area where he liked to go skin diving. This plan was called off, the CIA inspector general wrote, when it was determined that "none of the shells that might conceivably be found in the Caribbean area was both spectacular enough to be sure of attracting attention and large enough to hold the needed volume of explosives."[101] The most that the CIA accomplished in 1963 was to stage a few attacks on Cuban infrastructure. But such sabotage—"boom and bang," in CIA parlance—"never amounted to more than pinpricks," Richard Helms conceded. "The notion that an underground resistance organization might be created on the island remained a remote, romantic myth."[102]

◆

IT WAS unfair to blame Edward Lansdale for not toppling Castro when no one else had any better luck. And yet Mongoose had been a failure, and he had been responsible. His reputation inside the government went from that of a can-do covert-action specialist to a "nut," "a fantasist, a lucky amateur."[103] This was the view pushed in particular by Sam Halpern and Tom Parrott of the CIA, the sources of these damning descriptions. They nurtured a long-standing loathing of the "Ugly American," whose lack of traditional espionage credentials and disdain for CIA "tradecraft" was seen as an affront to career intelligence officers. Halpern had spent much of the 1950s working in the Far East Division alongside George Aurell, who resisted Lansdale's forays into nation building as an unwelcome diversion from traditional spying. Lansdale's apostasy grated all the more because of the high-level backing that he enjoyed. The very establishment of Mongoose outside the CIA's control was seen as a challenge to the entire intelligence establishment, whose competence had been called into question by the Bay of Pigs. If Lansdale succeeded where the CIA had failed, the CIA's very future could be in jeopardy. Mongoose's failure, therefore, occasioned some unseemly celebration at Langley.

Just days after the resolution of the Cuban Missile Crisis, George McManus, an aide to Richard Helms, wrote on November 5, 1962, "With a political solution to the Cuban problem in hand reflecting great credit on the part of the President, the A.G. [attorney general] will drop Lansdale like a hot brick." He professed himself delighted that Task Force W would no longer be "available to Lansdale as a 'whipping boy'" and would instead become "a normal part of our monolithic Agency structure." His only concern: "Lansdale's reaction to any reassignment is apt to be a violent one. He undoubtedly realizes that he never again will be in the position of a special adviser to the most powerful men in the country. Therefore ... he might be able to inflict serious damage to CIA's standing before his eventual demise." Psychologists would call this a case of projection. In reality, there was no evidence that the easygoing Lansdale ever displayed such vindictiveness—in contrast to his bureaucratic foes, who pursued their vendetta against him with increasing success.[104]

Having failed to achieve the Kennedys' most cherished desire, Lansdale lost their favor. He was left naked before his bureaucratic enemies, including his own boss, Robert McNamara. It was probably no coincidence that his military career ended less than a year after Mongoose did. "I think the thing that hurt me the most in the long run was the task that Kennedy gave me on Cuba," he reflected decades later. "I'm sorry I ever got mixed up in those Cuban things."[105]

His Cuban failure proved historically significant, not just for the future of that island nation but also for Indochina, because it ensured that he was cut out of American policymaking toward Vietnam even as relations between the Kennedy administration and the Diem government were reaching their sordid denouement.

24

"Washington at Its Nuttiest"

We essentially are pointing a gun at Diem's head and are asking him to commit suicide.

—EDWARD LANSDALE

THERE is not infrequently a disconnect, sometimes a large one, between developments on a distant battlefield and perceptions back home. Such divergence is especially prone to occur in a guerrilla war, where progress is notoriously difficult to measure. President George W. Bush earned widespread mockery for proclaiming "Mission Accomplished" in Iraq on May 1, 2003, just before the start of a massive insurgency. So, too, President Barack Obama was derided for claiming, in an interview published in early 2014, that the Islamic State was a "jayvee team," in no way comparable to Al Qaeda, just a few months before its black-clad fighters conquered Mosul, Iraq's second-largest city.

The disparity between perception and reality would prove especially acute during the Vietnam War, with the optimistic assessments of American political leaders and military officers often starkly at odds with the dismal reality that American correspondents could perceive with their own eyes. But in 1962–63, before America had sent hundreds of thousands of its own soldiers to fight in Vietnam, the problem was the reverse: not excessive official optimism but rather excessive pessimism. In those years, the Saigon government was making real progress against the Vietcong while also encountering undeniable problems, yet most American journalists and policymakers could perceive nothing but the shortcomings of the Ngo Dinh Diem regime while simply taking it on faith that any alternative would be preferable. This one-sided outlook—too distrustful of the incumbent president, too trusting of his would-be successors—would ultimately prove fatal to Diem's chances of survival.

◆

IN 1962, while Edward Lansdale was mired in his futile efforts to overthrow Fidel Castro, Ngo Dinh Diem launched an ambitious initiative to secure the countryside. The Strategic Hamlets program was overseen by the president's erudite brother, Ngo Dinh Nhu, the family intellectual, who had been inspired by the tactics employed by British counterinsurgents in Malaya and French counterinsurgents in Algeria to separate insurgents from villagers. Unlike agrovilles, a previous initiative that had failed because it required wrenching population resettlements, this program was designed to defend villagers where they lived. Hamlets would be surrounded by moats and barbed wire, and a hamlet militia would be armed to resist insurgent incursions. If the hamlet came under heavy attack, it would have a radio or field telephone to call for reinforcements from the Civil Guard, a regional militia that later became known as the Popular Forces, or from the Army of the Republic of Vietnam (ARVN). Inside the hamlets, villagers would be able to elect their own leaders so that they would have greater legitimacy, reversing a decision that Diem had made in 1956, without Lansdale's knowledge, to suspend village elections. The Ngos hoped that the hamlets would not only stymie Communist advances but also galvanize a new base of support for their regime among villagers, allowing them to lessen their reliance on the United States and the urban, Francophone elite, both of which they distrusted.[1]

Four thousand Strategic Hamlets were erected by the end of 1962—

well short of Nhu's goal of sixteen thousand but a substantial achievement nonetheless.[2] Not all of these hamlets were model developments; in many cases, local officials claimed more progress than they delivered, and sometimes they inflamed tensions by forcibly conscripting farmers to work on hamlet defenses. Moreover, many of the hamlet elections were rigged and many of the hamlets infiltrated by the Vietcong. Nevertheless, North Vietnamese historians later acknowledged that the Strategic Hamlets allowed Saigon to "gain control over more than two-thirds of the rural population."[3]

While these hamlets were blunting the efforts of the Vietcong to infiltrate villages, their fighters were coming under unrelenting assault from a South Vietnamese army newly equipped with advanced American military equipment. Their new arsenal included hulking M-113 armored personnel carriers weighing ten tons and capable of a top speed of thirty-seven miles per hour. Nicknamed the Green Dragon, each one was armed with a .50-caliber machine gun whose rounds could literally cut enemy fighters in half.[4] Also joining the ARVN arsenal were helicopters such as the H-21 Flying Banana (so called because of its awkward, angled shape) and the UH-1 Huey. The latter was to become a ubiquitous utility chopper that could transport an eleven-man infantry squad or six wounded soldiers on stretchers while also serving as a formidable gunship; its Gatling gun was capable of firing six thousand rounds a minute.

Airlifted by Flying Bananas and supported by M-113s and Huey gunships, South Vietnamese troops stormed through insurgent-controlled areas as if "hunting wild birds or driving rats from their holes," a South Vietnamese officer recalled.[5] Hanoi's official military history later lamented that "the enemy" had been able to launch a "vicious counterattack" utilizing "large numbers of troops, superior mobility, and heavy firepower" to occupy "portions of our liberated areas in the lowlands" and to "constantly" attack "our bases in the mountains."[6]

◆

AND THEN came the Battle of Ap Bac.

On January 3, 1963, readers of the *New York Times* awakened to read a front-page article by a skinny, bespectacled young reporter named David Halberstam: "Communist guerrillas armed with automatic weapons inflicted a major defeat today on United States helicopters carrying troops into an operation in the Mekong Delta." The next day, Halberstam wrote that, under "awesome air attacks," the "Vietcong simply refused to panic and they fired with deadly accuracy and consistency. The Vietnamese regulars, in contrast, in the eyes of one American observer, lost the initiative from the first moment and never showed much aggressive instinct."

The unnamed observer was Lieutenant Colonel John Paul Vann, a maverick officer assigned as an adviser to the ARVN's Seventh Division. Outspoken and opinionated, Vann was a favorite source for American reporters who did not know that he was about to be forced into retirement after perjuring himself to escape conviction on a statutory rape charge. (He had seduced a fifteen-year-old babysitter in Germany—a revelation made public only decades later with the publication of Neil Sheehan's blockbuster book *A Bright Shining Lie*.) He told Halberstam, Sheehan (then with the Associated Press), and other correspondents that the battle at Ap Bac had been "a miserable damn performance" on the part of South Vietnamese troops—they had lost at least eighty men killed and a hundred wounded against a smaller Vietcong force. Three American advisers also had died. Vann passed along rumors that Ngo Dinh Diem had told his commanders to avoid casualties at all costs, so as to maintain support among the troops for his government, even at the risk of letting the Vietcong escape. The events at Ap Bac seemed to confirm Vann's accusations, making this, as Sheehan would later write, "a decisive battle that would affect the course of the war."[7]

In recent works, however, two revisionist historians, Edward Miller and Mark Moyar, have argued that the reality of Ap Bac did not conform to the neat morality tale told by Vann. Miller has concluded that "Vann's understanding of the Ngos' thinking about military strategy was incorrect on almost every point."[8] While the Ngos were careful to select officers for their loyalty, they still expected the army to aggressively fight the Vietcong, which they viewed as a mortal threat to their regime. Moyar, meanwhile, has argued that Ap Bac was a much tougher

404 | THE ROAD NOT TAKEN

objective to capture than initial press reports had conveyed. The Vietcong had three hundred to four hundred crack troops dug in behind
zigzagging dikes, protected from aerial attack by thick forest and dense
undergrowth. Vann was furious that the ARVN troops would not
expose themselves and take more risks, but later in the war U.S. units
would behave in similar fashion when facing entrenched positions:
they, too, would prefer to reduce casualties by calling in air and artillery strikes. As Halberstam was to concede months later, after having
covered more battles, "A rice paddy deals an awesome advantage to a
well-armed defender."⁹

The South Vietnamese attack at Ap Bac had suffered from numerous defects and it was hardly an ARVN victory, but, as Miller notes,
neither was it evidence of "ARVN incompetence and cowardice."
That, however, was the story that reached the American public and
policymakers.¹⁰

◆

THE DAMAGE that Ap Bac did to Diem's reputation would be compounded by press coverage of the showdown between the regime and a
group of militant Buddhists. Before long, Buddhist monks were setting
fire to themselves in the streets of Saigon. Watching this confrontation
from afar, many Americans concluded that Diem, as a devout Catholic, was irrevocably at odds with the Buddhist majority. It was certainly
true that Diem was an autocrat whose popularity was waning. But most
Vietnamese were Confucianists, not Buddhists, and even among Buddhists, only a small, politicized minority actively sympathized with the
demonstrations. And although Catholics were overrepresented in the
lower rungs of the government bureaucracy, Diem had numerous Buddhists in his cabinet and the top ranks of the army.¹¹ But such details
tended to be forgotten in the sensationalistic media coverage of the
demonstrations.

Tensions between Washington and Saigon came to a head on
August 20, 1963, when Diem ordered the army to raid twelve pagodas
in Saigon and to arrest more than seven hundred Buddhist activists. He
was repeating the tactics that had worked for him in 1955 during his

confrontation with the sects.[12] But this time he did not have Edward Lansdale at his side to curb his brother Nhu's dictatorial instincts—or to save him from the backlash of an increasingly hostile American administration and press corps.

The anti-Diem faction in the administration was led by a trio of influential officials: W. Averell Harriman, a wealthy Democratic Party elder, former ambassador to Moscow, and governor of New York who was now under secretary of state for political affairs; Roger Hilsman, a veteran of Merrill's Marauders and the OSS who was assistant secretary of state for Far Eastern affairs; and Michael Forrestal, son of the first secretary of defense, a corporate lawyer from New York who was serving on the staff of the National Security Council. These three men strategized over the summer weekend of August 24–25, 1963, while more-senior officials were holidaying, to win approval for a cable authorizing the newly arrived American ambassador in Saigon, Henry Cabot Lodge, to offer support to the generals who were plotting to overthrow Ngo Dinh Diem.

When President Kennedy reconvened with his National Security Council on Monday, August 26, 1963, he discovered that many of his most-senior advisers—including General Maxwell Taylor, now chairman of the Joint Chiefs of Staff, Secretary of Defense Robert McNamara, and CIA Director John McCone—did not agree with a policy of overthrowing Diem. They felt that the cable had been approved in an underhanded fashion that made an end run around the normal policy-review process.[13] But in spite of the misgivings of many of its members, and even of the president himself, the administration did not, in the end, countermand the infamous missive authorizing Diem's ouster. The power of inertia proved too strong: having once endorsed an anti-Diem coup, Kennedy was loath to reverse himself when the man on the spot—the former senator and vice presidential candidate Henry Cabot Lodge—was so adamantly set on regime change. Overruling him would risk a political crisis at home that would endanger Republican support for the president's foreign policy, and could even lead Lodge to seek the presidency himself in the 1964 election, as he eventually would do. Thus Lodge was allowed to proceed.

The ambassador delegated the task of engineering the coup to Lansdale's old teammate, the hard-drinking, hell-raising Lou Conein, who had known most of the South Vietnamese generals for years. After a stint at the CIA station in Tehran, Luigi had returned to Saigon in 1961. Before long, he was deep into plotting with the generals.

◆

AND WHERE was Ngo Dinh Diem's foremost champion while these machinations were going on? Edward Lansdale had received a promotion to major general in February 1963, but that was little consolation for his frustrating inability to significantly influence top-level decision-making. The position that Lansdale had briefly occupied as the Pentagon's point man on Vietnam policy had been usurped by Marine Major General Victor "Brute" Krulak, adviser to the Joint Chiefs of Staff on counterinsurgency and special activities. A far more skillful bureaucrat than Lansdale, he spread a fictitious tale that he had been a wartime buddy of Jack Kennedy's to enhance his aura of power.[14] Official records show that in 1963 Krulak was at the White House at least a dozen times, Lansdale not at all.[15] (As we shall see, Lansdale may have had one off-the-books meeting with President Kennedy.) Cut out of Vietnam decision-making, Lansdale was left to take brief trips to Venezuela (March 8–16) and Bolivia (May 25–June 1) to study the state of Marxist insurgencies in those countries.

Even though he was cut out of the paper flow, Lansdale recalled,

I sensed something was going very wrong in Vietnam with Diem. I didn't know they were threatening to overthrow him. But I could tell that there was some sort of movement afoot, and I talked to McNamara, to Harriman, on the thing, as though they were going to overthrow Diem, and I explained: "There's a constitution in there. Please don't destroy that when you're trying to change the government. Remember there's a vice president [Nguyen Ngoc Tho] who's been elected and is holding office now, and if anything happens to the president he should succeed. Try to keep something sustained there."[16]

McNamara reacted by pretending that he didn't know what Lansdale was talking about. Rebuffed, Lansdale tried to get more information from Roger Hilsman, but he "refused to talk about Vietnam and kept switching the conversation to Australia, which he said he was planning to visit."[17]

Given the way he was frozen out in Washington, the fullest case that Lansdale made for continuing to support Diem was heard not by decision-makers in the councils of power but by *Life* magazine editors at a lunch in New York on Friday, February 23, 1962. The setting was the Time-Life Building, a forty-eight-story modernist masterpiece, all glass and steel and clean lines, which had opened just three years earlier, at 1271 Avenue of the Americas.

The editors asked Lansdale, "Can we win with Diem? Should a coup replace him?"

Lansdale replied that Americans "were trying to play God, by trying to pick a leader for Vietnam. If they were serious, as they seemed to be, then they needed a yardstick to measure up Diem and other Vietnamese, to compare them for the job." Lansdale went on to suggest some useful measurements, including "dedication to defeat the enemy," "executive ability," "moral courage," "constitutionality," "integrity," and "popularity." Diem was decidedly flawed, he argued, but by these metrics he was the best available alternative.[18]

While Lansdale thought it was important to leave Diem in power, he shared the widespread distaste for the president's Machiavellian brother, Ngo Dinh Nhu, and his wife, "the dragon lady," Madame Nhu. "I've always thought it was brother Nhu who got Diem roused up about the Buddhists and urged the reaction to them," Lansdale later wrote.[19] But Lansdale knew it would not be easy to get rid of Nhu, because Diem had pledged to their father on his deathbed that he would take care of his younger sibling.

In late August 1963, Lansdale had breakfast at Averell Harriman's spacious redbrick house in Georgetown, just down the street from the Kennedys' old place. Joining them was John Kenneth Galbraith, the Harvard economist and Kennedy friend who was serving as ambassador to India. Lansdale suggested that Harriman and Galbraith organize a sinecure for Nhu at Harvard. He told them, "Kick him upstairs. Tell him he's an intellectual. Listen to him and give him a job there. He'd come, and Diem would let him go. And once he's away, then Diem will be a very different person and be on his own and you won't have to worry so much about him." Harriman liked the idea, Lansdale recounted, but Galbraith took a "dim view" of it. "We don't do that at Harvard," he said dismissively.[20]

◆

YET IF Lansdale was ignored, he was not entirely forgotten. Diem, for one, continued to pine for his erstwhile adviser and champion as the summer wore on and the Buddhist crisis intensified, with more monks immolating themselves. On July 19, 1963, for example, he asked Rufus Phillips, who was in charge of USAID's Rural Affairs office in Saigon, if there would be "any objections to General Lansdale's coming out to Vietnam again, if this could be arranged."[21] There were, as usual, many objections within the U.S. government. But the idea of sending Lansdale to the rescue would not go away. It was raised directly to the president by Phillips at a White House meeting convened on September 10, 1963, to consider the findings of two high-level emissaries who had just returned from a four-day visit to South Vietnam—Major General Victor Krulak and the veteran diplomat Joseph Mendenhall. They gave conflicting accounts: Krulak was sure that the "shooting war" was being won, while Mendenhall was convinced that the war "could not be won" as long as Ngo Dinh Nhu and possibly even Ngo Dinh Diem remained in power. JFK quipped, "The two of you did visit the same country, didn't you?" Nervous laughter. Followed by an uncomfortable silence.[22]

For another perspective, the president turned to Rufe Phillips. Having just left Vietnam to see his dying father in Virginia, he was less optimistic than Krulak and less pessimistic than Mendenhall. Phillips said that on the whole the Strategic Hamlets program was succeeding, except in the Mekong Delta, where the hamlets were "being overrun wholesale," and that "most Vietnamese would like to see President Diem remain, but they are unalterably opposed to the Nhus." "We need a man," he counseled, "to guide and operate a campaign to isolate the Nhus," and there was only one man for that mission: Edward Lansdale.²³ When Phillips raised Lansdale's name, he saw McNamara shaking his head vigorously in opposition. The president, however, continued listening intently and taking notes. When he had finished, Kennedy said, in his inimitable Boston Brahmin accent, "Mr. Phillips, I want to thank you for your remarks, particularly for your recommendation concerning General Lansdale."²⁴ The meeting then moved on to an inconclusive debate about Vietnam, with no agreement among the "best and brightest" about whether the war was being won or lost or whether Diem should stay or go.

That evening, Phillips telephoned Lansdale at his home on MacArthur Boulevard to tell him what had transpired: "There was still an opportunity to get Nhu out of the country, I urged, but only he could do it. He said he would go if asked."²⁵ But would Lansdale be asked?

The next day, September 11, 1963, Roger Hilsman unexpectedly gave his endorsement to the dispatch of the "Ugly American" but in a way that neither Diem nor Lansdale was likely to accept. As part of a prospective deal to exile Ngo Dinh Nhu and Madame Nhu, he suggested, "We should be ready to inform Diem that we would place General Lansdale at his disposal, if requested, to assist in providing him political advice during the difficult period after the departure of his brother."²⁶ This was turning Phillips's recommendation on its head: instead of sending Lansdale to persuade Diem to part with his brother, he would be sent only after Diem had already done so. Neither Diem nor Lansdale would ever agree to such an ultimatum.

Two days later, on September 13, 1963, a top-secret, "eyes only" missive arrived in Washington from, of all people, Henry Cabot Lodge requesting Lansdale's presence in Saigon. The ambassador was upset with CIA station chief John "Jocko" Richardson for opposing a military coup. Bizarrely, Lodge thought that Lansdale would be the ideal candidate to take over the station and manage a coup d'état: "What I ask is that General Lansdale be sent over here at once to take charge, under my supervision, of all U.S. relationships with a change of government here." Lodge was right that "General Lansdale has outstanding qualifications" for this assignment, but he was wrong in thinking that Lansdale would accept it.[27]

It is possible, though far from certain, that President Kennedy personally asked Lansdale to go to Vietnam on his behalf. The sole and not entirely reliable source for this encounter is Daniel Ellsberg, the future Pentagon Papers leaker who, as we shall see, went to work for Lansdale in 1965. According to Ellsberg, during a late-night drinking session in Saigon, Lansdale shared with him the story of what happened when he was summoned to the Oval Office in September 1963 along with Secretary of Defense McNamara.

Supposedly Kennedy asked Lansdale whether he would return to Vietnam and try to persuade Diem to send Nhu and Madame Nhu out of the country.

Yes, Lansdale said.

"But if that didn't work out," Kennedy continued, "or if I changed my mind and decided we had to get rid of Diem, would you be able to go along with that?"

"No, Mr. President," Lansdale replied, sadly. "I couldn't do that. Diem is my friend."

In the limousine ride back to the Pentagon, McNamara scolded Lansdale: "You don't talk to the president of the United States that way. When he asks you to do something, you don't tell him you won't be able to do it."[28]

McNamara subsequently denied having any memory of this episode, but then McNamara had a penchant for forgetting inconvenient conversations, as, for example, when he had suggested killing Castro or bombing Cuba. On its face, the story is plausible and consistent with Lansdale's previous refusals to apply too much pressure to Diem when he thought that doing so would be counterproductive. The fact that there is no official White House record of this meeting, however, and that Ellsberg became known for telling tall tales calls into question whether it ever actually occurred.[29]

We do not need to posit an off-the-books meeting with the president to understand why Lansdale was not sent to Saigon. The official record notes a conversation that occurred at 12:01 p.m. on September 17, 1963, between Secretary of State Dean Rusk and CIA Director John McCone. McCone made clear that in the CIA "there would be insurmountable problems raised re this man [Lansdale]—no confidence at all in him and M [McCone] could assume no responsibility for the operation." As far as McCone was concerned, "they could replace Richardson if Lodge wants but not [with] someone from the outside."[30] McNamara, too, "flatly refused" to send Lansdale to Saigon.[31] The proposal to dispatch Lansdale died a few hours later at an NSC meeting that also enhanced Lodge's authority to deal with Diem as he saw fit.[32] In hindsight, this can be seen as the death knell for Diem and Nhu and for the government they led.

As the weeks of October, filled with intrigue in both Saigon and Washington, ticked off, Lansdale wrote to his old commander Hanging Sam Williams, now retired from the army, to tell him, "My volunteering to go out and give a hand, along with Diem's asking for me, got an emotionally negative response." Lansdale was in "agony," because he was "semi-close to the stumbling around on Vietnam without a chance to lend a hand in any way that was then heeded. At critical moments, I was cut out of the communications, so I couldn't even read about what was happening. . . . It was Washington at its nuttiest." He told Williams that, from what he could gather, "we essentially are pointing a gun at Diem's head and are asking him to commit suicide."[33]

Just a few days after Lansdale wrote those dire words, Diem called Rufus Phillips over to the presidential palace. The date was October 30, 1963. Phillips, who was back in Saigon after having buried his father in Virginia, recalled, "He inquired about General Lansdale: had I seen him, how was he? I said I had been busy with my father's funeral but had talked to Lansdale on the phone, and he was well. I regretted to tell him that despite all my efforts to get General Lansdale out to Vietnam to help him, particularly during my previous visit home, I had not been successful." The embattled Vietnamese leader let out a sigh. He did not exhibit the agitation he had shown during the height of the sect crisis in 1955 or during the Buddhist crisis over the past year. He seemed calm, philosophical, resigned to his fate, whatever that might be.

The two men sat in silence for a moment while Diem puffed on his "ever-present cigarette." Finally he looked directly at Phillips and asked softly, "Do you think there will be a coup?"

"I'm afraid so, Mr. President," Phillips replied. He felt like crying.

Diem tried to comfort *him* by putting a hand on his arm. As the burly American walked out, he felt (or so he later recalled, with the benefit of hindsight) that this might be the last time he would ever see the president of South Vietnam.[34]

◆

DIEM'S DAYS in power, which had begun nine years earlier, in the summer of 1954, were rapidly ticking down, and so were Lansdale's. In early September 1963, Deputy Secretary of Defense Roswell Gilpatric told Lansdale that McNamara was thinking of phasing out his Special Operations office. A few days later, Lansdale wrote an anguished and only recently declassified reply: "I assume that the underlying reason for my being appointed as Assistant to the Secretary of Defense was to help the U.S. to achieve some solid victories in the cold war. If this assumption is correct, then, unhappily, I have not succeeded." Lansdale was upset not only that he was cut out of the loop on Vietnam but also that, the Green Berets aside, his attempts to get the armed forces to focus seriously on counterinsurgency had failed. The army had created "airmobile" divisions equipped with helicopters to fight guerrillas rather than figuring out how to win "hearts and minds" as Lansdale favored. Some were calling him the "father" of counterinsurgency, but, he wrote, "I must disclaim any real kinship with much of the currently giant institution of counterinsurgency . . . and its massive conventional weaponry and operations. The program has borrowed many of my words, but has left out too much of the spirit and true meaning of what I have said." His seven-page *cri de coeur* ended with these words: "Sincerely, if there is no way for me to be truly effective in helping get some cold war wins, then I shouldn't stay on."[35]

This was the bureaucratic equivalent of a suicide note, and it duly produced the expected result. On September 30, 1963, Lansdale received notice that his office was being eliminated. "The mice finally gnawed through the work and got my office 'disestablished,'" Lansdale wrote to Colonel Ed Black, an army friend in Saigon.³⁶ Lansdale elected to retire effective October 31, 1963. His hair was still thick, his brush mustache still dark, his posture still military erect. He was just fifty-five years old and still vigorous, if battered by too many bureaucratic beatings to count.

Much as Lansdale might have liked to blame his downfall on the "impersonal bureaucracy," he was at fault, too, for incessantly making war on the powers that be. "He set himself up in such a way that he created waves of antagonism from within the more orthodox bureaucratic circles," Sam Wilson was to say, "and he kind of thrived on it, thumbed his nose at it. It would have been so easy for him to give just a little bit, sort of grease the skids." That's what Wilson himself did during the course of a long Army career that culminated in his appointment in 1976 as a three-star general to command the Defense Intelligence Agency. In his view, "a bureaucracy is a system which is necessary to get things done. Neither good nor bad. It exists for a purpose and the task is to make it work."³⁷ That is not a perspective Lansdale shared. He viewed the bureaucracy as an enemy and, by so doing, turned it into one.

The relentlessly upbeat Lansdale tried to put the best gloss on what had happened to him. He wrote to Pat Kelly in Manila,

> There was a lot of inside wrestling that went on, some of it emotional as could be, so part of my feeling is a big lift of spirit in dumping this load. I was trying to get in to help affairs in Vietnam before they got too bad, but was shoved hard to one side— completely out of being able to help as Diem made some clumsy moves and then Washington made some clumsy moves. Much the same thing was happening with a lot of other affairs. So, I said heck, if I'm not going to be able to help in any way that counts, let me out. And they did.³⁸

To Hanging Sam Williams, Lansdale wrote, "So, with a phew of relief and a considerable lift of spirits, I'm looking forward to retirement."³⁹

But Sam Wilson saw that, beneath his cheerful exterior, Lansdale was "upset" and "depressed" because "he felt he'd been treated unfairly for no reason." The final indignity occurred at Lansdale's retirement party in the Pentagon. It was held on October 31, 1963, in a meeting room connecting the suites of the secretary of defense and the deputy secretary. While various colleagues were delivering flowery toasts and speeches in honor of Lansdale, Robert McNamara walked in. And he kept on walking, striding purposefully forward, one polished wingtip after another, never looking at what was going on through his rimless spectacles, much less stopping to join in the tributes to a man who had left behind a successful advertising career to devote the last twenty-one years of his life to his country's service.[40]

◆

LATE THAT very Thursday evening—October 31 in Washington, November 1 in Saigon—Lansdale received a phone call at home from an old friend, Spencer Davis of the Associated Press. He had just gotten a flash cable from Saigon that a coup was starting and wondered whether Lansdale could help him flesh out a story. Wearing pajamas and sprawled in a comfortable chair with a book in his lap and a drink close at hand, Lansdale had to admit that he was now retired and knew nothing of what was occurring.[41] Fittingly, if coincidentally, his tenure in government had ended on the very day when his friend of nine years, Ngo Dinh Diem—the man who embodied all of his dreams for the future of Vietnam—was being overthrown at America's instigation, an act that Lansdale had been warning against for nearly a decade.

Once Lansdale heard the following day that Diem and Nhu had been not just overthrown but killed—butchered, while their hands were bound, in the back of an armored vehicle by a professional killer—his disappointment and sorrow turned to anger, even rage, not an emotion that this imperturbable operative often displayed. Roger Hilsman, David Halberstam, and Diem's other critics, he said bitterly, had "some touch of blood on their hands."[42] Before long, even many of those who had been responsible for Diem's overthrow came to see the enormity of their mistake. A few years later, when the hard-bitten Lou Conein got drunk in Saigon, Lansdale said, "He tearfully asked me to forgive him for the Diem action."[43]

It was not truly Conein's fault. He was just following orders. But there was much to ask forgiveness for. As Lansdale wrote decades later, "It was morally wrong and strategically stupid to divide our political base in Vietnam when that political base, small as it was, was facing an energetic and exploitive enemy. Napoleon had a maxim about not dividing your forces in the face of the enemy."[44] Because the Kennedy administration had violated this "truism," the anti-Communist forces were left demoralized, disarrayed, and divided. America would have no choice but to send its own sons to fight if it wanted to avert a Communist victory.

What made Lansdale's anguish all the greater was his belief that he might have averted this cataclysm if he had been dispatched to Saigon. And he was not the only one to think so. On December 11, 1963, Lansdale received an extraordinary letter from Dillon Anderson, Eisenhower's national security adviser, who had worked with him on the Draper Committee in 1958 to study American foreign aid programs. "First," Anderson wrote, "let me say that I think it's a damn shame that you are not in Viet-Nam where your unique talents (1) might have saved our nation the anguish and a flavor of the guilt for the bloody termination of the Ngo regime; and (2) your particular skills in dealing with political problems might help us save this salubrious corner of Asia from going down the drain. But there's nothing I can do about that."[45]

There was nothing Edward Lansdale could do about it, either, especially now that Diem, the one man who might have been able to hold the country together, had been cut down in a blaze of bullets. South Vietnam was careening into free fall, and it was going to drag America, tethered by an umbilical cord of commitments, down with it.

PART FIVE

BASTARD CHILD

(1964–1968)

Lansdale with Vice President Hubert Humphrey and Prime Minister Nguyen Cao Ky of South Vietnam, returning from the Honolulu Summit, 1966. Lansdale was close to both men, but they could exert only limited influence over their own governments. (Image Works)

25

"A Hell of a Mess"

I am not going to lose Vietnam.

—LYNDON JOHNSON

A T 12:34 p.m. Central Standard Time on Friday, November 22, 1963, just three weeks after Ngo Dinh Diem's death, the United Press International news service sent out the first intimation that something terrible had just happened in Dallas. Just seconds before, the UPI correspondent Merriman Smith, who was sitting in the press pool car trailing the presidential limousine, had seized a radio telephone to inform the UPI's Dallas bureau chief, "Three shots were fired at President Kennedy's motorcade in downtown Dallas."[1]

Only four minutes had elapsed since those shots had rung out, hitting not only President Kennedy but also Governor John Connally of Texas, who was in the same vehicle, along with their wives, Jacqueline Kennedy and Nellie Connally. The president's car, a 1961 Lincoln convertible, was even then bearing its occupants at high speed to Parkland Memorial Hospital. At 1:35 p.m., as William Manchester noted in his magisterial account of the shooting and its aftermath, "UPI bells chimed on teletype machines around the world: FLASH PRESIDENT KENNEDY'S DEAD." "Over half the population wept," Manchester wrote, quoting an opinion poll. "Four out of five, in the words of the report, felt 'the loss of someone very close and dear,' and subsequently nine out of ten suffered 'physical discomfort.'"[2]

The mourning and shock would continue—in some ways they would never end—as John F. Kennedy's body was borne back to Washington in the cargo hold of his own airplane, a Boeing 707 designated *Air Force One*. After his murder that Friday afternoon in Dallas, the hope and perceived innocence that had characterized the initial years of the Kennedys' mythical Camelot would never return, the vanquishing of a youthful president somehow symbolizing America's expulsion from an illusory Eden. On Saturday, November 23, the casket was placed on display in the East Room of the White House, where notables—senators, generals, former presidents—arrived to say their final goodbyes. On Sunday, November 24, an estimated three hundred thousand people lined up in silent respect along Pennsylvania Avenue to watch a caisson drawn by six matched gray horses pull the flag-draped casket from the White House to the Capitol building. Hundreds of thousands more stood in another line stretching for more than three miles, waiting in near-freezing temperatures for as long as ten hours for a chance to walk through the Rotunda to pass by the coffin. The poignant farewell concluded on Monday, November 25, with a funeral mass at St. Matthew's Cathedral attended by world leaders and royalty followed by burial at Arlington National Cemetery with full pomp and circumstance.

◆

MANY PEOPLE never accepted—and never will—the verdict rendered by numerous independent investigations, that Kennedy was killed by Lee Harvey Oswald acting alone. The murder of a beloved young president, an idol and an inspiration to millions, appeared too consequential an event to be the work of one deranged misfit, a disgraced former marine armed with a mail-order rifle. The fact that Oswald himself was killed shortly thereafter by a gunman with Mafia links only added to speculation that Kennedy had been the victim of a far-reaching plot. In the decades after Kennedy's murder, phrases such as "grassy knoll" and "the Zapruder film" would enter the popular culture, thanks to an industry of conspiracy-mongers, their work culminating in 1991 with the release of the director Oliver Stone's $40 million epic *JFK*.

The film features a shadowy character, played by Donald Sutherland and identified only as X, who claims that Kennedy was killed by the "military industrial complex" in a plot orchestrated by "General Y." The movie furnishes some telltale clues to Y's identity. X says that Allen Dulles was Y's benefactor and that Y was in charge of Operation Mongoose. In case there is any further doubt of Y's identity, the camera briefly pans to his office desk. His nameplate is obscured but the visible part reads "M/GEN. E.G." above the words "U.S. AIR." It does not take much imagination to infer that this is the desk of Major General E. G. Lansdale, U.S. Air Force. And just as the identity of Y was obvious, so too the identity of X was never in doubt either. Stone himself identified X at a press conference as L. Fletcher Prouty, a retired Air Force colonel who had worked as a liaison officer in the Pentagon's special operations office when it was run by Lansdale between 1961 and 1963.[3]

Stone held up Prouty as a fearless truth-teller—a man who, in his words, "will go down in history" for revealing the "Secret History" of the United States and uncovering "the ugliest nest of vipers the civilized world has probably seen since the dreaded Mongol raiders of the tenth and eleventh centuries."[4] (The Mongol invasions actually occurred in the thirteenth and fourteenth centuries.) In reality, Prouty was a crank with a febrile imagination—"a complete nut," in Rufus Phillips's words.[5] He was a "good pilot of prop-driven aircraft," Lansdale later said, "but had such a heavy dose of paranoia about CIA when he was on my staff that I kicked him back to the Air Force."[6]

Prouty would be associated after his retirement from the Air Force in 1964 with the white supremacist Liberty Lobby, the Church of Scientology, and the cult leader Lyndon LaRouche; he grandiosely compared LaRouche's federal prosecution for conspiracy and mail fraud to the trial of Socrates. He also claimed that the fall of the Berlin Wall was stage-managed by David Rockefeller to profit from "the rubles and the gold," that he had personally seen a UFO, and that "the Churchill gang" murdered Franklin D. Roosevelt.[7]

Prouty's old boss was a favorite target of his bizarre and inventive accusations. He claimed that Lansdale had concocted the entire Huk threat—that so-called Huk attacks were actually carried out by Philippine army special forces in order to elect Ramon Magsaysay president, although he never explained why Washington would want to elect Magsaysay if there was no Huk threat.[8] In a similar vein, he claimed that the members of Lansdale's Saigon Military Mission were "a band of superterrorists" who deliberately created the Vietcong by moving a million Vietnamese from the North to the South in 1954–55. Their goal, Prouty explained, was to spark a war that could profit the military-industrial complex.[9] (In reality, as we have seen, most of the refugees were Catholics who were staunchly anti-Communist.)

To back up his grave accusation that Lansdale was the mastermind of the Kennedy assassination, Prouty could offer but one piece of "evidence": a photograph taken on November 22, 1963, near Dealey Plaza, showing a man in a suit walking by three tramps who are being escorted by two police officers. The man is visible only from the rear, but Prouty nevertheless claimed that this was none other than Lansdale and that the "tramps" were actors hired by the conspirators.[10] Yet even Prouty insouciantly admitted, "The picture could be a hundred other people and I could be wrong."[11] He was definitely wrong about the tramps: they were finally identified by an enterprising reporter in 1992, who established they really were vagrants and not assassins in disguise.[12]

There is no reason to imagine that the man seen from the back was Lansdale—why, after all, would he have wanted to kill Kennedy? Prouty and Stone claimed JFK had mortally offended the "military-industrial complex" by embracing the cause of peace and trying to end the Cold War. In reality, while Kennedy contemplated reducing the number of U.S. advisers in Vietnam if conditions continued to improve, he also made clear that the "security of South Viet Nam is a major interest of the United States" and that "we will adhere to our policy of working with the people and government of South Viet Nam to deny this country to Communism."[13] Nor did Kennedy end attempts to overthrow or kill Fidel Castro, as *JFK* suggested. On November 22, 1963, at the very time that the president was being killed in Dallas, a CIA case officer was meeting in Paris with a disaffected Cuban military officer to give him a hypodermic syringe filled with poison, disguised as a Paper-Mate pen, which could be used to "eliminate" Castro.[14] And far from cutting the defense budget, Kennedy, as he boasted in a speech in Fort Worth on the very day of his demise, had increased defense spending by more than 20 percent.[15]

Even if Kennedy had actually been intent on reducing the U.S. presence in Vietnam, ending the plots against Castro, or cutting defense spending, Lansdale would hardly have objected. He was a critic, not an advocate, of the Americanization of the Vietnam War. He was never a proponent of expensive weapons systems; he argued that the best weapon was a well-trained soldier, diplomat, or spy who would deal sympathetically with the local populace. And, although he ran Operation Mongoose, he was happy to end his participation in what he viewed as a thankless task. A staunch advocate of spreading liberty abroad, Lansdale was scarcely likely to undermine liberty at home by participating in a military coup d'état against the lawfully elected president—a man he had worked for and respected, even if he was less enamored of the president's younger brother.

Far from plotting to kill John F. Kennedy, as numerous conspiracy-mongers continue to allege, Lansdale was as grief-stricken as the rest of the country by his shocking death and as uncertain about what would come next. Like most Americans, he must have wondered whether Lyndon Baines Johnson, who had been seeking power all his life, could rise to the challenge of exercising the supreme authority he had now inherited by dint of an assassin's bullets.

◆

BORN IN 1908 a few months after Edward Lansdale, Johnson had been raised in the dirt-poor Hill Country of central Texas. His mother dressed him in Little Lord Fauntleroy suits, just as Lansdale's mother did, and imbued him with a sense that he was superior to his impoverished classmates. When Lyndon was young, his father, Sam Ealey Johnson, was a considerable success; not only did he make a comfortable living trading in cattle, cotton, and land, but he also won election to the Texas legislature. Lyndon idolized his strong-willed father and was devastated when he lost all of his money and his 433-acre ranch in the recession of 1922, which also hit the Lansdale family hard. In an instant, as Johnson later said, he "dropped to the bottom of the heap," and his father went from a big man in the community to a laughing-stock.[16] The humiliation of his family's downfall gave him added impetus to succeed, while also infusing him with deep-rooted resentment of those who were more privileged than he was.

Johnson would first come to Washington in 1931, while Lansdale was moving from Los Angeles to New York, as the aide to a newly elected congressman. He soon became the "boss" of the hitherto inconsequential Little Congress made up of Hill staffers—a feat he achieved by stuffing the ballot box just as he had done as an under-graduate at Southwest State Teachers College to win student body elections. "My God," a future president of the organization wondered, "who would cheat to win the presidency of something like the Little Congress?"[17] By 1937, while Lansdale was moving to San Francisco to launch his advertising career, Johnson was already a congressman himself, having won a special election when he was only twenty-eight years old. His first attempt to win a Senate seat in 1941 failed after his adversary stole more votes than he did. Vowing never to be beaten in such a manner again, Johnson did just enough to squeak out an 87-vote victory in the 1948 Senate election. By 1953, while Lansdale was engineering Ramon Magsaysay's election as president of the Philippines, "Landslide Lyndon" had been elected leader of the Senate Democrats. Two years later, while Lansdale was fighting the "battle of the sects" in Saigon, Johnson became at the age of forty-six the youngest majority leader in Senate history—and the most powerful.

The "Leader," as he was known, became famous in Washington for giving senators, journalists, donors, civil servants, and anyone else who came into his orbit "the treatment." Johnson was physically imposing, at more than six feet three inches tall, with gangly arms and huge hands, giant ears jutting from his head, and coal-black eyes blazing with intensity. He would often put his face next to the face of someone he was talking to, almost nose to nose, while he draped a giant arm around his interlocutor. "You really felt as if a St. Bernard had . . . pawed you all over," the *Washington Post* editor Ben Bradlee recalled.[18] No one in Washington was better than Johnson at intimidating people, ferreting out their weaknesses, and bending them to his will. Hubert Humphrey compared him to a "tidal wave. . . . He went through the walls. He'd come through a door, and he'd take the whole room over. Just like that."[19]

The tidal wave was temporarily at low tide while Johnson was vice president—a job he hated because he was denied real power. He bristled at the condescension of Kennedy aides who called him "Rufus Cornpone" behind his back. His trademark energy, which throughout his life had led him to work brutally long hours and to eat, drink, and womanize on an equally prodigious scale, seemed to have dissipated. He was listless and had trouble getting out of bed. He wallowed in self-pity.

Everything changed the minute John F. Kennedy was struck down. LBJ's Boswell, Robert Caro, quotes one of his aides remarking that her boss was a "'changed man, transformed' . . . the very movements of his body were different; . . . instead of the awkward, almost lunging, strides and 'flailing' movements of his arms that had previously often characterized Johnson under tension, now his stride was shorter, measured, and his arms were staying by his sides, hardly moving at all; . . . 'there was no flailing.'"[20] Another aide, Bill Moyers, said after JFK's assassination, "I've never seen him as controlled, as self-disciplined, as careful and as moderate as he's been this week."[21]

Johnson plunged into the presidency with "cyclonic vigor."[22] Determined to outdo his hero, Franklin Delano Roosevelt, he launched a "war on poverty" that was to result in the creation of the Job Corps, the Community Action Program, VISTA (Volunteers in Service to America), Head Start, Food Stamps, Medicare, Medicaid, and many other idealistic and costly initiatives designed to foster a "Great Society." Johnson also won passage of the Civil Rights Act of 1964 and then of the Voting Rights Act of 1965, two landmark pieces of legislation that the less Machiavellian Kennedy had not been able to pass in the face of Southern filibusters. By the spring of 1964, Johnson's approval ratings were over 70 percent and his election as president in his own right—once far from assured—now appeared to be a foregone conclusion. The columnist Joseph Alsop wrote that "in the few short months since last Nov. 22," Johnson has been "making Washington and the government his own."[23]

◆

SOUTH VIETNAM, unfortunately, had no Lyndon Johnson of its own to take over from Ngo Dinh Diem—and given the newness and fragility of its national institutions, it needed a strong successor even more than the United States did. On November 4, 1963, just two days after Diem's death, the architect of the coup, Ambassador Henry Cabot Lodge, alerted Washington that "the Generals are quarreling among themselves" over the division of power and that if they "cannot come to an agreement within next day, then Marines who actually led the coup against the regime would lead a countercoup."[24] The generals just barely reached an agreement: General Duong Van Minh ("Big Minh"), the head of the 22-member Military Revolutionary Committee, would become president of South Vietnam. Nguyen Ngoc Tho, Diem's vice president, would serve as prime minister to give a patina of civilian legitimacy to the arrangement. But generals would occupy all of the key posts. These military men were utterly unschooled in governance, suspicious of one another, and deeply insecure. They immediately unleashed a reign of terror against officials who had served Diem. Most of the 42 province and 253 district chiefs, including officials known for being especially effective in fighting the Communists, were replaced, often by men who did not know the areas they were assigned to govern.

Dreams that South Vietnam would become a more liberal place were shattered as the new military dictators imposed strict censorship, shut down newspapers, and arrested anyone suspected of disloyalty. Martial law would be invoked far more often after Diem's demise than it had been while he was still in charge. Within weeks, thousands of students were marching in protests and more Buddhist monks than ever were immolating themselves in public. After years of nation building, South Vietnam was returning to the chaos of the 1954–55 period—just as Lansdale had warned would happen if Diem were removed.

This was a heaven-sent opportunity for the Vietcong. "Our enemy had been seriously weakened from all points of view, military, political and administrative. . . ," a leader of the National Liberation Front crowed. "The police apparatus set up over the years with great care by Diem is utterly shattered, especially at the base. . . . Troops, officers, and officials of the army and administration are completely lost."[25] The number of "violent incidents" across South Vietnam increased from four hundred per week before the coup to more than a thousand in the week after the coup.[26] The Strategic Hamlets program, the most promising counterinsurgency program initiated by Diem, was all but abandoned as hamlet after hamlet was overrun by attackers and not rebuilt. The Ho Chi Minh Trail was widened and improved to allow trucks to deliver supplies through Laos all the way to the border with South Vietnam, while seaborne shipments of weapons to transshipment points in Cambodia and to secret landing spots along the ill-patrolled South Vietnamese coast increased. (The South Vietnamese navy was all but immobilized after its chief was murdered during the 1963 coup.)[27] The quantity of supplies reaching Communist forces in the South would be four times greater in 1964 than in 1963.[28] Most ominously of all, in 1964 the first North Vietnamese regular troops began heading south. Le Duan and the hard-liners were intent on accelerating the conflict, regardless of the risk of American intervention.[29]

◆

IN THE early morning hours of January 30, 1964, another coup—the second in less than three months—occurred in Saigon. The instigator was General Nguyen Khanh, a member of the anti-Diem cabal who was aggrieved because he had been promised that no harm would come to the president and that he would get a handsome reward for his treachery. Neither promise had been fulfilled: Diem had been killed, and Khanh had been relegated to a corps command in the northwest. Khanh placed most of the leading generals responsible for the anti-

Diem coup under house arrest. Khanh also arrested Diem's killer (and Big Minh's bodyguard), Captain Nguyen Van Nhung, who was subsequently found hanging in his cell.

Just thirty-six years old, General Khanh "was a chunky man with a small, dark goatee and slightly protuberant eyes," noted an American press adviser, and he was given to wearing a "sharply creased field uniform" with boots polished to a mirrorlike sheen.[30] Now that he was prime minister, Khanh worked to improve his popularity by importing American-style campaign tactics. "From the way he button-holed passers-by on Saigon sidewalks," raved *Time* magazine, "the pint-sized Vietnamese officer in green fatigues could have been Nelson Rockefeller campaigning in the New Hampshire primary."[31] But Khanh did not prove any more adept at governing than Big Minh had been. He was not to be the Vietnamese LBJ.

◆

LYNDON JOHNSON had not been an advocate of the Diem coup; he thought it was "a tragic mistake."[32] Having inherited what Robert McNamara aptly described as "a hell of a mess" in Vietnam,[33] the new president struggled to find the right response.

Although a liberal in domestic affairs, Johnson was a foreign-policy hard-liner. He had spent long years on the House Naval Affairs and Armed Services Committees and then on the Senate Armed Services Committee championing a strong national defense and, not incidentally, ensuring that a disproportionate share of the defense budget found its way back to Texas in the form of bases and weapons contracts. Like most of his generation, Johnson was haunted by the failure of appeasement and isolationism in the 1930s. If Saigon fell, Johnson was terrified that he would be held politically responsible by Republicans as Truman had been held responsible for the Communist takeover of China. He would have recurring nightmares in which people kept shouting at him, "Coward! Traitor! Weakling!" Waking up "terribly shaken," he would vow, "I am not going to lose Vietnam. I am not going to be the President who saw Southeast Asia go the way China went."[34] He urged his aides, "Don't go to bed at night until you have asked yourself, 'Have I done everything I could to further the American effort to assist South Vietnam?'"[35]

Yet, determined as he was to save South Vietnam, Johnson hesitated to commit American forces to combat. He feared that a conflict would interfere with his Great Society agenda at home and that his popularity would suffer if he embroiled America in another land war in Asia like the Korean War.[36] Balancing these competing imperatives, Johnson quietly shelved plans to reduce the American advisory presence as Kennedy had considered doing. In May 1964, he increased aid to South Vietnam by $125 million and sent another fifteen hundred advisers.[37]

He also embraced Nguyen Khanh as tightly as he could. Before Secretary of Defense Robert McNamara and General Maxwell Taylor visited Saigon in March 1964, Johnson told them he wanted to see a picture "on the front pages of the world press" showing them holding up Khanh's arms as a show of support.[38] But far from strengthening Khanh, as LBJ expected, the resulting pictures strengthened the Vietcong narrative that Khanh was an American puppet. It did not help that McNamara, while grasping Khanh's hand, tried to say *Vietnam muon nam* ("Vietnam ten thousand years"). But his pronunciation was so atrocious that it sounded to many listeners as if he had said, "Ruptured duck wants to lie down."[39]

◆

WHEN HENRY CABOT LODGE finally left Saigon in June 1964 to seek the Republican presidential nomination, after having done so much to undermine South Vietnam's tenuous stability, Johnson named a high-powered replacement: Maxwell Taylor. Aloof, handsome, cerebral, the multilingual tribune of "flexible response" and advocate of "limited wars" had impressed Johnson as much as he had Kennedy. Assisting him as deputy ambassador would be one of the State Department's rising stars, U. Alexis Johnson, a former ambassador to Czechoslovakia and Thailand and most recently deputy under secretary of state.

MACV (Military Assistance Command—Vietnam) was also receiving new leadership. The relentlessly upbeat General Paul Harkins was replaced in June 1964 by another up-and-comer: General William Childs Westmoreland. Like Max Taylor, his mentor and friend, "Westy" was an Army golden boy with an airborne pedigree. A courtly native of South Carolina, Westmoreland had been an Eagle Scout as a boy. At West Point, where he transferred after beginning his college years at The Citadel, he was named first captain, the top cadet. He led an artillery battalion ashore in North Africa in 1942, and he landed in Normandy on D-Day. After the war, he joined the 82nd Airborne Division—a more glamorous assignment than staying in the field artillery. When the Korean War broke out, Westmoreland was dispatched as a regimental commander. Further promotions followed rapidly once his patron, Max Taylor, became chief of staff in 1955. Westmoreland became the army's youngest major general at age forty-two, assigned to command the storied 101st Airborne Division, Taylor's old outfit. In 1960, he was appointed Superintendent of West Point, his alma mater. By early 1964, he was in Vietnam as Harkins's deputy and successor-in-waiting.[40]

Fifty years old, tall, lean, vigorous, gray-haired, and handsome, Westy looked the very image of a "rugged, no-nonsense soldier"[41]—a "Tough Man" for a "Tough Job," as one magazine put it.[42] Some of those who knew him better were less impressed. Westy did little reading, and he had little interest in, or understanding of, Asia or counterinsurgency warfare. His level of intellectual sophistication was displayed when he told a visitor to Saigon—the Harvard professor Henry Kissinger—that the Americans in Vietnam were much better liked than the French had been because "when the French wanted a woman they simply grabbed her off the streets and went to bed with her," whereas "when an American soldier wants a woman he pays for her." "I thought at first he was kidding," Kissinger recorded in his diary, "but I then found out he was absolutely serious."[43]

A brigadier general who had served under Westmoreland warned the secretary of the army, Cyrus Vance, that "it would be a grave mistake" to send him to Vietnam. "He is spit and polish, two up and one back. This is a counterinsurgency war, and he would have no idea of how to deal with it."[44] Such prophecies were ignored by McNamara and Johnson, as was any unease that might have been stirred by one of Westmoreland's early directives. He demanded that all American advisers "accentuate the positive," "bring best thought to bear," and avoid "frustration and stagnation."⁴⁵ This was designed to instill a positive, can-do attitude, but it became a prescription for wishful thinking and the denial of certain grim realities.

◆

WHILE PRESIDENT JOHNSON was assembling a new team in Saigon, he was also authorizing a covert-harassment plan against the North cobbled together by an interagency committee chaired by Lansdale's old rival Major General Victor "Brute" Krulak. In outline, it was reminiscent of Lansdale's ineffectual Mongoose plans against Cuba: it called for increased intelligence collection, psychological operations such as leaflet drops and radio broadcasts, and a small number of "destructive undertakings," that is, hit-and-run raids that would be carried out by South Vietnamese personnel with American support. Operation Plan (OPLAN) 34A, approved by Johnson on January 16, 1964, was designed "to inflict increasing punishment upon North Vietnam and to create pressures, which may convince the North Vietnamese leadership, in its own self-interest, to desist from aggressive policies."⁴⁶

It did not occur to anyone that there might be a problem with staging OPLAN 34A raids along the North Vietnam coast at the same time that U.S. naval ships were offshore on intelligence-gathering patrols. The confluence of these two operations provoked North Vietnamese patrol boats on August 2, 1963, to stage an unsuccessful attack on the destroyer USS *Maddox* in the Gulf of Tonkin. The next day, the *Maddox* and another destroyer, the *Turner Joy*, reported a further attack. The two warships fired 372 shells and at least four depth charges while reporting that they had dodged multiple torpedoes and enemy gunfire. But American pilots flying overhead could not see any enemy vessels, and later analysis concluded that the second attack, unlike the first one, had not really occurred. "Hell, those damn, stupid sailors were just shooting at flying fish," Lyndon Johnson concluded a few days later. But such doubts did not prevent Johnson from sending to Congress, and Congress approving with near unanimity, a resolution giving the president the authority "to take all necessary measures to repel armed attacks against the forces of the United States and to prevent further aggression" as well as to aid any American ally in Southeast Asia "requesting assistance in defense of its freedom."

Neither the members of Congress nor Lyndon Johnson himself had any idea that the vague language of the Gulf of Tonkin Resolution would be used to justify a ground war that would eventually draw in half a million American troops. On both ends of Pennsylvania Avenue, there was fervent hope that South Vietnam's government would be able to fight its own battles. But with South Vietnam still buffeted by the divisive reverberations from the anti-Diem coup, and with North Vietnam continuing to ramp up its offensive, the pressure would build to prevent a total collapse through the introduction of American combat troops. There was nothing inevitable about the outcome, but in hindsight it is easy to see the course upon which America was now embarked toward the deadliest guerrilla conflict in its history.[47]

26

"Concept for Victory"

Are paddy farmers in a combat zone to be shot just because
they inadvertently are standing in the way of Vietcong targets
or are they to be protected and helped?

—EDWARD LANSDALE

WHILE South Vietnam was struggling with the destabilizing aftereffects of Ngo Dinh Diem's ouster and murder, Diem's greatest American champion was struggling to find a role for himself. Edward Lansdale was only fifty-six years old. Normally this would be the prime of a man's working life, but he was unemployed for the first time since 1942, when he had moved from advertising to the OSS. He had no desire to leave the fight for freedom, as he conceived of the Cold War, but also no firm idea of how he could continue to contribute. On his last day in the Pentagon, October 31, 1963, he wrote to Pat Kelly, "All I can think about is trying to catch my breath and catch up on some rest before even starting to think about what comes next."[1]

Publishers were approaching Lansdale to write a book. He told Pat that he kept "thinking of how nice it would be to get a house on the beach at maybe San F'do La U [San Fernando La Union, a beach town on Lingayen Gulf] and sit with a typewriter maybe a couple of hours a day, and the rest of the time really live again."[2] In this fantasy, writing a book would have provided an excuse for rekindling their romance. "My heart's with you," he told Pat. When he got word that her mother had died, he wrote, "I ached to comfort you. I know how much she meant to you, and the feeling of loss with someone you love. Doggone this distance between us when you need me!"[3]

But ultimately Ed decided against becoming an author, at least for the time being. "I am never about to write the truth of some past events—the way they turned out made nice history for the nations involved and I'm happy to keep history in the fiction class," he told his friend Peter Richards.[4]

Instead of writing a book, Lansdale wrote a five-page proposal for a new educational institution to "teach practical American political action, for export abroad." He called it Liberty Hall, and imagined it could be a "non-profit, public-service corporation" with a "center with offices and class rooms, probably in the area of Washington, D.C." The initial students would "be a carefully picked handful of U.S. official personnel, primarily from the Foreign Services." The instructors "would be a small group of experienced people"—obviously Lansdale had himself and his old colleagues in mind—who would also be available as "consultants to the U.S. government as well as to foreign governments."[5]

To turn his brainstorm into reality, Lansdale attracted the support of the American Security Council, a Chicago-based organization founded in 1954 by Robert E. Wood, a retired general and former president of Sears, Roebuck & Co., and Colonel Robert McCormick, the flamboyant publisher of the *Chicago Tribune*. Wood and McCormick had been prominent America Firsters before Pearl Harbor, and they became McCarthyites in the 1950s. The American Security Council, initially designed to root out supposed Communist infiltrators in the private sector, agreed in 1965 to support a revamped version of Lansdale's school to be called the Freedom Studies Center.[6] Lansdale grew disenchanted, however, as soon as he realized that the American Security Council was "almost a John Birch Society roll call" and that everyone involved in the project was "either Republicans or too far right to be Republicans."[7]

Although Lansdale was a staunch anti-Communist, he was no John Bircher or McCarthyite or, for that matter, even a Republican. Studiously neutral in domestic politics, like many other military officers, he nevertheless felt very much at home working with Cold War liberals who were determined to fight Communism abroad while striving to improve society at home.

◆

THE SPIRIT of Cold War liberalism was personified by Lansdale's friend Richard W. Reuter, a jowly, Brooklyn-born pacifist with a passing resemblance to J. Edgar Hoover. A conscientious objector, Reuter had worked during World War II for the American Friends Service Committee and after the war for CARE, a leading international charity based in New York. In 1962, he had been appointed by President Kennedy as director of Food for Peace, an eight-year-old agency created to send some of America's agricultural surplus to needy nations. While Lansdale, a career military man, and Reuter, a career aid worker, came from very different backgrounds, they shared a similar vision of promoting "civic action" to stymie Communist subversion.

Upon hearing that Lansdale was being forced out of the Pentagon, Dick Reuter offered him a job at Food for Peace working on long-range planning, and Lansdale accepted. He began work on December 3, 1963, in the Old Executive Office Building next door to the White House, as a consultant paid $68.96 a day.[8] When one of Reuter's aides asked for some biographical background to release to the media, Lansdale replied with his trademark wryness, "Moscow, Peking, and Hanoi (echoed by Phnom Penh) possibly will pick this up to say FFP is becoming a front for a U.S. spy or gangster organization, confirmed by my presence. On the other hand, maybe the news that I have retired from military service will cheer them up, since I doubt that this is known very widely."[9]

Although now working at Food for Peace, Lansdale was by no means convinced that providing more food to poor countries would result in more peace. "Just 50 years ago," he noted, "some remarkably well-fed people started World War I. . . . I'm thinking of the waistlines of those gentlemen in the Triple Alliance and the Triple Entente, the waistlines of the cheering crowds in the streets, the waistlines of the burghers in spiked helmets who went wheeling into Belgium on their bicycles, the waistlines of the Colonel Blimps who crossed the Channel into France. Man, they had food in those days! But, did it bring peace?"[10] Rather than giving out aid indiscriminately, Lansdale argued, it should be used to "cause fundamental strengthening of the rights of man in the receiving countries," with countries that promoted the "reign of law" receiving more assistance than those that did not.[11] Lansdale's idea of tying aid to human-rights reforms anticipated by four decades the Millennium Challenge Corporation created by President George W. Bush in 2004.

His other ideas would be stillborn, just as most of his ideas had been at the Pentagon. Lansdale kept on coming up with imaginative proposals—including a "Jules Vernian" concept for deploying an international corps of aquanauts to explore the ocean's depths[12]—yet he had to concede privately, "My heart really isn't in it."[13] His passion, as it had been for many years, was to return to Vietnam and help that nation in its crucible of agony.

◆

"WITH MORALE sagging like the mattress in a Bowery flop-house," Lansdale wrote of Vietnam in March 1964, shortly after Nguyen Khanh's coup, "some tangible victories are needed."[14] To figure out how to attain those victories, he joined forces with Rufus Phillips and Charles "Bo" Bohannan, both recently returned from working for USAID in Vietnam. In the spring of 1964, the three of them met in the Kensington, Maryland, home of Bo's mother to hash out ideas. By June 1964, they had produced two strategy papers intended for high-level circulation within the Johnson administration. In Phillips's recollection, Lansdale did almost all of the writing.[15]

The main paper, "Concept for Victory in Vietnam," warned that the "Communist insurgents have a firm political base which the Vietnamese people understand," with a "program to gain control of the people," "a strong belief in eventual victory," "iron discipline," and a "leadership skilled in subversive insurgency." These problems would remain "even if South Vietnam were isolated completely from North Vietnam or outside Communist help." Thus, Lansdale did not suggest bombing North Vietnam or sending more troops to South Vietnam. "Overt U.S. intervention against North Vietnam or Cambodia is neither necessary nor appropriate," he wrote. At a time when there were fewer than twenty thousand American advisers in South Vietnam, he concluded, "Military forces and equipment already in Vietnam should be more than sufficient to cope with most military aspects of the Vietcong insurgency."

Lansdale was more receptive to a foray into Laos to block the Ho Chi Minh Trail "if dramatic, positive acknowledged action seems required." But he preferred a covert campaign of subversion aimed at Hanoi. He suggested that "notable leaders from North Vietnam now residing in Saigon" could "form a Council of Liberty and issue a liberation policy for NVN." With his long-standing penchant for "black ops" and "psy-ops," he suggested "the publication of two 'black' newspapers, for distribution to the Vietcong, each espousing one side of the apparent Sino-Soviet split," the distribution of "contaminated ammunition" that would blow up in the faces of Vietcong fighters, and the promulgation of "black 'orders' to VC units" telling them to stop "collection from peasants."

As for military action in South Vietnam, Lansdale argued that the ARVN should be ordered to "vigorously seek to bring the enemy to battle, and to destroy him." But he also believed that the ARVN should be told, "No ordnance shall be expended from aircraft or artillery, unless both the officers in charge and any U.S. advisers or personnel present are satisfied that the target does not include non-combatant women or children. Mistakes mean court-martial."

No such rules would ever be implemented in Vietnam, and partly as a result untold numbers of civilians would be killed by South Vietnamese and American forces. The U.S. military would not recognize the utility of such restrictive rules of engagement, designed to avoid alienating the populace, until decades later in Afghanistan and Iraq.

To stabilize the turbulent South Vietnamese political situation, Lansdale suggested that the leaders of the government sign, "in their blood if need be," a declaration of liberty outlining "the principles of service to freedom and country essential for victory, with a pledge to uphold them or else suffer public shame." A new assembly of notables, including "representatives from all major patriotic political parties and groups," could then supervise the transition "from Junta to Constitutional government." Unlike more naïve exponents of democracy, Lansdale did not think that it made sense to hold early national elections; he argued that the electoral process should begin gradually, with elections for district chiefs in areas where "conditions are deemed secure enough."

The crux of Lansdale's paper was his suggestion, yet again, for the dispatch to Saigon of a "small team of winners" who "have proven their ability to defeat Asian Communist subversive insurgents." A second paper, just three pages long and titled "A Catalyst Team for Vietnam," explained that such a team would not need "elaborate logistics or separate headquarters," but it would need "the backing of the President or it will suffer the same fate as so many other well-intentioned efforts in Vietnam." Lansdale was seeking to recreate the kind of position of influence he had occupied in the Philippines from 1950 to 1953 and in South Vietnam from 1954 to 1956. He hoped to build up Nguyen Khanh as, in Rufus Phillips's words, a "national hero by leading the transition back to elected government,"[16] the way he had previously done with Ramon Magsaysay and Ngo Dinh Diem.

The problem was that Lansdale no longer had an influential position in the government or the support of those who did. He was stymied— until he met an eminent legislator who would shortly become the second most important elected official in America.

◆

IN FEBRUARY 1964, when he first met Edward Lansdale, Hubert Horatio Humphrey was the Senate majority whip, the number-two leadership position behind Majority Leader Mike Mansfield, and the unofficial leader of Washington's liberals. A onetime college professor, Humphrey had become mayor of Minneapolis, his first elected position, at the age of thirty-four in 1945. Three years later, he had electrified the delegates to the 1948 Democratic National Convention in Philadelphia with a fiery speech in favor of civil rights, urging them to "get out of the shadow of state's rights and walk forthrightly in the bright sunshine of human rights."[17] Thanks to Humphrey's emotional appeal, the convention narrowly approved a civil rights plank over the strenuous opposition of Southern delegates, many of whom walked out to endorse the Dixiecrat Strom Thurmond for president.

By the time Humphrey arrived in Washington in 1949 as a senator from Minnesota, he was thoroughly disliked by the Senate's crusty Southerners. To the Old Bulls, he seemed to be an overbearing, self-righteous know-it-all with a tendency to talk too much. Humphrey did not help matters when he insisted on lunching with a black aide in the Senate's once segregated dining room.[18] Almost as bad from the Southerners' perspective, he publicly attacked the Senate's cherished system of seniority, which allowed them to block civil rights legislation.[19] Senator Richard Russell of Georgia, dean of the Southerners, was heard to say within Humphrey's hearing, "Can you imagine the people of Minnesota sending that damn fool down here to represent them?" This scorn was especially painful for someone like Humphrey who, by his own description, "was a more than normally gregarious person, who wanted to be liked."[20]

Humphrey sought a bridge to the Southerners and found one in Senator Lyndon Johnson, who in 1951 began inviting him to his office to talk and drink. Johnson knew that he needed Northern support to pass legislation and to achieve his presidential ambitions; Humphrey knew he needed Southern support to break his isolation in the Senate and realize his own presidential dreams. Johnson promoted Humphrey within the Senate, but there was a price to be paid for acknowledging Lyndon Johnson as one's liege lord—a significant price. Robert Caro writes, "Once, after Johnson had given Hubert Humphrey an order on the Senate floor and he hadn't moved fast enough to suit the Leader, Johnson, snarling, 'Get goin' now!,' had kicked him—hard—in the shin to speed him on the way, and Humphrey had accepted the kick without complaint, had even pulled up his pant leg the next day to proudly show a reporter the scar."[21]

This was typical of Lyndon Baines Johnson: he could be saccharine with those he was cultivating, but once he was sure of their support, he would go out of his way to humiliate them, to make clear that they had to bend their will to his. Johnson made this explicit when, in August 1964, he asked Humphrey to be his running mate. "This is like a marriage with no chance of divorce," he told the vice presidential nominee. "I need complete and unswerving loyalty."[22]

Johnson insisted, as soon as the Democratic convention ended, that Humphrey and his wife, Muriel, accompany him and Lady Bird to his ranch in Johnson City, Texas. Once there, the president said they were going for a horseback ride. But first Humphrey had to be properly attired. "He called me into his bedroom," Humphrey recalled, "and pulled out an outfit that dwarfed me. The pants were huge, so big that I thought I could put both my legs in one pant leg and still dance a polka. The jacket draped like a tent over a shirt whose neck was several sizes too large. I looked ridiculous and felt ridiculous as I smiled wanly from under a cowboy hat that was made for his head and clearly not mine." The mortification only worsened once Johnson put Humphrey atop a "big and spirited horse" in spite of his running mate's total lack of riding experience. "There seemed to be an acre of cameramen and reporters grinning and clicking as the horse sort of reared," Humphrey wrote, "leaving me filled with fear and clutching that horse like a tiny child on his first merry-go-round ride, hanging on for dear life."

The president, Humphrey noted, "got a big kick out of it."[23]

◆

NINE MONTHS before the 1964 election, Humphrey would be introduced to Edward Lansdale and Rufus Phillips by Bert Fraleigh, a rural-development expert at USAID who had gotten to know Humphrey while working in Taiwan for Food for Peace, a program that Humphrey had sponsored. Fraleigh had subsequently gone to work at the Rural Affairs office in South Vietnam, where his boss, Rufus Phillips, found that, much like Lansdale, he "had a 'can-do' attitude, without a bureaucratic mindset."[24] Humphrey admired Fraleigh and took seriously his suggestion to invite Lansdale and Phillips in for a talk about

Vietnam. "Meeting Humphrey," Phillips later wrote, "was to encounter a human dynamo, brimming with energy and obvious intelligence but also human interest and curiosity." The senator listened intently—more intently than any other high-level official that Phillips ever encountered—and understood what he was hearing. He displayed "an instinctive feel for the unconventional people-based, political nature of the war, the 'x factor' that McNamara failed to comprehend."[25]

Humphrey was receptive to the unorthodox message being delivered by Lansdale and Phillips in large measure because it accorded so perfectly with his own view. Like Lyndon Johnson, Humphrey was a liberal at home and a hawk abroad—but one with more idealistic tendencies than the ruthless president. Humphrey was a supporter of the Truman Doctrine, NATO, and the defense budget, while also being the leading champion of Food for Peace, the Peace Corps (created in 1961), the Arms Control and Disarmament Agency (also created in 1961), and the 1963 Limited Nuclear Test Ban Treaty, the first arms control treaty between the United States and the Soviet Union. He was, in short, an advocate of standing up to the Soviet Union militarily while also an advocate of using peaceful means to promote American interests.

Those competing instincts carried over to Vietnam. A Humphrey aide, Ted Van Dyke, recalled, "Humphrey was always equivocal and a bit confused on Vietnam. He was torn two ways. On the one hand, he bought into the anti-Communist Cold War context at that time. On the other hand, he wanted everything limited to an advisory role only."[26] Edward Lansdale, with his "Concept for Victory," gave Humphrey a way to square the circle: to support South Vietnam without sending American boys into battle.

The Minnesotan became Lansdale's biggest booster in the U.S. government. When he did not have time to see Lansdale and Phillips himself, he delegated that task to his chief of staff, William Connell, a hard-liner on Vietnam who had served in the Navy in World War II and who was at odds with more dovish staffers like Van Dyke. Connell later said that Lansdale was "a very decent person, very intelligent" who was "obsessed with an idea . . . a revolutionary idea," and "proba-

bly sacrificed a career to try to get something done." He was "probably
a little nutty," but then, Connell reflected, "most people that get things
done and shake things up have to be a little nutty."[27]

Lansdale sent Connell an early draft of the "Concept for Victory"
and incorporated Connell's suggested changes.[28] With Connell's help,
Humphrey then drafted a memorandum to President Johnson, dated
June 8, 1964, extolling Lansdale's ideas and urging that Lansdale be
sent to Vietnam to implement them. He described Lansdale as "the key
American figure in Magsaysay's defeat of the Huk forces in the Philippines, the key figure in the development of counter-insurgency work
in the Defense Department, as well as being the key adviser to Diem
in the first two years of his reign." His letter concluded, "It is strongly
suggested that the President ask Lansdale to discuss this whole matter
with him."[29]

Such a strong suggestion coming from the Senate minority whip—a
man whom Johnson already had in mind as his vice president—could
not simply be ignored. But that did not mean that Johnson had any
intention of following his guidance. While Johnson valued Humphrey's skills as an orator, he had little respect for his future vice president's political or military acumen. Humphrey, he said disdainfully, is
"all heart and no balls."[30]

There is no evidence that Johnson even read Humphrey's proposal.
His aides, who did read it, delivered a withering assessment. Major
General Charles V. "Ted" Clifton, the president's senior military assistant, defended the use of "heavy weapons" as being necessary to defeat
North Vietnamese regulars, even at the cost of inflicting civilian casualties. And he dismissed calls for more civic action: "Our advisers have
as their primary mission stabilizing the insurgency and protecting
their own lives. I am afraid that the civic action effort will have to come
later or be performed by a separate group of people." This was a perfect reflection of the mindset that would relegate counterinsurgency—
"the other war," it would come to be called—to an irrelevant adjunct to
the big-war effort run by generals who shared Clifton's conventional
mindset.[31]

Instead of seeing Lansdale personally, as Humphrey had urged,

Johnson dismissed the whole matter with a handwritten scribble on a memo: "This is good. Carefully comb Humphrey for all ideas and then forward to appropriate officials."[32]

◆

LANSDALE'S IDEAS were not implemented by the "appropriate officials"—and there was never much hope they would be. On June 26, 1964, just as his "Concept for Victory" was getting a brush-off from the administration, Lansdale wrote presciently to Bill Connell that "the Taylor–Johnson team is only a better grade of Lodge . . . but doing the same old thing (even though doing more of the same old thing)." He was no more impressed by the well-turned-out Westmoreland or his key staff officers. "Deep down," they "look upon Vietnam as a limited war, not as a revolution." In Lansdale's view, the choice confronting the military was simple: "Are paddy farmers in a combat zone to be shot just because they inadvertently are standing in the way of Vietcong targets or are they to be protected and helped?"[33] Lansdale strongly suspected that Westmoreland would choose the former option, and events would vindicate his foreboding.

Once again, Lansdale's advice was being ignored by immodest officials who thought they had all the answers but lacked any grasp of on-the-ground reality in Vietnam. Denied yet again any semblance of power, Lansdale was relegated to his habitual role of observer and critic from the sidelines, even if his office was now located next to the seat of power. But then the disparity of influence between the White House and the Executive Office Building is infinitely wider than the few yards that separate those two structures. In Food for Peace, Lansdale had found a way to keep busy but not what he most wanted: a way to influence America's Vietnam policy.

27

Escalation

I'm scared to death of putting ground forces in, but I'm more
frightened about losing a bunch of planes from lack of security.
—LYNDON JOHNSON

AMBASSADOR Maxwell Taylor's tenure in Saigon began during the
tense summer of 1964, dominated by news of the disappearance
in rural Mississippi of three civil rights workers whose bullet-riddled
bodies were finally recovered after a six-week FBI manhunt. Upon
arriving in Saigon, the general-turned-diplomat soon apprehended that
the situation in southern Vietnam was even more volatile than in the
southern United States. Given the internecine political warfare that
had embroiled South Vietnam, he proved no more able than Henry
Cabot Lodge to work with the military junta or to ease it out of power.
The Johnson administration was still supporting General Nguyen
Khanh, but Taylor realized that he was "too clever for his own good."
Far from unifying the armed forces or rallying the country behind the
war effort, Khanh was alienating "his colleagues by his sudden turns
and dodges."[1]

In August 1964, emboldened by the Tonkin Gulf Resolution, Khanh
declared a state of emergency, cracked down on dissent, and introduced

a new constitution that would make him president, displacing the current chief of state, General Duong Van Minh. This power grab led to vocal protests from militant students, Catholics, and Buddhists. Khanh asked Taylor for support; Taylor infuriated Khanh by refusing to grant it. Khanh had to revoke the charter and return Big Minh as chief of state for the time being.

On September 13, 1964, just two months before the American presidential election, two lower-ranking generals who declared themselves to be Diem loyalists attempted yet another in a seemingly never-ending series of coups. "The sound of tank engines and the sudden appearance of unfamiliar troops at strategic points in Saigon had now become commonplace," noted an American diplomat.[2] Khanh just barely held on to power with the support of a new faction of generals nicknamed the Young Turks, led by Air Vice Marshal Nguyen Cao Ky and Army General Nguyen Van Thieu, two men who would loom larger in South Vietnam's future. A month later, in October 1964, Khanh ostensibly left politics altogether, appointing himself commander in chief of the armed forces while making Tran Van Huong, an aged former mayor of Saigon, the new prime minster. A High National Council of civilian worthies was formed to write a new constitution and oversee the transfer of power to civilians. This arrangement did not last any longer than those that had preceded it. In December 1964, shortly after Lyndon Johnson's landslide win over Barry Goldwater, the Young Turks tried to persuade the High National Council to retire all military officers with more than twenty-five years of service, thus eliminating their superiors and rivals. When the High National Council, itself packed with aging eminences, refused this request, Khanh and the Young Turks dissolved the council and sacked Huong.

Maxwell Taylor, brimming with a quasi-colonial arrogance that the Vietnamese had seen before, was irate. Utterly lacking in Lansdale's diplomatic skills, he called in a group of Vietnamese generals and lectured them: "I told you all clearly . . . that we Americans are tired of coups. Apparently I wasted my words." The generals did not appreciate being treated, in Ky's words, as if they were "errant schoolboys who had been caught stealing apples from an orchard,"[3] and they left "white-faced with fury."[4] Refusing to back down, the four-star ambassador soon was telling Khanh that he "had lost confidence in him as an ally."[5] Khanh retaliated by giving interviews accusing Taylor of wanting to reimpose a colonial regime.[6] In short, by the beginning of 1965, while Edward Lansdale was still laboring in obscurity at the Food for Peace program, relations between the leading American representative in Saigon and the leaders of the South Vietnamese government had become just as poisonous as they had been in the months leading up to the anti-Diem coup at the end of 1963.

Yet another coup broke out on February 18, 1965. This mutiny was suppressed, but by now the other generals had had enough of Khanh. He was luckier than Diem. Instead of being executed, he was merely sent into exile; he would wind up running a "shabby" Asian restaurant in West Palm Beach.[7] A new civilian government was appointed under Phan Huy Quat, a physician who had been a leading figure in the Caravelle circle which had plotted against Diem. But Quat was no more able to rule effectively than any of Diem's other successors had been, and in June 1965 yet another military coup occurred.

South Vietnam's latest rulers were the flashy Vice Marshal Ky as prime minister and the more reserved General Thieu as head of state. The 1963 coup had been good for them; while Diem was still in power, they were a lieutenant colonel and a colonel, respectively. The two of them, in charge of what was at least the tenth government since Diem's downfall, would now jockey for power to see who would emerge as South Vietnam's next strongman.

◆

EDWARD LANSDALE kept himself well informed about the dispiriting developments in South Vietnam through his regular contacts with South Vietnamese and Americans serving there. On November 26, 1964, for example, Edmund Navarro, a USAID officer stationed in Tay Ninh, the Cao Dai seat located fifty miles northeast of Saigon, wrote to him, "I am losing faith everyday in our ability to win." Echoing Lansdale's own opposition to a purely military response, Navarro wrote, "The military can send home 15,000 men right now and I honestly believe the other 6,000 can do a better job. You will find most of the former in and around Saigon only."[8]

A few days later, USAID's Bert Fraleigh, who had returned to Saigon, wrote to Lansdale, "These are sad days here. Rural Affairs morale has hit rock-bottom as has, in fact, all of USOM's morale [U.S. Operating Mission, the name for the USAID office]. We don't know what to expect next from either USOM, the Vietnamese or our own government."[9] Shortly thereafter, Fraleigh was fired by a capricious USOM director who refused to leave Saigon for more than a few hours to see for himself what was going on in the rest of the country. Another Lansdale friend, Lou Conein of the CIA, orchestrator of the 1963 coup, had been expelled a few months earlier by Ambassador Taylor, who unfairly blamed Conein, the embassy's main line of communications to the generals, for his strained relations with Khanh.[10]

Throughout the fall of 1964, in a series of speeches, letters, and policy papers, Lansdale tried to give voice to disaffected officials such as Navarro, Fraleigh, and Conein by hammering away at the basic theme that the only way to save South Vietnam was to implement his program for political action. His most high-profile foray into the debate was an article for *Foreign Affairs*, the country's premier foreign-policy journal. Lansdale's essay in the October 1964 issue, "Viet Nam: Do We Understand Revolution?," was essentially an unclassified version of the "Concept for Victory" paper minus the suggestion that he and his team be sent to Vietnam. The essay's most-quoted line was, "the Communists have let loose a revolutionary idea in Viet Nam and . . . it will not die by being ignored, bombed or smothered by us. Ideas do not die in such ways." In a "people's war," he explained, firepower was counterproductive: "When the military opens fire at long range, whether by infantry weapons, artillery or air strike, on a reported Viet Cong concentration in a hamlet or village full of civilians, the Vietnamese officers who give those orders and the American advisers who let them 'get away with it' are helping defeat the cause of freedom." Lansdale did not argue for leaving Vietnam, as some were already doing, but rather for "conducting a successful counter-insurgency campaign." Citing previous efforts in Malaya and the Philippines, he wrote, "The great lesson was that there must be a heartfelt cause to which the legitimate government is pledged, a cause which makes a stronger appeal to the people than the Communist cause."

At Yale University on November 23, 1964, Lansdale rejected any suggestion that victory was impossible: "It's not a question of *can* we win, but a resolve that we *must* win."[11] In a paper entitled "Thoughts on Vietnam," written on New Year's Eve and sent to Hubert Humphrey, he insisted that if his ideas were implemented the result "will be a definite win during the new U.S. Administration, a win credited to the leadership of President Johnson."[12]

For the first time, such importuning was finding a receptive audience in the Oval Office. On December 30, 1964, the president wrote to Ambassador Taylor suggesting that "we ought to be ready to make full use of the specialized skills of *men who are skillful with Vietnamese*, even if they are not always the easiest men to handle in a country team. . . . To put it another way, I continue to believe that we should have the most sensitive, persistent, and attentive Americans that we can find in touch with Vietnamese of every kind and quality"[13] (italics added). The original draft of Johnson's letter had included the words "of the general type of Lansdale and Conein" in place of "men who are skillful with Vietnamese"; McGeorge Bundy must have blown a gasket and taken the names out, but the meaning remained clear.[14] Coming from a president who placed such a premium on loyalty, Johnson's willingness to even consider sending advisers who "are not always the easiest men to handle" was a sign of how desperate he was becoming to find some answer to the challenge of Vietnam.

Taylor, predictably, brushed off this suggestion, replying to the president, "On the whole, the quality of our personnel in Vietnam is high and I believe they meet pretty well your description of 'sensitive, persistent, and attentive Americans.' "[15] Maybe so, but their insights were not informing American decision-making or influencing the Vietnamese themselves in a more constructive direction.

◆

JOHNSON, CONSUMED by his struggle to implement historic civil rights legislation, did not press to implement Lansdale's policy ideas any more than he pressed for Lansdale's dispatch to Vietnam. Rather than trying to improve the quality of South Vietnam's governance or to restrain its military, he was mulling the options spelled out for him by McGeorge Bundy in a January 27, 1965, memo: "The first [option] is to use our military power in the Far East and to force a change of Communist policy. The second is to deploy all our resources along a track of negotiation, aimed at salvaging what little can be preserved with no major addition to our present military risks." "Bob [McNamara] and I," Bundy added, "tend to favor the first course," that is, the military course.[16]

The argument for escalation finally became incontrovertible to Lyndon Johnson on February 7, 1965. That afternoon he received word from Bundy, who was visiting South Vietnam, that the Vietcong had just attacked an American air base and Special Forces camp at Pleiku in the Central Highlands. Ten American aircraft had been destroyed and fifteen more damaged; eight American soldiers had been killed and more than a hundred wounded. At a White House meeting, LBJ said, in that theatrical Texas way of his, "I have kept my shotgun over the mantel and the bullets in the basement for a long time now, but . . . the enemy is killing my personnel and I could not expect them to continue their work if I did not authorize them to take steps to defend themselves."[17]

On his flight home from Saigon, Bundy completed a memorandum advocating "the development and execution of a policy of *sustained reprisal* against North Vietnam." The intent was to convince Hanoi that the cost of attacking the South was too high without risking a wider war. So the air strikes would be "reduced or stopped when outrages in the South are reduced or stopped." Rather than mobilizing the American public for a war against North Vietnam, Bundy recommended that "we should execute our reprisal policy with as low a level of public noise as possible"—"we do not wish to boast about them in ways that make it hard for Hanoi to shift its ground."[18]

This was the genesis of Operation Rolling Thunder, a bombing campaign that over the next three years would dump more ordnance on North Vietnam than had been dropped on all of Europe in World War II.[19] But in keeping with the desire of the president and his advisers to exquisitely calibrate the level of violence, Johnson personally oversaw the selection of targets. A master negotiator, he viewed bombs not as instruments of destruction but rather, in the words of his biographer Doris Kearns Goodwin, as a way of "bargaining without words."[20] Hanoi, however, did not understand what Johnson was up to. To the Politburo, bombs combined with offers to negotiate simply looked like duplicity.

The commitment of American airpower brought with it the commitment of American ground forces, because, as numerous attacks had made clear, South Vietnamese troops could not adequately guard American bases. "I'm scared to death of putting ground forces in," Johnson confided to McNamara, "but I'm more frightened about losing a bunch of planes from lack of security."[21]

On March 9, 1965, the front page of the *New York Times* depicted Marines storming ashore from landing craft onto the beaches of Da Nang, a coastal city in central Vietnam, as if it were Iwo Jima. Thirty-five hundred leathernecks, two battalions' worth, were to provide security at the nearby American air base. They were not supposed to undertake offensive operations or engage in any combat at all unless first attacked. But it was not long before what a later generation would call "mission creep" set in. By August, despite growing unrest at home, there were more than 125,000 American troops in South Vietnam, and they were beginning to take the offensive against the Vietcong. By the end of what would become a pivotal year, the U.S. commitment would swell to 184,000 troops.

◆

THE AMERICAN military escalation was supported by almost all of Johnson's inner circle—but not by the liberal stalwart and vice president, Hubert Humphrey. He remained convinced that the Lansdale approach, focusing on political reform and advisers rather than firepower and combat troops, was still the way to go. At a National Security Council meeting on February 10, 1965, called to discuss a response to a Vietcong attack on a U.S. outpost, Johnson went around the room asking whether anyone dissented from the meeting's consensus that it was imperative to launch a retaliatory air strike. Humphrey, being his usual ebullient self, spoke up to express "doubts as to whether the strike should take place today" while Soviet Premier Alexei Kosygin was visiting North Vietnam. In fact, "he had mixed feelings about whether we should retaliate as Secretary McNamara had recommended." Johnson seemed to take such reservations seriously. He suggested that the United States send "a message to the Soviet officials as to why we have to react the way we are." The meeting then moved on, with the president authorizing "execution of the strike plan as revised" before everyone walked out.[22]

The vice president did not think that anything momentous had occurred: he had expressed his dissent, the president had heard him and decided to act anyway. In Humphrey's mind he was doing nothing more than what he had done before when he had worked with Lyndon Johnson in the Senate—nothing more than any good counselor would do for his commander in chief. The following day, he asked his aide John Reilly to "keep a good file on Vietnam. Shortly I shall be sitting down with the president, the secretary of state and others to discuss U.S. policy on Southeast Asia in all its implications." Reilly had to inform him what he had learned from another staffer: that Humphrey was not going to be sitting down anymore with anyone in power to discuss Vietnam. The president was now conducting top-level meetings on Vietnam without notifying the vice president.

Without realizing it, Humphrey had committed an unforgivable sin in the eyes of Lyndon Johnson by contradicting him in front of others. As far as the president was concerned, Humphrey had broken his pledge of "complete and unswerving loyalty." Johnson wanted Humphrey, as he told his intimates, "to kiss my ass in Macy's window at high noon and tell me it smells like roses." By that demeaning standard, the vice president was falling egregiously short.[23]

The president could not by statute bar the vice president from meetings of the National Security Council, so Johnson simply moved the key deliberations to Tuesday lunches where the invitation list did not include the vice president. For the rest of 1965—a crucial year in the Americanization of the Vietnam War—Humphrey would be almost as powerless as Lansdale. He was even cut out of domestic policy, in spite of his long and passionate advocacy of the president's civil rights and social-welfare initiatives. Johnson inflicted on Humphrey every petty humiliation he could think of. He stopped Humphrey from hiring assistants. He dictated that Humphrey ask his permission for the use of an airplane or the presidential yacht—and then he would capriciously turn down Humphrey's requests. And he not only demanded that Humphrey submit every one of his speeches for presidential approval; he took a meat ax to Humphrey's planned remarks, slashing them so brutally that Humphrey's friends thought he had lost his oratorical gifts.[24]

Yet Humphrey continued to be the good soldier in public, never letting slip any hint of dissent. So staunch a defender of Johnson's conduct did Humphrey remain that soon he began to alienate his own constituency—the liberals—who were turning against the war. They could not figure out what had happened to Hubert, and they started to look for other champions such as Robert Kennedy and Eugene McCarthy. This was the essential tragedy of Hubert Humphrey, a man publicly forced to defend a cause he did not believe in and suffer the resulting brickbats from his closest friends. Humphrey's old friend the novelist Saul Bellow, who had come to know him in the 1940s while Humphrey was mayor of Minneapolis and Bellow was teaching at the University of Minnesota, had thought of writing a newspaper or magazine article about the vice president but dropped the idea, "anticipating no pleasure . . . in writing about poor Hubert's misery as LBJ's captive."[25]

◆

WITH HUMPHREY's fall from grace, Lansdale had less influence over Vietnam policy than ever. "It's sheer agony to be shoved to the sidelines and watch the mistakes being made by the glory-grabbers," he wrote in May 1965 to Robert Shaplen of *The New Yorker*.[26]

Luckily for Lansdale, he did find another supporter: Senator Thomas Dodd, Democrat of Connecticut, a friend of Humphrey's, a former Nuremberg prosecutor, and a Cold War hawk who would soon experience a precipitous downfall—he would be censured by the Senate in 1967 for diverting campaign funds to personal use. (His son

Christopher would later follow him into the Senate.) Dodd wrote to the president on February 23, 1965, urging the dispatch of a "special liaison group" to help the embassy in Saigon "to establish the broadest and most effective possible liaison with the army leaders, with the Buddhists, with the intellectual community, and with the Vietnamese political leaders." Attached was a list of eight men whom Dodd suggested sending. The very first name on the list was Edward Lansdale, who "enjoys a near legendary reputation in the Far East."[27]

As normally happens, this missive wound up on the desk of the Vietnam expert at the National Security Council, a post formerly filled by Roger Hilsman and Michael Forrestal and now held by CIA officer Chester L. Cooper. His reaction was both wary and weary. "I know the President sometimes must get the feeling that he is being pursued by Lansdale or, at least, by the advocates of Lansdale," he wrote to National Security Adviser McGeorge Bundy. "For whatever it's worth, I am in close touch with the General and am on the receiving end of a considerable number of ideas and projects which he and his friends have advanced. Some of these are quite interesting, and we are exploring them. It may well be that Lansdale could be more effectively used than he is at present—either here or in Saigon. But Lansdale is one thing—a platoon of Lansdales is another."[28]

On July 27, 1965, five months after his first letter, Senator Dodd tried again, writing to the president, "Because of the very grave situation in Vietnam, I again wish to urge that some consideration be given to assigning Major General Edward G. Lansdale to Vietnam." This time, however, the response was not a curt dismissal. At the bottom of Dodd's letter, Lyndon Johnson scrawled, "Tell him I'm going to get Lansdale out to Viet Nam."[29]

◆

How HAD this miracle been wrought? How had Lansdale finally prevailed in his efforts to return to Saigon, a campaign that in the past had been met with nothing but frustration and derision? In an unexpected twist of fate, his savior was not the man he respected and even revered—Hubert Horatio Humphrey—but a man he viewed with contempt and held responsible for the death of his friend Ngo Dinh Diem: Henry Cabot Lodge Jr.

Maxwell Taylor had agreed to serve as ambassador for only one year, and when his time expired in July 1965 there was little inclination to extend his stay in Saigon. Increasingly President Johnson was listening not to Taylor but to his onetime protégé General William Westmoreland, who was determined to introduce American combat troops into South Vietnam. In a turnabout from Taylor's stance in 1961, when he had advocated sending combat forces under the guise of flood relief, he had now decided it wasn't a good idea after all to Americanize the war, that it would simply alienate the nationalist and xenophobic Vietnamese. When he saw that troops would be sent anyway, Taylor suggested confining them to a defensive role in coastal areas. Westmoreland rejected this "enclave strategy," which he viewed as "an inglorious, static use of U.S. forces in overpopulated areas with little chance of direct or immediate impact on the outcome of events."[30] Westy wanted American forces to gain the glory of seeking out and destroying the Communist Main Force units in the mountainous jungles of the Central Highlands. By opposing the big-unit approach, Taylor lost his standing with the president. Even though Johnson had little respect for the patrician Henry Cabot Lodge, he decided to send him as ambassador to Saigon for the same reason that John F. Kennedy had: to provide bipartisan cover for a controversial policy.

On July 27, 1965, shortly after his confirmation hearing, Lodge went to lunch with Lansdale at a restaurant in Georgetown and said he wanted to bring him back to Vietnam. As Lansdale recalled the conversation, Lodge said that this was President Johnson's idea. Rumor also had it that Senator Dodd had threatened to put a hold on Lodge's nomination unless he enlisted Lansdale's help.[31] Whether that was true or not (Lodge later denied it),[32] Lodge was an astute enough politician to realize it would be best to propitiate Lansdale's congressional supporters.

Lodge reprised the suggestion he had made in September 1963 for Lansdale to take over the CIA station in Saigon. Knowing that the CIA would oppose his appointment, Lansdale demurred.[33] He was no more amenable to Lodge's suggestion that he become the political adviser to a province chief in the hope of turning that province into a pacification showcase. Advising a mere province chief was beneath the dignity of a "king-maker" who had previously molded entire countries and would surely puzzle the Vietnamese, who would wonder whether he was grooming the province chief as the next ruler of South Vietnam.[34] Lansdale was more amenable when Lodge suggested that he "take over pacification"[35] for the entire country. *Now that was more like it!* Lodge even offered to let him bring along a team to help him.

Lansdale agreed on the spot. And why wouldn't he, after having lobbied so long for this very assignment? He would finally be going back to Saigon with a chance to implement his most deeply cherished beliefs.

◆

THERE WAS another, unspoken reason why Edward Lansdale was so eager to depart for South Vietnam: there was not much to keep him in the District of Columbia. He did not particularly like his job at Food for Peace, and his sons were grown and gone.

Now twenty-six years old, Ted Lansdale had graduated from the University of Arizona in the spring of 1964 and that fall entered the U.S. Air Force as a second lieutenant, eventually to specialize in public affairs. Ted had no interest in following in his father's footsteps: "I figured two Lansdales in counterinsurgency—with one not adept at it all—that wouldn't do."[36] He was already engaged and would marry the following year.

Ted's younger brother, Pete, twenty-three years old, had even less interest in following their father's path. He had joined the Army in 1963 as a private, seeking an alternative to the junior college where he was getting poor grades. (He would eventually get his bachelor's degree through part-time study at George Washington University.) He even volunteered for airborne training, but soon grew disenchanted. He later recalled, "I had experienced pneumonia in basic training due to cadre incompetence, and saw enough ineptness and incompetence at all levels and rank to make me realize that I had made a big mistake in enlisting."[37] Pete jumped at a chance to volunteer for duty with the Third

U.S. Infantry Regiment, better known as the Old Guard. Stationed at Fort Myer, across the river from his parents' house, the Old Guard took part in John F. Kennedy's funeral and other high-profile ceremonies; it would become particularly busy transferring the remains of dead servicemen as the war in Vietnam intensified. Pete would marry even before his older brother—in October 1965. The following year he would leave the Army to begin a successful career as a telephone company executive.[38]

Helen Lansdale remained at home, along with Koko, the poodle Ed had brought from Vietnam in 1956. But while Ed had to a large extent repaired relations with his wife, it was evident that spending time with her was not a priority that could compete with the allure of Asia.

As he prepared to set off for Vietnam, Lansdale's thoughts, predictably, were not of home but of adventures to come. Ed wrote excitedly to Pat Kelly, "In case you hear rumors about my rushing out to save a country again, they'll probably be true this time. Lodge has asked me to go along to Vietnam with him as his assistant, to help out in a lot of non-military things. It now looks as though this might get by all the knifings-in-the-back in Washington, and that I'll really go. I've asked for a staff—including some of the old gang—and this too looks like it will be a go."[39] In case he stopped in Manila on his way to Saigon, he asked, "Can I buy a martini at the airport on the way through so you can look at my gray hair while I look at your stretch pants? State Dept has to employ me for this job, so I might well be in striped trousers and sweat shirt."[40]

Lansdale had every reason to feel elated. Little did he suspect that he was about to enter the most frustrating and difficult period of his life. His proverbial dream job would turn out to be a nightmare. A few years later, he was to reflect ruefully, "Why did I go to Viet Nam in 1965 to help the murderers of my friend Ngo Dinh Diem? . . . I think that sentiment overcame judgment."[41]

28

The Impossible
Missions Force

*[Lansdale] was the leader of the cult and I was a member of
that cult.*

—Daniel Ellsberg

Edward Lansdale arrived in Vietnam in the late summer of
1965, at a time when Americans could already see glimmerings
of the antiwar protests and race riots that would soon convulse their
country. The Watts neighborhood of Los Angeles had become a veritable battle zone between August 11 and August 16. More sedately, if
ultimately of greater consequence for the war just beginning, at least
twenty thousand people picketed the White House on April 17 to
demand that "the U.S. get out of Vietnam." The protest was organized
by Students for a Democratic Society, a New Left group ("left-lean-
ing but non-Communist," in the words of a news report) that claimed
chapters at sixty-three campuses across the country. By later standards, the protest was polite and decorous. The *New York Times* noted,
"Beards and blue jeans mixed with Ivy tweeds and an occasional clerical collar in the crowd. The marchers seemed to be enjoying their holiday from exams." Most Americans still supported the president and the

war. This was no mass revolt, but it was the beginning of a movement that within two years would paralyze many American campuses and leave the president feeling under siege in the White House.[1]

Pop songs are often an accurate barometer of the national mood, and the release of a hit called "Eve of Destruction" by a former pipefitter named Barry McGuire captured the anxiety of the times. Its lyrics, proclaiming "The eastern world it is explodin' / Violence flarin', bullets loadin'," were particularly apt, given that the Marine Corps had just launched the first major battle of the American war in Vietnam.

◆

OPERATION STARLITE was intended as a preemptive assault on the First Vietcong Regiment, a Main Force unit, which, according to American intelligence reports, was planning to attack the newly established Marine air base at Chu Lai, sixty miles south of Da Nang. In reality, the Vietcong were not planning any such offensive; they preferred to wear down the Marines with hit-and-run raids. This was only the first sign of how faulty American battlefield intelligence in Vietnam would turn out to be. The Vietcong, on the other hand, consistently had accurate information about the ponderous movements of the increasingly bloated American war machine. They knew Starlite was coming, and they were ready for it.

The plan, drawn up by veterans of the Pacific island campaign of World War II, called for Marines to land simultaneously from sea and air on the Van Tuong Peninsula, taking advantage of a new technology—helicopters—that had not been available during the struggle against Japan. The amphibious assault force, equipped with M-48 tanks and armored amphibian tractors (amtracs), would drive the Vietcong into the blocking force, which was to be inserted inland by H-34 helicopters. And then heavy American firepower—delivered not only by the Marine infantry and armor, helicopter gunships, and fixed-wing aircraft but also by three warships offshore—would annihilate the fifteen hundred or so Vietcong caught in the vise.

Armed with mortars, machine guns, recoilless rifles, and small arms, the veteran Vietcong fighters were waiting when the Marines landed in the early morning hours of August 18, 1965. The fighting was especially intense around the hamlets of Nam Yen 3 and An Cuong 2, both honeycombed with "spider holes" and bunkers. The Marine infantrymen had to back off and let F-4 Phantoms and A-4 Skyhawks finish the job. These jet-powered aircraft swooped in to drop "snake and nape"—250-pound Snakeye bombs and 500-pound napalm canisters that were certain to kill civilians along with enemy fighters. When the Marines continued taking small-arms fire from Nam Yen 3, they called in tanks, which leveled all the remaining houses with their main guns. As an official Marine Corps history later noted, "Although attempts were made to avoid civilian casualties, some villages were completely destroyed by supporting arms when it became obvious the enemy occupied fortified positions in them." A few years later, at the height of the American war in 1968, an anonymous Army major would be quoted saying, "It became necessary to destroy the town to save it." The philosophy embodied in those chilling words was already evident in Operation Starlite.

The Marines could congratulate themselves that Starlite was "the first major U.S. battle victory of the Vietnamese war," and Ambassador Henry Cabot Lodge could gloat that it was a "milestone" that showed "that the U.S. can with relative certainty prevent the Viet Cong from ever becoming a regular army." But the cost of this "victory" was high. The Marines lost 54 men killed and 200 wounded out of 5,500 engaged, while claiming to have killed more than 600 of the enemy, an estimate that was likely as exaggerated as "body counts" always were. It was a foretaste of what was in store for other units, including the army's helicopter-borne First Cavalry Division (Airmobile), which three months later was to lose nearly 250 soldiers in a battle in the Ia Drang Valley of the Central Highlands against North Vietnamese regulars.

And to what end? The Marines, who thought they had destroyed the First Vietcong Regiment, were in for a nasty shock four months later during Operation Harvest Moon, when they encountered the very same Main Force unit again near Chu Lai—and once again it was back at full strength and in control of the area. This was a sign of how easily the Vietcong could replenish their losses from a population base they controlled and how quickly they could reinfiltrate territory from which they had been temporarily evicted by an American offensive. It was an early warning, a warning unheeded, that in this type of war conventional combat tactics could produce lots and lots of casualties—to Americans and Vietnamese, combatants and noncombatants alike—but not decisive results.[2]

◆

THESE EVENTS—an increasingly Americanized war in Vietnam, an increasingly divided nation at home—did not form an auspicious backdrop for Edward Lansdale's arrival in Saigon on August 29, 1965, after an absence of more than four years. Like any other airline passenger coming to Saigon in those days, he would have felt the turbulence of conflict even before landing: aircraft, both military and civilian, were now doing corkscrew turns and heading practically straight down like a cannonball falling out of the sky in order to avoid possible ground fire. Once he stepped onto the tarmac of Tan Son Nhut Airport and into the blast-oven heat that was characteristic of Saigon year-round, he would have seen, as did a young American officer named Larry Gwin, an airport teeming with military activity: "Small mountains of military hardware covered every available inch of the field's macadam surface. Jeeps and trucks and forklifts busted through the maze. Shirtless American GIs struggled and sweated, pulled and tugged, lifted and lugged. . . . Two camouflaged Phantom jets, their wings heavily laden with bombs, took off from an adjacent runway with a terrible roar."[3]

Proceeding into the teeming capital city, which he vividly remembered from more placid and pleasant days, Lansdale would have seen American military vehicles joining civilian traffic on the increasingly clogged streets. To make way for even more vehicles, the U.S. Military Assistance Command—Vietnam (MACV) had widened the streets, cutting down hundreds of Saigon's "grand, old" trees in the four and a half years since Lansdale had last been there.[4] By mid-1966, there would be thirty-six thousand Americans in and around Saigon.[5] These well-heeled newcomers drove housing prices through the roof. And because each American-occupied apartment required its own air conditioner and refrigerator, the demand for electricity far outstripped the capacity of the city's old power plant. Brownouts ensued. To meet the surging power demand, the U.S. military at first anchored generator barges in the Saigon River and then flew in thousands of small generators that could be installed outside each billet. Bert Fraleigh of USAID, who returned for another tour at roughly the same time as Lansdale, noted, "Within a few weeks, the quiet old city was filled around-the-clock with a strong, low-pitched hum from these generators, and the previously clear, perfumed, tropical air became a brown, diesel-fumed miasma, which curiously seemed to cling about forty feet off the ground."[6]

In search of female company, off-duty soldiers and contractors dressed in Hawaiian shirts would gambol around the bars spreading like a fungus from the city center all the way to Tan Son Nhut Airport—as they had once spread in Seoul, Tokyo, Manila, and other Asian cities with a large American military presence. Bar girls would beseech prospective clients: "GI, buy me one drink?" Actual prostitutes would be cruder: "Boom-boom, GI? Fuck-suck?" Pimps with pompadours would be hovering nearby, ready to skim part of the day's take. An entirely new argot developed between GIs and the profusion of Vietnamese eager to separate them from their piastres. "Gimme cigarette," kids would beg passing American troops. "You numbah one." (Number one meant "very good.") If the GIs refused, the street kids would denounce them: "Cheap Charlie, number-ten cheap Charlie." (Number ten meant "very bad.")[7]

The free-spending American ways were driving up inflation and creating an anomalous situation where prostitutes were making more than army majors.[8] Many Vietnamese soldiers succumbed to corruption to supplement their incomes. More honest officers would hang up their uniforms at the end of the day and use their personal cars or motor scooters to act as cab drivers for big-spending GIs out for a good time on the town, a necessity that was deeply humiliating to the proud Vietnamese, always mindful of their "face," or reputation, in this Confucian society.[9]

Americans were not the only newcomers. Refugees fleeing the fighting in the countryside were also inundating Saigon, transforming this once elegant French provincial capital into an urban gallimaufry of every possible ingredient. The ramshackle South Vietnamese government simply could not cope with the influx. Garbage was piling up, potholes were not being repaired, bus service was becoming unpredictable. Surveying the scene, the USIA's Howard Simpson concluded, "The sleepy colonial capital had become a crowded, dirty wartime metropolis."[10] Lansdale thought that "Saigon looks a bit run-down and war-weary right now but maybe," he added, with typical optimism, "we can put some spark back in."[11]

◆

THAT WAS a tall order—to revive the spirits of a deflated city and a country ravaged by war—but, then, great expectations accompanied Lansdale on his return to Vietnam. Upon hearing of his appointment, many friends wrote with some version of the sentiment expressed by retired Admiral Arleigh Burke: "I and a lot of other Americans took heart when we heard that you were returning to Viet Nam."[12]

Practically every major American newspaper—and most of the minor ones—ran breathless accounts of Lansdale's new role. Mentions of *The Quiet American* and *The Ugly American* were obligatory. There was even a new fictionalized version of the Lansdale legend to read: the English-language translation of *Yellow Fever*, a novel by the French journalist Jean Larteguy, came out in 1965. Its characters included an American colonel named Lionel Terryman, clearly based on Lansdale (*terre* means "land" in French), who is advising a Diem-like president named Dinh-Tu. Larteguy wrote of Terryman, "He could get hold of the most bigoted old scoundrel, the most inexperienced novice and, out of a gang leader, make a president of the republic; out of an odious and tyrannical old fogey, an all-powerful dictator."[13] Little wonder that the *New York Times* wrote that Landale had "made a rather legendary reputation in Asia in the nineteen-fifties."[14] Stanley Karnow of the *Washington Post* wrote that, like T. E. Lawrence, "Lansdale has inspired admiration, ridicule—and, above all, controversy." He quoted "one U.S. official" as saying, "If he doesn't produce a miracle, his friends will be disappointed and his enemies delighted."[15]

When Lansdale landed at Tan Son Nhut Airport, wearing a dark suit with a white shirt and skinny tie, he was met by a gaggle of fifteen reporters and photographers who surrounded him as if he were a visiting movie star—Cary Grant, perhaps, or John Wayne. He had been expecting this and delivered a brief statement he had prepared en route: "When Ambassador Henry Cabot Lodge asked me to join him on his mission to Vietnam, I had the happy feeling that he was asking me to come back home again. Vietnam and Vietnamese friends have been so much in my thoughts, so close to my heart, even while I was 10,000 miles away, that Vietnam truly seems like home to me. So now I am home again."[16]

It was a good statement; it struck just the right note to win over the Vietnamese. As Lansdale subsequently wrote in a diplomatic cable, "Arrival statement about being members of Great Vietnamese Family stirred heart-warming emotional acceptance among wide circle Vietnam."[17] His statement did not engender such warm feelings in Helen Lansdale, who was not amused to read a news clipping of her husband proclaiming that he was finally home when he was thousands of miles away from the house they shared in Washington. "You sounded as though hurt a bit," Ed wrote to her apologetically a few days later. In his defense, he pleaded insincerity: "I have to make like a real feather merchant to get us all set in here again just the right way, so I know you'll understand when I sound off, it's for a real cause."[18] ("Feather merchant" was old military slang for someone who talked a lot but said little.) In fact, there is every reason to think that Lansdale was being sincere in what he had said at the airport. He really felt Saigon was where he belonged.

◆

LANSDALE'S FIRST days back were predictably harried as he tried to make up for years away by insinuating himself into the labyrinthine structures of power in Saigon. He was confronted, he noted, by "all this tremendous seeming confusion and seemingly ineluctable problems that are flooding me from all quarters . . . with so many, many folks to see and so many demands on time." With no quarters prepared for him, Lansdale took refuge temporarily in a series of hotels, where he checked in under an assumed name: "My sleeping arrangements have to keep being changed, because all the publicity of course aroused the other side—who now have all sorts of pictures of me. So, I just keep moving fast."[19]

He was, in any case, not getting much shut-eye. Ten days after arriving, Ed wrote home, "Can't sleep. Or, maybe just wide awake at the wrong time. I just was trying to figure out what the date is . . . and was shocked to find out how many days have gone by since I was here. It's just sort of a blur to me, of seeing people, of moving around all the time, of getting our group in place and running, of security, and of having to be eternally diplomatic with Americans and Vietnamese who are artfully playing their dealings with us."

Not surprisingly, the last thing on his mind was his twenty-second wedding anniversary on September 3. "I know you might have been expecting some word from me on our Anniversary," he wrote to Helen ("Darling"), "but honest Injun, the day was just another 18-hour work grind of puzzling out a seemingly million loose ends here and how to fit them all together. But, my thoughts were on you during the day, and I'd sure have been happier home than here, to give you a big hug and kiss for the day. I miss being home! Miss you!"[20] One wonders whether the exclamation points were meant to convince Helen or himself.

◆

IN SEPTEMBER 1966, CBS would air a new show called *Mission: Impossible*. It featured a group of secret agents who would assemble every week to battle dictators, mobsters, and other enemies designated by their unseen supervisor, "the secretary," who would deliver their orders via a self-destructing tape-recording that threatened to "disavow" any knowledge of their actions if they were caught or killed. As if anticipating the series, Lansdale was then in the process of assembling his own Impossible Missions Force in Saigon, known as the Senior Liaison Office, made up largely of the same individuals who had served with him previously in South Vietnam and, in some cases, before that in the Philippines.

"It is worth noting," Rufus Phillips later wrote, "that for those with established government positions, going out to Vietnam with Lansdale was not going to enhance a career. It was obvious from prior experience that bureaucratic enemies would be generated. For those with families it was a considerable sacrifice, since dependents were no longer allowed in Saigon. For members of his original team, it was a display of loyalty based on firsthand knowledge of how effective Lansdale could be and how he dealt with those who worked for him."[21] Phillips himself joined the team only temporarily; he came to Saigon for the first month to help them set up operations before returning home to run his father's engineering firm, which was negotiating to build a new airport in Jeddah, Saudi Arabia. In the future, he would act as a Washington liaison for Lansdale.

Others came out for longer periods in spite of their misgivings. Joe Redick, the French-speaking CIA officer, reprised his role as translator. He earned the nickname Mother—"an appellation that he does not precisely cherish," wrote another team member[22]—because he showed "so much solicitude" toward his teammates. Lou Conein, the covert operator who had overseen the coup that toppled Diem, was looking forward to a promised new assignment as a military attaché in Venezuela when he was called in by the CIA's deputy director, Richard Helms, and told, "Lou, you are going to Vietnam." Lou replied that he didn't want to go. Helms put a stop to that: "This is a directed assignment and you cannot refuse and you cannot let the agency down."[23] Once in Saigon, the hard-drinking Luigi would be referred to by his teammates as "the I & I (Intelligence and Intoxication) Officer."[24]

Other Lansdale associates from his 1950s heyday included the eccentric archaeologist-turned-intelligence officer Charles "Bo" Bohannan, his onetime deputy in the Philippines; the cautious CIA operative Joe Baker, who left his posting in Paris to become the team's executive officer, or second in command; the Army colonel (and Christian Science practitioner) Sam Karrick, who had helped direct South Vietnamese pacification in 1955; the former Philippine army officer Napoleon Valeriano, who was now on the CIA payroll and had helped train the Bay of Pigs invasion force; the erstwhile Shanghai symphony conductor and

anti-Japanese guerrilla Bernie Yoh, "an extremely brilliant and energetic man," in Henry Kissinger's estimation;[25] the economist Michael J.
Deutch, a warmhearted Russian-Jewish refugee who had arrived in
America by way of Belgium in 1940 and helped the war effort by devel-
oping synthetic rubber out of petroleum; and Hank Miller of the U.S.
Information Agency, who at six feet six inches towered over the Viet-
namese. One of the few team members with whom Lansdale did not
have a long relationship was the white-shoe Boston lawyer Charlie
Choate, who had been recommended by Henry Cabot Lodge's son.
With no experience in Vietnam but lots of idealism, Choate arrived
bearing a letter of introduction from the president of the Boston Bar
Association to the president of the Saigon Bar Association.[26]

Lansdale's team was a good one, but, like Lansdale himself, it sometimes seemed trapped in the past. The gonzo war reporter Michael
Herr, then of *Esquire* magazine, called Lansdale and Conein—the best-
known team members—"spook deities," but added, "As sure as heat
rises, their time was over. The war passed into the hard hands of firepower freaks out to eat the country whole, and with no fine touches
either, leaving the spooks on the beach."[27]

◆

BY THE end of September 1965, all of the members of the Senior Liaison Office had arrived and settled in. Lansdale moved into "a big barn
of a house, really two flats, or a duplex," located at 194 Cong Ly, on the
road to the airport. The four bedrooms were used as living quarters
and offices and the large living room as a conference and entertaining
space. Joining Lansdale were Joe Redick, Michael Deutch, and Hank
Miller. The team commandeered another house at 35 Nguyen Thong
for Sam Karrick, Bernie Yoh, and Charlie Choate. Just as at Cong Ly,
they had a cook and a "houseboy" to take care of them. As a pet they
kept a ten-foot boa constrictor, named Baby, given to them by Father
Nguyen Loc Hoa, the "fighting priest" defending the village of Binh
Hung. Bo Bohannan took up residence with the Filipino workers at the
Eastern Construction Company compound in Cholon; Eastern Construction, or Eccoi, was the successor to the Freedom Company. No

longer CIA funded, it was now working as a contractor for the Saigon government.[28]

The only team member who got his own villa, oddly enough, was its youngest and least experienced member. Writing a letter home to the wives of the team members, Mike Deutch described him jocularly: "Now I don't want to alarm you girls unduly—but I cannot dissimulate from you the skeleton in the team's closet—a young, handsome, presently unmarried team member (in fact, brace yourself—he is divorced—but he's only one exception that confirms the good rule of married men on the team, and it will never happen again). He is Dan Ellsberg of Rand and the Pentagon. It is his first trip to Asia, and he is free to enjoy the sight of the alluring ao-dais [dresses], but he is beginning to learn, and in time we will get him married."[29] Deutch was more prophetic than he could have realized in describing Daniel Ellsberg as the "skeleton in the team's closet," since five years later he would gain worldwide notoriety as the leaker of the top-secret Pentagon Papers.

How did a future hero of the antiwar movement come to work for Major General Edward G. Lansdale, USAF (Ret.)? The answer to that question requires a brief recapitulation of Ellsberg's life up to that point, a story told not only by Ellsberg himself but also by his biographer Tom Wells. Then thirty-four years old, he had grown up in Highland Park, the same municipality within Detroit where Lansdale had spent part of his youth, to Jewish parents who had converted to Christian Science. Although he did not grow up to be a practicing Christian Scientist, this religious background as well as his childhood around Detroit gave him some common ground with Lansdale. His father even had the same first name as Lansdale's father and, like Harry Lansdale, a connection to the automobile industry: Harry Ellsberg was a structural engineer who had helped design Ford's vast Willow Run factory.[30]

The similarities, however, ended there. While Lansdale had been a mediocre student, Ellsberg was an intellectual standout. As a young man, he had been a musical prodigy who was relentlessly pushed by his mother, Adele, to practice the piano even though he displayed little enthusiasm for the instrument. He was only freed of the burden of musical practice by the great conductor in the sky. In 1946, the entire

Ellsberg family was on a long road trip when Daniel's father fell asleep at the wheel, and the car veered into a concrete bridge abutment. Daniel's thirteen-year-old sister and his mother were killed. Daniel himself was in a coma for thirty-six hours. When he woke up and learned that his mother had died, his first reaction was, "Now I don't have to play the piano anymore."[31] Daniel's father survived, but they never had a close relationship again, leaving him to seek out a series of surrogate father figures as mentors.

First at the Cranbrook Academy, an elite boarding school in Michigan, and then at Harvard College, Ellsberg's classmates discovered that he was brilliant, charming, fascinating—but also boastful, self-centered, and prone to exaggeration. An economics major, Ellsberg graduated third in his class at Harvard. He interrupted his postgraduate studies in economics to join the Marine Corps. He was drawn to the Corps because he was, in his own words, "a dedicated cold warrior"[32] and had, as one of his professors said, "a kind of macho way about him."[33] He served as a lieutenant from 1954 to 1957 and even extended his tour in the hope of seeing combat in the Suez Crisis of 1956. He later called his years in the Corps "the happiest time in my life."[34]

Ellsberg left the Marines in 1957 to assume a prestigious fellowship at Harvard and continue his graduate studies. Eventually, in 1962, he would complete his PhD. By then, he had already been working for three years at the RAND Corporation in Santa Monica, California, the nation's leading defense think tank, where intellectual heavyweights such as Albert Wohlstetter, Herman Kahn, Bernard Brodie, and Harry Rowen were becoming famous for applying social science methods to the study of nuclear deterrence. Even at RAND, where genius was common, Ellsberg stood out as a "supergenius," possibly a future Nobel Prize winner.[35] He was also a super-womanizer who openly bragged to colleagues about his conquests—and even passed around the RAND office nude photos of women he had slept with.[36] His family, including two young children, did not command the same level of attention. By the end of 1963, his wife, Carol, had had enough and demanded a divorce.[37]

Reeling from the separation, Ellsberg in 1964 moved to Washington, where he became a special assistant to John McNaughton, the assistant secretary of defense for international security affairs. Although, as he later acknowledged, his job was "a very lowly one," Ellsberg asked for and received a very high civil service grade, GS-18, equivalent to a two-star general. However, Ellsberg had trouble keeping up with the hectic pace of work in the Pentagon. By the summer of 1965, he was being encouraged to find employment elsewhere, the sooner the better.[38]

In August 1965, Ellsberg attended an interagency meeting at the State Department. William Colby, who was now in charge of the CIA's Far East department, introduced Edward Lansdale, who proceeded to speak about his upcoming mission to Vietnam. Ellsberg had heard of Lansdale, the Quiet American. Everyone had. He had, as Ellsberg later recalled, "a great reputation." After the meeting, Ellsberg approached Lansdale and offered to accompany him to Vietnam as a counterinsurgency "apprentice."[39] After checking him out, Lansdale decided there would be advantages to recruiting one of McNamara's "whiz kids." "I liked Ellsberg," Lansdale later said. "But I had a sort of underhanded motive for putting him on the team. I wanted somebody to keep the bureaucrats off my back in Saigon, and here was this bright young man who could talk a mile a minute."[40]

Because Ellsberg carried such a high civil service grade, he came in with rank and perquisites greater than Lansdale's own. (Ellsberg earned $37,678 a year, Lansdale $36,490.)[41] And he became the only team member to be given a villa to himself. He was not shy about flaunting his rank in spite of his lack of experience in Vietnam. "That didn't cut any ice with anybody else on his damn team," Rufus Phillips said. "He had a hyper ego."[42]

If Ellsberg could be arrogant with others, he was, however, deferential to Lansdale. "I loved Lansdale," he said decades later in his comfortable home in the hills near Berkeley, California, now white-haired but still handsome, voluble, and intense even in his eighties. "He was a father figure to me. I really revered him and continue to have the same warm feeling; that never changed. I felt just like the other members of the team did. It was a cult. He was the leader of the cult, and I was a member of that cult."[43]

After getting to know Lansdale, Ellsberg concluded that he was more impressive in private than in public:

Many people from their dealings with him got the impression that this guy is actually nutty, lightweight, stupid in his mind, crazy ideas and nothing else, just a salesman. I *know* that's not true. I experienced him very often as strikingly shrewd in his calculations and his understanding and his analysis. I also understood at the time that he was capable of dissembling to people that he did not want to reveal anything to, by sounding like a hick. . . . That is not the case. This was a very shrewd, smart guy.[44]

Shrewd and smart Lansdale may have been, but most of his bureaucratic rivals in the burgeoning American establishment in Saigon shared the pejorative view—"nutty, lightweight, stupid"—that Ellsberg ascribed to those who did not know him well. As the American war was reaching its full fury, with offensives larger than Operation Starlite becoming a routine occurrence, Lansdale would have the unenviable task of trying to overcome the suspicion and resentment of his colleagues in order to influence the course of American and Vietnamese policy.

29

Waging Peace in a
Time of War

*Most other elements of the country-team cordially dislike the
Lansdale operation.*

—Henry Kissinger

I N the American political system, the length of titles is usually in
inverse proportion to the importance of the title-holder. The most
powerful person of all is known simply as the president. His cabinet
members are known as the secretary of state or the secretary of the
treasury. Lesser officials, by contrast, are styled as under secretaries or
deputy secretaries or assistant secretaries or, worse, deputy assistants
or assistant deputies. It was, therefore, an ominous sign that Edward
Lansdale's formal title in Vietnam was quite a mouthful: he was to be
head of the Senior Liaison Office and chairman of the U.S. Mission
Liaison Group to the Secretary General of the Central Rural Reconstruction Council.

The council was, in theory at least, a powerful body within the
South Vietnamese government. It was chaired by none other than the
flamboyant prime minister, Nguyen Cao Ky, and it included the secretary of rural affairs, a cabinet-level official who would be Lansdale's

closest interlocutor within the Vietnamese regime. "Rural reconstruction" was the Vietnamese term for what Americans called "pacification." Thus the Rural Reconstruction Council would be responsible for the counterinsurgency program in the countryside. The problem lay with the U.S. Mission Liaison Group, the working group at the U.S. embassy composed of representatives from the Military Assistance Command—Vietnam (MACV) and the civilian agencies that had a role in pacification.

Ambassador Henry Cabot Lodge expected Lansdale to orchestrate these various agencies in order to get "an effective political-social program moving in Viet Nam." But Lansdale was authorized to act only in an "advisory capacity." He would have no power to compel compliance—the same problem that had handicapped him during Operation Mongoose. Somehow, he was supposed to find a way of "tactfully and persuasively braiding together the separate economic, social, information, military, and other programs as necessary."[1] The problem was that all of the American agencies that Lansdale was supposed to "braid together" had far more money, manpower, and mandates than his Senior Liaison Office had, and they were all headed by strong-willed personalities who were not inclined to cede him an inch. It was, in the words of Bert Fraleigh of USAID, "a relatively small pond filled with many large sharks gobbling up or chasing the pilot fish. Cabot [Lodge] is like the ponderous but happy porpoise in all this and can't tell the fish apart even with a program."[2]

◆

ONE OF the most ferocious man-eating "sharks" was Philip Habib, who was in charge of the embassy's political section. A generously proportioned, first-generation Lebanese American born in Brooklyn, he was in the midst of one of the most glittering careers in the history of the Foreign Service; he would eventually rise to become President Ford's under secretary of state for political affairs and President Reagan's special envoy for the Middle East. Phil Habib was good at his job and was, as a colleague recalled, "very skeptical of anyone who wasn't a career professional."[3] Colonel Sam Wilson, Lansdale's old Pentagon deputy who was now working for Lodge, recalled that Habib was "merciless" and "ruthless" in waging a struggle to minimize the influence of Lansdale, whom he viewed as a "charlatan."[4] Barry Zorthian, the chief of a burgeoning public relations bureaucracy known as JUSPAO (Joint U.S. Public Affairs Office), said, "Phil Habib didn't like Lansdale one bit. He regarded Lansdale as a meddler and, in Vietnam terms, almost as irrelevant. Phil belonged to the establishment—the conventional standard machine structured to carrying out State Department missions. He regarded Lansdale as an unprogrammed loose cannon, a maverick upsetting things without discipline, without acceptance or commitment to Washington direction."[5]

It was hard to tell whether Zorthian was describing Habib's feelings or his own, because he felt exactly the same way. He was especially resentful because Lansdale had brought in Hank Miller, another senior U.S. Information Agency officer, to work under him, potentially challenging JUSPAO's authority. An Armenian American, Zorthian had served as a Marine officer during the Pacific campaign and remained a colonel in the Marine Corps Reserve. He had spent his postwar career rising up the ranks of what became the USIA. Now, as head of JUSPAO, he presided over his own office building on Avenue le Loi, where, in a second-floor auditorium, his press section provided daily briefings for hundreds of reporters. They came to be known as the "Five O'Clock Follies" for their tone of excessive optimism. But if the press briefings were overly crude and propagandistic, "Zorro" was more subtle and persuasive in private meetings with selected journalists. As one reporter later wrote,

He would take a deep drag off his cigarette, look pensively out the window of his upstairs office, release a sigh of resignation with the smoke, and then speak to a reporter, softly, reluctantly, off-the-record and in all confidence of course, about poor Ed Lansdale, the hopeless romantic. There was always enough about Lansdale to provide evidence that he might be a well-meaning but slightly nutty soul, and Zorthian's interpretation of him found its way into the works of David Halberstam and Frances

FitzGerald, who were, ideologically, not overly resistant to the idea, and into the writings of other journalists. While Zorthian worked the media, Habib made sure that Lansdale got nowhere in the bureaucracy.[6]

Although Zorthian and Habib were to prove Lansdale's most inveterate foes, they were hardly alone in protecting their prerogatives from this interloper. Gordon Jorgensen, the chief of the CIA station (known for cover purposes as the Office of Special Activities), had started off working under Lansdale in the 1950s and might have been expected to be amenable to his former boss's arrival. In fact, when a reporter told him the news, he "damn near dropped his martini." The reporter he was talking with could tell that mentally Jorgy was "throwing up the barricades to protect his turf, and that's what everyone was doing out there at that time."[7] Charlie Mann, head of USAID's office, was no more amenable to Lansdale's intrusion. He controlled a substantial development-aid budget, and he damn sure wasn't going to let Lansdale tell him how to spend his money or direct his people.

The most important shark of all was General William Westmoreland. The U.S. embassy in Saigon may have become the biggest American diplomatic outpost in the world, with 782 personnel in 1965,[8] but it was dwarfed by the MACV bureaucracy, whose headquarters staff alone expanded from 1,100 officers and men at the end of 1964 to 3,300 by the end of 1967.[9] With its staff overflowing numerous office buildings in Saigon, MACV in 1966 would begin construction on a $25 million headquarters complex next to Tan Son Nhut Airport, complete with a barracks and mess hall, the largest air-conditioning plant in all of Southeast Asia, and four acres of parking lots, all surrounded by watchtowers, searchlights, and a twelve-foot-high cyclone fence. When it opened in the summer of 1967, the new complex was dubbed "Pentagon East."[10]

Whatever MACV did was by definition more important than whatever the civilians did, because most interactions with the local population were conducted by American troops. Lansdale could dream up imaginative programs to win "hearts and minds," but such schemes amounted to little while Westmoreland's troops were turning the countryside into a "free fire" zone. Philip Caputo, a junior Marine officer who landed with the first combat battalion at Da Nang on March 8, 1965, was later to write in his acclaimed memoir *Rumors of War*, "Our mission was not to win terrain or seize positions, but simply to kill: to kill communists and to kill as many of them as possible. Stack 'em like cordwood. Victory was a high body-count, defeat a low kill-ratio, war a matter of arithmetic."[11] Lansdale perceived that that was not a winning strategy, but he had no authority to alter what Westmoreland and his forces were doing.

◆

GIVEN HIS aversion to bureaucracy, Edward Lansdale had little patience for his duties chairing the Mission Liaison Group. In a letter home, he called the meetings a "sort of big formal deal once a week, which brings out my most impish nature," adding, "Maybe I'll teach everyone yet not to get me to attend formal meetings."[12] He preferred to spend his time, as he had done in the past, getting to know the key Vietnamese players—listening to them and winning their trust in his characteristic, low-key style. A young, Vietnamese-speaking USIA officer who met Lansdale for the first time in 1965 found that he had not lost his mastery of the art of conversation. "He was one of the few skilled conversational operators that I encountered over time," recalled Frank Scotton, "in that he was a sensitive listener who drew people's thinking and motivation forth, then when he wished, melded it with his own purpose, and fed back a homogenized version that the other person could digest. It was better than just telling someone."[13]

As soon as the Cong Ly house was open and functioning, Lansdale began hosting lunches and dinners for Vietnamese officials to foster the kind of conversations he enjoyed, gradually adding Americans into the mix to foster more "team work." His first buffet dinner, for twenty-six people, was held on the evening of September 12, 1965. "In a burst of enthusiasm," he wrote to Hubert Humphrey, "I invited the Presidency staff to meet with technicians from all the Ministries (Health, Agriculture, Forestry, etc) at my house for supper, to meet the team and even to get acquainted with one another." The language barrier that had previously stymied Lansdale was melting away—most of the conversation was conducted in English, "the really fashionable language here"—and he thought the talk was "amazingly frank and heartfelt." They spoke "in terms of love for our fellow man, which means as much to a lad brought up by his parents with Confucian principles as it does to one believing in Christian principles."[14]

Among those attending this love-in, in the jargon of the sixties, was Nguyen Tat Ung, the secretary of rural affairs. Lansdale felt he was making real progress in fostering a good relationship with Ung, whom he judged to be an "unusually capable person." Unfortunately a week later, on September 17, 1965, he received word that Ung and several of his aides had been killed in an airplane crash. This "tragic setback" would delay his attempts to reinvigorate a rural pacification program that had become largely moribund since Ngo Dinh Diem's downfall two years earlier.[15]

Ung's replacement was General Nguyen Duc Thang, a thirty-four-year-old officer who was widely seen as the most effective and most honest general in the entire army. Unlike most of his peers, he had a horror of political maneuvering and stayed aloof from coup plots. He spoke fluent English, having learned the language while attending artillery school at Fort Sill, Oklahoma. Sporting an olive-green GI uniform, tall and heavily built, he even "looked like an American," Dan Ellsberg thought. Thang liked to repeat the story of a little boy who came up to him, asking, "Hey, OK, you number one, give me cigarettes!" Thang gave him a tongue-lashing for begging and for using pidgin English rather than the proper Vietnamese greetings. The little boy, startled, blurted out, "You speak Vietnamese?"[16]

Thang, like Lansdale, believed that it was important to win "hearts and minds," and that a first step was to curb military abuses against the populace. By the beginning of 1966, Lansdale was writing that Thang "is a younger version of Ramon Magsaysay (even to the foot jingling), and we've become close friends."[17] But Thang started off "with practically no staff in his Ministry," thus occasioning yet another delay while he staffed up.[18] Even once he acquired a staff, he still faced the problem of trying to implement a pacification program on behalf of a government that was barely functional. A regime that could not pick up the garbage in Saigon was not likely to defeat an entrenched insurgency in the countryside.

◆

WHILE LANSDALE was cultivating Thang, he knew that it was even more important to strike up a good relationship with Nguyen Cao Ky, the ambitious air force general-turned-prime minister. A native of northern Vietnam, Ky had learned to fly under the French. Like Thang, he was only thirty-four years old, and he was, in many ways, a typical fighter pilot. Brave and impetuous, he would personally lead bombing missions against the North. He loved drinking, gambling, and womanizing. His fellow pilots knew he had fallen hard for an Air Vietnam stewardess named Dang Tuyet Mai when he ordered an entire squadron to fly at treetop level over her neighborhood.[19] Before long, he had divorced his first wife, a Frenchwoman he had met while training in France, and married Mai. Prime Minister and Madame Ky would tour the country wearing matching jet-black flight suits, flight boots, blue flying caps, and sunglasses. An American who saw them exclaimed, "Good God, they look like Captain and Mrs. Midnight."[20] (Captain Midnight was a fictional aviator in a popular radio and television series.)

Ky had a tendency to shoot from the hip; he got into trouble for comments such as expressing admiration for Hitler's "leadership and sense of discipline." He wanted to get things done, but he did not have the patience for tedious paperwork. Upon taking office, he threatened to shoot rice and salt "profiteers," but when the police arrested two suspects they had to be released because the evidence was inconclusive.[21]

"I'm rather taken by Ky," Lansdale wrote in the fall of 1965.[22] He found Ky to be "honest, intelligent, well-motivated" and gifted with the ability to "talk to people."[23] Ky and Lansdale developed a "close personal relationship," in the words of Rufus Phillips.[24] Lansdale and his team wrote a speech for the prime minister to commemorate his first one hundred days in office, and on October 1, 1965, Ky delivered "big chunks of it" as scripted.[25]

478 | THE ROAD NOT TAKEN

Lansdale had less luck wooing General Nguyen Van Thieu, Ky's nominal superior. At age forty-two, Thieu was the grand old man of the ruling junta known as the Directory—a name that sounds as if it had come out of one of Isaac Asimov's science-fiction paperbacks. While Ky made a bold splash from the beginning, Thieu preferred to bide his time in the background, quietly plotting to accumulate power. Ky was impetuous, Thieu reserved. He also worked harder and had a much higher tolerance for paperwork. But, as if to offset these virtues, he was intensely calculating and suspicious of others, even paranoid.

Lansdale met the head of state at a September 21, 1965, dinner arranged by the influential bureaucrat Bui Diem, a future ambassador to Washington. As an icebreaker, Lansdale was asked to recount his relationship with the legendary Cao Dai warlord Trinh Minh Thé, who had died in the battle of Saigon in 1955. The assembled Vietnamese, all younger by at least a decade than the fifty-seven-year-old Lansdale, did not know their own country's history. They asked Lansdale about French reports that he had bribed Thé with twelve million dollars. Repeating his selective account of what had occurred, Lansdale told them that Thé was a "pure patriot and would have scorned bribery as much as I. The only money we each spent was for the meals we shared. I still believe in his ideals of unity, morality and freedom in Vietnam." Thieu and the other dinner guests, Lansdale remarked, "seemed quite moved by the story." This shared history gave Lansdale an opening to tell Thieu that the people of South Vietnam were hungry for a government that would "care about the people" and "serve with morality." Thieu responded warmly, but, as Lansdale was to learn, what the general said was often far removed from what he did. [26]

Thieu had few, if any, confidants beyond his wife, and he was not about to take an American into his confidence; he remembered all too well the fate suffered by Diem, who had gone from pet to pariah with Washington. So it was impossible for Lansdale to create the kind of close relationship he had had with Magsaysay or Diem. Complicating the situation was the rivalry between Thieu and Ky: Lansdale's closeness to Ky made Thieu even more suspicious of him.

At the same time that he was reaching out to South Vietnam's lead-

Fidel Castro with Nikita Khrushchev. The Cuban leader's closeness to the Soviet Union led President Kennedy to put Lansdale in charge of Operation Mongoose to overthrow his regime. (Image Works)

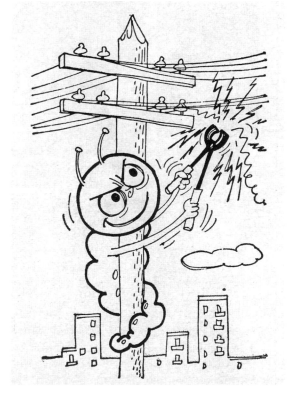

Gusano Libre (Free Worm), a cartoon image that the CIA concocted, at Lansdale's instigation, as a symbol of resistance to Castro. The CIA planned to deliver Gusano Libre "pins, armbands, seals, pencils, balloons, etc." to Cuba via helium-filled balloons. (NARA)

Attorney General Robert F. Kennedy was a relentless taskmaster. He told Lansdale, "Let's get the hell on with it. The President wants some action, right now." Lansdale's failure to topple Castro helped to sour the Kennedys on him. (AP)

General Maxwell Taylor and Secretary of Defense Robert McNamara confer with President John F. Kennedy. Lansdale did not see eye to eye with the more conventionally minded Taylor and McNamara about how to fight the Vietcong. But he did convince Kennedy to focus on the conflict early in his administration. (Image Works)

Major General Edward G. Lansdale in 1963, shortly before his retirement from the Pentagon. (Image Works)

Henry Cabot Lodge Jr., the patrician American ambassador who supported the overthrow of Ngo Dinh Diem in 1963 and returned for another tour, 1965–66. Although Lodge brought Lansdale back to Vietnam, he never gave him any real power. (MSFRIC)

Ellsworth Bunker replaced Lodge in 1967 and stayed until 1973. Lansdale trusted and liked Bunker more than Lodge, but Bunker did not grant him any more authority. (MSFRIC)

Lansdale held regular parties at his house in Saigon to bring Americans and Vietnamese together. Here Nguyen Cao Ky and General William Westmoreland listen to folk singing. (HI)

Lansdale poses in 1967 with General Nguyen Duc Thang (second from left) and his family. Lansdale aide Charlie Sweet is at far left, Calvin Mehlert at far right. Lansdale hoped that the honest and effective Thang could become a Vietnamese version of Ramon Magsaysay. (RPPP)

Everything that Lansdale tried to achieve in his second tour in Vietnam, 1965–68, was ultimately inconsequential compared to the "big unit" war fought by the American military. Lansdale warned that the enemy could not be bombed into submission, but he was ignored. (Image Works)

The former RAND analyst Daniel Ellsberg worked for Lansdale in Vietnam before leaking the Pentagon Papers in 1971. Lansdale "was the leader of the cult and I was a member of that cult," he later said. (AP)

Senator Frank Church led an investigation into the CIA in 1975. Testifying to the Church Committee "has all the charm and fun of going to a dentist to have root canals," Lansdale complained. (Getty)

Following Helen's death, Pat Kelly and Edward Lansdale married on the Fourth of July, 1973, and lived happily ever after. Here they are in the kitchen of their McLean, Virginia, home in 1979. (ECLPP)

ers, Lansdale and his team members were beginning to establish relationships with influential labor, religious, business, and ethnic minority leaders, in order to "get them to work in harmony with the GVN [Government of Vietnam], even though they will be independent of the government."²⁷ Lansdale was also taking quick trips outside of the capital, "away from the protocol," to talk to South Vietnam's rural cadres. "This just means," he told Helen, "that I stay up nights, working, when I get back to Saigon, to make up for the time I take out. Yet, I can't get a fix on the pulse of this place without getting around first-hand and easing into [the] local situation patiently."²⁸

◆

LANSDALE KEPT a stiff upper lip in public, but in private he was close to despair about the state of the war effort. In mid-October 1965, he wrote perceptively to Helen,

> I've analyzed the political situation here rather thoroughly by now—but migosh, what to do to construct something out of the horrible mess! I'm scared to tell everyone how really bad it is. . . . What has happened here is that after 20 years of war almost all the tensile strength has gone out of the social fabric. Military operations just make it limper. The village folks just don't seem to give a damn about anything except to please be left alone. The VC have an infrastructure in place throughout the villages—but the villagers are duly resentful of them, too—along with being disbelieving of the GVN. They've lost faith in themselves and tomorrow.²⁹

Reversing this dire state of affairs, Ed admitted, was "a whopping big, complex job. . . . The VC own the countryside, and we aren't going to defeat them by talking."³⁰ But talking was primarily what he did, because he lacked any real power.

Lansdale wanted to create a national consultative council to lead the transition to civilian rule and to focus counterinsurgency efforts on "revolutionary villages"—that is, villages such as Binh Hung populated by Hoa Hao, Cao Dai, Catholics or other anti-Communist minorities. These two programs would be united by allowing "revolutionary villages" to elect their own leaders as well as delegates to the national consultative council.[31] Caught up in the excitement of his initial months in Vietnam, Lansdale imagined that this plan "might well bring the turning point of the war here."[32] But while his proposal was embraced by Ky, it was vetoed by Lansdale's rivals at the U.S. embassy.[33]

In addition to these major proposals, Lansdale and his team spewed out a variety of lesser ideas. Recalling the propaganda coups he had carried out in the Philippines and Vietnam a decade or more earlier, he proposed air-dropping nearly five thousand captured Chinese Communist weapons over North Vietnam to show the peasants "how their government was working with the Chinese to threaten their compatriots in the South" and to force Hanoi to mount laborious and time-consuming searches for "'returned' armament."[34] He proposed building a "Rural Construction 'operations room' . . . in the vicinity of the Prime Minister's office" to make "the 'waging of peace' . . . as exciting as the waging of war."[35] He proposed investing in rural electrification and having Ky stage "fireside chats," both directly borrowed from Franklin Roosevelt, who was president when Lansdale was in his twenties and thirties.[36] He proposed bringing over Cuban exiles to address a shortage of "doctors, nurses, teachers, other professionals."[37] He proposed scholarships for Vietnamese students to study in American colleges.[38] He even proposed serving a traditional Tet holiday meal to encourage Vietcong fighters to surrender.[39] Few, if any, of these suggestions came to fruition.

◆

NOT SURPRISINGLY, given his famous proclivity for carrying a harmonica wherever he went, Lansdale was especially focused on using music to rally and unite the South Vietnamese—and to buck up the sagging spirits of the Americans helping them. In early September 1965, Lansdale renewed his friendship with Pham Duy, one of Vietnam's most famous folk singers and composers, whom he had first met in 1954. A forty-five-year-old former Vietminh fighter, Pham Duy (pronounced *fam zoo-ey*)[40] had grown disenchanted with Communist censorship and in 1951 moved south, where he became well-known for his prolific output of songs, especially "heart songs." He was also notorious for his womanizing ways; he claimed that he needed new "love partners" to inspire his creativity, and he did not allow his wedding in 1949 to slow down his search for fresh conquests. "Round-faced, intense and cheerful," he was a patriot who performed free for South Vietnamese troops—a "troubadour for freedom," in the words of the *Washington Post* columnist Mary McGrory, who was introduced to him by Lansdale.[41]

On November 25, 1965, Lansdale and his team hosted Pham Duy and Rural Affairs Minister Nguyen Duc Thang at the Cong Ly house for a Thanksgiving dinner. They brainstormed about how to "use music to popularize Rural Construction operations among villagers,"[42] and spent hours recording various songs, including new tunes that Pham Duy had written to inspire South Vietnamese troops.[43] A few months later, in March 1966, Pham Duy left for a three-month tour of the United States arranged by Lansdale and paid for by the U.S. government.[44]

Pham Duy was not the only musician that Lansdale promoted. He also took in hand a young army captain from Arkansas named Hershel Gober who would eventually became secretary of veterans affairs under President Bill Clinton. While serving as a military adviser in the Mekong Delta in 1965, Gober took to composing patriotic ditties such as "Look Over My Shoulder," written after Vietcong hiding on the bank of a canal fired at a sampan in which he was traveling with a district chief and a militiaman. Gober jumped out of the boat and waded to the canal bank, firing as he went, the two South Vietnamese right behind him. Hence the song's refrain: "Look over my shoulder and what do you see? / You see a nation fighting to be free!" Lansdale thought that "Hersh" had "an exceptional valuable quality as a man who can move others, in the idiom of folk music,"[45] and he persuaded Westmoreland to let him form a troupe of soldier-musicians, known as the Black Patches, to tour South Vietnam entertaining the troops. This was quite possibly the only proposal of Lansdale's that Westy ever adopted.[46]

Lansdale's insistence that "folk music is an effective medium of communication"[47] and his interest in using it to mobilize Vietnamese and Americans for the war effort was so unconventional that it struck other power brokers in Saigon as bizarre—all the more so because the most prominent folk singers in America, including Pete Seeger, Peter, Paul, and Mary, Bob Dylan, and Joan Baez, were associated with the peace movement. Barry Zorthian later spoke contemptuously of how "Ed and his team . . . were sitting in their house singing folk songs and doing what they had done so successfully in the Philippines," while "the war was moving toward conventional warfare again."[48]

◆

As if Lansdale didn't have enough problems with bureaucratic rivals, he also had to deal with problems within his own group among the strong personalities he had assembled. One recurring source of stress was Dan Ellsberg, who, having spent little time in the Third World, made the mistake shortly after his arrival of drinking water without first boiling it. The result was amoebic dysentery. "Dan was very, very naïve out there," Lansdale lamented.[49]

Even more dangerous was Ellsberg's decision to date a "sexy" Eurasian woman named Germaine who was the mistress of a Corsican gangster. When the Corsican found out, he threatened to slit Ellsberg's throat. Conein, who had been close to the Corsican mafia for years, told Ellsberg, "Listen, my friend. You are in much more trouble with the Corsicans than with the Vietcong. You know what they do when somebody fools with one of their women? They'll get you down on the pavement and whip your face with barbed wire." Lansdale and Conein had to go to the mafia don and plead for Ellsberg's life. Conein even threatened that if something happened to Ellsberg, he would come looking for the Corsican. Later, after Ellsberg leaked the Pentagon Papers, Conein regretted what he had done. "If I hadn't interceded, he might have been bumped off," he said wistfully.[50]

Another troublemaker on the team was Charles T. R. Bohannan, the temperamental counterinsurgency strategist who was nicknamed "Sandals" by irreverent young Foreign Service officers in Saigon for his habit of wearing leather sandals that were popular with the hippies of the era.[51] The irascible Bohannan had a habit of quarreling with even his closest friends. "Bo and I clashed hard the first night he was here," Ed wrote home in early September 1965, "and I haven't seen him since."[52] When Bo returned, he began intriguing to usurp Lansdale's position as team leader. He made plain his disagreement with the plan for "Revolutionary Villages," in which Lansdale invested such heavy (and unrealistic) hopes. When sent to embassy meetings, Bohannan would act bizarrely. "He'd sit over in a corner and wouldn't say a word," Rufus Phillips recalled. "Or if he did, he was very critical about what was going on."[53]

In January 1966, Bohannan wrote Lansdale a strange, rambling memorandum in which he complained, "I have been increasingly cut out from what is going on," and spoke of resigning not only from the team but "from the war and the human race."[54] He suggested various "cover stories" that could be used to explain his departure, ranging from "nervous exhaustion" to "habitual drunkenness." "If one of the more picaresque explanations appeals to you, I would be willing to discuss means by which it might be made credible, or, perhaps, true."[55] Lansdale would justify Bo's termination a couple of months later by citing not any of his suggested excuses but rather ill health—"He has a numbness in one hand and blanks out in eyesight."[56]

The real source of Bohannan's discontent was a feeling, well grounded in reality, that he and the team were being marginalized: "I have not felt that I was making any significant contribution to the 'team,' or to the U.S. effort," he complained.[57] Others on the team felt the same way. "Want to know the truth?" Lou Conein said. "I didn't know what [Lansdale] was doing. Nobody knew what they were doing. . . . Had no money, had no logistical support, except what we had glommed onto from the cookie factory [CIA] in the beginning. Nothing. We'd have VIPs like [LBJ aide Jack] Valenti come by, and we'd have things like that and would sit down and sing songs. I can only take so much of that."[58]

Lansdale and other team members were constantly overhearing derogatory descriptions of themselves—they were derided by other

Americans as "unstable" do-gooders, freewheelers "from a fly-by-night team," "suckers," Lansdale "spies," and so on.[59] Other Americans were even telling the Vietnamese not to talk with the "Lansdale team." "Rather than proceed further into what looked like an ugly rat's nest," Lansdale decided to slow down his attempts to cultivate labor unions, religious organizations, and other groups.[60] He even found that his radio messages to William Bundy—the assistant secretary of state, brother of McGeorge Bundy, and one of his few fans in Washington— were being "scrutinized minutely in the various U.S. agencies here, apparently mostly to discover trespass." The weekly activity reports that the Senior Liaison Office was filing were also generating too much "negative" reaction from colleagues. As a defensive measure, Lansdale decided to end the weekly reports and switch to either submitting memoranda that few saw or reporting orally to Ambassador Lodge and Deputy Ambassador William Porter.[61]

As if to add insult to injury, the very officials who were preventing Lansdale from exercising any authority were at the same time castigating him for not doing more to take control of the ponderous pacification bureaucracy. When the USAID administrator David E. Bell visited Saigon in early January 1966, he told SLO's Michael Deutch, "Dr. Deutch, I thought the Lansdale Group came here to coordinate and streamline this multiplicity of forces and activities in pacification—this apparently has not been done?" The mild-mannered Deutch recounted his response: "I am afraid that I lost for a moment control of myself and answered, 'Mr. Bell, I can assure you on behalf of General Lansdale that we will coordinate everything that your agency lets us coordinate.'"[62]

◆

No ONE did a more astute job of analyzing Edward Lansdale's anomalous position in Vietnam than a rising Harvard professor with horn-rim glasses, a German accent, and a tragic view of history who visited the country for the first time in the fall of 1965 as a consultant to Henry Cabot Lodge. "Lansdale is without doubt a man of extraordinary gifts," Henry Kissinger wrote to Lodge after spending three weeks in Vietnam. "He is an artist in dealing with Asians. He is patient, inspirational, imaginative. He has assembled an extraordinary group of individualists—each a remarkable personality in his own right. Anybody who could first collect such a group and then retain its loyalty over two decades is not an ordinary person."

Kissinger, however, also understood what Lansdale did not: that the Ugly American could be his own worst enemy. Kissinger noted:

> [T]he artistic and highly individualistic temperament of Lansdale and his group have caused them to cut themselves off—sometimes needlessly—from the other elements of the mission. Most other elements of the country-team cordially dislike the Lansdale operation. Some of this is an inevitable by-product of an unusual administrative arrangement. But some tensions could be avoided by greater tact on the part of Lansdale and his colleagues. They too often take the attitude that they will settle the pacification program singlehandedly, that Lansdale alone has the magic recipe and that the major contribution of other members of the mission should be to get out of the way.

Already a leading international relations scholar if not yet a policymaker, Kissinger also delivered an insightful assessment of Lansdale's shortcomings intellectually as well as bureaucratically. "Lansdale and his associates may be drawing too much on a precedent which is no longer fully relevant," he warned. "The Philippine Insurrection has as many points of difference from the Vietnamese civil war as similarities to it. In the Philippines the insurrection had never reached the scale of the war in Vietnam. There was no foreign base for the guerillas. The indigenous government was much stronger. There was a tradition of working with Americans. The situation in Vietnam is much more complex, much less susceptible to bravura, individual efforts."[63]

Kissinger recommended that Henry Cabot Lodge create "an administrative mechanism to plan, coordinate and follow-up" on the pacification program. While "Lansdale can and should play an important role in planning," Kissinger added, "he cannot, in my view, be the chief executive officer." Hardly devoid of self-knowledge, Lansdale was coming to the same conclusion. In a letter to Lodge, he noted that "it would require a strong administrator to manage [pacification] properly," and "I am not seeking this job." He suggested that "maybe my main usefulness today would be simply that of bringing Vietnamese together, overcoming their suspicions of one another. The good Lord knows, they are so split up into rivalries and jealousies that somebody or something has to bring them together into enough unity to save themselves. I don't understand it myself, but I seem to be able to do this."[64]

Many within the Johnson administration were concluding that Kissinger and Lansdale were right: a pacification czar was needed. That consensus translated into action at a conference in Honolulu that President Johnson, with typical impetuosity, convened on only a few days' notice from February 6 to February 9, 1966, while the First Cavalry Division was mounting the biggest search-and-destroy mission of the war so far, the aptly named Operation Masher. (This misbegotten offensive discharged 132,000 rounds of artillery, "1,000 rounds for every estimated enemy fatality," and yet failed to achieve any lasting success.)[65] The focus of the Honolulu meeting was to be on pacification, the not-so-hidden agenda being to distract attention from televised hearings that Senator J. William Fulbright was conducting in the Senate Foreign Relations Committee featuring witnesses who were highly critical of the Vietnam War. The president insisted on bringing half of his cabinet members along with 125 American and Vietnamese officials from Saigon, including Lodge, Westmoreland, Ky, Thieu—and Lansdale. To make way for this enormous entourage, the government took over the entire Royal Hawaiian Hotel, a beachfront property with stucco walls that was known as the "Pink Palace of the Pacific." The King Kalakaua Suite overlooking Waikiki Beach was specially equipped for the president's use with a "seven-ton air conditioner, a monarchic double bed, and several cases of Tab and low-calorie Dr. Pepper."[66]

Over the three frenetic days that followed, Lansdale reported getting perhaps five hours of sleep.[67] He had his first recorded meeting with Lyndon Johnson, albeit hardly a one-on-one, on February 7: Lansdale was one of many American and Vietnamese officials who gathered along with the president around a huge oval conference table at Camp Smith, the hilltop headquarters of the Pacific Command. Johnson, predictably, dominated the proceedings with his outsize personality and his stream of colorful colloquialisms. At one point, the mystified Vietnamese delegates conferred among themselves to figure out "just what is this gentleman talking about?" when the president demanded to see "coonskins on the wall."[68]

The conference produced the grandiose Declaration of Honolulu, in which Thieu and Ky pledged themselves to promote democracy and prosperity but with little in the way of specifics. One of the few concrete outcomes was the decision to formally designate Deputy Ambassador William Porter to run pacification. Lansdale would be relegated to working as a liaison to the South Vietnamese leadership.

◆

WHILE THE high-level focus on pacification led to Lansdale's being superseded within the Saigon bureaucracy, it also gave him a temporary boost, if only because Hubert Humphrey was now being allowed to play a role, however small, in the administration's Vietnam policy. Johnson summoned Humphrey out of his temporary political purgatory to fly back to Vietnam with Lodge, Thieu, Ky, and other American and Vietnamese officials, including Lansdale. Humphrey was terrified by Ky's habit of twirling his pistols "like a sheriff in a grade B Western," worried that the prime minister would blow someone's head off by accident.[69] Humphrey's physician was seated next to Thieu's wife, "an absolutely smashing Oriental beauty," who wanted to talk about nothing except her desire for plastic surgery to make her eyes look Caucasian.[70] Lansdale was too busy to notice what was going on around him. Working nonstop to arrange the vice president's unplanned visit, he felt like a "zombie" by the time they landed in Saigon.[71]

Showing Humphrey around an overcrowded Saigon and in particular around a couple of showcase pacification sites he had been working on with the Ministry of Rural Affairs, Lansdale was pleased to see how the Vietnamese reacted to him. "When Humphrey was talking to some veterinary researchers," Lansdale noted, "one of them looked up, saw me, and said to Humphrey—wait a minute, there's our best friend in Vietnam—and reached over to grab me and give me a hug." At the airport, with Humphrey preparing to leave for Washington, Lansdale told him that " 'we Vietnamese' had enjoyed his visit very much." Ky, who was standing nearby, laughed and told Humphrey that none of the Vietnamese leaders thought of Lansdale as a foreigner. "I guess he's taking quite an impression back," Lansdale said of Humphrey. All of this favorable attention, Lansdale added, "gave the team a shot in the arm . . . and helped me to cheer them up (sure puzzles me how quickly they slide into the gloom when I leave them alone a few days)."[72]

It also helped slightly when President Johnson, as a sort of consolation prize for not handing over control of pacification to Lansdale, appointed him as a "minister," one of the most senior ranks in the Foreign Service.[73] "No congrats from any Americans out here," Lansdale noted bitterly, "but many warm ones from the Vietnamese. What colleagues!"[74]

◆

GLOOM RETURNED soon enough as Lansdale and his team members grappled with their growing irrelevance amid the increasingly futile and destructive course that the war was taking. "The team went flat as a deflated balloon," Lansdale noted in late February 1966. "It was pure hell for some days."[75] Among the "disheartening news" that Lansdale received was that he had been kicked off the Mission Council, the top-level team at the embassy that included Lodge, Westmoreland, Habib, and other senior officials. Lansdale's old deputy Colonel Sam Wilson was the coordinator for the Mission Council, and he kept passing along its minutes to Lansdale—until Habib put a stop to it.[76] Lansdale approached Wilson to ask him to secretly continue providing the minutes. When Wilson refused, he recalled, Lansdale was "very, very upset."[77]

Lansdale's growing irrelevance became a matter of public knowledge following the publication in the *Washington Post* on February 25, 1966, of a scathing article by the correspondent Stanley Karnow, who had tangled with Lansdale in the past. Karnow noted that Lansdale had not performed the "miracles" expected of him: "His adversaries, who are numerous within the U.S. Mission, contend that Lansdale and his eleven-man team have failed to make the slightest impact on the Vietnam situation." The article was full of damning, if anonymous, quotes, both from rival Americans ("We are up against a superb Communist organization that must be uprooted by a better organization. This simply cannot be done by a few men of good will") and, even more dismaying, from Lansdale's own subordinates ("We haven't really done anything that couldn't have been done by any bureaucrat"). Lansdale suspected that the source of the internal leak was Bo Bohannan, who had just been fired from the team.[78]

Coming six months after Lansdale's arrival in Saigon, the *Washington Post* article represented a dirge for the once high hopes that had attended his return. Lansdale had made some progress in ingratiating himself with Vietnamese officials, from Prime Minister Ky on down, but he had failed to carve out for himself a powerful niche as he had previously done in the Philippines and in post-French Vietnam. Lansdale tried to shrug off the Karnow article "as evidence of petty spite," but the spite directed at him was potent.[79] By the spring of 1966, the only real question for Lansdale and his team members was whether they should stay in a diminished capacity or leave in defeat.

30

To Stay or to Go?

I'm not sure that I have any desire left to serve my country when its superior servants behave so cynically and so self-servingly as I now see them do.

—EDWARD LANSDALE

WHILE Edward Lansdale and his team were struggling to exert even the slimmest measure of influence in Saigon, the war in the countryside was raging out of control, an inferno consuming American and Vietnamese lives at an ever-quickening pace. American troop strength had climbed from 184,300 personnel at the end of 1965 to 385,300 by the end of 1966 and to 485,600 by the end of 1967.[1] North Vietnam matched America's escalation, feeding more regular forces into the South.

In the Mekong Delta, amid the rice paddies and rivers known on U.S. military maps as IV Corps, a classic guerrilla war was being waged, pitting Vietcong fighters against South Vietnamese forces and their American advisers. A Special Forces officer named Tobias Wolff, who spent a year in the delta, later wrote in his celebrated memoir *In Pharaoh's Army,*

Occasionally they combined for an attack on one of our compounds or to ambush a convoy of trucks or boats, or even a large unit isolated in the field and grown sloppy from long periods without contact, but most of the time they worked in small teams and out of sight. They blew us up with homemade mines fashioned from dud howitzer shells, or real American mines bought from our South Vietnamese allies. They dropped mortars on us at night—never very many; just enough, with luck, to kill a man or two, or inflict some wounds, or at least scare us half to death. Then they hightailed it home before our fire-direction people could vector in on them, slipped into bed, and, as I imagined, laughed themselves to sleep.[2]

Up north, in I Corps, the U.S. Marine area of operations located near the borders with North Vietnam and Laos, the fighting was heavier and more conventional. The enemy here was not shadowy guerrillas in black pajamas but tough PAVN (People's Army of Vietnam) soldiers wearing green or khaki uniforms and organized into regiments and divisions. In his searing novel *Matterhorn*, the Marine veteran Karl Marlantes, who received a Navy Cross and numerous other decorations as a young lieutenant, vividly evoked the kind of war the Marines fought. The title derives from the fictional Fire Support Base Matterhorn, a mountain peak "shrouded by cold monsoon rain and clouds" that was "flattened and shorn of vegetation to accommodate an artillery battery of 105-millimeter howitzers." Before long this hill had become "a sterile wasteland of smashed trees, tangled logging slash, broken C-ration pallets, empty tin cans, soggy cardboard containers, discarded Kool-Aid packages, torn candy wrappers—and mud."

Every night Matterhorn's mighty howitzers would unleash random "harassment and interdiction" fire into the jungle. Marlantes's protagonist and stand-in, Second Lieutenant Waino Mellas, asks his company commander, First Lieutenant Fitch, what happens if a Montagnard—one of the tribesmen who lived in the hills—got hit by an artillery shell. Fitch doesn't care. "You call off the H & I," he replies, "and the gooks have access to this mountain like a freeway ramp. It's my fucking troops over any lost mountain man, and it'll stay that way. I decided that a long time ago."

Every day Marine grunts would walk into the jungle on terrifying and tiring patrols to try to bring the elusive North Vietnamese Army (NVA) to battle. Simply hacking their way with machetes through the thick vegetation in the stifling heat and humidity, while carrying as much as a hundred pounds of gear, was an ordeal. In the "nearly impenetrable" bush, Marlantes wrote, "their eyes flickered rapidly back and forth as they tried to look in all directions at once," hoping to see the enemy a split second before they were seen. Once a patrol stumbled onto enemy troops, the jungle would reverberate with the screams of M-16s on full automatic, answered by "the slower, more solid hammering of the heavier-caliber NVA AK-47s."

The Marines would trudge back to Matterhorn punch-drunk with "stultifying fatigue," their legs covered with leeches, their hands "crisscrossed with infected cuts made by sharp jungle grasses," their bodies "drenched with sweat and rain." And then they would have to get "ready for the evening alert and the long night of watch," forgoing badly needed sleep to prevent the base from being overrun.[3]

It was hard to point to any real progress that all of this military activity was achieving. Lansdale wrote in mid-1966, "While the US military have been going great guns against large VC and NVA units, the hard fact is that the VC are still all over the landscape and their areas of control haven't diminished all that much."[4] He noted that when he arrived in August 1965, there were an estimated 150,000 Vietcong in South Vietnam. Now, a year later, there were 300,000. "I simply don't understand how anyone can figure that means we're winning."[5]

◆

To EDWARD LANSDALE and the rest of the Senior Liaison Office in Saigon, the war in the "bush" could seem almost as remote as the antiwar protests back home, which were growing in vehemence and volume along with the American military commitment. They spent most of their time in the relatively safe confines of the Cong Ly house and various government offices around the capital. The only member of SLO who spent much of his time in the field was Daniel Ellsberg, the former Pentagon whiz kid. He developed a fast friendship with John Paul Vann, the onetime army lieutenant colonel who had returned to Vietnam in 1965 as a USAID provincial adviser. Vann and Ellsberg would go for hair-raising trips through the countryside in Vann's International Harvester Scout, a four-wheel-drive utility vehicle, along roads that other Americans were too scared to traverse. Years later, Ellsberg wrote that "after years of reading cables and estimates," traveling with Vann to see the real war up close "was like breathing pure oxygen."[6]

Before long, Ellsberg was going off on his own, too, hefting a Swedish K SMG submachine gun, an unusual weapon that he carried as a status symbol. Those who encountered Ellsberg in combat recalled that he was often the most gung-ho person in the entire unit, urging the soldiers or Marines to get off their asses, to stay on the offensive, to get after "Charlie." The SLO team member Bernie Yoh described Ellsberg as a "shoot-them-dead superhawk."[7] Once out of the bush, Ellsberg would write up his adventures in vivid reports that were avidly read in Washington. While unhappy that his subordinate was off playing soldier, Lansdale praised him for having "an unusual talent for writing narrative based upon really sensitive observations of the scene around you,"[8] and for demonstrating a "rather unique skill at obtaining, digesting, and analyzing field problems that somehow hadn't come to light before."[9]

Ellsberg's skills, as well as his connections in Washington, caught the eye of Deputy Ambassador Bill Porter, who had been put in charge of pacification by the Honolulu conference. He asked for Ellsberg's services on his staff at the end of November 1966, and Lansdale agreed to let him go.[10]

By that point, most of the original SLO team had already drifted away. The most colorful departure was that of Lou Conein: after having transferred to the CIA station in Saigon, he got in trouble for having one Scotch too many and throwing flowerpots off a rooftop bar; hitting the pavement, they sounded like grenades going off. His punishment was to be transferred to a remote province called Phu

Bon, which Conein referred to as "Phu Elba," after the island where Napoleon had been exiled.[11] By the end of 1966, only Sam Karrick, Joe Redick, Napoleon Valeriano, and Hank Miller were left from the original squad. The smaller team consolidated its operations at the Cong Ly house, with Baby, the boa constrictor, moving into a big cage in the front yard. "I'm not sure I'm fond of the idea of a 12-foot rubber tube like that trying to get in bed with me evenings," Lansdale commented sardonically. "Maybe he'll sleep with Hank."[12]

Edward Lansdale contemplated getting out of Vietnam along with so many of his team members. He threatened to go public by "bugging out" and "blowing the whistle on the poor work of the U.S. in VN." Acting once again as the American Cassandra, he demanded of one State Department official visiting from Washington, "How long do you guys want to see the shit kicked out of the U.S. to serve the career ambitions of a handful of Americans? You don't seem to understand that, if the U.S. bureaucracies had done their work, we wouldn't have over 2,000 American kids killed in combat so far."[13] Lansdale wanted to change the direction of the war but felt powerless to do so: "It is senseless to ask me to throw myself or any of the team in the path of this thing, just to have a spectacle of a big 'spla-a-a-t,' which would be us."[14] "I'm getting to hate some of my fellow Americans," Ed wrote home, "and that's not good."[15] Lansdale vented his frustrations at the embassy's Fourth of July party in 1966 by trying to teach "some four-letter Anglo-Saxon words, ending in 'Cabot,'" to the ambassador's red-feathered parrots, an act of comical sabotage in which he was caught by one of the embassy staff.[16]

Writing from Washington, where he had returned, the former team member Mike Deutch urged Lansdale to stay in Vietnam. "However much you suffer, the alternative (coming back in defeat, retiring to a bit of writing on MacArthur Blvd., or getting entangled in domestic politics with Bo's political friends) is even less palatable." (Bohannon was a right-wing anti-Communist, Deutch a liberal anti-Communist.) The message of "stay the course" was reinforced by Pat Kelly: "I predict that if you did chuck it all and go back to Washington, within three months, the old fire-horse in you would have taken over completely and you'd be raring to get back and perhaps not able to do so. That frustration would dwarf what you now feel."[17]

Lansdale took this advice and in the summer of 1966 put off plans for his departure until after the American midterm election in November at the earliest. Why didn't he leave right away? There was, to be sure, the call of duty: Lansdale did not want to leave until he could place Vietnam, as he told Deutch, "on some kind of a sound enough political footing that even the heavy-handed Americans can't screw up for another decade or maybe a generation or two."[18] But Dan Ellsberg thought that the heart of the matter was that there was not much waiting for Lansdale in Washington. In Vietnam, Ellsberg dismissively said decades later, "he had a nice house, good cheap liquor. I think he had a more interesting life than he had back home."[19]

More generously, it might be said that the "magic potion" that Lansdale had imbibed when he first visited Vietnam in the summer of 1953 had not entirely worn off. As one of his aides from the 1950s was to say, "The whole thing was just elegant and romantic as hell. . . . My life in Vietnam was life in Technicolor. . . . It was always an enormous letdown to come back to the States."[20] The romance was no longer as strong in the rundown, overcrowded Saigon of the mid-1960s, but neither had it disappeared altogether. Nor had Lansdale's feeling of obligation to his country disappeared, in spite of how shabbily some of its representatives treated him.

◆

As LONG as he stayed in Vietnam, Ed Lansdale also had the hope of rekindling another kind of romance. He was now in his late fifties, Pat Kelly in her late forties. It was twenty years since they had met, ten years since she had broken off their relationship. Pat was starting to lose her slim figure. But a strong spark remained between them.

On the way back to Vietnam from a visit to Washington in early January 1966, Lansdale was allowed for the first time in years to visit the Philippines. After getting back to Saigon, Ed wrote to his "honeychile," "It was wonderful to be close to such beauty and sparkle again— you, rascal—and thank you too for the gifts." (Pat had given him a shirt and some nuts and guava jelly.)[21] Ed returned the favor by sending her a Vietnamese dog and cat for her birthday, knowing that she was an inveterate animal lover.[22]

Pat invited him to take a rest in the Philippines—with her. Ed sent back a flirtatious reply: "I'd love to get over for some R + R, but are there any quiet beaches left that could be reached without a big hassle about my passing through Manila? I'm ready to sleep for a week. Well, 48 hours anyhow. And I still dream of some of those beaches we've known. And dream about other things, too."[23] It was not hard to guess what "other things" he was dreaming of while living in a house that had been nicknamed "the Monastery." Yet Ed found that the press of business was too great to allow the getaway. In April 1966, he wrote to Pat, "So, honey-chile Pat, despite the great appeal of spending time with you doing what I most would want to do right now, in a country and with a person I love most, I have to say no, and have to stick to a course here which probably can only hurt me in the long run. Just chalk it down to my crazy stubbornness toward a belief which I cannot let down."[24]

As usual, Lansdale was working nonstop. "I'm sort of reeling from fatigue," he wrote to Helen. "I've just had a 20-hour work session, concentrated without a moment to blink an eye, after another longer session with only a quick nap in between—and that after a field trip and other flights up-country on something quite different. I'm dog-tired, but still wound up, can't seem to sleep, and want to visit with you." (By "visit," he meant "write.")[25] By early June 1966, Lansdale urgently needed a break from the pressure-packed atmosphere in Saigon. So he borrowed an embassy T-39 aircraft to take a weekend trip to Hong Kong with Joe Redick, Hank Miller, and Lou Conein. He found himself sitting in a room at the ultramodern President Hotel, which had opened just three years before (and has long since been torn down), sipping cognac, looking out at the harbor, and, he told Pat, "wishing to hell that you were with me, to make Hongkong just a really pleasant place for a guy trying to find life again, instead of a big city drowned out in rain + mud."[26]

Ed did finally manage to reunite with Pat in Hong Kong at the end of November 1966. He brought along his team members Joe Redick and George Melvin as quasi-chaperones, and Pat brought her grown daughter, Patricia, who was about to be married. Ed's older brother Phil, the ebullient owner of a chain of tire stores in Southern California, joined the party with his wife. "It was such a wonderful time for us that it made the descent into the maelstrom here all the harder on my return," Ed wrote to Pat from Saigon.[27] Pat's reply has not been preserved: she saved his letters, but he did not save hers—in part, one may surmise, because he did not want them discovered by Helen. But a letter she wrote him a few months later—one of the few that survives—makes clear that she had resumed the bantering tone that he had always found so attractive. "Write when you aren't too busy with your present Vietnamese preoccupation," she urged. "Just what was that all about anyway?"[28]

◆

IF ASKED to answer that question in the summer of 1966—"Just what was that all about anyway?"—Ed Lansdale would have answered that his top priority was ensuring a fair election for the Constituent Assembly on September 11, 1966. The assembly was supposed to draft a new constitution that would make possible a transition from military to civilian rule. It would replace the earlier constitution that Diem had crafted with Lansdale's help in 1956 and a more recent version promulgated by General Nguyen Khanh in 1964; both had become dead letters.

In late May 1966, Lansdale wrote to his team members describing the period leading up to the election in dramatic terms: "In every great human struggle, there comes a climactic point which prejudices the outcome. If seen for what it is, at the time, and properly exploited, the end of the struggle can be hastened. In my opinion, one of those vital moments of history lies just before us in Viet Nam—between now and September." In preparation, he instructed each member of SLO to "refresh himself on the principles expressed in the Declaration of Independence and the Bill of Rights," adding, "Texts are in the almanac at the office."[29]

When Lodge heard about Lansdale's plans to stage a free election, he launched into a lengthy diatribe about how he and Lyndon Johnson had spent most of their lives rigging elections. "Get it across to the press that they shouldn't apply higher standards here in Vietnam than they do in the U.S.," he instructed aides.[30] One of Lodge's closest aides believed that "Lansdale wanted the reality of elections, while Lodge was convinced we needed only the appearance of a democracy in order to do what we had to do. Which wasn't the same thing."[31]

Lansdale thought he could change the ambassador's attitude by enlisting the aid of Richard Nixon, Lodge's 1960 running mate, who was passing through Saigon. Jet-lagged and jowly, sporting the five o'clock shadow that was a cartoonist's delight, Nixon appeared at the Cong Ly house to meet Lansdale and his team. Going around the room, shaking hands with everyone, Nixon finally came to Lansdale and asked him, "Well, Ed, what are you up to?"

Lansdale got straight to the point: "Mr. Vice President, we want to help General [Nguyen Duc] Thang make this the most honest election that's ever been held in Vietnam."

"Oh, sure, honest, yes, honest, that's right," Nixon replied, *"so long as you win!"*

Daniel Ellsberg, who was present, noted that Nixon then "did three things in quick succession: winked, drove his elbow hard into Lansdale's arm, and, in a return motion, slapped his own knee. My colleagues turned to stone."[32]

Nixon's future national security adviser was no more supportive. At a White House meeting on August 2, 1966, following his second trip to Vietnam, Henry Kissinger said that Lansdale "was too much of a Boy Scout" and that Phil Habib should be put in charge of the elections instead.[33]

Such skepticism about the possibility of implanting democracy in Vietnam was understandable. But there was a hardheaded logic to what Lansdale was doing. It was not just a case of misapplied idealism on his part. As Tran Ngoc Chau, one of the most energetic and honest officers in the South Vietnamese army, explained, "Give villagers a way to get rid of a corrupt or abusive district chief other than having him killed by the VC, and they'll take to it very quickly."[34]

In spite of his lack of institutional backing, Lansdale plowed ahead. In July 1966—shortly after the South Vietnamese army had violently suppressed a Buddhist uprising in Hue and Da Nang led by Tri Quang, the same monk who had helped bring down Ngo Dinh Diem—there was a debate within the military junta over whether to rig the election. The prime minister, Nguyen Cao Ky, called in Lansdale to ask for his advice. Eschewing the cynicism of Lodge and Nixon, Lansdale urged him to think of "how he would look in the history books as the first Vietnamese to organize a truly honest election." This inspired Ky to make an impassioned plea before a conference of province chiefs to hold above-board balloting. A province chief commented "that he had come to the Seminar expecting to receive the usual cynical instructions, as in the past, but that he went away convinced that the Government truly wanted honest elections."[35]

The task of running the elections was assigned to Nguyen Duc Thang, the young minister of revolutionary development (as rural affairs had been renamed), to whom Lansdale had grown close. He readily adopted the suggestions made by Lansdale and his team. These included employing four thousand military cadets as poll watchers and loosening military censorship to make it possible for the press to provide extensive coverage of the campaign. Lansdale also persuaded MACV to substitute U.S. military aircraft for missions that would normally be flown by Vietnamese aircraft, freeing those airplanes to ferry ballots and election materials around the country.[36] No aspect of the campaign escaped Lansdale's attention. He even convened a meeting cohosted by Henry Cabot Lodge's wife to brainstorm about how to increase turnout among female voters.[37]

The result of Lansdale's efforts was that on September 11, 1966, 4.2 million voters (81 percent of those registered) turned out to choose among 542 candidates running for 117 seats. It was generally agreed that this was the freest and most honest election in the entire history of Vietnam. "I'm right proud of what was done,"[38] Lansdale said, and with good cause. Robert Komer, the top Vietnam expert on the National Security Council, wrote to him, "Everyone here from the top down has been immensely pleased with the elections. Few probably realize how much your constructive backstairs advice on how to play by the rules must have helped."[39]

◆

THE 1966 Constituent Assembly elections would turn out to be Lansdale's most important—and virtually sole—achievement during his second tour in Vietnam. But gaining a victory was like taking a powerful narcotic. Having done it once, Lansdale was eager to do it again. There would be a new constitution promulgated in 1967 and more elections to come—village and hamlet elections in the summer, a presidential election in September—and Lansdale was now eager to stick around and help to make them a success too. Although Colonel Sam Karrick, among others, urged him to leave when his reputation "is at a peak,"[40] he was rethinking his determination to disband his team and depart Vietnam in "late 1966." By the fall of 1966, he was talking to Henry Cabot Lodge about staying through September 1967 even though he professed himself to be "bone-weary from the past year."[41]

While Lansdale was generally far more realistic in his assessment of the situation than Westmoreland, Lodge, and other senior officials, and less prone to trumpeting illusory progress, he, too, had a weakness for imagining that his own initiatives could turn around a failing war effort. In a nine-page paper titled "The Battleground in 1967," he held out the hope that 1967 would prove "to be the turning point of the present war," not because American and South Vietnamese forces would win decisive battlefield victories (Lansdale was under no illusions on that score), but because they would succeed in wresting the initiative from the Vietcong in the "people's war."[42] Walt Rostow, who had replaced McGeorge Bundy as National Security Adviser, passed along Lansdale's memo to President Johnson with a glowing recommendation: "This is Ed Lansdale at his best—worth reading."[43]

Henry Cabot Lodge consented to let Lansdale stay on to pursue his quixotic vision. "I would like you to keep right on as you are, mingling with Vietnamese of all kinds, and maintaining your many friendships, thereby providing me with valuable information on which to base important judgments," the patrician Lodge, never one to mingle overmuch with the masses, told Lansdale in January 1967.[44] He did not, however, say anything about giving Lansdale any new power. "Either give the political ball entirely to the traditional U.S. Institutions; or give Ed a political charter," Rufus Phillips urged the State Department.[45] Lodge chose to do neither. Instead, he left Lansdale in the same perpetual limbo that he had been in ever since his arrival in Vietnam in August 1965: tasked with transforming Vietnamese politics but lacking the power to command the American pacification bureaucracy.

For all of Lansdale's complaints, he tacitly accepted this arrangement by agreeing to stay on without gaining any concessions about his role. It was a formula for more rage and frustration, and ultimately for defeat, even if Lansdale was momentarily blinded to this reality by the success of the 1966 Constituent Assembly election.

31

Waiting for the
Second Coming

The one place that a Vietnamese can afford to cry real tears.
—Visitor to Lansdale's house

B y 1967, the bipartisan consensus behind the Vietnam War—and the broader American role in the Cold War—was beginning to break down along with civil order in the United States. On April 15, the antiwar cause brought together a hundred thousand protesters in a march from New York's Central Park to the United Nations led by the Reverend Dr. Martin Luther King Jr., the pediatrician Benjamin Spock, and the singer Harry Belafonte, while that same day, on the other side of the continent, another forty thousand protesters massed in San Francisco. Prominent liberals, including Senators George McGovern, Eugene McCarthy, Mike Mansfield, and J. William Fulbright, broke with the president and expressed their opposition to the war. An anguished Bobby Kennedy, whose own brother had escalated the U.S. military involvement in Vietnam, now compared American actions to those of the Nazis, as did a growing chorus of academics.[1]

By October 1967, when nearly half of all Americans had concluded that getting into Vietnam was a mistake,[2] young men on one campus after another were burning draft cards and street battles were occurring in front of the Selective Service induction center in Oakland, California, between riot police swinging truncheons and thousands of "Stop the Draft" protesters.[3] On October 21, a hundred thousand antiwar protesters gathered at the Lincoln Memorial in Washington and marched on the Pentagon. Wherever Johnson and his appointees appeared in public, they were greeted by protesters. Some brandished signs such as "Lee Harvey Oswald, where are you now?" and "LBJ's father should have pulled out."[4] Vice President Humphrey was mobbed at Stanford University by antiwar protesters shrieking, "War criminal," "Murderer," and "Burn, baby, burn."[5]

Meanwhile, conservative Democrats and Republicans were getting fed up with the war for a very different reason: they were frustrated that Lyndon Johnson, who increasingly seemed unable to please anyone, chose to fight a "limited war" instead of bombing North Vietnam "into the Stone Age," as the retired Air Force general Curtis LeMay, a future vice presidential candidate on a ticket with George Wallace, had suggested in 1965. Some even called for invading North Vietnam or at least entering Laos and Cambodia to cut the Ho Chi Minh Trail. Senator Richard Russell of Georgia, Johnson's friend and the chairman of the Senate Armed Services Committee, spoke for many on the right when he said, "We should go in and win, or get out."[6] On both sides of the ideological divide, support for Johnson's war was plummeting.

◆

LYNDON JOHNSON knew that the war wasn't working, but he did not know what to do about it. Like many an embattled chief executive, his first instinct was to change the team while implementing the same old policy. First to go was Robert McNamara, who was looking increasingly haggard as he came to realize that the military's optimistic estimates of enemy killed and enemy strength were at odds with the dismal reality on the ground. McNamara's fetishistic zest for quantification, which Lansdale had warned against, predictably had led him astray. Once the picture of steely certitude, the defense secretary would now weep at work, leading fellow officials to worry that he was "a very disturbed guy" on the verge of a "nervous breakdown."[7] Worried that McNamara was "cracking up" and might "pull a Forrestal,"[8] Johnson eased him out at the end of November 1967 by announcing his appointment as president of the World Bank. Three months later, he would be replaced at the Pentagon by the consummate Democratic Party insider Clark Clifford, who was widely, if wrongly, believed to be more of a hawk.

Changes were also afoot in an increasingly bureaucratized Saigon. In 1967, "Blowtorch Bob" Komer, a master bureaucrat, moved from the National Security Council in Washington to Saigon to take charge of CORDS (Civil Operations and Revolutionary Development Support), the office in charge of all pacification programs. CORDS would fall under MACV, rather than the embassy; Komer would be General Westmoreland's deputy, and he would have command of military as well as civilian personnel. This would make him a far more powerful "pacification czar" than William Porter had been. At the same time, Westmoreland was getting a new deputy and successor in waiting—General Creighton "Abe" Abrams, who was widely seen as more capable and intelligent. Westy was not leaving quite yet, but Henry Cabot Lodge was. In April 1967, after less than two years in Saigon on his latest tour, he was replaced as ambassador by Ellsworth Bunker.

Bunker's father had been one of the founders of the National Sugar Refining Company (makers of the Jack Frost brand), and he spent his life until the age of fifty-six in the sugar business, rising to become president of his father's old firm. He did not enter government service until 1951, when, at the age of fifty-seven, he was appointed ambassador to Argentina by an old friend from his undergraduate days at Yale, Secretary of State Dean Acheson. He made enough of a name for himself as ambassador first to Argentina and then to Italy that, although he was a Democrat, President Eisenhower appointed him ambassador to New Delhi. John F. Kennedy and Lyndon Johnson, in turn, made him a diplomatic troubleshooter, sending him to resolve disputes between the Dutch and the Indonesians in West New Guinea, between the Egyptians and the Saudis in Yemen, and, most importantly, between various warring factions in the Dominican Republic following the U.S.

military intervention in 1965. Bunker's success in brokering Domini-can elections earned him Johnson's lasting gratitude.

Even though Bunker was already seventy-three years old, Johnson turned to him again to take charge in Saigon in 1967. Few could have predicted that he would remain in the job until 1973, long after Lyndon Johnson himself had left the White House. The Vietnamese nick-named him "Old Man Refrigerator" because of his aristocratic bearing and cool demeanor. While Bunker was invariably polite, dignified, and friendly, he also displayed a steely quality that marked him out as a man not to be trifled with. With his white hair, lean frame, and elegantly tailored three-piece suits, worn even in the tropical climate of Viet-nam, he looked like a casting director's conception of a CEO. He knew how to manage a large organization, and he would run the embassy far more effectively than the vain and imperious Lodge had done.[9]

After winning unanimous Senate confirmation, Bunker landed at Tan Son Nhut Airport on April 25, 1967, a few hours after Lodge had left. When he saw that Lansdale was part of the reception committee, he asked Ed to ride with him in his car back to the ambassador's resi-dence. En route, Lansdale mentioned that Lodge had said he had talked to Bunker about his future, and that Bunker wanted him to go. Not at all, Bunker said. He wanted Lansdale to be his guide to the byways of Vietnamese politics.[10] With Bunker's arrival, one of Lansdale's friends said, he got a "second wind."[11]

Indeed, Lansdale found that he liked Bunker better than Lodge: "He was a true, old-fashioned gentleman. His word was his bond, which wasn't true of Cabot Lodge."[12] But just because Lansdale related better to Bunker did not mean that the new ambassador, well aware of Lansdale's reputation as an independent and sometimes insubordinate operator, was going to cede him any more power than the old one had.

◆

By THE summer of 1967, shortly after the U.S. armed forces had con-cluded two of their most massive search-and-destroy missions yet (Operations Cedar Falls and Junction City), both characteristically indecisive, the rest of Lansdale's original team had left Vietnam. He replaced them with three newcomers, all with perfect backgrounds to become his protégés. Charles Sweet was a youthful-looking former USAID worker and volunteer in Vietnam with the International Voluntary Services, a private-sector nonprofit group founded by pacifist Mennonites, Quakers, and Brethren. Having first come to Vietnam in 1964, he was fluent in Vietnamese and would devote much of his time to organizing residents of Saigon's District Eight into opposing the Vietcong. David E. Hudson, who had been in Vietnam since 1961, was a "lean, intense man with close-cropped hair and wire-rimmed glasses" who had worked for Rufus Phillips at USAID's Rural Affairs Office in 1962–63.[13] The third newcomer, Calvin E. Mehlert, was a diminutive and quirky Foreign Service officer who was "sharp of mind, pen, and of tongue as well."[14] Fluent in French, Vietnamese, and Chinese, "Cal" would often wear Vietnamese-style black pajamas and blend into the background. He was widely considered one of the best—if not *the* best—American speakers of Vietnamese, a "consummate Foreign Service officer with dazzling linguistic ability."[15]

The diminished size of Lansdale's team—down from a dozen operatives to only three, supported by two embassy secretaries, two Filipino bodyguards, and a few Vietnamese household staff—was a sign of his reduced role in Vietnam. Mehlert later remembered how he and Lansdale would sit by themselves after dinner in the Cong Ly house for a game of dominoes and a glass of sweet vermouth. "It was a kind of ritual every night: sliced lemon and sweet vermouth," he said. "It was very quiet."[16] It makes for a rather melancholy image: Ed Lansdale and Cal Mehlert, rattling around a spacious villa by themselves, far removed from either the decision-making or the fighting in Vietnam. It suggests that, like a dusty Ming dynasty vase, Lansdale was increasingly seen as a relic of a bygone era.

And that was certainly the way it appeared to some of those who met Lansdale in this period. Michael Delaney, an International Voluntary Services worker, remembered that when Lansdale came to speak at the IVS compound in Saigon, he "seemed exhausted and rather sickly," and his "rah-rah presentation"—the war was winnable, he recalled Lansdale saying, "with sufficient will and morale"—"was just too unsophisticated, almost insultingly so, to pass muster at this stage of the game."[17] Delaney did not, of course, know what Daniel Ellsberg had long since discovered: that in private Lansdale could be far more realistic than "rah rah."

A White House aide who visited Saigon and met with Lansdale was even more scathing. John P. Roche was a blunt, blue-collar intellectual who was on leave from Brandeis University to work on the White House staff. On a trip to Vietnam, Roche was dazzled by Ambassador Bunker, "a superb human being with a backbone of tempered steel." He was considerably less impressed by Lansdale, whom he described as "essentially a public nuisance who has been waiting around in an alcoholic haze for the Second Coming of Magsaysay. Spends most of his time explaining to visiting firemen that if he had been listened to, the war would be over—and that he is responsible for whatever progress we have made. He should be kept in the United States and given a job that will keep him too busy to write a book."[18]

It was a caricature, but one with enough verisimilitude to sting. Even more stinging was LBJ's response. Instead of upbraiding Roche for insulting a distinguished public servant who had gone to Vietnam at his behest, the president told a secretary to "call John and tell him I liked his memo very much."[19]

◆

WHAT ROCHE and Delaney did not see was that, while his fellow Americans increasingly looked down on Lansdale, many Vietnamese still sought him out for guidance, even if they, too, were aware that he was no longer the power broker of old. "Every afternoon and evening," Cal Mehlert recalled, "someone would drop by, looking for encouragement from the one American they felt understood their situation."[20] The Cong Ly villa was, as one South Vietnamese journalist wrote in Lansdale's guest book, "the one place that a Vietnamese can afford to cry real tears." ("A moving description," Lansdale noted, "but so many do it these days that it sort of gets me down.")[21] They came because Lansdale remained unusual among American officials in Saigon in his attitude toward the Vietnamese. As he noted in a letter home, "Most of the other Americans just seem to ignore the fact that there are Vietnamese around—and that we ourselves cannot win here; it is going to take the Vietnamese to do so, regardless of how many U.S. casualties there are."²² Sensing that Lansdale was different, wrote the *New York Times* correspondent A. J. Langguth, "the Vietnamese continue to consult Lansdale, talk to him, trust him."²³

As a sign of how close Lansdale remained to so many Vietnamese, he was asked to stand in for the late Cao Dai warlord General Trinh Minh Thé at the wedding of his oldest son on July 27, 1967, an honor that would not have been accorded to any other American. Lansdale wrote an entertaining account of the ceremony for Ambassador Bunker and other officials. The wedding took place before the family shrine, piled high with "gifts of food from the groom, including a whole roasted pig. Bride and groom, side by side, made obeisance before the shrine. The bride sank prostrate before it, while the groom made four complete kowtows, bumping his forehead on the floor in front of the shrine. . . . Neither the groom, the bride's father, nor I kissed the bride after the ceremony. We chewed betel nut just before it, so maybe that's the reason why." The wedding party left amid a heavy rainfall. "A very good sign, the rain," one of the family members told Lansdale. "In the romantic stories of China," Lansdale explained to the ambassador, "the rain is used as poetic description of moments in the act of love."²⁴

It was a side of Vietnamese society that all too few Americans saw: one far removed from the sordid reality of bar girls and beggars, "free fire" zones and search-and-destroy missions.

◆

LANSDALE TRIED to create a release valve from wartime pressures by continuing to hold regular soirees at his Cong Ly villa. His goal was to bring "selected Vietnamese and Americans together to talk freely on current problems, exchange ideas, get opinions off the chest, and discover that we are all members of the human race."²⁵ Lansdale's soirees still drew a Who's Who of official Saigon. Photographs show Lansdale and his team laughing, relaxing, and singing with the likes of Henry Cabot Lodge, William Westmoreland, Nguyen Cao Ky, Nguyen Duc

Thang, Barry Zorthian, and distinguished visitors such as John Steinbeck, Richard Nixon, and Henry Kissinger. Scattered among them are a few women—mostly embassy secretaries with beehive hairdos typical of the era.

The bashes would start around seven o'clock in the evening and not end until midnight or later. Upon arrival, guests were invited to deposit their pistols in a chest near the door—"just like going into Tombstone," one attendee recalled.[26] A buffet supper was usually served along with drinks. Music was an invariable part of any evening, with guitar players such as Sam Wilson and Bernie Yoh accompanying singers such as Pham Duy and Hershel Gober. Lansdale sometimes would put down his cigarette—he often seemed to have one dangling out of his mouth—and join in on his harmonica. On occasion everyone would dance the tinikling, the Philippine pole dance. Lansdale later kidded the portly Barry Zorthian over his "skillful attempt to break up the bamboo poles we used to dance the tinikling."[27]

Even fellow Americans who generally thought Lansdale was an ineffectual nuisance were happy to accept invitations. "I couldn't for the life of me find a policy where Lansdale had an influence," said the Foreign Service officer Peter Tarnoff, a future under secretary of state, but the parties were a "relaxed" environment where "alcohol flowed freely although people were not dead drunk." For the "younger set," men like himself, the gatherings offered a place where they could share candid impressions of the war effort, most "fairly negative."[28]

◆

WHEN HE wasn't hosting these receptions, Lansdale's attention in 1967 was focused on the next set of Vietnamese elections. Village and hamlet elections were to be held from April to June, followed by an election for the presidency and the Senate in September and an election for the National Assembly in October. There were 660 candidates for the Senate elections alone,[29] but Lansdale held out the most hope for the local elections. "To my mind," he wrote early in 1967, "this can bring about the most revolutionary change in Viet Nam of the last 100 years, and be the real start of democracy—much more than the promulgation of a Constitution or election of a President. It will be the first time that village people will get power into their own hands, with their elected officials having the say on how village funds will be spent."[30] But the election of village chiefs would make little difference if the same corrupt and repressive military officers remained in power at the district, provincial, and national levels.

Lansdale argued that whoever was elected president must be able to compete with Ho Chi Minh in projecting the "image of a Confucian Vietnamese nationalist." The problem, he lamented, was that "there is no potential candidate for the Presidency in South Viet Nam who has an image to compare favorably with Ho's, in the minds of the electorate." The worst possible candidates, in his view, were generals who "are viewed for what they were before 1954 by most Vietnamese"—which is to say as "corporals or sergeants in the French forces fighting against the Vietnamese nationalists." The problem was exacerbated by the military's notorious corruption. "When a tarnish of colonialism is further clouded by personal behavior that goes against the Confucian ideal of leadership," Lansdale warned, "the problem becomes hard indeed."[31]

Fed up with the military dictatorship, Lansdale favored a transition to civilian rule. But Ellsworth Bunker continued Henry Cabot Lodge's policy of embracing the military junta because it offered stability and continuity. The only real question in the minds of American policymakers was which general should run for president. They favored Vice Marshal Nguyen Cao Ky, the "gregarious, impulsive, incautious and flamboyant" prime minister and air force commander, over the "withdrawn, suspicious, and highly cautious" head of state, General Nguyen Van Thieu.[32] But when the generals met among themselves, they selected Thieu for the presidency and Ky for the vice presidency. Thieu, cunning if boring, had defeated the flashy but erratic Ky in the only vote that counted.[33] The actual election was an afterthought: The Thieu–Ky slate won with a paltry 34.8 percent of the vote after two of the strongest civilian candidates were disqualified.[34] Once again, after a destabilizing interval of four years, South Vietnam had an autocratic Catholic president who had been born in the North.

Thieu's ascendance was grim news not only for Ky but also for Lansdale, who was closer to Ky. Lansdale offered to come in for "advisory talks," and Thieu agreed to see Lansdale for what Lansdale described as "quite candid sessions." Lansdale would challenge the president in a way that few others dared—asking, for example, "How can you make a speech about ending corruption in ARVN to a group of junior officers when you're standing next to General So-and-so whom you'd just put in charge of an operation—and all the junior officers know that he's the biggest crook in ARVN?"[35] Such sessions may have made Thieu think, but they did not make him follow Lansdale's guidance as Diem and Magsaysay had once done. In a conversation with a friend, the new president said that he was suspicious of Lansdale because of his reputation as a "kingmaker" and because Ky had "made plain to one and all" that Lansdale was "*his* friend."[36]

In truth, Lansdale was disappointed with both Thieu *and* Ky. "Thieu and Ky are very weak leaders at the moment," he wrote. "Given their natures, I doubt that they will improve much."[37]

◆

IF THE United States wanted to find a real leader in Vietnam, Lansdale suggested, it needed to look elsewhere—specifically to General Nguyen Duc Thang, the young minister of revolutionary development with whom he had become fast friends. Thang was, Lansdale said, "the only Vietnamese leader I have been permitted to work with closely over a long enough period," and he was "the only Vietnamese of stature who demonstrates inspired leadership."[38] Thang and Lansdale were, the latter wrote, "in close agreement on how to wage and win a 'people's war' against Asian Communists."[39]

Lansdale was hardly alone in his high estimation of Thang. It was a judgment almost universally shared. The *New York Times* correspondent Charles Mohr called him "the most effective administrator, innovator and inspirational leader South Vietnam has produced in seven years." Mohr accompanied Thang on one of his regular tours of the provinces, which he undertook at Lansdale's urging, making him the only senior government official whom most peasants ever encountered. The *Times* man was impressed by the general's conduct: "He invariably takes off his cap when he speaks to a village woman and invariably shakes hands with every man. He scolds policemen or hamlet officials who try to shoo children away or line people up in ranks." When an official ordered an old man to dismount from his bicycle until Thang passed, the general "showed a rare burst of anger." "I hate that," he exclaimed. "I want the people to have dignity."[40]

Lansdale had high hopes for Thang, and he thought they were beginning to be realized just before the September 3, 1967, presidential election, when Ky moved Thang from the revolutionary development ministry to become the army's vice chief of staff. In that position, he could impose the kind of practices upon the South Vietnamese army that Magsaysay had imposed on the Philippine army, persuading soldiers to embrace rather than to brutalize the peasantry. "Not quite in a Magsaysay position yet, but close to it," Lansdale wrote.[41] "My personal blue chips are on Thang—to reform the Vietnamese Armed Forces and to spark them into gaining a real win for us."[42]

But Thang did not turn out to be nearly as adept a politician as Magsaysay. In the summer of 1967, he made the fatal mistake of getting entangled in the internecine jockeying between Ky and Thieu. Although he refused Ky's entreaties to become his campaign manager and to utilize his ministry personnel to support Ky's candidacy, he did agree to see Thieu on behalf of Ky to ask the chief of state to withdraw from the presidential race. That sealed his fate as far as Thieu was concerned. The new president now regarded Thang as an enemy whose power had to be curbed. When Thang tried to prosecute a province chief and district chief in Binh Dinh Province for peculating "huge sums of piasters" intended to compensate local residents who were being resettled to make way for an American air base, Thieu sided with the II Corps commander, who had appointed the local officials and wanted the investigation blocked.[43] Lansdale wrote to Bunker that he did "not believe that the central government can truly strengthen its political position through effective programs capable of convincing the body politic that the government is both effective and honestly concerned about its citizens, until the political power of the Corps Commanders is eliminated."[44] Far from eliminating their power, Thieu was enhancing the hold of the corps commanders and undermining Thang. When Thang asked his fellow generals to adopt a code of conduct—stipulating, inter alia, that they live within their pay, limit themselves to only one house and one vehicle, and not use soldiers as domestic servants—his proposal was met with "stunned disbelief."[45]

In frustration, Thang resigned in January 1968, just before the Tet Offensive. American officials were irate, lamenting, as CIA Director Richard Helms wrote, the loss of a man who "has provided a quality of leadership and courage in his relationships with other senior leaders that, one can safely predict, will not be replaced."[46] Not wanting to alienate the Americans, Thieu gave Thang another post, appointing him commander of IV Corps in the Mekong Delta. Lansdale hoped that "as a Corps Commander, he will be free to initiate the desired reforms and reorganization in his own area, as rapidly as possible."[47] His agenda included indoctrinating troops on "why we fight," basing promotion purely on merit rather than personal connections, and demoting or dismissing "lax or incapable officers."[48]

But Thang could do little because Thieu consistently undercut him. He resigned again in June 1968 just as his staunchest American supporter, Edward Lansdale, was leaving the country. This time, the United States did not pressure Thieu to bring Thang back; Bunker had developed a close relationship with Thieu, and he did not want to spark a crisis over the fate of one general. Thang was appointed to a meaningless job as special assistant to the chairman of the Joint General Staff, "but," reported the *New York Times*, "he has no duties and he spends his time *o nha*—or 'at home'—studying mathematics for his own amusement."[49]

The system of corruption that Thang had tried to uproot long outlasted his tenure. Some province chiefs were rumored to pay ten million piastres for their posts ($50,000), with "the approved method of pay-off" being for "the wife of the nominee to 'lose' the money to the wife of the collector at poker or mah-jongg, which Vietnamese ladies of leisure play with a skill and ferocity—and for stakes even when the game is on the level—that would dazzle the sisterhoods of the Rockaways," wrote Tom Buckley of the *New York Times*. As a result of this system, founded on family connections, personal loyalties, and graft, Buckley noted, "incompetence and dishonesty are not necessarily punishable offenses, nor is merit often rewarded for its own sake."[50] Lansdale was virtually alone among senior American officials in perceiving that this was a major problem—that the corruption and unaccountability of South Vietnam's government could pose a fatal flaw in the American war effort.

◆

WITH THE 1967 elections concluded, however unsatisfactory the results, Edward Lansdale's thoughts turned once again to home. "Just plain tuckered out," he planned to leave Vietnam in early November and "loaf for a solid month in the U.S. before even starting to think again."[51] He did indeed go home for an extended period to spend the holidays with Helen, but he did not stay there. Come January 1968, he returned to Saigon. Ever the optimist, he still hoped that he could put in a few "licks" for the cause of freedom.

Lansdale expected that 1968 would be a pivotal year, and he did not want to be away. At the end of October 1967, he wrote to Ellsworth Bunker, "I believe that Hanoi is gambling on the climax of the war coming in 1968." He anticipated that North Vietnam's leaders would try to repeat their success against the French: "Hanoi policymakers and historians saw the defeat of the French forces as having reached its decisive point through the anti-war sentiment in Metropolitan France rather than on the field of battle in Viet Nam; Dien Bien Phu was fought by the Viet Minh mostly to shape public opinion in Paris, a bit of drama rather than sound military strategy. It worked and made a handful of Vietnamese leaders famous inside the Communist world." Now, he warned, Hanoi was going to implement a similar plan to "bleed the Americans" and "get the American public to force U.S. withdrawal," because "they believe the American public is vulnerable to psychological manipulation in 1968."[52]

It was an uncannily accurate prediction, which showed that, for all his inability to exert influence, Lansdale still had a better grasp than most Americans of what was happening in Vietnam.

32

The Long Goodbye

The emotional factor in the Viet-Nam war has grown to immense size since the shock of the Tet offensive. In the months ahead . . . it promises to become the real pivot factor.

—EDWARD LANSDALE

I N the early morning darkness of January 31, 1968, the *Washington Post*'s Saigon bureau chief, Peter Braestrup, received an urgent phone call from his colleague Lee Lescaze.

"They're attacking the city," Lescaze said.

"What city?" Braestrup groggily asked.

"This city," Lescaze said patiently. "Saigon."

"Ridiculous," replied Braestrup, a gruff, battle-hardened Marine veteran. "Just some incoming."[1]

And then he went back to sleep.

Edward Lansdale and his team at 194 Cong Ly—Charlie Sweet, Cal Mehlert, and Dave Hudson—were just as startled when they were woken out of a slumber around that same time by what Lansdale described as "some loud bangs nearby, followed by automatic weapons fire."

The Tet holiday is the biggest one on the Vietnamese calendar, and Lansdale and his colleagues had been up until four o'clock in the morning on the previous day reveling with Vietnamese friends. "We shot off giant strings of firecrackers . . . we ate Tet cakes and watermelons, and we drank rice and ginseng wine," Lansdale recalled, completely unconscious of the chaos that would envelop the city in a few hours. Then they had spent the afternoon of January 30 "delivering Tet gifts to various Vietnamese friends." Everyone was "a bit tuckered out when night came again."[2]

Roused out of bed around 3 a.m., Lansdale and the others grabbed weapons and went on guard duty in case the villa was attacked. It wasn't. But numerous other locations were. At 6 a.m., Ambassador Ellsworth Bunker's office called to say the embassy was under attack and not to go there. The two team secretaries, Reggie Miskovish and Martha Devlin (Lansdale referred to them, in the patronizing vernacular of the day, as "our two FS [Foreign Service] girls"), lived at the Park Hotel next to the embassy and called to report "heavy fighting next door." At virtually the same time, a South Vietnamese senator called to say that the Joint General Staff compound, the Vietnamese military headquarters located next to MACV at the airport, was under "infantry assault." Other frantic calls informed the team of "fighting all through the western part of Saigon–Cholon." It was, as Lansdale noted, "a booming way to start the day."[3]

Eighty thousand Vietcong troops had attacked 36 out of 44 provincial capitals, 64 of 242 district capitals, 5 of 6 autonomous cities, and numerous hamlets and villages.[4] Much of Hue, the nineteenth-century capital of Vietnam under the Nguyen dynasty, was seized by Communist forces, who systematically massacred at least 2,500 "class enemies"—mainly South Vietnamese military and political officials and their relatives. It would take U.S. Marines weeks of hard house-to-house fighting to dislodge the Vietcong from their final stronghold in Hue's Citadel, built in the style of Beijing's Forbidden City. Not until February 25 was the city declared secure.

Saigon had been infiltrated by more than four thousand Vietcong guerrillas in civilian clothes indistinguishable from the general population, hiding their weapons inside shipments of firewood, rice, and tomatoes. In the predawn darkness of January 31, they fanned out to attack the government radio station, the South Vietnamese military headquarters, the presidential palace, the U.S. embassy, and other targets. Their objective was to hold these locations for forty-eight hours until Main Force reinforcements could arrive in the city. At the six-story U.S. embassy on Thong Nhut (Reunification) Boulevard, completed only three months earlier, nineteen sappers wearing black pajamas and red armbands and armed with AK-47s, rocket-propelled grenades, and satchel charges managed to blast their way inside the perimeter, although they failed to penetrate the chancellery building itself. By morning, all the attackers had been killed or captured.

Lansdale and his team set out for the embassy shortly after the fighting ended. In scenes reminiscent of the battle with the sects in 1955, they drove down deserted streets, passing bullet-riddled cars; "one of them, a sedan with doors ajar, had a body sprawling from the seat onto the pavement," Lansdale noted. "An American in civilian clothes, dead."[5] At the embassy itself, he found that "broken glass and bits of masonry crunched underfoot. Along with holes in the new Embassy building and wall from VC rockets and a satchel charge . . . , the few cars in the parking lot had smashed windows, flat tires and bullet holes."[6]

Lansdale hoped to fetch his two secretaries at the Park Hotel but found himself unable to get through. A Vietcong sapper squad that had been repelled in an attack on the presidential palace had retreated to a nearby building under construction and held off one assault after another throughout the day. Finally the insurgents were cleared out, and Lansdale was able to rescue Miskovish and Devlin.

Back at Cong Ly, the team members took turns standing guard along with their two Philippine security men, Amador Maik and Joe Olan. As the siege continued day after day, the house took on, in Lansdale's words, a "gypsy air." Most of the household staff were not around because of the Tet holiday, so the Americans had to scrounge for food and cook for themselves. Cal Mehlert liberated a load of bread from the Brink's Hotel, which was being used as American bachelor officers' quarters. Most Saigon residents were trapped inside their houses, too afraid to go out, so Lansdale and his men visited their Vietnamese friends to bring them the contraband bread. Among those they saw was the family of General Nguyen Duc Thang, who were living in the garage, the most secure part of the house in case of a mortar hit. Mrs. Thang refused Lansdale's offer to move to the Cong Ly house, as did the family of Trinh Minh Thé, which had a new baby in an "amazingly brief period" after the big wedding the previous summer.

General Thang, who was spending his days helping to direct the defense of the capital, would drop by 194 Cong Ly at night, driving his own jeep, with "his old sergeant-driver sitting in the passenger seat, fondling a carbine, and looking glum," Lansdale noted. "I tell Thang that his sergeant looks that way thanks to Thang's driving, at which Thang whacks me on the back with such forceful good humor that I wonder why I don't learn to shut my mouth in time."[7]

Even without the Thang and Thé families, there was no shortage of newcomers at the Cong Ly house. Ambassador Bunker came with his security detail to spend a night after his own residence was deemed insecure. Lansdale noted that the ambassador, after taking a nap, "became acquainted with our FOV cognac from Hong Kong for the first time." Then came three Filipinos, one of them a friend of Amador Maik's, who had been driven out of their house by the fighting. Then Charlie Sweet spotted an old cook of his among a group of Vietnamese refugees, and she moved into the house along with her young daughter and niece, carrying their meager belongings on their backs. Lansdale and the rest of the team took up a collection to help these refugees make a fresh start.

"By the second day of alarums and excursions in Saigon," Lansdale wrote, "194 Cong Ly had started returning to its former habits of being a sort of Grand Central Station, with folks wandering in and out." To celebrate Ed's sixtieth birthday on February 6, Helen sent smoked oysters and other snacks from the Woodward & Lothrop department store in Washington, and his son Ted dispatched a "mammoth salami from California," while Filipino friends at the Eastern Construction Company delivered a plate of flan and San Miguel beer and Vietnamese friends presented him with "sugar baby" watermelons. "So," Ed wrote, "some of the meetings at Cong Ly lacked the usual Vietnamese spirit of grand tragedy, looking more like old-fashioned picnics."[8]

The Cong Ly house was relatively secure, given its proximity to various MACV offices "full of Americans and automatic weapons," and given the ample supply of munitions stockpiled in the house.[9] In addition, Lansdale had organized all of the Vietnamese families in a three- or four-block area into an intelligence network to warn him of strangers in the neighborhood.[10] The tragic dimensions of the offensive became apparent only when the team left the safety of their house to check on developments across the sprawling metropolis, where fighting continued for weeks. When Charlie Sweet ventured out to Saigon's District Eight, a seven-square-mile working-class area on the southern edge of the city, he found a war zone: "smoke billowed from burning houses ignited by rockets; fire trucks, ambulances and police cars made frequent runs to and from the combat area; helicopters hovered overhead; and scattered refugees emerged on foot and camped near the base of the Binh An bridge."[11]

In the end, the Tet Offensive did not succeed in igniting a general uprising against the South Vietnamese government. Official U.S. statistics showed 58,373 enemy dead between January 29 and March 1, 1968, compared with 3,895 American combat deaths, 214 allied troops (Australians, South Koreans, New Zealanders, Thais), 4,954 South Vietnamese troops, and 14,300 South Vietnamese civilians.[12] By coming out into the open, the Vietcong lost a great deal of their infrastructure in the South.

Lansdale noted that the enemy "has been crushed militarily,"[13] but, unlike more conventional military men, he warned Bunker that the offensive had the potential to achieve Hanoi's objectives: it could strike "fear into the hearts of the urban population by demonstrating the inability of the government to provide adequate security," and it could increase "pressure on the U.S. at home and abroad to withdraw, by seeking to demonstrate the hopelessness of victory and the immorality of our cause (for example, the image of U.S. firepower destroying friendly Vietnamese cities)."[14] "The emotional factor in the Viet-Nam war has grown to immense size since the shock of the Tet offensive," he wrote. "In the months ahead . . . it promises to become the real pivot factor."[15]

To counteract this psychological blow, Lansdale wanted the South Vietnamese government to stage a public relations "campaign built around the battle-cry of 'Remember Hue!'" modeled on American slogans such as "Remember the Alamo" and "Remember the *Maine*." President Thieu admitted that Lansdale's idea "had merit," given popular outrage over Vietcong massacres of civilians in Hue, but did not implement it.[16] It would be Hanoi, not Saigon, that would reap the psychological benefits of the Tet Offensive.

◆

"ED, WE are going through a tremendously traumatic experience here in the States," Bill Connell, Vice President Humphrey's chief aide, wrote to Lansdale on March 20, 1968. "The success of the Tet offensive has been most dramatic here at home. Many who were with us have fallen away, and the television stations and newspapers are in full cry against the President and his policies."[17]

In a sense, the Johnson administration was a victim of its own clumsy and overeager efforts to bolster public support for the war effort. Throughout 1967, the administration had rolled out General Westmoreland to reassure Americans that "we are making progress" and "the end begins to come into view." In his most memorable phrase, Westy claimed to see "some light at the end of the tunnel."[18]

Such Pollyannaish views appeared impossible to reconcile with the capabilities the Vietcong had displayed in the Tet Offensive. "What the hell is going on?" Walter Cronkite of CBS News exclaimed. "I thought we were winning the war."[19] In the aftermath of the Tet Offensive, Cronkite journeyed to Vietnam and produced a bleak half-hour special report that aired on CBS on February 27, 1968. "It seems now more certain than ever that the bloody experience of Vietnam is to end in a stalemate," he proclaimed with his typical gravity. Imperturbable, bland, and authoritative, Cronkite was, according to polls, the most trusted man in America. "If I've lost Cronkite, I've lost Middle America," Lyndon Johnson said.[20]

Always desperate for affection and approbation, LBJ was finding his growing unpopularity to be literally unbearable. The energy that had infused him when he had assumed the presidency in 1963 was now draining out, almost as if he were a wind-up toy frozen in midgesture. In the week after the Tet Offensive began, he hardly slept. In a private meeting with Senator Richard Russell, he cried "uncontrollably."[21] "The pressure grew so intense," wrote the new secretary of defense, Clark Clifford, "that at times I felt the government itself might come apart at the seams."[22]

On February 28, 1968, Westmoreland had requested 206,000 more troops, in addition to the 492,000 who were already in Vietnam. Johnson asked Clifford what he should do. Clifford, a onetime hawk who was beginning to change his ornithological coloration, believed that the best course was to "cut losses & get out."[23] That was also the dominant view of the Wise Men, a group of elder statesmen whom Johnson convened to advise him on the war. Johnson accordingly rejected Westmoreland's request for 206,000 more troops and decided to bring the general back to Washington to become Army chief of staff. He would be replaced in Saigon by his gruff and cerebral deputy, General Creighton Abrams, who had never liked Westy's big-unit search-and-destroy strategy; Abrams preferred employing smaller-size units for a "clear and hold" strategy focused on securing the population rather than chasing the enemy's forces around the jungles.

Johnson's refusal to send any more reinforcements, coupled with his announced intention to reduce bombing of the North while launching peace talks, represented a turning point in the war. There would be no more hopes of an American military victory. The only question now was the terms and pace of withdrawal. Like the French in 1953, the Americans were simply looking for "an honorable way out." It would be a long goodbye: the war would drag on for five more years, and more Americans would be killed after the Tet Offensive than before it.

◆

LBJ WAS acutely aware that the steps he was taking, however momentous, might come too late to rescue him politically. The leak of Westmoreland's request for 206,000 troops, which appeared on the front page of the *New York Times* on March 10, 1968, reinforced public perceptions that the war was being lost. (Why would Westy need more troops if he was winning?) Two days later, on March 12, an antiwar challenger, Senator Eugene McCarthy, took 42 percent of the vote in the Democratic New Hampshire primary. When Senator Robert F. Kennedy entered the race four days later, Johnson realized he would have a bruising fight on his hands simply to secure the Democratic nomination.

Johnson tried to regain the initiative by announcing that he would deliver a televised address to the nation on Sunday evening, March 31, 1968. That morning, he stopped by Vice President Humphrey's residence—a modest two-bedroom apartment in southwest Washington overlooking the Potomac River—and showed him the text of a speech announcing that he would stop bombing most of North Vietnam and appoint Averell Harriman as special envoy for peace talks.

Then Johnson whipped out an alternative ending: "I shall not seek, nor will I accept, the nomination of my party for the Presidency of the United States."

"You're kidding, Mr. President," a shocked Humphrey exclaimed. "You can't do this, you can't just resign from office. You're going to be reelected."

Johnson said that he hadn't made up his mind, but he was afraid that unless he bowed out of the race "nobody will believe that I'm trying to end this war."

The vice president then left for a scheduled trip to Mexico City. Not until just minutes before Johnson began delivering his speech on live television from the Oval Office did Humphrey receive word of which ending he would use. When Hubert's wife, Muriel, heard the news, she burst into tears. Both Humphreys were "very shaken and emotionally upset."[24]

Much of the country, having had nary a hint that this was not to be more of Johnson's usual truculence about the war, was equally shaken—yet hardly upset. From Berkeley, California, to Madison, Wisconsin, students spilled out into the streets, honking horns and celebrating the imminent departure of the man they had come to hate over the past two years.[25] The president received more praise than he had seen since the heady early days of his presidency for what Bobby Kennedy called his "truly magnanimous" decision.[26]

◆

YET DESPITE Johnson's announcement, the war went on, with troop levels peaking later in the year at 536,000. So, too, the antiwar movement continued, as vociferous as ever. Columbia University was shut down from April 23 to April 30, 1968, by demonstrators seizing the offices of top administrators. Meanwhile, an epidemic of political violence was convulsing the land. On April 4, 1968, the Reverend Martin Luther King Jr. was assassinated in Memphis, triggering riots in 110 cities around the country, including Washington. On June 5, 1968, it was Robert F. Kennedy's turn: he was gunned down in Los Angeles in the wee morning hours shortly after winning the California primary. "Pressures here have mounted almost hour by hour, as the U.S. seems to be crumbling as a nation," Lansdale wrote, "and as the Vietnamese start wondering if we're going to abandon millions of people to be enslaved or murdered." The Cong Ly house was "filling with Vietnamese who needed some hand-holding and encouragement."[27]

On May 4, 1968, the Vietcong struck again across the South in what came to be known as mini-Tet. "As during the Tet attacks," Lansdale wrote, "all the flowering trees and shrubs are still in bloom. Somehow, their beauty just makes the rest of it more ugly than ever."[28] This time, American and South Vietnamese forces were better prepared. The Vietcong lost thirty-six thousand men without achieving any of their objectives, while American and South Vietnamese forces lost nine thousand. The Vietcong suffered even more heavily during another wave of attacks in August, losing another seventeen thousand fighters. These multiple waves of attacks were, in the words of the historian John Prados, "a military disaster" for Hanoi.[29] They were also a disaster for the South Vietnamese civilians caught in the crossfire.

On May 11, 1968, just a week after the start of mini-Tet, Charlie Sweet visited his old friends in District Eight. He was startled by "the deep anger against all Americans" because of the heavy firepower that U.S. forces were employing against the two hundred or so Vietcong guerrillas who had infiltrated their neighborhood and were launching mortar attacks against central Saigon. "Two hundred houses were being destroyed for every Viet Cong killed," one man complained. The fighting in District Eight would destroy more than five thousand buildings, kill more than two hundred civilians, wound two thousand more, and create forty thousand refugees.[30] "I hope we never use these tactics in riots in the U.S.," Lansdale wrote, "or we will lose all of our cities."[31]

Sweet's memo about District Eight "resonated," Defense Secretary Clark Clifford later wrote, with the president and with him. The defense secretary sent Sweet's memorandum to General Earle "Bus" Wheeler, chairman of the Joint Chiefs of Staff, with his endorsement, noting "that we must find a way to reduce civilian deaths without increasing American casualties." After an initial spasm of pique, General "Abe" Abrams decreed there would be no more air or artillery strikes inside Saigon without his personal authorization. As a result, there were far fewer civilian casualties during the mini-Tet of May than there had been during the original Tet Offensive.[32]

Abrams also took steps to end the Vietcong rocketing of Saigon. In June 1968, enemy rockets crashed into Saigon on twelve consecutive days, much as London had been targeted by German V-1 and V-2 rockets in 1944–45. With terrifying explosions occurring at random throughout the metropolitan area, hundreds of civilians were being killed and wounded. As Lansdale noted, "The blind caprice of enemy gunners . . . made each inhabitant feel that he might be the next target."[33] Westmoreland did not think it was a big deal; the rocketing, he said, "is of really no military consequence." Abrams disagreed. He understood that allowing the capital to be attacked was deeply demoralizing. So he instituted various measures to stop the barrage, including having helicopter gunships orbit at night over likely launch points and sending out patrols to ambush the rocket crews. An American colonel observed that "it was almost like somebody just turned the volume down."[34]

Still with a modicum of influence, Lansdale urged Abrams to

modify the way he visited with the chief of Vietnam's Joint General Staff, General Cao Van Vien. Westmoreland, in the manner of a head of state, would visit Vien's headquarters in his sedan accompanied by a flotilla of motorcycle outriders and a truckload of bodyguards. Vien, in turn, would be waiting to receive him with an honor guard. Westy would ask him, "How are you this morning, general? How are things going?" "Everything is fine," Vien would reply. Westmoreland would tell him that things were going fine with the American forces too. And then he would return to his colleagues to report that "everything's going well with the Vietnamese." Of course, Lansdale said, "Half their troops have deserted or something, but they aren't about to tell Westmoreland."

The always informal "Ugly American" suggested to Abrams that he escape the deadly formalities. "Do you drive?" he asked the general. "Of course I do," Abrams replied.

> So why don't you go over in a jeep and take an aide if you want, but you don't really need an aide. Cao Van Vien will be there with all his troops lined up and you say, General, can I park my jeep somewhere around here? Be a human being. Say I'm worrying about something—pick something that your troops aren't doing right—and Vien'll say, "You haven't heard anything yet. Let me tell you what's happened with mine." And you get down to the truth pretty quickly. And maybe you can help each other a bit. . . . It's about time we got this thing on the basis of humans talking to each other![35]

Westmoreland had ignored such advice from Lansdale before. Abrams took it as part of the process of creating what the historian Lewis Sorley described as "a better war." But Lansdale would not stay long enough to see the changes for himself. He was scheduled to leave in mid-June 1968 and, despite pressure he was receiving from some Vietnamese, including President Nguyen Van Thieu, to stay on,[36] he was determined that this time he would leave for good.

◆

By now, Lansdale had all but given up any hope of significantly influencing the turn of events. Promoting General Nguyen Duc Thang had been his last hope to make an impact, and as Thang's influence waned, so did Lansdale's. He was left to become more an analyst of Vietnamese society than a political player in his own right, as he had been in the 1950s.

Already Lansdale had become known within the U.S. government for issuing memoranda that were more anthropological than political. In 1967, for example, he had compiled a two-and-a-half-hour recording of songs performed at the Cong Ly villa. It was billed as "In the Midst of War: Folk Music, Viet Nam, 1965–1967," and featured both Vietnamese and GI tunes. "These tapes tell the story of a human side of war that should be told," Hank Miller, the narrator, intoned.[37] This was, as the anthropologist Lydia Fish later noted, "perhaps the only example known to military history of folklore being used for the transmission of intelligence." Lansdale also issued many memoranda along the lines of his description of the Trinh Minh Thé family wedding or a lexicon of Vietnamese slang, which Fish has described as "models of ethnographic field notes." Lansdale sent copies of the tape recording to President Johnson, General Westmoreland, Ambassador Bunker, and other prominent personages. All he got back in return were form letters. "It was very disappointing to me," Lansdale said a few years later, "and I don't know to this day whether they ever listened to them or not."[38]

Undaunted by the apathy of his superiors, Lansdale pressed on with his well-intentioned, but ultimately futile, mission of trying to get his fellow Americans to better understand the place where they were fighting. As a grand finale to his time in Vietnam—a total of almost seven years spread across two tours a decade apart—Lansdale produced a series of lengthy memoranda. One memo on "Vietnamese Soothsaying" included a classified annex with the names of "certain soothsayers," which had been omitted from the main report, "in case there is ever a desire for some clandestine operational use of these persons."[39]

Who but Ed Lansdale would ever think to make "operational use" of soothsayers? Another memo detailed the history and politics of the Cao Dai, whose temple in Tay Ninh Province he had first visited in the summer of 1953.[40]

His pièce de résistance was a study of South Vietnam's convoluted politics. "If I'm not present in VN as a sort of living conscience for our Mission," he told Helen, "this can be a substitute."[41] The resulting study was so long, at sixty-eight pages plus six annexes, that Lansdale told Walt Rostow, the national security adviser, "Be not dismayed by the bulk of this document, although I admit that it looks to be the heft of the leaflet I'd like to drop on Ho Chi Minh's head from 10,000 feet up."[42] The report's findings were not sanguine. Lansdale wrote that the government had "dominant political influence" over no more than half the population, primarily city dwellers and government employees and dependents. The remaining people, including most rural residents, were either controlled by the Communists or in areas of disputed control. "It seems evident that our nationalist friends will have to create much more dynamic polarity than they have been able to do since 1963, if they are to win a political struggle against the Communists," Lansdale concluded.[43]

As he regularly did with Lansdale's memoranda, Rostow forwarded this paper to President Johnson with his recommendation: "This is Ed Lansdale's bare-knuckled account of Thieu's political problems and what we face in Vietnamese politics, including how corruption works. It is worth reading."[44] Whether Johnson read the memo or not, he continued to support Thieu without pressing him to make his rule more popular and effective.

◆

By mid-June 1968, when Edward Lansdale was due to leave Vietnam for the last time, the "traditional *bong-mai* blossoms, the chrysanthemums called *bong-cuc*, the *van-tho* Buddha flowers, *mong-ca* rooster combs, mandariniers, and dahlia were withered and gone," he poetically noted, with remembrances of things now past. "Masses of barbed wire, now rusting under the rains that had come with May, clogged streets here and there about the town. Trash and garbage were being heaped on the pavements, as public services slowed."[45] Because of the mini-Tet fighting, the streets were full of kids. "The primary schools are filled with refugees, so this means that the kids cannot go to school and now have to play at home or in the streets," Lansdale observed. "And what do you think they play? Just what you think they play. They have made guns out of sticks, with tin cans and wire stuck on to show that they are up to date with the more Buck Rogerish looking weapons of the Americans and of the enemy's imports from Czechoslovakia."[46]

Given "so much suffering among the people in the urban areas," Lansdale thought of not holding a farewell party. Vietnamese friends persuaded him to go ahead but "without the usual singing and dancing." So a more "subdued" gathering convened, only two days after Robert F. Kennedy's assassination in Los Angeles, at the Cong Ly house at 4 p.m. on June 8, 1968, the early start necessitated by the curfew in post-Tet Saigon. Three hundred guests packed the second floor, Lansdale wrote, "to test whether or not the floor actually will collapse according to dire predictions in the past."[47]

At another farewell party, hosted by the attorney Dinh Thach Bich, a mob of political leaders gathered to pay tribute to Lansdale. Bich's wife had to move to a neighbor's house to find room to cook lunch; the heaping platters were then carried back to their house by neighborhood children. Lansdale accused the politicos of not having a vision for their country. "All you want to do is to be president and have everybody bowing and cheering and you smile and wave your hand at them and everything, but it doesn't go beyond that." Chastened, the politicians began making stirring speeches about the good they wanted to accomplish. Lansdale was moved and encouraged. "Well goddamn it, you people better start working together or you're going to lose your country," he said.[48]

South Vietnam's congenitally suspicious president, Nguyen Van Thieu, heard a distorted version of what had happened at Bich's house. When he called in Lansdale for a farewell visit on June 13, he said, "The police tell me that you're trying to start a revolution with all these politicians."

"Goddamn it, Thieu," Lansdale snapped (or so he later recalled). "You know what I'm doing? I am doing your job. I'm a foreigner and you should never let a foreigner do your job as president. You should do what I was doing."[49] He then told Thieu that he should get out of his office more and talk with both ordinary people and politicians. He should also "encourage political leaders to band together," and set an example of honest and moral leadership. The meeting concluded with Lansdale telling Thieu he needed to be "much closer to the people to win the struggle."[50]

It was, as Rufus Phillips wrote, "vintage Lansdale—no one else could have talked to a Vietnamese leader that way and be listened to."[51]

◆

As Edward Lansdale departed one last time from the always bustling Tan Son Nhut Airport on June 16, 1968, never to return, he tried to put a brave face on the situation. In a valedictory letter to current and former team members, he admitted, "We took some clobbering," but then went on to say, "There are a lot more Vietnamese having a much bigger say about their future today than there were when we arrived in 1965. We did our bit to bring this about. So, if we didn't do all the important things we had in mind originally—we sure did a whale of a lot of them!"[52] In truth, Lansdale knew he had not accomplished nearly as much as he or his most enthusiastic backers had hoped.

The good news was that the nonstop coups of the immediate post-Diem period had yielded to the more stable rule of General Thieu and his military junta, and their government had attained more popularity in the wake of Communist atrocities during the Tet Offensive. There was even a semblance of a functioning parliament, although its role was largely symbolic. Lansdale's greatest triumph on his second tour was the honest legislative elections of 1966. But, despite a patina of democracy, the Saigon regime was still a long way from realizing the lofty principles of the Declaration of Independence and Constitution that Lansdale cited as his lodestars. Corruption and factionalism, in particular, remained cancers eating away at the state. When Clark Clifford visited Saigon shortly after Lansdale's departure, he found "a group of squabbling and corrupt Generals, selfishly maneuvering for their own advantage while Americans and Vietnamese continued to die in combat."[53]

The larger problem was that America was no closer to winning the Vietnam War than it had been when Lansdale arrived in 1965. Although the North Vietnamese had suffered serious losses, most recently during the Tet Offensive, Hanoi's will to win remained as strong as ever, while America's was eroding by the day. Lansdale's warnings about the futility of a conventional military strategy had been ignored, along with his advice to strengthen the South Vietnamese state.

A sign of Lansdale's spectacular fall from grace was the lack of media attention to his departure. His arrival in August 1965 had been a major story covered by every newspaper and broadcast network in America. His departure in June 1968 was covered by only one newspaper, the *New York Times*, which buried a small item headlined "Lansdale Retires from Saigon Post" on an inside page next to a giant advertisement for patio furniture.[54] The *Washington Post* waited more than three months, until late September 1968, to run an interview with Lansdale. The *Post* account noted that he had tried to carve out a niche as a thought leader and catalyst for action. The problem was that "in a situation where everyone considers himself to be his own expert after a two-month stay, the post of thought leader is held at a discount."[55]

In the final analysis, *everything* that Lansdale had done on his second tour—from studying Vietnamese customs to overseeing the 1966 elections to cultivating his would-be Magsaysay, General Nguyen Duc Thang—had been "held at a discount" by the decision-makers in Washington and Saigon. The United States was being beaten in a war for the first time in its history, in political if not military terms, and Lansdale was returning home a beaten man.

PART SIX

THE BEATEN MAN

(1968–1987)

Lansdale at home with Canbo in the 1970s. (ECLPP)

33

The War at Home

What hurts me most is that friends whom I love, innocent,
decent ones, got hurt through me.

—EDWARD LANSDALE

NINETEEN SIXTY-EIGHT was destined to be remembered, like 1789, 1848, and 1989, as a year of revolution. It was not just the year of the Tet Offensive and of Lyndon Johnson's stepping down. It was also the year of the Prague Spring followed by a Red Army invasion of Czechoslovakia. The North Korean capture of an American intelligence ship, the *Pueblo*. The assassinations of Martin Luther King Jr. and Robert Kennedy. Riots in more than a hundred American cities and smoking ruins in Washington. Student protests not only across the United States but also in Britain, Mexico, Germany, France—in Paris most spectacularly. The rise of African American militants led by the Black Panthers and the Nation of Islam and of leftist militants led by the Students for a Democratic Society and the Weathermen. A chaotic Democratic National Convention in Chicago—tear gas and nightsticks, cracked heads and watery eyes. To many who lived through it, 1968 appeared to be the start of a final showdown between the Establishment and the counterculture for the future of America—or, as the radicals spelled it, "Amerika." "We spoke of smashing the State," the radical organizer turned sociologist Todd Gitlin wrote years later; "the State of smashing us."[1]

Edward Lansdale got a small taste of the unrest convulsing America's campuses when he returned from Vietnam in June 1968 feeling, as a friend put, "very low in spirits" after years of frustration and defeats.[2] Instead of going straight to Washington, he spent a few weeks in California visiting with his son Ted and his daughter-in-law Carol; Ted was stationed at Hamilton Air Force Base in Marin County. Helen even overcame her fear of flying to join him.[3]

While on the West Coast, Lansdale gave talks at UCLA, Stanford University, and the University of California at Berkeley. Berkeley, in particular, was an eye-opener. Ever since the Free Speech Movement in 1964–65, it had been the epicenter of student protest. On June 28–29, 1968, just before Lansdale's arrival, the Trotskyist Young Socialist Alliance held a rally on Telegraph Avenue in support of French student protesters. A riot ensued that left a dozen police officers and thirty-one protesters hospitalized. An underground newspaper headlined the event, "WAR DECLARED. . . . Enemy Troops Deploying on Telegraph Avenue, Allies Put Up Fierce Resistance, Then Fell Back,"[4] and millions of Americans had a distinct feeling that a domestic war, partly brought on by objections to the Vietnam War, had indeed been declared.

Lansdale's talk at the university produced what he described as a "wild session." Even if he was hardly a conventional hawk, insofar as he believed the United States should reduce its military presence in Vietnam, he was not willing to simply abandon South Vietnam, as many of the antiwar protesters demanded. He found that the students were actually better behaved than the faculty, who offered him lunch at the Faculty Club. Some of the scholars, Lansdale noted, "left the luncheon in anger over some of my jibes at them; I gathered that they wanted to do all the verbal knifing and hadn't expected me to return the blows." By contrast, Lansdale wrote, he managed to disarm the undergraduates with a clever psychological ploy: "When I gathered with the mob of students, I told them that I probably was a dirty old man, but I'd been away from the U.S. a long time and hadn't had a chance to see girls in mini skirts, and would they mind if the girls sat in the front rows where I could see them? Which the gals did. And, when the lads started acting up, the girls turned around and shut them up. So, it turned out well, with the mob finally giving me a chance to have my say."[5]

In dealing with these radicalized students—separated from him by vast disparities of age, experience, and beliefs—the by-now elderly Lansdale showed the same deft touch that he had habitually displayed with Filipinos and Vietnamese and that mysteriously eluded him in dealings with his own government colleagues.

◆

ONCE HIS West Coast swing was concluded, Lansdale planned to return to Washington, D.C., with Helen only briefly to pack their belongings and sell their house. He was intending to move to Honolulu, where the University of Hawaii had offered him a fellowship to write his memoirs and train emerging Asian leaders. But sometime in October 1968 he changed his mind and decided to stay in Washington. It is unclear why, although the explanation may have been his wife's reluctance to move.

Helen was getting along in years (she was now sixty-seven years old, while Ed was sixty), and understandably preferred to stay in the Washington area where their son Pete and his wife and children lived, rather than move far away to an unfamiliar place. Although Ed had maintained his lines of communication with Pat Kelly, he had grown more devoted to his wife with the passage of time. Some of his last letters from Vietnam communicated more passion for Helen than any of his previous extant correspondence. On March 15, 1968, for example, he wrote, "I love you. I need you."[6] A month later: "I love you and miss you, even though it doesn't go into words all the time."[7] Now they were together again, settling into the contented domesticity of which she had long dreamed. It is understandable if, after finally having come home, Ed did not want to move again.

There was only one problem. The Lansdales had already sold their house at 4503 MacArthur Boulevard in anticipation of the move to

Hawaii. They had to move temporarily into a high-rise apartment before buying a four-bedroom house at 1917 Wakefield Street in Alexandria. The hometown of both George Washington and Robert E. Lee, Alexandria had been a busy Potomac River port in the late eighteenth and early nineteenth centuries, but by 1968 it had become a bedroom community for workers from Washington. As a retired federal employee, Ed Lansdale fit right in. His house on Wakefield Street was built of brick and wood and resembled a farmhouse, an impression heightened by the many trees and bushes that surrounded it. Ed took charge of cooking the meals and tending the vegetable garden—and of walking his seventy-five-pound black poodle, Canbo (Vietnamese for "cadre"), who had replaced the deceased Koko, the dog he had acquired after the end of his last stint in Vietnam in 1956.

◆

IN THE wood-paneled study of the house, with a window affording a view of his front lawn, Lansdale would work on a memoir that he agreed in September 1968 to write for Harper & Row. Lansdale warned Cass Canfield, the legendary publishing executive who commissioned the book, that it would not be a "tell all": "I was privileged to be a sharer of some of our national policy 'secrets,' some of which remain alive and a potential danger to courageous people who are allied with America's larger interests. I'm not about to cause harm to them, if I can help it. This means that, if I were to write memoirs, there would be odd and obvious gaps in the telling."[8] Lansdale's reticence would reduce the book's marketability, but Canfield was undaunted and went ahead with the contract.

Lansdale's initial target date for delivery of the manuscript was September 1969, but like countless other authors, he would miss his deadline.[9] Lansdale found writing "much harder than [he] had contemplated."[10] By the beginning of 1970, a year and a half after starting, he was complaining to his agent, "Ouch! I didn't know it was going to be such a long, long grind when I started. I hereby give permission to hit me over the head and stop me if I ever get to thinking of doing this again."[11]

At first, the narrative started in the Philippines in 1950 and ended with his departure from Vietnam in 1956. His subsequent activities in the Pentagon and again in Vietnam he found so "full of frustrating might-have-beens that it would be sheer agony for me to write about."[12] But his editor, Genève Young, insisted that he prune back his account of the 1950s and add in a narrative of his work up to 1968. This Lansdale did—in multiple versions—only to have his next editor, Ann Harris, tell him that the book was too long. Acting very much like a Christian Scientist denying the unpleasant realities of the physical world, he took advantage of these instructions to expunge all mention of his second tour in Vietnam. He called it "a sordid epoch, I must still be bleeding emotionally from it. . . . I didn't write about it too lucidly."[13]

◆

WHILE PRIMARILY engaged in recounting his past exploits, Lansdale did not give up hope of influencing future policy toward Vietnam under the administration of Richard Nixon, who had beaten the Democratic nominee, Lansdale's old champion Hubert Humphrey, in a closely fought election. Scrupulously nonpartisan, "neither hawk nor dove,"[14] Lansdale had not supported either candidate, while maintaining links to both. He gathered in October 1968 with Rufus Phillips and other old teammates from Saigon to work on an agenda for the next administration similar to the "Concept for Victory" paper they had produced in 1964. Also participating were two current, if low-level, government officials: Sven Kraemer of the National Security Council and Ted Cantrell of the State Department.

The paper's starting point was bleak: "(1) A politically viable South Viet-Nam does not yet exist. (2) North Viet-Nam retains the military initiative and an imposing military capability. (3) The American people are tiring quickly of the war." In assaying a way forward, Lansdale and his friends counseled against both withdrawal and escalation, recommending instead that further aid to the South Vietnamese be made contingent "upon their doing their utmost to live up to the ideals and precepts contained in their own Constitution."[15]

Taking to the pages of *Foreign Affairs* for the first time since 1964,

Lansdale used the October 1968 issue to advance an even more daring idea in an article entitled "Viet Nam: Still the Search for Goals." He suggested that "a peace settlement might provide for the division of Viet Nam into three parts: a communist North, a free South and a coalition Center. The people throughout Viet Nam would be given an appropriate period to move to the area governed by the regime of their choice." He hoped that millions of Vietnamese would "vote with their feet," as they had done in 1954–55, and leave the North for freedom in the South. But the idea was impractical and attracted unfavorable attention in South Vietnam. As Ellsworth Bunker noted in a cable back to Washington, "Widespread critical reaction to the 'Lansdale Solution' has been noted here in the press, among members of the National Assembly, and from other opinion leaders. Emphasis is often placed on the fact that the Vietnamese people want unity, not further division."[16]

Lansdale's *Foreign Affairs* essay got no traction with the incoming Nixon administration. Neither did the policy paper that he and his friends prepared. Nixon and his national security adviser, Henry Kissinger, had their own ideas of how to handle Vietnam and, despite their personal acquaintance with, and even admiration for, Lansdale, there was scant overlap between their thinking and his.

◆

Richard Nixon might have been expected to sympathize with Edward Lansdale, like him a middle-class Southern Californian and an outsider to the political establishment who was often looked down upon by those with more distinguished pedigrees. Both had been raised in small religious sects—Lansdale a Christian Scientist, Nixon a Quaker. Neither man had had much use for government bureaucrats, and both reserved special disdain for the State Department, which Nixon believed to be full of "snobs in striped pants."[17] And both men were, of course, famous for their staunch anti-Communism. During the Eisenhower administration, Nixon had been a booster of Lansdale's and remained a supporter even after leaving the vice presidency. But, in the final analysis, the differences between Lansdale and Nixon were more significant than their similarities.

Lansdale was, like Hubert Humphrey, optimistic, sunny, and gregarious. Nixon, on the other hand, was a grim loner, an introvert who had turned himself into a successful politician—an extrovert's business—through sheer force of will. Like his predecessor Lyndon Johnson, he was intensely resentful of those he perceived to be his social betters and vindictive toward his self-designated "enemies." "Can you imagine what this man would have been like if somebody had loved him?" wondered Henry Kissinger.[18]

Nixon was often restrained from taking precipitate actions by Kissinger, his chief foreign policy adviser. He later wrote that those closest to the president "were expected, we believed, to delay implementing more exuberant directives"—such as bombing foreign countries on a whim—"giving our President the opportunity to live out his fantasies and yet to act, through us, with the calculation that his other image of himself prescribed."[19] But if Kissinger held Nixon back in some ways, he only encouraged Nixon in his Machiavellian tendencies.

Heinz Alfred Kissinger was a Jewish refugee from Nazi Germany who had arrived in New York in 1938 at the age of sixteen. He became a dazzling writer and speaker of English, with a talent for witty aperçus ("Nobody will ever win the battle of the sexes. There's just too much fraternizing with the enemy"), but he never lost his Teutonic accent or gravitas. As a boy, he had witnessed the collapse of the Weimar Republic. Most of his extended family perished in the Holocaust. As a sergeant in the U.S. Army, he would return to Germany with an army of occupation where he would see the price that Germany had paid for the rise of Nazism. He would be particularly anguished when, along with other GIs, he liberated a concentration camp near Hanover. A friend of his emerged from a hut to say, "Don't go in there. We had to kick them to tell the dead from the living." According to the biographer Niall Ferguson, young Kissinger commented in an unpublished essay written shortly thereafter, "That is humanity in the 20th century."[20]

Given his life experience, it is understandable that Kissinger emerged with limited faith in democracy, a deep fear of instability, and a pessimistic view of history. Kissinger was not given to enthusing, as Lansdale did, about the brotherhood of man. He preferred to pursue stability and to defend America's narrow strategic interests rather than to promote democracy and human rights. Having written his doctoral thesis on European diplomacy after the Napoleonic Wars, Kissinger imagined himself to be another Metternich or Bismarck—another brilliant, cold-blooded statesman shrewdly moving pieces around the geostrategic chessboard with scant regard for the human cost.

Neither Nixon nor Kissinger had much interest in fostering representative government in South Vietnam—a goal that Lansdale believed was imperative if the Saigon regime was ever to stand on its own. They had already made their disdain for democracy plain when, separately, each had denigrated Lansdale's plans to hold free and fair National Assembly elections in 1966. In 1971, with South Vietnam scheduled to hold a presidential election, they ignored pleas from Ambassador Ellsworth Bunker not to let Nguyen Van Thieu rig the results. Thieu wound up running unopposed with tacit approval from the White House. Following the example of Ngo Dinh Diem, he even formed his own ruling party, known ironically as the Democracy Party. Bui Diem, South Vietnam's ambassador to Washington, thought that the United States was making a fundamental mistake: "Kissinger invited the blossoming of one-man rule. Eventually, this would prove the most destructive and destabilizing factor of all."[21]

Lansdale agreed with his friend Bui Diem, writing in a letter to the *Washington Post*, "Only if the Vietnamese have a free chance to determine their future now, and use it, will there be any point to all the sacrifices we have made in Vietnam or any rationale to our present withdrawal with which we Americans can live with ourselves afterwards here at home." But his views were mocked by the *Post*'s editors, who argued that "this is the time to stop pursuing causes in Vietnam and instead to take whatever gains can be perceived, cut losses, and come home."[22] That reflected the mood of the Nixon administration, too, and helps to explain why it did not seek Lansdale's guidance. Lansdale had hoped for more influence, but wasn't especially surprised to be excluded. "I know that I've become too big a boogeyman to too many people to be really effective anymore," he acknowledged.[23]

◆

WHILE NIXON and Kissinger knew they did not want to adopt the idealistic—if also practical—reform agenda that Lansdale advocated, they fumbled around for other ways to achieve their goal of "peace with honor." Their desire was to extract U.S. troops without leaving Nixon open to the charge that he was the first president to lose a war—the same accusation that had haunted Lyndon Johnson.

Nixon thought at first that he could scare North Vietnam into ending the conflict within his first year in office, employing what he called the "Madman Theory": "We'll just slip the word to them that, 'for God's sake you know Nixon is obsessed with Communists. We can't restrain him when he's angry—and he had his hand on the nuclear button'—and Ho Chi Minh himself will be in Paris in two days begging for peace."[24] But his early 1969 ultimatum failed to spook Le Duan, who, long before Ho Chi Minh's death in September, had taken charge of North Vietnam's war effort.[25]

Nixon and Kissenger wound up adopting willy-nilly a multipronged approach toward ending the war. Their first and most important priority was reducing the total number of troops—from 536,000 when Nixon took office to 475,000 by the end of 1969, to 334,000 in 1970, to 156,000 in 1971, to 24,000 in 1972, and eventually, in 1973, to zero. Given plummeting morale in the ranks, the troop drawdown came none too soon; by the end of the 1960s, the U.S. armed forces, mired in an unpopular and ruinous war that they did not appear to be winning, were afflicted with rampant drug use, racial tensions, and even "fraggings"—troops killing their officers.

The second part of the administration's approach was to change the strategy of the troops on the ground. In truth, this was the doing more of General Creighton Abrams than of the president. Acting on his own initiative, he scaled back big-unit search-and-destroy operations to focus on securing South Vietnam's population, although he still sent troops to fight costly clashes such as the Battle of Hamburger Hill in May 1969. In the meantime, the CIA's William Colby in 1968 took over the pacification bureaucracy known as CORDS, focusing his efforts on a controversial intelligence-sharing program known as Phoenix that would "neutralize" 81,740 Vietcong cadres between 1968 and 1972, with roughly a third killed and the rest either captured or defected.[26]

The third prong of Nixon's strategy was to disrupt North Vietnamese base camps in Cambodia and Laos. When the secret bombing of Cambodia in 1969–70 accomplished, as the president put it, "Zilch,"[27] he ordered a ground "incursion"—the word "invasion" was studiously avoided. A total of 19,300 U.S. and 29,000 South Vietnamese troops moved into Cambodia beginning on April 30, 1970, backed by massive American aerial and artillery bombardment, but, as a South Vietnamese general admitted, "The Cambodian incursion proved, in the long run, to pose little more than a temporary disruption of North Vietnam's march toward domination of all of Laos, Cambodia, and South Vietnam."[28] An incursion into Laos—Operation Lam Son 719—the following year, undertaken by ARVN troops with American airpower and logistical support but no American ground troops, was even less successful. The operation would last only forty-two days, not the planned ninety days, and pictures of South Vietnamese troops hanging onto helicopter skids to escape would prove an international embarrassment.[29]

While the American and South Vietnamese armed forces were trying to increase the military pressure on Hanoi, Nixon and Kissinger were also pursuing an ambitious agenda to secure a peace deal. Starting in early 1970, the national security adviser would steal away to Paris to conduct secret negotiations with Le Duc Tho, a member of North Vietnam's Politburo, in the working-class neighborhood of Choisy-le-Roi.[30] The talks were stalemated over American demands for a mutual pullout of North Vietnamese and U.S. forces until Nixon and Kissinger decided to make a major concession in May 1971. It was billed as a "cease-fire in place," but, as Kissinger admitted to Nixon in an Oval Office conversation, "It's a unilateral withdrawal. We're not asking them to pull out."[31] Nixon and Kissinger continued to hope that South Vietnam could hold out on its own without any American military presence, even while North Vietnamese troops remained in the South, but they were realistic enough to know this might not be possible and cynical enough not to care.[32]

Thus was born what became known as the "decent interval" strategy, with Nixon and Kissinger signaling to North Vietnam and its patrons in Moscow and Beijing that Washington wanted a face-saving way out of the conflict regardless of the consequences for America's allies in Saigon. As Kissinger explained to Premier Zhou Enlai of China on July 9, 1971, "If the [South Vietnamese] government is as unpopular as you seem to think, then the quicker our forces are withdrawn, the quicker it will be overthrown. And if it is overthrown after we withdraw, we will not intervene." Zhou inquired what time period would suffice between the American withdrawal and the Communist conquest of South Vietnam. Kissinger's answer: "Say eighteen months."[33]

◆

THE EXISTENCE of the Kissinger–Le Duc Tho talks remained confidential until January 1972, when Nixon announced that they were going on, but even then the extent of the American concessions was not revealed. By contrast, there was no hiding the body bags that kept coming home. More than twenty thousand American troops would die and more than fifty thousand would be seriously wounded during the Nixon administration's slow-motion disengagement from Indochina. News of this continuing stream of casualties, along with the attacks on Laos and Cambodia, induced despair in many Americans and convinced them that Nixon really was the war-loving madman that he only pretended to be. Domestic opposition surged after panicky National Guardsmen opened fire on demonstrators at Kent State University on May 4, 1970, killing four students and wounding nine. More than 4.3 million students across the country demonstrated against the invasion of Cambodia and the Kent State shootings, forcing the temporary closure of 20 percent of America's colleges.

Among those radicalized by the invasion of Cambodia and the shootings at Kent State was Daniel Ellsberg, the former member of the Senior Liaison Office who, after a stint working in Saigon for Deputy Ambassador Bill Porter, returned in July 1967 to RAND's headquarters in Santa Monica. Like his old boss Edward Lansdale and his close friend John Paul Vann, Ellsberg had long been critical of the way the war was being conducted. But, unlike them, he now gave up hope that the war effort could be reformed, embracing immediate withdrawal as the only solution.[34] On April 15, 1971, he left RAND, a Pentagon contractor, liberating himself to come out publicly against the war. Ellsberg now opposed the conflict with the same zeal with which he had once supported it. He began to claim that everyone associated with the conflict, including himself, was a "war criminal" and that anyone who did not actively try to stop the war was a "good German."[35]

Ellsberg decided to strike a blow for peace—and to realize his own thwarted ambitions for fame—by releasing a secret study of the war's history that he had helped to compile, along with numerous other researchers, at the behest of the then defense secretary Robert McNamara. Known as *United States–Vietnam Relations, 1945–1967*, it consisted of forty-seven volumes totaling seven thousand pages. Only fifteen copies were printed, and three went to RAND for safekeeping. Ellsberg sneaked this massive study out of the building to photocopy it in an operation that would have done the CIA proud. Ellsberg was convinced that once the public read this classified history, it would conclude that Lyndon Johnson and other leaders had deceived them. After trying and failing to interest antiwar lawmakers in releasing the study with the benefit of legislative immunity from prosecution, Ellsberg shared most of the material with the *New York Times* reporter Neil Sheehan, a veteran war correspondent, who published it without Ellsberg's explicit permission beginning on June 13, 1971. Before long, Ellsberg was identified as the leaker and charged with a variety of offenses, including espionage and conspiracy, which carried a maximum punishment of 115 years in prison.

Nixon was not overly concerned at first about these disclosures, which concerned preceding administrations, not his own. Kissinger, however, was more alarmed, and his paranoia, in turn, fed Nixon's own.

Kissinger warned the president that he would be perceived as a "weakling" if he allowed this breach of security to go unchallenged, knowing that Nixon wanted above all to be seen as a "tough guy." At the president's insistence, the Justice Department went to federal court and won a temporary restraining order on June 15 to prevent the *Times* from publishing any more documents—the first time that such a thing had ever happened in U.S. history. The *Times* complied while it appealed the judge's order. To get around this roadblock, Ellsberg slipped some of the documents to the *Washington Post*, which began publishing them by the end of the week. On June 30, the Supreme Court ruled, six to three, in a landmark First Amendment case, that the *Times* and the *Post* had a right to publish the Pentagon Papers.[36]

On July 1, 1971, the *New York Times* ran excerpts from a classified memorandum Edward Lansdale had written in July 1961 to General Maxwell Taylor. Titled "Resources for Unconventional Warfare, SE Asia," the memo listed as assets not only various covert American and allied units but also two Philippines-based organizations that Lansdale had personally set up while working for the CIA: Eastern Construction Company (formerly Freedom Company) and Operation Brotherhood. The memorandum punctured their cover story as private groups by making clear that they received "U.S. support (on a clandestine basis)."

And that was only the start of the revelations. Four days later, on July 5, 1971, Lansdale found himself mentioned in a front-page article focused on the U.S. role in Indochina in 1954. In the view of the *Times*, the Pentagon Papers contradicted "the repeated assertion of several American administrations that North Vietnam alone was to blame for the undermining of the Geneva accords." One document, in particular, showed "how the Eisenhower Administration sent a team of agents to carry out clandestine warfare against North Vietnam from the minute the Geneva conference closed." That team was "headed by the legendary intelligence operative Col. Edward G. Lansdale." Inside the newspaper was a full page of quotations from Lansdale's Saigon Military Mission report. The excerpts amounted to only a fourth of the entire report and for some reason did not include one of the juiciest revelations—that Lansdale had given Ngo Dinh Diem money to facilitate the murder of the Hoa Hao rebel Ba Cut. (That would not become known until the declassification of the full report in 2014.) But what was published was titillating enough, including details of how Lou Conein and his team had infiltrated North Vietnam to conduct sabotage operations. These actions were not as damning as the *Times* made them out to be: the U.S. could hardly be accused of violating an accord it had never signed, and Lansdale's small-scale covert operations hardly compared with the massive scale of Vietcong subversion in South Vietnam. Nevertheless, the publication of the Pentagon Papers exposed to public view some of the most sensitive aspects of Lansdale's first deployment to Vietnam.

In a letter to "The Old Team," written on the day his memo to Maxwell Taylor was published, Lansdale called Ellsberg "a loon with a martyr complex." "I like Dan personally," Lansdale wrote, "but I feel strongly that he broke a trust when he purveyed the papers. They simply weren't his to play God with and neither he nor any of us can tell the extent of harm that might result to those who trusted us."[37] Lansdale was particularly "heart-sore" about the impact of Ellsberg's revelations on the Filipinos he had worked with. He wrote to Oscar Arellano, founder of Operation Brotherhood, after Arellano came under attack in the Philippines for his association with the CIA: "What hurts me most is that friends whom I love, innocent, decent ones, got hurt through me—the last damn thing I'd ever want to have happen. Please forgive me. I apologize. Want me to bend over for a swift kick?"[38]

Yet in spite of his disgust at Ellsberg's actions, Lansdale continued to maintain friendly, if distant, relations with him. Later he was to say, "His heart was in the right place when he was with me and he was always trying hard, so I excused all sorts of things."[39]

Few others could keep such a balanced perspective on such a polarizing figure. Ellsberg was admired by the left as a hero—the Beatles lined up to get *his* autograph[40]—while the right pilloried him as a traitor. Richard Nixon particularly overreacted to the Pentagon Papers leaks, and his actions contributed to his own downfall. Paranoid about more leaks, Nixon ordered the creation of the infamous Plumbers Unit, whose actions would lead to the Watergate scandal. The former FBI agent G. Gordon Liddy and the former CIA agent E. Howard Hunt burglarized the office of Ellsberg's psychiatrist in Los Angeles to dig up dirt on him. They also concocted wilder plots, redolent of earlier anti-Castro plans that Lansdale had overseen at Operation Mongoose, such as slipping Ellsberg LSD to make him appear "incoherent" in public.[41] While the White House operatives did not actually feed Ellsberg hallucinogenics, they did illegally wiretap the home telephone of Morton Halperin, a former National Security Council staffer who had joined Ellsberg's defense team. And to try to get the federal judge overseeing Ellsberg's trial to suppress the evidence of White House illegality, the Nixon aide John Ehrlichman offered to have him appointed FBI director.

The White House's blatant attempts to interfere with the court proceeding backfired: Ellsberg's case was dismissed and Nixon's actions formed a significant part of the articles of impeachment against him. Ellsberg's release of the Pentagon Papers did not hasten the end of American involvement in the Vietnam War as he had hoped—Nixon and Kissinger were already ending the war—but it did hasten the end of the Nixon presidency itself.

◆

IN HIS memoirs, Henry Kissinger pithily summed up the change that had occurred during the sixties. "A decade that had begun with the bold declaration that America should pay any price and bear any burden to ensure the survival and success of liberty," he noted, "had ended in an agony of assassinations, urban riots, and ugly demonstrations."[42]

Edward Lansdale watched the agonizing end of the stormy sixties and its bleed over into the louche seventies as a retiree quietly living in the suburbs of northern Virginia, composing his memoirs and offering advice that was ignored. As if he were a real-life version of Saul Bellow's Moses Herzog, writing unsent letters to famous recipients (and indeed he had now taken to expressing his views in letters to the editor of the *Washington Post*), he could not in the slightest affect the troop drawdown in Vietnam (of which he approved), the forays into Cambodia and Laos (of which he was less approving), the neglect of South Vietnamese democracy (of which he was bitterly critical), or the secret negotiations with Hanoi (of which he was ignorant). The process begun in the Kennedy administration, of Lansdale's gradual fall from power, had been completed by that revolutionary year of 1968. All that remained was to reckon with the cost of the policies he had opposed without effect—and to reckon, too, with the cost to himself and others of his secret past, now brought into the open by the actions of an erstwhile friend and subordinate.

34

A Defeat in Disguise

*I suspect that we're going to wind up with the twelve Politburo
guys dictating the peace, while we cover up the fact with all
sorts of face-saving statements and devices.*

—EDWARD LANSDALE

I N hindsight there was something fitting about the way that 1972,
the momentous year that would see a break-in at the Democratic
Party headquarters in the Watergate complex, began in the Lansdale
household. On February 12, a fire broke out in Ed's book-lined, wood-
paneled study. He was out of the house when it happened. Helen was
alerted by Canbo's barking. She immediately shut the door to the study
to keep the flames from spreading and called the fire department.[1] By
the time the firefighters put out the blaze, many of Ed's books, pictures, and papers had burned; others were left a "charred mess."[2] (Some
of the papers he later donated to the Hoover Institution still have burn
marks around the edges.) Even his typewriter was destroyed; all that
was left was a "melted glob."[3]

Lansdale never did figure out how the fire started. And he never
noticed, or at least never commented, on the symbolism of what had
occurred: many of his papers—the records of his past—were literally

going up in flames just as his greatest achievements in the Philippines and Vietnam were about to meet a similar fate.

◆

LUCKILY FOR Lansdale, by the time that the fire broke out, his memoir was finished. It was published by Harper & Row on March 15, 1972. The title had changed as often as its contents. Contemplated titles included "The Good Fight," "There Is My Country," "Yankee Do," "On Common Ground," "The Juan and Dan Wars," and "Memoirs of a Cold Warrior." Harper & Row opted for "Mission in Southeast Asia," which Lansdale didn't like—he felt it was too "stodgy."[4] So the book came out as *In the Midst of Wars: An American's Mission to Southeast Asia*, a title borrowed from a study of Vietnamese folk songs that Lansdale had completed in 1967.

One thing that did not change even after the publication of the Pentagon Papers was the author's quixotic refusal to come clean about his work for the CIA between 1950 and 1956. What Lansdale wrote was generally accurate as far as it went, but it was far from the whole truth. When he mentioned Operation Brotherhood and Freedom Company, for example, he made them sound as if they had been started by Filipinos. Besides his desire to cloak his secret agent past, Lansdale had another motive to rewrite history: he wanted to enhance the status of the Asians he had worked with. "Our friends come out smelling like roses, untainted and heroic in it and against a proper background," Lansdale told Charles "Bo" Bohannan. "As you know from long ago, I decided that Asia needed its own heroes—so I've given them a whole bookful of them, with us 'uns merely being companionable friends to some great guys."[5]

Other emendations were done for more personal reasons. To spare Helen's feelings, Ed left out any mention of his relationship with Pat Kelly, an omission all the more glaring because she had played such a central role in leading him to empathize with Filipinos and Vietnamese and to understand the nature of their societies. Yet for appearance's sake she needed to be blotted out of the official portrait of his life, her name appearing only once in the entire book—in the acknowledgments, tucked into a lengthy list of other people.[6]

Lansdale's decisions about what to include and what to exclude were understandable, but they came at a cost of lost credibility. Reviewing *In the Midst of Wars* for the *Saturday Review*, an influential weekly magazine, the historian Jonathan Mirsky wrote that "there is only one difficulty" with the book: "from the cover to the final page it is permeated with lies."[7] In the *New York Times*, the war correspondent Peter Arnett criticized Lansdale for ending his account in 1956 when Diem was "firmly in power in Saigon." "With all we know of the later dramatic developments of the war, and with all Lansdale knows," Arnett wrote, "his memoirs are like reading a history of the American Civil War that ends with the first election of Abraham Lincoln to the presidency."[8] In the daily *Washington Post*, the former NSC aide Chester L. Cooper criticized Lansdale for refusing to admit that his friends could do any wrong and for sheathing his heroes, Magsaysay and Diem, in a "mist of nostalgic affection."[9] In the *Post*'s Sunday "Book World," the foreign correspondent Sherwood Dickerman complained that "the national mood nowadays calls for either repentance or justification," but that Lansdale provided neither.[10]

Not even Pat Kelly thought that Lansdale's book had succeeded, and not only because any mention of their long liaison had been left out. Writing from Manila, she told the first-time author, with her typical honesty, that *In the Midst of Wars* "should have sounded more like you and not like an edited, censored document that has been declassified." She demanded to know, "Why don't you write a book just like you write your letters???"[11]

Given the negative reviews and the antiwar mood of the day, it was hardly surprising that *In the Midst of Wars* was far from a best seller. Harper & Row printed 16,100 copies but managed to sell only 3,100 in the first month, worse than any of its other lead titles.[12] The book did little to burnish Lansdale's reputation, which increasingly was that of a dreamer and an idealist out of touch with the hard realities of Asia. His approach to the Cold War, focused on winning "hearts and minds" to beat the Communists at their own game, had once been considered revolutionary but now was judged hopelessly passé. A different approach, focused on coexistence with Communism, was being pioneered by, of all people, the onetime scourge of Alger Hiss, Nikita Khrushchev, and Helen Gahagan Douglas.

◆

ON THE cold and hazy morning of February 21, 1972, *Air Force One* landed in Beijing. Waiting to greet President Richard Nixon and his party was an honor guard accompanied by China's premier, Zhou Enlai, and a gaggle of American journalists. Zhou was wearing a gray Mao suit and blue overcoat; Nixon, like a photographic negative, wore a blue business suit and gray overcoat. Photographers' shutters clicked and television cameras whirred as the two men shook hands. "How was the flight?" Zhou asked. "Very pleasant," Nixon said. The formalities over, the two leaders climbed into big black limousines for a journey into the city down a road cleared of other cars. Like Prince Potemkin preparing for a visit from Catherine the Great, the Chinese had arranged everything in advance. As the motorcade drove by, pedestrians and bicyclists hardly looked up; they had been ordered to act as if there were nothing out of the ordinary about the president of the United States dropping by for a visit.[13]

Nixon's visit to China, which would last until February 28, had taken three years to arrange and was the pinnacle of his presidency. As he loved to do, Nixon had confounded expectations: an inveterate Cold Warrior, he had pierced the "Bamboo Curtain." His intent was partly to put pressure on Moscow, and he succeeded in persuading the Soviets to launch "détente," an easing of tensions with the United States symbolized by the president's visit to Moscow from May 22 to May 30, 1972. But Nixon also wanted to put pressure on Hanoi to settle the Vietnam War; "if we don't get any Soviet breakthrough, if we don't get the Chinese, if we can't get that ensemble, we can't get anything on Vietnam," the president told Kissinger.[14] By this measure, the "opening to China" backfired. Le Duan, North Vietnam's leader, was furious that Beijing had thrown a lifeline to the "drowning" Nixon and feared that this presaged a sellout of North Vietnamese interests comparable to the 1954 Geneva Accords. To prevent this from occurring, and to take advantage of a more favorable strategic situation in South Vietnam brought about by the drawdown of U.S. forces, North Vietnam's Politburo ordered an all-out offensive to overrun South Vietnam.[15]

Beginning on March 30, 1972, First Secretary Le Duan and General Vo Nguyen Giap committed 120,000 troops and 1,200 armored vehicles to the three-pronged assault that became known as the Easter Offensive.[16] The attack enjoyed initial success, leading to concerns in Washington that South Vietnam would collapse. That catastrophe was averted with American aid. While B-52s pounded North Vietnam, other American aircraft came to the support of embattled South Vietnamese forces. The role of U.S. advisers, numbering just 5,300 men,[17] was crucial in calling in air strikes and stiffening the resistance of the ARVN (Army of the Republic of Vietnam). South Vietnamese soldiers were capable of fighting doggedly and skillfully, but the officer corps remained riddled with corruption and cronyism—the problems that Lansdale had decried and against which his protégé General Nguyen Duc Thang had unsuccessfully fought. But in 1972 embedded American advisers were able to make up for these shortcomings; they, in effect, provided the leadership that many ARVN units otherwise lacked.

The situation in II Corps, a vast area encompassing the Central Highlands, was typical. The South Vietnamese commander was Lieutenant General Ngo Dzu, a pleasant enough man and not especially corrupt by South Vietnamese standards but primarily a staff officer of scant value as a combat leader. His deputy commander, General Nguyen Huu Hanh, was a Communist sympathizer who had no desire to fight the North.[18] Luckily the senior American adviser was the indefatigable John Paul Vann, a civilian who had once been a lieutenant colonel and now occupied a major general's billet. Only five feet eight inches tall and 150 pounds, he was a small man with an outsize command presence. Vann and his fellow advisers orchestrated a crescendo of air strikes by American pilots flying Cobra gunships, various fighter-bombers, B-52 bombers, and AC-130 gunships. Other American aircraft—Huey and Chinook helicopters and C-130 transport aircraft—delivered supplies, evacuated the wounded, and moved units around the battlefield. "Wherever you dropped bombs, you scattered bodies," Vann exulted.[19] By early June 1972, the Northern attacks had been repulsed with heavy casualties. The People's Army of Vietnam lost an estimated forty thousand men, while their South Vietnamese counterparts lost eight thousand.[20]

The battle was all but over on the evening of June 9, 1972, when John Paul Vann set out on a short hop from Pleiku to Kontum aboard his Kiowa helicopter. He did not have with him his regular pilot, an experienced old warrant officer who had burned out after taking one risk too many with the fearless Vann. At the controls was a twenty-six-year-old U.S. Army lieutenant who was not used to the rain squalls and fog they encountered. Apparently overcome by vertigo, he became disoriented and flew the little helicopter straight into a clump of trees. It disintegrated in an orange fireball. As told by Neil Sheehan in his peerless chronicle, *A Bright Shining Lie*, Vann died instantly along with the pilot and a passenger.[21]

His death marked the end of an era in Vietnam. The American war was drawing to a conclusion after the death of fifty-eight thousand personnel. Vann and his fellow advisers had rendered invaluable assistance in stopping the Easter Offensive, playing the kind of low-visibility role that Lansdale had long advocated in place of massive combat formations. South Vietnam had been denuded of American ground troops and survived the test of 1972. But it was unlikely to survive in the future if the advisers—and the aircraft they could summon—were withdrawn.

◆

JOHN PAUL VANN was buried at Arlington National Cemetery on June 16, 1972. The Old Guard, the regiment to which Pete Lansdale had once belonged, assembled in the muggy heat in their dress-blue uniforms and white gloves to conduct the coffin to its final resting spot on a horse-drawn caisson. In attendance, in silent testimony to Vann's outsize influence, was a Who's Who of Washington, including Secretary of Defense Melvin Laird, Secretary of State William Rogers, General William Westmoreland, the former CORDS director Robert Komer, and his successor, William Colby, soon to become the CIA's director. Vann had touched all of them with his fire and zeal. Lou Conein came too, and so did Daniel Ellsberg, who flew in from Los Angeles, where he was about to go on trial in the Pentagon Papers case. This counter-cultural icon tried to blend in by wearing a blue pinstripe suit, but his presence, in a pew right behind Vann's family, caused a stir.

Less noticed was Edward Lansdale. Neil Sheehan thought that, in his "light brown business suit," he looked "unstylish" and exhausted. His "habitual smile" was still there, but his "throaty voice . . . was now tired and old."[22] If Lansdale appeared dejected and beaten, there was a good reason for it. The spring of '72 had been for him a time of mourning.

In late April, Lansdale had learned that his old aide Dave Hudson, who had worked with him in Saigon in 1967–68, had committed sui-cide. After leaving Vietnam, Hudson had started a dry cleaning store in La Mesa, California, but just before his death he told Lansdale that he intended to sell the business "and devote his time to helping the people of Viet Nam."[23] Lansdale was left to speculate that the unmarried and childless Hudson had killed himself out of grief over the fate of Viet-nam compounded by grief for his recently deceased mother. George Melvin, another member of Lansdale's old team, spoke for all of them when he wrote, "Dave Hudson's death hurt. America has lost a most conscientious American in Dave. Dave was a loner, but aren't we all?"[24]

At the same time that he was receiving the sad news about Dave Hudson, Edward Lansdale was also seeing his wife take a turn for the worse. "She went into a rather unexpected decline around the first of May," he noted.[25] The exact nature of her illness was impossible to ascer-tain because, as a Christian Scientist, Helen refused medical care. But it was obvious that both her heart and lungs were giving out. A long-time smoker, she had finally quit the habit, but the fire in their home on February 12 might have triggered emphysema—or so her husband and children speculated. Unable to take her to the hospital, Lansdale called in Christian Science practitioners and nurses to look after her. Their sons, Ted and Pete, came over to help, too, and they were all with her when the end came on May 14, 1972. "I gather," Ed wrote, "that Helen liked the idea of having all her menfolk present—and fell into a natural and peaceful sleep the last night, simply not awaking."[26] Sam Karrick, a former member of Lansdale's Vietnam team who was a Christian Science practitioner, conducted the funeral service.

Helen was seventy-one years old, and she had been married to Ed for thirty-eight years. The small-town secretary with "brilliant blue" eyes had met the handsome young aspiring cartoonist in New York in 1932, and they had succored each other in dealing with the misery of the Great Depression and the wreckage of their broken families. Within a few years their union had produced two sons, and by now they were doting grandparents. Most of their marriage, admittedly, had been not a fulfilling one. They had spent long years living apart and only narrowly avoided divorce. But they had drawn closer during the four years of Ed's retirement. Now she was gone, and there was a hole in his life. "It hit me pretty hard," Ed wrote a couple of months later, "and I'm taking my time about getting myself oriented again."[27]

Even nearly half a year later, Lansdale still sounded disoriented. In October 1972, he wrote that he was struggling to find his "balance again."[28] Stanley Karnow, who profiled him toward the end of the year for the *Washington Post*, described him as "lonely and dispirited" and living a "rather secluded existence" since his wife's death.[29] This "very lonely period," as Ed described it, was not destined to last long.[30] What Lansdale took care to conceal from Karnow and others, as carefully as any covert operation he had ever supervised, was that within weeks of Helen's demise he was taking steps to rekindle an old romance.

◆

As SOON as Pat Kelly heard about Helen's death, she penned a letter of condolence. Ed wrote back less than a month after Helen's death, "Patching—Bless you for your letter, which reached out and touched me so at a time of need. It's a strange period for a person to go through and a bit of affection from someone who means so much to me really helps."[31] Soon the letters between Ed and Pat began to fly with the frequency of 747s back and forth across the vast expanse of the Pacific.

There was no longer any need to limit the relationship to an epistolary one. Ed was a recent widower, Pat a longtime widow. She was now contemplating retirement from her job at the U.S. Information Agency in Manila, where her current boss was Lansdale's old friend Hank Miller. Her grown daughter, Patricia, and her family were still living in Manila, but they did not require her constant presence. Sensing an opportunity at long last for the life that she had dreamed of ever since she first met Ed, Pat announced in August 1972 that she was going to apply for a special immigrant visa available only to those who had rendered valuable service to the United States. "Hurray!" Ed wrote as soon as he found out. "It's great news—and a great and wonderful surprise to me."[32]

Ed began to dream of showing Pat the United States. "I've seen your country," he told her, "but you haven't seen mine and I can't think of anything that would thrill me more than to see it with you. We might even get into more trouble than we ever did in the Philippines. Entice you?"[33] A few days later, Pat wrote back to thank him for all his "tempting propositions." "I have never had such lures dangled over my nose in all my life [so] that perhaps one crazy day when I can hear the rain on the tin rooftops and I am lonely as all get out, I will go straight to the airline office and get me a ticket instead of getting to the Embassy for work, provided I have my special immigrant's visa by then."[34]

Pat admitted to harboring nostalgia, as did Ed, for their days together: "I can never look at a setting sun beyond the mountains or the sea, without thinking of you and those beach trips." Before long she began to imagine their life together: "You don't like shopping? Is that the message? I will shop for groceries (bacon and toast for breakfast?). How dull! How about smoked herring and fried eggs and rice, and diced tomatoes or vinegar? That's what I eat Saturdays and Sundays, sometimes replacing the smoked fish with pork sausage or the cured meat from Tarlac." She even asked him to go shopping to help her acquire a wardrobe suitable for America: "I dare you to buy me a couple of good bras, preferably Warners (stock #22998 or similar) white, and 34-B. If you are going to dress me up, you might start from the basic. Am I starting to frighten you?"[35]

Ed not only went bra shopping; he sent Pat money to finance her trip to America. "I am looking forward so much to this trip and the world it will open for this provinciana from Tarlac," she wrote. But her anticipation was tinged with nervousness. She was worried about living in a cold, strange country and having to do without some of the comforts that even middle-class Filipinos were used to. "Living in Asia, with maids and drivers around, makes living in the U.S. a little difficult at first, or so I heard," she wrote.[36]

Unspoken was an even bigger reason for concern: could she and Ed finally make a go of it as a proper couple after a decade-long liaison followed by sixteen years of intermittent contacts? What would Ed's boys, whom she had never met, think about his embrace of an old flame so soon after their mother's death? And, for that matter, what would their neighbors, friends, and complete strangers say about an interracial romance between a white man of English ancestry and a woman with darker skin and an accent? America had turned more tolerant on matters of race since the forties, when Ed and Pat had first met, but anti-miscegenation statutes had not been invalidated by the Supreme Court until 1967 (in a case originating in Ed's new home state of Virginia). With her ticket finally purchased—she was due to fly from Manila to Honolulu on February 19, 1973, and from there to San Francisco— Pat understandably found herself getting "cold feet and thinking up excuses to delay."[37] To shield herself against disappointment, she talked of visiting other friends and getting a job in the United States, thus creating an independent life for herself.

Ed flew out to San Francisco to meet Pat. For propriety's sake, she stayed with a couple of female friends from the Philippines while Ed stayed at a motel. They got together to visit the wineries of Napa and Sonoma.[38] They found each other a bit aged—she was fifty-eight, he sixty-five—and she now wore giant eyeglasses that seemed to engulf her face like a diving mask. But both were still in good health and their feelings for each other had remained undimmed by all the years that had passed since their first meeting in 1946.

By June, Pat was living with Ed in Alexandria and, after a few job interviews, had given up any thought of finding employment. Instead, they had agreed "to get married quietly one of these days before a justice of the peace." "Since we're both grandparents, and have known each other more than 27 years now," Ed explained to his younger brother Ben, "it's far from being an impulsive, blind thing. She's a lovely, witty woman whom it's a sheer joy to have around close by, as well as an old comrade who shared dangers in the Huk country—in the unwritten chapter I left out of my book. The only rub, a minor one now, is our religious backgrounds. She is Catholic, although dismayed by the materialistic trend of that church these days. We've agreed to let each other alone on the subject."[39]

The simple ceremony took place, fittingly enough given Ed's devotion to the Declaration of Independence, on the Fourth of July 1973. The setting was the Good Shepherd Catholic Church in Alexandria, Virginia, located near their house; Pat, who wore a flowing white wedding dress, had won the religious point, as women usually do. Ed's younger son, Pete, was his best man; the maid of honor was Hank Miller's wife, Ann. Ed's older son, Ted, and his wife, Carol, remained in Florida, where Ted was teaching at an Air Force ROTC summer camp. The boys were taken aback that their father was remarrying little more than a year after their mother's death, and they knew that his long-standing relationship with Pat had poisoned their parents' marriage. But they could not begrudge their father his newfound happiness. "This was an uncomfortable event for Dad's sons and their wives, in many respects," Pete recalled many years later. "I was there to support Dad in his decision to marry Pat, but could not completely shed my feelings about past issues."[40]

Ed and Pat took Amtrak's then new Auto-Train down to Florida for their honeymoon, which they combined with some lectures that Ed was giving and with a visit to see Ted and Carol. Canbo came along too: "The dog, a giant 75 lb French poodle, crowded Pat out of her place at the train window, insisting he wanted to see where we were going," Ed wrote to his English friend Peter Richards. "When he tried to crawl into her train bunk one night, I kicked him out. Who in hell does he think married the gal?"[41]

A couple of months after the wedding, Lansdale told Richards, "We are a couple of very happy people," "busily enjoying each day" together. The American lifestyle was "new and different to Pat," who had no idea "that Americans could get so much done on their own without a bunch of servants and helpers." But they managed, with Ed doing the cooking and Pat taking responsibility for housekeeping and laundry.[42]

Edward Lansdale had accomplished an improbable transformation. After coming home depressed, dejected, and defeated from Vietnam, after weathering the embarrassment of the Pentagon Papers and the humiliation of savage reviews for his book, after the deaths of two old friends and betrayal by a third, and, most importantly, after the agonizing demise of his wife of nearly four decades—after all of that, he had found contentment again with an old flame, a woman who had already shared many adventures with him and had now walked back into his life sixteen years after breaking off their illicit romance. His sons may have been understandably uneasy, but Ed was to be more content with Pat than he had been in a long time—possibly ever.

Sadly, neither of the two countries that Lansdale loved so well, the Philippines and South Vietnam, was destined to have as happy a time of it in the 1970s.

◆

FERDINAND MARCOS had been elected president of the Philippines in 1965, eight years after the death of Ramon Magsaysay, and reelected in 1969. By the early 1970s, the country was facing growing student protests, crime, and two insurgent uprisings—one by the Muslim separatists of the Moro National Liberation Front, the other by a Communist group called the New People's Army, a successor to the Huks. On September 21, 1972, Marcos imposed martial law under the rationale of restoring law and order.

Many Filipinos, including Lansdale's old friends, welcomed the move. Lansdale was skeptical—and with good cause. In a letter to the American defense attaché in Manila, who gushed about the "amazing progress" that was being made under martial law, Lansdale pointed out, "One man can improve physical conditions and make some immediate reforms. Along with it, though, is a power climate surrounding the top that is infectious in terms of corruption and paranoia which ultimately taints and then destroys the ideal of the beginning. I sure hope that

Marcos proves the exception and that his acts bring ultimate benefit to the people. I'm far from being convinced of this yet."[43]

Lansdale's concerns were well warranted. Marcos did not succeed in suppressing the insurgencies. Instead, he presided over repression and legitimized a welter of extravagant corruption that finished undoing the good government reforms that Magsaysay and Lansdale had implemented.

◆

IN NORTH VIETNAM, the failure of the Easter Offensive revived interest in the Paris peace talks. By then the negotiations had moved out of the dingy old house in Choisy-le-Roi, which the press had found out about, to a new location, a pleasant white stucco house in the quiet country town of Gif-sur-Yvette which had once belonged to the cubist painter and Communist Party member Fernand Léger.[44] With Léger's abstract paintings and tapestries as a colorful backdrop, Le Duc Tho formally dropped his demand that Nguyen Van Thieu be toppled as part of a peace deal. This made possible the outlines of a deal that was reached by the end of October 1972.

At the core of the agreement was a one-sided bargain: Washington would pledge to withdraw all of its forces from Vietnam, while Hanoi would not have to withdraw more than 150,000 of its troops from the South. Now the North Vietnamese would be in a better position to mount a fresh offensive from inside South Vietnam without having to worry, as during the Easter Offensive, about American air strikes or American advisers. Nguyen Van Thieu understandably was livid over what he viewed as a "surrender" and "sell-out."[45]

After the 1972 election, in which Nixon defeated George McGovern in a historic, forty-nine-state landslide, Nixon and Kissinger pressed for changes to appease Saigon, and when these were not forthcoming, they launched another bombing blitz against the North—Operation Linebacker II. Nixon and Kissinger later argued that the Christmas bombing forced the North to sign a peace treaty on America's terms. In fact, the changes between the preliminary agreement in October 1972 and the final version in January 1973 were minor. John Negroponte, one of Kissinger's aides, quipped, "We bombed the North Vietnamese into accepting our concessions."[46]

To bring Thieu around to support this agreement, Nixon offered a combination of threats—including a cutoff of American aid—and reassurances that the United States would rescue South Vietnam if the North attacked. South Vietnam's president had no choice but to comply. "We were doomed to failure," he reflected gloomily, "but we could not do otherwise."[47]

◆

THE PARIS PEACE ACCORDS brought precious little peace. On the very morning when the cease-fire was to go into effect, the *New York Times* reported, "Communist troops cut Route 14, the one road that connects Kontum [in the Central Highlands] with the rest of the world, and a few days later attacked a string of hamlets just west of the city."[48]

Edward Lansdale was not, of course, privy to the secret conversations of the president and his closest aides, but he knew long before the signing of the treaty that South Vietnam was being abandoned. In August 1972, he wrote, "I suspect that we're going to wind up with the twelve Politburo guys dictating the peace, while we cover up the fact with all sorts of face-saving statements and devices."[49]

Lansdale took to the op-ed page of the *New York Times* to warn that a "bloodbath" could occur after an American pullout that would cause millions of South Vietnamese to flee their country. "It is all too likely that they would turn to us Americans and plead for a way out. What would we do then? Set up refugee camps for maybe five million or so people in Southern California or the Black Hills or Cape Cod?" Lansdale warned his fellow Americans that they were mistaken to "think that our morality will permit us to isolate ourselves from postwar Vietnam" or "that generous United States economic programs for postwar rehabilitation and development will buy political solutions."[50]

Lansdale's Cassandra-like warning went unheeded—again. By 1973, after a decade of costly and seemingly futile conflict, most Americans were heartily sick of Vietnam and eager to shed the commitments made by administrations stretching back to Harry Truman's day. Nixon and

Kissinger were as war-weary as anyone. In their haste to disengage, they would set in place the conditions for the very bloodbath—and the mass exodus of refugees—that Lansdale had predicted. But just as Lansdale had been ignored when he warned about the consequences of toppling Ngo Dinh Diem in 1963, so a decade later he was ignored when he warned about the consequences of a peace treaty that would render meaningless the sacrifice of fifty-eight thousand American lives.

Lansdale's newfound marital bliss would provide scant diversion from the tragedy that was about to engulf Indochina.

35

The Abandoned Ally

It is so easy to be an enemy of the United States, but so difficult to be a friend.

—Nguyen Van Thieu

The final reckoning for South Vietnam was to come in the spring of 1975, a little more than two years after the conclusion of the Paris Peace Accords. By then, Richard Nixon had been disgraced, while the mood of self-confidence and optimism that had led America into Vietnam in the first place had been discarded as thoroughly as the fedoras and pillbox hats of the early sixties.

Facing the threat of impeachment over the Watergate scandal, Nixon had become the first president to resign from office. On the morning of August 9, 1974, Dick and Pat Nixon left the White House for the last time, walking down a red carpet onto the South Lawn to climb aboard a drab, olive-colored army helicopter that would begin their journey to exile in California. "Goodbye, Mr. President," Nixon said to his successor, Gerald R. Ford, who had assumed the vice presidency less than a year earlier after the resignation of Spiro Agnew amid a corruption probe.

"Goodbye, Mr. President," Ford replied, in the republican version of "The king is dead, long live the king!"

Then the new president and the new first lady, Betty Ford, walked back into the executive mansion, holding hands, to take part in a hastily arranged inauguration ceremony. At noon, Chief Justice Warren Burger administered the oath of office in the East Room. Ford, standing in a blue suit in front of a heavy yellow drape, delivered a short inauguration address. "In all my public and private acts as your President," he said, "I expect to follow my instincts of openness and candor with full confidence that honesty is always the best policy in the end. My fellow Americans, our long national nightmare is over."[1]

In truth, the nightmare was just beginning. Americans were dealing with runaway inflation, rising oil prices, increasing crime, and divisions over fundamental issues such as legalized abortion and school busing. The whole country seemed to be going through a crisis of confidence. In early 1974, as his brother, Stewart Alsop, lay dying of cancer, the columnist Joseph Alsop, a paladin of the Eastern Establishment, wrote to a friend, "I have begun to think that the '70s are the very worst vintage years since the history of life began on earth—with the possible exception of such intervals as the wanderings of Attila in Europe."[2]

◆

GIVEN THE multiple crises on the home front, it was hardly surprising that few Americans, with the exception of old Vietnam hands like Edward Lansdale, had any sympathy for the plight of America's allies in South Vietnam. North Vietnam had taken advantage of the withdrawal of American forces in 1973 to broaden and improve the Ho Chi Minh Trail. It was now easy for Hanoi to move large numbers of troops and weapons south, including tanks and howitzers imported from the Soviet Union and China, to make up for losses suffered in the Easter Offensive. A cadre likened the experience of driving the Ho Chi Minh Trail after 1973, with the threat of American air strikes lifted, as being "not much different from what I would later experience heading into the suburbs of an American city during rush hour."[3]

As North Vietnam was getting stronger, South Vietnam was visibly attenuated. Although the South Vietnamese armed forces appeared formidable on paper, numbering more than a million men, the bulk of them were in low-quality militia units, the Regional and Popular Forces, tied down in static defensive positions. The ground combat units of the Army of the Republic of Vietnam (ARVN) numbered only 210,000 men—fewer than the total number of North Vietnamese forces left in the South after the signing of the Paris Peace Accords. Desertion further depleted South Vietnamese ranks, as did commanders' habit of inflating their paper strength to claim the salaries of nonexistent soldiers.[4] The problem was exacerbated by declining support from Washington. The United States had provided $1.53 billion in military aid in 1973, $1.069 billion in 1974, and $583 million in 1975—half the level judged necessary even in the absence of a major North Vietnamese offensive. At the same time, a global epidemic of inflation eroded the buying power of the dollar and the piastre. In early 1975, the chairman of South Vietnam's Joint General Staff, General Cao Van Vien, issued a directive to his forces: "From this moment on we must conserve and economize on the use of each individual bullet, each drop of gasoline."[5]

"We would like to be on the side of freedom," President Nguyen Van Thieu lamented. "How can the free world abandon us?"[6] Very easily, as it turned out—all the more so because Thieu's country was hardly a democracy. Although North Vietnam was far more repressive, the lack of representative government in the South convinced many Americans that South Vietnam was not worth saving. Even many South Vietnamese came to question whether such a corrupt and ineffectual state was worth fighting for, although few showed any desire to live under Communism. By January 1975, Lansdale was writing, "With the new Congress apparently coming to the conclusion to sharply curtail aid to Vietnam, looks as though the U.S. will wind up with no options on doing anything to help our Vietnamese friends. Ouch."[7]

◆

THE UNITED STATES did not, in fact, have any good options when the North Vietnamese armed forces launched another major offensive on March 10, 1975. The attackers swiftly captured the town of Ban Me Thuot, the key to the entire Central Highlands. Rather than trying to regain control, Thieu ordered a hasty redeployment of the ARVN from the northern part of the country, intending to consolidate around Saigon and the Mekong Delta, where most of the population and agricultural land was located. This was a fatal miscalculation that led to the collapse of the South Vietnamese armed forces and, with them, the whole state. "A redeployment of forces during a slack period would have been extremely difficult—but to do so under pressure was all but impossible," noted Ira Hunt, an American general based in Thailand who provided logistical support to Saigon.[8]

By April 21, despite staunch and even suicidal resistance by some ARVN units, the last remaining defenses had collapsed around Saigon. Staffers at the U.S. embassy and the CIA annex next door began frantically shredding and burning files. The embassy roof, with smokestacks belching flames from the incinerators, looked like a funeral pyre.[9]

The U.S. ambassador, Graham Martin, who had succeeded Ellsworth Bunker in 1973, was suffering from bronchial pneumonia. "Drawn" and "pasty-faced," he looked, in the words of the CIA officer Frank Snepp, "like a walking dead man."[10] Martin had held out hope until the very end that South Vietnam could survive. Finally, on the morning of April 29, 1975, he agreed to launch Operation Frequent Wind, the helicopter evacuation of the final remaining Americans along with South Vietnamese who had worked closely with them. Americans throughout the city knew the end had come when that morning the American Radio Service interrupted its regular programming to announce, "It's a hundred and five degrees in Saigon and the temperature is rising." This was followed by the playing of Bing Crosby's "White Christmas"—the signal to skedaddle.[11] The U.S. embassy turned into a "complete mob scene": "It was surrounded," an American correspondent noted, "by a huge, frantic crowd of Vietnamese trying to get in, trying to climb over the walls."[12]

By the afternoon of April 29, a parade of Marine CH-46 Sea Knight helicopters were landing on the roof of the embassy and the larger CH-53 Jolly Green Giants in the parking lots. The helicopter flights went on all afternoon on April 29 and into the night. Finally, in the early morning hours of April 30, the order came directly from President Ford: the ambassador had to get on a helicopter and the evacuation had to end. The sickly Graham Martin, clutching the embassy's flag, took off with his remaining staff at 4:47 a.m.

There were still at least four hundred frantic Vietnamese and third-country nationals sitting in neat rows in the parking lot. "Don't worry," the Marines told them, "there's a big helicopter coming and we're all going. . . . Nobody's going to be left behind." Then the Marines sneaked away one by one to enter the embassy through a back door, barring the entrance behind them. When the panic-stricken Vietnamese saw what was happening, they smashed through the door. It was too late. At 7:53 a.m., the final helicopter took off with the final load of Marines—the last American troops out of the 2.7 million who had served in-country to leave Vietnamese soil.[13]

The passengers on those last helicopters saw a doomed city beneath them. "It looked like the countryside was exploding in flames," the ABC correspondent Ken Kashiwahara said. "That's no exaggeration. The ammunition dump at Long Binh, which was just outside Saigon, was exploding, and the sun was setting, and in several parts of the city there were big fires and flames going into the sky. It was just incredible."[14] In the distance could be seen highways crowded, Frank Snepp noted, with "literally thousands of trucks and tanks, presumably North Vietnamese, inching their way forward, their headlights blazing."[15]

◆

ON APRIL 21, Nguyen Van Thieu resigned the presidency after a decade in power. Seven days later, the Republic of Vietnam swore in its last president—General Duong Van Minh ("Big Minh"), the leader of the anti-Diem coup that had plunged the country into chaos in November 1963. He claimed that he could make a peace deal because one of his brothers was a Vietcong general. But with victory in sight, the North Vietnamese had no interest in negotiating. At 10:45 a.m. on April 30, 1975, a T-59 tank from the 203rd Tank Brigade crashed through the gates of the modernist Independence Palace (built on the site of the old Norodom Palace), where Minh and his cabinet were waiting. A few minutes later, the Communist flag was raised over the building. When the news reached Hanoi, the Vietcong leader Truong Nhu Tang noted, "the ordinarily grim and stoic Hanoiese were cheering, singing, hugging each other—many of them sobbing with a force of emotion unimaginable to anyone who had not endured and suffered as they had."[16]

What Americans call "the Vietnam War" and Vietnamese "the American War" had finally concluded in one last spasm of violence. This was the end of a thirty-year civil war between competing factions of Vietnamese over control of their country, each side aided by outside sponsors, each claiming to be the sole legitimate representatives of nationalist aspirations. The conflict had claimed the lives of 58,000 Americans and 3.6 million Vietnamese.[17] Rare was the family in either South or North Vietnam that did not have an altar set up in a corner of their house with a picture of a child, a parent, or another close relative who had been killed.

For the Communists, it was a glorious victory, the culmination of their struggle to reunite their country. "We were celebrating the advent of a new world," Truong Nhu Tang said.[18] From the American vantage point, it was the worst military defeat in their country's history, representing a profound rupture with what most (save partisans of the doomed Confederacy) perceived as an unsullied record of martial success. South Vietnam, the state that Edward Lansdale had done so much to create and sustain, had ceased to exist. Saigon was literally wiped off the map; it was renamed Ho Chi Minh City. Cambodia fell at virtually the same time to the Khmer Rouge, while Laos fell to the Pathet Lao.

All that remained for America was to succor those able to escape.

◆

EVEN BEFORE the fall of Saigon, Edward Lansdale had sprung into action to try to help his old friends in South Vietnam. In March 1975, he wrote to Hubert Humphrey, now back in the Senate, to suggest "bipartisan action to save those people who have had to flee from their homes." He invoked his experience in 1954–55, when he had helped nearly a million refugees move from North to South Vietnam, warning, "The problem today is even a heavier one."[19]

Lansdale's desperation increased as he received frantic pleas from South Vietnam. Pham Duy, the famous balladeer, sent him a particularly heartrending, handwritten note on April 3: "You know what happens to me and my family if the Communists arrive. We are now, 8 children, my wife and myself, ready to go anywhere we can live decently. . . . I never want to leave Vietnam illegally, but it's now a question of life and death! Can you help us?"[20]

Lansdale joined a group of Vietnamese friends on the evening of April 6, 1975, in front of the White House for a prayer vigil. As "an unseasonal April wind storm" chilled them and blew out their candles, "they prayed that Americans would help save their families left behind in Vietnam," Lansdale wrote in an article for the *New York Times*. "As the wind whisked away their words and tears, it seemed that nobody was listening."[21] The public may have been indifferent to the fate of South Vietnam, but Congress and the Ford administration did agree to spend $405 million to resettle 130,000 refugees in the United States.

Many of Lansdale's old Vietnamese friends asked him to help them find a new job, a new home, a new car—a new life. He arranged for Pham Duy to stay with a friend from the Air Force; eventually the singer moved to California and began giving concerts and selling records.[22] Nguyen Duc Thang, the incorruptible general who had once been seen by Lansdale as the savior of South Vietnam, escaped with his family on a small boat just before the fall of Saigon. Eventually, with the help of Lansdale and other friends, he went to work for IBM, employing his formidable mathematical skills.[23] Another friend, Bui Diem, a former South Vietnamese ambassador to the United States, wound up working, improbably enough, at a kosher deli in Washington called Goldberg's.[24] Lansdale spent Christmas week 1975 "playing a modest Santa Claus to Vietnamese families in need, giving them presents of holiday food (fruit cakes, candies, etc) to feed their big families."[25]

As for the last leaders of South Vietnam: the flashily bedecked

Nguyen Cao Ky, the air marshal and former prime minister and vice president, opened a liquor store in Orange County, California, where he worked fourteen hours a day. After the failure of his store in 1984, he went into the shrimp-fishing business in Louisiana. He died in 2011 after having moved back to Vietnam.[26] His old rival, President Nguyen Van Thieu, moved to London and then to the Boston suburbs. He became a controversial figure in the Vietnamese American community, with many of his countrymen blaming him for the collapse of South Vietnam. He died ten years before Ky. In his exile, Thieu offered a pithy summation of the South Vietnamese experience: "It is so easy to be an enemy of the United States, but so difficult to be a friend."[27]

◆

THERE WAS nothing in Vietnam comparable to the horrors of the "killing fields" of Cambodia, where an estimated two million people lost their lives after the takeover of the Khmer Rouge in 1975. But the Vietnamese Communists did carry out more limited executions of "enemies of the people," and they sent at least three hundred thousand South Vietnamese—including civil servants and politicians, artists and writers, army and police officers—to hellish "re-education camps," where they had to engage in manual labor with inadequate rations and without medical care while being subjected to Communist indoctrination and made to write "self-criticism" reports confessing their ideological sins. Those who broke the rules were subject to confinement in "tiger cages," beatings, and executions.[28] More than a million people were forced to move out of the cities and into the countryside to work on collective farms. Private businesses and property were confiscated. Anyone whose family was associated with the *ancien régime*—roughly a third of the population—suffered discrimination in employment and education. Books were burned, newspapers and broadcasters closed, and a stifling Marxist-Leninist orthodoxy imposed in the schools and the media.

Conditions took another turn for the worse in 1978 when the Vietnamese army invaded Cambodia to depose China's genocidal client, Pol Pot, beginning an eleven-year occupation of that neighboring country. The following year, 1979, Chinese troops invaded northern Vietnam, only to be defeated and humiliated by the battle-hardened Vietnamese army. There had been only a four-year respite between the end of the Second Indochina War and the outbreak of the Third. The new war—combined with the misery of collectivization and expropriation, drought and flooding, and international sanctions—sparked an economic crisis. In 1978–79, some 700,000 people fled Indochina on leaky, overcrowded boats; as many as 200,000 of these "boat people" died at sea. The rest reached squalid refugee camps in other Southeast Asian countries. In all, more than 1.4 million people left Laos, Cambodia, and Vietnam following the Communist takeover of Indochina.[29]

◆

EDWARD LANSDALE expressed "a deep-seated feeling of grief over my failure to accomplish enough in my 1965–1968 service in Vietnam to have helped the people there prevent the tragedy which eventually overcame them."[30] He and his old teammates continued to believe until their dying days that his program of political action could have saved South Vietnam. As Charles "Bo" Bohannan wrote in 1982, "Had Lansdale remained in Vietnam in the late 50s and early 60s the story would have been far different. Had we been permitted to advise Nguyen Cao Ky as he desired, again the story might have been far different."[31] And it was not just Lansdale and his circle who thought so. William Conrad Gibbons, one of the foremost chroniclers of the Vietnam War, was to say, "I think one of the tragedies of the whole thing was that [Lansdale] was never put in charge. . . . He had more of an ability to deal with the people there than almost any American—certainly any American of note. . . . Of all the people involved, he had the best understanding of what we ought to do."[32]

Would the course of the conflict have been different if Lansdale's advice had been heeded? There is, of course, no way to know. Historical counterfactuals—"could have beens" and "might have beens"—must always remain a matter of speculation.

Lansdale was at his least convincing when he regretted the American failure to do more to undermine the Hanoi regime. Washington did try to paint the North as the aggressor, but that hardly lessened its success at destabilizing the South. Nor did it lessen opposition to the war on the home front, which was primarily driven by anger at American casualties and the lack of progress by American troops on the ground. Lansdale was downright delusional when he suggested that an American-led information campaign could have so discredited the Politburo that it "could well have lost its control of the people and been overthrown."[33] He should have known better given his experience with Operation Mongoose and with his operations to destabilize North Vietnam itself in 1954–55. The only realistic way to topple the Hanoi regime would have been an American invasion. But this was an option Lansdale opposed, and for good reason. It is unlikely that it would have led to a quick and complete victory, as so many right-wingers of the Curtis LeMay type imagined. More likely, it would have resulted in an endless guerrilla war, of the kind the French had previously endured, with the Communists retaining the advantage of secure supply lines from China. Even worse, an American invasion of North Vietnam could have sparked a war with China, just as the American invasion of North Korea had done in 1950. Mao Zedong had 300,000 troops in North Vietnam, manning antiaircraft batteries and building roads, and he made clear that an American move across the seventeenth parallel would trigger a Chinese response.[34]

Lansdale was on considerably firmer ground in arguing that the Kennedy administration made a tragic mistake in backing the over-throw of Ngo Dinh Diem. Admittedly Diem was deeply flawed—he was not a man of the people like Lansdale's other protégé, Ramon Magsaysay—but there was no better alternative on offer. As Lansdale had warned, the rulers who succeeded Diem shared his shortcomings while lacking his strengths—in particular, his incorruptibility and his nationalist record. Whereas Diem had managed to achieve at least a tenuous stalemate against the Communists, his successors presided over a rapid unraveling that, for the Johnson administration, necessitated the Americanization of the war. Diem might have been even more popular if Lansdale had succeeded in the mid-1950s in his attempts to limit the authoritarian tendencies that Diem's paranoid brother, Ngo

Dinh Nhu, only encouraged. But it would have been difficult to persuade Diem under any circumstances to rule in more consensual fashion and impossible without Washington's support, which Lansdale lacked in this case.

Lansdale had a good point in arguing that the American authorities, from Eisenhower to Nixon, had erred in disregarding his advice to strengthen the accountability and reduce the corruption of the South Vietnamese regime. He may have been overly idealistic in imagining that democracy could blossom in the tropical soil of South Vietnam even as a war raged all around, but his critics were overly cynical in imagining that the unpopularity and the corruption of the regime did not matter or that there was absolutely nothing the United States could do to constructively influence a regime so dependent on American aid. Unfortunately, Lansdale's attempts to use his patented methods of friendly persuasion were effectively stillborn after 1956 in large part because he was persistently undercut by bureaucratic rivals—and after 1965, all other considerations were subordinated to the military imperatives of the American war machine. The result, as Lansdale later wrote, was that "the political rot in the selfish corruption of GVN [Government of Vietnam] and ARVN leaders . . . grew worse and worse in the post-1968 period."[35] In the end, that political rot left only the husk of a state that rapidly collapsed under the pressure of the 1975 invasion.

In fairness, South Vietnam might not have survived even if Lansdale had enjoyed more success in implementing his agenda; North Vietnam would have been a tough and determined adversary under any circumstances, with more will to win than the United States had. But at the very least the war's loss would have been less painful all around if Lansdale's advice had been heeded. He had never wanted to see half a million American troops thrashing around Vietnam, suffering and inflicting heavy casualties. His approach, successful or not, would have been more humane and less costly.

36

The Family Jewels

The visit to Senator Church's committee is what every red-blooded American boy should dream of doing some day. It has all the charm and fun of going to a dentist to have root canals.

—EDWARD LANSDALE

THE year 1975 was an annus horribilis for Edward Lansdale. It saw not just the fall of Saigon but also the fall of the CIA, at least as it had existed since its founding in 1947, as a freewheeling organization with no accountability to any outsider other than the commander in chief.

Senator Leverett Saltonstall, a Republican from Massachusetts, summed up the prevailing attitude during the CIA's early years when he said, "It is not a question of reluctance on the part of CIA officials to speak to us. Instead, it is a question of our reluctance, if you will, to seek information and knowledge on subjects which I personally, as a member of Congress and as a citizen, would rather not have."[1] By the time Saltonstall spoke those words in 1966, the outlook he described was already changing. The bungled Bay of Pigs landing in 1961 had dented the CIA's aura. The Vietnam War and the Watergate scandal further tarnished all governmental institutions, including the CIA.

The depiction of spies in the popular media moved from the glamour days of James Bond, *Mission: Impossible*, and *The Man from U.N.C.L.E.* to the paranoia of *The Parallax View* (1974), *Three Days of the Condor* (1975), and *The Osterman Weekend* (1972 novel, 1983 film), which depicted American agents as murderous villains.

Embarrassing revelations about the real-life CIA began to emerge in the mid-1960s and continued into the mid-1970s. In 1964, the journalists David Wise and Thomas B. Ross published *Invisible Government*, which provided details about CIA involvement in coups in Guatemala, Iran, South Vietnam, and Indonesia. In 1967, the radical magazine *Ramparts* revealed that the National Student Association and other private groups had taken CIA funds. In 1971, Daniel Ellsberg's leak of the Pentagon Papers revealed CIA operations in Vietnam. Soon thereafter, the CIA turncoats Victor Marchetti and Philip Agee published unauthorized accounts of their careers. The CIA was able to redact the most sensitive information out of Marchetti's 1973 book, *The CIA and the Cult of Intelligence*, but Agee published his 1975 book *Inside the Company: CIA Diary* in Britain, where it appeared full of the names of CIA officers and agents.

The CIA was even caught in the periphery of the Watergate scandal. Although CIA officials had refused to help Nixon with a cover-up (a decision for which CIA Director Richard Helms paid with his job), they had supplied, at White House request, equipment, including disguises and cameras, that was used by the Plumbers to break into the Watergate building and into the offices of Daniel Ellsberg's psychiatrist. CIA experts then worked up a psychological profile of Ellsberg for the White House. When the CIA connection emerged during Ellsberg's trial in May 1973, the newly appointed CIA director, James Schlesinger, and his deputy director for operations, William Colby, launched an investigation into what other activities outside its charter the agency might have been involved in. The result was what came to be known as the "family jewels": a 693-item list of questionable CIA operations. It was all there: opening international mail to and from the Soviet Union, reading international cables, LSD experiments on unwitting subjects, surveillance of antiwar activists to establish possible foreign connections, wiretaps of journalists implicated in leaks of classified documents, and, most embarrassing of all, unsuccessful assassination plots against foreign leaders, including Fidel Castro, Patrice Lumumba, and Rafael Trujillo. Colby was later to write "that the most remarkable thing about the list was that it was not more serious, that it did not include more widespread dangers to the lives and liberties of our citizens."[2] But it was still explosive material—and it blew up in his face eighteen months later, by which time he had succeeded Schlesinger as CIA director.

On Sunday, December 22, 1974, the *New York Times* splashed a big article by the investigative reporter Seymour Hersh across its front page. It began, "The Central Intelligence Agency, directly violating its charter, conducted a massive, illegal domestic intelligence operation during the Nixon Administration against the antiwar movement and other dissident groups in the United States, according to well-placed Government sources." The article, based on the information contained in the "family jewels" memo, went on to note "evidence of dozens of other illegal activities of the C.I.A. inside the United States, beginning in the nineteen-fifties, including break-ins, wiretapping and the surreptitious inspection of mail."[3]

There was no mention of assassination plots, but those could not stay hidden for long. President Ford worried—and he was not the only one—that "the CIA would be destroyed" if this secret came out.[4] In fact, the leak was Ford's own doing. On January 16, 1975, the president mentioned at an off-the-record lunch with editors and writers from the *New York Times* that the CIA had been involved in assassinations. On February 28, Daniel Schorr of CBS News took to the airwaves with this blockbuster revelation.[5]

By this time, Ford had already appointed an eight-person commission headed by Vice President Nelson Rockefeller to study the CIA's dubious activities. In early 1975, both the House and the Senate created select committees to hold hearings on the intelligence community: the Senate panel under Senator Frank Church of Idaho, its House counterpart under Congressman Otis Pike of New York.

All of these investigations, coming in the wake of the Watergate scandal, would combine to make 1975 the "Year of Intelligence," that is, the year when the future of the intelligence community hung in the balance. At the start of the year, it hardly seemed far-fetched to imagine that the result could be the abolishment of the CIA. Ed Lansdale was not alone among old CIA hands in thinking that, as he wrote to Charles "Bo" Bohannan, "We are seeing the subtle wreckage of some national necessities that we hold dear, being done by a new breed of terrible infants. Hardly a noble sight."[6] In March 1975, he foresaw a "witch hunt on intelligence": "I suspect we're in for a lull before the storm, the latter coming when the Hill committees start vying for publicity. I imagine that our friend Luigi [Lou Conein] might get caught up in their meshes then. I doubt that I will."[7]

Lansdale was right to expect a storm ahead. But he was wrong in thinking that he could avoid being drenched.

◆

WITHIN WEEKS of writing that letter, Lansdale was summoned in March 1975 for his first, informal interview with David W. Belin, a bow-tied attorney from Iowa who was the executive director of the Rockefeller Commission. "Seems he wanted to know what I know about assassination attempts on Fidel Castro," Lansdale wrote afterward. "I told him I knew of contingency planning, but no actual operations being attempted. . . . It struck me as a bit of Alice in Wonderland narrative. As far as I know, nobody seriously tried to bump off Castro under U.S. orders."[8]

Lansdale was probably displaying ignorance rather than duplicity in denying that anyone "tried to bump off Castro." Even though Lansdale had been executive director of Operation Mongoose, the CIA's gun-toting liaison officer William King Harvey had kept Lansdale in the dark about his attempts to induce mobsters to assassinate Castro. Few would believe, however, that Lansdale was innocent in this whole disreputable business. He would spend the next several months, as South Vietnam was in its death throes, being repeatedly questioned not only by Rockefeller Commission investigators but also by reporters and the Church Committee about his role in plots against Castro.

Two weeks after the fall of Saigon, on May 16, 1975, Lansdale was questioned again by David Belin, this time under oath. The deposition took place at 712 Jackson Place, an ornate townhouse across the street from the White House that was being used by the Rockefeller Commission as its offices. The questioning centered on a memorandum Lansdale had written on August 13, 1962, listing among various policy options the "liquidation of leaders"—words that Lansdale had excised from subsequent drafts after Bill Harvey became incensed at this breach of security. Lansdale told Belin, "I just don't recall anything at all on liquidation of leaders," but he did not deny that "there might well have been" a request for such an option. As for where such a request could have come from, Lansdale said, "Probably the president of the United States."[9]

The Rockefeller Commission finished its work on June 6, 1975, with a public report that found that "the great majority of the CIA's domestic activities comply with its statutory authority" but that it had "engaged in some activities that should be criticized and not permitted to happen again."[10] The topic of assassination was relegated to a secret annex. The commission then turned over the entire assassination file to the Senate Select Committee to Study Government Operations with Respect to Intelligence. Its eleven members and 150 staff were more than happy to take this information and run with it.

◆

THE COMMITTEE chairman, Frank Church, was only fifty-one years old and still had a boyish, slightly puffy face and a thick head of hair. But he had already served in the Senate for nineteen years and was preparing to seek the Democratic presidential nomination in 1976. Like Lansdale, he had joined Army intelligence during World War II and shipped out to Asia in 1945—in his case, China rather than the Philippines. From this experience he drew conclusions very different from those of the "Ugly American." Lansdale believed that the United States had to help the people of Asia maintain their freedom from Communism. By contrast, Church was convinced that nationalism, rather than communism, was "the great force of our times" and that the United States should not repeat the mistakes of the old colonial powers in opposing nationalist movements. In 1961, Church wrote an article arguing that the ideals of the Declaration of Independence were not transportable abroad—the very opposite of what Lansdale believed. "We are an alien in Asia," he warned, "a suspect, rich power, the only one that remains after the others have fled."[11] Lansdale was an idealist and interventionist. Church was a progressive isolationist in the mold of his boyhood hero, Senator William Borah of Idaho, a fixture in Washington from 1907 to 1940.[12]

First elected to the Senate at the age of thirty-two, in 1956, Church acquired a reputation as a gifted orator and a devoted family man—but also for being egotistical and self-righteous, constantly seeking the spotlight, and being aloof from his colleagues. He was no Lyndon Johnson–style backslapper, and he was not well liked in the clubby atmosphere of the Upper House. During the 1960s, he became an increasingly vocal opponent of the Vietnam War—much to the consternation of President Johnson. He introduced a series of amendments that gradually forced an American military pullout from Southeast Asia. But Church frustrated those of more radical views, including his own son, by being willing to work within the system for change and seeking compromise with Republicans where possible.

Church and the committee's vice chairman, Senator John Tower, Republican of Texas, negotiated an agreement with Bill Colby, who agreed to provide virtually unlimited information from the CIA as long as the committee took appropriate safeguards to keep it secret. The committee's cavernous offices in the Dirksen Senate Office Building were guarded around the clock by armed Capitol police and stocked with heavy combination safes.[13]

Being as eager for publicity as the average senator, if not more so, Frank Church focused the committee's initial inquiries on the sexiest topic available: assassinations. On Monday, July 7, 1975, Lansdale met for hours with the committee staff to discuss his participation in anti-Castro plots. The following day, it was time for the main event—a hearing in which Lansdale would testify before the senators. This spectacle would not be televised or even open to the public. It would take place in executive session in room S407, a small, out-of-the-way hearing room located directly beneath the Capitol dome. "The low ceiling, windowless walls, and heavily insulated silence—disturbed only by the hum of fluorescent lights—gave S407 a bunkerlike atmosphere," noted one of the committee staffers. The senators "sat in red leather armchairs around a curved bench." The witness sat at a small table in the middle.[14] Lansdale took his place at the witness table, which previously had been occupied by Bill Colby, Bill Harvey, and Lou Conein, among others, shortly before 2 p.m. on Tuesday, July 8. He would not leave until nearly 6 p.m.

The initial questioning was conducted by the committee's chief counsel, F. A. O. "Fritz" Schwarz, an "aggressive and strongly opinionated" litigator from a major New York law firm and scion of the toy store dynasty that had been founded by his grandfather.[15] Soon, committee members joined in. Particularly aggressive were Senator Richard Schweiker of Pennsylvania, a liberal Republican, and Senator Howard Baker of Tennessee, a more conservative Republican who had gained fame on the Watergate committee for asking witnesses, "What did the president know and when did he know it?"

Lansdale testified that neither President Kennedy nor his brother Robert F. Kennedy had ever spoken to him about assassinating Castro. He admitted to having asked the CIA to investigate the "feasibility of the assassination of Castro," but denied that anyone had ever told him that an operation to kill the Cuban leader was actually under way.

The major difficulty that Lansdale encountered came when the senators asked him about interviews he had given to the press suggesting that he was aware of Bobby Kennedy's complicity. On July 3, the *Washington Star* had run a headline: "Lansdale Names RFK in Castro Plot." The story, by the reporter Jeremiah O'Leary, confirmed an interview Lansdale had given to the Associated Press reporter David Martin on May 31. The AP article quoted him as replying "in the affirmative to the specific question of whether assassination was one of the means he considered." It also quoted him as saying, "I was working for the highest authority in the land. . . . It was the president." Lansdale told Martin that he did not deal directly with JFK but rather through an intermediary. Asked whether that intermediary was National Security Adviser McGeorge Bundy, Lansdale replied, "No, it was someone much more intimate." He told Martin, off the record, that he was referring to Robert Kennedy.

Asked by the Church Committee to reconcile those interviews with his sworn statement that Bobby Kennedy had not ordered him to kill Castro, Lansdale claimed the reporters misquoted him. "I never did receive any order from President Kennedy or from the Attorney General, Robert Kennedy—no order about taking action against Castro personally."[16] The committee subsequently called in both O'Leary and Martin to swear under oath that the accounts they had written were accurate. How to reconcile Lansdale's divergent statements?

He was telling the truth, but not the whole truth, when he told the Church Committee that neither of the Kennedy brothers had directly ordered him to kill Castro. They would never do something so . . . gauche! But the bulk of the evidence suggested that, as Lansdale told O'Leary and Martin, the Kennedy brothers were aware of the plots and did not object. It is unclear why, in testifying before the committee, Lansdale recoiled from drawing the obvious inference about the Kennedys' complicity, but he may have been trying to tamp down the outrage he heard from Kennedy partisans after his interviews were published. Robert McNamara, who had never cared for Lansdale, blasted him in his own testimony to the Church Committee "for what I consider loose and irresponsible and at times contradictory testimony in the press. . . . I am damn annoyed at the damage he has done to dead people."[17] McNamara was, of course, being less than truthful in denying his own support and the Kennedys' for Castro's assassination. The myth of Camelot died hard.

Joseph diGenova, a future U.S. attorney for the District of Columbia who was then a young lawyer on the Church Committee's minority staff, recalled that Lansdale "did a good job," although he was not as much of a showman as Bill Harvey had been during his testimony. "Lansdale did not want to be there, but he came," diGenova said. "I don't remember anyone pouncing on him or grilling him. He was treated very respectfully."[18] Lansdale's own recollection was less favorable:

The visit to Senator Church's committee is what every red-blooded American boy should dream of doing some day. It has all the charm and fun of going to a dentist to have root canals. I had two long days of it—the first with staff and the committee's legal counsels and the second with the committee itself—with questions being shot at me by the majority and minority counsels as well as the 13 senators. I think some of them had been watching too many Perry Mason shows on TV or the old Watergate trials. From the way they tried to badger and intimidate me about minutia from 13 years ago—getting sarcastic when I couldn't remember who said what at a meeting, I must admit I did a little lecturing in return, although I barely kept my temper at some of the nastier questions.[19]

It was hardly surprising that Lansdale had such a negative reaction. It was the first time he had testified to Congress since leaving his Pentagon position in 1963, and in those days he was used to far more genteel treatment at the hands of deferential lawmakers.

◆

THE CHURCH COMMITTEE continued its investigation into the fall. On September 16, 1975, it held its first televised hearing. The highlight was Chairman Church, in the glare of klieg lights, holding up a dart gun that Colby had obligingly provided to him from the CIA's vaults—a weapon that could have been, but never was, used to kill someone. This caused a media sensation, but by the third day public interest had waned, with Church's biographers noting that "seats in the huge room were half empty, and many reporters had turned to other stories."[20]

The committee's report, entitled "Alleged Assassination Plots Involving Foreign Leaders," was publicly released on November 21, 1975, over the protests of President Ford. The major finding was incontrovertible: "The evidence establishes that the United States was implicated in several assassination plots."[21] On the crucial issue of whether these assassination attempts had been authorized by the president, the committee equivocated; the hallowed doctrine of "plausible deniability" made it impossible definitively to ascribe ultimate responsibility for the CIA's most sensitive operations.[22]

From Lansdale's standpoint, the major interest in the committee report lay in the fact that it provided the fullest public accounting yet of Operation Mongoose and his role in it—something that he had tried to keep hidden from even his closest associates. Given that Mongoose had been a failure, the details that now emerged were hardly flattering. A footnote on page 143 of the committee report, which was to be much quoted in newspaper accounts, recounted the CIA officer Tom Parrott's sarcastic testimony about Lansdale's "Elimination by Illumination" scheme—that is, having a U.S. submarine surface off the coast of Cuba to shoot star shells into the night sky to convince Cubans that "the Second Coming of Christ was imminent and that Christ was against Castro." Lansdale indignantly fired off a letter to Church assuring him "that this is absolutely *untrue*."[23] In fact, as we have seen, it *was* true. Lansdale had either forgotten, or was lying about, a classified memorandum he had written on October 15, 1962, that proposed just such a scheme. The publicity that this scheme received did further damage to Lansdale's already frayed reputation. By 1975, at the height of détente, few remembered how prevalent such "nutty schemes" had been during World War II and the early days of the Cold War, when a feeling of wartime necessity prevailed. Lansdale was suffering the public humiliation that could just as easily have been meted out to numerous others.

After digesting the Church Committee report, Lansdale wrote to Bohannan, "It's fascinating reading—even astonishing reading in some places since it made me squirm to see some of the things in public print that are in this. Nauseating to see how far some of our politicos and journalists go to serve their own selfish interests and to hell with our country's needs!"[24]

Many Americans shared Landale's misgivings about the exposure of the intelligence community's darkest secrets. The chorus of indignation grew when Richard Welch, the CIA station chief in Athens, was assassinated by Marxist terrorists on December 23, 1976, after having been publicly outed in Greek newspapers and in Philip Agee's magazine *CounterSpy*. Critics of the Church Committee accused it of contributing to Welch's death, even though it had been careful not to publicly name any clandestine operatives. "In the Washington area, the swing is definitely that Congress and the press have been naïve, stupid, and unfair," Lansdale wrote in January 1976.[25] The House, appalled at the Pike Committee's indiscriminate release of classified information, voted against publicly releasing its report on the CIA. (It wound up being leaked to the *Village Voice*.) The Church Committee released a final report on April 26, 1976, but it had, as the *New York Times* noted, "few disclosures."[26] In a rebuke to CIA critics, the committee concluded that the CIA "is not 'out of control.' "[27]

The thrust of the committee's findings was that there needed to be better controls on the intelligence agencies. This led the House and Senate in 1976 to set up permanent intelligence oversight committees— an arrangement that wound up working reasonably well. The "Year of Intelligence" led to other reforms, including legal limitations on domestic surveillance and an executive order prohibiting political assassinations, that, with some modifications, have stood the test of time. But the cost of these convulsions was real—and it would only grow when veteran operatives were sent into the cold.

Sensitive operations that were perfectly legal, such as the construction of a ship called the *Glomar Explorer* to raise a Russian submarine off the ocean floor, were blown and morale at the CIA plummeted. The swashbuckling spirit displayed by Lansdale and other early Cold Warriors gave way to what Henry Kissinger described as "cramped caution": "It became far easier and safer to bury oneself in bureaucratic paperwork than to stick one's neck out in a profession in which the risks at home sometimes exceeded those in the field."[28] The CIA's capacity for both covert action and intelligence gathering declined, with Lansdale lamenting in 1979, the year of the Iranian hostage crisis, "We no longer seem to have any operators worth their salt left in the old Company."[29]

It would take the CIA years to recover. But that was no longer Lansdale's direct concern. Having retired for good, he was now out in the cold himself.

37

The End of the Road

We shall not see his like again, but his ideas shall never die.

—Rufus Phillips

THE Church Committee hearings in 1975 represented Edward Lansdale's last painful turn in the public spotlight.

At the instigation of his new wife, now known as Pat Lansdale, he tried halfheartedly to land the job of ambassador to the Philippines from Jimmy Carter, who narrowly defeated Gerald Ford in the 1976 election. In early 1977, Lansdale wrote to the Democratic Party elder W. Averell Harriman, one of the leaders of the anti-Diem faction in the Kennedy administration, "Although I've just turned 69, I'm in good health and spirits—and would welcome a chance to serve our country among the Filipino people, for whom I have a deep affection." But even Lansdale was aware of how radioactive he was, especially in light of the revelations about Operation Mongoose. An ambassadorial appointment, he conceded, might stir a contentious confirmation battle and could even "strengthen the suspicions of President Marcos that Americans have been behind the plots to assassinate him and were sending me out to supervise such a task." Accordingly, Lansdale suggested, he would be satisfied to be a special envoy or assistant to the ambassador— or to take any other job that "could make honorable use of my long-time ties among the Filipino people."¹

The lack of reply to his letter was a clear indication of the fact— hardly surprising—that the Carter administration had no use for his services. Lansdale took the hint and refrained from trying to gain any other governmental position.

◆

IN THE midst of the Church Committee investigations, Pat and Ed, living comfortably, if hardly luxuriously, on their government pensions, moved in June 1975 from Alexandria to 2008 Lorraine Avenue in McLean, Virginia, a home on a winding street located closer to Washington. Founded in 1910, McLean was one of Washington's wealthiest suburbs. Its close proximity to the CIA's headquarters in Langley, which had opened in 1961, had turned it into Spook Central, with bars such as O'Toole's (jocularly referred to as the McLean Cultural Center) that were frequented by active-duty and retired intelligence officers.² Lansdale fit right in among old friends such as Rufus Phillips, Lucien Conein, Joseph Baker, and Nick Arundel.

Ed's Filipina bride was rapidly adjusting to life in the United States, although she was still thrilled by new experiences such as snowfalls. "Wonder if Pat will ever get her fill of seeing snow?" Ed wrote during the winter of 1975. "She's like a little kid every time it snows."³ Whereas Ed's first wife, Helen, had never learned to drive, Pat approached the task with gusto, learning behind the wheel of a 1975 Mustang II that Ed bought for her. "[Ed] secretly hopes that with a car to take me around shopping, I will be out of his hair and leave him alone with Vietnam problems," Pat wrote to friends in the Philippines. "As usual, he is wrong about me."⁴

Ed and Pat traveled regularly, taking long drives across the country—to the South, West, Midwest, New England—so that Ed could give speeches at institutions such as the Air Force Academy or Air War College, and they could take in the sights. There were also annual reunions of Ed and his three brothers along with their spouses and children. And there were weeks spent at a small beach cottage that Ed and Pat built in Kitty Hawk, North Carolina, where the Wright Brothers had launched the age of aviation.

While Pat did not play the role of grandmother to Ed's five grandchildren—she had four grandchildren of her own in the Philippines—he was a doting grandfather who tried to make up for all the time he had been absent during his own boys' lives. Pat, for her part, spent a few months every year in the Philippines visiting with her daughter and grandchildren. Ed joined her only once, in 1974. Having spent so much of his career overseas, he now preferred to stay at home.

While apart, Pat and Ed wrote touching letters about how much they missed each other. On July 4, 1977, their fourth wedding anniversary, Ed surprised Pat in Manila with the gift of an anniversary cake and two dozen yellow roses—along with an overseas phone call, which was still an expensive luxury in those days. "Your voice is still the same as the very first time I heard it on the phone, a million years ago . . . ," she wrote back. "I love you very much, just as I have all these past years and instead of waning, it's getting to be more and more strong."[5]

Back home, recalled Pete Lansdale, the married couple would get up late, spend a "quiet, lazy morning" together, play Scrabble for an hour or two, walk their dog, Canbo, and generally enjoy each other's company.[6] Ed spent the rest of his time either preparing for lectures, meeting with friends from the Philippines and Vietnam to swap stories about the "old days," or answering a flurry of questions from historians, documentary filmmakers, and even a biographer—Cecil Currey, a chaplain in the Army Reserves and professor of history at the University of South Florida, who, at Pat's urging, secured Ed's cooperation to work on a biography in the 1980s. "One of the graduate students who write me letters noted that there is poison in some of the writing about Vietnam," Ed wrote to Pat in 1979. "I guess maybe that's why I keep working at trying to get a straight account of it made. I sure see the poison of some of the things said about me. Maybe I'll never be able to get it all antidoted with truth."[7] He never did get the truth out to his satisfaction.

◆

THE HISTORIC election of Ronald Reagan in 1980 inaugurated a renewed push to win the Cold War. In the process there was revived interest in Edward Lansdale and his teachings, with some Reaganites eager to apply lessons from his days in the Philippines and Vietnam to fresh fights against Communist forces in Latin America—specifically, the FLMN (Farabundo Marti National Liberation Front) in El Salvador and the Sandinista government in neighboring Nicaragua.

Lansdale's chief champion was a Special Forces reservist, Major F. Andy Messing Jr., who had served in Vietnam. He started a lobbying group called the National Defense Council, whose motto was "In Defense of Free Enterprise, Country and Constitution"; its chairman was "B-1" Bob Dornan, a hawkish Republican congressman from Orange County, California. Messing had read *In the Midst of Wars*, and on a whim in 1980 he called Lansdale up—he was listed in the phone directory—and then, at Lansdale's invitation, drove out to McLean to meet him. Pat served finger sandwiches and soft drinks, and they began talking. "Whatever he said was brilliant and on-target," Messing recalled, and "it was like E. F. Hutton, everyone listened."[8] Messing became a ceaseless preacher for Lansdale's methods of fighting "low-intensity conflict," the preferred name at the time for wars involving guerrillas. "The key to solving such conflicts," he wrote, "is to address simultaneously the social, political, economic and military concerns of the countries in conflict."[9]

Messing was a well-connected player within the Reagan administration. His friends included an obscure, square-jawed Marine officer, Lieutenant Colonel Oliver North, then laboring quietly on the National Security Council staff, and retired Major General John K. "Jack" Singlaub, like Lansdale a graduate of UCLA and a onetime OSS operative who had been relieved of duty in 1977 after publicly criticizing President Jimmy Carter's call to withdraw U.S. forces from South Korea. Through Messing, Lansdale met both North and Singlaub. "I considered Lansdale a real hero," Singlaub later said.[10] North, too, was an admirer, and the attraction was mutual. When North was

fired from the NSC in 1986 for his part in the Iran-contra affair—
selling arms to Iran to win the release of American hostages and using
the proceeds to fund the Nicaraguan insurgents, known as the con-
tras, in violation of the Boland Act—Lansdale lamented, "He's a very
decent guy and used good initiative on the NSC staff. Friends of mine
have claimed that he is simply a current copy of me in today's government."[11] But whereas Lansdale had also been a maverick, he had not
violated the law and lied about his activities; if anything, he had a tendency to be too honest.

In 1984, Fred Iklé, the under secretary of defense for policy, asked
Singlaub to convene a panel of outside advisers to provide advice on
counterinsurgency in El Salvador. Lansdale, by then seventy-six years
old, was among the ten experts who spent a couple of days at the Pentagon, May 22–23, 1984, getting briefed on the situation and providing
their recommendations.[12] Lansdale argued, as did other panel members,
against sending U.S. combat forces or heavy weapons. "I don't think conventional forces work," he said.[13] He and other panel members advocated
keeping U.S. Special Forces in the lead and pressuring the government
in San Salvador to crack down on corruption and human-rights abuses to
address the "potent political element of the guerrillas." "Ideas, not bullets, are needed to defeat this element of any Communist insurgency,"
Lansdale counseled, just as he had in Vietnam and the Philippines.[14]

This time, the government was listening, in no small part because
everyone was so eager to avoid the trauma of "another Vietnam." The
Reagan administration implemented the recommendations of the Singlaub panel to sell to El Salvador slow-moving, highly precise AC-47
gunships rather than speedy A-37 jets, whose bombs risked more collat-
eral damage, while also training a disciplined police force and putting
much greater emphasis on civic action. Most importantly, the administration backed the democratically elected president, José Napoleón
Duarte, who took office in 1984. The El Salvadoran version of Ramon
Magsaysay, Duarte curbed abuses by right-wing "death squads" while
implementing the policies that, with American aid, led to the end of
the civil war in 1992.

◆

ONE OF the inescapable burdens of aging is to watch one's boon companions disappear. In August 1983, Edward Lansdale had to euthanize his beloved poodle, Canbo. "He had a hard time standing up, with legs not working well, and had even about given up eating," Ed wrote to his brothers. "Gallantly, he tried hard to keep going, but it just didn't work out. . . . It sure was hard to say good-bye to him."¹⁵ No new dog took Canbo's place. For the first time in decades, Ed would be without a canine companion.

The news about Charles "Bo" Bohannan, Lansdale's eccentric former subordinate, was no more encouraging. On June 28, 1982, Bo wrote laconically from Manila, "Got my PCS orders to the wild blue yonder or Fiddler's Green, depending on whether you take the flyboy view or the traditional yellow leg." ("PCS" was the military acronym for Permanent Change of Station; "yellow leg" is the slang for cavalry.) He was suffering from esophageal cancer, and the doctors at Clark Air Base gave him only four to eight months to live.¹⁶ Ed wrote back promising to visit the Philippines over Christmas to see him and trying to buck him up: "Aren't you just too ornery to believe the docs? A truly splendid American like you still has the fighting spirit for the tough ones."¹⁷ Lansdale never did get to see Bohannan again. He died on September 7, 1982.

◆

BY THIS time, Ed's own health was failing. In the summer of 1981, he discovered that he had trouble signing checks. His son Pete insisted that he go for a checkup. The doctors discovered that, at the age of seventy-three, he had suffered a ministroke. He was released after a couple of days and "shocked" the doctors by driving out to Colorado with Pat to give a talk at the Air Force Academy.¹⁸

On the evening of August 25, 1983, Lansdale collapsed in the hallway of his McLean home. He told Pat he would go to the hospital in the morning. But the next morning, while getting out of bed, he blacked out. "I . . . must have hit all the furniture in the room on the way down, as well as ripping the blanket off Pat and waking her up abruptly," he said. "I came to on the floor with a bloody head and banged up body and Pat kneeling over me. . . . I was a sight. Two black eyes, a broken nose, broken ribs, and a black and blue chest."[19]

Lansdale was rushed by ambulance to Fairfax Hospital, one of the top teaching hospitals in the country, where doctors discovered that he was suffering from an irregular heartbeat—technically a type of cardiac arrhythmia known as torsades de pointes. His years of hard living— working too long, suffering too much stress, smoking and drinking too much—had taken their toll. He had to be repeatedly defibrillated, with doctors sending three hundred jolts of electricity through his chest fifteen or twenty times a day in order to get his heart pumping normally. "It's a horrific experience. Most people never forget it for the rest of their lives," recalled Dr. Douglas Israel, a cardiologist who was then a third-year medical student assigned to the team treating Lansdale. "His reaction was just, 'Ow'—very understated, very impressive." Lansdale was to remember that the "electronic paddles kicked like a mule"—"a great scene on TV doctor shows, but lousy in real practice."[20]

Dr. Israel would spend three days at his patient's side. Like others who dealt with Lansdale over the decades, Israel found him to be a "good listener," "friendly and open," and, above all, informal. He called Lansdale "sir" or "general." His patient insisted on being called just plain "Ed," something that the young physician could not bring himself to do.[21]

The doctors restored Lansdale to a semblance of health by implanting first a temporary pacemaker in his groin and then a permanent one in his shoulder. "There's a lump in my shoulder that wasn't there before," he wrote to his college friend Hubert "Pooley" Roberts the following year. "I feel like the Tin Man of Oz, not the Million Dollar Man."[22]

By the fall of 1986 Lansdale was suffering from "heavy lethargy," which made it hard for him "to form the sentences" when he tried to write.[23] Marc Leepson, a journalist who visited him on September 22, 1986, reported, "When you meet Ed Lansdale today, it's difficult to conjure visions of the daring risk-taker who starred in one of the most fascinating espionage dramas of the Vietnam War." Leepson found that Lansdale "speaks matter-of-factly about his adventures, an intermittent cough betraying the signs of a recent illness. Lansdale still wears his trademark mustache, but it is now dull gray, faded. He sometimes forgets names and dates, but talks willingly and with conviction about his long military career and the legend that has grown up around him."[24]

Not long before Leepson's visit, Ed and Pat had gone to California to see his brother Phil Lansdale and his wife along with other friends such as Calvin Mehlert and Daniel Ellsberg. Afterward Ed wrote to Phil, "It's hard to admit, but I came close to crying when we said goodbye in Cupertino." It was almost as if he could sense that he would never see his brother again.

◆

EDWARD LANSDALE celebrated his seventy-ninth birthday on February 6, 1987, as a survivor from a world that no longer existed. Having been born in 1908 when aviation and automobile travel were still in their infancy, in a pre–World War I age when the Romanovs were presiding over an empire that was crumbling beneath their feet, he had lived into an era where television and jet travel had become humdrum, and one in which Mikhail Gorbachev was presiding over the dissolution of a *second* Russian empire in under a century. Coming into the world only a decade after the American victory in the Spanish-American War—that "splendid little war," in Secretary of State John Hay's words—he had witnessed the agonies of two world wars followed by a stalemate in Korea and a defeat in Vietnam.

Little more than two weeks after Lansdale's birthday, Washington, D.C., was battered by a massive winter storm on the evening of Sunday, February 22, 1987, that paralyzed much of the northeastern seaboard. By sunrise on Monday, eighteen inches of snow had fallen in the suburbs. The "thick, wet snow . . . snapped hundreds of tree limbs and power lines in the Washington area," the *Washington Post* reported, "leaving residents in more than 200,000 homes and businesses shivering from what some utility officials called the worst power outage in the region's history."[25]

Pat Lansdale awakened that frosty morning to see the heavy accumulations outside. Turning to Ed, she saw that he was not waking up. He had died sometime during the night, his many infirmities having finally caught up with him: congestive heart failure, cardiac arrest, and coronary artery disease would be listed as the causes of death.

In characteristic fashion, Ed Lansdale's exit from the world was quiet and unobtrusive. He was forever the "Quiet American," eschewing histrionics even in his death throes. In her grief, Pat phoned Ed's son Pete, who lived in the Washington area. He and his wife Carolyn drove as fast as they could through the blizzard. They had to park a mile away and walk over unplowed streets to reach the house where Pete's father lay as stiff as the icicles outside.[26]

Ed's other son, Ted, got the news in New York. He had by then retired as a lieutenant colonel from the Air Force and was working in public relations. When his colleagues heard that his father had died and that he had been a general of some kind, one of them said, "Look, I've got some media contacts. Maybe we can get an obit in the *Times* or something like that." Knowing his father's outsize reputation, Ted replied there was no need: "I think that's taken care of."[27]

As Ted had expected, the next morning the *New York Times* ran a front-page obituary that commemorated his father as a "dashing Californian ... whose influential theories of counterinsurgent warfare proved a success in the Philippines after World War II but failed to bring victory in South Vietnam."[28] The *Washington Post* ran not only a lengthy obituary but also an editorial that called him a "disappointed but unapologetic" advocate of winning "the 'hearts and minds' of the people" in order to combat communism.[29] News articles about his death appeared in many other magazines and newspapers around the world. The *Nation* magazine called Lansdale "the Quiet American and the Ugly American made one flesh," and preposterously claimed, "His tools were civic action and death squads."[30] Far from employing "death squads," Lansdale had always counseled against excessive violence.

This was but one more myth added to the Lansdale legend by critics and supporters alike.

◆

IF THERE is one thing that the American armed forces know how to do well, it is conducting funerals with full military honors. The long line of twentieth-century wars—the Philippines, World War I, World War II, Korea, Vietnam—provided, alas, plenty of practice. Veterans from all those conflicts, and more, are laid to rest in Arlington National Cemetery. The onetime home of General Robert E. Lee, this sprawling plantation across the Potomac River from the federal capital was turned into a burial place in 1864. Its more than six hundred gently rolling acres already contained headstones and monuments commemorating many of the people with whom Edward Lansdale had been associated during his long career—an illustrious list, including Wild Bill Donovan, John F. Kennedy, Robert F. Kennedy, Creighton Abrams, John Paul Vann, and John Foster Dulles. In death, as in life, Lansdale would take his place among them.

The service began at 1 p.m. on February 27, 1987, at Fort Myer, adjoining the cemetery. It was "a cold, dreary, cloudy day"[31] and the grass, a brilliant, immaculately tended green in the summer, was hidden underneath a coating of grayish-white snow. The dark wooden pews of the colonial-style redbrick chapel, topped with a white steeple, were packed that afternoon. Bill Colby, the former CIA director, who a few years earlier had anointed Lansdale one of the "Ten Greatest Spies of All Time,"[32] was there. So were many other colleagues from the spy world. Also in attendance were many members of Lansdale's old teams, the Saigon Military Mission and the Senior Liaison Office, including Joe Baker, Lou Conein, Joe Redick, and Bernie Yoh, and, of course, a number of Vietnamese friends, among them the former South Vietnamese ambassador to Washington, Bui Diem. Both of Edward Lansdale's sons were there with their families.

Pat Lansdale was the grieving widow, having lost a man she had fallen for forty-one years earlier, when she was an attractive war widow and he was an advertising whiz turned intelligence officer with a movie-star mustache and an intense interest in all things Huk. Together they had shared adventures in the Philippine boondocks, and had somehow stayed connected during the rocky decades that followed, in spite of Ed's refusal to leave his first wife. Helen's premature death had vouchsafed them fourteen happy years together as husband and wife, a period of late-life contentment now brought to an end.

Pat "looked bewildered and bereft but did her best to put a brave face on things," one mourner, the biographer Cecil Currey, observed.[33] It would have been hard for her to hide her exasperation that her late husband was about to be buried alongside her predecessor—a woman she had spent years resenting for keeping them apart—underneath a substantial marble tombstone inscribed "Edward G. Lansdale, Major General, U.S. Air Force, 1908–1987" and "Beloved Wife Helen Lansdale, 1901–1972." Eventually, after Pat Lansdale's own death in 2006, at the age of ninety-one, she too would take her place in the same grave. It was somehow fitting that Pat, for so long the hidden "other woman," was not to receive any notice on the tombstone, her presence commemorated only with a small plaque set unobtrusively into the nearby lawn.

Ed Lansdale's funeral service was conducted by Sam Karrick, a Christian Science practitioner and retired army colonel who had served with Lansdale in Vietnam. Many of the attendees were surprised to learn that Lansdale had been a Christian Scientist; he was not demonstratively religious, nor had he abstained from alcohol, tobacco, or aspirin.

There were only two eulogies. One was delivered by Spencer Davis, an old newsman who had known Lansdale since they had met in the Philippines in 1947; it had been Davis who on October 31, 1963, the very date of Lansdale's enforced retirement from the Pentagon, had delivered the news that a coup had taken place in Saigon against Ngo Dinh Diem. He ended with a tribute to "unconventional Ed Lansdale— the good American. We salute you!"[34]

The other eulogist was Rufus Phillips, Lansdale's onetime protégé who had first met him as a twenty-four-year-old Yale graduate sent by the CIA to Saigon in 1954. Now Phillips was fifty-eight years old and nearing his own retirement. In the years since leaving government service in 1963, he had run his father's engineering firm and sought political office in Virginia, winning a race for the Fairfax County Board of Supervisors but losing contests for the U.S. House and U.S. Senate. If Lansdale was the revealer of the counterinsurgency gospel, as many of his teammates believed, then Phillips was his foremost apostle—the Saint Paul of the movement. In his soft Virginia accent, Phillips paid tribute to the "selflessness" of his mentor's "ideas": "Ed had a simply elegant premise that the only way to win a people's war was to give the people a government they could trust and be willing to fight for. It worked in the Philippines, it worked for a time in Vietnam before we and the Vietnamese strayed too far into the thicket in which the force of numbers, material and money seemed to equal victory."

Choking up, Rufe Phillips concluded, "We shall not see his like again but his ideas shall never die."[35]

The rest of the service was a far smaller but equally touching version of the send-off John F. Kennedy had received twenty-four years before. A caisson pulled by six horses carried Lansdale's flag-draped casket to its final resting spot on a snow-covered hill on the southern edge of Arlington National Cemetery. A black riderless horse, empty boots reversed in the stirrups, joined the funeral cortege—an honor first given to Alexander Hamilton in 1804 and ever since reserved for presidents and high-ranking officers. The U.S. Air Force brass ensemble played "Nearer My God to Thee" and "Amazing Grace." A bugler blew the melancholy strains of taps. Soldiers from Pete Lansdale's old regiment, the Old Guard, resplendent in their dark blue uniforms, fired three crisp volleys over the grave. "It was all very somber and elegant and full of military symbolism," Cecil Currey wrote.[36]

This was a poignant, if slightly incongruous, farewell for a general who during his lifetime had always eschewed pomp and formality. "I almost expected Ed to sit up in his bier momentarily," Currey wrote, "and exclaim, 'Jeez! You mean all this is for me?' "[37]

◆

FOUR YEARS after Edward Lansdale's death, following the lightning-fast American victory in the 1991 Gulf War, President George H. W. Bush proclaimed, "By God, we've kicked the Vietnam syndrome once and for all." That same year, the Cold War, the conflict to which Lansdale had devoted much of his life, came to an unexpected end with the peaceful dissolution of the Soviet Union. Four years after that, in 1995, President Bill Clinton restored diplomatic relations with Hanoi.

By then, Le Duan, the hard-liner who had displaced Ho Chi Minh and guided North Vietnam to victory, was long dead; he had predeceased Lansdale in 1986. His successors had pulled Vietnamese troops out of Cambodia and adopted a market-based economic policy known as Doi Moi that was unveiled just months before Lansdale's death. The traumas of the Vietnam War were at long last evanescing, the wounds finally healing. Vietnam and America were on a long and winding path—a road not previously taken, if you will—that by the twenty-first century would lead them to become de facto allies against North Vietnam's erstwhile backer, the People's Republic of China.

Lansdale did not live long enough to see this improbable twist of fate. But he would hardly have been surprised to learn that the American ideology of freedom, in which he had believed with boundless devotion ever since as a boy he had read green leather-bound books on the American Revolution in his father's library, had prevailed over the illiberal forces of Communism. Ed Lansdale had been serenely confident all along about the universal appeal of the Declaration of Independence and its "self-evident truths."

AFTERWORD

Lansdalism in the Twenty-First Century

Perhaps Americans will never learn the simplicity of fighting a political war.

—EDWARD LANSDALE

E DWARD LANSDALE spent much of his career trying to convince America's military and political leaders that there was more to defeating insurgencies than killing insurgents. As he put it near the end of his life, "Damn hard for guerrillas to get the people to help them throw down a government that the people feel is their very own."[1] This was a seemingly obvious insight but one that was strongly resisted by most American military commanders and their civilian masters during the Vietnam War. As Lansdale observed, "We mostly sought to destroy enemy forces. The enemy sought to gain control of the people."[2]

A future generation of American military leaders would turn out to be just as averse to Lansdale's arguments. As soon as the Vietnam War was over, the military services threw out all of the lessons of counter-insurgency, learned at such high cost. After a visit with Special Operations Forces at Eglin Air Force Base in Florida in 1980, Lansdale noted sadly, "The only remnant of the old days is a brief, one-week course on special operations—counter-guerrilla, counter terror, counter revolution—just as a little familiarization course. Apparently the last remnant of counterinsurgency. How times have changed."[3]

The loss of interest in counterinsurgency and an insistence on pursuing a conventional, firepower-intensive strategy led the United States to the brink of defeat in Iraq from 2003 to 2006. No matter how many insurgents American forces killed, more seemed to pop up. Finally, in desperation, in 2007 the Bush administration tried a different approach under General David Petraeus. Shortly before going to Iraq to take command, Petraeus had coauthored Field Manual 3-24, the U.S. Army/Marine Field Manual on Counterinsurgency.[4] Published in late 2006, FM 3-24 did not mention Lansdale's name—it cited instead other theorists such as David Galula and T. E. Lawrence who by that point were better known, in no small part because they had produced books that had stood the test of time—but, whether the authors knew it or not, his ideas permeated its pages. One can imagine Lansdale nodding in accord if he had been alive to read passages such as "Long-term success in COIN depends on the people taking charge of their own affairs and consenting to the government's rule," or "It is vital for commanders to adopt appropriate and measured levels of force and apply that force precisely so that it accomplishes the mission without causing unnecessary loss of life or suffering." The application of these tenets in Iraq helped to produce the impressive, if impermanent, success of the "surge" in 2007–08.

Lansdale would have been cheered to see American troops finally getting closer to the people, even if he would have disapproved of any large-scale American troop commitment to begin with. "Visually," he wrote of South Vietnam, "we the donors seemed to overwhelm the recipients with large headquarters complexes and warehouses, hordes of staff personnel, fleets of vehicles, and extensive housing complexes for Americans engaged in economic and social programs as well as in military aid. A journalist aptly commented that it was as though the whole Court of Versailles had come along with Lafayette, Rochambeau, and the French troops in the American Revolution." The result, he continued, was that "can do" Americans often wound up "stifling the initiative of local Vietnamese" and inadvertently lending credence to enemy claims that "the Americans had designs eventually to seize the whole country for themselves."⁵ Substitute "Iraqis" or "Afghans" for "Vietnamese" and this would be a valid description of the massive American commitments in those countries long after Lansdale's death.

Lansdale wanted Americans to operate in a more modest fashion, as he had done in the Philippines and in South Vietnam in the 1950s. He would have been cheered by the success of American advisory missions in countries such as El Salvador in the 1980s and Colombia in the 2000s, and he would have been particularly satisfied to see the Army's Green Berets taking the lead in such operations, because he had been instrumental in giving them the counterinsurgency mission in the first place.

◆

For all the superficial resurgence of "Lansdalism" in the twenty-first century, there were also strong countervailing pressures that led the United States to eschew the kind of political action that the "Ugly American" had advocated. The costly and drawn-out wars in Iraq and Afghanistan led many policymakers to prefer drone strikes and Special Operations raids to kill terrorist leaders. Yet while such operations were more precise and lethal than ever before, groups such as Al Qaeda and the Taliban were able to survive the loss of their leaders. As Lansdale had warned, "kinetic" action could not be decisive in a war among the people. The United States did take steps to promote democracy in both Iraq and Afghanistan—but only up to a point. In both countries real power continued to be exercised by corrupt warlords and sectarian power brokers. Most American representatives preferred to work with these strongmen in order to kill insurgents, turning a blind eye to abuses of power that drove more recruits into the insurgents' ranks.

Back in 1971, three years after his disheartening return from Vietnam, where his advice had been all but ignored, Lansdale had despaired "that perhaps Americans will never learn the simplicity of fighting a political war, as our forefathers knew so well in the American Revolution and even in the Civil War. Maybe our schooling in power politics à la Disraeli, Metternich, et al and our marriage to the computer have disabled us from acting within our own heritage."⁶ If Lansdale had lived to see the wars of the twenty-first century, his sense of frustration would only have deepened.

The key American shortcoming, in the early twenty-first century as in the 1960s, was the inability to constructively guide the leaders of allied states in the direction desired by Washington. The Kennedy administration had seen a downward spiral into a hostile relationship with Ngo Dinh Diem after Lansdale's return home at the end of 1956. Something similar happened with Afghanistan's President Hamid Karzai and Iraq's Prime Minister Nouri al-Maliki under the Bush and Obama administrations. What was missing was a high-level American official who could influence those allies to take difficult but necessary steps such as fighting corruption without risking a blowup or backlash. Lansdale believed that such tricky tasks could be accomplished only by "a person who was selflessly dedicated to the ideal of man's liberty, was sustained by spiritual principles of his own faith, was demonstrably sensitive to the felt needs of the people of a foreign culture and had earned their trust, was an expert in one or more skills necessary for close-in struggle against the subtleties and brutality of Communist operations, and who was known to behave rationally and purposively in the face of chaos and terror."⁷

Needless to say, there were few people aside from Lansdale himself who combined all of these characteristics. He was a master—right up there with the legendary Lawrence of Arabia—at what he called "the art of friendly persuasion." Lansdale explained that this skill was "based upon a realistic assessment of the enlightened self-interests of the one being persuaded and the needs of the persuader. In other words, it's the ideal operation of friendship or alliance. Admittedly it takes unusual skill in communicating between humans. It's on a higher skill level than the rather pedestrian and unimaginative use of 'leverage' and is on a higher ethical plane than thoughtless generosity to a friend—the two bases upon which the U.S. seemed to operate in Saigon."⁸

Unlike T. E. Lawrence, who in 1917 produced an influential essay, "Twenty-Seven Articles," for guiding military advisers, Lansdale was not enough of a systematic thinker to commit his methods of "friendly persuasion" to paper. When a friend asked him in 1976 how a foreigner could "generate an impact" in an environment such as Latin America, he replied,

> Years ago [in 1954], both Admiral [Arthur] Radford and Allen Dulles asked me to write a handbook on the subject. I had only a limited time during home leave to work on it. I remember I got as far as the first rules, filled a couple of pages with exceptions to the first rules, and then my wife jumped me for my first rule, which was to get to know the inhabitants intimately, through picking a mistress with the right background or moving in with a family, etc.—just to get a firm grasp of customs, emotions, etc. Anyhow I discovered then how complex a subject it was. Much of my own behavior abroad was instinctive rather than rational.[9]

We may nevertheless extrapolate from Lansdale's experiences a few rules worth studying for anyone intent on exerting influence abroad. Call them "the three L's":

1. ***Learn.*** Lansdale familiarized himself with the lands to which he had been dispatched. He did indeed, to Helen's consternation, take a local mistress in the Philippines, if not in Vietnam. In both countries, he traveled widely, made many friends, and talked to many different people. William Colby was later to say, "I think his greatest legacy was his belief that you have to enter into a foreign society and understand how it works, what its motivations are, and what its aspirations are, and then relate a policy to that. Rather than stomp in there and proceed to tell people what to do."[10]

   Lansdale's lack of language skills was more of an obstacle in Vietnam than in the Philippines, where English was more commonly spoken. But he believed that there was more to communicating than speaking the local tongue, and he was able to make a connection even if he had to employ sign language with the

Stone Age tribesmen of Luzon. Even some Americans who could speak Vietnamese, he said, "had the wrong attitude—of haughtiness or brusqueness or even disinterest—when interpreting, which of course subtly spoiled the intention of the U.S. official dealing with the Vietnamese." Although Lansdale commended Americans such as Calvin Mehlert, who combined "language skill" with "evident empathy for the Vietnamese," he made clear that the latter was more important than the former: "I know that I had great difficulty myself, thanks to lack of language skill, but tried to make up for it by careful selection of interpreters that Vietnamese would respect, along with empathy and patience in hearing out everything the Vietnamese had to say."[11]

2. ***Like***. In the process of talking and traveling widely, Lansdale identified and cultivated influential individuals sympathetic to American interests. In the Philippines, his principal agent of influence was Ramon Magsaysay; in South Vietnam, Ngo Dinh Diem. Lansdale won the loyalty of both men by showing himself to be a devoted and sympathetic friend—one who was utterly devoid of condescension and racism. Knowing that Lansdale liked them personally made Magsaysay and Diem open to Lansdale's advice.

3. ***Listen***. Rather than lecturing his friends, as Westerners in the developing world are still wont to do, Lansdale listened intently to what they had to say. When Magsaysay would stop talking and look into the distance, lost in thought, Lansdale did not feel compelled to fill the silence. He would simply sit there "silently, companionably" until Magsaysay was ready to resume talking, leading the Philippine president to wonder why others felt compelled to talk nonstop in his presence.[12] Lansdale's patience would be tested by Diem, given his penchant for rambling, hours-long monologues, but Lansdale professed to find the Vietnamese leader's lectures fascinating. He then would reformulate what he had just heard, subtly changing his summary to get across more

of his own message. Lansdale made sure that his protégés got full credit for his own ideas.

Because of his congenital contempt for bureaucracy and its irksome demands, Lansdale's skill at "strategic listening" failed him when it came to working with other American officials. Rather than win them over, he tended to get their backs up—and as a result his influence was less than it might have been. But when it came to Asians, his sure touch seldom deserted him. As Joe Redick, Lansdale's longtime translator, put it, "He was actually a genius at it. . . . A lot of the things he did or said seemed to be really rather simple, even simplistic. But they seemed to go down, they seemed to work. He was good, there was no question about it."[13] Or as Fritz Kraemer, Henry Kissinger's mentor and a longtime Pentagon official, put it, "Lansdale was a mystic. . . . He didn't say very much . . . [but] he radiated this personal influence."[14]

This same low-key approach might have been effective with Karzai, Maliki, and others if only the United States had had more "operators" as skilled as Lansdale in the lost art of "friendly persuasion." The United States and its allies would be well advised to cultivate this skill set in a world where insurgency, now of the Islamist rather than Communist persuasion, continues to threaten their interests.

The American public will not often support massive military interventions abroad. But few will notice if Washington sends to a distant and embattled land a skilled political operative—someone well versed in the country, able to establish an intimate connection with its leaders, and cognizant of the all-important X Factor, the feelings of the local populace—to subtly influence the course of an important, if obscure, conflict. Such an operative could do far worse than to study the life of Edward G. Lansdale for lessons on what to do—and what not to do.

ACKNOWLEDGMENTS

THIS IS a Council on Foreign Relations book. I cannot imagine a more congenial or supportive work environment, thanks to my superb bosses—Council President Richard Haass and the director of studies, James Lindsay. I have also been blessed to work alongside many other distinguished colleagues and Council members—I must mention in particular Amy Baker, Patricia Dorff, Irina Faskianos, Victoria Harlan, Janine Hill, Lisa Shields, and Iva Zoric—who continue to make the Council what it has been since its inception in 1921: a vibrant intellectual community for advancing America's engagement with the world. I am honored to be a small part of it.*

While toiling on this book between 2013 and 2017, I have been aided by a succession of first-rate young research associates. While I did all of my own research and writing, my RAs—first Greg Roberts, then Harry Oppenheimer, and finally Sherry Cho—helped by tracking down books, contacting archives, making logistical arrangements, acquiring illustrations, preparing budgets, and performing myriad other tasks.

I am grateful for the financial, intellectual, and moral support of Roger Hertog and the Hertog Foundation, Dianne J. Sehler and the Bradley Foundation, and other supporters who prefer to remain anonymous.

I am also grateful to the archivists and librarians all over the world that my RAs and I worked with. Trang Nguyen helped me to conduct research in Vietnam; Alice Le Clezio in France; and Kathryn Blankenberg at the Hoover archives at Stanford. Henry Kissinger was kind enough to grant me permission to quote from his papers at Yale.

Special thanks to the family members of Ed and Pat Lansdale who shared with me letters and photos that have not been seen by any previous author: Pat's grandchildren, Patricia Pelaez-Yi, Leah Pelaez-Ramos, Manny Pelaez, and Francisco Kelly; Ed's children, Ed and Pete Lansdale, and their wives, Carol and Carolyn, respectively; and Ed's niece Ginger Lansdale Brodie, and her husband, Robert. All of them also shared their memories during the course of extended interviews and email exchanges. I could not have written this book without their generosity and help.

Many of the people who worked with Lansdale—a full list is in the bibliography—took the time to sit down with me and share their recollections. The journalist Marc Leepson shared interviews he conducted for a book about Lansdale that was never written. The late Cecil Currey interviewed Lansdale and many of his associates, now long gone, for his own biography. I am grateful for his spadework, and have drawn on the transcripts he left behind.

Rufus Phillips, one of Lansdale's closest friends, not only spent many hours reminiscing with me but also made himself available to answer a plethora of questions via email. Once I had a manuscript ready, he read it over carefully and pointed out ways to make it more precise. The manuscript was also read by two anonymous academic reviewers commissioned by the Council as well as by two retired generals—Sam Wilson and Victor Hugo—who worked with Lansdale. They made many suggestions that I incorporated. Finally, the novelist Karl Marlantes not only offered kind words of praise but also gave me the nudge that I needed to conduct some final tightening of the text.

It is a privilege to be represented by one of the best and most thoughtful literary agents in the business, Tina Bennett of William Morris Endeavor. I am deeply grateful for all of her help, as I am for all that my editor, Robert Weil of Norton/Liveright, has done for this book and for me personally. As far as I am concerned, Bob is the second coming of Maxwell Perkins; I cannot imagine a more skillful or supportive editor. He not only persuaded me to write this book but also consistently elevated my prose. Bob's assistant, Marie Pantojan, has also been a pleasure to work with, as has the whole team at Norton/Liveright—Phil Marino, Anna Oler, Steve Attardo, Bill Rusin, Peter Miller, and Cordelia Calvert. All of them care deeply about books, not just about the business of publishing. David Lindroth once again drew the beautiful maps.

Finally I must thank my loved ones—especially my partner, Sue Mi Terry; my stepchildren, Alexander and Zachary; and my children, Victoria, Abigail, and William; along with my mother and stepfather, Olga and Yan Kagan; and my father and stepmother, Alexander Boot and Penelope Blackie Boot—for enriching my life and being a constant source of inspiration. Sue, in particular, has been both a perceptive critic and a staunch champion, and I have benefited immeasurably from both characteristics.

* The Council on Foreign Relations (CFR) is an independent, nonpartisan membership organization, think tank, and publisher dedicated to being a resource for its members, government officials, business executives, journalists, educators and students, civic and religious leaders, and other interested citizens in order to help them better understand the world and the foreign policy choices facing the United States and other countries. Founded in 1921, CFR carries out its mission by maintaining a diverse membership, with special programs to promote interest and develop expertise in the next generation of foreign policy leaders; convening meetings at its headquarters in New York and in Washington, D.C., and other cities where senior government officials, members of Congress, global leaders, and prominent thinkers come together with CFR members to discuss and debate major international issues; supporting a Studies Program that fosters independent research, enabling CFR scholars to produce articles, reports, and books and hold roundtables that analyze foreign policy issues and make concrete policy recommendations; publishing *Foreign Affairs*, the preeminent journal on international affairs and U.S. foreign policy; sponsoring Independent Task Forces that produce reports with both findings and policy prescriptions on the most important foreign-policy topics; and providing up-to-date information and analysis about world events and American foreign policy on its website, www.cfr.org. The Council on Foreign Relations takes no institutional positions on policy issues and has no affiliation with the U.S. government. All views expressed in its publications and on its website are the sole responsibility of the author or authors.

NOTES

ABBREVIATIONS
(For all other abbreviations, see the bibliography)

CTRB: Charles T. R. Bohannan
EGL: Edward G. Lansdale
FRUS: *Foreign Relations of the United States*
HCL: Henry Cabot Lodge
HL: Helen Lansdale
NYT: *New York Times*
PK: Pat Kelly
PP: Pentagon Papers
RG: Record Group
RP: Rufus Phillips
SMM: Saigon Military Mission
SLO: Senior Liaison Office
WP: *Washington Post*

EPIGRAPH

1 George Orwell, "Benefit of Clergy: Some Notes on Salvador Dali," available at http://orwell.ru/library/reviews/dali/english/e_dali.

PROLOGUE: *The Day of the Dead*

1 http://stardate.org/nightsky/riseset.
2 Hovis, *Hospital*, 49.
3 Ibid., 50.
4 *Reporting Vietnam*, 1.91.
5 McAllister, "Religions."
6 Jacobs, *Mandarin*, 149.
7 *FRUS 1961–1963, Vietnam*, 3.628.
8 After the fall of South Vietnam, its name would be changed to Tan Son Nhat.
9 Berman, *Hubert*, 109.
10 Blair, *Lodge*, 43–44.
11 *FRUS 1961–1963, Vietnam*, 4.21.
12 Ibid., 3.645.

13 Ibid., 4.140–43.
14 Ibid., 4.255.
15 Ibid., 4.442–46.
16 Ahern, *Ngo*, 203; Tran Van Don, *Endless*, 98.
17 Higgins, *Nightmare*, 208.
18 Henry Kissinger, "Vietnam trip, 1965—diary 1/4," HKP, box 100, file 14.
19 *FRUS 1961–1963, Vietnam*, 4.517.
20 Hovis, *Hospital*, 77–84.
21 *FRUS 1961–1963, Vietnam*, 4.513.
22 RP, *Vietnam*, 19.
23 Herr, *Dispatches*, 233.
24 Ahern, *Ngo*, 203.
25 Miller, *Misalliance*, 210, 282; Tran Van Don, *Endless*, 83.
26 Ahern, *Ngo*, 203.
27 *Reporting Vietnam*, 1.94.
28 Tran Van Don, *Endless*, 87.
29 Grant, *Phoenix*, 211.
30 MFF/TLC.
31 Hammer, *Death*, 298.
32 Taylor, *Swords*, 301.
33 McNamara, *Retrospect*, 85.
34 http://whitehousetapes.net/clips/1963_1104_jfk_vietnam_memoir.swf.
35 Lodge, *Storm*, 214.
36 Hammer, *Death*, 314.
37 Colby, *Lost Victory*, 158.
38 PP, Part IV.B.5, p. viii.
39 Colby, *Honorable Men*, 203; Jacobs, *Mandarin*, 186.

INTRODUCTION: *The Misunderstood Man*

1 JFKPL/VHKOH.
2 Halberstam, *Brightest*, 128.
3 Karnow, *Vietnam*, 236, 458.
4 Weiner, *Ashes*, 213.
5 Sheehan, *Lie*, 138.
6 http://www.youtube.com/watch?v=5ATbhCUZxjQ.

CHAPTER 1: *In Terrific Flux*

1 Great White Fleet: *WP*, Dec. 17, 1907 ("blue of the sky," "top hat"); Crawford, *Great White Fleet*; Reckner, *Great White Fleet*.
2 London, *Iron*, 104.
3 Phil Lansdale to Gary May, April 18, 1978, HI/EGL, box 5.
4 Ginger Brodie, "Edward Philips and Sarah Adelaide Walker Family Time Line," GBPP.

5   Ibid.
6   Ibid.
7   Phil Lansdale to Ed, Ben, Dave, Dec. 25, 1971, GBPP.
8   Phil Lansdale to Dave Lansdale, Oct. 11, 1987, GBPP.
9   EGL, "The Lansdale Family," Nov. 1971, ECLPP; David Lansdale, "Some Side Lights on Henry Lansdale," GBPP.
10 EGL, "The Lansdale Family," Nov. 1971, ECLPP.
11 *Detroit News*, March 7, 1896.
12 Keep, *Guide*, 36.
13 EGL interview, Feb. 15, 1984, CCP.
14 EGL, "There Is My Country," HI/EGL, box 75.
15 Dallek, *Unfinished*, 29; Schlesinger, *Robert Kennedy*, 14.
16 EGL to family, Jan. 20, 1976, GBPP; EGL, "There Is My Country," HI/EGL, box 75.
17 EGL interview, Feb. 15, 1984, CCP.
18 EGL, memoir draft, HI/EGL, box 76, file 265.
19 EGL, "The Lansdale Family," Nov. 1971, ECLPP.
20 I am grateful to the Yale graduate student Michael D. Hattem, an expert in early American history, for identifying the volumes in question as *American Archives*.
21 Apocryphal: Morgan, "Pleasures of Paine." EGL cited: EGL, *Midst*, xxi; AI/RP.
22 EGL interview, Feb. 18, 1984, CCP.
23 Phil Lansdale to David Lansdale, Jan. 4, 1988, GBPP.
24 EGL interview, Feb. 15, 1984, CCP.
25 David Lansdale interview, Nov. 11, 1985, CCP.
26 David Lansdale, unpublished memoir, Feb. 20, 1991, GBPP.
27 Ben Lansdale to Gary May, April 28, 1978, HI/EGL, box 5.
28 Lederer, *Ugly American*, 110.
29 Ben Lansdale to Gary May, May 5, 1978, HI/EGL, box 5.
30 Gottschalk, *Christian Science*, 79.
31 Henry Lansdale to David Lansdale, March 6, 1956, GBPP.
32 Butler, *Religion*, 296.
33 Gottschalk, *Christian Science*, 206.
34 EGL interview, Feb 15, 1984, CCP.
35 David Lansdale interview, Nov. 11, 1985, CCP.
36 Takaki, *Strangers*, 181.
37 Dallek, *Unfinished*, 112.
38 USAFA/EGLOH.
39 Fogelson, *Fragmented*, 82.
40 Hubert "Pooley" Roberts interview, July 13, 1985, CCP.

CHAPTER 2: *Enfant Terrible*

1   Boot, *Invisible*, 286.
2   Ibid., 285.
3   *Los Angeles Times*, June 12, 1925.
4   http://www.lausd.k12.ca.us/Los_Angeles_HS/Archives/History/History.htm.

5 Ben Lansdale to Gary May, April 28, 1979, HI/EGL, box 5.
6 EGL transcript, Los Angeles High School.
7 Roberts interview, July 13, 1985, CCP.
8 Roberts interview, July 13, 1985, CCP.
9 German: *College Humor* (reprint from *The Claw*), July 1930. Ratings, Hubbard: *The Claw*, Oct. 10, 1932.
10 *The Claw*, Oct. 1928.
11 Roberts interview, July 13, 1985, CCP.
12 Roberts interview, July 13, 1985, CCP.
13 *California Daily Bruin*, Jan. 5, 1931.
14 Ben Lansdale to Gary May, April 28, 1975, HI/EGL, box 5.
15 Dundjerski, UCLA, 59.
16 EGL transcript, UCLA Registrar's Office.
17 Caro, *Power Broker*, 323.
18 Wilson, *Thirties*, 156–57.
19 Williams, *Ambition*, 91.
20 Ibid., 135.
21 Ibid., 159.
22 https://livingnewdeal.berkeley.edu/us/ny/.
23 EGL interview, Feb. 15, 1984, CCP.
24 Dorothy Bohannan interview, July 27, 1985, CCP.
25 EGL interview, Feb. 15, 1984, CCP; Currey, *Lansdale*, 10.
26 Helen Batcheller Lansdale death certificate, Commonwealth of Virginia, ECLPP.
27 EGL personnel file, CCP.
28 Roberts interview, July 13, 1985, CCP.
29 John Doran interview, Nov. 11, 1985, CCP.
30 Marriage certificate, HI/EGL, box 69.
31 EGL to PK, Nov. 7, 1949, PCLPP.
32 EGL to HL, Nov. 1951, PCLPP.
33 AI/ELCL.
34 David Lansdale interview, Nov. 15, 1985, CCP.
35 Pooley Roberts interview, July 13, 1985, CCP.
36 Phil Lansdale interview, Sept. 20, 1985, CCP.
37 AI/EC.
38 David Lansdale interview, Nov. 15, 1985, CCP.
39 HL: Carolyn and Pete Lansdale, email to author, Jan. 20, 2014; Dunkirk *Evening Observer*, Aug. 23, 1909 (Nellie's death), Aug. 15, 1927 (Mary Jane's death); *Centennial History*, 444, 450; Dunkirk Historical Museum (town history); Pierce, *Genealogy*, 588; 1917 draft registration card, Ancestry.com; 1910 census, Ancestry.com.
40 Ethel's age: Findagrave.com. Hotel cashier: Phil Lansdale to David Lansdale, Nov. 2, 1987, GBPP.
41 David Lansdale, "A Sad Period in My Young Life," March 2000, GBPP.
42 Phil Lansdale to David Lansdale, Nov. 2, 1987, GBPP.
43 Gottschalk, *Christian Science*, 124.
44 *New Republic*, Aug. 20, 1919.
45 U.S. WPA, *San Francisco* ("The City": 3; "monument": 161; "quality": 177; "Mediterranean": 236; "Canton": 220).

46 James, *Treasure Island*, 106–13; Starr, *Endangered*, ch. 13.

47 EGL interview, Feb. 15, 1984, CCP.

48 Personnel Placement Questionnaire, Dec. 12, 1941, EGL personnel file, CCP.

49 RSPP.

50 EGL, "Application for Commission," 1947, CCP; 1940 census.

51 AI/AI.

52 EGL interview, Feb. 15, 1984, CCP.

53 Ibid.

54 Currey, *Unquiet*, 16, erroneously has Lansdale living in Larkspur in 1941. EGL's military records indicate the family did not move to Marin County until 1942, first to Kentfield and then, in 1943, to Larkspur.

55 Temperature: National Climatic Data Center.

56 EGL to Cecil Currey, July 10, 1984, CCP, 10/190.

57 EGL to MIS, Nov. 10, 1943, NARA, RG 226, box 43, folder 698.

CHAPTER 3: *An Institution Run by Its Inmates*

1 "Temporary Assignment," Feb. 22, 1943, HI/EGL, box 70, file 5.

2 AI/AI.

3 EGL interview, Feb. 15, 1984, CCP.

4 EGL to Cecil Currey, July 10, 1984, CCP.

5 Ibid.

6 EGL to PK, 1948 (n.d.), PYPP.

7 Phil Lansdale to Gary May, April 28, 1979, HI/EGL, box 5.

8 Hall, *Cloak*, 188.

9 EGL interview, Feb. 15, 1984, CCP; EGL to Lt. Col. Charles Drake, chief, San Francisco office M.I.S., "Trip to Washington and New York," Dec. 21, 1943, HI/EGL, box 32, file 706.

10 Dunlop, *Donovan*, 306.

11 Waller, *Wild Bill*, 93.

12 EGL to Cecil Currey, July 10, 1984, CCP.

13 Smith, *OSS*, 4.

14 Dunlop, *Donovan*, 426.

15 Smith, *OSS*, 26.

16 "Short," "soft," "manner": Alsop, *Sub Rosa*, 9. "Pudgy," "neck": Lovell, *Spies*, 16.

17 Smith, *OSS*, 4.

18 Lovell, *Spies*, 17, 84–85, 56.

19 Weiner, *Legacy*, 4–5.

20 Lovell, *Spies*, 61–63.

21 Waller, *Wild Bill*, 127–28.

22 Smith, *OSS*, 26–27.

23 Waller, *Wild Bill*, 96.

24 EGL to Cecil Currey, July 10, 1984, CCP.

25 USAFA/EGLOH.

26 EGL, "From the Serpent's Mouth," 1943, HI/EGL, box 31, folder 694.

27 EGL to M.I.S., Nov. 10, 1943, NARA, RG 226, box 43, folder 698.

28 EGL to Melvin F. Meyer, Feb. 1, 1972, HI/EGL, box 1.
29 USAFA/EGLOH.
30 O. J. "Mac" Magee letter, March 3, 1947, EGL personnel file, CCP.
31 EGL service record, CCP, box 8, file 183.1.
32 USAFA/EGLOH.
33 USAFA/EGLOH.
34 *NYT*, Aug. 15, 1945.
35 *NYT*, Sept. 9, 1945.
36 EGL, "Comrades," Bulletin of the American Historical Collection, April–June 1984. HI/EGL, box 74.

<h3 style="text-align:center">CHAPTER 4: The Time of His Life</h3>

1 Herring, *Colony*, 598.
2 Ed Navarro interview, July 25, 1985, CCP.
3 Karnow, *Image*, 16–25; Marquez, *Blood* ("paint": loc. 4434).
4 EGL, "The True American," June 3, 1960, HI/EGL, box 96.
5 Joaquin, *Manila*, 185.
6 Karnow, *Image*, 295.
7 Ephraim, *Escape*, 161–62.
8 James, *Years*, 2.653–55.
9 Arrival in Manila: all quotations from Lansdale's diary, Oct. 9–15, 1945, GBPP.
10 EGL to HL, Oct. 20, 1945, PCLPP.
11 Ben Lansdale to Gary May, April 28, 1978, HI/EGL, box 5.
12 O. J. Magee letter, March 3, 1947, EGL personnel file, CCP.
13 EGL, "Comrades," Bulletin of the American Historical Collection, HI/EGL, box 74.
14 Intelligence Report No. 27, Headquarters, U.S. Army Forces Western Pacific, June 20, 1946, HI/EGL, box 74.
15 Ryukyus: all quotations from EGL diary, PCLPP, unless otherwise noted; EGL interview, Feb. 15, 1984, CCP ("take a shot," "Geez," "dirty pictures," "look"); "Intelligence Report No. 30: Northern Ryukyus," HI/EGL, box 33, file 717 ("subsistence," "wiped out," "frequency").
16 EGL interview, Dec. 17, 1984, CCP.
17 Sunday: all quotations from Lansdale's journal, Oct. 30, 1946, HI/EGL, box 83, file 8.
18 USAFA/EGLOH.
19 Frank Zaldarriaga interview, July 26, 1985, CCP.
20 Spencer Davis interview, March 24, 1987, MLEPP.
21 EGL interview, May 16, 1984, CCP.

<h3 style="text-align:center">CHAPTER 5: In Love and War</h3>

1 EGL journal, Jan. 11, 1946, HI/EGL, box 83, file 8.
2 EGL, "Comrades," Bulletin of the American Historical Collection, HI/EGL, box 74.

3   EGL, *Midst*, 364.

4   EGL to PK, Feb. 12, 1949, PYPP. 1946: EGL to PK, Feb. 25, 1949, PYPP.

5   Bernstein, *Sex*, 37.

6   Ibid., 46.

7   Ibid., 115–16.

8   EGL to PK, April 14, 1949, PYPP.

9   Dorothy Bohannan interview, July 27, 1985, CCP.

10 Samuel V. Wilson, email to author, April 2, 2014.

11 AI/RP.

12 Manny Pelaez, email to author, Jan. 14, 2014.

13 AI/LPR.

14 EGL to PK, 1948 (n.d.), PYPP.

15 Joaquin, *Aquinos.*

16 AI/LPR.

17 PK interview, June 23, 1985, CCP; Palaez to author, email, Jan. 14, 2014.

18 "Brightest," "legs": EGL to PK, 1948 (no date), PYPP. "Intensely": EGL to PK, Feb. 12, 1949, PYPP. "Uncanny": EGL to PK, 1949 (undated). "Fanny," "glint": EGL to PK, May 3, 1949. "Knee": EGL to PK, June 30, 1949, PYPP.

19 EGL to PK, 1949 (n.d.), PYPP.

20 EGL to PK, May 5, 1949, PYPP.

21 EGL to PK, Sept. 28, 1949, PYPP.

22 EGL to PK, dated Sept. 18, 1945 (an inaccurate date), PYPP.

23 EGL to PK, 1948 (n.d.), PYPP.

24 EGL to PK, Feb. 12, 1949, PYPP.

25 EGL to PK, Feb. 18, 1949, PYPP.

26 EGL to PK, April 5, 1949, PYPP.

27 EGL to PK, Jan. 24, 1949, PYPP.

28 EGL interview, Dec. 17, 1984, CCP.

29 EGL journal, March 19, 1947, HI/EGL, box 83, file 8.

30 EGL interview, Dec. 17, 1984, CCP.

31 EGL journal, March 19, 1947, HI/EGL, box 83, file 8.

32 EGL interview, Dec. 17, 1984, CCP.

33 EGL journal, June 10 1947, HI/EGL, box 83, file 8; "Armed Robbery," June 28, 1947, Headquarters, Philippine-Ryukyus Command, HI/EGL, box 70, file 5.

34 Karnow, *Image*, 339.

35 Taruc, *Tiger*, 33.

36 EGL interview, Dec. 17, 1984, CCP.

37 *WP*, Jan. 27, 1975.

38 Valeriano, *Counter-Guerrilla*, 79.

39 EGL journal, March 30, 1947, HI/EGL, box 83, file 8.

40 Ibid.

41 EGL journal, June 10, 1947, HI/EGL, box 83, file 8.

42 EGL journal, Aug. 24, 1947, HI/EGL, box 83, file 8.

43 EGL journal, Feb. 29, 1948, HI/EGL, box 83, file 8.

44 Dorothy Bohannan interview, July 27, 1985, CCP.

45 AI/RP.

46 EGL interview, May 17, 1984, CCP.

47 Ibid.

48 EGL journal, Jan. 4, 1948, HI/EGL, box 83, file 8.

49 Peter C. Richards interview, July 23, 1985, CCP.

50 EGL, *Midst*, 5.

51 EGL, memoir draft, HI/EGL, box 76, file 265.

52 EGL to HL, Oct. 30, 1946, HI/EGL, box 83, file 8.

53 James, *Years*, 3.193–217.

54 EGL to HL, Oct. 30, 1946, HI/EGL, box 83, file 8.

55 EGL interview, May 16, 1984, CCP.

56 EGL journal, Jan. 4, 1948, HI/EGL, box 83, file 8.

57 EGL interview, May 16, 1984, CCP.

58 Ibid.

59 "Headquarters PHILRYCOM Check Sheet," July 10, 1947, HI/EGL, box 33, file 733.

60 "Public Relations Objectives," HI/EGL, box 34, file 735.

61 EGL interview, May 16, 1984, CCP.

62 EGL to Leo D. Kowatch Jr., March 13, 1978, HI/EGL, box 70, file 4.

63 EGL journal, Aug. 3, 1948, HI/EGL, box 83, file 8.

64 EGL journal, July 5, 1948, HI/EGL, box 83, file 8.

65 Ibid.

66 EGL, *Midst*, 11.

67 EGL, "Personal History Statement," May 12, 1949, HI/EGL, box 70.

CHAPTER 6: *The Knights Templar*

1 EGL to PK, Dec. 3, 1949, PYPP.

2 EGL to PK, Sept. 6, 1949, PYPP.

3 EGL to PK, 1948 (n.d.), PYPP.

4 Ibid.

5 Ibid.

6 EGL to PK, Dec. 12, 1948, PYPP.

7 EGL to PK, 1948 (n.d.), PYPP.

8 EGL to PK, Dec. 12, 1948, PYPP.

9 EGL to PK, April 15, 1949, PYPP.

10 EGL to PK, Feb. 8, 1949, PYPP.

11 EGL to PK, Feb. 18, 1949, PYPP.

12 EGL to PK, April 15, 1949, PYPP.

13 EGL to PK, March 1959, PYPP.

14 EGL to PK, July 5, 1949, PYPP.

15 DiFonzo, "No Fault."

16 EGL to PK, Sept. 11, 1949, PYPP.

17 EGL to PK, April 15, 1949, PYPP.

18 EGL to PK, Feb. 27, 1949, PYPP.

19 EGL to PK, Feb. 20, 1949, PYPP.

20 EGL to PK, May 1, 1949, PYPP.

21 EGL to PK, July 5, 1949, PYPP.

22 EGL to PK, June 9, 1949, PYPP.

23 EGL to PK, June 30, 1949, PYPP.

24 EGL to PK, May 18, 1949, PYPP.

25 EGL to PK, Feb. 10, 1949, PYPP.

26 EGL to PK, June 27, 1949, PYPP.

27 EGL to PK, Sept. 6, 1949, PYPP.

28 EGL to PK, 1949 (n.d.), PYPP.

29 EGL to PK, Jan. 13, 1949, PYPP.

30 EGL to PK, May 8, 1949, PYPP.

31 *Foreign Affairs*, July 1947.

32 Nicolson, *Years*, 155.

33 *Wheeling Intelligencer*, Feb. 10, 1950.

34 *NYT*, Feb. 12, 1950.

35 Oshinsky, *Conspiracy*, 56.

36 Ibid., 339.

37 Ibid., 197.

38 Ibid., 140.

39 EGL to PK, Sept. 26, 1949, PYPP.

40 EGL to PK, Feb. 15, 1949, PYPP.

41 EGL to PK, April 14, 1949, PYPP.

42 http://history.state.gov/milestones/1945-1952/NSC68.

43 Powers, *Intelligence*, 17.

44 Wisner, OPC: Thomas, *Best Men*, 17–23, 40 ("candy"); Helms, *Look*, 114 ("intelligent"); "Biographical Sketch," Wisner personnel file, NARA, RG 263, box 7 ("urgency," "demanding," "intense"); Colby, *Honorable*, 73 ("knights"); Weiner, *Legacy*, 32 (bigger than rest); Warner, *CIA*, 235–36 ("independently," "direction"); *FRUS*, *1945–1950*, *Intelligence*, 713–15 (NSC 10/2); Senate Church Committee, *Final Report*, 4.31–32 (OPC growth); Herken, *Georgetown*, loc. 163 ("aristocracy"), loc. 1442 ("washerwomen").

45 "Academic Record," Nov. 23, 1949, EGL personnel file, CCP.

46 EGL to PK, Oct. 12, 1949, PYPP.

47 George A. Chester to Air Adjutant General, Jan. 2, 1951, EGL personnel file, CCP.

48 EGL to PK, Dec. 3, 1949, PYPP.

49 Graham, *Washington*, 242.

50 Friedman, *Covert*, 30–31.

51 EGL interview, Dec. 17, 1984, CCP.

52 EGL to PK, Jan. 16, 1950, PYPP.

53 EGL to PK, March 6, 1949, PYPP.

54 EGL to PK, Nov. 2, 1949, PYPP.

CHAPTER 7: *"A Most Difficult and Delicate Problem"*

1 Karnow, *Image*, 341.

2 Taruc, *Tiger*, 38.

3 EGL to PK, April 29, 1949, PYPP.

4 Karnow, *Image*, 344.

5 *NYT*, Aug. 27, 28, 1950; Ismael D. Lapus, "The Communist Huk Enemy," Fort Bragg, June 15, 1961, CCP; EGL, *Midst*, 26.

6 EGL to PK, Aug. 28, 1950, PYPP.

7 Romulo, *Magsaysay*, 104.

8 *FRUS 1950, East Asia*, 6.1442.

9 Cullather, *Illusions*, 83.

10 *FRUS 1950, East Asia*, 6.1495.

11 Ibid., 1519–20.

12 Ibid.

13 Bell, *Report*.

14 *FRUS 1950, East Asia*, 6.1436–37.

15 EGL to PK, Feb. 2, 1950, PYPP.

16 EGL interviews, Dec. 17, 1984, Nov. 12, 1985 ("the guy"), CCP; EGL, *Midst* ("husky," "practicality": 13–14); USAFA/EGLOH.

17 Magysaysay: Abueva, *Magsaysay*; Romulo, *Magsaysay*; Martinez, *Magsaysay*; Charles T. R. Bohannan, "Revisionism in Philippine History," Sept. 17, 1979, CCP ("anti-intellectual"); Myron G. Cowen, Memorandum, Jan. 8, 1952, HSTPL/MMC ("nothing"); Smith, *Portrait*, 101 ("repeal"); Cullather, *Illusion*, 100 (Perez).

18 EGL interview, Dec. 17, 1984, CCP; USAFA/EGLOH.

19 EGL interview, Nov. 12, 1985, CCP.

20 Abueva, *Magsaysay*, 154.

21 EGL interview, Dec. 17, 1984, CCP.

22 EGL interview, Nov. 12, 1985, CCP.

23 NWC/EGL.

24 EGL interview, Nov. 12, 1985, CCP.

25 EGL, *Midst*, 31; Pacific Stars and Stripes, via Ancestry.com.

26 EGL, "The Good Fights," HI/EGL, box 77, file 272.

27 EGL, *Midst*, 32 ("love"); EGL to Obituary Editor, *WP*, Sept. 24, 1982, HI/EGL, box 2 ("tough"); McCoy, *Policing*, 377.

28 AI/VH.

29 EGL interview, Nov. 12, 1985, CCP.

30 EGL to PK, June 1, 1950, PYPP.

31 Deed, Feb. 22, 1950, HI/EGL, box 70.

32 AI/FAS.

33 EGL, *Midst*, 15.

34 Ibid.

35 EGL to PK, Aug. 28, 1950, PYPP.

36 EGL, *Midst*, 1–2.

37 https://www.youtube.com/watch?v=v92U2F9gbUo.

38 EGL, *Midst*, 1–2.

CHAPTER 8: *"All-Out Force or All-Out Friendship"*

1 EGL to PK, Oct. 12, 1950, PYPP.

2 EGL's first days: EGL, *Midst*, 17–30.

3   EGL, "A Case History of Insurgency," National War College, March 25, 1964, HI/EGL, box 96.

4   EGL, *Midst*, 34–35.

5   EGL to Jose Abueva, Nov. 5, 1962, HI/EGL, box 36.

6   AI/RM.

7   EGL to Jose Abueva, Nov. 5, 1962, HI/EGL, box 36.

8   Ibid.; EGL, "Comrades," Bulletin of the American Historical Collection, April–June 1984, PCLPP.

9   EGL, *Midst*, 47; USAFA/EGLOH; EGL, "The Philippines," Foreign Service Institute, July 3, 1962, NSA/EGL, box 1.

10 Inspections: EGL, *Midst*, 37–45 (all quotations unless otherwise specified); EGL, "Notes on Magsaysay," HI/EGL, box 80, file 295 (carbine, corn, corned beef, fish); Valeriano, *Counter-Guerrilla*, 167 ("shampoo"); EGL, "The Philippines," Foreign Service Institute, July 3, 1962, NSA/EGL, box 1; USAFA/EGLOH ("empower").

11 EGL, *Midst*, 60–65.

12 Pomeroy, *Forest*, 81–82.

13 EGL, *Midst*, 66–67.

14 EGL, *Midst*, 70; Grant, *Phoenix*, 113.

15 Laurie, *Propaganda*, 193 ("refusing"), 196 (League).

16 Wilford, *Wurlitzer*, 7.

17 Boot, *Invisible*, 333.

18 EGL, *Midst*, 70.

19 Ibid., 71.

20 Napoleon Valeriano, "Counter-Guerrilla Operations," Ft. Bragg, June 15, 1961, HI/EGL, box 73.

21 Boot, *Invisible*, 378–88.

22 EGL, *Midst*, 52–59; Kerkvliet, *Huk*, 239 (250 resettled).

23 EGL, "Counter-Guerrilla Operations," Ft. Bragg, June 15, 1961, HI/EGL, box 73.

24 EGL, *Midst*, 79.

25 *FRUS 1951, Asia*, 6.1550.

26 CTRB, "Counter-Guerrilla Operations," Ft. Bragg, June 15, 1961, HI/EGL, box 73.

27 Pomeroy, *Forest*, 161.

28 EGL, "A Case History of Insurgency—the Philippines," National War College, March 25, 1965, HI/EGL, box 96.

29 EGL, "Notes on Magsaysay," HI/EGL, box 80, file 295.

30 EGL, *Midst*, 72–73 (source of all quotations); EGL, "Military Psychological Operations: Part Two," Lecture to the Armed Forces Staff College, Norfolk, Virginia, March 29, 1960, HI/EGL, box 73, file 1.

31 Johnson, *Tree*, 61.

32 EGL, *Midst*, 73–75.

33 Ibid., 75.

34 Pomeroy, *Forest*, 164.

35 *FRUS 1951, Asia*, 6.1566–67.

CHAPTER 9: *The Power Broker*

1 Italy: Brogi, *Cold War*, 101–10; Miller, "Taking Off"; Platt, "Foreign Policy"; *NYT*, April 23, 1948 ("roughhouse"); Mistry, *Waging*, 127–53.

2 AI/FSJ.

3 1951 election: EGL, *Midst*, 90–92; EGL to Helen, Nov. 1951, PCLPP ("feather"); Smith, *Portrait*, 107 ("Jewish"), 265 (cigars), 267 ("trust"); *NYT*, Sept. 18, 1968; Karnow, *Image*, 349–51; EGL, "Military Psychological Operations: Part Two," Armed Forces Staff College, March 29, 1960, HI/EGL, box 73, file 1; Satoshi, "Gabriel L. Kaplan."

4 EGL to HL, May 19, 1952, PCLPP.

5 EGL to HL, April 1952, PCLPP.

6 AI/FSJ.

7 Trip: EGL, "There Is My Country," HI/EGL, box 77, file 274 ("babies," "shocked"); EGL interview, Nov. 12, 1985, CCP ("ranting," "a T," "Daddy"); NWC/EGL (Sternberg, "hack"); Abuevo, *Magsaysay*, 213 (praise); Romulo, *Magsaysay*, 166 (Constellation), 169 ("Caesar"); Karnow, *Image*, 349 (Sternberg); HI/EGL, box 34 (text of Mexico City speech).

8 Abueva, *Magsaysay*, 225.

9 EGL to Allen Dulles, Nov. 23, 1953, HI/EGL, box 34, file 764.

10 Buell, *Quiet*, 407–8.

11 Abueva, *Magsaysay*, 235.

12 HI/EGL, box 34, file 753.

13 EGL, "The Good Fights," HI/EGL, box 77, file 272.

14 EGL to HL, May 18, 1953, PCLPP.

15 EGL to HL, April 26, 1952, PCLPP.

16 EGL to HL, Aug. 22, 1952, PCLPP.

17 EGL to HL, April 26, 1953, PCLPP.

18 EGL to HL, Aug. 22, 1953, PCLPP.

19 Richard R. Ely, June 15, 1964, NWC/RASP.

20 EGL to HL, April 26, 1952, PCLPP.

21 EGL to HL, Aug. 19, 1953, PCLPP.

22 EGL to HL, May 14, 1953, PCLPP.

23 Ibid.

24 Press release from Malacañang Palace, March 28, 1953, Peter Richards Collection, CCP.

25 EGL to HL, May 18, 1953, PCLPP.

26 Abueva, *Magsaysay*, 246.

27 Romulo, *Magsaysay*, 213–14.

28 EGL to HL, Aug. 22, 1952, PCLPP.

29 EGL to HL, April 29, 1953, PCLPP.

30 *FRUS 1952–1954, Asia*, 12.521.

31 "Covert Operations," May 9, 1961, CREST 5076DE59993247D4D82B5B68; Grose, *Gentleman*, 445–46.

32 Smith, *Portrait*, 106 ("comfortable," "hell"), 253 ("social engineering"), 255 ("crusader").

33 EGL, *Midst*, 105.
34 EGL to Allen Dulles, Nov. 23, 1953, HI/EGL, box 34, file 764.
35 *NYT*, July 13, 1986.
36 Colby, *Honorable*, 102.
37 Grose, *Gentleman*, 18.
38 Ibid., 106.
39 Ibid., 155.
40 Ibid., 318.
41 Ibid., 386.
42 Ibid., 410.
43 Ambrose, *Eisenhower*, 2.111.
44 Grose, *Gentleman*, 341.
45 Allen Dulles to Raymond Spruance, Jan. 19, 1953, SGMML/AWDP, box 50, file 5.
46 Spruance to Hugh Bain Snow Jr., April 8, 1967, NWC/RASP; Helms, *Shoulder*, 102.
47 EGL to HL, Aug. 22, 1953, PCLPP.
48 EGL to Thomas Buell, April 17, 1972, NWC/RASP.
49 *FRUS 1952–1954, Asia*, 12.522.
50 EGL to HL, Sept. 30, 1952, PCLPP.
51 Embassy Manila to Secretary of State, March 14, 1953, NARA, RG 84, box 84.
52 EGL interview, Nov. 12, 1985, CCP; Currey, *Unquiet*, 121.
53 EGL to HL, May 14, 1953, PCLPP.
54 EGL to HL, April 29, 1953, PCLPP.
55 EGL, *Midst*, 108.
56 Ibid., 116.
57 EGL to HL, May 14, 1953, PCLPP.
58 EGL to HL, April 29, 1953, PCLPP.
59 EGL to HL, May 14, 1953, PCLPP.

CHAPTER 10: *"A Real Vindication"*

1 Quezon, *Good*, 149; *Philippine Free Press*, Aug. 19, 1942.
2 Romulo, *Magsaysay*, 226.
3 Abuevo, *Magsaysay*, 253–54.
4 Cullather, *Illusion*, 110.
5 Romulo, *Magsaysay*, 219.
6 Abueva, *Magsaysay*, 259.
7 Romulo, *Magsaysay*, 225.
8 EGL to Myron Cowen, June 11, 1953, HSTPL/MMC.
9 Smith, *Portrait*, 263.
10 EGL to Allen Dulles, Nov. 23, 1953, HI/EGL, box 34, file 764.
11 NWC/EGL.
12 EGL to Allen Dulles, Nov. 23, 1953, HI/EGL, box 34, file 764.
13 EGL to Stephen Shalom, May 20, 1975, CCP.
14 EGL to Jose Abueva, Nov. 5, 1962, HI/EGL, box 36, file 817.

15 EGL to Roswell Gilpatric, July 27, 1961, NSA/EGL.
16 NWC/EGL.
17 EGL to Stephen Shalom, May 20, 1975, CCP.
18 EGL to Myron Cowen, June 11, 1953, HSTPL/MMC. $250,000: *Time*, Nov. 23, 1953.
19 EGL, *Midst*, 115.
20 NWC/EGL.
21 EGL, *Midst*, 119–20 ("skulduggery"); EGL to Dulles, Nov. 23, 1953, HI/EGL, box 34, file 764 ("emulation").
22 EGL to Allen Dulles, Nov. 23, 1953, HI/EGL, box 34, file 764.
23 Election Day: EGL to HL, Nov. 12, 1953, PCLPP (all quotations unless specified); EGL to HL, Nov. 23, 1953, PCLPP ("constructively").
24 Smith, *Portrait*, 103.
25 EGL, "The Good Fights," HI/EGL, box 77, file 272; EGL, *Midst*, 123.
26 NARA/CREST CIA-RDP79-00498A0005000300008-5; HI/EGL, box 71.
27 EGL interview, Nov. 30, 1984, CCP.
28 EGL to HL, Nov. 23, 1953, PCLPP.
29 EGL to HL, Dec. 5, 1953, PCLPP.
30 Ibid.
31 https://weatherspark.com/#!dashboard;ws=33313.
32 *Time*, Jan. 11, 1954.
33 http://www.gov.ph/1953/12/30/inaugural-address-of-president-magsaysay-december-30-1953/.
34 Taruc, *Tiger*, 121.
35 EGL to Magsaysay, May 24, 1954, HI/EGL, box 97, file 6.
36 Romulo, *Magsaysay*, 277.
37 Karnow, *Image*, 354; *Time*, May 31, 1954.
38 EGL interview, Sept. 17, 1986, MLEPP.

CHAPTER 11: La Guerre sans Fronts

1 Greene, *Ways*, 161.
2 EGL was to write in *Midst*, 110, that he spent "about six weeks" in Indochina, but the O'Daniel mission, which included EGL, left Saigon on July 10, meaning the trip lasted three weeks ("Note of Captain Feral," CHA, box 10H 155, file O'Daniel Mission).
3 Fall, *Street*, 252.
4 Greene, *Ways*, 161.
5 1953 trip: All quotations, unless otherwise noted, from EGL to HL, June 24, July 4, 1953, PCLPP; EGL to "Folks," July 16, 1953, PCLPP; EGL to PK, June 21, July 3, 1953, PYPP.
6 Sainteny, *Memoir*, 20.
7 Duiker, *Ho*, 15.
8 Ibid., 64; Logevall, *Embers*, 14.
9 "Stalinist": Duiker, *Ho*, 95. "Goodness": 94.
10 Sainteny, *Memoir*, 51–52.

11 Duiker, *Ho*, 167.
12 Sainteny, *Memoir*, 48.
13 Duiker, *Ho*, 251.
14 Ibid., 289.
15 Logevall, *Embers*, 83.
16 Ibid., 97.
17 Fall, *Street*, 32–33; Logevall, *Embers*, 238–52.
18 Bodard, *Quicksand*, 137.
19 *FRUS 1952–1953, Indochina*, 13.643.
20 Morgan, *Valley*, 168.
21 *WP*, March 30, 1975 ("jut jawed," "hit," "slum"); Atkinson, *Day*, 430 ("inch"); Atkinson, *Guns*, 209 ("axe").
22 EGL, "The Good Fights," HI/EGL, box 77, file 272.
23 EGL to HL, June 24, 1953, PCLPP.
24 EGL to "folks," July 16, 1953, PCLPP.
25 Ibid.
26 Commander, Jacquelot Battalion, July 5, 1953, CHA, box 10H 155, file O'Daniel Mission.
27 *FRUS 1952–1954, Indochina*, 13.683–89.
28 Ibid.
29 LBJPL/EGLOH.
30 EGL, *Midst*, 111.
31 "Psychological Warfare," n.d., HI/EGL, box 35.
32 EGL to O'Daniel, "Unconventional Warfare," June 23, 1953, HI/EGL, box 35; EGL to O'Daniel, "Guerrilla Warfare," June 25, 1953, HI/EGL, box 35; "Guerrilla Warfare," n.d., NSA/EGL.
33 Fall, *Street*, 267–79.
34 EGL to "Folks," July 16, 1953, PCLPP.
35 EGL to PK, July 3, 1953, PYPP.
36 "Report of U.S. Special Mission to Indochina," Feb. 5, 1954, NARA, RG 330, EGL office files, box 3, Indo-China file.
37 Windrow, *Last*, 233.

CHAPTER 12: *A Fortress Falls*

1 Windrow, *Last*, 238.
2 Morgan, *Valley*, 232.
3 Fall, *Hell*, 127.
4 Morgan, *Valley*, 228.
5 EGL to PK, Jan. 20, 1954, PYPP.
6 EGL interview, May 17, 1984, CCP.
7 AI/ELCL.
8 Ibid.
9 Ibid.
10 AI/PLCL.
11 RP, email to author, Jan. 12, 2017.

12 Pete Lansdale interview, Nov. 11, 1985, CCP.
13 AI/PLCL.
14 AI/ELCL.
15 Ted Lansdale, email to author, Nov. 17, 2014.
16 EGL to HL, Jan. 11, 1954, PCLPP.
17 Smith, *Eisenhower*, xi.
18 *FRUS 1952–1954, Indochina*, 13.949.
19 Ibid., 1016.
20 Ibid., 1006.
21 Nashel, *Lansdale's*, 1; Currey, *Unquiet*, 136.
22 HI/EGLOH/CRS.
23 EGL interview, May 16, 1984, CCP.
24 HI/EGLOH/CRS.
25 EGL to CIA Director, March 21, 1954, HI/EGL, box 97, file 6.
26 HI/EGLOH/CRS.
27 Lansdale, *Midst*, 127–28.
28 EGL to HL, May 3, 1954, PCLPP.
29 EGL to HL, May 29, 1954, PCLPP.
30 EGL to HL, May 31, 1954, PCLPP.
31 EGL to HL, May 3, 1954, PCLPP.
32 *Manila Bulletin*, April 22, 1954.
33 EGL to HL, April 24, 1954, PCLPP.
34 *FRUS 1952–1954, Indochina*, 13.1271.
35 Logevall, *Embers*, 454–509.
36 Fall, *Hell*, 344.
37 Windrow, *Valley*, 592.
38 Ibid., 591.
39 Ibid., 616.
40 EGL to HL, May 29, 1954, PCLPP.
41 EGL, *Midst*, 128; EGL to Allen Dulles, Nov. 15, 1961, HI/EGL, box 37.
42 EGL to HL, May 31, PCLPP; EGL, *Midst*, 128–29.

CHAPTER 13: *"I Am Ngo Dinh Diem"*

1 EGL, *Midst*, 131.
2 Ibid., 134.
3 EGL to HL, June 1, 1954, PCLPP.
4 LBJPL/EGLOH. In this interview, EGL did not identify the Air Force attaché. His identity comes from U.S. State Department, *Foreign Service List*.
5 Emmett J. McCarthy, OSS personnel file, NARA, RG 226, box 498.
6 EGL interview, May 17, 1984, CCP.
7 EGL to PK, June 2, 1954, PYPP; EGL to HL, June 1, 1954, PCLPP.
8 EGL to HL, Nov. 1954 (n.d.), PCLPP.
9 Cyclo, "loved": EGL, *Midst*, 135–36. "Vacuum": EGL to PK, July 14, 1954, PYPP.
10 EGL to PK, July 14, 1954, PYPP.
11 EGL, draft memoir, HI/EGL, box 76, file 263.

12 EGL, *Midst*, 150.
13 Ibid.
14 EGL to PK, June 2, 1954, PYPP.
15 Ibid.
16 EGL to HL, June 4, 1954, PCLPP.
17 EGL to PK, June 5, 1954, PYPP.
18 EGL to HL, July 5, 1954, PCLPP.
19 EGL to HL, June 4, 1943, PCLPP.
20 EGL to PK, June 2, 1954, PYPP.
21 EGL to PK, June 18, 1954, PYPP.
22 EGL to HL, June 13, 1954, PCLPP.
23 EGL to HL, June 4, 1954, PCLPP.
24 EGL interview, Dec. 17, 1984, CCP.
25 EGL, *Midst*, 142.
26 EGL to PK, June 5, 1954, PYPP.
27 EGL to family, Feb. 26, 1956, PCLPP.
28 Chapman, *Cauldron*, 15; author's visit to Cao Dai Holy See, 2016.
29 Chapman, *Cauldron*, 26; Miller, *Misalliance*, 92.
30 EGL to HL, June 20, 1954, PCLPP.
31 Greene, *Ways*, 162.
32 EGL, *Midst*, 147.
33 EGL to HL, June 20, 1954, PCLPP.
34 EGL, *Midst*, 147; *FRUS 1952–1954, Indochina*, 13.1722.
35 EGL to HL, June 27, 1954, PCLPP.
36 Ibid.
37 RP, *Vietnam*, 21.
38 Chapman, *Cauldron*, 33.
39 Simpson, *Tiger*, 14.
40 EGL, *Midst*, 148–49.
41 Ibid., 149.
42 EGL to HL, July 5, 1954, PCLPP.
43 NSA/EGL/SMM, 3.
44 EGL, *Midst*, 137–39.
45 CIA, "Weekly Indochina Report," June 2, 1954, NARA/CREST, CIA-RDP91T01172R000300190004-6.
46 EGL, *Midst*, 154–55.
47 Miller, *Misalliance*, 24.
48 Jacobs, *Mandarin*, 19.
49 Shaplen, *Lost*, 107.
50 Hammer, *Death*, 50.
51 Ibid., 51.
52 Shaplen, *Lost*, 110.
53 Jacobs, *Mandarin*, 31.
54 *FRUS 1952–1954, Indochina*, 13.553–55.
55 Logevall, *Embers*, 590.
56 EGL to HL, Aug. 4, 1954, PYPP.
57 EGL, *Midst*, 156–57.

58 Miller, *Misalliance*, 4.
59 Ahern, *Declassified*, 10; "Courses of Action Which the United States Should Adopt to Ensure Survival of Free Vietnam," NARA, RG 84, box 1, file 22.
60 EGL, *Midst*, 158–59.
61 NSA/EGL/SMM, 5.
62 EGL, *Midst*, 159.
63 WGBH, pt. 1.
64 Mecklin, *Mission*, 40.
65 WGBH, pt. 2.
66 EGL to Roswell Gilpatric, April 25, 1961. NARA, RG 330, EGL office files, box 5.
67 Mecklin, *Mission*, 42.
68 USAFA/EGLOH.
69 VCA/OWOH.
70 EGL interview, Dec. 19, 1985, CCP.
71 EGL, "Thoughts concerning Diem," n.d., HI/EGL, box 80, file 298.
72 WGBH, pt. 2.
73 USAFA/EGLOH.
74 EGL, *Midst*, 362.
75 EGL interview, Dec. 19, 1984, CCP.
76 EGL, *Midst*, 160.

CHAPTER 14: *The Chopstick Torture*

1 AI/TN.
2 NSA/EGL/SMM, 8.
3 "Courses of Action Which the U.S. Should Adopt to Ensure Survival of Free Vietnam," NARA, RG 84, box 1, file 22. Internal evidence indicates this was written by EGL in late July 1954.
4 EGL, *Midst*, 165.
5 EGL to HL, July 5, 1954, PCLPP.
6 NSA/EGL/SMM, 2.
7 *NYT*, Jan. 3, 1999.
8 RP, *Vietnam*, 19.
9 AI/VH.
10 *Kansas City Star*, Sept. 20, 1998.
11 Conein's CIA personnel file, NSA.
12 Grant, *Phoenix*, 48.
13 Conein's CIA personnel file, NSA.
14 Conein interview with Lydia Fish, July 30, 1989, CCP.
15 *NYT*, Jan. 3, 1999.
16 Grant, *Phoenix*, 104–5.
17 RP, *Vietnam*, 19.
18 EGL to Bohannan, Jan. 23, 1957, CCP.
19 NSA/EGL/SMM, 2.
20 EGL, *Midst*, 161.
21 RP, *Vietnam*, 11–12.

22 Ibid., 13.

23 Ibid., 14.

24 Grant, *Phoenix*, 104.

25 EGL, draft memoir, HI/EGL, box 78, file 281.

26 RP, *Vietnam*, 17.

27 Ibid., 16.

28 *NYT*, July 25, 1962.

29 EGL to HL, Aug. 2, 1955, PCLPP.

30 Richard W. Smith to Cecil Currey, May 15, 2000, CCP.

31 EGL interview, Dec. 17, 1984, CCP.

32 EGL to PK, Sept. 12, 1954, PYPP.

33 Simpson, *Tiger*, 121.

34 *FRUS 1952–1954, Indochina*, 13.1922.

35 EGL to Smith Simpson, Jan. 19, 1973, HI/EGL, box 28, file 639b; EGL interview, May 17, 1984, CCP.

36 EGL, draft memoir, HI/EGL box 76, file 263.

37 HI/EGLOH/CRS.

38 Simpson, *Tiger*, 128–30.

39 Jacobs, *Mandarin*, 45.

40 Dooley, *Deliver*, 119.

41 *NYT*, Jan. 19, 1961.

42 Fisher, *Dr. America*, 80.

43 *Los Angeles Times*, Dec. 15, 1991.

44 Simpson, *Tiger*, 127.

45 NSA/EGL/SMM, 11.

46 Ibid., 12.

47 EGL, "Military Psychological Operations," Armed Forces Staff College, Jan. 7, 1960, CCP.

48 NSA/EGL/SMM, 23.

49 RP, *Vietnam*, 39–40.

50 NSA/EGL/SMM, 12.

51 EGL interview, May 17, 1984, CCP.

52 EGL, *Midst*, 138–40; EGL interview, May 17, 1984, CCP.

53 Grant, *Phoenix*, 109.

54 Fall, *Two*, 153.

55 Smith, *Portrait*, 179.

56 EGL to Smith Simpson, Jan. 19, 1973, HI/EGL, box 28, file 639b.

57 NSA/EGL/SMM, 48.

58 *FRUS 1952–1954, Indochina*, 13.2074.

59 Fall, *Two*, 153.

60 AI/RWS.

61 NSA/EGL/SMM, 11.

62 RP, *Vietnam*, 14.

63 Nick Arundel interview, April 2, 2001, CCP.

64 FitzGerald, *Fire*, 76–77.

65 Halberstam, *Best*, 126.

66 Grant, *Phoenix*, 108.

67 NSA/EGL/SMM, 12.
68 Ibid.
69 Conboy, *Spies*, 7–10; Tourison, *Secret*, 9.
70 NSA/EGL/SMM, 32.
71 EGL, *Midst*, 168.
72 AI/RWS.
73 Conboy, *Spies*, 13–15.
74 AI/DG.
75 Berman, *Perfect*, loc. 948.
76 Ibid., loc. 961.
77 Bass, *Spy*, 87, 95, 97.

CHAPTER 15: *Pacification*

 1 Porter, *War*, 12.
 2 NSA/EGL/SMM, 9. In his memoir, written two decades later (EGL, *Midst*, 172), Lansdale said the lighter came from Nasser, who by then was more famous than Naguib.
 3 NSA/EGL/SMM, 13–14.
 4 RP, *Vietnam*, 30–31; EGL, *Midst*, 173; NSA/EGL/SMM, 8–9.
 5 RP, *Vietnam*, 31.
 6 EGL interview, May 17, 1984, CCP.
 7 NSA/EGL/SMM, 13–14.
 8 EGL, *Midst*, 175.
 9 Ibid.
10 EGL to HL, Oct. 25, 1954, PCLPP.
11 EGL, *Midst*, 175.
12 PP, Part IV.A.3, p. 13.
13 Ahern, *Ngo*, 49.
14 *FRUS 1952–1954, Indochina*, 13.2157.
15 Simpson, *Tiger*, 135.
16 EGL interview, Dec. 17, 1984, CCP.
17 Ahern, *Ngo*, 47.
18 *WP*, Sept. 13, 1987.
19 Jeffers, *Command*, 3.
20 Simpson, *Tiger*, 136.
21 EGL, *Midst*, 203.
22 Collins to State, Nov. 25, 1954, DDEPP/JLCP, box 25.
23 EGL, *Midst*, 204; Grant, *Phoenix*, 121; RP, *Vietnam*, 32; LBJPL/EGLOH, pt. II. I have not been able to locate a contemporaneous record, and Collins later said he could not recall the incident (see WGBH/JLC). But "it was common knowledge among Lansdale's team at the time" (RP, *Vietnam*, 322). See also Joe Baker interview, June 23, 1985, CCP.
24 Grant, *Phoenix*, 122.
25 LBJPL/EGLOH, pt. II.
26 EGL, *Midst*, 205–7.

27 Ibid., 207.
28 EGL to PK, Aug. 4, 1954, PYPP.
29 EGL to PK, Aug. 10, 1954, PYPP.
30 RP, email to author, Dec. 17, 2014.
31 EGL to PK, Sept. 3, 1954, PYPP.
32 PK to EGL, Sept. 21, 1954, PYPP.
33 Richard Smith to Cecil Currey, May 15, 2000, CCP.
34 EGL to family, Oct. 31, 1956, PCLPP.
35 LBJPL/KBOH.
36 EGL to HL, Dec. 27, 1954, PCLPP.
37 Ibid.
38 EGL to PK, n.d., PYPP.
39 AI/VH.
40 Grant, *Phoenix*, 122.
41 EGL, *Midst*, 169.
42 NSA/EGL/SMM, 14, 46; Ahern, *Ngo*, 52; Ahern, *Declassified*, 19.
43 EGL to Rockefellers, April 12, 1957, RAC, Series O, RG 2, box 22, folder 220.
44 AI/FSJ.
45 EGL, *Midst*, 214.
46 EGL to J. Lawton Collins, Dec. 29, 1954, DDEPL/JLCP, box 28 (Lansdale).
47 Mojica and Maik to PK, March 3, 1987, CCP.
48 NSA/EGL/SMM, 51.
49 EGL to PK, n.d., PYPP.
50 EGL to PK, Jan. 12, 1955, PYPP; EGL to James Douglas, Feb. 12, 1963, HI/EGL, box 37.
51 EGL to HL, Dec. 27, 1954, PCLPP.
52 EGL to HL, April 5, 1956, PCLPP.
53 EGL to family, Feb. 6, 1955, PCLPP.
54 Fishel to EGL, April 15, 1955, HI/EGL, box 35, Vietnam 1954–66 file.
55 EGL to HL, Sept. 5, 1955, PCLPP.
56 EGL, *Midst*, 229–31.
57 NSA/EGL/SMM, 17.
58 *FRUS 1955–1957, Indochina*, 1.8.
59 EGL to HL, Feb. 6, 1955, PCLPP.
60 EGL to Robert Shaplen, May 30, 1965, HI/EGL, box 40.
61 Spector, *Advice*, 240.
62 EGL to PK, Jan. 12, 1955, PYPP.
63 EGL to HL, Jan. 11, 1955, PCLPP.
64 EGL to PK, Jan. 29, 1955, PYPP.
65 EGL to HL, Feb. 10, 1954, PCLPP.
66 EGL to PK, Jan. 29, 1955, PYPP.
67 EGL, *Midst*, 218.
68 Ibid.
69 "Bulletin," Deuxieme Bureau, May 14, 1955, CHA, group 10, box 4198.
70 Joe Baker to Cecil Currey, Feb. 18, 1988, CCP.
71 Joe Redick interview, Dec. 18, 1984, CCP.
72 EGL to HL, Oct. 25, 1954, PCLPP.

73 EGL, *Midst*, 235.

74 RP, email to author, Jan. 12, 2017.

75 RP, *Vietnam*, 45; NSA/EGL/SMM, 24.

76 EGL, *Midst*, 234.

77 Ibid., 232–33.

78 RP, *Vietnam*, 42.

79 NSA/EGL/SMM, 24.

80 EGL, *Midst*, 237–38.

81 EGL to Lionel McCarr, Oct. 2, 1961, NARA, RG 330, EGL office files, box 5, Vietnam #3 file.

82 NSA/EGL/SMM, 7.

83 RP, *Vietnam*, 53–55, 5861, 67–70.

84 NSA/EGL/SMM, 47.

85 Ahern, *Declassified*, 18.

86 *FRUS 1955–1957, Vietnam*, 1.65; Grant, *Phoenix*, 127.

87 EGL interview, Nov. 29, 1984, CCP.

88 RP, *Vietnam*, 71.

CHAPTER 16: *The Viper's Nest*

1 Sherry, *Greene*, 2.434.

2 Ahern, *Ngo*, 67.

3 EGL, *Midst*, 184.

4 EGL to HL, Feb. 13, 1955, HI/EGL, box 83, file 1.

5 EGL, *Midst*, 189–90; EGL, draft memoir, HI/EGL, box 78, file 281.

6 Ahern, *Ngo*, 41–42.

7 EGL, *Midst*, 190–94.

8 Ibid., 196–99.

9 Ibid., 199–201.

10 EGL to HL, Feb. 13, 1955, HI/EGL, box 83, file 1.

11 LBJPL/EGLOH, pt. II.

12 EGL to Karl H. Cerny, 1965, HI/EGL, box 37.

13 EGL to Lt. William P. Dickey, April 14, 1965, HI/EGL, box 37.

14 EGL to Helen, May 2, 1955, HI/EGL, box 83, file 1.

15 EGL to family, Aug. 15, 1955, PYPP.

16 Boot, *Invisible*, 280–81.

17 NSA/EGL/SMM, 10.

18 Logevall, *Embers*, 642; Fall, *Two*, 246.

19 Ahern, *Ngo*, 69; EGL to Karl H. Cerny, 1965, HI/EGL, box 37.

20 NSA/EGL/SMM, 45.

21 Chapman, *Cauldron*, 76.

22 EGL to Collins/O'Daniel, March 13, 1955, DDEPL/JLCP, box 28, Lansdale file 1.

23 EGL, *Midst*, 244.

24 EGL to Collins/O'Daniel, March 23, 1955, DDEPP/JLCP, box 28, Lansdale file 2.

25 EGL, *Midst*, 253–54.
26 *FRUS 1955–1957, Vietnam*, 1.143.
27 EGL to Collins/O'Daniel, March 13, 1955, DDEPP/JLCP, box 28, Lansdale file 2. A CIA estimate on March 31 (NARA/CREST CIA-RDP79R00890A000500030066-7) listed 16,000 Cao Dai, 19,600 Hoa Hao, 3,500 Binh Xuyen.
28 EGL to Collins/O'Daniel, March 13, 1955, DDEPL/JLCP, box 28, Lansdale file 2.
29 Ahern, *Ngo*, 68.
30 EGL, *Midst*, 257.
31 EGL to Roswell Gilpatric, April 25, 1961, NARA, RG 330, EGL office files, box 5.
32 EGL, *Midst*, 262–64.
33 Ibid., 265–66.
34 EGL to PK, April 26, 1955, PYPP.
35 Simpson, *Tiger*, 144–45.
36 *FRUS 1952–1954, Indochina*, 13.2250.
37 EGL to Robert Shaplen, May 30, 1965, HI/EGL, box 40.
38 *FRUS 1955–1957, Vietnam*, 1.168–71.
39 Ibid., 235.
40 Ibid., 237.
41 Ibid., 250.
42 EGL, *Midst*, 276–77.
43 *FRUS 1955–1957, Vietnam*, 1.294–98.
44 Ibid., 301.
45 Ibid., 301–2.
46 RP, *Vietnam*, 65, 77.
47 EGL, *Midst*, 282–83.
48 Ibid., 300.
49 Anderson, *Trapped*, 111; Miller, *Misalliance*, 120.
50 U.S. Embassy, Paris, to Secretary of State, May 2, 1955, SGMML/JFDP, box 8, file 12.
51 EGL, *Midst*, 286.
52 Ibid., 288–89.
53 EGL to PK, June 10, 1955, PYPP.
54 NSA/EGL/SMM, 40.
55 Ibid., 34.
56 RP, *Vietnam*, 64.
57 Charles W. Sandman to Cecil Currey, Aug. 2000, CCP.
58 *FRUS 1955–1957, Vietnam*, 1.303.
59 RP, *Vietnam*, 64.
60 *FRUS 1955–1957, Vietnam*, 1.307–12.
61 EGL to PK, April 26, 1955, PYPP.
62 RP, *Vietnam*, 65.
63 EGL, *Midst*, 294.
64 EGL to Dorothy Bohannan, Nov. 18, 1982, HI/EGL, box 2.
65 EGL, *Midst*, 297.
66 Ahern, *Ngo*, 80.
67 Ibid.

68 Simpson, *Tiger*, 148.
69 EGL to Collins, May 3, 1955, DDEPL/JLCP, Lansdale file 1; NSA/EGL/ SMM, 43.
70 EGL to Robert Shaplen, May 30, 1965, HI/EGL, box 40; EGL, *Midst*, 309; EGL, "Memo for the Record," May 3, 1955, DDEPL/JLCP, Lansdale file 1; NSA/EGL/ SMM, 44.
71 Blagov, *Honest*, 173–95.
72 EGL to PK, May 15, 1955, PYPP.
73 EGL to PK, Sunday, n.d., 1955, PYPP.
74 Logevall, *Embers*, 645.
75 Chapman, *Cauldron*, 141–45.
76 Simpson, *Tiger*, 150.
77 *FRUS 1955–1957, Vietnam*, 344–45.
78 Collins, *Lightning Joe*, 405.
79 Anderson, *Trapped*, 112.
80 Collins to EGL, May 13, 1955, HI/EGL, box 35, Vietnam 1954–56 file.
81 Ahern, *Ngo*, 88.
82 EGL to PK, May 15, 1955, PYPP.
83 Fall, *Two*, 245.
84 Ahern, *Ngo*, 83.
85 Gibbons interview, Jan. 14, 1987, MLEPP.

CHAPTER 17: *"Stop Calling Me* Papa*!"*

1 EGL to PK, n.d., PYPP.
2 EGL, *Midst*, 316.
3 AI/RWS; Smith to Cecil Currey, May 15, 2000, CCP.
4 RP, *Vietnam*, 77.
5 EGL to PK, June 1955 (n.d.), PYPP.
6 EGL, *Midst*, 318.
7 RP, *Vietnam*, 77–78; AI/EC; Grant, *Phoenix*, 125–26.
8 Jacobs, *Mandarin*, 93; Nguyen, *Hanoi's War*, 40.
9 LBJPL/KBOH.
10 EGL to family, June 17, 1955, PCLPP.
11 "Ngo Dinh Diem—Summarized Biographical Report," 1957, SGMML/JFDP, box 5, folder 5.
12 EGL, *Midst*, 328–30.
13 Miller, *Misalliance*, 138.
14 Ahern, *Ngo*, 90.
15 Ibid., 23.
16 Thomas Ahern, email to author, March 4, 2015.
17 *FRUS 1955–1957, Vietnam*, 1.415.
18 PP, Part IV.A.5, p. 17.
19 Miller, *Misalliance*, 132–33.
20 Ahern, *Declassified*, 21–23.
21 EGL to HL, Feb. 24, 1956, PCLPP.

22 *NYT*, Oct. 26, 1999.
23 EGL to family, June 17, 1955, PCLPP.
24 "Memorandum of Conversation with the President," June 7, 1955, SGMML/JFDP, box 77.
25 EGL to HL, July 31, 1944, PCLPP.
26 EGL to PK, July 23, 1955, PYPP.
27 NSA/EGL/SMM, 52–53.
28 EGL to family, Aug. 15, 1955, PCLPP.
29 Dulles to Eisenhower, July 26, 1955, CCP.
30 EGL to Magsaysay, Aug. 10, 1955, HI/EGL, box 35, file 784.
31 EGL to HL, July 31, 1955, PCLPP.
32 EGL to family, Aug. 15, 1955, PCLPP.
33 Meyer, *Hanging Sam*, 88, 91–92, 108.
34 LBJPL/STWOH.
35 Ibid.
36 EGL, *Midst*, 336.
37 RP, *Vietnam*, 85.
38 EGL to HL, Feb. 18, 1956, PCLPP.
39 Tran Van Don, *Endless*, 60.
40 EGL to HL, March 31, 1956, PCLPP.
41 EGL, *Midst*, 333–34.
42 *FRUS 1955–1957, Vietnam*, 590; Chapman, *Cauldron*, 154, 165–67.
43 Simpson, *Tiger*, 151.
44 EGL to family, Feb. 26, 1956, PCLPP.
45 EGL, *Midst*, 349–51; Ahern, *Ngo*, 104–5; Miller, *Misalliance*, 147.
46 EGL, *Midst*, 356; Ahern, *Declassified*, 26.
47 EGL to PK, Aug. 6, 1955, PYPP.
48 EGL to HL, Jan. 12, 1956, PCLPP.
49 EGL, *Midst*, 343–44.
50 Greene, *Quiet*, 52.
51 EGL to HL, Jan. 12, 1956, PCLPP.
52 EGL to HL, Feb. 18, 1956, PCLPP.
53 EGL interview, May 16, 1984, CCP.
54 Pratt, *Text*, 319.
55 Greene, *Ways*, 170.
56 Wise, *Works*, 31; Sherry, *Greene*, 2.417.
57 Halberstam, *Best*, 125; Karnow, *Vietnam*, 236; Reeves, *Kennedy*, loc. 706.
58 Logevall, *Embers*, 681.
59 Geist, *Pictures*, xii.
60 EGL to HL, Jan. 30, 1956, PCLPP.
61 EGL to HL, Feb. 6, 1956, PCLPP.
62 EGL to Mankiewicz, March 17, 1956, HI/EGL, box 35.
63 Ahern, *Ngo*, 102.
64 EGL to Diem, Oct. 28, 1957, HI/EGL, box 39.
65 EGL to O'Daniel, Oct. 28, 1957, HI/EGL, box 39.
66 *Times of Viet Nam*, Jan. 25, 1958, VCA/DPC.
67 EGL, *Midst*, 360–63.

68 EGL to HL, July 30, 1956, PCLPP.
69 EGL to HL, Nov. 25, 1956, PCLPP.
70 EGL service record, CCP.
71 USAFA/EGLOH.
72 *Life*, May 13, 1957.
73 Ahern, *Ngo*, 108.
74 Ibid., 111.
75 RP, *Vietnam*, 92.
76 Ahern, *Declassified*, 28.

CHAPTER 18: *Heartbreak Hotel*

1 EGL to HL, March 31, 1956, PCLPP.
2 EGL to HL, Nov. 26, 1955, PCLPP.
3 EGL to family, Sept. 15, 1956, PCLPP.
4 EGL to CTRB, Jan. 23, 1957, CCP.
5 AI/FSJ.
6 EGL to PK, Jan. 29, 1955, PYPP.
7 EGL to PK, April 13, 1956, PYPP.
8 EGL to PK, n.d., PYPP.
9 EGL to PK, April 13, 1956, PYPP.
10 http://www.azlyrics.com/lyrics/elvispresley/heartbreakhotel.html.
11 NWC/EGL.
12 EGL to HL, Feb. 6, 1956, PCLPP.
13 Abuevo, *Magsaysay*, 484; *NYT*, March 18, 1957; *WP*, March 18, 1957; Martinez, *Magsaysay*, ch. 11.
14 AI/RM.
15 *NYT*, March 23, 1957.
16 EGL, *Midst*, 377.
17 EGL to CTRB, March 19, 1957, CCP.
18 EGL to CTRB, April 16, 1957, CCP; EGL to Rockefellers, April 12, 1957, and J.D. Rockefeller III to EGL, June 13, 1957, RAC, Series O, RG 2, box 22, folder 220.
19 EGL to CTRB, March 28, 1957, CCP.
20 Smith, *Portrait*, 253.
21 Ibid., 254.
22 EGL to Roswell Gilpatrick, July 27, 1961, NSA/EGL.

CHAPTER 19: *Guerrilla Guru*

1 EGL to HL, Jan. 12, 1956, PCLPP.
2 EGL to PK, n.d., PYPP.
3 EGL to Samuel T. Williams, Oct. 28, 1957, HI/EGL, box 42.
4 [Name redacted] to Villiers, July 26, 1956, NSA/EGL.
5 EGL to PK, n.d., PYPP.
6 EGL to CTRB, Jan. 23, 1957, CCP.

7   EGL to CTRB, May 8, 1957, CCP.

8   Ahern, *Ngo*, 105.

9   NSA/EGL/SMM.

10 Bird, *Good*.

11 "The Pentagon," HI/EGL, box 48.

12 Vogel, *Pentagon*, loc. 5884.

13 EGL to Romy Espino, Oct. 10, 1960, HI/EGL, box 37.

14 "Biographical Sketch," MCA/GBE; *WP*, May 23, 1973; *NYT*, May 23, 1973.

15 EGL interviews, Nov. 30, Dec. 17, 1984, CCP.

16 EGL interview, Nov. 30, 1984, CCP.

17 AI/JTF.

18 EGL to PK, April 7, [1958?], PYPP.

19 EGL to PK, Sept. 3, 1957, PYPP.

20 AI/JTF.

21 EGL, "A Cold War Program for Defense," Sept. 1957, NARA/CREST CIA-RDP80R01731R000300160011-.

22 Ibid.

23 PK to EGL, June 9, 1958, PYPP.

24 EGL, "The Free Citizen in Uniform," Nov. 1, 1960, HI/EGL, box 96.

25 "Resume of OCB Luncheon Meeting," April 1, 1959, CIA-RDP80B01676R0027000 30035-4.

26 EGL, "Leadership Training in Africa," Aug. 25, 1960, HI/EGL, box 43.

27 EGL, "Military Assistance," April 27, 1959, VCA/DPC, box 19, folder 11.

28 EGL, "OSD Working Paper," Sept. 10, 1958, NSA/EGL.

29 HI/EGL, box 73, file 1.

30 "Informal Discussion with Col. Lansdale, USAF," Feb. 27, 1957, U.S. Army War College, HI/EGL, box 80, file 292.

31 AI/SVW.

32 *New York Herald Tribune*, Sept. 1, 1965.

33 AI/SVW.

34 Ibid.

35 "Counter Insurgency Operations Officer Course," U.S. Army Special Warfare School, Oct. 11, 1961, NARA, RG 330, EGL office files, box 2, CG file.

36 AI/SVW.

37 Jones to EGL, May 9, 1961, HI/EGL, box 38, file 969.

38 Rostow, *Diffusion*, 265.

39 Lederer to EGL, Dec 3, 1957, WJLP.

40 Lederer to Ivan Von Auw, Aug. 16, 1957, CU/WWN, box 161, 1957 file, WJLP.

41 Lederer, "Revisited."

42 Swenson to Burdick/Lederer, Dec. 3, 1957; Burdick to Wesley Price, April 29, 158; Burdick to Swenson, Dec. 7, 1957. CU/WWN, box 161, 1957 file.

43 Lederer, *Ugly*, 12.

44 Ibid., 84–85.

45 Ibid., 110–14.

46 Ibid., 181.

47 EGL to Peter McInerney, Sept. 4, 1980, CCP.

48 NWC/EGL.

49 Lederer to "Fritz," April 1959, in Palm, *American Pie*.

50 Klein, *Orientalism*, 87.

51 *NYT*, July 12, 2009.

52 PK to EGL, April 26, 1963, HI/EGL, box 38.

53 EGL, "Pakse-Kontum Road," NARA/CREST CIA-RDP80R0R01731R0003001
80001-3.

54 "A Program of Action to Prevent Communist Domination of South Vietnam,"
April 26, 1961, NARA, RG 330, EGL office files, box 5.

55 Nashel, *Cold War*, 179–80.

56 Schlesinger, *Robert Kennedy*, 476.

57 EGL to S. R. Davis, April 16, 1961, HI/EGL, box 37.

58 *FRUS 1958–1960, Vietnam*, 1.144.

59 AI/CW.

60 PK to EGL, June 9, 1958, PYPP.

61 EGL to HL, Feb. 3, 1959, PCLPP.

62 EGL, draft memoir, box 76, file 264.

63 EGL to Diem, Jan. 6, 1959, HI/EGL, box 42.

64 EGL to Diem, April 2, 1959, HI/EGL, box 42.

65 *FRUS 1958–1960, Vietnam*, 1.138–44.

66 AI/CW.

67 Ladejinsky to EGL, April 22, 1959, HI/EGL, box 4.

68 Sihanouk, *My War*, 107–8.

69 *Wall Street Journal*, Nov. 15, 1968; Nashel, *Cold War*, 195.

70 EGL, *Midst*, 113.

71 EGL to Gen. McGarr, Aug. 11, 1960, NARA, RG 330, EGL office files, box 6,
Vietnam Correspondence file.

72 Woods, *Shadow Warrior*, 126; Thomas, *Best*, 190.

73 EGL to HL, Feb. 11, 1959, PCLPP.

74 *FRUS 1958–1960, Foreign Economic Policy*, 4.469–72.

75 EGL to PK, April 7, 1959, PYPP.

CHAPTER 20: *A New War Begins*

1 Nguyen, *Hanoi's War*, 17.

2 Military History Institute, *Victory*, 50.

3 Larteguy, *Yellow*, 62.

4 Military History Institute, *Victory*, 53.

5 Elliott, *Vietnamese*, 135.

6 Ibid., 86.

7 Miller, *Misalliance*, 178–83.

8 Hammer, *Death*, 77; Jacobs, *Mandarin*, 115; Frankum, *Rat*, ch. 4.

9 Colby, *Lost*, 76.

10 Ibid., 74.

11 *FRUS 1958–1960, Vietnam*, 1.575–79.

12 Ibid., 637, 649.

13 Ibid., 667–68.

14 Ibid., 581–82.
15 *NYT*, May 23, 1997.
16 Winik, *1944*, 309.
17 *FRUS 1958–1960, Vietnam*, 1.409.
18 Ibid., 426.
19 EGL personnel file, CCP.
20 EGL to Eugene M. Zuckert, Oct. 25, 1963, HI/EGL, box 42.
21 *FRUS 1958–1960, Vietnam*, 1.457–59.
22 Ibid., 691–92.
23 Felt to EGL, Dec. 11, 1960, HI/EGL, box 49, file 1376.
24 EGL to Williams, Dec. 23, 1960, HI/EGL, box 49, file 1376.
25 PK to EGL, Jan. 25, 1961, PYPP.
26 *Manila Bulletin*, Jan. 3, 1961.
27 EGL to PK, Jan. 14, 1961, PYPP.
28 Trimble to Secretary of State, Jan. 3, 1961. HI/EGL, box 49, file 1376.
29 EGL to HL, Jan. 8, 1961, PCLPP.
30 "Far East Itinerary for General Lansdale," HI/EGL, box 47, file 1330.
31 Logevall, *Embers*, 702–4.
32 EGL to PK, Jan. 14, 1961, PYPP.
33 Colby, *Lost*, 88.
34 Colby interview, June 24, 1985, CCP.
35 LBJPL/EGLOH.
36 EGL to PK, Jan. 14, 1961, PYPP.
37 EGL to Secretary of Defense, Jan. 17, 1961, HI/EGL, box 49, file 1376.
38 EGL to Secretary of Defense, Jan. 6, 1961, HI/EGL, box 49, file 1376.
39 HI/EGLOH/CRS.
40 EGL to HL, Jan. 8, 1961, PCLPP.
41 EGL to PK, Jan. 14, 1961, PYPP.
42 LBJPL/EGLOH; EGL interview, May 16, 1984, CCP; EGL to Diem, Jan. 30, 1961, HI/EGL, box 39.
43 LBJPL/EGLOH.
44 *Reader's Digest*, July 1963.
45 Binh Hung: EGL, "Visit to Fifth Military Region," Jan. 13, 1961, NARA, RG 330, EGL office files, box 5, Vietnam file #1; EGL, "Binh Hung: A Counter-Guerrilla Case Study," Feb. 9, 1961, HI/EGL, box 73, file 2; EGL to PK, Jan. 14, 1961, PYPP.
46 EGL to PK, Jan. 14, 1961, PYPP.
47 "Far East Itinerary for General Lansdale," HI/EGL, box 47, file 1330.

CHAPTER 21: *The Ambassador Who Never Was*

1 *Time*, Jan. 27, 1961.
2 Schlesinger, *Thousand*, 1.
3 *NYT*, Jan. 21, 1961.
4 Dallek, *Unfinished*, 398.
5 Caro, *Passage*, loc. 1110.
6 Dallek, *Unfinished*, 152.

7 http://www.jfklibrary.org/Asset-Viewer/BqXIEM9F4024ntFl7SVAjA.aspx.

8 EGL to PK, Jan. 14, 1961, PYPP.

9 Newman, *JFK*, 3; Currey, *Unquiet*, 223.

10 JFKPL/EGLOH.

11 RP, *Vietnam*, 331.

12 EGL, "Vietnam," Jan. 17, 1961, HI/EGL, box 49, file 1376.

13 EGL, "Binh Hung: A Counter-Guerrilla Case Study," Feb. 1/9, 1961, HI/EGL, box 73, file 2.

14 EGL to Robert Komer, May 30, 1971, HI/EGL, box 4.

15 Schlesinger, *Thousand*, 672.

16 Rostow, *Diffusion*, 264–65; LBJPL/WWROH.

17 Bundy to McNamara, Rusk, Dulles, Jan. 27, 1963. JFKPL, NSF, box 193, Vietnam General 1/61–3/61 file.

18 Schlesinger, *Thousand*, 672.

19 http://www.jfklibrary.org/Research/Research-Aids/Ready-Reference/JFK-Fast-Facts/Items-in-the-Oval-Office.aspx; Caro, *Passage*, loc. 10727–56.

20 *FRUS 1961–1963, Vietnam*, 1.16.

21 JFKPL/EGLOH.

22 Ibid.

23 EGL interview, Nov. 28, 1984, CCP.

24 JFKPL/EGLOH; EGL, draft memoir, HI/EGL, box 76, file 264. Except where noted, all quotations from Jan. 28 meeting are from *FRUS 1961–1963, Vietnam*, 1.13–19.

25 EGL interview, May 16, 1984, CCP.

26 Shaplen, *Lost*, 148.

27 EGL to Robert Komer, May 30, 1971, HI/EGL, box 4.

28 EGL interview, May 16, 1984, CCP; JFKPL/EGLOH.

29 Ahern, *Declassified*, 72–73.

30 EGL to Redick, May 18, 1961, NARA, RG 330, EGL office files, box 5, Vietnam File #1.

31 EGL, "OSO/OSD," n.d., CCP.

32 EGL to Nguyen Dinh Thuan, April 17, 1961, NARA, RG 330, EGL office files, box 5, Vietnam File #1.

33 Nguyen to EGL, April 22, 1961, NARA, RG 330, EGL office files, box 5, Vietnam File #1.

34 *FRUS 1961–1963, Vietnam*, 1.78.

35 LBJPL/WWROH.

36 *FRUS 1961–1963, Vietnam*, 1.72–73.

37 Ibid., 68; PP, Part IV.B.1, p. 24.

38 PP, Part IV.B.1, p. 23.

39 PP, Part V.B.4, bk. 1, pp. 22–34.

40 EGL to McNamara/Gilpatric, Aug. 1, 1961, NSA/EGL.

41 *FRUS 1961–1963, Vietnam*, 1.74.

42 LBJPL/RLGOH; McClintock, *Instruments*, 200.

43 EGL personnel file, CCP.

44 PP, Part IV.B.1, pp. 24–29.

45 *FRUS 1961–1963, Vietnam*, 1.132–34.

46 PP, Part V.B.4, bk. 1, p. 78.
47 PP, Part IV.B.1, p. 50.
48 Ibid., 36.
49 EGL to Robert Komer, May 30, 1971, HI/EGL, box 4.
50 EGL to Lionel McGarr, Oct. 2, 1961, NARA, RG 330, EGL office files, box 5, Vietnam #3 file.

CHAPTER 22: *"The X Factor"*

1 Hoopes, *Patriot.*
2 McNamara, *Retrospect*, 32.
3 RP, *Vietnam*, 104.
4 *Life*, Nov. 30, 1962.
5 HI/EGLOH/CRS.
6 Ibid.
7 Shapley, *Promise*, 13.
8 Ibid., 102.
9 Ibid., 65.
10 Ibid., 82.
11 Ibid., 103.
12 EGL to McNamara/Gilpatric, July 7, 1962, HI/EGL, box 47, file 1374.
13 AI/SVW.
14 HI/EGLOH/CRS.
15 AI/SVW.
16 McNamara, *Retrospect*, 32.
17 PP, Part IV.B.1, p. 72.
18 *Time*, July 28, 1961.
19 *NYT*, April 21, 1987.
20 Bissell, "Report of Counter Guerrilla Task Force," Dec. 13, 1961, NARA/CREST CIA-RDP89B00552R000100040005-0; *FRUS 1961–1963, National Security Policy*, 8.229–30.
21 Halberstam, *Best*, 161
22 Milne, *Rasputin*, 67.
23 Halberstam, *Best*, 156.
24 *Time*, July 28, 1961.
25 EGL to Robert Shaplen, May 30, 1965, HI/EGL, box 40.
26 *Life*, Oct. 27, 1961.
27 EGL interview, Dec. 17, 1984, CCP.
28 Ibid.
29 LBJPL/EGLOH.
30 "Concept of Border Control," Oct. 25, 1961, HI/EGL, box 49, file 1372.
31 LBJPL/EGOLH.
32 Taylor, *Swords*, 229.
33 Ibid.
34 Ibid., 239.
35 *FRUS 1961–1963, Vietnam*, 1.429.

36 PP, Part IV.B.1, pp. 99–100.

37 EGL to Roswell Gilpatric, May 10, 1961, JFKPL/NSF, box 231, folder 1.

38 *FRUS 1961–1963, Vietnam*, 1.419.

39 Ibid., 477.

40 Schlesinger, *Thousand*, 547.

41 EGL to McNamara, Nov. 6, 1961, NARA, RG 330, EGL office files, box 5.

42 *FRUS 1961–1963, Vietnam*, 1.421,

43 Ibid., 433.

44 Ibid., 643.

45 EGL to Samuel T. Wilson, Nov. 28, 1961, in Newman, *JFK*, 146.

46 EGL to McNamara/Gilpatric, Nov. 25, 1961, HI/EGL, box 49, file 1374.

47 *FRUS 1961–1963, Vietnam*, 1.719.

48 JFKPL/MGB.

49 Rostow, *Diffusion*, 279.

CHAPTER 23: *"Worms of the World Unite"*

1 EGL, Bay of Pigs: EGL to James Douglas, June 21, 1976, HI/EGL, box 3; EGL to Peter H. Wyden, Feb. 18, 1976, HI/EGL, box 10; Douglas to EGL, April 26, 1973, HI/EGL, box 3; LBJPL/EGLOH; EGL interview, Nov. 29, 1984, Dec. 17, 1984, CCP; Wyden, *Bay*, 71–73.

2 Draper, "Cuba," 6.

3 Goodwin, *Remembering*, loc. 3453–64.

4 *FRUS 1961–1963, Cuba*, 10.314.

5 Bissell, *Reflections*, 201.

6 "Memorandum for the Record," March 21, 1962, CCP.

7 Thomas, *RFK*, 30.

8 Ibid., 20.

9 Ibid., 26–27.

10 Ibid., 38.

11 Ibid., 62.

12 Thomas, *RFK*, 81; Caro, *Passage*, loc. 1843.

13 Caro, *Passage*, loc. 1804.

14 Ibid., loc. 1823.

15 *FRUS 1961–1963, Cuba*, 10.666.

16 AI/RNG.

17 Bohning, *Castro*, 81; Corn, *Ghost*, 81; Fursenko, *Gamble*, 146–47.

18 Schlesinger, *Robert Kennedy*, 480.

19 *FRUS 1961–1963, Cuba*, 10.721.

20 Helms, *Look*, 205.

21 Weiner, *Legacy*, 199.

22 Thomas, *RFK*, 20.

23 JFKPL/EGL.

24 RP, email to author, Nov. 6, 2014.

25 Goodwin, *Remembering*, loc. 3475.

26 AI/SVW.

27 Ted Lansdale, email to author, May 12, 2015.

28 RP, email to author, Nov. 6, 2014.

29 Helms, *Look*, 200.

30 EGL to Samuel T. Williams, Oct. 10, 1964, HI/STW, box 20, folder 15.

31 EGL to SG (A), May 7, 1962, CCP.

32 Bohning, *Castro*, 85.

33 *FRUS 1961–1963, Cuba*, 10.692.

34 EGL interview, Dec. 19, 1984, CCP.

35 *FRUS 1961–1963, Cuba*, 10.710–18.

36 William H. Craig, "Memorandum for the Special Group," March 13, 1962, MFF/
    TEGL; EGL, "Task 33," Jan. 19, 1962, CCP.

37 MFF/TRH13, 26.

38 MFF/RSM, 93.

39 MFF/TTP, 49–50.

40 EGL to Frank Church, Jan. 1, 1976, HI/EGL, box 10.

41 EGL to Peter Richards, Dec. 26, 1975, CCP, box 13, file 200; EGL to Bohannan,
    Nov. 22, 1975, CCP, box 13, file 198.1.

42 JFKPL/NSF, NLK-90-51, 12/95.

43 AI/SVW.

44 MFF/IG, 10–13, 21; Elliston, *Psywar*, 15–19.

45 Craig to EGL, Jan. 30, 1962, MFF/TEGL; Elliston, *Psywar*, 84–86.

46 MFF/TEGL, 26.

47 Craig to EGL, Feb. 2, 1962, NSA/CMC; Elliston, *Psywar*, 87–90.

48 Bohning, *Castro*, 101–2.

49 Lemnitzer to Secretary of Defense, March 13, 1962, NSA/CMC.

50 EGL, "The Cuba Project," Feb. 20, 1962, NARA/JFKARB, 176-10011-10046.

51 EGL to RFK, Jan. 27, 1962, MFF/TEGL.

52 EGL lecture, Nov. 29, 1984, CCP.

53 MFF/TEGL.

54 EGL, "The Cuba Project," Feb. 20, 1962, NARA/JFKARB, 176-10011-10046.

55 *FRUS 1961–1963, Cuba*, 10.765.

56 Martin, *Wilderness*, 129 ("ducklike"); MFF/TEGL, 70, 81–82.

57 Thomas, *Best*, 131.

58 Martin, *Wilderness*, 34, 38.

59 Ibid., 48.

60 Weiner, *Legacy*, 186; MFF/TRH13, 49–50.

61 Weiner, *Legacy*, 186.

62 Dallek, *Unfinished*, 479; Bohning, *Castro*, 181–82.

63 Helms, *Look*, 197.

64 MGG/TEGL, 80.

65 EGL interview, Dec. 30, 1976, NYPL/ASP.

66 MFF/IG, 113; *FRUS 1961–1963, Cuba*, 10.923–25; MFF/TRSM.

67 MFF/TEGL, appendix.

68 Ibid., 23.

69 EGL to David Lansdale, July 20, 1975, GBPP.

70 Church Committee, *Plots*, 151; MFF/TRH13, 137; MFF/TRH17, 18.

71 MFF/TSH, 5, 9–10; Helms, *Look*, 204; Corn, *Ghost*.

72 Bohning, *Castro*, 130; Corn, *Ghost*, 74.

73 Branch, "Secret War."

74 *FRUS 1961–1963, Cuba*, 10.844.

75 Harvey to EGL, July 24, 1962, JFKPL/NSF, box 319, folder 8.

76 *FRUS 1961–1963, Cuba*, 10.864–72; "Consequences of US Military Intervention in Cuba," Aug. 8, 1962, JFKPL/NSF, box 319, file 9.

77 Elliston, *Psywar*, 114, 207.

78 *FRUS 1961–1963, Cuba*, 10.896–97.

79 Ibid., 922.

80 Harvey to EGL, July 24, 1962, JFKPL/NSF, box 319, folder 8.

81 *FRUS 1961–1963, Cuba*, 11.944–46.

82 Martin, *Wilderness*, 137.

83 MFF/TWE, 13.

84 Corn, *Ghost*, 82.

85 MFF/TEGL, 84.

86 MFF/TP.

87 Ibid., 51.

88 MFF/TRH17, appendix.

89 Thomas, *RFK*, 114.

90 Schlesinger, *Robert Kennedy*, 239.

91 Helms, *Look*, 207.

92 Ibid., 208.

93 Stern, *Memory*, 17.

94 Ibid., 2.

95 Ibid., 6.

96 Bohning, *Castro*, 112.

97 Rasenberger, *Disaster*, 364.

98 Bohning, *Castro*, 122–23.

99 *FRUS 1961–1963, Cuba*, 11.648.

100 Ibid., 670.

101 MFF/IG, 75–77.

102 Helms, *Look*, 202.

103 Fursenko, *Gamble*, 145.

104 MFF/TRH17, appendix.

105 EGL interviews, Dec. 19, Nov. 29, 1984, CCP.

CHAPTER 24: *"Washington at Its Nuttiest"*

1 Catton, "Counter-Insurgency."

2 Miller, *Misalliance*, 248.

3 Military History Institute, *Victory*, 110.

4 Rottman, *Browning*, 5.

5 Miller, *Misalliance*, 248.

6 Military History Institute, *Victory*, 109.

7 Sheehan, *Lie*, 205.

8 Miller, *Misalliance*, 252.

9 Moyar, *Triumph*, 186–205.

10 Miller, *Misalliance*, 250.

11 Ibid., 264.

12 Ibid., 277.

13 *FRUS 1961–1963, Vietnam*, 3.638–41.

14 Coram, *Brute*.

15 White House diaries at millercenter.org.

16 EGL interview, May 17, 1984, CCP.

17 EGL to Phil Lansdale, Jan. 12, 1983, HI/EGL, box 28, file 639.

18 EGL to McNamara, Feb. 26, 1962, NARA, RG 330, box 4.

19 EGL to Roger Allen, Nov. 12, 1983, HI/EGL, box 28, file 639.

20 HI/EGLOH/CRS; RP, *Vietnam*, 190; "Non-Violent Alternatives," RMNPL, White House Special Files, Ehrlichman, box 30, Vietnam 1963–64; *Honolulu Star-Bulletin*, Jan. 7, 1984.

21 RP, "Memorandum for the Record," July 25, 1963, VCA/RPP, box 2, file 1.

22 RP, *Vietnam*, 184.

23 *FRUS 1961–1963, Vietnam*, 4.161–67.

24 RP, *Vietnam*, 192, 185.

25 Ibid., 187.

26 *FRUS 1961–1963, Vietnam*, 4.179.

27 Ibid., 205.

28 Jones, *Death*, 364–65; Langguth, *Vietnam*, 245; AI/DE; RP, *Vietnam*, 193–94; Hersh, *Dark Side*, 426–28.

29 Wells, *Wild*, ix.

30 *FRUS 1961–1963, Vietnam*, 4.240–41.

31 Blair, *Lodge*, 88.

32 Ahern, *Ngo*, 188.

33 EGL to Samuel T. Williams, Oct. 24, 1963, HI/EGL, box 42.

34 RP, *Vietnam*, 201–2.

35 EGL to Gilpatric, Sept. 6, 1963, HI/EGL, box 97, file 6.

36 EGL to E. F. Black, Oct. 14, 1963, HI/EGL, box 36.

37 AI/SVW.

38 EGL to PK, Oct. 31, 1963, PYPP.

39 EGL to Samuel T. Williams, Oct. 24, 1963, HI/EGL, box 42.

40 AI/SVW.

41 EGL to William J. Rust, April 21, 1982, HI/EGL, box 8; EGL interview, May 17, 1984, CCP; EGL, draft memoir, HI/EGL, box 76, file 264.

42 EGL to Rust, April 21, 1982, HI/EGL, box 8.

43 EGL to Samuel T. Williams, Oct. 8, 1963, HI/EGL, box 8.

44 EGL to Phil Lansdale, Jan. 12, 1983, HI/EGL, box 28, file 639.

45 Dillon Anderson to EGL, Dec. 11, 1963, HI/EGL, box 36.

CHAPTER 25: *"A Hell of a Mess"*

1 Manchester, *Death*, loc. 3568.

2 Ibid, loc. 4023.

3 Prouty, *JFK*, xiv.

4 Ibid., vii.

5 AI/RP.

6 EGL to CTRB, March 2, 1975, July 2, 1975, CCP, box 13, file 198.1.

7 Epstein, "Second Coming."

8 Prouty, *JFK*, 33.

9 Ibid., 66–67.

10 http://www.ratical.org/ratville/JFK/USO/appD.html.

11 https://www.youtube.com/watch?v=wA-3navQ-_E.

12 Bugliosi, *Reclaiming*, 929–34; Posner, *Case*, loc. 5657.

13 *FRUS 1961–1963, Vietnam*, 4.353–54.

14 Thomas, *RFK*, 272.

15 http://www.presidency.ucsb.edu/ws/?pid=9538.

16 Caro, *Means*, 5.

17 Ibid., 8.

18 Dallek, *Giant*, 5.

19 Ibid., 4.

20 Caro, *Passage*, loc. 9905.

21 Ibid., loc. 9913.

22 *Time*, Dec. 13, 1963.

23 Caro, *Passage*, loc. 14500.

24 *FRUS 1961–1963, Vietnam*, 4.557.

25 Hammer, *Death*, 309.

26 *FRUS 1961–1963, Vietnam*, 4.722.

27 Moyar, *Triumph*, 300.

28 Military History Institute, *Victory*, 127.

29 Nguyen, *Hanoi's War*, 65.

30 Simpson, *Tiger*, 167.

31 *Time*, Feb. 14, 1964.

32 Beschloss, *Taking*, 366.

33 Dallek, *Giant*, 99.

34 Goodwin, *Johnson*, 253.

35 Dallek, *Giant*, 99.

36 Beschloss, *Taking*, 368.

37 Moyar, *Triumph*, 293.

38 Taylor, *Swords*, 309.

39 RP, *Vietnam*, 230; Bui Diem, *Jaws*, 114–15.

40 Sorley, *Westmoreland*; Westmoreland, *Soldier*; Zaffiri, *Westmoreland*.

41 *NYT*, April 27, 1964.

42 *Time*, May 5, 1964.

43 Henry Kissinger, "Vietnam trip, 1965—diary 1/4," HKP, box 100, file 14.

44 Sorley, *Westmoreland*, 67.

45 Ibid., 74.

46 PP, IV.C.2.a, pp. 1–4.

47 Moise, *Tonkin Gulf* ("flying fish": 210); *FRUS 1964–1968, Vietnam*, 1.589–663.

CHAPTER 26: *"Concept for Victory"*

1 EGL to PK, Oct. 31, 1963, PYPP.
2 EGL to PK, n.d., PYPP.
3 Ibid.
4 EGL to Richards, Jan. 14, 1964, CCP, box 13, file 200.
5 EGL, "Liberty Hall," Nov. 29, 1963, SGMML/AWDP, box 37, folder 1.
6 Frank J. Johnson to EGL, Nov. 30, 1965, HI/EGL, box 50, file 1396.
7 EGL interview, May 17, 1984, CCP.
8 Joseph M. Robertson to Reuter, Dec. 2, 1963, HI/EGL, box 71.
9 EGL to Reuter, Dec. 17, 1963, LBJPL, White House Central Files, box 52.
10 EGL to Reuter, July 31, 1964, JFKPL/RWR, box 11, file 6.
11 EGL to Reuter, Dec. 12, 1963, JFKPL/RWR, box 11, file 4.
12 EGL to Reuter, May 1, 1964, HI/EGL, box 73, file 1.
13 EGL to PK, n.d., PYPP.
14 EGL to Sam Karrick, March 5, 1964, JFKPL/RWR, box 11, file 5.
15 RP, email to author, Sept. 14, 2015.
16 RP, *Vietnam*, 233.
17 Solberg, *Humphrey*, 8.
18 Ibid., 137.
19 Caro, *Master*, 447.
20 Humphrey, *Education*, 87.
21 Caro, *Passage*, loc. 4610.
22 Humphrey, *Education*, 224–25.
23 Ibid., 229.
24 RP, *Vietnam*, 108.
25 Ibid., 231.
26 AI/TVD.
27 LBJPL/WJCOH.
28 EGL to Connell, June 4, 1964, MNH/HHH, Senate political files, box 74.
29 *FRUS 1961–1963, Vietnam*, 4.477–84.
30 Berman, *Hubert*, 88.
31 Clifton to LBJ, June 25, 1964, LBJPL/NSF/VCF, box 195.
32 Douglas Cater to LBJ, June 23, 1964, LBJPL/NSF/VCF, box 54.
33 EGL to Connell, June 26, 1964, MHS/HHH, Senate political files, box 74.

CHAPTER 27: *Escalation*

1 Taylor, *Swords*, 328.
2 Simpson, *Tiger*, 186.
3 Nguyen, *Twenty Years*, 53–55.
4 Simpson, *Tiger*, 187.
5 Taylor, *Swords*, 331.
6 Karnow, *Vietnam*, 399.
7 Ibid., 351.

8 Navarro to EGL, Nov. 26, 1964, HI/EGL, box 5.
9 Fraleigh to EGL, Dec. 6, 1964, HI/EGL, box 37.
10 RP, *Vietnam*, 239–40.
11 EGL, "Talk at Yale University," Nov. 23, 1964, HI/EGL, box 96.
12 EGL, "Thoughts on Vietnam," Dec. 31, 1964, VCA/RPP, box 2, file 13.
13 *FRUS 1964–1968, Vietnam*, 1.1057–59.
14 Gibbons, *U.S. Government*, 3.26.
15 *FRUS 1964–1968, Vietnam*, 2.23.
16 Ibid., 95–97.
17 Ibid., 159.
18 Ibid., 174–85.
19 McNamara, *Retrospect*, 174.
20 Goodwin, *Johnson*, 269.
21 Beschloss, *Glory*, 193–95.
22 *FRUS 1964–1968, Vietnam*, 2.216–20.
23 Garrettson, *Humphrey*, 185, 188.
24 Solberg, *Humphrey*, 279.
25 Ibid., 277.
26 EGL to Shaplen, May 30, 1965, HI/EGL, box 40.
27 Dodd to LBJ, Feb. 23, 1965, LBJPL/NSF/VCF, box 14.
28 Cooper to Bundy, March 1, 1965, Ibid.
29 Dodd to LBJ, July 27, 1965, LBJPL, Handwriting File, box 9.
30 Westmoreland, *Soldier*, 130.
31 Karnow, "On Duty."
32 Lodge, "Comment on Profile of Maj. Gen. Edwin Lansdale," MHS/HCL, Part V,
     reel 21.
33 EGL interview, May 17, 1984, CCP.
34 EGL to HCL, July 29, 1965, HI/EGL, box 58, file 1532.
35 LBJPL/EGLOH.
36 AI/ELCL.
37 Pete Lansdale, email to author, Nov. 3, 2015.
38 AI/PLCL.
39 EGL to PK, Aug. 8, 1965, PYPP.
40 AI/SVW.
41 EGL to Peter Richards, July 23, 1971, CCP, box 13, file 200.

CHAPTER 28: *The Impossible Missions Force*

1 *NYT*, April 18, 1965.
2 Starlite: Lehrack, *First Battle* (intel: 64; "spider holes": 104; casualties: 181; VC
     reconstituted: 177); *NYT*, Aug. 19–20, 1965, Feb. 8, 1968 ("save"); *Newsweek*, Aug.
     30, 1965 ("victory"; "carried out"); Gibbons, *U.S. Government*, 4.68 ("milestone,"
     "destroyed").
3 Gwin, *Baptism*, 18.
4 Neese, *Prelude*, 125–26.
5 Cosmas, *MACV*, loc. 5523.

6 Neese, *Prelude*, 125.
7 Caputo, *Rumor*, 139–43.
8 EGL to Bill Bundy, Oct. 23, 1965, HI/EGL, box 55, file 1485.
9 RP, *Vietnam*, 273.
10 Simpson, *Tiger*, 165.
11 EGL to HL, Aug. 31, 1965, PCLPP.
12 Burke to EGL, Aug. 25, 1965, HI/EGL, box 50, file 1392.
13 Larteguy, *Yellow*, 204–5.
14 *NYT*, Aug. 19, 1965.
15 *WP*, Aug. 20, 1965.
16 Saigon embassy to State Department, Aug. 29, 1965, CCP.
17 Lodge to State, Sept. 17, 1965, HI/EGL, box 53, file 1419.
18 EGL to HL, Sept. 8, 1965, PCLPP.
19 EGL to HL, Sept. 4, 1965, PCLPP.
20 EGL to HL, Sept. 8, 1965, PCLPP.
21 RP, *Vietnam*, 353.
22 Michael Deutch to "Wives," Nov. 22, 1965, HI/EGL, box 53.
23 LBJPL/LCOH.
24 Deutch to "Wives," Nov. 22, 1965, HI/EGL, box 53.
25 Henry Kissinger, "Vietnam trip, 1965—diary 2/4," HKP, box 100, file 15.
26 LBJPL/KBOH.
27 Herr, *Dispatches*, 50–51.
28 Michael Deutch to "Wives," Nov. 22, 1965, HI/EGL, box 53.
29 Ibid.
30 Wells, *Wild*, 39.
31 Ibid., 73.
32 Ellsberg, *Secrets*, 4.
33 Wells, *Wild*, 108.
34 Ibid., 119.
35 Ibid., 133.
36 Ibid, 179.
37 Wells, *Wild*, 187; Ellsberg, *Secrets*, 34.
38 Wells, *Wild*, 224.
39 AI/DE.
40 Grant, *Phoenix*, 259.
41 Sam Karrick, "SLO Budget," Oct 13, 1966, HI/EGL, box 56, file 1494.
42 AI/RP.
43 AI/DE.
44 AI/DE.

CHAPTER 29: *Waging Peace in a Time of War*

1 Lodge to EGL, Aug. 9, 1965, MHS/HCL, Part V, reel 20.
2 Fraleigh to RP, Nov. 1, 1965, HI/EGL, box 52, file 1414.
3 AI/PT.
4 AI/SW.

5 Grant, *Phoenix*, 264.

6 Ibid., 265. See also Critchfield, *Charade*, 168 (Zorthian said Lansdale "was a 'straw man' who was 'on his way out'").

7 LBJPL/KBOH.

8 State Department, Foreign Service List, Oct. 1965.

9 Cosmas, *MACV*, loc. 5450–51.

10 Traas, *Engineers*, loc. 5974.

11 Caputo, *Rumor*, xix.

12 EGL to HL, Sept. 9, 1965, PCLPP.

13 AI/FS.

14 EGL to Humphrey, Sept. 19, 1965, HI/EGL, box 55, file 1484.

15 Lodge to State, Sept. 17, 1965, HI/EGL, box 53, file 1419.

16 Ellsberg, *Secrets*, 106.

17 EGL to HL, Feb. 27, 1966, PCLPP.

18 EGL to Wallace M. Greene Jr., Nov 13, 1965, HI/EGL, box 55, file 1486.

19 *Weekly Standard*, Aug. 8, 2011.

20 *Time*, Feb. 18, 1966.

21 Ibid.

22 EGL to HL, Sept. 8, 1965, PCLPP.

23 RP to EGL, Oct. 8, 1965, HI/EGL, box 50, file 1392.

24 RP, *Vietnam*, 263.

25 EGL to HL, Sept. 26, 1965, PCLPP.

26 EGL to Lodge, Sept. 21, 1965, HI/EGL, box 58, file 1532.

27 EGL to McNamara, Nov. 30, 1965, MHS/HCL, Part V, reel 20.

28 EGL to HL, Sept. 24, 1965, PCLPP.

29 EGL to HL, Oct. 17, 1965, PCLPP.

30 EGL to HL, Sept. 26, 1965, PCLPP.

31 Lodge to EGL, Oct. 30, 1965, MHS/HCL, Part V, reel 20.

32 EGL to HL, Oct. 29, 1965, PCLPP.

33 EGL to Robert Komer, May 30, 1971, HI/EGL, box 4.

34 EGL to Lodge, Sept. 29, 1965, HI/EGL, box 55, file 1484.

35 EGL to State, n.d., HI/EGL, box 55, file 1486.

36 *FRUS 1964–1968, Vietnam*, 3.458–60.

37 EGL to Bundy/Unger, Oct. 6, 1965, HI/EGL, box 55, file 1485.

38 EGL to William Bundy/Leonard Unger, Sept. 27, 1965, HI/EGL, box 55, file 1484.

39 EGL to State, Nov. 26, 1965, HI/EGL, box 53, file 1419.

40 EGL to HL, March 24, 1966, PCLPP.

41 Schafer, "Pham Duy"; *WP*, April 4, 1966.

42 "Weekly Report," Nov. 28, 1965, HI/EGL, box 55, file 1487.

43 EGL to William Bundy, Dec. 3, 1965, HI/EGL, box 52, file 1415.

44 Timeline, HI/EGL, box 95, file 5.

45 EGL to Westmoreland, Aug. 2 1966, HI/EGL, box 56, file 1491.

46 AI/HG; Westmoreland to EGL, Aug. 20, 1966, HI/EGL, box 56, file 1491.

47 EGL to Tom W. Hoffer, Feb. 7, 1974, HI/EGL, box 3.

48 VCA/BZOH.

49 EGL interview, Dec. 17, 1984, CCP.

50 Wells, *Wild*, 235–36; Grant, *Phoenix*, 268.

51 AI/FS.

52 EGL to HL, Sept. 8, 1965, PCLPP.

53 AI/RP.

54 CTRB to EGL, Nov. 29, 1965, HI/CB, box 35, file 19.

55 Ibid.

56 EGL to HL, Jan. 20, 1966, PCLPP.

57 CTRB to EGL, Nov. 29, 1965, HI/CB, box 35, file 19.

58 LBJPL/LCOH.

59 Mike Deutch to EGL, July 26, 1966, HI/EGL, box 53,

60 EGL, "Memorandum," March 4, 1966, HI/EGL, box 55, file 1480.

61 EGL to William Bundy, Dec. 17, 1965, HI/EGL, box 52, file 1415.

62 Deutch to EGL, Jan. 6, 1966, NSA/EGL.

63 Kissinger to Lodge, Dec. 3, 1965, HKP, box 99, file 22.

64 EGL to Lodge, Dec. 2, 1965, HI/EGL, box 58, file 1532.

65 Gibbons, *U.S. Government*, 4.189.

66 *Time*, Feb. 18, 1966.

67 EGL to HL, Feb. 13, 1966, PCLPP.

68 Bui Diem, *Jaws*, 162.

69 Humphrey, *Education*, 246–47.

70 Berman, *Hubert*, 108.

71 EGL to HL, Feb. 13, 1966, PCLPP.

72 Ibid.

73 LBJ to EGL, March 17, 1966, LBJPL, White House Central Files, box 52, file L.

74 EGL to HL, March 24, 1966, PCLPP.

75 EGL to HL, Feb. 22, 1966, PCLPP.

76 RP, *Vietnam*, 266.

77 AI/SW.

78 EGL to HL, March 2, 1966, PCLPP.

79 Lodge to State, March 1966, HI/EGL, box 55, file 1480.

CHAPTER 30: *To Stay or to Go?*

1 http://www.americanwarlibrary.com/vietnam/vwatl.htm.

2 Wolff, *Pharaoh's Army*, 6–7.

3 Marlantes, *Matterhorn* ("sterile": 9; "eyes": 49; "cuts": 29; "sweat": 12; "fatigue": 56; "H&I": 52).

4 EGL to Deutch, June 22, 1966, HI/EGL, Box 53.

5 EGL to HL, Aug. 7, 1966, PCLPP.

6 Ellsberg, *Secrets*, 110.

7 Wells, *Wild*, 246–70.

8 EGL to Ellsberg, Sept. 15, 1972, HI/EGL, box 3.

9 EGL, "Talk with Amb. Porter," April 20, 1966, HI/EGL, box 55, file 1481.

10 Wells, *Wild*, 263.

11 RP, *Vietnam*, 358; Grant, *Phoenix*, 269–70.

12 EGL to HL, March 16, 1966, PCLPP.

13 EGL to Deutch, May 15, 1966, HI/EGL, box 53.

14 EGL to Deutch, June 22, 1966, HI/EGL, box 53.
15 EGL to HL, June 4, 1966, PCLPP.
16 EGL to HL, July 5, 1966, PCLPP.
17 PK to EGL, n.d., HI/EGL, box 53.
18 EGL to Deutch, June 8, 1966, HI/EGL, box 53.
19 AI/DE.
20 VCA/OWOH.
21 EGL to PK, Feb. 5, 1966, PYPP.
22 EGL to PK, Feb. 28, 1966, PYPP.
23 EGL to PK, March 19, 1966, PYPP.
24 EGL to PK, April 4, 1966, PYPP.
25 EGL to HL, April 1, 1966, PCLPP.
26 EGL to PK, June 12, 1966, PYPP.
27 EGL to PK, Dec. 10, 1966, PYPP.
28 PK to EGL, March 1, 1967, HI/EGL, box 38.
29 EGL to SLO Staff, May 26, 1966, HI/EGL, box 59, file 1537.
30 Ellsberg, *Secrets*, 107.
31 Grant, *Phoenix*, 266.
32 Ellsberg, *Secrets*, 108.
33 *FRUS 1966, Vietnam*, 4.547.
34 Ellsberg, *Secrets*, 106.
35 RP to William Jorden, "The Vietnam Elections—Ed Lansdale's Key Role," Sept. 22, 1966, HI/EGL, box 59, file 1549.
36 EGL to Lodge/Porter, Aug. 19, 1966, NSA/EGL, box 2.
37 "Notes on Meeting at 194 Cong Ly, 10 August 1966," HI/EGL box 56, file 1491.
38 EGL to Joseph Baker, Sept. 14, 1966, HI/EGL, box 53.
39 Komer to EGL, Sept. 16, 1966, NSA/EGL, box 2.
40 Karrick to EGL, Sept. 20, 1966, HI/EGL, box 56, file 1493.
41 EGL to Lodge, Feb. 18, 1967, NSA/EGL, box 2.
42 EGL, "The Battleground in 1967," Nov. 8, 1966, HI/EGL, box 58, file 1525.
43 Rostow to LBJ, Nov. 17, 1966, LBJPL/NSF, box 11.
44 Lodge to EGL, Jan. 24, 1967, MHS/HCLP, Part V, reel 21.
45 RP to Leonard Unger, Nov. 10, 1968, HI/EGL, box 59, file 1550.

CHAPTER 31: *Waiting for the Second Coming*

1 Shapley, *Promise*, 438.
2 Gitlin, *Sixties*, loc. 6601.
3 Wells, *War*, 194.
4 Dallek, *Flawed*, 452.
5 Solberg, *Humphrey*, 303.
6 Gibbons, *U.S. Government*, 4.549.
7 Shapley, *Promise*, 426.
8 Dallek, *Flawed*, 495; Goodwin, *Johnson*, 321.
9 Schaffer, *Bunker*.
10 LBJPL/EGLOH.
11 AI/ML.

12 EGL interview, Dec. 17, 1985, CCP.

13 RP, *Vietnam*, 130.

14 AI/FS.

15 AI/ML.

16 AI/CM.

17 Michael Delaney, email to author, Dec. 19, 2015.

18 Roche to LBJ, Nov. 13, 1967, LBJPL, Handwriting File, box 26, 1967 folder.

19 Ibid.

20 AI/CM.

21 EGL to HL, Aug. 30, 1966, PCLPP.

22 Ibid.

23 *NYT*, April 28, 1968.

24 EGL to Bunker, "Wedding," July 27, 1967, CCP, box 5, file 118.

25 EGL to SLO Staff, Nov. 3, 1966, HI/EGL, box 52, file 1415.

26 AI/GB.

27 EGL to Zorthian, March 20, 1967, HI/EGL, box 52, file 1407.

28 AI/PT.

29 EGL to Napoleon Valeriano, July 6, 1967, HI/EGL, box 52, file 1409.

30 EGL to William Connell, March 10, 1967, HI/EGL, box 57, file 1499.

31 EGL to Lodge, Feb. 21, 1967, HI/EGL, box 56, file 1498.

32 Shaplen, *Road*, 155.

33 Ibid., 156–57.

34 McAllister, "Fiasco."

35 EGL to Sam Wilson, March 24, 1976, HI/EGL, box 8.

36 EGL, "Talk with Phong," Sept. 28, 1967, NSA/EGL, box 2.

37 EGL to Sam Karrick, Sept. 22, 1967, HI/EGL, box 57, file 1505.

38 EGL to Bunker, Oct. 11, 1967, HI/EGL, box 57, file 1506.

39 EGL to William Connell, Oct. 4, 1967, HI/EGL, box 53.

40 *NYT*, April 1, 1967.

41 EGL to Karrick, Sept. 22, 1967, HI/EGL, box 57, file 1505.

42 EGL to William Connell, Oct. 4, 1967, HI/EGL, box 53.

43 EGL to Bunker, Sept. 15, 1967, HI/EGL, box 57, file 1505.

44 EGL to Bunker, Oct. 28, 1967, HI/EGL, box 57, file 1506.

45 EGL to Bunker, Sept. 15, 1967, HI/EGL, box 57, file 1505.

46 McAllister, "One Man."

47 EGL, "Talk with Thang," Jan. 20, 1968, HI/EGL, box 57, file 1509.

48 EGL to Bunker, Sept. 15, 1967, HI/EGL, box 57, file 1505.

49 McAllister, "One Man."

50 *NYT*, Oct. 12, 1969.

51 EGL to Alan Berg, Sept. 30. 1967, HI/EGL, box 53.

52 EGL to Bunker, Oct. 28, 1967, HI/EGL, box 57, file 1506.

CHAPTER 32: *The Long Goodbye*

1 Braestrup, *Big Story*, 94.

2 EGL to "The Old Team," Feb. 10, 1968, HI/EGL, box 57, file 1510.

3 Ibid.

4   Duiker, *Road*, 292; Prados, *Vietnam*, 239.
5   EGL, draft memoir, HI/EGL, box 77, file 268.
6   EGL to "The Old Team," Feb. 10, 1968, HI/EGL, box 57, file 1510.
7   Ibid.
8   Ibid.
9   Ibid.
10 EGL interview, Dec. 17, 1984, CCP.
11 EGL to Bunker, Feb. 4, 1968, HI/EGL, box 57, file 1510.
12 Oberdorfer, *Tet*, 329–30.
13 EGL to Bunker, Feb. 27, 1968, HI/EGL, box 57, file 1510.
14 Ibid.
15 EGL to Bunker, March 27, 1968, HI/EGL, box 58, file 1511.
16 EGL to Bunker, March 1, 1968, HI/EGL, box 58, file 1511.
17 Connell to EGL, March 20, 1968, HI/EGL, box 53, Connell file.
18 *NYT*, Nov. 30, 1984.
19 Braestrup, *Big Story*, 49–53.
20 Dallek, *Flawed*, 506.
21 Ibid., 526.
22 Clifford, *Counsel*, 476.
23 Ibid., 511.
24 Solberg, *Humphrey*, 321–22.
25 Gitlin, *Sixties*, loc. 6831.
26 Dallek, *Flawed*, 531.
27 EGL to HL, April 9, 1968, PCLPP.
28 EGL to HL, May 6, 1968, PCLPP.
29 Prados, *Vietnam*, 255.
30 RP, *Vietnam*, 287.
31 EGL to HL, May 12, 1968, PCLPP.
32 Clifford, *Counsel*, 542–44; Sorley, *Better*, 28–29.
33 EGL, draft memoir, HI/EGL, box 76, file 265.
34 Sorley, *Better*, 24–27.
35 EGL interview, May 16, 1984, CCP; LBJPL/EGLOH.
36 EGL to HL, May 6, 1968, PCLPP.
37 HI/EGL, box 73, file 2.
38 Fish, "Folksongs."
39 EGL to Bunker, June 4, 1968, HI/EGL, box 58, file 1514.
40 EGL to Bunker, May 1968, HI/EGL, box 58, file 1513.
41 EGL to HL, May 25, 1968, PCLPP.
42 EGL to Rostow, June 1, 1968, HI/EGL, box 58, file 1519.
43 EGL to Bunker, June 7, 1968, HI/EGL, box 58, file 1527.
44 Rostow to LBJ, June 11, 1968, LBJPL/NSF, Memos to the President, box 35.
45 EGL, "There Is My Country," HI/EGL, box 75.
46 Ibid.
47 EGL, draft memoir, HI/EGL, box 76, file 265; EGL to "The Old Team," June 8, 1968, HI/EGL, box 59, file 1535.
48 LBJPL/EGLOH.
49 Ibid.

50 EGL to Bunker, June 14, 1968, HI/EGL, box 58, file 1514.
51 RP, *Vietnam*, 290.
52 EGL to "The Old Team," June 8, 1968, HI/EGL, box 59, file 1535.
53 Clifford, *Counsel*, 551.
54 *NYT*, June 16, 1968.
55 *WP*, Sept. 29, 1968.

CHAPTER 33: *The War at Home*

1   Gittlin, *Sixties*, loc. 6462.
2   Bernie Yoh interview, March 25, 1987, MLEPP.
3   Ted Lansdale, email to author, March 3, 2016.
4   Gittlin, *Sixties*, loc. 7089.
5   EGL to PK, Nov. 11, 1972, PYPP.
6   EGL to HL, March 15, 1968, PCLPP.
7   EGL to HL, April 30, 1968, PCLPP.
8   EGL to Cass Canfield, Sept. 30, 1968, HI/EGL, box 75.
9   Carol Brandt to EGL, Nov. 4, 1968, HI/EGL, box 2.
10 EGL to David G. Marr, Jan 7, 1970, HI/EGL, box 5.
11 EGL to Carol Brandt, March 4, 1970, HI/EGL, box 2.
12 EGL to Edwin O. Learnard, July 17, 1972, HI/EGL, box 1.
13 EGL to Peter Richards, July 23, 1971, CCP.
14 EGL to Lee C. Hanson, Oct. 24, 1974, HI/EGL, box 73.
15 "Viet-Nam: Problems and Prospects," VCA/RPP, box 2, file 25.
16 Bunker to State, Sept. 29, 1968, CCP, box 9, file 68.
17 Black, *Nixon*, 78.
18 Thomas, *Nixon*, 10.
19 Kissinger, *Memoirs*, loc. 58847.
20 Ferguson, *Kissinger*, 167.
21 Bui Diem, *Jaws*, 292.
22 *WP*, May 26, 1971.
23 EGL to Peter Richards, Nov. 6, 1971, CCP, box 13, file 200.
24 Thomas, *Nixon*, 218, 235.
25 Burr, *Nuclear*, 326.
26 Moyar, *Phoenix*, 236.
27 Woodward, *Last*, 114.
28 Sorley, *Better*, 208–13.
29 Kimball, *Nixon's*, 246–47; Sorley, *Better*, 256–63.
30 Kissinger, *Memoirs*, loc. 9123–78.
31 Hughes, *Fatal*, 27.
32 Ibid., 27–28.
33 Ibid., 35.
34 Wells, *Wild*, 316.
35 Ibid., 387.
36 Rudenstine, *Day*; Prados, *Inside*; Wells, *Wild*.
37 EGL to Bob Burns, July 20, 1971, HI/EGL, box 2.

38 EGL to Arellano, Oct. 20, 1971, HI/EGL, box 2.
39 EGL interview, Dec. 17, 1984, CCP.
40 Wells, *Wild*, 542.
41 Ibid., 509.
42 Kissinger, *Memoirs*, loc. 1391.

CHAPTER 34: *A Defeat in Disguise*

1 *WP*, Feb. 13, 1972.
2 EGL to Lawrence Houston, March 14, 1972, HI/EGL, box 2.
3 EGL to Jack [Wachtell?], March 14, 1972, box 2.
4 EGL to Ann Harris, Oct. 9, 1971, HI/EGL, box 75.
5 EGL to CTRB, July 18, 1971, CCP, box 13, file 198.1.
6 EGL, *Midst*, vii.
7 *Saturday Review*, April 1, 1971.
8 *NYT*, April 9, 1972.
9 *WP*, March 15, 1972.
10 *WP*, March 19, 1972.
11 PK to EGL, Aug. 23, 1972, PYPP.
12 "Current Titles and Sales Figures," April 1972, CU/HR, Series II, box 228.
13 MacMillan, *Nixon*, 23–27.
14 Kimball, *Files*, 162–63.
15 Nguyen, *Hanoi's War*, 241–43.
16 Willbanks, *Thiet Giap*, 3–4.
17 Ibid., 11.
18 Randolph, *Brutal*, loc. 1710.
19 Sheehan, *Lie*, 790.
20 Sorley, *Better*, 342.
21 Sheehan, *Lie*, 785–89.
22 Ibid., 8.
23 EGL to W. E. Thacker, May 9, 1972, HI/EGL, box 2.
24 Melvin to EGL, June 2, 1972, box 5.
25 EGL to Peter Richards, July 11, 1972, CCP, box 13, file 200.
26 Ibid.
27 Ibid.
28 EGL to Donald H. McLean Jr., Oct. 21, 1972, HI/EGL, box 5.
29 *WP*, Dec. 10, 1972.
30 EGL to Philip Flammer, Jan. 18, 1974, HI/EGL, box 73.
31 EGL to PK, June 8, 1972, PYPP.
32 EGL to Hank Miller and PK, Aug. 15, 1927, PYPP.
33 EGL to PK, Aug. 29, 1972, PYPP.
34 PK to EGL, Sept. 8, 1972, HI/EGL, box 4.
35 PK to EGL, Oct. 31, 1972, HI/EGL, box 4.
36 PK to EGL, Nov. 16, 1972, HI/EGL, box 4.
37 PK to EGL, Feb. 2, 1972, HI/EGL, box 4.

38 EGL to Bohannan, March 15, 1973, CCP, box 13, file 198.1.
39 EGL to Ben Lansdale, June 12, 1973, HI/EGL, box 83, file 1.
40 Pete Lansdale, email to author, March 8, 2016.
41 EGL to Peter Richards, Sept. 12, 1973, CCP, box 13, file 200.
42 Ibid.
43 EGL to Charles F. Baker, HI/EGL, box 1.
44 Kissinger, *Memoirs*, loc. 27445.
45 Nguyen, *Palace*, 83.
46 Ibid., 146.
47 Ibid., 103.
48 *NYT*, Feb. 25, 1973.
49 EGL to Glen W. Martin, Aug 5, 1972, HI/EGL, box 1.
50 *NYT*, Sept. 5, 1972.

CHAPTER 35: *The Abandoned Ally*

1   Ford, *Heal*, 39–40.
2   Merry, *World*, 525.
3   Truong, *Memoir*, 242.
4   Hunt, *Losing*, 28.
5   Veith, *Black*, 144.
6   Ibid., 119.
7   EGL to Bohannan, Jan. 16, 1975, CCP, box 13, file 198.1.
8   Hunt, *Losing*, 132.
9   Snepp, *Interval*, 556.
10 Ibid., 498.
11 Engelmann, *Tears*, 174.
12 Ibid., 164–65.
13 Ibid., 101–2.
14 Ibid., 166.
15 Snepp, *Interval*, 548.
16 Truong, *Memoir*, 258–59.
17 *NYT*, Aug. 10, 1997.
18 Truong, *Memoir*, 259.
19 EGL to Humphrey, March 24, 1975, HI/EGL, box 4.
20 Pham Duy to EGL, April 3, 1975, HI/EGL, box 6.
21 *NYT*, April 12, 1975.
22 EGL to CTRB, June 1, 1975, CCP, box 13, file 198.1.
23 EGL to Robert De Vecchi, May 20, 1975, HI/EGL, box 5.
24 EGL to CTRB, March 23, 1981, CCP, box 13, file 198.1.
25 EGL to CTRB, Dec. 26, 1975, CCP, box 13, file 198.1.
26 *NYT*, July 23, 2011; Nguyen, *Child*, 350–60.
27 Nguyen, *Palace*, 333.
28 Nguyen, *Communism*, 206–25.
29 Goscha, *Vietnam*, 372–98.

30 EGL to Gary May, Oct. 10, 1977, HI/EGL, box 5.
31 EGL to Douglas Blaufarb, June 3, 1982, HI/EGL, box 2.
32 Gibbons interview, Jan. 14, 1987, MLEPP.
33 EGL, "Comments on Limited War," U.S. Air Force Academy, Oct. 20, 1978, HI/EGL, box 79, file 290a.
34 Goscha, *Vietnam*, 323–24.
35 EGL to Lawrence E. Grinter, Dec. 12, 1975, HI/EGL, box 3.

CHAPTER 36: *The Family Jewels*

1 Frum, *70s*, 39.
2 Colby, *Honorable*, 341.
3 Ibid., 389–91.
4 Weiner, *Legacy*, 338.
5 Colby, *Honorable*, 409–10.
6 EGL to CTRB, Feb. 24, 1975, CCP, box 13, file 198.1.
7 EGL to CTRB, March 13, 1975, CCP, box 13, file 198.1.
8 EGL to CTRB, March 28, 1975, CCP, box 13, file 198.1.
9 MFF/DEGL.
10 Kissinger, *Memoirs*, loc. 70186.
11 Ashby, *Odds*, 217.
12 Ibid., 24–25, 33, 140.
13 Johnson, *Inquiry*, 19.
14 Ibid., 41.
15 Ibid., 21.
16 MFF/EGL.
17 MFF/RSM.
18 AI/JD.
19 EGL to CTRB, July 12, 1975, CCP, box 13, file 198.1.
20 Ashby, *Odds*, 478.
21 U.S. Senate, *Plots*, 1.
22 Ibid., 265.
23 EGL to Church, Jan. 1, 1976, HI/EGL, box 10.
24 EGL to CTRB, Jan. 31, 1976, CCP, box 13, file 198.1.
25 Ibid.
26 *NYT*, April 27, 1976.
27 U.S. Senate, *Final Report*, 427.
28 Kissinger, *Memoirs*, loc. 70475.
29 EGL to CTRB, Jan. 9, 1979, CCP, box 13, file 198.1.

CHAPTER 37: *The End of the Road*

1 EGL to Harriman, Feb. 26, 1977, HI/EGL, box 3.
2 Friedman, *Covert*, 90; AI/FV.

3 EGL to CTRB, Feb. 5, 1975, CCP, box 13, file 198.1.

4 PK postscript, EGL to CTRB, May 23, 1975, CCP, box 13, file 198.1.

5 PK to EGL, July 4, 1977, PYPP.

6 AI/PLCL.

7 EGL to PK, May 12, 1979, PYPP.

8 AI/AM.

9 *Los Angeles Times*, Jan. 14, 1986.

10 AI/JKS.

11 EGL to brothers, Nov. 29, 1986, GBPP.

12 OSD to OSD Security, "Memo for the Record," May 16, 1984, HI/EGL, box 5.

13 *Nation*, July 7–14, 1984.

14 EGL interview, *Journal of Defense & Diplomacy*, July 1983.

15 EGL to brothers, Aug. 17, 1983, GBPP.

16 CTRB to EGL, June 28, 1982, CCP, box 13, file 198.1.

17 EGL to CTRB, July 17, 1982, CCP, box 13, file 198.1.

18 EGL to CTRB, Jan. 9, 1982, CCP, box 13, file 198.1.

19 EGL to Peter Richards, Dec. 14, 1983, CCP, box 13, file 200.

20 EGL to Hubert Pooley, Oct. 4, 1983, CCP, box 5, file 103.

21 AI/DI.

22 EGL to Hubert Pooley, Oct. 4, 1983, CCP, box 5, file 103.

23 EGL to Cecil Currey, Jan. 8, 1986, CCP, box 10, file 190.

24 *VVA Veteran*, Dec. 1986.

25 *WP*, Feb. 24, 1987.

26 AI/PLCL.

27 AI/ELCL.

28 *NYT*, Feb. 24, 1987.

29 *WP*, Feb. 26, 1987.

30 *Nation*, March 7, 1987.

31 Currey to Dorothy Bohannan, March 11, 1987, CCP, box 13, file 198.1.

32 Colby to EGL, Nov. 1, 1982, HI/EGL, box 2.

33 Currey to Dorothy Bohannan, March 11, 1987, CCP, box 13, file 198.1.

34 "Edward Geary Lansdale Memorial Service," GBPP.

35 Phillips, "A Eulogy for Ed Lansdale," Feb. 27, 1987, GBPP.

36 Currey to Dorothy Bohannan, March 11, 1987, CCP, box 13, file 198.1.

37 Currey to Peter Richards, April 15, 1987, CCP, box 13, file 200.

AFTERWORD: *Lansdalism in the Twenty-First Century*

1 EGL to Rose Kushner, March 21, 1983, HI/EGL, box 4.

2 EGL, Foreword, in Millett, *Short*, ix.

3 EGL to CTRB, March 10, 1980, CCP, box 13, file 198.1.

4 http://usacac.army.mil/cac2/Repository/Materials/COIN-FM3-24.pdf.

5 EGL, Foreword, in Millett, *Short*, ix.

6 EGL to Robert Komer, May 30, 1971, HI/EGL, box 4.

7 EGL, draft memoir, HI/EGL, box 76, file 264.

8 EGL to Lawrence E. Grinter, Jan. 17, 1975, HI/EGL, box 3.

9 EGL to Stacy Lloyd, Feb. 26, 1976, HI/EGL, box 1.

10 Colby interview, March 5, 1987, MLEPP.

11 EGL to Lawrence E. Grinter, Jan. 17, 1975, HI/EGL, box 3.

12 EGL, draft memoir, HI/EGL, box 76, file 264.

13 Joe Redick interview, March 19, 1987, MLEPP.

14 Kraemer interview, March 19, 1987, MLEPP.

SELECT BIBLIOGRAPHY

AUTHOR INTERVIEWS

AI: Ann Ingram
AM: Andy Messing Jr.
BD: Bui Diem
BP: Barbara Phillips
CM: Calvin Mehlert
CP: Clarita C. Pagulong
CW: Charles Wolf Jr.
DE: Daniel Ellsberg
DG: Donald Gregg
DI: Douglas Israel
DN: Don North
EC: Elyette Conein
EJE: Edward Jay Epstein
ELCL: Edward R. Lansdale and Carol H. Lansdale
FAS: Frank and Arden Staroba
FS: Frank Scotton
FSJ: Frisco San Juan
FV: Francisco Valeriano
FW: Frank G. Wisner II
GB: Ginger Brodie
HG: Hershel Gober
HK: Henry Kissinger
HS: Harvey Segall
JD: John Deutsch

JED: Joseph E. diGenova
JKS: John K. Singlaub
JRB: James R. Bullington
JTF: Jerome T. French
LHG: Leslie H. Gelb
LPR: Leah Pelaez-Ramos
ML: Mark Lynch
MLE: Marc Leepson
NVC: Nguyen Van Canh
PLCL: Peter Lansdale and Carolyn Lansdale
PT: Peter Tarnoff
RM: Ramon B. Magsaysay
RNG: Richard N. Goodwin
RP: Rufus Phillips
RVA: Richard V. Allen
RWS: Richard W. Smith
SK: Sven Kraemer
SVW: Samuel V. Wilson
TN: Thai Nguyen
TNC: Tran Ngoc Chau
TVD: Ted Van Dyk
VH: Victor Hugo
VHL: Vu Hoang Linh

ARCHIVES

AM: Ayala Museum, Manila.
    EQP: Elpidio Quirino Papers.
    CRP: Carlos Romulo Papers.
ADST: Association for Diplomatic Studies and Training, Arlington, Virginia.
    THOH: Theodore J. C. Heavner Oral History, 1997.
CCP: Cecil Currey Papers, Fort Hays State University, Kansas.
CHA: Centre Historique des Archives à Vincennes, France.

CU: Rare Book and Manuscript Library, Columbia University, New York City.
    HR: Harper & Row Records.
    WWN: W. W. Norton & Co. Records.
DDEPL: Dwight D. Eisenhower Presidential Library, Abilene, Kansas.
    JLCP: J. Lawton Collins Papers, Special Mission to Vietnam, 1954–1955.
ECLPP: Edward R. and Carol H. Lansdale Personal Papers, Garden City, New York.
GBPP: Ginger Brodie Personal Papers, Maple Shade, New Jersey.
HI: Hoover Institution, Stanford University, Palo Alto, California.
    CB: Charles T. R. Bohannan Papers.
    EGL: EGL Papers.
    EGLOH/CRS: EGL Oral History, Congressional Research Service, box 79, file 285.
    RVA: Richard V. Allen Papers.
    STW: Samuel T. Wilson Papers.
HKP: Henry A. Kissinger Papers, Part II, Series I, Manuscripts and Archives, Yale University Library, New Haven, Connecticut.
HSTPL: Harry S. Truman Presidential Library, Independence, Missouri.
    MMC: Myron M. Cowen Papers.
    JFMOH: John F. Melby Oral History Interview.
JFKPL: John F. Kennedy Presidential Library, Boston.
    EGLOH: EGL Oral History.
    JCT: James C. Thomson Personal Papers.
    MGB: McGeorge Bundy Oral History.
    NSF: National Security Files.
    POF: President's Office Files.
    RG: Richard Goodwin Papers.
    RWR: Richard W. Reuter Papers.
    VHKOH: Victor H. Krulak Oral History.
LBJPL: Lyndon Baines Johnson Presidential Library, Austin, Texas.
    EDOH: Elbridge Durbrow Oral History.
    EGLOH: EGL Oral History.
    KBOH: Keyes Beech Oral History.
    LCOH: Lucien Conein Oral History.
    NSF/VCF: National Security Files, Vietnam Country Files.
    RHOH: Richard Helms Oral History.
    RLGOH: Roswell L. Gilpatric Oral History.
    STWOH: Samuel T. Williams Oral History.
    WJCOH: William J. Connell Oral History.
    WWP: William Westmoreland Papers.
    WWROH: Walt W. Rostow Oral History.
LOC: Library of Congress, Washington, D.C.
    CVWS: EGL Collection of Vietnam War Songs.
    NS: Neil Sheehan Papers.
MCA/GBE: Graves B. Erskine Papers, Marine Corps Archives and Special Collections Branch Library, Gray Research Center, Quantico, Virginia.
MFF: Mary Ferrell Foundation, Ipswich, Massachusetts.
    DEGL: Deposition of EGL, May 16, 1975.
    IG: Report on Plots to Assassinate Fidel Castro (1967 Inspector General's Report)

TEGL: Testimony of EGL, July 8, 1975.

TLC: Testimony of Lucien Conein.

TRH13: Testimony of Richard Helms.

TRH17: Testimony of Richard Helms.

TRH18: Testimony of Richard Helms.

TRSM: Testimony of Robert S. McNamara.

TSH: Testimony of Samuel Halpern.

TTP: Testimony of Thomas Parrott.

TWE: Testimony of Walter Elder.

TWH: Testimony of William Harvey.

MHS/HCL: Henry Cabot Lodge Papers, Massachusetts Historical Society, Boston.

MNH/HHH: Hubert H. Humphrey Papers, Minnesota Historical Society, St. Paul, Minnesota.

MLEPP: Marc Leepson Personal Papers, Middleburg, Virginia.

MMM: MacArthur Memorial Museum, Norfolk, Virginia.

MSFRIC/EGL: EGL Papers, Muir S. Fairchild Research Information Center, Maxwell Air Force Base, Montgomery, Alabama.

MSU/WRF: Wesley R. Fishel Papers, Michigan State University Archives and Historical Collections, East Lansing, Michigan.

NARA: National Archives and Record Administration, College Park, Maryland.

CREST: CIA Records Search Tool.

JFKARB: JFK Assassination Review Board, Part I: Kennedy Administration Policy toward Cuba.

RG 84: State Department.

RG 226: OSS.

RG 263: CIA.

RG 330: Secretary of Defense.

RG 541: Kennedy Assassination Records Review Board.

NSA: National Security Archives, George Washington University, Washington, D.C.

CMC: Cuban Missile Crisis, 1962.

EGL: EGL Papers.

EGL/SMM: Saigon Military Mission report.

RGD: Raymond Garthoff Donation Relating to the Cuban Missile Crisis.

NWC: Naval War College, Newport, Rhode Island.

EGL: EGL Interview.

RASP: Raymond A. Spruance Papers.

NYP: New York Public Library, New York, New York.

ASP: Arthur Schlesinger Jr. Papers.

PCLPP: Peter and Carolyn Lansdale Personal Papers, Ponte Verde Beach, Florida.

PYPP: Patricia Yi Personal Papers, McLean, Virginia.

RPPP: Rufus Phillips Personal Papers, Arlington, Virginia.

RAC: Rockefeller Archives Center, Sleepy Hollow, New York.

RMNPL: Richard M. Nixon Presidential Library, Yorba Linda, California.

RMP: Ramon Magsaysay Papers, Magsaysay Award Foundation, Manila.

RSPP: Rebekka Slone Personal Papers, Lindenhurst, New York.

SGMML: Seeley G. Mudd Manuscript Library, Princeton University.

AWDP: Allen W. Dulles Papers.

JFDP: John Foster Dulles Papers.

UCLA: UCLA University Archives, Library Special Collections, Los Angeles, California.
  CCNOH: Cyril C. Nigg Oral History.
USAFA/EGLOH: EGL Oral History, U.S. Air Force Academy, Colorado Springs, Colorado.
VCA: Vietnam Center and Archives, Texas Tech University, Lubbock, Texas.
  BZOH: Barry Zorthian Oral History.
  DPC: Douglas Pike Collection.
  LBC: Larry Berman Collection.
  OWOH: Ogden Williams Oral History.
  RPP: Rufus Phillips Papers.
VNA: Vietnam National Archives No. 2, Ho Chi Minh City, Vietnam.
  OPFR: Office of the President of the First Republic.
  PA: Photo Archives.
WGBH: Stanley Karnow interviews for WGBH's *Vietnam: A Television History*, 1979, http://openvault.wgbh.org/catalog/vietnam-the-vietnam-collection.
  EGL: EGL Interview.
  JLC: J. Lawton Collins Interview.
WJLP: William J. Lederer Papers, Special Collections and University Archives, University of Massachusetts, Amherst.

BOOKS AND MAGAZINE ARTICLES

Abueva, Jose V. *Ramon Magsaysay: A Political Biography*. Manila: Solidaridad Publishing, 1971.
Ahern, Thomas L., Jr. *CIA and the House of Ngo: Covert Action in South Vietnam, 1954–63*. Washington, DC: CIA History Staff, 2000.
———. *Vietnam Declassified: The CIA and Counterinsurgency*. Lexington: University Press of Kentucky, 2010.
Alsop, Stewart, and Thomas Braden. *Sub Rosa: The O.S.S. and American Espionage*. New York: Reynal & Hitchcock, 1946.
Ambrose, Stephen E. *Eisenhower*. Vol. 2, *The President*. New York: Simon & Schuster, 1984.
Ashby, LeRoy, and Rod Gramer. *Fighting the Odds: The Life of Senator Frank Church*. Pullman: Washington State University Press, 1994.
Atkinson, Rick. *The Day of Battle: The War in Sicily and Italy, 1943–1944*. New York: Henry Holt, 2007.
———. *The Guns at Last Light: The War in Western Europe, 1944–1945*. New York: Henry Holt, 2013.
Bass, Thomas A. *The Spy Who Loved Us: The Vietnam War and Pham Xuan An's Dangerous Game*. New York: PublicAffairs, 2009.
Bell, Daniel, et al. *Report to the President by the Economic Survey Mission to the Philippines*. Washington, DC: Department of State, Oct. 9, 1950.
Berman, Edgar. *Hubert: The Triumph and Tragedy of the Humphrey I Knew*. New York: G. P. Putnam's Sons, 1979.
Berman, Larry. *Perfect Spy: The Incredible Double Life of Pham Xuan An, Time Magazine Reporter and Vietnamese Communist Agent*. New York: HarperCollins, 2008.

Bernstein, Richard. *The East, the West, and Sex: A History of Erotic Encounters*. New York: Alfred A. Knopf, 2009.

Beschloss, Michael, ed. *Reaching for Glory: Lyndon Johnson's Secret White House Tapes, 1964–1965*. New York: Simon & Schuster, 2002.

———. *Taking Charge: The Johnson White House Tapes, 1963–1964*. New York: Simon & Schuster, 1997.

Bird, Kai. *The Good Spy: The Life and Death of Robert Ames*. New York: Crown, 2014.

Bissell, Richard M. *Reflections of a Cold Warrior: From Yalta to the Bay of Pigs*. New Haven: Yale University Press, 1996.

Black, Conrad. *Richard M. Nixon: A Life in Full*. New York: PublicAffairs, 2007.

Blagov, Sergei. *Honest Mistakes: The Life and Death of Trinh Minh Thé (1922–1955): South Vietnam's Alternative Leader*. Huntington, NY: Nova Science, 2001.

Blair, Anne. *Lodge in Vietnam: A Patriot Abroad*. New Haven: Yale University Press, 1995.

Bodard, Lucien. *The Quicksand War: Prelude to Vietnam*. Boston: Little, Brown, 1967.

Bohning, Don. *The Castro Obsession: U.S. Covert Operations Against Cuba, 1959–1965*. Washington, DC: Potomac Books, 2005.

Boot, Max. *Invisible Armies: An Epic History of Guerrilla Warfare from Ancient Times to the Present*. New York: Liveright, 2013.

———. *The Savage Wars of Peace: Small Wars and the Rise of American Power*. 2nd ed. New York: Basic Books, 2014.

Braestrup, Peter. *Big Story: How the American Press and Television Reported and Interpreted the Crisis of Tet 1968 in Vietnam and Washington*. Novato, CA: Presidio Press, 1994.

Branch, Taylor, and George Crile III. "Our Secret War on Cuba." *Harper's*, Aug. 1975.

Brinkley, Douglas, and Luke A. Nichter, eds. *The Nixon Tapes: 1971–1972*. Boston: Houghton Mifflin Harcourt, 2014.

———. *The Nixon Tapes: 1973*. Boston: Houghton Mifflin Harcourt, 2015.

Brogi, Alessandro. *Confronting America: The Cold War between the United States and the Communists in France and Italy*. Chapel Hill: University of North Carolina Press, 2011.

Buell, Thomas B. *The Quiet Warrior: A Biography of Admiral Raymond A. Spruance*. Boston: Little, Brown, 1974.

Bugliosi, Vincent. *Reclaiming History: The Assassination of President John F. Kennedy*. New York: W. W. Norton, 2007.

Bui Diem, with David Chanoff. *In the Jaws of History*. Bloomington: Indiana University Press, 1999.

Burr, William, and Jeffrey P. Kimball. *Nixon's Nuclear Specter: The Secret Alert of 1969, Madman Diplomacy, and the Vietnam War*. Lawrence: University Press of Kansas, 2016.

Butler, Jon, Grant Wacker, and Randall Balmer. *Religion in American Life: A Short History*. 2nd ed. New York: Oxford University Press, 2011.

Caputo, Philip. *A Rumor of War*. New York: Henry Holt, 1996.

Caro, Robert A. *The Power Broker: Robert Moses and the Fall of New York*. New York: Vintage Books, 1975.

———. *The Years of Lyndon Johnson*. Vol. 2, *Means of Ascent*. New York: Alfred A. Knopf, 1990.

———. *The Years of Lyndon Johnson*. Vol. 4, *The Passage of Power*. New York: Alfred A. Knopf, 2012.

Catton, Philip E. "Counter-Insurgency and Nation Building: The Strategic Hamlet Program in South Vietnam, 1961–1963." *International History Review*, Dec. 1999.

———. *Diem's Final Failure: Prelude to America's War in Vietnam*. Lawrence: University Press of Kansas, 2002.

The Centennial History of Chautauqua County. Vol. 2. Jamestown, NY: Chautauqua History Co., 1904.

Chapman, Jessica M. *Cauldron of Resistance: Ngo Dinh Diem, the United States, and 1950s Southern Vietnam*. Ithaca: Cornell University Press, 2013.

Clifford, Clark, with Richard Holbrooke. *Counsel to the President: A Memoir*. New York: Random House, 1991.

Colby, William, with James McCragar. *Lost Victory: A Firsthand Account of America's Sixteen-Year Involvement in Vietnam*. Chicago: Contemporary Books, 1989.

Colby, William, and Peter Forbath. *Honorable Men: My Life in the CIA*. New York: Simon & Schuster, 1978.

Collins, J. Lawton. *Lightning Joe: An Autobiography*. Baton Rouge: Louisiana State University Press, 1979.

Conboy, Kenneth, and Dale Andrade. *Spies & Commandos: How America Lost the Secret War in North Vietnam*. Lawrence: University Press of Kansas, 2000.

Cooper, Chester L. *The Lost Crusade: America in Vietnam*. New York: Dodd, Mead, 1970.

Coram, Robert. *Brute: The Life of Victor Krulak, U.S. Marine*. New York: Little, Brown, 2010.

Corn, David. *Blond Ghost: Ted Shackley and the CIA's Crusades*. New York: Simon & Schuster, 1994.

Cosmas, Graham A. *MACV: The Joint Command in the Years of Escalation, 1962–1967*. Washington, DC: Center of Military History, 2006.

Crawford, Michael, ed. *The World Cruise of the Great White Fleet*. Washington, DC: Naval Historical Center, 2007.

Critchfield, Richard. *The Long Charade: Political Subversion in the Vietnam War*. New York: Harcourt, Brace & World, 1968.

Cullather, Nick. *Illusions of Influence: The Political Economy of United States–Philippines Relations, 1942–1960*. Palo Alto, CA: Stanford University Press, 1994.

Currey, Cecil B. *Edward Lansdale: The Unquiet American*. Washington, DC: Brassey's, 1998.

Dallek, Robert. *Flawed Giant: Lyndon Johnson and His Times, 1961–1973*. New York: Oxford University Press, 1998.

———. *Lone Star Rising: Lyndon Johnson and His Times, 1908–1960*. New York: Oxford University Press, 1991.

———. *An Unfinished Life: John F. Kennedy, 1917–1963*. New York: Little, Brown, 2003.

DiFonzo, J. Herbie. "No Fault Marital Dissolution: The Bitter Triumph of Naked Divorce" (1994). http://scholarlycommons.law.hofstra.edu/faculty_scholarship/242.

Dooley, Thomas A. *Deliver Us from Evil: The Story of Viet Nam's Flight to Freedom*. New York: Signet, 1956.

Draper, Theodore. "Cuba and United States Policy." *New Leader*, June 5, 1961.

Duiker, William J. *The Communist Road to Power in Vietnam*. 2nd ed. Boulder, CO: Westview Press, 1986.

———. *Ho Chi Minh: A Life*. New York: Hyperion, 2000.

Dundjerski, Marina. *UCLA: The First Century*. Los Angeles: Third Millennium, 2011.

Dunlop, Richard. *Donovan: America's Master Spy*. Chicago: Rand McNally, 1982.

Elliott, David W. P. *The Vietnamese War: Revolution and Social Change in the Mekong Delta, 1930–1975*. Armonk, NY: M. E. Sharpe, 2007.

Elliston, Jon. *Psywar on Cuba: The Declassified History of U.S. Anti-Castro Propaganda*. Melbourne: Ocean Press, 1999.

Ellsberg, Daniel. *Secrets: A Memoir of Vietnam and the Pentagon Papers*. New York: Penguin, 2002.

Engelmann, Larry. *Tears before the Rain: An Oral History of the Fall of South Vietnam*. New York: Da Capo Press, 1997.

Ephraim, Frank. *Escape to Manila: From Nazi Tyranny to Japanese Terror*. Urbana: University of Illinois Press, 2008.

Epstein, Edward Jay. "The Second Coming of Jim Garrison." *Atlantic*, March 1993.

Fall, Bernard B. *Hell in a Very Small Place: The Siege of Dien Bien Phu*. New York: Da Capo Press, 2002.

———. *Street without Joy*. Mechanicsburg, PA: Stackpole Books, 1994.

———. *The Two Viet-Nams: A Political and Military Analysis*. New York: Frederick A. Praeger, 1963.

Ferguson, Niall. *Kissinger*. Vol. 1, *1923–1968: The Idealist*. New York: Penguin Press, 2015.

Fish, Lydia. "Edward G. Lansdale and the Folksongs of Americans in the Vietnam War." *Journal of American Folklore*, Oct.–Dec. 1989.

Fisher, James T. *Dr. America: The Lives of Thomas A. Dooley, 1927–1961*. Amherst: University of Massachusetts Press, 1997.

FitzGerald, Frances. *Fire in the Lake: The Vietnamese and the Americans in Vietnam*. New York: Little, Brown, 2002.

Fogelson, Robert M. *The Fragmented Metropolis: Los Angeles, 1850–1930*. Berkeley: University of California Press, 1993.

Ford, Gerald R. *A Time to Heal: The Autobiography of Gerald R. Ford*. New York: Harper & Row, 1979.

Frankum, Ronald Bruce, Jr. *Vietnam's Year of the Rat: Elbridge Durbrow, Ngo Dinh Diem, and the Turn in U.S. Relations, 1959–1961*. Jefferson, NC: McFarland, 2014.

Friedman, Andrew. *Covert Capital: Landscapes of Denial and the Making of U.S. Empire in the Suburbs of Northern Virginia*. Berkeley: University of California Press, 2013.

Frum, David. *How We Got Here: The 1970s: The Decade That Brought You Modern Life (for Better or Worse)*. New York: Basic Books, 2000.

Fursenko, Aleksandr, and Timothy Naftali. *"One Hell of a Gamble": Khrushchev, Castro, and Kennedy, 1958–1964*. New York: W. W. Norton, 1997.

Garrettson, Charles Lloyd, III. *Hubert H. Humphrey: The Politics of Joy*. New Brunswick, NJ: Transaction, 1993.

Geist, Kenneth L. *Pictures Will Talk: The Life and Films of Joseph L. Mankiewicz*. New York: Charles Scribner's Sons, 1978.

Gibbons, William Conrad. *The U.S. Government and the Vietnam War*. 4 vols. Princeton: Princeton University Press, 2014.

Gittlin, Todd. *The Sixties: Years of Hope, Days of Rage*. New York: Bantam Books, 1993.

Goldberg, Arthur, ed. *History of the Office of the Secretary of Defense*. Vol. 4, *Into the Missile Age, 1956–1960*. Washington, DC: Office of the Secretary of Defense, 1997.

Goodwin, Doris Kearns. *Lyndon Johnson and the American Dream*. New York: St. Martin's Griffin, 1991.

Goodwin, Richard. *Remembering America: A Voice from the Sixties*. New York: Open Road Media, 2014.

Goscha, Christopher. *Vietnam: A New History*. New York: Basic Books, 2016.

Gottschalk, Stephen. *The Emergence of Christian Science in American Religious Life*. Berkeley: University of California Press, 1973.

Graham, Katharine, ed. *Katharine Graham's Washington*. New York: Alfred A. Knopf, 2002.

Grant, Zalin. *Facing the Phoenix*. New York: W. W. Norton, 1991.

Greene, Graham. *The Quiet American*. New York: Penguin, 2004.

———. *Ways of Escape*. New York: Simon & Schuster, 1980.

Grose, Peter. *Gentleman Spy: The Life of Allen Dulles*. Boston: Houghton Mifflin, 1994.

Gwin, Larry. *Baptism: A Vietnam Memoir*. New York: Ballantine Books, 1999.

Halberstam, David. *The Best and the Brightest*. New York: Random House, 1969.

Hall, Roger. *You're Stepping on My Cloak and Dagger*. Annapolis, MD: Naval Institute Press, 1957.

Hammer, Ellen. *A Death in November: America in Vietnam 1963*. New York: Oxford University Press, 1987.

Helms, Richard, with William Hood. *A Look over My Shoulder: A Life in the Central Intelligence Agency*. New York: Random House, 2003.

Herken, Gregg. *The Georgetown Set: Friends and Rivals in Cold War Washington*. New York: Alfred A. Knopf, 2014.

Herr, Michael. *Dispatches*. New York: Vintage Books, 1977.

Herring, George C. *From Colony to Superpower: U.S. Foreign Relations since 1776*. New York: Oxford University Press, 2008.

Hersh, Seymour M. *The Dark Side of Camelot*. Boston: Little, Brown, 1997.

Higgins, Marguerite. *Our Vietnam Nightmare*. New York: Harper & Row, 1965.

Hoopes, Townsend, and Douglas Brinkley. *Driven Patriot: The Life and Times of James Forrestal*. Annapolis, MD: Naval Institute Press, 1992.

Hovis, Bobbi. *Station Hospital Saigon: A Navy Nurse in Vietnam, 1963–1964*. Annapolis, MD: Naval Institute Press, 1991.

Hughes, Ken. *Fatal Politics: The Nixon Tapes, the Vietnam War, and the Casualties of Reelection*. Charlottesville: University of Virginia Press, 2015.

Humphrey, Hubert H. *The Education of a Public Man: My Life and Politics*. Minneapolis: University of Minnesota Press, 1991.

Hunt, Ira A., Jr. *Losing Vietnam: How America Abandoned Southeast Asia*. Lexington: University Press of Kentucky, 2013.

Jacobs, Seth. *Cold War Mandarin: Ngo Dinh Diem and the Origins of America's War in Vietnam, 1950–1963*. Lanham, MD: Rowman & Littlefield, 2006.

James, D. Clayton. *The Years of MacArthur*. 3 vols. Boston: Houghton Mifflin, 1970–85.

James, Jack, and Earle Weller. *Treasure Island: "The Magic City," 1939–1940*. San Francisco: Pisani Printing, 1941.

Jeffers, H. Paul. *Taking Command: General J. Lawton Collins from Guadalcanal to Utah Beach and Victory in Europe*. New York: New American Library, 2009.

Joaquin, Nick. *The Aquinos of Tarlac: An Essay on History as Three Generations*. 3rd ed. Manila: Solar Publishing, 1986.

——. *Manila, My Manila: A History for the Young*. Manila: City of Manila, 1990.

Johnson, Denis. *Tree of Smoke*. New York: Picador, 2007.

Johnson, Loch K. *A Season of Inquiry Revisited: The Church Committee Confronts America's Spy Agencies*. Lawrence: University Press of Kansas, 2015.

Jones, Howard. *Death of a Generation: How the Assassinations of Diem and JFK Prolonged the Vietnam War*. New York: Oxford University Press, 2003.

Karnow, Stanley. *In Our Image: America's Empire in the Philippines*. New York: Random House, 1989.

——. *Vietnam: A History*. New York: Penguin Press, 1983.

Keep, Helen E., and M. Agnes Burton. *Guide to Detroit*. Detroit: Detroit News, 1916.

Kerkvliet, Benedict J. *The Huk Rebellion: A Study of Peasant Revolt in the Philippines*. Lanham, MD: Rowman & Littlefield, 1977.

Kimball, Jeffrey. *Nixon's Vietnam War*. Lawrence: University Press of Kansas, 1998.

——. *The Vietnam War Files: Uncovering the Secret History of Nixon-Era Strategy*. Lawrence: University Press of Kansas, 2004.

Kissinger, Henry. *The Complete Memoirs: E-Book Boxed Set*. New York: Simon & Schuster, 2013.

Klein, Christina. *Cold War Orientalism: Asia in the Middlebrow Imagination, 1945–1961*. Berkeley: University of California Press, 2003.

Langguth, A. J. *Our Vietnam: The War, 1954–1975*. New York: Simon & Schuster, 2000.

Lansdale, Edward G. *In the Midst of Wars: An American's Mission to Southeast Asia*. New York: Fordham University Press, 1991.

Larteguy, Jean. *Yellow Fever*. New York: Avon, 1967.

Laurie, Clayton D. *The Propaganda Warriors: America's Crusade against Nazi Germany*. Lawrence: University Press of Kansas, 1996.

Lederer, William J., and Eugene Burdick. *The Ugly American*. New York: W. W. Norton, 1999.

——. "The Ugly American Revisited." *Saturday Evening Post*, May 4, 1963.

Lehrack, Otto J. *The First Battle: Operation Starlite and the Beginning of the Blood Debt in Vietnam*. New York: Ballantine Books, 2006.

Lodge, Henry Cabot, Jr. *The Storm Has Many Eyes: A Personal Narrative*. New York: W. W. Norton, 1973.

Logevall, Fredrik. *Choosing War: The Lost Chance for Peace and the Escalation of War in Vietnam*. Berkeley: University of California Press, 1999.

——. *Embers of War: The Fall of an Empire and the Making of America's Vietnam*. New York: Random House, 2012.

London, Jack. *The Iron Heel*. New York: Regent Press, 1908.

Lovell, Stanley P. *Of Spies and Stratagems*. Englewood Cliffs, NJ: Prentice-Hall, 1963.

MacMillan, Margaret. *Nixon in China: The Week That Changed the World*. New York: Penguin, 2006.

Manchester, William. *The Death of a President: November 20–November 25, 1963*. New York: Little, Brown, 2013.

Marlantes, Karl. *Matterhorn: A Novel of the Vietnam War*. New York: Atlantic Monthly Press, 2010.

Marquez, Adalia. *Blood on the Rising Sun: The Japanese Occupation in the Philippines*. New York: Tanko Publishers, 1957.

Martin, David C. *Wilderness of Mirrors: Intrigue, Deception, and the Secrets That Destroyed Two of the Cold War's Most Important Agents*. Guilford, CT: Lyons Press, 2003.

Martinez, Manuel F. *Magsaysay: The People's President*. Makati City: RMJ Development, 2004.

McAllister, James. "A Fiasco of Noble Proportions: The Johnson Administration and the South Vietnamese Election of 1967." *Pacific Historical Review*, Nov. 2004.

———. "The Lost Revolution: Edward Lansdale and the American Defeat in Vietnam 1964–1968." *Small Wars and Insurgencies*, Summer 2003.

———. "'Only Religions Count in Vietnam': Thich Tri Quang and the Vietnam War." *Modern Asian Studies*, July 2008.

———. "What Can One Man Do? Nguyen Duc Thang and the Limits of Reform in Vietnam." *Journal of Vietnamese Studies*, Summer 2009.

McClintock, Michael. *Instruments of Statecraft: U.S. Guerrilla Warfare, Counterinsurgency, Counter-Terrorism, 1940–1990*. New York: Pantheon, 1992.

McCoy, Alfred W. *Policing America's Empire: The United States, the Philippines, and the Rise of the Surveillance State*. Madison: University of Wisconsin Press, 2009.

McNamara, Robert S. *In Retrospect: The Tragedy and Lessons of Vietnam*. New York: Vintage Books, 1995.

Mecklin, John. *Mission in Torment: An Intimate Account of the U.S. Role in Vietnam*. Garden City, NY: Doubleday, 1965.

Merry, Robert W. *Taking on the World: Joseph and Stewart Alsop, Guardians of the American Century*. New York: Viking, 1996.

Meyer, Harold J. *Hanging Sam: A Military Biography of General Samuel T. Williams, from Pancho Villa to Vietnam*. Denton: University of North Texas Press, 1990.

Military History Institute of Vietnam. *Victory in Vietnam: The Official History of the People's Army in Vietnam, 1954–1975*. Translated by Merle L. Pribbenow. Lawrence: University Press of Kansas, 2002.

Miller, Edward. *Misalliance: Ngo Dinh Diem, the United States, and the Fate of South Vietnam*. Cambridge, MA: Harvard University Press, 2013.

Miller, James E. "Taking Off the Gloves: The United States and the Italian Elections of 1948." *Diplomatic History*, Jan. 1983.

Millett, Allan R., ed. *A Short History of the Vietnam War*. Bloomington: Indiana University Press, 1978.

Milne, David. *America's Rasputin: Walt Rostow and the Vietnam War*. New York: Hill & Wang, 2009.

Mistry, Kaeten. *The United States, Italy and the Origins of the Cold War: Waging Political Warfare, 1945–1950*. Cambridge, UK: Cambridge University Press, 2014.

Moise, Edwin E. *Tonkin Gulf and the Escalation of the Vietnam War*. Chapel Hill: University of North Carolina Press, 1996.

Morgan, Edmund S. "The Pleasures of Paine." *New York Review of Books*, April 13, 1989.

Morgan, Ted. *Valley of Death: The Tragedy at Dien Bien Phu That Led America into the Vietnam War*. New York: Random House, 2010.

Moyar, Mark. *Phoenix and the Birds of Prey: The CIA's Secret Campaign to Destroy the Viet Cong*. Annapolis, MD: Naval Institute Press, 1997.

———. *Triumph Forsaken: The Vietnam War, 1954–1965.* Cambridge, UK: Cambridge University Press, 2006.

Nashel, Jonathan. *Edward Lansdale's Cold War.* Amherst: University of Massachusetts Press, 2005.

Neece, Harvey, and John O'Donnell, eds. *Prelude to Tragedy: Vietnam, 1960–1965.* Annapolis, MD: Naval Institute Press, 2001.

Newman, John M. *JFK and Vietnam: Deception, Intrigue, and the Struggle for Power.* New York: Warner Books, 1992.

Nguyen Cao Ky. *Twenty Years and Twenty Days.* New York: Stein & Day, 1976.

Nguyen Cao Ky with Marvin J. Wolf. *Buddha's Child: My Fight to Save Vietnam.* New York: St. Martin's Press, 2002.

Nguyen, Lien-Hang T. *Hanoi's War: An International History of the War for Peace in Vietnam.* Chapel Hill: University of North Carolina Press, 2012.

Nguyen Tien Hung and Jerrold L. Schechter. *The Palace File.* New York: Harper & Row, 1986.

Nguyen Van Canh. *Vietnam under Communism, 1975–1982.* Palo Alto, CA: Hoover Institution Press, 1983.

Nicolson, Harold. *Diaries and Letters.* Vol. 3, *The Later Years: 1945–1962.* New York: Atheneum, 1968.

Nixon, Richard M. *No More Vietnams.* New York: Arbor House, 1985.

Oberdorfer, Don. *Tet! The Turning Point in the Vietnam War.* Baltimore: Johns Hopkins University Press, 2001.

Oshinsky, David M. *A Conspiracy So Immense: The World of Joe McCarthy.* New York: Oxford University Press, 2005.

Palm, Edward F. *An "American Pie": Lansdale, Lederer, Dooley and Modern Memory.* Lexington, KY: CreateSpace Independent Publishing Forum, 2013.

Phillips, Rufus. *Why Vietnam Matters: An Eyewitness Account of Lessons Not Learned.* Annapolis, MD: Naval Institute Press, 2008.

Pierce, Frederick Clifton. *Batchelder, Batcheller Genealogy.* Chicago: W. B. Cunkey, 1898.

Platt, Alan A., and Robert Leonardi. "American Foreign Policy and the Postwar Italian Left." *Political Science Quarterly,* Summer 1978.

Pomeroy, William J. *The Forest: A Personal Record of the Huk Guerrilla Struggle in the Philippines.* Quezon City: University of Philippines Press, 2010.

Porter, Bruce D. *War and the Rise of the State: The Military Foundation of Modern Politics.* New York: Free Press, 1994.

Posner, Gerald. *Case Closed: Lee Harvey Oswald and the Assassination of JFK.* New York: Open Road, 2013.

Powers, Thomas. *Intelligence Wars: American Secret History from Hitler to Al-Qaeda.* New York: New York Review of Books, 2004.

———. *The Man Who Kept the Secrets: Richard Helms & the CIA.* New York: Alfred A. Knopf, 1979.

Prados, John. *Vietnam: The History of an Unwinnable War, 1945–1975.* Lawrence: University Press of Kansas, 2009.

Prados, John, and Margaret Pratt Porter, eds. *Inside the Pentagon Papers.* Lawrence: University Press of Kansas, 2004.

Pratt, John Clark, ed. *The Quiet American: Text and Criticism.* New York: Penguin, 1996.

Prouty, L. Fletcher. *JFK: The CIA, Vietnam, and the Plot to Assassinate John F. Kennedy.* New York: Skyhorse Publishing, 2011.

———. *The Secret Team: The CIA and Its Allies in Control of the United States and the World.* New York: Skyhorse Publishing, 2011.

Quezon, Manuel L. *The Good Fight: The Autobiography of Manuel Luis Quezon.* New York: D. Appleton-Century, 1946.

Quirino, Elpidio. *The Memoirs of Elpidio Quirino.* Manila: National Historical Institute, 1990.

Randolph, Stephen P. *Powerful and Brutal Weapons: Nixon, Kissinger, and the Easter Offensive.* Cambridge, MA: Harvard University Press, 2007.

Rasenberger, Jim. *The Brilliant Disaster: JFK, Castro, and America's Doomed Invasion of Cuba's Bay of Pigs.* New York: Scribner, 2011.

Reckner, James R. *Teddy Roosevelt's Great White Fleet.* Annapolis, MD: Naval Institute Press, 1988.

Recto, Claro M. *My Crusade.* Manila: Pio C. Calica & Nicanor Carag, 1955.

Reedy, George. *Lyndon B. Johnson: A Memoir.* New York: Andrews and McMeel, 1982.

Reeves, Richard. *President Kennedy: Profile of Power.* New York: Simon & Schuster, 1993.

Reporting Vietnam. Pt. 1, *American Journalism, 1959–1969.* New York: Library of America, 1998.

Romulo, Carlos P., and Marvin M. Gray. *The Magsaysay Story.* New York: John Day, 1956.

Rostow, W. W. *The Diffusion of Power: An Essay in Recent History.* New York: Macmillan, 1972.

Rottman, Gordon L. *Browning .50 Caliber Machine Guns.* Oxford, UK: Osprey, 2010.

Rudenstine, David. *The Day the Presses Stopped: A History of the Pentagon Papers Case.* Berkeley: University of California Press, 1996.

Safer, Morley. *Flashbacks: On Returning to Vietnam.* New York: Random House, 1990.

Sainteny, Jean. *Ho Chi Minh and His Vietnam: A Personal Memoir.* Translated by Herma Briffault. Chicago: Cowles, 1972.

Satoshi, Nakano. "Gabriel L. Kaplan and U.S. Involvement in Philippine Electoral Democracy: A Tale of Two Democracies." *Philippine Stud*ies, 2004.

Schafer, John C. "The Curious Memoirs of the Vietnamese Composer Pham Duy." *Journal of Southeast Asian Studies,* Feb. 2012.

Schaffer, Howard B. *Ellsworth Bunker: Global Troubleshooter, Vietnam Hawk.* Chapel Hill: University of North Carolina Press, 2003.

Schlesinger, Arthur M., Jr. *A Thousand Days: John F. Kennedy in the White House.* New York: Mariner Books, 2002.

Schmitz, David F. *Richard Nixon and the Vietnam War.* Lanham, MD: Rowman & Littlefield, 2014.

Scotton, Frank. *Uphill Battle: Reflections on Viet Nam Counterinsurgency.* Lubbock: Texas Tech University Press, 2014.

Shaplen, Robert. *The Lost Revolution: The U.S. in Vietnam, 1946–1966.* New York: Harper & Row, 1966.

———. *The Road from War: Vietnam, 1965–1970.* New York: Harper & Row, 1970.

Shapley, Deborah. *Promise and Power: The Life and Times of Robert McNamara.* Boston: Little, Brown, 1993.

Sheehan, Neil. *A Bright Shining Lie: John Paul Vann and America in Vietnam*. New York: Random House, 1988.

Sherry, Norman. *The Life of Graham Greene*, Vol. 2, *1939–1955*. New York: Penguin, 1994.

Sihanouk, Norodom, and Wilfred Burchett. *My War with the CIA: The Memoirs of Prince Norodom Sihanouk*. New York: Pantheon, 1973.

Simpson, Howard R. *Tiger in the Barbed Wire: An American in Vietnam, 1952–1991*. Washington, DC: Brassey's, 1992.

Singlaub, John K., with Malcolm McConnell. *Hazardous Duty: An American Soldier in the Twentieth Century*. New York: Summit Books, 1991.

Smith, Jean Edward. *Eisenhower in War and Peace*. New York: Random House, 2013.

Smith, Joseph Burkholder. *Portrait of a Cold Warrior*. New York: G. P. Putnam's Sons, 1976.

Smith, Richard Harris. *OSS: The Secret History of America's First Central Intelligence Agency*. Guilford, CT: Lyons Press, 2005.

Snepp, Frank. *Decent Interval: An Insider's Account of Saigon's Indecent End Told by the CIA's Chief Strategy Analyst in Vietnam*. Lawrence: University Press of Kansas, 2002.

Solberg, Carl. *Hubert Humphrey: A Biography*. St. Paul, MN: Borealis Books, 2003.

Sorley, Lewis. *A Better War: The Unexamined Victories and Final Tragedy of America's Last Years in Vietnam*. New York: Harcourt Brace, 1999.

———. *Westmoreland: The General Who Lost Vietnam*. Boston: Houghton Mifflin, 2011.

Spector, Ronald H. *Advice and Support: The Early Years of the U.S. Army in Vietnam, 1941–1960*. New York: Free Press, 1985.

Starr, Kevin. *Endangered Dreams: The Great Depression in California*. New York: Oxford University Press, 1996.

Stern, Sheldon. *The Cuban Missile Crisis in American Memory: Myths versus Reality*. Palo Alto, CA: Stanford University Press, 2012.

Stone, Oliver, and Zachary Sklar. *JFK: The Book of the Film*. New York: Applause Books, 1992.

Takaki, Ronald. *Strangers from a Different Shore: A History of Asian Americans*. Rev. ed. New York: Back Bay Books, 1998.

Taruc, Luis. *He Who Rides the Tiger: The Story of an Asian Guerrilla Leader*. London: Geoffrey Chapman, 1967.

Taylor, John M. *An American Soldier: The Wars of General Maxwell Taylor*. San Marin, CA: Presidio Press, 1989.

Taylor, Maxwell D. *Swords and Plowshares*. New York: W. W. Norton, 1972.

Thomas, Evan. *Being Nixon: A Man Divided*. New York: Random House, 2015.

———. *Robert F. Kennedy: His Life*. New York: Simon & Schuster, 2000.

———. *The Very Best Men: The Daring Early Years of the CIA*. New York: Simon & Schuster, 2006.

Tourison, Sedgwick. *Secret Army, Secret War: Washington's Tragic Spy Operation in North Vietnam*. Annapolis, MD: Naval Institute Press, 1995.

Traas, Adrian G. *Engineers at War*. Washington, DC: Center of Military History, 2010.

Tran Van Don. *Our Endless War: Inside Vietnam*. Novato, CA: Presidio Press, 1978.

Truong Nhu Tang with David Chanoff and Doan Van Toai. *A Viet Cong Memoir:*

An Inside Account of the Vietnam War and Its Aftermath. New York: Vintage Books, 1986.

U.S. Department of Defense. *U.S.–Vietnam Relations, 1945–1967* [The Pentagon Papers]. Washington, DC: Department of Defense, 1969. http://www.archives.gov/research/pentagon-papers.

U.S. Department of State. Foreign Service List. Washington, DC: Government Printing Office, 1819–. http://catalog.hathitrust.org/Record/001719572/Home.

U.S. Senate [Church Committee]. "Alleged Assassination Plots Involving Foreign Leaders: An Interim Report of the Select Committee to Study Governmental Operations with Respect to Intelligence." Washington, DC: Government Printing Office, 1975.

———. "Final Report of the Select Committee to Study Governmental Operations with Respect to Intelligence." Washington, DC: Government Printing Office, 1976.

U.S. Senate. "Executive Session of the Senate Foreign Relations Committee." Vol. XVII. 89th Congress, 1st sess., 1965. Washington, DC: Government Printing Office, 1990.

U.S. Works Progress Administration. *Los Angeles in the 1930s: The WPA Guide to the City of Angels.* Berkeley: University of California Press, 2011.

———. *San Francisco in the 1930s: The WPA Guide to the City by the Bay.* Berkeley: University of California Press, 2011.

———. *The WPA Guide to New York City.* New York: New Press, 1939.

Valeriano, Napoleon D., and Charles T. R. Bohannan. *Counter-Guerrilla Operations: The Philippine Experience.* Westport, CT: Praeger Security International, 2006.

Veith, George J. *Black April: The Fall of South Vietnam, 1973–1975.* New York: Encounter Books, 2012.

Waller, Douglas. *Wild Bill Donovan: The Spymaster Who Created the OSS and Modern American Espionage.* New York: Free Press, 2011.

Warner, Michael, ed. *The CIA under Harry Truman.* Washington, DC: CIA Center for Study of Intelligence, 1994.

Weiner, Tim. *Legacy of Ashes: The History of the CIA.* New York: Doubleday, 2007.

Wells, Tom. *Wild Man: The Life and Times of Daniel Ellsberg.* New York: Palgrave, 2001.

Westmoreland, William C. *A Soldier Reports.* New York: Da Capo Press, 1989.

Wilford, Hugh. *The Mighty Wurlitzer: How the CIA Played America.* Cambridge, MA: Harvard University Press, 2009.

Willbanks, James H. *Thiet Giap! The Battle of An Loc, April 1972.* Fort Leavenworth, KS: U.S. Army Command and Staff College, 1993.

Williams, Mason B. *City of Ambition: FDR, La Guardia, and the Making of Modern New York.* New York: W. W. Norton, 2014.

Wilson, Edmund. *The Thirties: From Notebooks and Diaries of the Period.* Edited by Leon Edel. New York: Farrar, Straus & Giroux, 1980.

Windrow, Martin. *The Last Valley: Dien Bien Phu and the French Defeat in Vietnam.* New York: Da Capo Press, 2004.

Winik, Jay. *1944: FDR and the Year That Changed History.* New York: Simon & Schuster, 2015.

Wise, Jon, and Mike Hill, eds. *The Works of Graham Greene: A Reader's Bibliography and Guide.* New York: Continuum, 2012.

Wolff, Tobias. *In Pharaoh's Army: Memories of the Lost War*. New York: Vintage Books, 1994.

Woods, Randall B. *Shadow Warrior: William Egan Colby and the CIA*. New York: Basic Books, 2013.

Woodward, Bob. *The Last of the President's Men*. New York: Simon & Schuster, 2015.

Wyden, Peter. *Bay of Pigs: The Untold Story*. New York: Simon & Schuster, 1979.

Zaffiri, Samuel. *Westmoreland: A Biography of General William C. Westmoreland*. New York: William Morrow, 1994.

Zhai, Qiang. "Transplanting the Chinese Model: Chinese Military Advisers and the First Vietnam War, 1950–1954." *Journal of Military History*, Oct. 1993.

INDEX

Page numbers in *italics* refer to illustrations.